P9-DCM-447

THE COURT TV CRADLE-TO-GRAVE LEGAL SURVIVAL GUIDE

THE COURT TV CRADLE-TO-GRAVE LEGAL SURVIVAL GUIDE

A COMPLETE RESOURCE FOR ANY QUESTION YOU MIGHT HAVE ABOUT THE LAW

BY THE EDITORS OF 

The American Lawyer/Little, Brown and Company

Little, Brown and Company
Boston New York Toronto London

First Edition

An *American Lawyer* / Little, Brown and Company book

Library of Congress Cataloging-in-Publication Data

The Court TV cradle-to-grave legal survival guide: a complete resource for any question you might have about the law / by the editors of Court TV and The American Lawyer. — 1st ed.
p. cm.
"An American Lawyer / Little, Brown and Company title" — T.p. verso.
Includes index.
ISBN 0-316-03699-4 (hc)
ISBN 0-316-03663-3 (pb)
1. Law — United States — Popular works. I. Court TV (Television network) II. American Lawyer (New York, N.Y.:1979)
KF387.C62 1995
349.73 — dc20
[347.3] 94-24900

10 9 8 7 6 5 4 3 2 1

RRD-OH

Published simultaneously in Canada by Little, Brown & Company (Canada) Limited

Printed in the United States of America

BOARD OF EDITORS

CONTRIBUTING EDITORS

CONTENTS

CONTENTS

CONTENTS

INTRODUCTION

Dear Reader,

The document appended herewith offers an explanation of the law insofar as it affects the everyday life of your person, your heirs, your tangible personal property, your real property, and any interrelationships between and among the aforementioned.

Don't panic! The sentence above contains the first and last incomprehensible legalisms you'll find in this book. What you'll discover instead is an easy-to-read, in-depth guide to the law as it affects you in all aspects of your daily life — whether you're buying or selling a house, loaning money to a friend, applying to college, going to the doctor, pursuing a personal injury claim, facing a criminal charge, or doing any number of other things.

Consider a few scenarios:

- Your new designer leather jacket is stolen from a restaurant cloakroom. The manager apologizes profusely but claims to have no obligation to reimburse you.
- You order an expensive set of exercise videos from a pushy door-to-door saleswoman. ("Another body part transformed every month," she promises.) You decide to cancel the order the next day. "Sorry, too late," you're told.
- You're driving home from a business dinner when a cop signals you to pull over. "We're doing spot checks for drunk driving," he says. "Would you mind stepping out of the car and singing the national anthem?"

What do you do? What do you say? What are you entitled to demand and receive? We answer these questions and guide you through hundreds of other scenarios. Our goal is to introduce you to the important legal issues you're likely to encounter, outline your rights and responsibilities, and give you a clearly organized explanation of the law in language you can understand.

Which doesn't mean we don't throw in some legal terms. We do, because we think it's important for legal consumers to be familiar with them and because our purpose here is to demystify the law and the legal system and make it less intimidating.

In this book you'll meet the Goodfriend family: Grace and Gordon; their four children, Beatrice, Bartholomew, Blossom, and Bradley; and many of their friends, work colleagues, and other relatives. We expect (and hope) that you won't ever encounter a group of people beset by so many problems. But we also expect (and hope) that their problems, humorous as some of them may be, illustrate and illuminate how our legal system works.

You'll read over and over again that the law varies from state to state. It's true. In many instances we tell you exactly what the law is in your state on a particular issue. When we don't do that, we direct you to various sources — from government agencies to nonprofit organizations — that can be of further help. We also tell you the best ways to find a lawyer when you need one.

That noted, we must state clearly that while you may turn to this book for guidance, it's in no way meant to substitute for professional legal advice. In fact, while we often suggest strategies for solving a problem without going to a lawyer, we don't believe you should pursue litigation, sign an important contract, or face criminal charges without the assistance of an attorney. Unless you're bringing a case in small-claims court, we don't advocate representing yourself in court.

In fact, we don't encourage you to rush to court at all, unless you're in immediate need of what's called a protective order because someone is threatening you. Going to court is tedious, time-consuming, and expensive and should be reserved for truly serious grievances that cannot be resolved in any other way. Dealing with a conflict directly by trying to negotiate an amenable solution often yields more satisfactory results than taking a case to a jury.

If you do need to hire a lawyer, we have a section to guide you through that process — from finding the best person to negotiating the fee to dealing with disagreements that arise in the handling of your case. And if you have a problem with your lawyer, we've provided a list of state bar associations that can advise you where to register your complaint.

A word about format. The book is arranged chronologically, following the legal issues a person confronts throughout life — from birth to death. If you have a particular problem, you can look it up in the table of contents or in the index at the back of the book. Or you may want to browse through the chapters to learn more about subjects that interest you or to chuckle at the problems that never stop for the Goodfriends. And if a big case is making headlines, the book can help you understand the legal issues involved.

A final note: This book includes many hypothetical situations involving the Goodfriend family and their acquaintances. Any similarity to real people or actual events is purely coincidental.

THE COURT TV CRADLE-TO-GRAVE LEGAL SURVIVAL GUIDE

BEING BORN

1

VITAL STATISTICS

Birth Certificates and Social Security Numbers

Grace Goodfriend gave her husband Gordon Goodfriend a nudge. "I think it's happening," she said.

"What's happening?" he asked.

"You know," she said, pointing at her bulging stomach.

"Holy moly mother of my brother," said Gordon in a panic. It was the Fourth of July, and they were downtown, along with a few thousand of their friends and neighbors, to watch fireworks. The festivities had just started, and the car was several blocks away.

Gordon tried to clear a path through the crowd. "I'm not going to make it," said Grace, doubling over from the pain of a contraction. An hour later Grace had given birth to their first baby, a daughter, on the lawn of the town's Civic Center. Two men dressed as Uncle Sam held up an American flag to give her some privacy.

Later at the hospital, people joked that there was no question the new baby was a true American. "You should name her Betsy Ross," suggested one nurse. Gordon realized that he had no idea what paperwork, if any, was necessary to get his new daughter started in life.

■ Does everyone have to have a birth certificate?

Yes, since many things in life, such as obtaining a passport, getting a driver's license, or registering for school may require a person to have one. The health officials you deal with at the time you give birth will provide you with the forms you need to obtain a birth certificate. Otherwise, you can obtain the necessary forms from the appropriate government office in your municipality, sometimes called the registrar of vital statistics.

■ Should a new baby get a Social Security number?

Yes. A Social Security number has become one of the most important means of identifying your child. Although there is no requirement to apply, you will be unable to claim a child over age one as a tax exemption on your income taxes if you don't. (You can note that you have "Applied For" a number on your return and claim the exemption, but you must then indeed apply for, and receive, the number.) You can apply for a Social Security number by contacting the Social Security Administration in your area.

Names

Grace and Gordon could not agree on a name. She liked Lily and Magnolia. He liked Hope and Joy. Mostly, however, they called their new baby Miss Firecracker. Still, they had to put something on the birth certificate, so they settled on Beatrice Rose (their variation of Betsy Ross).

■ Can parents keep changing their baby's name?

Most states have a period of time within which the child must be named on the birth certificate. You can contact your local registrar of vital statistics to find out the specifics that apply in your area. Once the child is named, the birth certificate can be amended at a later date, but you will probably have to go through some bureaucratic procedures and pay fees before you can do so. You should bear in mind that, regardless of the name that is on one's birth certificate, every individual has a right to use any first or last name so long as it is not done for the purpose of deceiving creditors, committing fraud, or avoiding criminal prosecution.

Still, if you want to avoid problems and lots of questions like "Why is your name different from that on your birth certificate?," you may want to make your name change official. You can change your name legally upon reaching adulthood, which in most states is age eighteen.

Grace's sister, an actress, had kept her own last name when she got married. Now that she and her husband were about to have their first baby, she was unsure how to deal with the last-name issue.

■ Does a baby have to be given the father's last name?

Most states have laws that govern the naming of a child. Traditionally, a man's wife and children were required to have the same last name as he had. The modern trend is to permit the parents to give the child whatever name they choose, whether it is the name of the father, the mother, or some combination of the two, such as a hyphenated name. You can find out what the law is in your state by asking the registrar of vital statistics when you fill out the birth certificate.

■ Can a woman give her baby the father's last name if she's not married to him?

Probably. Traditionally, the father's name was not given to an illegitimate child, because that was considered to be a stigma to the father as well as to the child. The world is changing, however, and statutes have been enacted in many states that give a parent the right to give a child any last name, be it the mother's, the father's, or something totally different.

BEING A KID

2

The Goodfriend kids were a handful. While Bartholomew was off spray painting graffiti on a neighbor's house, Blossom was out charging gourmet groceries to her parents without permission. Bradley was always getting beat up by big kids, and Beatrice had a little problem with shoplifting.

Grace and Gordon could hardly keep up.

■ Does the law treat children and adults differently?

Yes. In general, a **minor** does not have the legal rights of an adult. A minor is usually defined as a person who has not yet reached the age of **majority**. In most states, a person reaches majority and acquires all the rights and responsibilities of an adult when he or she turns eighteen.

Basically, the law views children as incompetent to make important decisions about their lives and unable to take care of themselves. So if a minor enters into a contract, it may be voidable because the minor (in the eyes of the law) does not have the capacity to understand what he or she is undertaking. Similarly, criminal law gives a lot of deference to juveniles, mostly in the belief that it is more likely that a juvenile can be rehabilitated and outgrow the mishaps of youth. Thus, a juvenile's criminal record is sealed, because it is believed that what someone does as a child should not be held against him or her later in life. (For more on juveniles and crime, see page 11.)

There are, of course, circumstances in which a minor has achieved independence from his or her parents, and is thus considered **emancipated**. Emancipation can occur

- **when a child gets legally married prior to the age of eighteen**
- **when a child moves out on his or her own, gets a job, and becomes fully self-supporting**
- **when a child joins a branch of the military**

PARENTAL CONSENT

Marriage

Beatrice was in love. She was fifteen, and her boyfriend Jason was seventeen. They hung out after school, cruising around in Jason's old Mustang. Bea's parents approved, and thought Jason was a "nice boy." Little did they know that when Beatrice said she was sleeping over at her friend Jennifer's, she was actually staying with Jason at his brother's college apartment. Grace hardly took it seriously when Beatrice told her she and Jason planned to get married. "That's lovely, dear," she said.

Gordon was less sanguine. "No way. Over my dead body," he shouted. "Don't even think about such nonsense. You're just a stupid kid. Get out of here, clean up your room, and do your homework so that you'll get into a good college."

■ Does a minor need parental permission to get married?

All states have a minimum age for marriage, but it is not always eighteen. In some states, persons as young as fourteen or fifteen years of age can get married even without parental consent. In others, persons younger than the minimum age can be married if they get the permission of their parents or of a judge. In one state, Mississippi, the minimum age differs for boys and girls. There, parental consent is required for boys under age seventeen. Consent is required for girls only under age fifteen. (This distinction is almost surely unconstitutional.) Puerto Rico requires parental consent for marriage up to age twenty-one.

Most of these laws make exceptions for female minors who are pregnant or who have already had a child. Also, in many cases, it may be possible for a determined minor to travel to a state that has a lower minimum age.

> **Mother, May I . . .**
>
> Thirty-six states, including Massachusetts, Michigan, and Pennsylvania, have laws requiring young women to notify or get the consent of one or both parents prior to an abortion. In several states, such as Arizona, California, and Florida, enforcement of the laws has been blocked by federal or state court order. Thirteen states, including New York, New Jersey, and Texas, have no laws requiring parental involvement or permission.

Birth Control and Abortion

When Beatrice told her parents that she and Jason wanted to get married, she had left out a crucial fact: she thought she might be pregnant. Of course, she did really love Jason and want to marry him, but she knew her father was right that she was too young. She did want to go to college and maybe even on to graduate school. Having a baby would probably derail that plan. And how well could she and Jason support a family at their age? She thought it might be best to get an abortion — something she definitely did not want to tell her parents.

■ Does a minor have to get parental permission for an abortion?

It depends on the state she lives in. In several states, minors can obtain abortions without the knowledge of their parents, but many states have placed restrictions on their ability to do so. Some states require a minor to *notify* one or both of her parents before obtaining an abortion. Other states require a minor to get the *consent* of one or both of her parents. (In both procedures, parents are usually asked to sign a document that says they've been informed. Some doctors require that the signature be notarized.)

While one or both parents may refuse to provide consent, they cannot veto the minor's right to have an abortion. The U.S. Supreme Court has ruled that states that require parental notification or consent must provide an option of "judicial bypass" for minors who cannot (or choose not to) inform their parents before obtaining an abortion. In the "judicial bypass" process, the minor appears before a judge and presents her case. If the judge determines that the young woman is mature enough to understand all the consequences of her situation and her decision to have an abortion, the judge can grant her permission to proceed. (For more on abortion, see page 138.)

If the woman can show that she is an emancipated minor, she may be able to get an abortion without notifying her parents, because she has all the rights of an adult.

■ Can a doctor prescribe birth control without a minor's parent's consent?

This is an area of the law that varies from state to state — and that is frequently in dispute in the courts. But, in general, minors may seek the services of a doctor or clinic for the purposes of obtaining birth control, usually without their parents' consent.

ENTERING INTO CONTRACTS

Bartholomew, eleven, was snooping through the junk mail his mother had tossed in the trash when he found an offer for a twelve-volume set of books called "The Human Sexual Experience Throughout History." Each volume contained articles and photos on intimacy and relationships. ("Wow, pictures," thought Bart.) The first volume, *Forging Closeness in the Middle Ages*, was available for just $2.00. Bart signed up, putting eight quarters in the return envelope and ignoring the small print, which stated that the purchaser agreed to buy at least three more volumes during the next year at a price of $16.95 each.

Can a minor enter into a contract?

Yes, but in general a contract entered into by a minor is not valid or binding. (For more on contracts, see page 51.) That means that if a minor rented an apartment, took out a loan, or agreed to buy a car from a neighbor, the minor would not actually be bound to carry out the transaction. In some circumstances, such as when the minor's parent agreed to co-sign, then the deal would be valid. Also, the minor could back out of the contract, but the adult could not, since the adult is supposed to know better.

There is one exception. If a minor enters into a contract and then turns eighteen without trying to rescind the contract, the contract then becomes binding on the minor. For example, suppose when you were seventeen years old you agreed to buy a car from your neighbor. Up until you turned eighteen, you could legally rescind that contract because as a minor you are not considered capable of entering into a binding contract.

However, say you turn eighteen the week after signing the contract. Once you are eighteen, you pay for the car, accept it from your neighbor, start to drive around in it, and take it to be registered in your name. You have, in essence, agreed to the terms of the contract, *and* you are no longer a minor. So you would not be able to rescind the contract if, for instance, you suddenly realized you didn't really have enough money to cover the costs of owning a car. On the other hand, if you turn eighteen a week after signing the contract but haven't accepted the car yet or started payments, you can probably still back out of the deal.

CASE IN POINT

Bodily Pride

While a contract entered into by a minor can be invalidated, it's not so easy when the minor's *parent* signs an agreement on behalf of the minor. Such was the case for actress Brooke Shields, who tried to stop a photographer from selling nude photos he had taken of her. The problem? Shields's mother had signed a consent agreement authorizing the pictures.

The case began in 1975, when Shields was ten years old and working as a child model. With the permission of her mother, photographer Garry Gross took a series of photos of the young girl posing nude in a bathtub. The series was financed by the Playboy Press, which printed them in a publication called "Sugar and Spice." The photos were also reprinted, with the knowledge of both Shields and her mother, in several other publications.

Five years later, in 1980, a more mature Shields learned that the pictures had been republished in a French magazine and that there were plans to print them elsewhere. She sued and won a court order prohibiting the use of the photos in pornographic magazines. Her reason? She was embarrassed by them because "they are not me now," notes a court opinion. Shields argued that she, as a minor, had the right to "disaffirm" the unrestricted consent her mother gave for republication of the photos. The photographer argued that the consent was valid.

In 1983, the New York Court of Appeals ruled in favor of the photographer, noting that Shields didn't actually contend that the pictures were obscene or pornographic. The court ruled that Shields had no standing to prohibit the use of the photographs.

In a dissent, Judge Matthew Jasen disagreed with the decision, noting that the state has a compelling interest to protect children, and that it had long been a rule in New York that a minor can "disaffirm" a contract, even when it was entered into by the minor's parent on the minor's behalf.

Gregory K's Story

While the case of Gregory Kingsley, more widely known as Gregory K, may have inspired disgruntled children throughout the country, it did not actually establish the right of a child to "divorce" his parents.

Gregory was born in Florida in 1980 to Ralph and Rachel Kingsley. After they separated in 1983, Gregory spent the next few years shuttling between various social service agencies and the homes of Ralph, allegedly an abusive alcoholic, and Rachel, who was sporadically employed.

By 1989, Rachel could no longer take care of Gregory, and he subsequently lived in various state-run group homes and with several foster families. During this time Rachel moved to Missouri. In 1991, Gregory's third foster family, the Russes, decided to adopt him, believing it would not be a problem, since Rachel had ignored him for years.

Not so. When Rachel learned of the adoption plans in 1992, she decided she wanted her son back. Gregory, then age eleven, filed a lawsuit to terminate the parental rights of his parents, and he also filed a complaint asking to be adopted by his foster parents. Shortly after he filed, several additional petitions to terminate the parental rights were filed on Gregory's behalf: by his foster parents, by the court-appointed guardian ad litem, and by the state agency in charge of the welfare of children.

In July 1992, a Florida trial court judge ruled that Gregory had the right to bring his lawsuit even though he was an unemancipated minor. A trial was held to consider the issue of termination and adoption, and the judge ruled that Rachel's rights could be terminated and that the Russes could adopt Gregory.

However, the adoption decision was overturned in August 1993 by a midlevel Florida appeals court, which ruled that the trial court had erroneously entered an order finalizing the adoption before Rachel had exhausted her appeals. The appeals court also ruled that it was erroneous to allow Gregory to petition to terminate his parent's rights on his own behalf. However, because the additional petitions had been filed on Gregory's behalf, the error was found to be harmless, so the court let stand the ruling terminating Rachel's parental rights.

Still, in a partially concurring and partially dissenting opinion, Judge Charles Harris did not mince words about whether a minor should be able to sue in his or her own behalf. "While the child has the right not to be abused, neglected or abandoned," he wrote, "there is no right to change parents simply because the child finds substitutes that he or she likes better or who can provide a better standard of living."

The case ended in early 1994, when Florida's highest court rejected Rachel's petition to review the lower court's decision, thus letting it stand. Because the Russes' adoption of Gregory had been ruled procedurally incorrect, it was carried out in the appropriate manner and finalized in March 1994.

"DIVORCING" YOUR PARENTS

When Gordon found out about the book purchase, he grounded Bart, cut off his allowance for a month, and ordered him to read the *Oxford Guide to Every Last Detail of Historical Significance in the Past Two Thousand Years.* (Bart had claimed he ordered the books only because he was interested in history.) Bart told his father he was a spiteful old man with no sense of humor. Gordon responded by slugging Bart in the face so hard it broke his nose. Bart ran out of the house screaming, "You're terrible. I hate you. I'm never coming back."

■ Can children "divorce" their parents?

Not usually. When a child asks to "divorce" his (or her) parents, he essentially is asking a judge to end their right to be parents. This can happen only if the judge determines that the parents are unfit to care for their children. An isolated incident of abuse or neglect is not necessarily enough to justify termination of parental rights, though that would probably trigger an investigation by the appropriate state agency. While the specific definition of an unfit parent varies from state to state and from case to case, the overall question is whether or not the parent can care for the child. (While Gordon's behavior very well might be considered abusive, his parental rights probably would not be severed without more evidence of a pattern of abuse or neglect. However, if he had attempted to kill Bart with a gun, that might well be considered enough evidence of abuse.)

A minor cannot usually start a termination proceeding alone, because children do not have the power to bring lawsuits on their own behalf. Such a lawsuit would have to be initiated by a state agency that has determined that the parents are unfit. Even if a minor finds a lawyer who wants to represent him or her, that lawyer may have to file a motion asking the court to appoint a **guardian ad litem** for the child. The guardian ad litem is a person who looks out for the best interests of the child during the course of legal proceedings. It would be up to this person to decide whether it would be appropriate to pursue an action to terminate the parents' rights.

■ What's the procedure?

The actual process of terminating parental rights varies from state to state, but in general, it starts with the filing of a **complaint** or **petition** in a family court by a state agency on behalf of the child. Usually, this does not happen until after the family has already been under investigation for some time and the children are probably already in foster care.

Parents who are in danger of having their parental rights terminated should have a lawyer, and one usually will be appointed for them if they are unable to afford it themselves. In fact, the parents may each need to be represented by a different attorney if their interests are very different. For example, if one parent is accused of abusing the other, or if they are each fighting for custody of the child, they should have separate lawyers.

Also, a child can terminate his relationship to his parents by seeking to be declared an emancipated minor (see page 5).

Note: Many states now allow children to sue their parents when there has been abuse. Generally, such lawsuits seek money to compensate for physical injury, emotional distress, and attorneys' fees, and it is hoped that such suits will help deter parents from abusing their children. However, a child almost always must have an adult guardian or representative who brings the lawsuit on his or her behalf.

BABYSITTERS

As a teenager Blossom babysat almost every weekend. One night while she was watching a neighbor's two children, the bouncy three-year-old toddler accidentally tripped and hit his head on a table and needed several stitches.

■ Is a babysitter who is a minor liable for accidents suffered by the children in her care?

Possibly, if the babysitter negligently allows her charges to do dangerous things without trying to stop them. A babysitter — whether a minor or an adult — is obligated to exercise reasonable care for the children. This includes preventing unusually dangerous activities and providing adequate supervision. But a babysitter does not guarantee the safety of her charges. Running, including the risk of tripping, is a normal activity for young children, and ensuring that a child will not be hurt in a fall is not possible.

There are different expectations for adult and minor babysitters. A thirteen-year-old might not be held liable for failing to realize that a child's abdominal pain might be appendicitis, but a forty-year-old nanny may well be. As a practical matter, neither is likely to be insured, or to have enough money to warrant a suit. However, many agencies provide child-care workers who are "bonded" — insured in case of accident.

CHILD LABOR

Beatrice, like a typical fifteen-year-old, spent a lot of time hanging out at the mall. But unlike some of her friends, she did not have her mother's credit card in hand to pay for purchases. That created a problem, since Beatrice's allowance didn't cover much more than snack food after school. So she decided to find a job (in a store at the mall, of course).

■ At what age can a child start working?

A person must be at least fourteen years old, although some states do not allow children to start working until they are sixteen. In addition, many states restrict the kinds of jobs that children can hold in order to protect the well-being of minors and to prevent overwork and exposure to dangerous or unhealthful conditions. For instance, a fourteen-year-old cannot be employed in a job that involves manufacturing or mining (the minimum age for those jobs is sixteen), and the job cannot have an adverse effect on the child's health or education. That means that unless the worker is a child actor (see page 124), he or she cannot usually take a job that conflicts with going to school. (See the Case in Point opposite.)

■ Must a child have work papers?

It depends on the state. Many states require an employer hiring a minor under age sixteen or eighteen to have a "permit to employ" on file for the duration of the minor's employment. The permits are usually available from the state department of employment or labor.

■ Are the work hours restricted?

Yes, under federal law, minors under the age of sixteen are not allowed to work during school hours or later than 7 P.M. on a school night, except during the summer (from June 1 to Labor Day), when they may work until 9 P.M. In addition, some states restrict the hours even further. You can find out the rules in your state by calling your state department of employment or labor.

Beatrice got a job working afternoons and weekends as a sales clerk at The Groove, a hip clothing store owned by the parents of her classmate Alexis. She took the job because they were offering minimum wage and many of the other stores weren't.

■ Aren't all workers entitled to minimum wage?

In general, yes. However, under federal law, full-time students with part-time jobs in retail, agriculture, and service industries may be paid less than minimum wage if the employer has obtained authorization from the wage and hour division of the Department of Labor. Taxes and social security will be withheld from a minor's wages as they are from any other employee's check, although a minor is likely to qualify for a refund at the end of the year.

Also, the law in most states allows a parent to take the money earned by his or her children.

Beatrice had wanted to work on weekdays from 5 to 9 (so she could have Saturday free to roam the mall), but the owners wouldn't let her because of the 7 P.M. law. However, they did let their daughter Alexis work past 7 P.M.

Are the rules different if the employer is the child's parent?

Yes. Child labor laws do not apply to children under sixteen if they are employed by their parents in occupations other than manufacturing, mining, or other fields that have been declared hazardous by the Secretary of Labor.

CHILDREN'S CRIMINAL BEHAVIOR

Being Charged with a Crime

Two young boys in Beatrice's neighborhood, Jimmy, seven, and Timmy, five, were playing. "I'll be the cop and you be the robber," said Jimmy, opening up his mother's nightstand drawer and pulling out a small handgun, which he aimed at Timmy. "Stop or I'll shoot," he shouted menacingly. "Pow pow," he added before pulling the trigger. Timmy died of the bullet wounds. Timmy's parents were distraught and tried to get the district attorney to prosecute, but she told them that, under their state law, Jimmy was too young to be charged.

At what age can a child be charged with a crime?

Each state has its own laws concerning crimes committed by children. In most states, a child under the age of seven or eight is usually considered to be lacking the mental capacity to commit a crime. Older children will generally not be charged with a crime unless a prosecutor can prove to a juvenile court judge that the child knew or should have known that he was committing a crime. However, great deference is paid to the prosecutor's decision to file a case, and as a general rule children over the age of eight will be fair game for criminal prosecution in juvenile court.

Can a juvenile be prosecuted as an adult?

Yes. Many states allow minors over the age of sixteen to be prosecuted as adults if they commit serious felonies like robbery or murder. Some states set the age at seventeen, and some go as low as age fourteen when a homicide is committed. Because of rising crime rates, many other states are trying to lower the age at which a child can be tried as an adult (usually from eighteen to sixteen).

In some states and under some circumstances, it takes a judge's approval, at a hearing, to "transfer" a juvenile's case to adult court. There are many factors that a juvenile court judge has to take into account when deciding whether a juvenile should be prosecuted as an adult, including

- **the nature of the child's actions**
- **psychiatric evaluations**
- **past criminal record**

CASE IN POINT

It's Ten O'Clock . . .

In 1993, a major supermarket chain agreed to pay the U.S. government $490,000 for more than 900 alleged violations of federal child labor law.

The case was brought against the Great Atlantic and Pacific Tea Company, Inc. (A & P), by the U.S. Department of Labor. It charged that A & P had unlawfully employed twelve- and thirteen-year-olds and had employed older teens during prohibited hours. The company was also accused of allowing minors to operate, load, unload, or clean hazardous equipment, including meat-cutters and power-dough mixers. In addition, minors allegedly operated scrap-paper balers — dangerous machines used to crush cardboard into tight masses.

The settlement included the promise that A & P would comply with all provisions of federal child labor laws in the future. Lawyers for A & P and the Department of Labor said that only one A & P store had employed twelve- and thirteen-year-olds and that most of the alleged violations had to do with letting older teens load balers and work during impermissible hours. The case was settled, said the A & P lawyer, to avoid the burden of litigation.

The Rights of Juveniles

Ralphie, a thirteen-year-old classmate of Bart's, was picked up by the cops for vandalism at a shopping mall; he was breaking windows with a baseball bat. The police called his parents, who came and picked him up, and he was given a citation to appear in juvenile court the following Monday. His parents couldn't afford a lawyer, and were anxious to find out whether the state would appoint one and whether Ralphie would have to go before a jury.

■ What rights does a juvenile have?

Juveniles have many of the same rights as others accused of a crime, including the right to remain silent, the right to be free from unreasonable searches and seizures (see page 210), and the right to a state-appointed lawyer. However, a juvenile usually doesn't have to offer the same level of proof of indigence as an adult would, although some states will consider the assets of the parents and decide whether they can afford to pay for an attorney.

However, other rights available to adults, such as the right to a jury trial, do not necessarily apply to juvenile proceedings. In many states such cases are heard by a judge alone at a hearing, not a trial.

■ How do juvenile proceedings differ from those for adults?

A juvenile court proceeding is called a hearing, not a trial, and is held before a judge, not a jury. A juvenile has the same right as an adult to be released on bail, although first-time defendants and those charged with nonviolent offenses are often released to their parents' custody with no bail posted.

Juvenile hearings are usually closed to the public, and the names of the offenders are usually withheld from the press. In many states the probation officers who supervise juveniles also play an important role in deciding on charges and making recommendations to the judge.

■ How are juveniles sentenced?

In juvenile court, unlike adult court, the main guide for the judge at sentencing is not supposed to be punishment. Rather, the judge, in theory, is supposed to consider what is in "the best interests of the child." Most juveniles who commit minor crimes are placed on probation and must report regularly to a juvenile probation officer. This differs from adult probation in that it is meant to rehabilitate and counsel, more than to punish. To that end, supervision may be closer, and is conducted by a special agency that works only with juveniles. The court will usually use probation instead of imprisonment as a form of sentencing. The sentence and probation may include ordering the juvenile

- **to go to school regularly**
- **to report to a counselor regularly**
- **to hold down a steady job**
- **to adhere to a curfew**

A violation of these terms may mean incarceration in a juvenile home for the offender.

■ What are prisons for juveniles generally like?

Juveniles who commit more serious crimes or who are repeat offenders may be sent to a juvenile detention facility. While these facilities generally have looser regulations than a prison, they are far more regimented than living at home. Some innovative "boot camps" for juveniles may actually be stricter than most jails. Many states have created a broad variety of juvenile institutions, which range from fairly open and comfortable to extremely confining and very strict. In this way, the juvenile court can best fit the child into an appropriate institution.

Juveniles who are tried as adults usually face far heavier consequences. Depending on the state, they may be sentenced to a juvenile detention center until reaching age eighteen, at which time they may be moved into an adult prison. In many states, a juvenile tried as an adult can be punished as an adult — meaning going to an adult prison. However, a juvenile tried as a juvenile cannot be sent to an adult prison. There are, however, a number of high-security juvenile homes for violent youths convicted of the most serious crimes, such as rape, assault with a weapon, and murder.

Juvenile Records

After Ralphie had served his probation, his parents were worried that his juvenile record would haunt him for the rest of his life. They wondered if there was anything they could do to clear his name.

■ What happens to the records of a juvenile case?

It depends on the state. In some states it is up to the judge. Some may agree to issue an order forever sealing records of a juvenile arrest once probation has been successfully completed. This is the exception, however, and most courts will make juvenile records confidential but not seal them. This means that the public at large (including journalists and employers) will be blocked from access to these records, but certain governmental agencies, such as the state police, the FBI, or the U.S. State Department, may gain access to them.

Some states, however, will allow a juvenile record to be erased or destroyed upon successful completion of probation.

Capital Punishment and Minors

A schoolmate of Beatrice's was abducted, raped, and killed by a fifteen-year-old boy. He was tried as an adult, found guilty, and sentenced to death, causing a storm of protest.

■ Can a minor be executed?

In certain states, yes. While it is very rare for a minor to face execution, statutes allowing it have been upheld by the U.S. Supreme Court, which has ruled that they do not violate the Eighth Amendment prohibition against cruel and unusual punishment.

Of the fifty states, thirty-six allow capital punishment. Of those, twelve do not execute minors. The states that do execute minors set varying minimum ages, from fourteen to seventeen.

CHILDREN'S MONEY

See Chapter 17, Paying Taxes; Chapter 24, Having Money; and "Minors and Their Money" on page 363.

GOING TO SCHOOL 3

DRESS CODES

The principal of Beatrice's public high school decided that the students needed more discipline. So she instituted a dress code:

- **All boys must wear ties**
- **All girls must wear skirts**
- **No hair below the shoulders on boys**
- **No earrings on boys or girls**

■ Can a public school impose dress or hair codes on students?

The U.S. Supreme Court has not yet addressed that question, and the lower courts that have dealt with the issue have handed down conflicting decisions. Some have allowed all dress or hair codes instituted by schools, finding that there is no constitutional right for students to dress or wear their hair as they please. Other courts say that students do have a right to dress as they want. For these courts, the question is whether the school officials have an adequate reason to justify the infringement of the students' rights to free expression.

■ Are the rules different for private and parochial schools?

Yes. Private and parochial schools can impose dress or hair codes on students because they are private and not run by the government. The Constitution is designed to protect citizens only against the actions of government and thus is no bar to private schools requiring any kind of dress or hair code.

STUDENT SEARCHES

Several of Bradley's classmates were suspected by the principal of selling drugs. She decided to search their purses and backpacks at random every day.

■ Is the principal or other official of a public school allowed to search a student's purse or backpack?

Yes, under certain circumstances. If the official has a good reason to suspect a particular student, then a search of the student's belongings may be justified. However, students can't be singled out at random for a search. That's the rule established in a 1985 Supreme Court case, *New Jersey v. T.L.O.* That case found that even though teachers and administrators are entitled to maintain discipline in the classroom and on school grounds, students are entitled to some measure of privacy.

■ Can a public school official search a student's locker?

The Supreme Court has not ruled on what standards apply to searches of school lockers. In rulings on the issue by lower courts, some say that schools have an unbridled right to inspect lockers, while others assert that students have a right to expect that their lockers are private. Such searches — as well as searches of desks or other school property provided for storage of student supplies — raise the same question of how much weight to give the student's right to privacy. An important difference, however, is that a locker or desk is school property given to the student for use during the school year, but a purse or backpack is the student's own property. Therefore, if the Supreme Court ever gets the opportunity to decide the issue, it is likely to find that an official's search of a locker or desk requires less justification than the search of a purse or backpack.

■ What about searches at private or parochial schools?

There is an important difference between public and private or parochial schools because the Constitution was written to protect individuals from actions by the government. Therefore, a search can violate the Constitution only if the person conducting it is acting "on behalf" of the government, and the Supreme Court has decided that public school officials are acting on behalf of the government when they search students' belongings. Private school faculty and administrators are not usually acting on behalf of the government and thus are not subject to constitutional prohibitions. They would thus be free to conduct a search any time they wanted to without violating the Constitution. If they were requested to conduct a search by the police, though, that would be a different story, since they would then be acting "on behalf" of the government.

STUDENTS' RIGHT TO FREE EXPRESSION

Bradley wasn't worried about being caught with drugs, since he didn't use any. He was, however, worried about what would happen when the principal read his article for the school paper about the challenge of being a gay teenager. The principal reviewed every issue of the paper before publication, and Bradley feared his story would be censored.

■ Don't public school students have a right to free expression?

Yes, but school officials generally have the right to impose reasonable restrictions. The Supreme Court has ruled that the free speech rights of students in public schools are not necessarily as extensive as the rights of adults in other settings and that a school newspaper is not automatically a forum for public expression — especially if the paper is produced as part of the educational curriculum. If a school authority believes that a student's expression will substantially interfere with the rights of other students or the work of the school, then the expression can be limited.

■ Are these rules the same for private and parochial schools?

No. Once again, because private and parochial schools are not government entities, they may impose regulations more freely than public schools.

THE PLEDGE OF ALLEGIANCE

Bradley announced to his homeroom teacher that he was no longer going to stand up with the rest of the class and say the pledge of allegiance. "My country has shown no loyalty to me," he said. "So I'm through showing loyalty to it." The teacher, a disabled war veteran, was disgusted and told Brad he had no idea what it meant to be patriotic.

■ Are students required to say the pledge of allegiance?

No, nobody is. In 1943, the Supreme Court ruled that it is unconstitutional for federal, state, or local governments to force citizens to salute or pledge allegiance to the flag. In a famous passage of that opinion, *West Virginia State Board of Education v. Barnette,* the court said: "[But if] there is any fixed star in our constitutional constellation, it is that no official, high or petty, can prescribe what shall be orthodox in politics, nationalism, religion or other matters of opinion or force citizens to confess by word or act their faith therein."

PRAYING IN SCHOOL

Grace noticed that Beatrice was singing a song about angels. "Where did you learn that?" she asked. "In Bible class," said Bea. "We sing songs, and then we say a prayer."

■ Are praying and other religious activities allowed in public schools?

No, not during class time and not when such activities are organized or led by public school officials. The Supreme Court has ruled that violates the section of the First Amendment known as the **Establishment Clause**, which prohibits government from "establishing" a religion. The Constitution does not, however, prevent students from meeting on their own to pray. In fact, in 1984, Congress passed a law called the **Equal Access Act**, which requires public schools to allow students who want to do so to meet before and after classes for religious purposes, including prayer. (If all extracurricular activities are prohibited by a school, it can also nix the prayer meetings. Otherwise, it has to allow them if students so desire.)

Note: Some states, including Georgia, have enacted or considered legislation to allow "quiet reflection" by students during school. The constitutionality of such laws is not settled and is likely to face many court challenges.

■ What should a parent do if a public school teacher is giving students Bible lessons?

The first step should be to discuss the matter with either the teacher or the school principal. During such discussions you should point out that the Supreme Court has ruled that teaching Bible lessons in public school classes is prohibited by the Constitution. If the teacher continues to teach these lessons, bring the matter to the attention of the local school board or some other local authority that could influence the teacher to stop. If that doesn't work, you should consider bringing a legal challenge to the teacher's activities, in which case you should consult with a lawyer or with a local chapter of the American Civil Liberties Union to learn what this would entail.

INJURIES AT SCHOOL

When Beatrice was thirteen, all she wanted was to be a star gymnast. She longed to do all the tricks she saw Cathy Rigby do at the Olympics, and she practiced hard. Her favorite event was the trampoline, and she became so good at the forward double flip that she decided to try a back flip without using a safety harness. Her coach was in another part of the gym when the accident happened. Beatrice didn't tuck enough and landed on her neck, causing a severe sprain that put her in a neck brace for six weeks — an eternity of embarrassment for an adolescent.

■ Is the school liable if a child is injured on the premises? Are teachers personally liable?

All school personnel must generally exercise reasonable care at all times. This duty includes maintaining the building, equipment, and playgrounds in reasonably safe condition. However, schools are not required to *guarantee* the safety of students.

In addition, teachers are considered agents of the school and are covered by a school's insurance. In most cases, the school, not the teacher, will be sued for injuries arising from the teacher's acts while working for the school. And in some states, individual teachers are viewed by the law as "standing in" for the parents and thus are protected from negligence actions, including failure to supervise, because in most states, children can't sue their parents for negligence.

When Beatrice recovered, she went back to training with fresh hopes, practiced hard, and made the gymnastic team. On a trip to an away meet, the team's bus swerved as it rounded a corner in the rain, hitting a telephone pole. The girls were thrown against the seats, and some were cut and bruised; the worst injury was one broken arm. Several girls reported to their parents that the driver couldn't have been watching the road carefully because he had been joking and laughing with the students behind him.

■ Is the school liable when children are hurt during an outing?

Possibly. When an injury occurs during a class outing, the school may be liable for failing to supervise students adequately. Again, in some states, teachers are considered to be acting as parents and are therefore protected — as parents are in those states — from negligence actions.

When bus accidents occur, the school may be liable for the negligence of its driver and for its own negligence in hiring a negligent driver. In addition, whoever holds the insurance policy for the bus may be sued, which is often a private bus company, if it is not the school district.

TEAM SPORTS

Much to her mother's surprise (and dismay), Beatrice loved sports — especially football. Her dream, she confided to Grace, was to make the high school varsity team. Grace tried to dissuade her, mostly out of fear of what a bunch of brutes in helmets would do to her sweet Beatrice. Grace didn't need to worry so much, though. It turned out that the coach, Nelson Porterhouse, laughed Beatrice out of the locker room. "A girl on my team? See you later, sweetheart. Go back to home economics. I've got enough sissies as it is."

■ Can a school coach refuse to allow a girl to try out for a sports team?

Maybe. If the sport involved is a noncontact sport, like tennis, federal regulations say that schools that receive federal funds (which includes most public schools and some private schools) generally may sponsor single-sex teams so long as they offer one team for each sex. In other words, it's usually okay to have a boys-only team, so long as the school also has a team for girls. However, if it's not feasible for the school to sponsor a girls' team because there aren't enough students interested in participating, it may not be required to do so.

If a girl wants to try out for an all-boys team in a contact sport like football, her best hope is the Equal Protection Clause of the Fourteenth Amendment to the Constitution, which generally prohibits gender discrimination by government institutions, including public schools. Under the clause, any regulation that does discriminate by gender must be "substantially related" to an "important government interest." The Supreme Court has not decided whether the clause mandates that girls be allowed to try out for school football teams, but many lower courts that have ruled on the issue have said that it does.

Of course, even when the courts have determined that a girl is entitled to try out for the football team, she is not guaranteed a spot on the team if she does not make the cut for reasons that have nothing to do with her gender.

DISABLED CHILDREN

Grace's niece Tanya, eight, had learning disabilities. She could participate in classes, but needed extra attention. However, her school was overcrowded, and her second-grade teacher was unable to give her adequate attention. Tanya flunked and had to go through second grade again.

■ Do disabled children have the right to special classes?

Yes. Under the Individuals with Disabilities Education Act, the federal government supplies funding to help states provide special education. Every state accepts these funds and is required to offer a "free appropriate public education" for all children who have physical, mental, or severe emotional impairments or developmental or learning disabilities. The act requires that the special education for each handicapped child be tailored to the unique needs of that child. If the child's local school district does not offer special classes, the state may also have to bear the costs of transporting the child to a public school that can accommodate the needs of the child.

For more information regarding special education, you can contact:

Disability Rights, Education and Defense Fund
2212 6th Street
Berkeley, CA 94710
510-644-2555

COLLEGE APPLICATIONS

Beatrice was applying to colleges (two state schools and one Ivy). The process was tedious: collecting high school transcripts, getting recommendations, writing essays. She thought she had a good chance of getting into all three schools, but she didn't understand why each application wanted to know her race and religion.

CASE IN POINT

Bakke: "Reverse Discrimination" Reversed?

The most famous of all Supreme Court "reverse discrimination" suits was brought by a would-be medical student named Allen Bakke. In 1973, Bakke had applied to the University of California medical school at Davis. His admissions file showed that he was close to getting in, and might well have made it if he hadn't applied relatively late in the process, when many of the admissions slots had already been filled. His interviewer considered him "a very desirable applicant to the medical school."

At the time, however, several admissions slots had been earmarked for racial and ethnic minorities. While many minority applicants had been admitted through the regular process, Davis had a program in which minority group members could be evaluated by a separate admissions committee. This special committee was allocated sixteen of the one hundred class slots, to fill with people whom they believed would make good doctors, but who were "disadvantaged" in the eyes of the committee. Though a number of whites from disadvantaged backgrounds applied under the program, not one was admitted.

Bakke had applied as a regular candidate, not as a "disadvantaged" one. By the time he applied, no "regular" slots were open, though four of the special minority slots remained. He was rejected. Bakke wrote to the chairman of the admissions committee, protesting that the special program operated as a racial and ethnic quota. He reapplied early the next year, but was rejected a second time. He filed a lawsuit charging that Davis's two-track admissions policy had discriminated against him because he was white.

The case reached the United States Supreme Court. A divided court gave something to both sides. Bakke got his wish: he was admitted to medical school, and the Davis two-track admissions program was declared unconstitutional. The court found that the program completely excluded some people from competition for sixteen slots in the class on the basis of their race, and declared that using race as a requirement was a "suspect classification" and an impermissible one, because it denied equal protection to all applicants under the law.

However, the court stopped short of the blanket ruling against affirmative action programs that Bakke and many of his supporters had argued for. The court did not rule that admissions must be completely colorblind. On the contrary: The court held that racial and ethnic diversity was a permissible goal for universities, and cited Harvard University's admissions program as one in which race or ethnicity could be used to *bolster* a candidate's case for admission, so long as everyone who applied was openly competing for all the possible slots.

As a result, the controversial and often misunderstood case known as *Bakke* moved the goal of affirmative action programs from that of repairing past discrimination through quotas to a goal of diversity without quotas.

Are colleges allowed to ask an applicant's race or religion?

Yes. So long as a college does not discriminate in its admissions policies, it is permitted to ask an applicant's race or religion. Colleges may ask for this information in order to create diverse student bodies. (Colleges are not generally required to have affirmative action programs.) So long as a college considers race or religion as only one admissions factor among many, its decisions will probably not be considered discriminatory.

If you are a minority and a state university — or a private university that receives federal funds — rejects you solely on the basis of your race or religion, you may have a viable claim for discrimination (although it will probably be difficult to prove that race or religion was the *only* reason you were rejected). And if you are a qualified white applicant who is rejected by a college that has a certain number of places reserved in its entering class for members of certain races, you may have a viable claim for reverse discrimination, because the Supreme Court has rejected strict numerical quotas to achieve diversity.

DRIVING

4

GETTING A LICENSE

As the youngest of four siblings, Bradley had been relying on his older brother and sisters for rides everywhere, and he was sick and tired of it, especially since he was always having to do them favors just to get a lift to the movies. So he had big plans for his sixteenth birthday: he was going to the Department of Motor Vehicles to get his driver's license. Or was he? Beatrice and Bart had been teasing him, telling him that people who wear glasses aren't allowed to drive. Was it true? Or maybe it was like the time when he was starting kindergarten and they told him he had to jump on the school bus when it approached their corner, since it wouldn't stop for him.

■ Does everyone have the right to a driver's license?

Driver's licenses are regulated by the states, and each state has its own restrictions. In general, if you pass the tests set up by your state, you get the license. The usual requirements are

- **you must be a certain age (sixteen in most states if you have taken a driver's education course and have parental consent)**
- **you must pass a vision test**
- **you must pass a written test about the laws of the state**
- **you must pass a road driving test**

Most states will allow you to get a learner's permit before you are old enough to get a license.

A driver's license can be revoked or suspended for a number of reasons. Most are driving related (too many traffic violations or drunk driving, for instance), but in some states, like New York, you can also lose your license for advocating the overthrow of the United States government.

Generally, there is no upper age limit on who can be issued a license. However, if a person fails to pass the required tests, the state can deny a renewal.

Many states have agreed to share information about drivers and to honor other states' decisions. Therefore, if you have lost your license in one state, you will probably not be issued another one by any other state.

Registering in a New State

When Beatrice left home to go to college, she was very nervous. She had barely been away from home and suddenly she was driving to the next state to live in a small room with someone she had never met. She had so many details to worry about, but still came up with a new one the week before she left: Would her license be valid in another state? Would she be breaking the law by driving there?

■ Does a person have to get a new license if he or she moves to another state?

It depends. You generally are required to have a license from the state in which you are legally a resident, though many states will honor a license until it expires. But in some, like Virginia, new residents have thirty days to apply for a new license. After that, they are considered to be driving without a license.

HAVING AN ACCIDENT

The Fault and No-Fault Systems

Max and Beatrice got into a fender-bender while they were having a heated argument over directions. Max knew that he had taken the left turn without looking carefully enough at the traffic, and now the angry driver of a red BMW with a broken headlight was coming up to them

with a notebook, ready to chew him out and take down his name, address, registration, and insurance numbers.

Does the person who causes a fender-bender always have to pay for the other party's damages?

No. States have developed two main ways of dealing with damages arising from such comparatively minor run-ins: **fault** and **no-fault** systems. Under a no-fault system, it doesn't matter which driver made the crucial mistake that caused an accident. Instead of recovering from the other driver's insurance carrier, you recover from your own insurance company, *regardless of who caused the accident.* Under a fault system, one side admits to (or is proved to bear) the blame for an accident, and any damages are paid for by his or her insurer or by the negligent individual.

What kinds of accidents are covered by no-fault?

No-fault systems vary widely. Most states that use no-fault rely on it for minor property damage and personal injury claims and then revert to a fault system for serious injuries. No state is entirely no-fault.

CASE IN POINT

An "Accident" That Never Really Happened

When a drunken sailor leans out of his car and intentionally shoots and injures the driver of another car, does that constitute an "accident" under the sailor's automobile liability insurance policy? That was the question in a 1993 California case involving the State Farm Mutual Automobile Insurance Company, the drunken sailor and his cohorts, and the unfortunate victims of the shooting.

The events began when Charles Keukelaar was driving on a California highway with his pregnant wife, Shellie. Their trip in late November of 1984 should have been uneventful, but they had the misfortune of passing a van containing three inebriated Marines.

During the trip, one Marine, Walter Davis, had been firing his gun at various objects along the road. When he spotted the Keukelaars' black Corvette, he told Brian Painter, the driver, to overtake it. As Painter pulled up behind the Corvette, Davis blasted a single shot into the rear window, hitting Charles Keukelaar in the head and seriously wounding him. Keukelaar's unhurt wife was able to steer the car to a stop.

The three Marines were subsequently arrested, and Davis and Painter were convicted of felony assault. The Keukelaars then brought a civil suit against them for damages and won. They agreed not to pursue payment directly from Davis and Painter so long as Davis would assign them the right to collect the damages from his car insurer, something he could do if he had injured them in an automobile accident.

There was one slight glitch, however. The insurer, State Farm Mutual Automobile Insurance, refused to pay, contending that, under the policy's language, Davis (and Painter, as an additionally insured driver) was covered only for accidents. Driving drunk on an interstate and brazenly shooting unsuspecting motorists was no accident, State Farm contended.

In 1993, nearly nine years after the shooting, a California federal appeals court upheld a lower court's dismissal of the case, agreeing with State Farm that once the Marines were convicted there was no way the incident could be labeled accidental. Indeed, a California state appeals court, in upholding Painter's assault conviction, noted that he had "deliberately pursued another vehicle at the behest of a companion he knew to be armed, drunk and dangerous . . . Having chosen to risk making the crime possible, he cannot escape responsibility."

■ How does a no-fault claim work?

Claims under no-fault are submitted to your own auto insurance company. The guidelines and limitations of coverage vary from state to state. Generally speaking, you can collect from your insurer even if the other party caused the accident and is insured. Whether you can recover for totaling your car depends on the no-fault limits in your state.

■ How does a fault system work?

Most states use a fault system. If you are involved in an auto collision caused by the negligence of another driver, your damages are paid by that driver's liability insurer. Of course, you may not agree about whose fault the accident was. In such cases, the question may have to be determined by a judge or a jury if you cannot settle it with the other party.

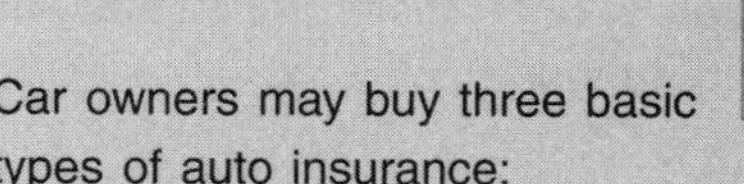

Types of Auto Insurance

Car owners may buy three basic types of auto insurance:

Collision insurance. Covers loss or damage to *your* vehicle caused by accidental collision with another vehicle or object.

Liability insurance. Covers property and personal injury damages to *someone else* when you are at fault.

Medical expense insurance. Covers hospital and doctor bills for *your own injuries.* These may also be covered by your health insurance provider. (The latter insurer can then turn around and sue another insurer or individual who might be liable for your injuries; this prerogative is called a "subrogation right" in your contract with your provider.)

Most states require all drivers to have a certain level of *liability* insurance. Collision and medical coverage are optional. Of course, these laws do not fully protect drivers from people who are irresponsible and drive with no insurance or with insurance that has expired.

(For general insurance information, see Chapter 8, INSURANCE.)

If the other driver proves that *you* are at fault for the collision, his or her damages will be paid by *your* insurer, up to the limits of your policy. Your own damages are covered by other portions of your insurance policy, such as collision insurance (see the box at left).

■ What happens when the insurance of the person at fault doesn't fully cover the other person's damages?

It depends on whether the negligent person has enough assets to cover the damages. If you think he or she does, you can sue the person directly and attempt to recover, but that entails hiring a lawyer, and the case may not be worth the expense. If the person is partially insured and poor, you're probably out of luck.

You can also protect yourself in advance by getting "underinsurance coverage" in your own insurance policy, which pays for uncovered damage by other drivers who take out only bare-minimum insurance. This will fill the gap between what the other guy can pay and what you're shelling out for repairs or medical bills.

Uninsured Drivers

Max was in a second accident. This time, the other driver had run a stop sign and was clearly at fault. However, she also was uninsured. (Actually, she just hadn't bothered to renew her policy.) Max couldn't believe she was so blasé.

■ What happens when an insured driver has an accident with an uninsured person, and the accident is the other's fault?

In a no-fault state, your insurer automatically covers you. In other states, there are different sanctions for not having insurance. In some states, it is illegal not to have any insurance. If you have a collision with an uninsured driver and the police are called, the state may fine or even arrest the person.

You can protect yourself against such expensive run-ins by making sure that your own policy contains "uninsured motorist coverage," which allows

If You're Involved in an Access Accident

- Stay calm. Make safety your primary concern.
- After a minor accident, pull off the road. Don't block traffic.
- In a serious accident, when a car is disabled or there are injuries, leave vehicles in place.
- Administer first aid and call an ambulance, if needed.
- Call the police whenever there is personal injury or serious damage to the vehicles.
- Use flares and flag traffic away from the scene until police arrive.
- Drivers should exchange key information: name, address, insurance company, policy number, driver's license number, license plate number, and registration.
- Do not make any admission of fault to police or other drivers.
- Cooperate with the police if they are on the scene.

Should the police be called to the scene? You're almost always better off doing so, but it's not a legal requirement. In any significant accident, drivers are required by law to file a report with their state motor vehicle bureau. If someone is injured in the accident, you definitely should call the police to the scene and get a written report.

Sometimes, of course, people settle minor fender-benders — especially those that incur less damage than is included in their insurance deductibles — by themselves. If you do this, however, be sure to get the other party to sign a letter releasing you from any further liability.

you to make a claim for damages by the uninsured. Some states also maintain an uninsured motorist fund, which you can apply to if you have damages that are not covered. There will, however, be a limit to how much you can collect.

■ If a driver's insurance payment is overdue, and he gets in an accident, is he covered?

Probably. While coverage depends on the terms of an individual contract, insurance regulations require the insurer to continue coverage until you receive notice of cancellation. Even after notice, state law may impose additional requirements on the insurance company before it can cancel your coverage.

Suing Your Spouse

Max backed out of the garage too quickly — right into the side of Beatrice's car. Repairing the damage to the door cost $300.

■ Can one spouse sue the other for damages?

Yes. A majority of states have eliminated the rule that one spouse may not sue the other. (A growing number of states have also eliminated the rule prohibiting suits between parent and child.) *However,* automobile insurance policies frequently contain family or household exclusion clauses, which prohibit a family member from collecting on a claim from the same company against another family member. A few states have invalidated these clauses, enabling a couple who go through an accident together to collect more insurance than they could have if only one was permitted to file a claim. So, in those states, if a husband is driving with his wife as passenger, and he stops short and she is injured, she can file a claim to recover her damages from their insurance company.

When You Lend Your Car to a Friend

Blossom wanted to impress the owners of a company she was hoping to do business with, so she borrowed her friend Anne's Porsche to drive to an interview. The meeting was a success, but on her way home Blossom was involved in a minor accident that caused several hundred dollars' worth of damage to the front end of the car. Blossom insisted it was the other driver's fault; he blamed her.

■ **Who's responsible when a person has an accident while driving a friend's car?**

The owner's auto insurance coverage extends to use of the car by a friend *if* the friend was driving with the owner's permission. Generally, this includes liability, collision, and medical expense coverage.

When Your Passenger Is a Friend or Relative

Beatrice, Blossom, and her friend Anne were on the way to the movies in Blossom's beat-up Buick. She was gunning to make a yellow light, when a dog ran into the road, causing her to stomp on the brakes. Anne's head smashed into the windshield, causing a concussion, and Beatrice slammed against the back door, dislocating her shoulder.

■ **Can a passenger recover damages against the driver for negligence if they are friends or relatives?**

Usually. In most states, there is no prohibition against negligence suits between friends or relatives, so they can recover damages against each other. (In a few states, however, spouses cannot sue their partners, nor can parents and children sue each other. Therefore, they cannot claim damages against each other, either.)

CASE IN POINT

Love Means Never Having to Say "I'm Suing" — Or Does It?

The right to sue a member of your immediate family varies from state to state. In most of these cases, the relatives aren't mad at each other, nor are they seeking revenge: they simply want to collect insurance money and are forced to sue to recover.

In the 1978 case of the colliding Coffindaffers, however, a West Virginia couple crunched cars during a tense period in which they were awaiting the outcome of their divorce suit. Even though Mr. Coffindaffer was apparently at fault, he got out of his car and allegedly assaulted his injured wife, causing (she claimed) even more injuries. She sued him, but he argued that he was shielded by "interspousal immunity," which prevents spouses from suing each other. Her complaint was dismissed, but she appealed and won before the state supreme court, which allowed her to proceed with her suit.

Many other states, such as Nevada, have also overturned old laws that prevented such lawsuits. In 1974, the Nevada Supreme Court considered two related cases: In one, a wife sued her husband after being injured in an accident in which she was the passenger and he was the driver. In the other case, a minor child sued his own mother after being injured in a car she was driving. The state supreme court reversed previous cases which held that family members could not sue each other, and allowed the cases to proceed.

But there is another factor to consider. Some states have acted to limit the liability of all drivers to all passengers, not just relatives or friends. To accomplish this, some states have lowered the **standard of care** owed by drivers to passengers — that is, the degree of care a reasonable person would take to prevent an injury to another. In these states a passenger might be required to prove that the accident was caused by **gross negligence**, such as reckless driving or willful disregard for safety. For example, an injury caused by drivers drag racing on a public highway is likely a case of gross negligence, while one caused by skidding on a slippery road would be merely **negligent**.

Courts are divided as to the constitutionality of this type of statute that protects drivers from their own passengers. But whenever a state legislature has attempted to abolish all lawsuits by guest passengers against drivers, these statutes have been held unconstitutional.

Seatbelts

Blossom was also hurt in the accident (she sprained her arm), but she was worried that the insurance company wouldn't pay her medical expenses if they found out she hadn't been wearing her seatbelt.

Can a driver or passenger recover money damages if he or she was not wearing a seatbelt?

Yes. Judges have generally ruled that failure to use a seatbelt does not cause accidents and therefore could not have been the primary cause of a person's injury. However, a significant number of states do consider the failure to wear a seatbelt as one factor when setting the amount of damages. The reasoning is that a person's injury would not have occurred or would have been significantly less if he or she had buckled up.

Comparative and Contributory Negligence

Within one month of buying a new car, Beatrice had a dent. It was small, but costly and annoying, all the more so because she knew she was partly at fault. While driving in the country on a beautiful fall afternoon, she and another driver had crunched into each other at low speed in an uncontrolled intersection while gazing at the foliage. Both admitted being at fault.

What happens if both drivers involved in an accident were negligent?

If it's a no-fault state, each driver collects from his or her own insurer. In a fault state, it depends on whether the state where it occurred applies the rule of **contributory** negligence, which prevents recovery, or the rule of **comparative** negligence. In a contributory negligence state, one driver cannot recover from the other unless he or she bore no fault whatsoever for the accident. If both were partly at fault, neither driver can recover from the other. Their only recourse would be their own insurance, which may or may not cover such a situation, depending on how the policy is written.

Comparative negligence is more flexible, allowing drivers to recover some portion of the damages caused by the other's negligence. Usually the case will go to trial and a jury will decide how much each person will receive in damages, or the lawyers for each side will work out a settlement with the insurers.

Warning: Pedestrian Crossing

Gordon and Grace were walking to the park with their old dog, Terry. The dog was getting impatient and pulled at the leash so hard that Gordon crossed against the light. As Grace looked on horrified, a car swerved to avoid the dog and hit Gordon, who sustained a broken rib and some bruises.

■ Is a driver negligent if he hits a pedestrian who crosses against the light?

A pedestrian crossing a street is required to exercise reasonable care for his or her own safety. Although disregard of a crossing signal is not automatically negligent, a walker who, like Gordon, ignores a signal may be found partly or even totally negligent depending on the circumstances.

■ What if the pedestrian crosses in the middle of the street where there is no crosswalk or signal?

Generally, pedestrians are entitled to cross in the middle of the street. However, they are required to exercise a greater degree of care when doing so. Where there are laws prohibiting jaywalking — which the dictionary defines as "crossing the street carelessly or in an illegal manner" — some courts have ruled that a violation automatically constitutes negligence. Most states take the position that the jaywalker may be found partly negligent, depending on the circumstances surrounding the accident.

GETTING STOPPED BY THE POLICE

Blossom was driving with some friends to a bluegrass festival way out in the country. They were having a fine old time until a police car pulled them over. Blossom was confused: she hadn't been speeding, and there was nothing wrong with her car. What did he want?

It turned out that the policeman was looking for something. After he took her driver's license and registration, he looked them all up and down carefully and even shined his flashlight into the back windows for a long time, as though he knew something illegal was there. Blossom realized — as they all did — that he suspected them of having drugs in the car. But why them? All they'd been doing was smoking cigarettes, laughing, talking, and singing along with the radio. Surely that wasn't enough to stop and search anyone, or arrest them? She became very scared, and her friends, who had all been so uproariously happy, looked at each other in terror.

■ Can a driver be stopped for no reason — say, the officer was bored or felt like issuing a ticket?

No. The stopping of a motor vehicle is considered a "seizure" under the Fourth and Fourteenth Amendments to the U.S. Constitution. Therefore, a vehicle may be stopped and its occupants detained only if the officer has a "reasonable belief" that a crime is being (or has been) committed by the driver or passengers. Once these reasonable grounds exist, the officer may stop and approach the vehicle in order to investigate. A "crime" doesn't have to be something major, like a robbery. Even a burned-out headlight is enough justification for a pull-over unless you can somehow prove it was used just as a pretext to search you for another crime.

■ Can the police search a person's car without permission?

Not unless they have probable cause (see page 210 and the box on page 211), which is harder to prove than reasonable belief. The Fourth Amendment area of police searches and seizures is complex and detailed, and is in a constant state of flux. Many state courts apply different standards of probable cause and reasonable belief.

With that said, it is possible to make a few generalizations. In order to search your car, an officer must have probable cause to do so. He may look in through the windows all he wants, but he can't get inside and rummage around or demand that you open your trunk (see the Case in Point on page 213). To arrest you, he must have probable cause, and he must also have probable cause to make you open your trunk.

However, anything suspicious that the officer sees, such as an open beer can or a baggie with white powder in it, may be seized without a warrant if it is in "plain view" when the officer looks through the window. Also, the officer is free to ask you to open the trunk of the car. If you agree, you have consented to a search. However, if the officer has no warrant or probable cause, you are free to refuse.

CASE IN POINT

Why Your Car Is Not Your Castle

While citizens have a high degree of privacy rights in their homes, they have far fewer protections when they get into their cars. Since 1925, the police have been allowed to stop, search, and seize on the roads without a warrant — *if* they have a clearcut reason to be suspicious. Nevertheless, thousands of defendants contest police actions in such searches, arguing that the circumstances in their cases did not justify the police search.

For instance, can a police officer open a closed container found in a car without getting a warrant? That was the issue in a 1991 U.S. Supreme Court case, *California v. Acevedo.* After the Santa Ana police department and the Drug Enforcement Administration had intercepted a Federal Express package containing marijuana, they set up a sting that caught one of the buyers of the marijuana, Charles Steven Acevedo, as he drove away from an apartment where he had apparently bought the drug. The police observed him putting a sealed paper bag the same size as the shipment into his trunk. Without obtaining a warrant, they stopped Acevedo, searched his trunk, and opened the bag, which was indeed full of marijuana. The Supreme Court later held that the police had established probable cause to search his trunk and the sealed bag. Key to that finding was the fact that Acevedo's bag was the same size as the specific drug shipment.

The police do not have the blanket right to search *any* closed container found in a car, however. For example, in a 1993 Colorado case, a car was stopped for a routine traffic violation. The officer spotted a syringe on the floor and asked the occupants if either of them had diabetes. When they replied no, he searched the car and opened the purse of one of the passengers, where he found illegal drugs. The owner of the purse was arrested, tried, and convicted for possession of a controlled substance. An appeals court later found that the search was illegal, ruling that while there was probable cause to permit a general search of the car, the officer did not have a particular reason to believe there were drugs in that particular purse.

DRUNK DRIVING

It was very late, and there were few cars on the road. Bart was in a great mood as he drove home from an office Christmas party. There had been a lot of Christmas cheer — so much in fact that Bart was swerving the car from side to side in time to the radio's sounds of "Jinglebell Rock."

To his dismay he saw the telltale flash of red behind him. He pulled over, and the officer approached with his mouth set in a grim line. Bart sat up straight, smoothed down his hair, and tried to look as calm and sober as possible.

In those few moments before the officer reached his car Bart tried to recall how many drinks he'd had — was it one, two, three, or more? What about that punch — had it been more spiked than he'd realized? He thought dimly that he wasn't sure whether he could pass a breath test.

Bart hated drunk drivers. A friend's daughter had been killed by one. He also hated the thought of losing his license, and he was planning to run for public office. He couldn't afford any bad publicity. He couldn't think straight as his anxiety mounted.

■ What is the legal definition of "drunk driving"?

The legal definitions of "driving" and "drunk" are open to many interpretations, which vary subtly from state to state. In some places, "driving" can include sitting still in a parked vehicle with the motor off or starting up a car in a driveway. Police can and do arrest people whom they believe are drunk before they get on the road and even when they've pulled off to "sleep it off," if they're in the driver's seat.

As for the definition of "drunk," there are several major factors to consider. You can be "legally impaired" in the eyes of the law without ever taking a drink, if you have taken other substances (including prescribed medication) that affect your ability to drive. You can also be found drunk even when you have all your faculties in perfect working order.

In short, you can be found guilty of drunk driving, also called driving while intoxicated (DWI) or driving under the influence (DUI), if the state can prove one of two things:

- that you are **legally intoxicated** while driving, meaning that your body shows alcohol levels above a state-mandated limit. The most common level is **.10 percent**, as determined by a blood test or breath test, although in some states the level is lower. (In Colorado, for instance, you are legally impaired if your alcohol level is .05 percent.) For drivers of commercial vehicles, the level may be even lower. (See the box at left.)
- that you have been driving while your faculties are **impaired** by alcohol or a drug — that is, that your ability to see, hear, walk, talk, and judge distances is below normal as set by the state you're arrested in. Even if your alcohol level is lower than the legal intoxication level, you can still be convicted if the state can show your abilities were impaired.

What's the Legal Limit?

Blood tests measure the number of grams of alcohol per 100 milliliters of blood, and breath tests measure grams of alcohol per 210 liters of breath. In most states, you can be convicted of drunk driving when either level is at .10 percent or higher. But remember, you can be convicted based on other factors even if you don't take the test.

State legislatures have justified these levels on the basis of scientific testing, which has concluded that persons having a blood alcohol content at or above .10 percent are impaired. (In some states, such as California and Florida, the level of impairment is .08 percent, and many other states are considering adopting this standard.) So, if the state can prove that at the time a person operated a motor vehicle his or her blood alcohol level was above the legal limit, a conviction for drunk driving may be possible.

The police also may sometimes be able to require that you take a blood test to determine if you have been using drugs. Even if you have taken a legally prescribed dose of medication, you can be convicted if you are found to be impaired.

Roadside Tests

The cop asked Bart to get out of the car. Bart hesitated, thinking how he'd heard once that you don't have to take any tests if you absolutely don't want to. And he wondered if the police could really make him do all those silly things he'd seen on TV, like try to touch his nose or walk a straight line.

What kinds of tests for impairment can the police ask a person to take by the side of the road?

Any type they want. They could, for instance, ask you to sing the national anthem. However, the commonly used types of "field sobriety tests" include

- **the "one-leg stand" (the driver must stand on one leg for approximately thirty seconds)**
- **the "heel-to-toe" test (walking heel to toe in a straight line)**
- **the "bend test" (the driver must bend forward or backward with eyes closed)**

Some police will ask a driver to recite the alphabet or count backward. These and other tests may be conducted again at the police station in greater detail.

In most states, including Colorado and Florida, you can refuse to take the roadside tests without suffering any penalty. Even so, if the officer observes the smell of alcohol, bloodshot eyes, bad balance, slurred speech, or other signs of intoxication, he usually has enough **probable cause** to believe you are impaired, and therefore can arrest you on a charge of drunk driving. (For more on probable cause, see page 196.) However, in some circumstances, your refusal to take roadside tests could be used against you in court, although it will not be evidence enough to convict you.

■ Can a person be arrested on the road merely because the police officer claimed to smell alcohol on his or her breath?

While the odor may not be enough to warrant an arrest, that fact combined with others, such as bloodshot or watery eyes, slurred speech, or the manner of driving prior to the stop, may give the officer probable cause to arrest the driver.

■ What happens when an officer asks a person to take a roadside breath test?

In a roadside test, also known as a preliminary breath test, an officer gets an immediate measurement of your alcohol level by asking you to breathe into a specially designed bag or a tube. The test does not usually substitute for a formal blood or Breathalyzer test, but it can be used to determine that enough probable cause exists to arrest you. You may refuse to take the test, but that won't prevent the officer from arresting you if there is enough other evidence that you are drunk.

Breathalyzer Tests

The police officer took Bart to the station and into a room, where he was told he'd be taking a Breathalyzer test. Another officer put a plastic tube into his mouth and asked him to breathe out. Bart, who was pretty scared, hesitated for a second before letting out his breath. Should he risk saying no and angering the officer? Would he stand a better chance with a court if he didn't take the test? Should he call a lawyer?

■ Can a person refuse to take the Breathalyzer test at the station?

You can, but it is not a good idea. Your refusal may make it harder for the prosecution to obtain a conviction, but because of the trend to greater stringency you can still be convicted on the basis of the roadside tests and other police testimony. You don't even have the right to a lawyer at this point in the process, because a breath or blood sample is considered "nontestimonial" evidence.

In an attempt to ensure compliance, all states have adopted what are known as **implied consent**

Biking Under the Influence

You don't have to be operating a car to be guilty of driving under the influence. So learned Lee Brown, the defendant in a 1993 Pennsylvania case.

Brown was riding her bicycle the wrong way up a one-way street in Clairton when she hit a car that had swerved to avoid her. After the officer at the scene smelled alcohol on her breath, Brown consented to a blood alcohol test, which revealed that she was severely intoxicated. She was charged with driving a vehicle while intoxicated, but a local judge dismissed the charge on the ground that a bicycle was not a "vehicle" within the meaning of state law. The Superior Court of Pennsylvania reversed, however, holding that a bicycle did qualify as a vehicle and noted that the law prohibited the operators of all vehicles, not just motorized ones, from driving under the influence of alcohol.

(also called **express consent**) laws that apply to testing for alcohol in the blood, breath, or urine, and most states also have such laws that apply to testing for the use of drugs. The principle underlying these laws is that any licensed driver who operates a vehicle has *implicitly* (that is, without stating it) consented to submit to approved tests for purposes of detecting alcohol or other chemical substances to show intoxication.

Nonetheless, even with these "implied consent" laws, you may still refuse to take a breath, blood, or urine test, *but* the state can punish you for such a refusal with higher fines or jail terms. In many states you also risk having your license revoked quickly, after a summary hearing, simply because you refused. You can be convicted even if you were sober and refused to cooperate because you objected to the police show of power.

The drawbacks of refusal don't stop there: If you refuse, go to trial, and are convicted, your penalty often will be harsher than if you agreed to cooperate and take the test. You will probably lose your driving privilege for six to eighteen months, depending on whether it is your first refusal or not.

■ Under what circumstances would the police ask for a blood or urine sample rather than a breath test?

Whenever there is serious injury or death as the result of an accident, police will want to get a blood sample from drivers because such tests are more scientifically solid than breath tests and will stand up better in court. State statutes and judicial interpretations of an individual's right to due process generally require that blood be drawn by medical personnel — usually at a hospital or other medical facility.

Because drugs are more easily traced in urine than in blood, someone arrested on suspicion of impairment through drugs may be asked to take a urine test. Since this is not an "invasive procedure" like a blood test and does not require special training to administer, it may sometimes be done at the police station rather than at a hospital.

CARS, ALCOHOL, AND PUNISHMENT

Bart's friend Jill lost a daughter in a drunk driving accident. Jill had told him that both the driver and her daughter were taken from the scene to the hospital; her daughter died en route. The driver, still drunk, had fought the police tooth and nail and had to be held down to allow the nurse to get his blood sample.

■ Can a driver involved in an accident where someone is injured or killed refuse a blood test?

In these instances, a person's right to refuse a test is severely restricted. If the police have probable cause to believe that a driver is impaired, they can and do use a reasonable amount of force to require the driver to submit to a blood test. While this test must be performed by medical personnel, the fact remains that the police have the right in this situation to apply force.

In addition to drunk driving penalties, a driver involved in a fatal accident could face criminal charges of assault, manslaughter, and even homicide. There may also be civil penalties.

■ What are the typical penalties for drunk driving?

A conviction for drunk driving usually carries with it some stiff penalties. And while these penalties will vary from state to state, they will generally entail the loss of a driver's license for a specified amount of time, a fine, and possibly jail time (see the box on page 32). Other penalties may include probation, community service, driver rehabilitation school, and substance abuse counseling.

The high-profile get-tough policy has developed because drunk driving has been targeted as a terrible social problem that has potential for improvement. Organizations such as Mothers Against Drunk Driving (MADD), led by parents who have lost children in drunk driving accidents, have been extremely effective in stirring public outrage and lobbying for tougher laws.

Drunk Driving Penalties

Penalties vary sharply by state, but in all cases they are highest for accidents in which others are injured or killed, and for repeat offenders. Sometimes a driver is jailed on a manslaughter charge immediately after a fatal crash, if there is probable cause to believe the driver was drunk.

As for postconviction sentences, some states have statutes requiring mandatory jail time — ranging from forty-eight consecutive hours to two years — for a drunk driving conviction for anyone whose drinking caused a death or an injury. Some states also require driving school and alcohol or drug rehabilitation, and in some cases judges may sentence offenders to do community service in emergency rooms and morgues.

The following shows a general range of penalties imposed after conviction on drivers who were arrested in accidents or in incidents *in which there were no injuries or major damage:*

For a first conviction with no injury or major damage:

1. A fine ranging from $100 to $5,000, and/or
2. Imprisonment for up to two years, and/or
3. Loss of driving privilege for a certain period of time (usually ranging from thirty days to three years)

For a second conviction on a similar charge:

1. A fine ranging from $200 to $5,000, and/or
2. Imprisonment up to two years, and/or
3. Loss of driving privilege for up to five years

For a third conviction on a similar charge:

1. A fine ranging from $300 to $150,000 and/or
2. Imprisonment for up to six years, and/or
3. Loss of driving privilege for 180 days to a permanent revocation.

Their success has been aided by the fact that possessing a driver's license and operating a motor vehicle is *not a right* of every citizen, but a privilege extended by the state in which you live. The license is issued under a state's regulation, and a state may revoke it. The courts have given police wide discretion when dealing with the enforcement of motor vehicle laws. A citizen usually has fewer rights when driving a car than when walking on the street or residing at home.

Insurance Rates

In addition to all his other woes — his license was suspended for six months, he paid a $500 fine, and he had to go to a rehabilitative driving school — Bart found out a few weeks after his conviction that his insurance company was raising his rates! He was incensed. Surely that was unconstitutional?

Can an insurer legally raise a person's rates because of a drunk driving conviction?

Yes. A very costly aspect of a conviction for drunk driving is the price of insurance. Basically, insurers can charge sky-high fees and raise the rates of convicted drivers. In some states — New Jersey, for example — a person convicted of drunk driving must pay a mandatory $1,000 per year auto insurance payment for three consecutive years, in addition to any court-imposed penalties and fines. This is added to the increase that will inevitably — and legally — occur in a driver's automobile insurance premiums.

Your Rights When You're Stopped by the Police

A police officer is motioning you to pull over. What are your rights?

You may refuse to

- take a roadside test in most states without suffering a penalty. In some states, though, a refusal can be presented as evidence against you in court.
- take a breath test — but in many states refusal will result in automatic suspension of your license. And in every state, you can still be convicted of drunk driving on other grounds (see page 28).
- give permission for a search of your trunk or car interior if the police have no probable cause to conduct the search (see also page 27). You should not be intimidated by the police into giving consent when you really don't want them to do a search — even if you've got nothing to hide. If the police ignore your refusal and search anyway, you will have a strong argument that anything they found cannot be used against you.

You may not refuse to

- stop your car.
- give blood or urine samples when you have been involved in an accident with major damage or injury. The police may apply force to help medical personnel take the sample (see page 31).

You have no say at all when

- the police have probable cause to search your car. In this case, they won't ask permission (see page 27). An unopened six-pack on the front seat usually won't give them probable cause to search, but the smell of marijuana will.
- the police search the interior from the outside with their flashlights, see something illegal, and seize it (see page 27).
- the police stop and frisk you *if* they have a "reasonably articulable suspicion" that you may be carrying weapons, drugs, or other contraband (see the Case in Point on page 213).

Challenging a Drunk Driving Charge

Bart had some regrets about how he'd handled his case. He had decided not to plead guilty, had defended himself, and had lost. Afterward, he wondered what else he could have done. He most regretted not hiring a lawyer.

What is the best way to prevent a conviction?

There are ways to challenge a drunk driving charge, but it will be difficult to prevail and will require expensive legal advice and possibly the payment of an expert. Success in court is rare. As a result, most drunk driving charges result in guilty pleas.

For those who decide to take it to the mat, it is important to remember that if you fight and lose, a judge will sometimes impose higher penalties. But if after hearing all this, you still want to fight (you may, after all, be not guilty), here are some ways that others have occasionally succeeded:

- You can challenge the Breathalyzer test you took, alleging it was improperly administered or malfunctioned. However, be aware that this is becoming much more difficult to do because the test, which used to be mechanical, is now digital and more reliable.
- You can challenge a roadside test as improperly performed or inconclusive, or offer it as proof that you were sober.
- You can argue that your alcohol level was rising, not falling, at the time of your Breathalyzer test at the station. This is generally a last-ditch attempt at defense by repeat offenders; after a driver has had two or three convictions, is in danger of

losing his license, and faces serious jail time, he or she may decide it's worth it to fight with this tactic, which is costly but sometimes meets with success.

Here is the logic behind this defense: The body metabolizes alcohol at varying rates. Levels fall and rise with time as the effects wear off. If your level at the station was just a tad over the legal limit of .10 percent — say, .12 percent or .11 percent — you can argue that it had *risen* in your blood in just the time it took to go from roadside to the station. So you argue that it was *lower* than the legal limit when you were stopped, and you were not drunk driving on the road. You will in all likelihood need an expert to testify whether the Breathalyzer level showed a rising or falling level, and the state will enlist its own expert to refute yours. These freelance experts can be very expensive; one well-known expert in Florida flies around the country on these cases and charges $10,000 to a defendant for an appearance.

Drunk Driving Accidents

Beatrice and Max spent New Year's Eve at a local nightclub with several of their friends. One of them, Bob, had been drinking heavily, encouraged by the bartender, whose favorite line was "Go ahead, have one more. Tomorrow's a holiday." As Bob was driving home, he swerved into another car, severely injuring the driver and killing her six-year-old son.

Is a nightclub liable if a drunk patron causes an accident?

Yes. Many states impose liability on commercial vendors of alcohol, including package stores, bars, and taverns, for injury to others caused by drunk patrons. In some states, a vendor has a duty to withhold liquor to prevent a customer from injuring himself or others.

CASE IN POINT

Am I My Drunken Friend's Keeper?

This case might make you think twice about getting your friends loaded at your next party — especially if you live in New Jersey. After work one night, Donald Gwinnell drove over to the home of his friend Joseph Zak in northern New Jersey and had a few drinks with Zak and his wife. Afterward Zak walked Gwinnell out to his car and watched as he drove off. About twenty-five minutes later, Zak called Gwinnell's home to see whether he had gotten home safely. Mrs. Gwinnell told him that her husband had been involved in a head-on collision with someone who had been seriously injured, named Marie Kelly. Gwinnell's injuries were minor.

Kelly later sued Gwinnell and the Zaks for damages, charging that the Zaks had negligently allowed Gwinnell to drive home drunk. Gwinnell's blood showed a blood alcohol concentration of .286 percent after the accident — an amount equal to thirteen drinks, according to the plaintiff's expert. Despite this, the case against the Zaks was dismissed.

Kelly appealed, and in a two-part ruling the New Jersey Supreme Court in 1984 found that the Zaks were indeed liable because they had known, or should have known, that letting Gwinnell drive home drunk would endanger others. Second, the court ruled for the first time ever that a social host serving liquor has a duty to the public at large not to allow guests to drive away drunk. If he does so, he can be held liable for any damages. The decision did not spell out what a host must do if a guest ignores a host and insists on driving home, as one judge pointed out in his dissent.

Many other state courts, however, have rejected New Jersey's rule, leaving it up to state legislatures to write new laws concerning social hosts.

Known as "dram shop" laws, these types of rules also establish limits to liability by spelling out what a plaintiff must prove to file suit. They require that a plaintiff establish "proximate cause" between an injury and a specific act of drinking at the establishment being sued. In most cases, the plaintiff must also prove that alcohol was served or sold to a visibly intoxicated patron. The burden is less if it is proved that the alcohol was sold to a minor, which is, of course, illegal.

■ What if the drunk driver was served alcohol at a friend's house, not a bar?

A few states impose liability on social hosts, but only for injuries on the premises. In other states, people who serve alcohol to drivers who then injure others on the road may be held liable as well.

If a drunk person injures *himself* at a party, the host won't be liable for damages. But if the drunk person hurts someone else or damages the house, the host may be liable. These kinds of cases, while highly publicized, are still rare, and it should be noted that most of them have been decided in favor of the host.

RENTING A HOUSE OR AN APARTMENT 5

THE LEASE

After finishing college, Beatrice and her friend Renata decided they would get an apartment together. They found a sunny, two-bedroom unit owned by Ray and Sue, a friendly older couple, who lived on the ground floor of the three-story building. Ray and Sue thought the two young women were perfectly charming, well-scrubbed college graduates and agreed to rent them the apartment for one year at $600 a month. They shook hands and drank a wine cooler toast.

■ Should a lease be in writing?

Yes. It's possible that a landlord-tenant relationship can be totally harmonious and that there will never be any dispute about what each side's rights and responsibilities are. Possible, but rare. A month after Beatrice and Renata moved in, for example, Sue presented them with utility bills for heat and electricity. Beatrice said she was sure Ray had said that utilities were included in the rent. Sue then noticed Renata's pet poodle. "No way," said Sue. "No pets."

A written lease could have saved everybody a lot of problems. It doesn't need to be a fancy document, but it should address all the issues that are important to both landlord and tenant. At a minimum it should include

- **the names of the landlord and tenant(s)**
- **a description of the leased premises ("123 Broadway, Apt. 2, Anycity, Anystate, Anyzip")**
- **the duration of the lease**
- **the amount of the rent**

It's best, however, if the lease deals with other issues too, such as when the rent is due, how much is required for a security deposit (see page 46), not to mention who pays the utilities and whether pets are allowed.

You can write a lease on a piece of scrap paper. Most of the time, though, landlords have preprinted form leases (often available at stationery stores). These are typically long, wordy documents with lots of scary-looking language (although many states now prohibit the use of legalese and complicated phrases). However, a lot of it makes sense if you read it carefully. If you don't understand something, ask the person who gave you the lease. If you disagree with something, see if it's possible to negotiate. (You can then cross out or reword a provision — just have each party initial the changes.) Most important, if the form lease doesn't address an issue at all, write in your own provision.

If a dispute lands you in court (see page 41), will the court require that the lease be in writing? The answer to this question depends on the term of the lease and also on the laws of your jurisdiction. While your tenancy may be governed by an oral agreement, in most states an agreement to lease property must be in writing if it is for one year or more. And if an agreement is not in writing, all sorts of disputes over its terms are possible. For instance, is the rent to go up every six months? Are dogs prohibited, but cats and canaries allowed? When does the lease actually expire? The point is that both in court and out, a written document that spells out what each side must do makes resolving disputes much easier. So it's not the law that matters most, it's common sense.

YOUR RIGHT TO A LIVABLE HOME

Beatrice and Renata moved into their new apartment in October. As winter set in and the temperature regularly dropped below freezing at night, they often woke up to find the pipes were frozen, cutting off water in the bathroom. Meanwhile, the radiator in Beatrice's room knocked and banged all night, forcing her to sleep on the couch in the living room. Even there it wasn't very quiet.

When Beatrice complained to Ray and Sue, they said that it would cost them thousands of dollars to reroute the bathroom pipes so they'd be insulated. Besides, they said, no one needs to bathe much in the winter, and what's wrong with using the kitchen sink for brushing teeth? As for the radiator banging, they shrugged, noted that it was an old heating system, that there was nothing "wrong" with it, and that Beatrice should get earplugs.

If an apartment or house becomes unlivable, is the tenant stuck?

Probably not, but it may depend where he or she lives. In most states, residential leases are covered by what is called an **implied warranty of habitability**. That means that regardless of what a lease says, the landlord must provide premises that are safe and livable — or "habitable" — at some basic level. Problems with essential building services and cleanliness are often breaches of the implied warranty and the landlord will be required to correct them. The implied warranty applies not only to the leased apartment, but also to common areas such as a lobby, a stairway, or a yard. What a court will consider a violation depends on the law of each state and, of course, on the particular facts at issue.

Beatrice and Renata will have to hope that they don't live in one of the few states that have not adopted the implied warranty of habitability. In these states — Alabama, Colorado, Kansas, and South Carolina — the tenant takes a house or an apartment "as is," and the landlord has no obligation to provide anything unless it is written into the lease. (See the Case in Point opposite.)

REPAIRS: WHEN THE LANDLORD WON'T MAKE THEM

Beatrice and Renata were pretty frustrated by Ray and Sue's flippant attitude about the plumbing and heat. They weren't prepared to move out, but they didn't think they were getting their money's worth.

Landlord and Tenant Obligations

In most states a landlord must

- **comply with building and housing codes**
- **repair broken plumbing, heating, and ventilation systems and appliances**
- **maintain garbage facilities**
- **keep common areas (lobbies, elevators, hallways) clean**
- **provide heat and hot water**

Tenants shouldn't expect landlords to provide even modest accommodations that are considered "conveniences," because they don't have to. Conveniences include

- **use of a rooftop**
- **parking space**
- **additional storage room**
- **air-conditioning, if the windows are openable (however, if a landlord does provide an air-conditioning unit, it must be operable unless the lease states that it's the tenant's responsibility to make it work)**

However, if a lease promises luxuries such as a doorman or swimming pool, the landlord generally can't cancel them. They must be provided for the entire lease.

A tenant has the obligation

- **to take reasonable care of the premises (wild parties may cause damage that you're responsible for)**
- **to avoid violations and to pay any fines that may result from them (you'll have to pay for dumping the garbage from your parties out the window)**
- **to avoid neglect or abuse by guests (watch your rowdy friends)**

Tenants have the right to the quiet use and enjoyment of their homes. You may decorate according to your own taste — so long as you don't create any lasting damage. Be prepared to spackle any holes before you move out or else risk losing some of your security deposit.

■ **Can a tenant stop paying rent if the landlord won't make repairs?**

Sure, but you risk losing the apartment. First, you should make sure that the landlord knows about the problem. Even if you already complained in person, put it in writing and hand-deliver the letter or send it via certified mail with a return receipt requested. (Tenants who live in large apartment buildings may notify the managing agent, superintendent, or janitor instead of the landlord.) Keep a record of all correspondence.

If the landlord fails to act within a reasonable amount of time, tenants have several options. They may

- **withhold rent (which can be risky — see the box on page 40).**
- **report the disrepair to the appropriate local agency to determine whether it violates a housing or safety code, and ask to have a copy of the inspection report (some states require an inspection of the dwelling prior to the case being heard in court).**
- **make the repairs and ask the landlord for repayment. However, it's usually not a good idea to pay for a costly repair, since the landlord may determine that the repair was unnecessary or too expensive and refuse to reimburse the tenant. Be sure to keep all receipts.**
- **go to court (see the box on page 41).**

REPAIRS: WHEN THE LANDLORD DOESN'T HAVE TO MAKE THEM

Beatrice complained to Ray that the bathtub wasn't draining properly. A plumber (hired by Ray) found an unusually large clump of dark hair was clogging the pipe. Beatrice admitted that Renata

CASE IN POINT

For Rent: Rotted Floors and Peeling Plaster

In 1987 a Salt Lake City, Utah, building inspector found over forty housing code violations in the residence rented by Cathy Oliver, the mother of eight children. The violations included rotted floors around the toilets; holes in other floors; collapsed ceilings in a bathroom and bedroom; uncovered electrical outlets; exposed wiring; inoperable light fixtures; leaking toilets and faucets; a deteriorated shower stall; roof leaks; and peeling plaster in every room. In addition, cracked and broken windows made it difficult to heat the structure, resulting in monthly heating bills that ran as high as $235.

When Oliver withheld her rent, the landlord, P. H. Investment, tried to evict her, and in 1989 the Court of Appeals of Utah ordered Oliver to move out and pay the rent owed — even though it was obvious the landlord had not maintained the dwelling.

Why the harsh decision? Because at the time, Utah was one of the few states that had not established that rentals are covered by an implied warranty of habitability. That meant Oliver had agreed to take her dwelling "as is" and that her landlord had no obligation to bring it up to standard.

The judges who ruled in Utah were not insensitive to Oliver's dilemma, and one of them noted that the state's laws governing rundown housing were outdated. "Those rules are exceptionally senseless," wrote the judge, David Dee. He urged the Utah legislature to enact an implied warranty of habitability.

To a large extent, that's exactly what Utah lawmakers did in 1990 when they passed the Utah Fit Premises Act, which imposes some basic building maintenance requirements on landlords and provides tenants with various remedies when violations are not repaired. However, if housing is deemed unfit for occupancy, the owner has the option of terminating the lease and boarding up the dwelling rather than repairing it.

regularly washed her poodle in the tub. Ray insisted that Beatrice and Renata pay the plumber's bill.

■ Can tenants be billed for repairs?

Yes, since landlords generally aren't responsible for problems that are caused by a tenant's carelessness. However, problems that arise as part of the normal wear and tear of daily life are usually the landlord's responsibility — especially if a failure to make repairs would leave the residence unlivable. For instance, if the drain had been clogged with human hair that had accumulated naturally over several years, it probably would be considered ordinary wear and tear. Ray and Sue would then have to pay the plumber's bill. (But, remember, in those states without an implied warranty of habitability, the tenant takes the apartment as it is.)

■ If the tenant hired a plumber to repair a clogged drain, could the landlord refuse to reimburse her?

Yes — if the tenant did not notify the landlord about the problem and give him a reasonable amount of time to fix it. For instance, if Beatrice called the plumber herself without first telling Ray, she probably wouldn't get her money back — even if the clog was not caused by the poodle hair. However, if the situation is an emergency (say the toilet won't stop overflowing and the landlord is nowhere to be found), then the tenant may take reasonable action, and the landlord will have to reimburse her — so long as the problem was not caused by the tenant's neglect.

PEST CONTROL

Although they had a few bad habits, Beatrice and Renata actually kept their apartment very clean and tidy. So when they started noticing roaches, they asked Ray and Sue to hire an exterminator.

Should You Withhold the Rent?

When a landlord fails to provide the essential services (such as heat and hot water) that make an apartment or house habitable, it may be acceptable to withhold the rent. But you do take a risk in doing so, because the landlord may move to evict you for nonpayment. That would put you on the defensive to show that you were justified in not paying.

Before withholding the rent, you should document the problem and give your landlord sufficient time to solve it. It's okay to make a phone call to the landlord, but you should follow up with a letter delivered in person or sent via certified mail. Your letter should state clearly the nature and scope of the repairs you want the landlord to make. Keep a record of all communications.

If the landlord fails to act within a reasonable period of time, a second letter is in order. This letter should outline your previous requests for repairs and should detail the problems once again. This letter should advise that landlord that you will withhold future rent payments if the repairs are not made.

If you do withhold the rent, you should set up a separate savings account and deposit the full rent into it each month (that is, if you want to lessen the risk that you will be forced to move for nonpayment). You could also deposit the money in an account set up and monitored by a lawyer (that's called an escrow account), although you don't really need to do this.

If the landlord does sue you for nonpayment and you go to court, the judge may require that you pay your rent into a court-monitored account until your dispute is settled.

What Happens If Your Dispute Goes to Court?

Many states have special housing courts to handle landlord-tenant disputes, and they often have forms available for tenants and landlords to file complaints. The judges in these civil courts are specially trained, and the proceedings are designed in theory to move quickly.

In practice, however, housing court cases can move very slowly, and the experience can be a bureaucratic nightmare. Because of this, tenants rarely initiate cases by going to court. Instead, if there is a problem, a tenant typically withholds the rent and waits to see if the landlord fixes the problem.

The landlord, of course, may also go to court and sue the tenant for nonpayment, thus initiating the legal process. Generally, before a landlord starts such a legal proceeding, he or she must first give the tenant notice that a "wrongdoing" exists (such as nonpayment of rent or violation of other rules in the lease). If the landlord wants to evict, the tenant must also be notified that the lease is being canceled. Then the landlord files a complaint in court and notifies the tenant, who will have the right to appear and argue his or her case.

If a tenant does decide to initiate a court action, the landlord must be given proper notice that a legal proceeding has been enacted.

An individual is not required to hire a lawyer for housing matters, although an attorney who handles landlord-tenant disputes will be in a good position to advise you of your rights and the best strategy for resolving your situation. In many places, law schools and community organizations provide advice for tenants in their legal disputes against landlords. Landlord groups may provide this service for dwelling owners. (See Chapter 30, FINDING AND USING A LAWYER.)

■ **Who is responsible for dealing with problems like roaches and mice?**

In states where tenants are entitled to a habitable dwelling, the landlord has to pay for an exterminator. However, if the landlord can show that the pests invaded because of the tenant's sloppy habits (like allowing garbage to accumulate or leaving food uncovered), then the tenant could be forced to deal with the problem.

In states where a dwelling is rented "as is," it is the tenant's responsibility to cope with the pests.

FEES FOR LATE RENT

Beatrice and Renata now had a written lease that required them to pay rent by the first of the month. The tenants were always several days late with the payment, leaving Sue nervous about whether she'd ever get paid. Finally Sue told Beatrice and Renata that she was going to charge them if the rent wasn't paid on time.

■ **Can a landlord demand a late fee if the rent is overdue?**

Yes, but only if a provision of the lease permits it. If the lease fails to specify it, the landlord can't collect a late fee.

"VISITORS" WHO MOVE IN

Beatrice's boyfriend, Max, was a constant visitor to their new apartment and before long he had moved his clothes in and was sleeping over four or five nights a week. Ray and Sue found this relationship just a bit too "modern" for their tastes. They told Beatrice and Renata that they'd decided they'd rather rent the apartment to someone else ("a nice married couple") and that Beatrice and Renata had to move out in thirty days.

■ **Can the landlord break the lease if an additional tenant moves in?**

Yes, if the lease designates that only a specific tenant (or tenants) may live in a dwelling, then the landlord can break it — even if the new person is a spouse. Some states, however, have roommate laws that allow an additional tenant to move in so long as the original tenant remains in the residence. Some states also require that a new spouse's name automatically be added to the lease.

ROOMMATE OBLIGATIONS TO PAY RENT

Renata disliked Max almost as much as Ray and Sue did, but for different reasons (he drank orange juice right out of the container and used her shampoo without asking). She told Bea she'd be moving out, even though they had several months left on the lease.

If a roommate moves out, is she still responsible for the rent?

If she has signed the lease (or agreed to an oral lease), then yes. In fact, when two or more roommates sign a lease, a landlord can look to each roommate for full payment of the rent, not just his or her share. Moving out doesn't end that obligation.

BREAKING A LEASE

The strains between Renata and Beatrice were mounting. Renata wouldn't stop complaining about Max's bad habits, and Beatrice had grown tired of coming home and finding that Renata had once again borrowed some cherished item of clothing and then returned it stained or unironed. The roommates thought they would be better friends if they no longer lived together.

If tenants move out before their lease expires, can the landlord make them pay for the remaining time?

Yes. A tenant can't just up and decide to break a lease, and some leases have "acceleration clauses" that allow a landlord to collect the rent for the time remaining on the lease in one lump sum. Most often, though, the landlord can only collect the rent owed as it becomes due each month that remains on the lease. In some places, however, landlords cannot collect unpaid rent on a broken lease if they haven't made a reasonable effort to find a new tenant.

Are there circumstances that would justify a tenant breaking a lease?

Yes, when

- **the premises are destroyed beyond repair by fire or flood**
- **the landlord fails to disclose hidden defects in the property**
- **the premises become uninhabitable**
- **the landlord does not comply with an important term of the lease (such as keeping kitchen appliances in working order)**

EVICTIONS

Ray and Sue were getting increasingly impatient with the constant problems. Finally, when the rent was three weeks overdue (for the fourth month in a row), they decided to kick out Beatrice and Renata.

How does a landlord evict a tenant?

Generally, the landlord must first warn the tenant, usually with a written notice, that a condition of the lease has been violated. Then the landlord must wait to see if the tenant corrects the problem. If the tenant fails to respond, the landlord may go to court (see the box on page 41) seeking an eviction. The procedure varies from state to state, but ordinarily the landlord sends a notice to the tenant and then files a petition or complaint in court. Although it's less common, a few jurisdictions allow the landlord to enter the premises and remove the tenant's property without going to court. The landlord, however, must do so peacefully.

How should a tenant respond to an eviction notice?

The tenant usually has the opportunity to appear before a judge and present his or her version of

Evictions

Landlords may be allowed to evict tenants who

- **fail to pay rent**
- **use the premises for illegal purposes, such as prostitution or gambling**
- **run a business in a residence-only zone**
- **sublet without permission**
- **overcharge a subtenant**
- **make structural changes without prior written consent**
- **fail to provide the landlord with access to make required repairs**
- **install appliances (dishwasher, washing machine, air conditioner, etc.) without the landlord's permission**
- **overcrowd the apartment**

events. You should bring documents to support your case. For example, Beatrice and Renata had paid the rent as soon as they got the eviction notice, and when they went to court they brought the canceled check. (The judge gave them a reprieve, but warned that if they were late again, he would grant an eviction.)

If you fail to appear in court, the judge may be able to order an eviction based on your default.

When an eviction order is obtained, some states allow the landlord to enter the premises and personally move out the tenant's possessions — though the landlord usually has to give the tenant notice beforehand. Other states require a sheriff or marshal to carry out the actual eviction after notice of the eviction has been served on the tenant.

CAN YOU RUN A BUSINESS AT HOME?

Beatrice was having trouble making ends meet on her salary as an entry-level computer programmer, so she posted several notices on college bulletin boards offering her services as a word processor. Several students called to hire her to type up their class papers. Several others wanted help with their résumés. They usually came to the apartment for a consultation in the early evening or on weekends, and Beatrice did the work on the computer she had set up in the living room. (She bought a used laser printer, so the actual work made very little noise.)

Sue, the landlady, reminded Beatrice that their neighborhood was strictly zoned as residential and that the lease clearly stated that no business was allowed in the apartment. If Beatrice continued, Sue threatened, she would be out.

■ Can a landlord evict a tenant who is running a business from the house?

Yes, although the kind of "business" Beatrice is running is usually not considered a violation of a residential-use-only rule. That means that so long as she is actually living in the apartment and her work is minor in nature and does not bother the neighbors or transform the apartment into an office, a judge would probably rule in favor of Beatrice and find that the business is "incidental" to her residency.

When ruling on whether an in-home business violates a zoning code (or a prohibition in the lease), a judge is likely to consider the nature of the operation and its effect on other tenants and services in the building. If, for example, a tenant hires five employees, sets up several phone lines, and wheels in six computers, a dozen file cabinets, and a copying machine, it is likely that the judge would find that she is running a substantial business — not just an incidental one. She would be found in violation, and her landlord would be allowed to evict her.

THE LANDLORD'S FAMILY

Six months into the lease, Ray told Beatrice and Renata they'd have to move out because his daughter was getting divorced and needed a place to live with her two children.

Regulated Rent

Rent control dates back to World War II, when the federal government moved to regulate the prices of various goods and services, including rents. (Some places, like New York State and the District of Columbia, had regulated rents even earlier.) The federal rent control law expired in 1950, but rent-controlled apartments still exist, since the laws in some states allow them to be kept in a family from generation to generation. Rent increases in these dwellings are set by the government. (See the Case in Point opposite.)

What is Rent Stabilization?

Several states have passed another, more "modern" rent regulation scheme. Rent stabilization laws were enacted in response to a shortage of affordable housing. These laws typically cover buildings with several rental units and exempt one- and two-family houses. The laws

- **regulate how much rent can be increased**
- **specify that landlords must provide essential services**
- **de^a ne how and why a lease may be terminated**

To find out the rules where you live, contact the agency that oversees housing matters in your state. A tenant's group or landlord's rights organization may also have helpful information.

Can a landlord break the lease if he wants to rent it to a member of his family?

No, unless the lease specifically states that he may do so. However, in most states where rents are not regulated, a landlord may refuse to *renew* (but not break) the lease for *any* reason. Even if an apartment or house is covered by rent regulations, some states allow the landlord to refuse to renew the lease if he truly intends to use the premises for his own use or that of a family member.

WHEN YOUR APARTMENT IS FOR SALE

Beatrice and Renata thought they had it bad with Ray and Sue. Then they met Barbara. She lived in a high-rise apartment building with a swimming pool and parking lot (a place Renata often thought would be much better than their little dump). But Barbara complained that the owner was converting it into condominiums and was trying to evict her.

Can the landlord break the lease if the building is going condo or co-op?

It depends on where the building is. Some states allow evictions, usually when the lease runs out. In other states, tenants like Barbara get first choice to buy the apartment (as an "insider") before it can be offered to an "outsider." Many states allow a tenant who chooses not to buy the apartment to continue living in it, although usually not forever.

HOME IMPROVEMENTS

Renata, a graphic designer, thought the apartment needed a lift. She wanted to paint the rooms to give them atmosphere: bright yellow for the kitchen, aqua with pink trim in the living room, and deep blue in the bedrooms (to create a restful effect). Beatrice and Renata were willing to shell out their own money for the redecorating.

Is a tenant allowed to paint at her own expense if she wants to?

If the lease does not specifically address the issue, tenants may paint (or wallpaper), but if they do so without getting the landlord's permission, they will probably be required to restore the apartment to its original condition when they leave. If they don't, they may lose all or part of their security deposit.

Is the landlord required to paint?

Only when

- **local law requires it**
- **it is written into the lease**
- **the dwelling is in such bad shape (holes in the walls, peeling paint, etc.) that a failure to paint would leave the apartment uninhabitable and in violation of the implied warranty of habitability**

Tenants usually have limited choices about the color or quality of the paint a landlord uses. Tenants, like Renata, who want to create special effects usually must do so at their own expense.

NOISY NEIGHBORS

The man who lived downstairs from Beatrice and Renata was getting tired of the late-night parties the young women held — especially since they kept his young son awake at night. He pointed out to Ray and Sue that his lease specifically promised him the "quiet use and enjoyment" of the apartment. He threatened to move out if Ray and Sue couldn't tame the wildness.

What can a tenant do about noisy neighbors?

You can try to resolve the problem neighbor to neighbor, but since emotions usually run hot, the amicable approach is rarely successful. Even though a lease promises quiet use and enjoyment of the premises, the landlord is not responsible for the acts of other tenants. However, the landlord has a duty to try to alleviate a troubling situation. If the landlord does offer to evict your bothersome neighbors, it would be helpful if you had a diary that notes the dates and times of the rowdy activity as well as tape recordings of the noise. In general, however, judges are hesitant to authorize such an eviction unless the situation has become extremely unpleasant.

BREAK-INS

Thieves broke into Beatrice and Renata's apartment, stealing the stereo (which thrilled the downstairs tenants), the television, and several pieces of jewelry. The thieves walked right into the building through the unlocked front door and then easily pried their way into the apartment. Several tenants had asked Ray and Sue to put a permanent lock on the front door and to install

CASE IN POINT

More Than Mere Roommates

Two men, Miguel Braschi and Leslie Blanchard, lived together as a couple for more than ten years in a rent-controlled apartment in New York City. When Blanchard, who held the lease, died in 1986, the landlord tried to evict Braschi, citing the state law that allows only a spouse or family member to retain possession of a rent-controlled apartment.

The New York Court of Appeals ruled in favor of Braschi, finding that under the circumstances "family includes two adult lifetime partners whose relationship is long term and characterized by an emotional and financial commitment and interdependence," wrote Judge Vito Titone.

The controversial decision gave several reasons why the relationship could be regarded as one of "family." The two men, Titone noted, shared all obligations. They maintained joint checking and savings accounts as well as credit cards. They attended family functions together as a couple, and Braschi was named as the beneficiary of Blanchard's life insurance policy and co-executor of his estate. A court "could reasonably conclude that these men were much more than mere roommates," Titone wrote.

dead bolts in their individual apartments. Ray and Sue had shrugged off the requests.

■ Can the landlord be held responsible for break-ins?

Generally not. However, in some places local law requires landlords to take certain security measures — such as making sure that doors lock properly. If a lock was broken and the landlord knew about the problem but failed to fix it, then he might be found negligent and thus responsible for the tenant's losses.

Landlords should make certain that doors close properly, hallways are well lighted, and security intercoms are operable.

CRIMINAL ACTS BY THE TENANTS

Ray and Sue finally figured out what that funny oregano smell was, and they began to suspect that Beatrice and Renata were selling marijuana. Ray considered sneaking into the apartment to look for evidence.

■ If a landlord suspects a tenant of criminal activity, can he use his keys to enter the apartment and look around?

No. A landlord is not a police officer. He is entitled to inspect his property periodically to make sure everything is in order, but he must give the tenant reasonable notice before doing so. Entering the apartment in a nonemergency situation without the tenant's permission could be considered trespassing.

DAMAGE DEPOSITS

When Beatrice and Renata moved in, Ray insisted they pay a deposit of one month's rent.

■ Can landlords do whatever they want to with a tenant's deposit?

Not usually. Many states require landlords to place security deposits in a separate, interest-bearing bank account and notify the tenant of the name and address of the bank where the money is held. The interest is calculated annually, but usually is not paid until the tenant moves out. But if the tenant wants it, the landlord does have to pay the interest at the end of each year.

Sometimes a landlord is entitled to withhold a fee (usually 1 percent of the deposit) for the work involved in setting up the bank account.

RETRIEVING YOUR DEPOSIT

After their one-year lease ended (which seemed like much longer to everyone involved), Beatrice and Renata moved out. Because they wanted their deposit back, they cleaned the apartment thoroughly — and dutifully repainted the walls with the original chalky white color. But when they asked for the deposit back two weeks after they moved out, Ray refused, stating that he had to hire a cleaning service after they left. And he informed Beatrice and Renata that he also found numerous repairs that needed to be made, including a broken light fixture in the bathroom, burns in the living room carpet that required replacement of the entire

How large a damage deposit can a landlord require?

It varies from state to state. The customary amount is one month's rent, but some places allow the landlord to ask for as much as he wants. Also, when an apartment or house is rented with furnishings, the landlord may request an additional deposit to cover the value of the furnishings.

The landlord should return the deposit — minus deductions for repairs or cleaning — within a reasonable time after the tenant moves out, usually one month. In some states, a landlord will be penalized (sometimes with a fine and sometimes even with a criminal action) if the security deposit is not handled according to the law.

carpet, and a missing cabinet door in the kitchen.

Beatrice and Renata were shocked. These problems had all existed when they moved in. Now Ray was blaming them.

■ Can the landlord refuse to return the deposit?

Yes, when the tenant has neglected or damaged the premises in a way that devalues the property. However, if the problems existed when the tenant moved in, the landlord can't deduct for them later. And if the problems are considered normal wear and tear, the tenants can't be penalized. When a tenant does leave behind a damaged apartment, the landlord should take photographs to document the problems.

In this case, Beatrice and Renata should have notified the landlord in writing of the problems when they first moved in.

■ How should a tenant protest when a landlord refuses to return the deposit?

As usual, the first step is to put the complaint in writing and include any photographs that document your position (making sure to keep copies for your records). If Beatrice and Renata had taken photographs, they could have shown that they left the apartment spanking clean — and that Ray was not justified in withholding a cleaning payment.

If a letter and photographs do not help resolve the problem, you can go to small-claims court (see page 431).

Actually, Bea and Renata suspected they'd have trouble getting their money back from Ray and Sue, so they had considered not paying the last month's rent.

■ Does a tenant have to pay the last month's rent if the landlord has a deposit worth that much?

Yes. But a landlord may, as a courtesy, agree to inspect the premises before the tenant moves and then apply the deposit to the last month's rent. However, the landlord has no obligation to do so, and Ray and Sue clearly weren't about to do any favors for Beatrice and Renata.

DISCRIMINATION

Beatrice and Renata wanted to get a place in the apartment complex where their friends Rick and Elly lived. The building had laundry facilities, a rec room with ping-pong tables, and an outdoor swimming pool. A sign in the window of the manager's office stated "Apartments for Rent."

Renata, who is black, called the manager to set up a time to see an apartment. He said several units were available, but when she arrived, he apologized and said the last one had just been rented.

■ Can landlords discriminate?

No, but it seems that may have happened in Renata's case — if there were indeed still apartments available. In all states, discriminating against a tenant (or, in this case, a potential tenant) on the basis of color, creed, race, national origin, religion, and sex is prohibited by the Fair Housing Act. Federal civil rights laws also protect certain minority groups against race discrimination in housing. In some states, discriminating on the basis of a person's profession, sexual preference, or marital status is also against the law. (See the Case in Point on page 49.)

■ So when, if ever, can a landlord refuse to rent to someone?

The rules vary from state to state, but in general a landlord must have a tangible reason for turning away a prospective tenant. For instance, a landlord could reject a tenant who wanted to share a two-bedroom apartment with five other people. When all other things are equal (such as finances, credit, and prior rental history), a landlord usually cannot refuse to rent to a single parent with a child if he would accept a married couple with a child.

Landlords are also permitted to turn away prospective tenants who do not agree to comply with the landlord's rules and regulations. But it's not as if landlords can create any rules they want. The rules must be reasonable (no pets, for example) and must apply to all tenants equally. If a tenant breaks the rules, then the landlord will have grounds for eviction.

SUBLETS

Renata's friend Richard was offered a job working for a year on an archaeological dig in Egypt. He had a dilemma, because only six months earlier he had moved into a gorgeous two-bedroom apartment with a three-year lease. He didn't want to lose the place (because he had no intention of spending extra time in Egypt), so he asked Renata if she and Beatrice wanted to rent it for one year.

■ What is a sublet?

In a **sublet,** a third party (in this case, Beatrice and Renata) agrees to rent a house or apartment for a portion of the time remaining on the lease. The original tenant (Richard) retains control of the lease and usually is responsible for paying the rent and for any problems that arise. So the sublettor becomes the tenant of the leaseholder. But the landlord may agree to accept the rent directly from the sublettor.

If Richard had decided to give up the apartment and let Beatrice and Renata take over the entire two and a half years left on the lease, it would have been called an **assignment**.

But Beatrice and Renata were thrilled to get even one year in a place as nice as Richard's (it had a fireplace, a terrace, and a swimming pool). They agreed to rent it at his cost of $650.

■ Does the landlord have to go along?

Yes, unless state law allows the landlord to insert a no-sublet clause into the lease, which many do. The landlord may reject individual applicants if he determines that their finances are insufficient to pay the rent or if they are unsavory characters. In fact, Richard's landlord was happy to approve a sublet. "No problem," he said. "It's a deal at $750 a month." Beatrice and Renata were upset, because that price was out of their range.

■ Can the landlord raise the rent of a sublettor?

Possibly. A lot depends on what the lease says. If the lease requires the landlord's approval for a sublet, which most do, the landlord may indeed be able to require additional rent before approving the sublet. However, in many states that have rent stabilization laws, the landlord can only charge the sublettor an amount equal to what he could have charged if a new tenant entered into a new lease. (So if the law allowed him to raise the rent for a new lease only 5 percent, he could charge a sublettor only 5 percent over the current rent.) In states with no rent regulation, the landlord could charge as much as he wanted so long as the lease did not specifically restrict him.

■ Can the leaseholding tenant charge the sublettor more than he pays the landlord — and pocket the difference?

Not usually. Leases don't typically give the tenant much flexibility to set a sublet rate. In the rare case when a lease doesn't address the issue and the rent is not regulated, the tenant could charge whatever he wants.

RENTER'S INSURANCE

Instead of an apartment, Beatrice and Renata decided to rent a small house. Everything was great until the day Renata rushed out on her way to work and forgot to turn off the iron. A small fire started in her bedroom and quickly spread to the living room. Luckily a neighbor noticed the smoke and called the fire department before the blaze caused any structural damage. Nevertheless, the living room furniture, carpet, and drapes were all destroyed.

As if that weren't bad enough, Beatrice and Renata were dismayed when the landlord later presented them with a bill for replacing the carpet and drapes (which came with the house). Attached to the bill was a copy of their rental lease that specified that the tenants were supposed to purchase fire insurance. Beatrice and Renata had ignored that instruction.

Can a landlord require a tenant to buy fire insurance?

Yes. In house rentals such as Beatrice and Renata's, the lease often requires the tenants to do so — and leaves them liable for any damage if they fail to do so. In apartment rentals, the landlord usually insures the premises (but not a tenant's possessions) against fire or other natural disasters.

It would have been a good idea for Beatrice and Renata to have insurance — and not just because their lease required it.

What is renter's insurance?

Typically, a renter's policy covers several things, including

- **loss of personal property**
- **living expenses incurred if your home becomes uninhabitable**
- **medical expenses for injuries sustained on the premises**
- **claims by others for injuries they sustain while on the premises**

However, when the insured person is negligent (as Renata was), the insurance may not cover the damages.

CASE IN POINT

Just Living Together? Not in His House

In 1988, a Minnesota landlord refused to rent a house to an unmarried woman who planned to live there with her fiancé. The landlord, Layle French, told the potential tenant, Susan Parsons, that he would not rent the property to her because it was against his religious beliefs for unmarried adults of the opposite sex to live together.

In Minnesota, it is unlawful for landlords to turn away tenants because of their marital status, and Parsons filed a suit charging French with discrimination. Nevertheless, in 1990, the Supreme Court of Minnesota ruled that marital status protections apply to individuals, not their relationships with a partner. The judges ruled that French, a member of the Evangelical Free Church, had the right to exercise his freedom of religion.

The law prohibiting discrimination, wrote Justice Lawrence Yetka, did not intend "to penalize landlords for refusing to rent to unmarried, cohabiting couples."

BUYING AND SELLING

6

CONTRACTS AND CONTRACTORS

Gordon and Grace's fiftieth wedding anniversary was approaching. Beatrice, Blossom, Bradley, and Bartholomew decided to chip in and have formal portraits made of each one of them and the grandchildren. Joe, a friend of someone Blossom knew at work, had recently opened his own photography business — Snappy Times — and she decided to use him. Because he had just struck out on his own, Joe offered her a good deal: $1,000 for all the portraits, plus he would shoot the party itself. He seemed like a nice enough guy, and talented too. Blossom was in charge of making the arrangements with Joe, and the two of them shook hands on the deal.

■ What is a contract?

A contract is an agreement that can be formal, informal, written, oral, or just plain understood. It can be between individuals, between two or more companies, or between different combinations of individuals and organizations. Basically, a contract is formed when there is an offer and an acceptance of terms in which each party benefits. (Agreeing to buy a new car for a specific amount of money is a contract.) The parties must be specific enough in their agreement for the contract to be enforceable. For example, in the sale of merchandise, the terms have to identify the goods and the price: "Tube Socks: 3 pairs for $5.00." "Sock Sale — Everything Must Go" is not a contract.

Sometimes a contract is formed by actions. When you drive into a gas station, see a sign that states the price, and then pump gas into your car, you have entered into a contract. By pumping gas into your car, you have accepted the gas station's offer to sell gas at the posted price.

Sometimes the parties *do not* have to spell out the essential terms in order to form a contract. Say, for instance, a man with a snowplow drives by your house after a big blizzard.

"Want me to plow?" he shouts.

"Sure, go ahead!" you holler back, and he cuts a neat path up your driveway.

He has provided goods or services, and you have accepted them knowing they are not a gift, so he is entitled to receive *quantum meruit* — the reasonable value. In other words, you have to pay him. If, however, he had just plowed without first asking you, no contract would be formed and you would owe him nothing.

■ Does a contract have to be in writing?

It depends. Some, but not all, contracts *must* be in writing to be enforceable. Most states have laws known as **statutes of fraud**, which were designed to protect against false claims for payment from contracts that were not, in fact, agreed upon. The specific laws vary from state to state, but most require that the following contracts be in writing:

- **the sale of land**
- **the sale of goods valued over $500**
- **contracts that require more than one year to perform (such as an agreement to work for an employer for two years)**
- **promises to guarantee someone else's debt**

The basic premise is that you should have written documentation of your transaction, but that doesn't mean you always need a lengthy agreement. For example, simply signing a check with the notation "For Car Purchase" may be sufficient to meet the "in writing" requirement. Even when you're not required by the statute of frauds to put your agreement in writing, it is still good practice for all significant transactions.

Who Can Enter Into a Contract?

For a contract to be valid, the parties must have the legal capacity to enter into it. In most states, that means that anyone who has reached the age of majority (usually eighteen) and who is considered to be mentally competent can enter into a contract. In general, minors can enter into binding, or enforceable, contracts only for necessities — food, clothing, and the like. In other words, if a sixteen-year-old puts $100 down and signs a contract to buy a $1,000 stereo system on credit, he cannot be held to that contract. He can return the stereo and reclaim his deposit for no other reason than not being able to pay for it. The only catch is that he has to return the stereo in the same condition in which he bought it.

Mentally handicapped persons can also enter into contracts, as long as they have not been declared incompetent (see page 322), and they understand the nature and consequences of their actions.

Changing Your Mind

Joe's cousin Joan, a lawyer, advised him to put all his work agreements into writing. So he asked Blossom to come to Snappy Times and sign a simple contract before the first photo shoots, which were scheduled to begin in three days. But Blossom was having doubts about the whole project. She and her siblings had been fighting endlessly about whether the photos should be in color (Bart and Beatrice's preference) or black-and-white (more artistic, argued Blossom and Brad). The one thing they agreed on was that all the portraits should be the same — either black-and-white or color. Still, Blossom was wondering if maybe they should just forget the whole idea.

Can a person enter a contract and then change his or her mind?

Yes, but only in very limited circumstances. The whole purpose of a contract is to create a binding obligation for both parties. If you simply have changed your mind about the terms of the contract (for instance, you can no longer afford the services, or on the other side, you realize that the work will be more expensive, difficult, or time-consuming than you anticipated), you are still bound by the agreement.

There are some reasons that do justify release from a contract, however. If the contract was obtained by the fraud of the other party — let's say the photographer had shown Blossom samples of his work that convinced her to hire him, and then she learned that the pictures were actually taken by someone else — you can be released from the contract. If the other party fails to perform a significant part of the contract, or lets you know that part of the contract will not be performed, you would no longer be bound by the agreement.

Blossom ran into Joe's cousin (and lawyer) Joan at the supermarket. She explained the whole situation about the pictures and the family fight. "Can't I get out of this?" Blossom asked. "After all, Joe and I haven't put anything in writing yet."

"Forget it," Joan said. "You and Joe have a deal. Besides, just relax. He'll do a great job."

Can a person back out of a deal before the papers are signed?

Maybe. If a contract is required to be in writing by your state's statutes of fraud (see page 51), and if the agreement has not yet been signed, either party probably can still back out. However, if a party admits that a verbal contract for the sale of goods was made, it will still be enforceable in almost all states. (Other types of contracts covered by statutes of fraud, such as for the sale of land, often can be nullified if they're not yet in writing.)

Beatrice and Bart won the argument. Against their better judgment, Blossom and Bradley agreed to have the pictures done in color. Blossom scheduled a time with Joe to sign the contract, squeezing it in between work and her aerobics class. (She had to lose ten pounds before the party!) Later, while doing leg lifts, Blossom had an idea: Instead of photos, why not hire someone to make a videotape about their parents' lives? When she got home, she called Bradley, who responded enthusiastically. They decided she should cancel the photo order. Because she had been pressured into the color picture idea by Bart and Beatrice, she figured she could get out of the contract.

■ What happens if a person signs a contract under duress?

Duress can be grounds for getting out of a contract. But duress is considered to be "extreme improper influence" that prevents you from asserting your own free will. Financial concerns or strong persuasion do not legally constitute duress. But if a burly guy threatens to burn your house down if you don't hire his son's band to play at your party, that would be duress.

Joe convinced Blossom that it was too late to back out of their agreement. After all, they signed a contract. But a week later, the whole family was in an uproar because Bart's wife had posed nude for a magazine. They wanted to delay the party.

■ What if unexpected circumstances prevent a person from fulfilling the terms of a contract?

In some cases unexpected circumstances can excuse you from the contract. However, this is generally limited to two types of situations:

- **the subject of the contract is destroyed (a party hall burns down or someone dies)**
- **circumstances arise that make it impossible or extremely difficult to perform the contract (if you canceled the party, that generally wouldn't excuse you)**

In Blossom's case, a delay of the party would not release her from the contract to have the photos taken.

The nude photo crisis passed, and they all posed for their (clothed) photos with Joe as scheduled. But when Blossom picked up the finished portraits, she was furious. Not only did she hate the effect of the color, but the pictures were totally unflattering. She looked like she had a double chin. Beatrice looked like she hadn't slept for a week. Bradley's pallor was extreme. Some of the pictures also seemed to be all scratchy. Blossom wanted a refund. These pictures were expensive!

■ What can consumers do if the services they contract for are defective?

Most states require that providers of services meet reasonable standards of competency in their field. Though workers will sometimes include provisions in their contracts to renounce any liability for their failure to perform the services properly, most state courts have frowned on such disclaimers. If the services are totally defective, you usually have the right to refuse to pay anything at all. If the work can be corrected, you can deduct the reasonable cost of getting it fixed. Some states have specific laws governing disputes over car and home repairs and certain other services. For more information on your state's laws, you can call your state attorney general's office or your local Better Business Bureau.

■ What can a contractor do if the consumer says that the services were inadequate?

If you provided services and the other party refuses to pay, you can bring a claim in court to recover your money. In many states, if the services were performed on a car, boat, house, or other property, you can file for a **lien** (a claim against the person's property) to secure your payment. (See the box on page 54.)

How to Get a Lien

You can secure a lien on someone's property by filing the appropriate papers at your local courthouse. If you have performed services on someone's house — painted it, for example — and they refuse to pay you for your work, you can put a lien on their house. They then will be unable to sell the house without paying you.

The rules for filing a lien vary from state to state, but often it's as easy as filling out a form. You are then required to notify the homeowner that you're filing a lien, and the homeowner has the right to a hearing to contest it. If you make a request for a lien purely out of maliciousness, you could be penalized.

If you are in possession of property that you have serviced or repaired, many states allow you to keep it if the owner will not pay you for the work. This is known as a "possessory lien," and you don't have to file anything in court to do it. You just keep the property until the owner pays you.

Contracting for Home Repair

When Blossom met her "significant other," Jeremy, she realized that the way to this man's heart *was* through his stomach, and their courtship flourished over *Live to Eat* magazine. With a shared serious interest in food, they had become quite a tag-team of gourmet cooks, but their skills had outgrown the "functional fifties" appliances and space of their kitchen. They decided to renovate. A convection oven, top-of-the-stove grill, and marble work surface were at the top of their list, but there were other changes they wanted to make as well. They interviewed several contractors and finally chose James, based on a combination of personality and cost. They had found someone with whom they felt they could communicate, and his written estimate looked good.

Is a contractor bound to a written estimate?

Not unless you can show that you were quoted an exact, fixed price or that an estimate was given in bad faith as a way to lure you into the contract. Such improper tactics aside, an owner is usually contracting to pay for needed goods and services at a price that will vary depending on the number of hours needed to get the job done. The owner will often be quoted an hourly rate, which must be honored. If no rate is set out, the owner is contracting to pay for the goods and services at the fair market value.

Blossom and Jeremy were deep into their renovation. The original kitchen had been demolished, and they were living on pizza and take-out Chinese food, knowing that, in a few weeks, they would have their dream kitchen. Neither of them had ever done a project like this where they had workers in their house for an extended period. They were a little uncomfortable with some of the contractor's behavior. James seemed to be making himself more "at home" than Blossom and Jeremy liked, regularly helping himself to food and drinks in the refrigerator.

Are contractors free to make themselves "at home" when doing renovations?

No, not unless you tell the contractor that this is okay. While it may not be possible for you to stay home while the work is being done, bear in mind that the number of problems and misunderstandings drops dramatically when someone is there to keep an eye on the situation. At the very least, be clear with the contractor what is acceptable behavior in your house.

There was trouble in paradise. James, the contractor, originally said the job would take two months and cost $15,000. But after three months, he told Blossom he needed at least four more weeks. Four more weeks? Blossom was beside herself.

What can you do if the contractor keeps needing more time?

It really depends on the details of the contract.

- **Was the completion date guaranteed, or was the date given as an estimate?**
- **Was there an agreement with the contractor about the consequences of a delay?**
- **If so, did you make that agreement orally or in writing?**
- **Is the delay due to the contractor's failure to do the work, or is it due to the nature of the job?**

If you made an explicit agreement about a completion time, then that agreement provides the basis for any settlement or renegotiation. In the absence of an explicit agreement, the contractor is required to meet *reasonable* completion times comparable to average contractors.

A written agreement carries a lot more legal weight than an oral agreement, especially when the two parties differ on what that agreement was. You may be able to sue and collect damages if a written provision explicitly states that there will be a penalty for lateness. Even without such a provision, you may still be able to recover damages if you told the contractor that the completion date was critical.

The completion date *was* critical. Blossom and Jeremy were hosting Blossom's parents' golden wedding anniversary party — a surprise buffet dinner for sixty-five people. They had spent the months of the renovation poring over recipes and planning the menu. The invitations had already gone out!

If the contractor is late, can a person get a refund?

Maybe. If the contractor knew the date was critical, you may be able to recover all reasonably foreseeable damages that result from the delay. You may also hire someone else to finish the work promptly, and you can deduct the cost from your payment to the first contractor. Generally, you will have to make at least a partial payment to your original contractor, except when

- **that contractor's work is useless**
- **your damages exceed the value of the contractor's work**
- **the contract expressly states that you do not have to pay at all for late work**

The party was in three weeks. The contractor agreed to finish on time, but only if Blossom and Jeremy would pay an additional $2,500. They had already broken their budget with that irresistible Italian marble for the counters. This extra money would mean that they'd have to postpone having a baby for yet another year.

What should a person do if a contractor says the job can't be finished without additional payments?

If the contractor asks for more money, be careful. It's a judgment call. You have to decide whether this request is being made in good faith, or if you should find someone else to finish the job. If you dispute this additional charge, but decide to pay it so the job will get done, note on your check that you dispute the payment. That way the contractor will not be able to claim later that your additional payment shows that you obviously agreed to a modification of the original contract.

Some contractors juggle their business by using cash from one job to pay for materials on another job. If you have any doubts about how this additional money will be used, pay it only upon proof of purchase of materials for your job (and keep the receipts). Or if you have the time and inclination, you can oversee the use of your money by buying the materials yourself.

It is essential to check out a contractor and do business only with one you trust. But even if you like and trust your contractor, protect yourself: be explicit about whether the price and completion dates are commitments or merely estimates.

Jeremy, a waiter at the All-Star Bar and Grill, had been moonlighting by painting houses and apartments. He and Blossom had signed up with Jungle Fever to take a trip to the Amazon (before it completely disappears), and they needed some extra money.

Malcolm, a fellow waiter at the All-Star Bar and Grill, hired Jeremy to paint his house. When Jeremy was two-thirds of the way through the job, Malcolm decided he hated the color, which *he* chose. He refused to pay extra for Jeremy's having to redo the job.

■ What can a contractor do when a client is fickle?

A client's change of heart or mind does not require you to redo your work. You are entitled to refuse to do further work unless the client agrees to pay you extra, and you have the right to be paid for all the work you have already performed. You can recover payment for your work through small-claims court (if it is within the dollar limits for these courts) or through a regular court.

In almost all states, you also have the right to attach a lien against the client's house to secure your payment (see page 54). But if you pursue this route, you should make sure that you yourself have complied with any state and local license and permit requirements for your profession. If a license is required — for housepainting, for example — and if you failed to obtain it, some states will not allow you to recover payment.

Malcolm's wishy-washiness notwithstanding, Jeremy's reputation quickly spread, and he soon had more work than he could handle. A friend of a friend asked him to paint her hallway to create a faux marble effect. Jeremy decided to hire Blossom's teenage nephew, Vinny, to help him out, after Vinny demonstrated that he could handle this technique. The next thing Jeremy knew, the client was calling and refusing payment, saying that Vinny's work was not up to par, especially since he spilled paint on her parquet floor.

■ What can a client do if the contractor's work is sloppy and unacceptable?

It depends on how badly the work was done. Unless you have agreed to other rules, the contractor is not entitled to payment when poor work is performed. But you have to prove that the work has no value at all. If the work is so bad that it has to be completely redone (and especially if you have made it clear that first-class work was required), then you probably can show that the work has zero value to you. At a minimum, you are entitled to require the worker to correct the defects. Or you can hire someone else to correct the defects at a reasonable price. You can then deduct that amount from the original contractor's payment.

Catering Contracts

Blossom and Jeremy abandoned all hope of their kitchen being finished on time for the party. But instead of changing the date, they simply changed the location to Bradley's apartment. Since there was no way they could prepare their menu in his ill-equipped kitchen, they broke down and hired a caterer.

But tragedy struck! John and Jane were exposed to *Polly Tinctuvulgaris,* a rare and highly communicable virus that their pet parrot contracted. They had to be quarantined for two months, and could not be in the same room as anyone else. Because the party had to be postponed, Blossom and Jeremy wanted to resuscitate their menu and revert to Plan A: host the party and do all the cooking themselves. But the caterer was insisting on full payment.

■ Is a person obligated to pay a caterer if it's necessary to cancel a week in advance?

Yes, you do have to pay, but not necessarily the full price. By canceling your order with the caterer, you are breaching your contract, and the catering company is entitled to be in the same financial position it would be in were the contract fulfilled. But the caterer is obligated to limit its damages in two ways:

- **by not ordering or preparing any further food**
- **by making reasonable efforts to find substitute work**

If the caterer finds another job and could not have done both jobs, you're in luck. The profits from the new job will be subtracted from what you owe. That doesn't mean you pay nothing, but your costs are lower.

Often a contract will specify a cancellation fee. If it does, and if it's reasonable, you probably will have to pay it.

WARRANTIES

Alena's sixteenth birthday was approaching, and she laughed at Beatrice's idea of a sweet-sixteen party: "Mom, you're so old-fashioned!" Still, Beatrice wanted to get her a really special gift, but she was somewhat daunted by Alena's wish list, which included a video camera, mountain bike, and portable compact disc player. What if she bought one of these big-ticket items and it broke? The salesman at her local Stereos 'N Stuff gave her a lot of unreassuring mumbo-jumbo about warranties.

■ What is a warranty?

A warranty is a promise about a product that can be made by either a manufacturer or a seller. "Satisfaction guaranteed" is a broad warranty that is often offered. A confusing aspect of warranties is that both the manufacturer *and* the seller can make a warranty. Usually the warranty of one is not binding on the other. As a result, the consumer has to determine which guarantees are given by the manufacturer and which by the seller.

Even more confusing is the fact that you don't automatically get a warranty when you buy something. In most states, manufacturers have no obligation to offer warranties to you — although most of them do. Sellers, on the other hand, usually must guarantee that the products you buy from them will work as directed. However, sellers often can *disclaim* (a legal term that means they can free themselves of the obligation) the warranty by posting a sign conspicuously or otherwise informing you that there is no guarantee being offered.

The sale of goods is generally governed by federal law and by a standard set of statutes that is in effect in almost all states — the **Uniform Commercial Code**. The Uniform Commercial Code consists of guidelines covering things like the sale of goods, credit, and bank transactions. All states have adopted and adapted the entire UCC, with the exception of Louisiana, which adopted only parts of it.

Also, because you typically have a direct relationship only with the seller, not the manufacturer, you may have no recourse against the manufacturer. Generally, a manufacturer has a legal obligation to you only under the following circumstances:

- **the manufacturer has specifically offered a warranty**
- **the manufacturer has sold you a service contract**
- **the product physically harmed you (see page 343)**

■ What is an implied warranty?

An **implied warranty** is a guarantee imposed by law in a sale. Even though the seller may not make any explicit promises, you (the buyer) still get some protection. Two important implied warranties apply to sales:

- **the implied warranty of merchantability**
- **the implied warranty of fitness for a particular purpose**

The **implied warranty of merchantability** guarantees that goods are reasonably fit for their ordinary purpose. If you buy a camera from a store, the camera should not fall apart quickly in regular use.

What Is Caveat Emptor?

Caveat emptor is Latin for "buyer beware." Before the modern law of warranties was developed, the rule of caveat emptor prevailed. This rule gave the *buyer* full responsibility for determining the quality of the goods in question. The seller had no duty to offer warranties or to disclose defects in the goods. In sales between individuals, caveat emptor generally still applies.

As the name suggests, this warranty applies only when you buy something from a person in business (typically either a store or a door-to-door salesman). It does not apply to sales between private individuals.

The **implied warranty of fitness for a particular purpose** applies when a sale is made by both private individuals and merchants. This warranty exists when a seller should know that a buyer is relying on the seller's expertise. For example, a homeowner who needs an air conditioner will most likely (unless he or she is an expert) ask the salesperson's advice on the correct size for the house. The seller implicitly guarantees that the recommended model is the appropriate size for the buyer's particular purpose, and violates the implied warranty of fitness if it is not.

Merchants often attempt to nullify implied warranties by printing disclaimers on their packages or sales forms. However, if a merchant gives any written warranty about consumer goods, the merchant also honors implied warranties for *at least* a minimum amount of time. Under federal law, if a consumer product costs more than $15, you are entitled to see any written warranty covering the product before you buy it. If the warranty is not displayed along with the product, you may ask to see it before you buy.

An important thing to know is that, in most states, if a store has a conspicuously placed disclaimer and doesn't sell you a service contract, then there is no implied warranty. So it could be possible that the manufacturer and the seller have decided to disclaim *all* warranties. In this case, you will have to decide whether the price is reasonable enough for you to take a chance or whether you would rather find similar goods that have a warranty. (Maryland, Massachusetts, Mississippi, Vermont, and the District of Columbia do not allow stores to disclaim implied warranties, although in Mississippi, used cars are sold "as is.")

■ What is an express warranty?

An **express warranty** is an assertion or promise concerning goods or services. Statements such as "This air conditioner will cool a five-room house" or "We will repair any problems in the first year" are express warranties. Even saying that the item is in good condition can create an express warranty, although some courts have required more specific statements. Statements announcing only the seller's opinion — "It's a fabulous deep-fryer" or "This hot air popcorn popper is an awesome buy" — are considered mere "puffing" by the seller, not express warranties.

When a manufacturer offers you a ninety-day (or one-year, or three-year) guarantee on the parts and labor, that is an express warranty. Again, although many manufacturers offer such warranties, they are under no legal obligation to do so.

Warranties on Used Goods

When Beatrice went mountain bike shopping, she practically went into shock. The store wanted $900 for a red Climbing Rocket, the model Alena had her heart set on. Beatrice thought she might be able to get a used one.

■ Is a warranty transferable?

Sometimes. The manufacturer or seller of consumer goods can limit the warranty to the original purchaser, but the written warranty must state that clearly. If the warranty is labeled "Full," as opposed to "Limited," then the warranty must be honored for all subsequent owners.

Get It in Writing

If you have a dispute over a salesperson's oral promises, it will be your word against the seller's. That means it could be very difficult to prove your case. Also, a written contract or warranty may specifically exclude the promises made by the salesperson. To best protect yourself, make sure any verbal guarantees are put in writing.

If the warranty has expired and the appliance breaks down, does the previous owner have to pay for the repair or give a refund?

When you buy used appliances from private individuals, you get no guarantees. However, if the seller made an express warranty (a specific promise about the product), you might be protected if the item breaks. The seller would then be responsible for the cost of repair or a refund. Practically speaking, however, it may be difficult to get reimbursement from a private individual. Your case probably would qualify for small-claims court (see page 431), but you may decide that pursuing what you are justly entitled to is not worth the time, expense, or trouble.

You don't have to get promises in writing, but you may find it hard to prove that someone made an oral guarantee.

Replacement of Shoddy Merchandise

After the downstairs neighbors complained for the umpteenth time about his piano practicing, Bradley decided to get wall-to-wall carpeting installed. The Carpet Caravansary salesman promised that the carpet would still look like new in five years. Bradley had his doubts, and sure enough, after less than a year the carpet was a mess and needed to be replaced.

Is a store obligated to replace shoddy merchandise for free?

The salesman's assurance that a carpet "will look like new after five years" creates an **express warranty**, which protects the buyer (see page 58). Even without that statement, a new carpet that needs replacing in less than a year of normal home use probably violates the **implied warranty of merchantability** (see page 57). The fact that you did not believe the salesman's promise does not invalidate these warranties.

In most states you would be entitled to a new carpet, although you might have to pay for a portion of the replacement.

We can't come to the phone; so . . . leave us a greeting after the tone . . ."

Vinny recorded the message for their new phone answering machine, but two days after Beatrice bought it, the device stopped working. She stomped into the store where she had bought it and demanded a replacement. The manager just shrugged. "It's your problem now, lady," he said.

Is a store responsible for problems with the products it sells?

The answer to this question is that there is no automatic answer, and that's the crux of most consumer nightmares. It highlights the benefits of dealing with reputable merchants who value service to their customers. Whether or not a store is responsible for the products it sells depends on a number of things, including what state the store is in, whether or not the seller made any promises about the product or "Satisfaction Guaranteed," and whether or not the store made any disclaimers about its responsibility for the merchandise it sells.

Even if the store is not responsible for the problems, the manufacturer very well could be, especially if it made any warranties. A machine that breaks within a few days would probably violate almost all warranties (assuming you used it more or less the way you should have). If it breaks down later, you may be out of luck. So if the store specifically made a promise to you about how long the item would last or failed to disclaim implied warranties, it would have to stand behind the goods.

However, in most states, the store would be allowed to repair the item, rather than replace it.

If the store disclaimed any implied warranty and did not make any specific promises about the product, then you probably will have to deal directly with the manufacturer. However, a few states prohibit stores from disclaiming implied warranties, and in these states the store would be responsible for the goods.

BILLS OF SALE

Beatrice found the deal she had been looking for: the Climbing Rocket for half its retail price. It was slightly used, but the seller assured her the bike was ridden only on weekends by his grandmother. Beatrice decided to buy it for Alena.

■ When should individuals buying and selling merchandise from each other write up a bill of sale?

Casual sales of small items between individuals, such as at a yard sale, do not call for a bill of sale or a written contract. But for more substantial items, including cars and boats, a short written record of the terms of sale is useful to prevent misunderstandings. Many states require written contracts for any sale of goods over $500. The law, though, usually recognizes that any completed transaction is valid even if you have no written documentation.

If, however, you make a deal to buy your neighbor's recreational vehicle, but won't pay or take possession of it for two weeks, then you must put the agreement in writing. It's no crime not to, but without a written document your neighbor could decide to sell to someone else and you may be left with no recourse. Your written document can be informal and doesn't even have to include all the specific terms of your agreement. However, the more inclusive your written proof is, the better off you will be if a dispute arises.

■ What should a bill of sale between individuals include?

- **the names of the buyer and seller**
- **the price of the goods**
- **any special terms, such as delayed payment or responsibility for delivery of the goods**

The most frequent disputes are over goods that fail. If the seller does not want to guarantee the goods, he or she should include the notation "as is" in the bill of sale. That basically says, "I make no guarantee of the quality or performance of the goods." On the other hand, the buyer should demand that any guarantee that the seller *is* offering be put in writing.

Besides a bill of sale, if you are buying or selling a car, any certificate of title for the car must also be transferred to the buyer (see page 64).

PRICING

Allegra thought that a "little black dress" would be the most elegant choice for her in-laws' anniversary bash, but when she searched her closet, she found nothing suitable. After spending a whole Saturday shopping, she came home with just the right thing. Even she had to admit that she looked fabulous in it. When she modeled it for Bart, he agreed. But when he found out how much she had paid for it, he hit the roof.

"Five hundred dollars?" he bellowed. "For a few scraps of black silk?"

■ Is there such a thing as a price that is too high?

Generally not. In a few cases, courts have suggested that the price of goods can be so excessive as to be "unconscionable" (shocking to a civilized conscience) and therefore illegal and unenforceable. (The price of a party dress, no matter how high, would probably never be considered unconscionable, because it is not an essential item like a refrigerator.) Many states prevent the scalping of tickets, which often are priced unconscionably high, and a few states prohibit price gouging during emergencies.

Most important, states often set maximum limits on interest charges, late fees, and insurance premiums. Other than these exceptions, though, buyers are bound by the price in a contract.

RETURNS AND REFUNDS

Allegra decided Bart was right: $500 was way too much for a little dress. What was she thinking? Her friend Samantha was a seamstress and could whip something together just as nice in an afternoon, for a fraction of the cost. But when she took the dress back to the store, they refused to give her a refund.

■ When, if ever, can a store refuse to allow a customer to return a product?

A store is under no obligation to allow returns unless

- **the store publicizes a right to return**
- **the store offers a "satisfaction guaranteed" promise**
- **the buyer finds that the goods were defective at the time of sale**

If a customer simply changes his or her mind, a store is not required to take an item back. As a matter of good customer relations, however, many stores do allow returns. Even if a warranty is breached, a seller or manufacturer usually is required only to repair or replace the item — not give a refund.

As she regretfully examined the dress on her way out of the store, Allegra discovered a small hole near the zipper. But when she showed the hole to the saleswoman, the woman accused Allegra of having torn the dress after she took it home.

■ What are a buyer's rights when a piece of clothing has a defect?

The law in most states says that buyers are responsible for discovering defects in goods before buying them, as long as they had the opportunity to examine the goods. Obvious defects are not usually covered by warranties. If a hole in a dress would have been noticeable at the time of sale, the store would not be obligated to accept the return unless the store had a "Satisfaction Guaranteed" policy. Even without such a policy, though, if the hole was so small or in such a location that it was hard to detect, any warranties would still apply and the dress could be returned.

To qualify for a refund or repair, it's up to the buyer to prove that it was more likely than not that the item was defective at the time of sale or delivery.

Alena and Vinny sat Beatrice down one afternoon and told her straight out: "Mom, we are too embarrassed to invite our friends over. That couch is disgusting." Beatrice had to admit that ever since Fluffy had her kittens right on the middle cushion the couch hadn't been the same. The next day, the three of them went shopping and picked out a brand-new white couch (and decided to ban Fluffy — and the kittens — from the living room). The salesman promised delivery in six weeks, but after twelve weeks there was no sign of a new couch.

■ When can a customer cancel an order?

If you are promised a delivery date and the seller fails to meet that date, you may have the right to cancel the contract. Generally, there has to be a significant delay. If the delivery date is just an estimate or if no date is given, the seller is obligated only to deliver within a reasonable time (which varies according to the standards of each particular industry). In either case, when a reasonable delivery date is not met, the buyer has the right to cancel the contract and receive a full refund. To find out what is considered "a reasonable time," you can consult a comparable furniture store.

If you had agreed on a specific date and informed the seller that time was of the essence, then you may have more freedom to cancel as soon as the order is delayed. And even if you had not specified a date, but the seller knows that time is of the essence, then you may have the right to cancel an order and refuse payment. For instance, when a caterer is hired to serve a party that starts at a specific hour, it's pretty clear when the delivery of the services is expected.

Beatrice canceled the couch order and bought one from a different store. This time, the couch arrived on time but was the wrong color. Beatrice had ordered ivory, and this was pumpkin.

■ **If a piece of furniture is not what the customer ordered, can it be returned at the store's expense?**

Yes. If a couch is a different color from the one you ordered, you can refuse to accept it. The company or store is required to pay the return shipping expense.

If you accepted the goods and then discovered there was a problem, you can cancel the contract and "revoke your acceptance" only if

- **you accepted the goods under an agreement that the seller would correct any problems**
- **you could not reasonably discover the defect at the time of acceptance (for example, the couch was boxed)**

In these circumstances you can still cancel the contract and return the goods at the seller's expense. But you must act promptly after you discover the problem. Additionally, the defect must substantially reduce the value of the couch to you. The wrong color probably meets this test, while a minor scratch might not.

MAIL-ORDER GOODS

Mail Fraud

Beatrice had never been a great sleeper. One of her favorite activities when she was up in the middle of the night was retail therapy: catalog shopping using toll-free phone numbers. But when she received a chartreuse crushed-velvet robe in the mail with her initials embossed on it, she was stymied. She never ordered it, and it was delivered COD (cash on delivery).

■ **Does a person have to pay for something she receives in the mail if she didn't order it?**

Sending unordered goods in the mail is prohibited by federal law (39 U.S.C. Section 3009) unless the goods are accompanied by a notice that the consumer may treat the goods as a gift. You neither have to return the goods nor pay for them.

Beatrice refused to pay for the robe, and the mail carrier assured her that she was not responsible for payment. A few weeks later, however, she started receiving unpleasant notices from Cozy Comfort, the manufacturer of the robe.

■ **What should a person do if a company insists on payment for something he didn't order?**

Any threats by the company that sent the goods are illegal. You should report the company to the mail fraud division of the U.S. Postal Service and to the Federal Trade Commission.

Credit Card Purchases

Beatrice *did* order some flannel pajamas for herself and the kids. (She was determined to lower her heating bills.) But the nights were getting colder and the pjs still hadn't arrived.

■ **What should a person do if she orders something from a catalog (and pays by credit card) and never receives it?**

In general, the Federal Trade Commission requires mail-order sellers to deliver goods within the time promised. If no time is stated, then the seller has thirty days to get you the goods. If the seller can't meet this deadline, the company must notify you and offer a full refund if you don't want to accept a delayed delivery.

Federal law also gives consumers specific rights when they buy something with a credit card, and in many circumstances you are entitled to withhold payment to the credit card company while it investigates your dispute with the store or company that sold you something. The law considers charges for goods that were not delivered, or that you reject because they are defective, as "billing errors." Within sixty days of the first billing of the charge on your credit card statement, you should notify the credit card company (in writing) of the error. When you dispute a charge, the federal Fair Credit Billing Act requires the credit card company to investigate, and the company may have to delete the charge from your bill unless it determines it was valid. It is the card company's duty to conduct the investigation. You cannot be assessed finance charges on the disputed amount if it is deleted.

Consumers also have specific rights that apply to all claims connected with credit card purchases (not just "billing errors"). Generally, if you have problems with something you bought with a credit card, you can complain to the credit card company, although you must usually try first to resolve the problem with the seller or the manufacturer.

In certain circumstances, a credit card company is essentially in the same shoes as a seller would be, so you can make the same claims against the credit card company as you could against the store. When you receive defective goods or services, you have the right to refuse payment to the credit card company if

- **you charged an item on a credit card issued directly by a store**
- **ads for the product you have problems with were sent with your credit card statement**
- **the charge is greater than $50 and the seller is in the same state or within 100 miles of your address**

When you dispute a charge, you should do so in writing.

Even if the credit card company is not legally required to delete a disputed charge, it may still be worthwhile to raise your claim. That's because all credit card companies have contracts with sellers that allow the credit card companies to get reimbursement from the seller when a charge is in dispute. If you have a dispute with a merchant, you are often better off challenging the charge with the credit card company, since it very well may delete a contested charge. It is much more difficult to go ahead and pay the credit card company for the disputed charge and then try to get a reimbursement from the seller.

(For more on credit cards, see page 370.)

DOOR-TO-DOOR SALES

Canceling an Order

"Have the world at your fingertips . . . from A to Z," said the salesman standing at Beatrice's front door. It sounded good to Beatrice, so she signed up to buy a set of encyclopedias. That night she had second thoughts: the kids needed new shoes and winter coats, not a big set of books they might never open. When she called to cancel the order the next day, the company told her it was too late. "Sorry, lady," said the office manager. "A deal's a deal."

■ Can a customer cancel an order from a door-to-door salesman?

Yes. Special consumer protections apply to home solicitation sales. Because you neither initiated the contact nor can simply walk away, a salesperson at your home can exert additional pressure on you to buy. Under both federal and state law, you have three business days to cancel the sale and receive a full refund. Under federal law and in most states, the salesperson is required to give you a form explaining this right, and your right to cancel does not usually begin until you have received the notice. (The notice must be in the same language as that principally used in the oral presentation. So if the sale was in Spanish, the notice must also be in Spanish.) If you cancel within the three-day time frame, the seller must take back the goods. In most states, if the items are not picked up from you, at the seller's expense and within a reasonable time, they are yours to keep without obligation. The seller must also refund any payment you already made for the goods.

Selling a Used Car

To sell a used car, you are required by law to provide the buyer with two documents:

- **the title certificate**
- **an odometer statement (which shows the mileage of the car)**

The following *are not* required, but are documents you may want to turn over:

- **the warranty, if it is transferable (see page 58)**
- **service records, especially if you have followed the manufacturer's recommendations**

While no law requires you to write a receipt to the buyer indicating that you are selling the car "as is," it is a good idea to protect yourself by doing so — unless you intend to guarantee the car.

You also are not required to disclose any apparent defects to the buyer. It is the buyer who has to inspect the car and discover such problems. However, you do have a duty to disclose any *hidden* defects that a buyer cannot reasonably be expected to discover, such as a knock that starts after the car has been running for an hour, or problems with overheating in warm weather. You should also be careful not to make positive statements about the condition of the car. ("It'll never break down on you." "These tires will last another 50,000 miles.") This type of statement can create an enforceable express warranty.

BUYING AND SELLING USED CARS

For years Beatrice had been driving an orange hatchback she bought from her cousin, and she loved her little car. But the poor thing had gone 150,000 miles and was beginning to knock ominously. Beatrice started reading the car ads in *The Gazette,* but she was a little nervous about buying a used car from a stranger.

■ **Is there a special procedure to follow when buying a used car?**

Yes. Make sure you know the condition of the car and don't just take the owner's word for it. Always take the car to an independent mechanic for a thorough checking out. You will have to pay the mechanic, but you need to know what you are buying. Also, make sure that you receive clear title to the car, especially if you are buying from an individual. Ownership of a car is transferred with a title certificate, which is a document issued by the state's department of motor vehicles and often labeled something like "certificate of title." The holder of that piece of paper owns the car under the law. Any **liens** (financial claims) against the car — such as bank loans — will appear on the title. These liens should be marked "Satisfied" before you buy. (You can call the lien holder to verify that it hasn't been marked falsely.) If the lien has not been paid, the lien holder could still seize the car from you, since a change of ownership does not eliminate the lien.

Many states also have certificate-of-title laws for boats and other motor vehicles besides cars.

Dealing with an Individual

Beatrice went to look at a used station wagon being sold by a guy named Bob. It seemed to be a good deal, but when Beatrice asked Bob to put something in writing, he looked at her as if she had just dropped down from Mars.

■ **Should a used car buyer have a contract?**

Most individual sellers do not want to give you a warranty for the condition or performance of a car. And they are under no obligation to be liable for any future problems. But if the seller does agree to give you a warranty, make sure to get it in writing. If you're the seller, you definitely should note in writing that you are selling the car "As Is" to avoid future problems (unless you want to guarantee the goods).

Buying a Used Car

A private individual is not required to offer a warranty, but all sellers must answer questions truthfully. Ask lots of them, including

- **Has the car ever been in an accident or otherwise damaged?**
- **Are there any current or prior mechanical problems?**
- **How many owners have there been, and who are they?**
- **Why is the person selling the car?**
- **Is the car still under the manufacturer's warranty?**
- **Is the warranty transferable?**
- **Does the seller have service records to show that warranty requirements have been met and the car properly maintained?**

In addition, *Consumer Reports* publishes research showing which years and makes of cars have the most and the fewest problems.

Beatrice's friend Shirley learned that her beautiful used car (which she had owned only three weeks) needed a new transmission. She called Dan, the previous owner. "Sorry, baby, you are on your own," he told her before hanging up.

■ **What recourse does a buyer have when a used car has problems?**

Not much, unless the seller made an express guarantee or lied about the condition of the car. Otherwise your only possible recourse would be the manufacturer's warranty if it still applies.

Shirley was furious about her car and decided to have it towed to Dan's driveway. She even paid a little extra to have it done in the middle of the night. When Dan tried to leave for work the next morning, he couldn't get out. Shirley had blocked his garage. "It's a lemon!" she yelled at him when he called her, enraged.

■ **What are lemon laws?**

Lemon laws require *manufacturers* to repair defective cars. If the repairs are not made within a reasonable amount of time and number of attempts, the manufacturer is required to refund the purchase price, less a reasonable amount for the use of the car.

While almost all states have lemon laws that cover new cars, only a few states have lemon laws covering used cars. The laws for used cars typically require the dealer (not the manufacturer) to refund the purchase price, less a reasonable allowance for the use of the car. The dealer usually gets a specified number of chances or days to fix the car.

Most lemon laws apply only if the defect arises during the period of the manufacturer's express warranty or for one year, whichever is longer. Some manufacturers have a "mandatory dispute resolution procedure." That means you may not be able to go directly to court without first trying to resolve the problem under this procedure.

While the lemon laws apply to situations where the dealer cannot fix your car in a reasonable amount of time, they are not your only protection. Consumers are also guarded by warranties, unfair-trade laws, and fraud laws. These warranties and laws are relevant if the dealer made false statements to sell you the car, or if the dealer fails to honor the car's warranties.

Dealing with a Dealer

After Shirley's disaster buying from an individual, Beatrice decided to buy her car from a dealer. She visited Turnpike Jerry's Used Car Lot. She'd heard that Turnpike Jerry was supposed to be honest — and he was. He told her flat out that he didn't offer warranties on any of his cars. "But I can get you a great deal on a great car," he promised.

■ **Do used car dealers have to offer warranties?**

Only a handful of states require dealers to provide warranties on used cars. But even these laws are limited — some of them have exceptions for high-mileage and inexpensive cars. Under federal law, the dealer is required only to post a notice in the window of a used car stating whether or not it is being sold with a warranty. However, when the dealer sells a service contract with the car, that usually triggers an implied warranty that lasts for the duration of the service contract.

Odometer Regulations

Well, I guess Turnpike Jerry wasn't as honest as he made out to be," sighed Beatrice to her mechanic. She had decided to buy a powder blue wagon and had taken it for a routine inspection. Turnpike Jerry had tried to talk her out of even inspecting it: "Take a look. It only has 5,300 miles on it. It's practically brand new!" The truth was more like 53,000, the inspector told Beatrice.

Is odometer tampering illegal?

Yes. It constitutes general fraud, and federal and state laws prohibit it and require truthful disclosure of a car's mileage. If the odometer has been doctored, the dealer must refund your money, and very well may be liable for punitive damages, which under federal and state odometer laws could include triple the amount of damages awarded plus attorneys' fees.

CASE IN POINT

Cars from Hell

When is a car actually "accepted" by a buyer: when a deposit is put down, or when the buyer gets the keys and drives off? The question is an important one in cases of buyers discovering their new pride and joy is a lemon.

The Smiths, a New Jersey couple, put down a deposit for a new 1966 Chevrolet Biscayne sedan. Just before picking up the car, Mr. Smith gave the dealer a check for the balance. When Mrs. Smith tried to drive the car home, it stalled several times and then limped home at 10 miles per hour. Furious, her husband called his bank and canceled the check. The Smiths then refused to accept the dealer's offer to repair the transmission and rejected the car outright. Two suits resulted: the dealer sued for the balance, and the Smiths countersued for return of the deposit and incidental charges.

A key issue at the trial and on appeal was the timing: when was the car officially accepted by the Smiths, and was there a stated or implied warranty that protected them? The court found that the Smiths had not yet accepted the car when Mrs. Smith drove it away — because neither she nor her husband had had "a reasonable opportunity to inspect" the vehicle, which the appeals court decided would take more time than their test spin. Even if they had accepted the car, the defective vehicle "breached the implied warranty of merchantability," the court ruled. The Smiths were vindicated.

A Maryland couple had a similar experience with their brand-new 1978 Ford Granada. Six days after paying cash for the vehicle, the Levines were shocked when its engine conked out after only 109 miles. They towed it to the dealer, who took the engine apart, found major defects, and offered to rebuild it. The Levines declined, insisting on a new car. The dealer and the carmaker refused. A lawsuit ensued when the dealer would not refund their purchase price.

The trial jury found that the seller's offer to repair did not adequately rectify the problem, and awarded the Levines the lemon's purchase price plus damages equal to the price of their replacement car. On appeal the payment for the replacement car was reversed as improper. The Levines did, however, win a ruling that the defendants would have to pay their attorneys' fees.

BUYING AND SELLING NEW CARS

Returning a Car

Great news! Beatrice was promoted at her job. Her new position and new salary helped her decide that she should have a *new* car. When she went to the dealer, he didn't have the color she wanted in stock, so she put it on order. Beatrice was excited when she heard that it had finally arrived. But her excitement died when she actually saw it. She thought aquamarine would match her eyes.

■ **Can a customer reject a car if it's not what was expected?**

It depends. If the car fails to match the description or specifications of the car you ordered, or if it is actually defective, you have the right to reject it and recover your deposit. Once you take the car home, you can later reject it only if

- **there are substantial defects that you could not reasonably find when the car was delivered (such as difficulty starting in cold weather)**
- **there are defects (perhaps a rattling muffler) that you reasonably believed the seller would correct**

Under either of these circumstances, you must reject the car promptly after you discover the defects or discover that the dealer will not correct them. Be aware that once you accept the car (or any other consumer item), it will be much more difficult to return it. For instance, if you find a big scratch on the door two days after you get the car, you will be hard pressed to prove that the scratch happened before you took possession of the car. Thus, you should examine the goods very carefully before accepting them. In a situation where you can return the car, you will be able to get your deposit refunded.

If you simply change your mind about buying the car, backing out of the deal would be a breach of contract. In that case, there is probably a clause in your contract that states what your financial obligation to the dealer is. The more special your order is, the more you are likely to have to pay if you have a change of heart.

(Also see "lemon laws" on page 65.)

LEASING A CAR

After the fiasco with her used car, Beatrice's friend Shirley decided to look into leasing. Not surprisingly, she wanted the least risky arrangement she could possibly make.

■ **Can a leased car be returned if it's a lemon?**

In most states, probably not. In only a few states do lemon laws specifically cover leased cars. More states are moving in this direction, though, because of the increasing popularity of car leasing. Even if the lemon law does not cover your leased car, the leasing company may be required to responsibly perform any repairs on the car. It's typical, though, for the person leasing the car to be responsible for any repairs not covered by the manufacturer's warranty.

Shirley signed a leasing contract and was soon tooling around town in her new luxury sedan. Quite a switch from her little sports car, but *that* was a lemon. And the great thing was, she could never afford to own this car. Unfortunately, Shirley — a real estate broker — was having a bad year. She began falling behind on her payments.

■ **Can a person cancel the lease without having to pay for the entire term?**

Yes, but if you terminate a car lease early, you will still owe additional money, just not the full amount of the remaining payments. It would be an unfair windfall for the lessor to have both the car and all the lease payments.

But because the value of a new car drops rapidly when it is driven (whether bought or leased), this drop in value is usually reflected in the early-termination charge. Thus, it can be very expensive for consumers to lease cars and terminate the lease early. The federal Consumer Leasing Act requires leasing companies to disclose the charges for early termination, and requires this charge to be reasonable. At present, no definition of "reasonable" charges exists, but the growing car-leasing business is due for regulation soon. In any case, whenever you return the car, you will be liable for excess mileage and any damage beyond normal wear and tear.

CAR REPAIRS

Kachunk! Kachunk!

No doubt about it, the muffler on Beatrice's car was on the blink. Beatrice left the car at the repair shop on her way to work. When she returned at the end of the day, the muffler had been fixed, but so had a few other things. The mechanic had replaced the brake fluid and realigned the tires.

"I'm not paying for this!" Beatrice fumed.

Is a person obligated to pay for unauthorized car repairs?

Probably not. About half the states have laws regulating car repairs. These laws usually require protections for the customer, such as written estimates and explicit authorization for repairs. If you didn't authorize the repairs, then, most likely, you don't have to pay for them. If you make an oral agreement, look around to see if any signs say that the garage is "Authorized to do any necessary work." If you have a written agreement, read the fine print carefully before signing. Guard against problems by

- **choosing a reputable mechanic**
- **being explicit with the mechanic that you want to be called before any additional work is performed**
- **reading the fine print, which may authorize any "necessary work"**

Getting an Estimate

Fluffy had another litter of kittens, this time in the backseat of Beatrice's new car. After finding homes for all the kittens, Beatrice dropped Fluffy at the vet to be spayed, and then dropped the car at the shop to have the upholstery replaced.

"No cleaning fluid will get out that mess," the mechanic asserted. He told her it would cost $300, including labor, to redo the seats, but when she returned to pick up the car, he handed her a bill for $559.

Does a customer have to pay the difference between the quoted price and the bill?

Many states that regulate car repairs require written estimates *and* customer approval before the estimate can be exceeded by a specified percentage, usually 10 percent. (In other words, if the estimate is $300, and the billed cost is $310, you probably *would* have to pay this nominal difference.) In states with these rules, you are not liable for charges that exceed the limit.

In other states, your liability depends on the particular facts. Was the mechanic's price fixed, or was it just an estimate? If it was a fixed price, the mechanic must honor it. If it was just an estimate (which is more common), you have agreed to pay an hourly labor rate plus parts. In these circumstances, you would be liable for all charges for work that was necessary. As long as the estimate was made in good faith, and the extra charges are not a result of the mechanic's error, you would have to pay.

It is illegal for a mechanic to "lowball" an estimate, knowingly getting you to agree to a low estimate and then charging you a much higher rate. But it can be very difficult to prove such a case in court. As with all consumer complaints, you can call your state attorney general's office, the state consumer protection department, or the local Better Business Bureau to report the incident. While none of these offices will act as your personal attorney, sometimes they will contact the merchant. If so contacted, many reputable merchants will want to resolve the dispute so as not to go on record for having bad business practices.

Bad Repairs

Whenever Blossom hit the brakes, her van pulled to the left. Four hundred dollars later, the problem still existed. In fact, Blossom was wondering if it had gotten worse. When she took the car back to the shop, the mechanic said, "Sure I can fix it. But it'll cost you."

That wasn't quite the way Blossom saw it. "I already paid you to fix my car," she said. "Now get it right."

■ Does a customer have to pay for additional repairs if the problem wasn't fixed the first time?

The law in most states requires mechanics to provide services in a workmanlike manner. That means the mechanic must possess and use reasonable skill in performing the work. Liability for additional charges depends on whether a reasonably careful mechanic would have fixed the original problem for the original charge. If the mechanic failed to use reasonable care in performing the repair and this is the cause of the additional expense, you would not be responsible for additional charges. If the mechanic is not at fault — for instance, the problem is just a difficult one to diagnose or fix — you *would* be responsible for the additional charges. In reality, these disputes can be difficult to handle since people often don't have the expertise to know whether or not a mechanic used reasonable care. Often, your best bet is to get a second opinion from another repairman.

Some car repair companies, usually national chains, advertise guarantees for their work. They have to honor these guarantees. All these cases can be difficult to prove, however, because they frequently depend on technical expertise.

> **How Can You Avoid Repair Nightmares?**
>
> The best way to avoid car repair problems is to choose a skilled and reputable mechanic. Your local Better Business Bureau and state regulatory agencies can tell you if any complaints have been filed against a particular mechanic. But the best resource of all is a personal reference from someone you trust.

Disputing Repair Charges

After a second shot at fixing the car, the mechanic took Blossom for a drive to demonstrate that the problem was really gone. But since Blossom was still refusing to pay extra, the mechanic wouldn't release her car. And, in addition, he was threatening to charge *her* a daily rate for *his* storage of *her* car!

■ What should a consumer do if a mechanic refuses to return a car until a disputed bill is paid?

Under the statutes of most states, a garage has the right to keep a car until the repair charges are paid. This is called a "possessory lien." Also, many lien statutes and repair agreements allow the garage to charge storage fees for a certain time after the car is repaired — even when there is no dispute over the repair costs. So it's usually in your interest to pick up your car as soon as possible to avoid such charges.

When there's a dispute over repair costs, a few states have special laws that allow consumers to pay the charges directly to a court clerk (or other specified person), thereby putting the money in **escrow**. That way you can get your car back while the dispute is being settled. But, in most cases, you either will have to pay the charge or go to court to get possession of your car. When you dispute a charge, you may want to document your disagreement on the bill by writing "Paid Under Dispute" or "I object to/disagree with this charge."

Another strategy when your car is being held hostage is to pay the bill with a credit card and then file a complaint with the credit card company and withhold payment to the credit card company (see pages 62 and 370). As a last resort, you can sue the garage in small-claims court to get the improper part of your bill refunded (see page 431). If you take this approach, you'll likely need to recruit another mechanic (whom you'll probably have to pay) to testify on your behalf to help prove your case. Otherwise you may have difficulties with the technical specifics of the dispute.

FOR FURTHER REFERENCE

For the number of your local Better Business Bureau:

Council of Better Business Bureaus, Inc.
4200 Wilson Boulevard, Suite 800
Arlington, VA 22203
703-276-0100

Consumer advocacy groups:

Consumer Federation of America
1424 16 Street NW, Suite 604
Washington, DC 20036
202-387-6121

Consumers Union
1666 Connecticut Avenue, Suite 310
Washington, DC 20009
202-462-6262

National Consumers League
815 15 Street NW, Suite 928
Washington, DC 20005
202-639-8140

If you have complaints in specific areas:

Credit Cards
Bankcard Holders of America
560 Herndon Parkway, Suite 120
Herndon, VA 22070
703-481-1110

Travel Agents
American Society of Travel Agents
1101 King Street
Alexandria, VA 22314
703-739-2782

United States Tour Operators Association
211 East 51 Street
New York, NY 10022
212-750-7371

The above organizations can help if the specific travel agent is a member. If not, try your local state consumer protection agency. For addresses and phone numbers, see page 71.

Car Trouble
Center for Auto Safety
2001 S Street NW
Washington, DC 20009
202-328-7700

National Automobile Dealers Association
8400 West Park Drive
McLean, VA 22102
703-821-7000

American Automobile Association's
Autosolve/Arbitration Division
1000 AAA Drive
Heathrow, FL 32746
407-444-7740

American Arbitration Association
140 West 51 Street
New York, NY 10019
212-484-4000

Better Business Bureau's Auto Line
(check with your local chapter)

Mail Order
Mail Order Action Line
c/o Direct Marketing Association
1101 17 Street NW
Washington, DC 20036-4705
202-347-1222

Brokers and Other Financial Advisers

National Association of Securities Dealers
33 Whitehall Street
New York, NY 10004
212-858-4477

Securities and Exchange Commission
Consumer Affairs Office
450 Fifth Street
Washington, DC 20549
202-942-7040

Certified Financial Planners
Board of Standards
attention: Legal Department
1660 Lincoln Street, Suite 3050
Denver, CO 80264
303-830-7543

Local state boards of accountancy handle complaints about certified public accountants

Home Improvement

Contractors should be licensed by the state. Individual state consumer protection agencies can help with complaints (see list at right for addresses and phone numbers).

Insurance

National Insurance Consumer Organization
P.O. Box 15492
Alexandria, VA 22309
703-549-8050

Also check local state insurance commissions (for listing, see page 103).

Real Estate

National Association of Realtors
777 14 Street NW
Washington, DC 20005
202-383-1000

They can direct you to the government agency that oversees realtors in your state.

Federal government offices that handle consumer complaints:

U.S. Consumer Product Safety
Commission Hotline:
800-638-2772

Food and Drug Administration
Office of Consumer Affairs
5600 Fishers Lane
Rockville, MD 20857
301-443-3170 (for consumer complaints)

FDA also has the following specific consumer complaint hotlines:

800-332-4010: seafood hotline
800-532-4440: breast implant hotline
800-332-1088: Medwatch — for complaints about medical products

Federal Trade Commission
Correspondence Branch
Room 692
6 Street and Pennsylvania Avenue NW
Washington, DC 20580
202-326-2222

Consumer Information Center
Pueblo, CO 81009
719-948-3334

This is an office of the federal government that publishes "The Consumer's Resource Handbook," listing several hundred consumer representatives and federal and state agencies that handle consumer complaints.

State Government Consumer Protection Offices

Alabama

Consumer Assistance Division
Office of Attorney General
11 South Union Street
Montgomery, AL 36130
205-242-7334
800-392-5658 (toll-free in AL)

Arizona

Consumer Protection
Office of the Attorney General
1275 West Washington Street, #259
Phoenix, AZ 85007
(for consumer information and complaints)
602-542-5763
800-352-8431 (toll-free in AZ)

Consumer Protection and Antitrust Section
Office of the Attorney General
402 West Congress Street, Suite 315
Tucson, AZ 85701
602-628-6504

Arkansas

Consumer Protection Division
Office of the Attorney General
200 Tower Building
323 Center Street
Little Rock, AR 72201
501-682-2341
800-482-8982 (toll-free in AR)

California

California Department of Consumer Affairs
400 R Street, Suite 1040
Sacramento, CA 95814
916-445-0660 (complaint assistance)
916-445-1254 (consumer information)
916-522-1799 (TDD)
800-344-9940 (toll-free in CA)

Office of Attorney General
Public Inquiry Unit
P.O. Box 944255
Sacramento, CA 94244-2550
916-322-3360
800-952-5225 (toll-free in CA)
800-952-5548 (toll-free TDD in CA)

Colorado

Consumer Protection Section
Office of Attorney General
11525 Sherman Street
Denver, CO 80203
303-866-5189
800-332-2071 (toll-free in CO)

Delaware

Consumer Protection Unit
Office of the Attorney General
820 North French Street, 4th Floor
Wilmington, DE 19801
302-577-3250 (for New Castle County)
302-739-4000 (for Kent County)
800-443-2179 (toll-free for Sussex County only)

District of Columbia

Department of Consumer and Regulatory Affairs
614 H Street NW
Washington, DC 20090
202-727-7000

Florida

Department of Agriculture and Consumer Services
Division of Consumer Services
The Mayo Building
Tallahassee, FL 32399-0800
904-488-2221
800-321-5366 (toll-free lemon law in FL)

Consumer Litigation Section
The Capitol
Tallahassee, FL 32399-1050
904-488-9105

Consumer Division
Office of Attorney General
4000 Hollywood Boulevard
Suite 505 South
Hollywood, FL 33021
305-985-4780

Georgia

Governors Office of Consumer Affairs
2 Martin Luther King Jr. Drive SE
Plaza Level — East Tower
Atlanta, GA 30334
404-651-8600 (for consumer complaints)
404-656-3790 (administrative #)
800-869-1123 (toll-free in GA)

Hawaii

Office of Consumer Protection
828 Fort St. Mall, Suite 2000B
P.O. Box 3767
Honolulu, HI 96812-3767
808-586-2630
800-468-4644 x62630 (toll-free in HI)

Idaho

Office of the Attorney General
Consumer Protection Unit
P.O. Box 83720
Boise, ID 83720-0010
208-334-2424
800-432-3545 (toll-free in ID)

Illinois

Governor's Office of Citizen's Assistance
222 South College
Springfield, IL 62706
217-782-0244
800-642-3112 (toll-free in IL)

Consumer Protection Division
Office of the Attorney General
100 West Randolph, 12th Floor
Chicago, IL 60601
312-814-3580
312-814-3374 (TDD)

Indiana

Consumer Protection Division
Office of the Attorney General
219 State House
Indianapolis, IN 46204
317-232-6330
800-382-5516 (toll-free in IN)

Iowa

Consumer Protection Division
Office of the Attorney General
1300 East Walnut Street, 2nd Floor
Des Moines, IA 50319
515-261-5926

Kansas

Consumer Protection Division
Office of the Attorney General
301 West 10th
Topeka, KS 66612-1597
913-296-3751
800-432-2310 (toll-free in KS)

Kentucky

Consumer Protection Division
Office of the Attorney General
P.O. Box 2000
1024 Capitol Center Drive
Frankfort, KY 40602
502-573-2200
800-432-9257 (toll-free in KY)

Louisiana

Consumer Protection Section
Office of the Attorney General
State Capitol Building
P.O. Box 94095
Baton Rouge, LA 70804-9095
504-342-9638

Maine

Consumer and Antitrust Division
Office of Attorney General
State House Station No. 6
Augusta, ME 04333
207-289-3716 (9 A.M.–1 P.M.)

Maryland

Consumer Protection Division
Office of the Attorney General
200 St. Paul Place
Baltimore, MD 21202-2022
410-528-8662
800-969-5766 (toll-free in MD)

Massachusetts

Consumer Protection Division
Office of the Attorney General
131 Tremont Street
Boston, MA 02111
617-727-8400

Michigan
Consumer Protection Division
Office of the Attorney General
P.O. Box 30213
Lansing, MI 48909
517-373-1140

Minnesota
Office of Consumer Services
Office of the Attorney General
1400 NCL Tower
445 Minnesota Street
St. Paul, MN 55101
612-296-3353
800-657-3787

Mississippi
Consumer Protection Division
Office of the Attorney General
P.O. Box 22947
Jackson, MS 39225-2947
601-354-6018

Missouri
Office of Attorney General
Consumer Complaints or Problems
P.O. Box 899
Jefferson City, MO 65102
314-751-3321
800-392-8222 (toll-free in MO)

Montana
Department of Commerce
Consumer Affairs Unit
1424 Ninth Avenue
Helena, MT 59620
406-444-4312

Nebraska
Consumer Protection Division
Department of Justice
2115 State Capitol
P.O. Box 98920
Lincoln, NE 68509
402-471-2682

Nevada
Consumer Affairs
Department of Business and Industry
1850 East Sahara, Suite 120
Las Vegas, NV 89104
702-486-7355
800-992-0900 (toll-free in NV)

New Hampshire
State of New Hampshire
Department of Justice
Consumer Protection and Antitrust Bureau
33 Capitol Street
Concord, NH 03301
603-271-3641

New Jersey
Division of Consumer Affairs
P.O. Box 45027
Newark, NJ 07101
201-504-6200

New Mexico
Consumer Protection Division
Office of the Attorney General
P.O. Drawer 1508
Santa Fe, NM 87504
505-827-6060
800-678-1508 (toll-free in NM)

New York
New York State Consumer Protection Board
99 Washington Avenue
Albany, NY 12210-2891
518-474-8583

Bureau of Consumer Frauds & Protection
Office of Attorney General
State Capitol
Albany, NY 12224
518-474-5481

North Carolina
Consumer Protection Section
Office of Attorney General
Raney Building
P.O. Box 629
Raleigh, NC 27602
919-733-7741

Ohio

Consumer Protection Division
Office of Attorney General
30 East Broad Street
State Office Tower, 25th Floor
Columbus, OH 43215-3428
614-466-4986 (complaints)
800-282-0515 (toll-free in OH)

Oklahoma

Consumer Protection Division
Office of Attorney General
4545 North Lincoln, Suite 260
Oklahoma City, OK 73105-3498
405-521-4274

Oregon

Financial Fraud Section
Department of Justice
Justice Building
Salem, OR 97310
503-378-4320

Pennsylvania

Bureau of Consumer Protection
Office of the Attorney General
Strawberry Square, 14th Floor
Harrisburg, PA 17120
717-787-9707
800-441-2555 (consumer hotline toll-free in PA)

Rhode Island

Consumer Protection Division
Department of Attorney General
72 Pine Street
Providence, RI 02903
401-277-2104
800-852-7776 (toll-free in RI)

South Carolina

Consumer Fraud and Antitrust Section
Office of the Attorney General
P.O. Box 11549
Columbia, SC 29211

Department of Consumer Affairs
P.O. Box 5757
Columbia, SC 29250-5757
803-734-9452
800-922-1594 (toll-free in SC)

South Dakota

Office of Consumer Protection
Office of the Attorney General
500 East Capitol, State Capitol Building
Pierre, SD 57501-5070
605-773-4400
800-300-1986 (toll-free in SD)

Texas

Consumer Protection Division
Office of Attorney General
P.O. Box 12548
Austin, TX 78711-2548
512-463-2070
800-337-3928 (toll-free in TX)

Tennessee

Division of Consumer Affairs
Department of Commerce and Insurance
500 James Robertson Parkway, 5th Floor
Nashville, TN 37243-0600
615-741-4737
800-342-8385 (toll-free in TN)

Utah

Division of Consumer Protection
Department of Commerce
160 East 3rd South
P.O. Box 45804
Salt Lake City, UT 84145-0804

Vermont

Consumer Assistance Program
104 Morrill Hall
University of Vermont
Burlington, VT 05405
802-656-3183
800-649-2424 (toll-free in VT)

Virginia

Department of Agriculture and Consumer Services
Division of Consumer Affairs
Room 101, Washington Building
1100 Bank Street
Richmond, VA 23219
mailing address:
P.O. Box 1163
Richmond, VA 23209
804-786-2042

Washington

Consumer Protection
Office of the Attorney General
905 Plum Street
Building 3
P.O. Box 40100
Olympia, WA 98504-0100
206-753-6210
800-551-4636 (toll-free in WA)

West Virginia

Consumer Protection Division
Office of the Attorney General
812 Quarrier Street, 6th Floor
Charleston, WV 25301
304-558-8986
800-368-8808 (toll-free in WV)

Wisconsin

Division of Trade & Consumer Protection
Department of Agriculture, Trade and Consumer Protection
801 West Badger Road
P.O. Box 8911
Madison, WI 53708-8911
608-266-9836
800-422-7128 (toll-free in WI)

Wyoming

Consumer Affairs Department
Office of the Attorney General
123 Capital Building
Cheyenne, WY 82002
307-777-7874

BUYING AND SELLING A HOME

7

Just as Beatrice was rushing out of the house one morning, the phone rang. She was surprised to be hearing from Isabel at House and Home Realtors, a broker who sold her the small house she bought a few years before she and Max were married.

"Bea, have you thought about moving?" Isabel queried. "I think if we put your place on the market right now, we could make you some money. A lot of money. And now that you and Max are married, it might be time to move into a house you could raise kids in. Think about it, hon, and let me know."

Beatrice mulled over the proposition. That night she dreamt she was moving into a new house, and it kept getting bigger and bigger and better and better. Maybe this *was* the right time to make the dream come true. On the other hand, she wasn't quite prepared to undertake such a massive project.

What happens when a person buys or sells a house?

The legal aspects of buying and selling property vary from state to state, but the basic transaction is the same — and in many ways is very simple: The owner of a property transfers ownership by delivering the **deed**, a written legal document, to the buyer in exchange for an agreed-upon sum of money. The deed formally grants the buyer **title** (ownership) to the property. That's it.

But of course that simple transaction has many steps leading up to it, which can become very complicated and can take months to complete. The parties must agree on the price and sign a **contract** that states the date when the exchange will take place. The buyer usually must obtain financing. The property should be physically inspected and the title searched to confirm the seller's legal ability to convey it. Finally, when everything is in order, the exchange takes place during a process known as the **closing**.

Sometimes problems arise along the way: a buyer or seller backs out; an inspection reveals serious structural problems; or restrictions on the property are revealed that make it less attractive. You're also likely to encounter a lot of legalese in the process of a real estate transaction. We've tried to demystify this process, define the basic terms, and explain as much as we can about your rights and responsibilities and the different things you should keep in mind whether you are the buyer or the seller.

BROKERS

Who Pays?

Beatrice was beginning to think that maybe it would be a good time to sell the house. After all, she and Max were planning to have children soon, and his music equipment was beginning to overrun the house. Still, she wasn't quite sure she wanted to share the proceeds of her house sale with Isabel or any other broker.

Does the seller always pay the real estate broker?

Yes, almost always. Of course, sellers don't have to use brokers, but they often do. Residential real estate brokers earn a commission, which generally is a percentage of the sales price and is set by a written agreement — the "listing agreement" — between the seller and the listing broker. (See the box on page 80.)

If the buyer finds the property through a different broker (known as a "cooperating" or "procuring" broker), the two brokers will share (usually split) the commission that is specified in the listing agreement. At the time of signing the purchase contract, the buyer is often asked to sign a document indicating that she understands that all the real estate brokers — listing as well as procuring

Real Estate 101

These are some legal terms you may encounter when buying or selling a home:

Title
The title shows who owns the property. There are several types of ownership. Joint ownership by spouses is very common and is called a **tenancy-by-the-entirety** in many states. You can also own property with other people (including your spouse) in different arrangements known as **tenancy in common** and **joint tenancy with right of survivorship.** The main difference between the two types arises when one owner dies. With a "survivorship" title, the deceased's share of the property goes to the surviving owner or owners. With a "tenancy in common," the deceased's interest goes to whomever the deceased named in his or her will, if there was one. (For more, see Chapter 11, WILLS AND TRUSTS.)

You want to be sure you are buying property with "clear title," that is with no financial or other claims against it. (See page 88.)

Deed
The deed describes the property, outlining its boundaries. There are different kinds of deeds. Some guarantee, or "warrant," that no other parties have any claims against the property. These are the most desirable types. A **quit-claim** deed, on the other hand, might spell trouble, since it gives no assurance about the nature of title. Thus, you could be acquiring a property along with all its debts.

Easement
An easement gives one party the right to go onto another party's property. For example, utilities often get easements that allow them to run pipes or phone lines beneath private property.

Lien
A lien is a financial claim against property. (See page 88.)

Encumbrance
Any claim or restriction on the property's title.

Escrow Agent
In some states, mostly in the West, escrow agents, rather than lawyers, collect the money due the respective parties and conduct the closing.

Contract
The formal agreement to buy the property. (See page 80.)

Closing
The final procedure, when the deed and title and purchase money change hands. (See page 86.)

— are acting as agents for the seller. State and local real estate boards require this disclosure as a way of protecting buyers. Buyers otherwise might assume that the broker who introduced them to the property is acting as *their* agent.

When an Offer Is Rejected or Falls Through

Bea and Max decided to sell their house. Doing so turned out to be a big drag. After six weeks of brokers and potential buyers peeking into closets and tramping through the bedroom, Beatrice was exhausted. Keeping the house presentable was challenging, especially since housework had never been Bea's idea of a good time. Max wasn't exactly enthusiastic about it, either.

When Isabel called to relay an offer from a buyer, Bea was jubilant. She and Max had listed the house at $200,000, but were willing to accept $175,000. The buyer was offering $180,000. Beatrice and Max told Isabel to accept it, but then had second thoughts. The next morning Max called Isabel (before she had contacted the buyer). "The deal is off," he said. "We decided we want at least $190,000."

Checklists for Buyers and Sellers

Buyer's List

- Exactly what property is included in the sale?
- What kind of deed are you getting? (See the box opposite.)
- If you're buying a condo or a new home, check on the number of units already sold and the developer's reputation and financial stability.
- What's the neighborhood like? Are there any local development plans that will affect the property?
- What are the property taxes?
- What other taxes are there?
- What is the physical condition of the property? Any termite, radon, asbestos, lead paint, or water-quality problems?

Seller's List

- Will you use a broker? If so, what kind of commission will the broker get?
- What's included in the sale?
- What's your asking price?
- Are there any defects you are required to disclose by the laws of your state?
- Do you have debts that will affect your ability to sell the home?

Does the broker have to be paid if the seller rejects an offer?

It depends on the language of your listing agreement. As the seller, it is in your best interests for the agreement to state that the commission will be paid only upon *completion* of the sale of the property. But many listing agreements require you to pay the commission if a "ready, willing, and able" purchaser is found, whether or not the sale is completed. In that case, you are legally obligated to pay the commission whenever an offer is presented that meets all the requirements stated in the listing agreement — including your full asking price. The flip side of that obligation is that, until all the conditions in the listing agreement are met, you do not owe the commission, no matter how much work the broker has done.

Let's say you agree to pay a commission of 6 percent on a sales price of $200,000. If you reject an offer of $180,000 (because it's less than the listing agreement price), you do not have to pay the commission. However, if the offer had been for $200,000 and all the other conditions of your agreement with the broker were met, then you *would* owe the commission, even if you changed your mind later and did not want to go through with the sale. If you decide to accept the $180,000 offer, the broker still earns the commission, but it will be 6 percent of $180,000 rather than of $200,000.

What if the buyer withdraws the offer?

If you are buying a property, you are free to withdraw an offer at any time *before it is accepted.* But in some cases, if the buyer backs out after acceptance, the seller may still owe the commission, depending on the wording of the agreement between the broker and the seller. In an attempt to recover the money lost by your change of heart, the seller might then sue you for breaching the agreement to buy the property.

When the Sellers Find a Buyer

Beatrice and Max were in a bind. Isabel had insisted on being the only broker for the house, which seemed fine at the time. But then Bea's friend Derek told her he wanted to buy the place. He had ambitious plans for an herb garden, and the backyard's southern exposure was just perfect.

"Let's just make a deal and skip the broker's fee," Derek suggested.

If the sellers find a buyer without using the broker, do they still have to pay a commission?

Maybe. It depends on the terms of your listing agreement. If you wish to place your home on the market, but think that someone you know may be interested in buying the house, you should specify that individual in the contract as an exception to paying the commission. This is commonly done.

What Is a Listing Agreement?

A listing agreement is simply a contract between a property owner and a broker. It typically includes

- **the length of the listing period**
- **the desired sales price**
- **the amount of the commission**
- **any exceptions to paying the commission (such as when the owner sells directly to a friend)**

The agreement does not need to follow the form that the broker presents. All matters are open to negotiation.

Naturally, your broker will prefer to have no exclusions, but will generally agree to reasonable requests. Exclusions of this nature, however, must be made at the time the listing agreement is signed.

If you make a deal to sell to your friend during the period of the listing, but did not exclude the friend from the listing agreement, you will still owe the broker the commission even though the broker did no work. If you do list your friend as an exclusion and then he sends his cousin to look at the place and she decides to buy, you will have to pay the commission, since the cousin would not have been named in your contract as an exclusion.

You might negotiate with the broker to include a statement in the agreement that says that if you find a buyer without the broker's assistance then the commission will be a lower percentage, perhaps half the full fee or even less.

MAKING A DEAL

Binders and Contracts

Beatrice and Max shook hands with Derek on the deal, and Bea and Max began househunting for themselves. Two days later, Derek called to tell them that Hot Stuff, one of the country's leading salsa producers, had offered him a job. The only problem is that the company's headquarters were 1,000 miles away. He hadn't decided whether or not to take the job, but he wondered if they would keep the house off the market while he decided. Beatrice was worried. Maybe she should have gotten a commitment from Derek in writing.

Should an agreement be in writing?

Absolutely. According to every state's laws, an agreement for the sale of real estate is not binding unless it is in writing. Occasionally, sales are consummated without a written agreement, but that puts both parties at risk. All parties preparing for real estate transactions incur expenses, and without a written agreement, you have no recourse if the other party backs out of the deal. If you enter an oral agreement with respect to property, put it down in writing as soon as possible.

What is a binder?

A binder is an outline of the basic terms of a proposed sales contract between a buyer and a seller. It includes

- **the property address**
- **names of the parties**
- **proposed closing date**
- **purchase price, including financing**
- **what happens if a buyer can't get a mortgage or if an inspection reveals serious problems with the dwelling**

The use of a binder is a matter of "local custom." In most areas, binders aren't used and a standard form completed with the realtor's assistance serves as the final, binding contract. But in certain parts of Connecticut and New York, among other places, it is customary to draw up a binder and collect a small deposit from the buyer (usually $500 or 1 percent of the agreed price), often in cases where the homes are more expensive. In most states, a binder is considered evidence of the intention to enter into a contract, but is not itself an enforceable contract. Thus signing a binder does not give either party the right to sue if the other one decides not to go ahead with the transaction. Only a real estate contract — also called a purchase and sale agreement

— gives parties enforceable rights against each other. These rights are specified in the contract.

What is the contract?

The contract, also known as the purchase and sale agreement, lays out the key issues of the sale. To be enforceable, a contract must clearly identify

- **the exact property to be sold**
- **the purchase price**
- **the proposed closing date**
- **the names of the parties**

Both the seller and the prospective buyer must sign the contract. The buyer usually signs first, and sometimes, an agent or fiduciary (a person who is authorized to act for one of the parties) will sign the contract. The contract can be circulated through the mail to get the necessary signatures. It's not required to have a "sit-down" meeting to sign it.

Is a lawyer needed?

It varies greatly from state to state. In many states, particularly in the West, a buyer may never see a lawyer, because the whole closing process is handled through an escrow agent or a closer for a title insurance company. These are impartial people who represent neither the buyer nor the seller. Their duties are to carry out the closing. In those states, a lawyer might be involved only if a dispute arises between buyer and seller as to the requirements of the contract, or the condition of the title to the property. In other states, however, buyers may want to hire an attorney for any of the following reasons:

- **to review (or prepare) the contract before it is signed**
- **to negotiate issues raised by a seller's counteroffer**
- **to coordinate the miscellaneous payments that get made at the closing**
- **to advise on the best means to comply with any special requirements of the lender**
- **to represent the mortgage lender at the closing in some states (There are often a lot of mortgage documents to sign at the closing, and some lenders allow the buyer's attorney to represent them at that proceeding. This arrangement usually reduces the buyer's closing costs.)**
- **to review the deed from the seller**
- **to review or prepare the title insurance policy (see page 88)**
- **to record title documents on the land records, including releases of old mortgages and other liens**

A seller may want to retain a lawyer for the following reasons:

- **to prepare the deed**
- **to make sure that all papers necessary to provide clear title to the buyer are received**
- **to make arrangements to pay off any liens or mortgages on the property**

When entering a real estate transaction, you should ask a broker or friend when it is customary in your area to involve a lawyer. But you should always see a lawyer if you expect any parts of the transaction to be difficult or to require special treatment.

How are legal fees calculated?

As always when you retain a lawyer, you should discuss fees in advance (see Chapter 30, FINDING AND USING A LAWYER). Most lawyers charge a fixed fee for a residential closing. That fee may include one or more of the following:

- **contract negotiation and preparation**
- **contract review**
- **representation of the lender**
- **review of loan documents**
- **review a title search**
- **attendance at closing**
- **preparation of documents needed for the closing**
- **preparation of a postclosing statement and gathering your documents for storage**

Contract Checklist

What the Buyer Wants

The contract should include a standard clause that enables the buyer to have inspections made of the property. The contract should also allow you to terminate the agreement and get your deposit refunded under a range of circumstances, including

- **your inability to obtain financing for the purchase within an agreed-upon time and at prevailing rates**
- **the discovery of mechanical problems or environmental hazards (such as radon or lead paint)**
- **discovery of other problems that you could not have found before signing the contract**

Many states now have laws requiring sellers to disclose to buyers the existence of any problems relating to the property. But there are still many questions about a property that the seller may not be able to answer. For example:

- Does the property comply with the local building and zoning rules?
- Are there any proposed developments near the property that might affect your use of it?
- Is there a possibility of a proceeding by the city or town to widen or build a road?
- If you are buying a condominium or cooperative apartment, is the building or development financially secure?

Your best protection as a buyer is to find answers to your questions about the property *before* you enter into the contract, although some information, like an inspection report, probably won't be obtainable until after you have a contract. The contract should also specify what personal property, such as appliances, is included in the sale. It should also address how damages will be determined if either party defaults on the agreement.

What the Seller Wants

If you are the seller, you want the contract to specify that

- **you are entitled to receive damages (usually the amount of the deposit) if the buyer does not fulfill his or her end of the agreement**
- **any statements you made about the property are accurate to the best of your knowledge**
- **any of the buyer's contingencies — such as getting financing or having inspections made of the property — be satisfied in the least amount of time that is reasonable**

It is important to remember that if you give a buyer sixty days to obtain mortgage financing, on the fifty-ninth day after signing the contract the buyer may advise you that he or she has been turned down for financing. As long as the buyer is within the bounds of the contract, you will have to return her deposit, and will have lost sixty days in trying to sell your home.

BREAKING A DEAL

Beatrice and Max made a deal with Derek and "went to contract." Ten days later, Derek got another call from Hot Stuff. The salsa maker had sweetened the offer with a company car and a moving allowance.

"I think I should take it," Derek told Bea. "Working in salsa is my dream!"

"We've got a contract," Beatrice reminded him.

When can a contract be broken?

A contract typically will specify what conditions allow for it to be broken with no financial consequences. Sometimes a buyer may terminate simply because she is not "satisfied" with the inspection report, but the more typical reasons a contract may be broken include

- **the buyer cannot get financing and informs the seller before the deadline imposed by the contract**
- **incurable environmental hazards are discovered in the property**
- **there are defects in the title or survey results**
- **irreparable mechanical problems are revealed upon inspection**

If you're a buyer, you're responsible for making sure that the seller receives timely notice of any problems that may result in a termination of the contract. For instance, the contract may state that you have thirty days to notify the seller of an inability to get mortgage financing. If, on day thirty-one, you tell the seller that you could not get a mortgage, you will have lost the right to break the contract without forfeiting the deposit.

It is important to read the contract carefully and make sure you understand what it says, and that it covers all matters that concern you. *The words of*

CASE IN POINT

Boo! Buyers Beware of Ghosts

When Jeffrey Stambovsky made a $32,500 down payment and entered into a contract to buy a riverfront Victorian house in the suburban village of Nyack, New York, in 1989, he was unaware that the home was widely reputed to be haunted by ghosts. And the seller, Helen Ackley, who had reportedly seen the poltergeists on numerous occasions, made no effort to tell him.

So when Stambovsky, a New York City resident, learned of his future home's ghoulish reputation, he was horrified and sued to cancel his contract to buy, arguing that since he was not informed of the phantasmal nature of the house, the contract was not legally fair. Ackley countered that buyers take a house "as is," so she had no duty to inform him of the home's spiritual qualities.

The trial court dismissed Stambovsky's case, ruling that no legal remedy was available for his ghoulish problem. In a 1991 decision, a New York state appellate court ruled that the contract could be rescinded and Stambovsky could recover his down payment. The decision noted that while most home buyers know that they're supposed to send a structural engineer or termite expert to inspect a dwelling before agreeing to buy it, few would think to hire a psychic to inspect whether the house was also inhabited by ghosts. From the perspective of a buyer, wrote Judge Israel Rubin, "a very practical problem arises with respect to the discovery of a paranormal phenomenon: 'Who you gonna call?' as the title song to the movie 'Ghostbusters' asks."

Rubin also noted that the presence of ghosts implied that Ackley was not delivering the premises "vacant" as she was required to do under the contract.

the contract govern the relationship and rights of the parties, and have nothing to do with what either party may have been told by the broker. Frequently, a standard-form contract will be used, with amendments made to meet the needs of each party. You should not assume that the standard-form contract will be fair to you as a buyer. That is why it might be helpful to have a lawyer review the contract before you sign it, especially if you don't understand it or feel comfortable with it.

While customs vary from state to state and even within a state, in all states attorneys will be used from time to time to draft the contract when the buyer has special concerns or is especially careful — particularly if the high price of a house justifies the additional legal expense. In cases where the closing (see page 86) is not handled through an escrow or title company, lawyers will prepare the closing documents, such as the title insurance policy (see page 88) and deed (see page 78) and will supervise the signing of any mortgage documents required by the lender.

Finding Defects in the Property

Derek was torn. He really did love the house and didn't particularly want to relocate to another state. But salsa . . .

Maybe instead of planting herbs, he'd plant peppers and do some experimenting of his own. Maybe someday he could have his own line of hot sauce!

In the meantime, he had only six weeks left to get his mortgage and do all the necessary inspections of Beatrice and Max's house. When Derek read the inspector's report, he was shocked. The faucets leaked in every sink; there was only one electrical outlet in the kitchen; and the soil sample revealed a high level of clay that he feared could be disastrous for his pepper plants.

■ What happens if the buyer discovers defects in the property?

It depends on the wording of the contract's "inspection contingency clause." To induce the buyer

CASE IN POINT

Home Is Where the Bugs Are

The great thing about termites, from the point of view of a house seller, is that they are silent and usually invisible. Home buyers, obviously, have a different point of view. When Neil Swinton found out in 1942 that his new home was infested with the wood-eaters, he sued the seller, who'd taken his money without bothering to mention that unpleasant fact. But Swinton was out of luck: the Supreme Judicial Court of Massachusetts ruled that it was up to the buyer to inspect for termites. Mere "nondisclosure," ruled the court, didn't rise to the level of fraud.

The Swinton case attracted wide notoriety and has now become mostly a relic in the casebooks read by first-year law students. Today, courts are more inclined to take pity on clueless buyers, who are rarely treated as harshly as the Swintons were. Take, for instance, the case of Donald and Estella Krobatsch, who had signed a contract to buy a New Jersey house. In 1971, before closing the deal, they went to visit the house one evening. Turning on the lights, they saw what they later described in a document as an appalling scene — "roaches literally running in all directions, up the walls, drapes, etc."

When the couple called off the deal, the seller and broker sued to keep the deposit and collect the broker's fees, and won. But the Krobatsches appealed and won in the New Jersey Supreme Court, which held that when it's proven that the seller and broker had knowledge of a significant problem not immediately apparent to the buyers, and knowingly failed to disclose it, then the buyers could break the contract.

to go ahead with the transaction, many sellers agree to make repairs or give a cash adjustment for problems disclosed by inspections. The inspection contingency clause determines what will happen if the seller refuses to repair defects that are revealed by the inspections. This clause sometimes gives the buyer the right to terminate the contract if he or she is "not satisfied" with the results of the inspection. In some contracts, the clause allows the buyer to terminate only if the inspection reveals "substantial structural or mechanical defects."

For example, if you learn that a windowpane is cracked, a closet door is not hung properly, and the bathtub faucet leaks, the inspection contingency clause may let you break the contract, since you are "not satisfied." But these defects would not generally be considered "substantial." However, if the inspector reports that the furnace needs replacing, the electrical system is dangerous, or the house is about to slide down the cliff on which it is built, these problems would definitely qualify as substantial defects, and the contract most likely could be canceled.

In addition, you should examine the property just before closing to make sure that no damage has occurred since the last inspection, and to see that the seller has fully complied with the contract by doing any specified cleaning, leaving fireplace screens, or repairing a broken furnace, for example. If there are problems in this regard, the seller and buyer usually work out some financial arrangement at, or preferably before, the closing to compensate the buyer or ensure that the repairs will be made.

Unexpected Damage to the Property

It had been raining steadily for twelve days. Bea had never seen such a deluge. On the thirteenth day when she went to the garage to get her car, she couldn't believe her eyes. The garage was flooded, and water was leaking everywhere through the roof. And it was only four weeks until they were supposed to close on the deal with Derek. Beatrice had gone inside to call Max when she heard a deafening crack of thunder and then a loud crash. She looked out the window just in time to see an old oak tree crashing onto the roof of the garage.

"Guess I don't have to worry about the leaking anymore," she thought.

■ What if some damage happens unexpectedly to the property after the contract is signed?

The contract will determine who is liable for the repairs. Most often the sellers, usually through their homeowner's insurance, bear the cost of repairing weather-related damage and other damages, too. If the repairs are not completed by the closing date, the contract usually gives the buyer a choice: wait until the repairs are made; accept the money from the insurer in lieu of the repairs; or terminate the contract. If you are the buyer, you want the contract to give you a wide range of options on this issue. In general, it is the seller's responsibility to deliver the property to you in the same condition as when you entered into the contract.

Can the Sellers Cancel?

As the date of the closing approached, Beatrice began to feel sentimental. After all, Max proposed to her in the kitchen over breakfast on New Year's Day. And she and her girlfriends had some wild Halloween parties here. How quickly the time had passed. As she house hunted with Isabel, she was having a hard time finding her dream home or even imagining what it would look like. Maybe she and Max should just stay put.

■ If the sellers change their mind about moving, can they cancel the contract?

It would be very unusual for a contract to give the sellers the right to cancel. The contract typically describes specific rights the buyer has if the seller refuses to close. In general, the buyer can sue the seller for "specific performance" of the contract. That means that the buyer can take the seller to court, to require him or her to transfer the title to the buyer in exchange for the purchase price. In addition, the buyer can block a proposed sale to anyone else by filing a notice on the land records that warns other potential buyers that you have a claim to the title.

When the Sellers Haven't Moved Out Yet

Isabel convinced Beatrice that she had more to gain by moving than not. But time was running out. Derek had given notice on his apartment and would want to move into the house soon after the closing. They had better speed up their house hunt.

■ **What if the sellers are not ready to move by the date of closing?**

It depends on your contract and it depends on the length of the delay. Many contracts do not cover the issue of short delays. Quite often the two parties work out alternative closing dates because of delayed mortgage approval, the movers' schedule, the sellers' inability to close on a new home, or the buyers' inability to close on the home they are selling. Frequently, there is inconvenience and cost to the party who is ready, willing, and able to close on the exact date in the contract. If the contract does not cover the question of short delays, then that party will have to bear those costs. If the contract specifically states that "time is of the essence" as to the closing date, then you would have the right to sue for failure to close. As a practical matter, though, it does not make sense to sue when it is clear that the other party is making every effort to close and will do so within a relatively short period of time.

However, if the delay of either party goes beyond thirty days and extensions have not been granted, the party causing the delay is considered to be in default. Your contract should provide a full range of remedies for this type of default, including a daily charge to be paid by the seller for failing to close or move out by the deadline.

THE CLOSING

Beatrice was singing under her breath when she walked into the closing. Derek had agreed to let her and Max stay in the house for an extra two months. All they had to do was pay him rent and let him work in the garden whenever he wanted. He was already busy mulching the soil. And she and Max had signed a binder on the house of her dreams (well, not exactly of her dreams — their new house didn't keep getting bigger).

Bea and Derek hugged before they sat down at the table. Bea even hugged Evelyn, her lawyer.

■ **What happens at a closing?**

Not usually so much hugging, but always a lot of signing of documents relating to the buyer's mortgage financing, title insurance, and transfer taxes. Transfer taxes are paid to the state or local government and are based on the sales price or new mortgage amount. Basically, what's happening at the closing is that the deed transfers the title to the property from the seller to the buyer in exchange for the purchase price (part of which has already been paid as a deposit). In addition to the purchase price, the buyer also pays the seller for

- **miscellaneous expenses such as the remaining oil in the oil tank**
- **previously agreed-on purchases such as appliances and furniture**
- **that portion of taxes (such as real estate and sewer) that the seller has prepaid**

The seller uses the money from the sale to pay off any mortgages or liens on the property.

TAXES

Beatrice and Max sent Isabel a large, beautiful flower arrangement to thank her for initiating the real estate transaction. Isabel had been right, and they had made a nice profit on the house. Bea told Isabel she planned to make some long-term investments and maybe start a college fund for the kids she and Max wanted to have.

"Talk to an accountant about it," warned Isabel. "You may have to pay a hefty tax on your capital gains."

What kind of taxes must a person pay on the profit from a real estate deal?

If you do not buy a new place to live within two years of your sale, you will have to pay tax on your *capital gain* as follows:

- First calculate your adjusted "basis" or investment. This is the amount you originally paid for the property (including any costs associated with closing the original transaction) plus the cost of any capital improvements, such as a new kitchen.
- Then calculate your profit, or "capital gain," from the sale. This is the amount by which the sale price (minus the broker's commission and other expenses associated with the sale) exceeds the "basis."
- If you made a profit (and don't reinvest in a new home), you will have to pay federal (and probably state) tax on your capital gain. If you lost money in the sale, you won't owe anything.

If you buy and occupy a more expensive home than the one you sold within two years, federal tax codes allow you to "roll over" all the gain from the sale and postpone paying the tax. You can avoid paying the capital-gain tax indefinitely, so long as the cost of the replacement residence is greater than that of the old residence and so long as you have reinvested the profits into your *new principal* dwelling (vacation homes don't count). If you are fifty-five years of age or older, you get a one-time capital-gain tax exemption of $125,000.

LIENS

Beatrice and Max were all set to celebrate when their mortgage was approved, but then some unexpected delays developed. Apparently, the sellers of the house had some unresolved differences with the contractor who renovated their kitchen years earlier. He subsequently got a lien on the property for their failure to pay him for his services.

How Are Property Taxes Figured?

Property taxes are based on the local government's estimate of the value of a property. Most states require that all real estate be reassessed at regular intervals. In many states, the reassessment takes place automatically upon any sale, and the property is reassessed at a value equal to the sale price. (This is a good argument for making a separate agreement with the seller for any additional purchases such as appliances, rather than including them in the sale price.) Home improvements requiring a building permit are also likely to generate an increased tax assessment.

If you have reason to think that the assessed value of your property is too high (based, for instance, on your knowledge of the assessments of other properties in your area), you should contact your local tax assessor's office to find out how to protest the assessment. Usually, assessors specify a period of time each year during which such protests can be made.

If the market value of your specific property has gone down (for example, from a fire), you might get some tax relief from your protest. If property values have gone down uniformly in your area, your own tax bill probably will not be reduced, even if your property is reassessed at a lower level, since the local government still needs to raise the same amount of revenue from property taxes.

What other taxes might a homeowner expect?

Homeowners might also be assessed fire district taxes, school taxes, water district taxes, sewer taxes, and beach taxes, just to name a few.

What is a lien?

A lien is someone's financial claim on your property. The most common form of lien is a mortgage, but there are other types of liens, including liens by contractors who have not been paid and liens for unpaid taxes. If you are buying a house, it is the seller's responsibility to pay off the mortgage and any other liens through the closing, so that you will receive "clear title" to the property. As a seller, as long as you use the closing proceeds to pay off all such obligations and a release of each lien is recorded on the land records, you will have conveyed good title to the buyer as far as the liens are concerned. (See also page 54.)

How does a buyer find out if there is a lien against the property he wants to purchase?

Through a **title search**, a review of the land records that will determine the ownership and description of the property. Title searches are performed by lawyers, private searchers, or title insurance companies. The title search reveals restrictions that might affect the buyer's use of the property, such as

- **mortgages of the seller or a prior owner of the property**
- **other related debts, such as a failure to pay taxes (known as a tax lien), unpaid utilities (a sewer lien, for instance), or a claim by a contractor (known as a mechanic's lien)**

The title search tells you which, if any, liens must be released in order to convey good title. If you're the buyer, it's very important to discover any unresolved liens against the property, because the liens will affect your title to the property and your ability to sell it in the future.

TITLE AND MORTGAGE INSURANCE

"Another bill?" asked Max as he plopped onto the couch. "I can't believe all these closing costs."

Beatrice frowned. "Take your feet off the couch," she ordered. "And tell me if we need to buy this insurance."

Max folded the bill into a paper airplane and sailed it into the garbage. "What does the bank say?" he asked.

What is title insurance?

Owner's title insurance covers you if a problem arises that was not discovered in the title search. For instance, if documents had been forged or if a title transfer was made by an incompetent person (such as a minor), your title and thus your ownership of the property could be jeopardized.

With owner's title insurance, you are covered for all costs (including attorneys' fees) of defending claims against the title, even those that might arise years after you sell the property to someone else.

There is also a second kind of title insurance, known as lender's title insurance. A loan title policy essentially insures that there are no liens or encumbrances having priority over the mortgage. Lenders almost always require the borrower to buy this kind of title insurance before they agree to finance a first mortgage. Title insurance premiums are paid in one installment, usually at the closing.

Title problems arise infrequently, but when they do, an owner risks losing the value of the house. For that reason, many people choose to buy owner's title coverage.

What is mortgage insurance?

Mortgage insurance protects the lender (usually a bank) against the risk of nonpayment by the buyer. The buyer does not benefit from mortgage insurance, but lenders frequently require it from "higher-risk" borrowers — people who borrow more than 80 percent of the value of the property. Because mortgage insurance has no value for the buyer, there is no reason to buy it unless your lender insists upon it.

DISCOVERING FLAWS IN YOUR NEW DREAM HOUSE

On moving day, Max and Bea had a nasty shock. One of their favorite details of the house were the cut glass antique door handles that had been so lovingly restored. But when they arrived with the movers, they found that all the doorknobs had been replaced with fake brass handles.

Max was livid and drove straight to the nearest pay phone to call their lawyer. "Evelyn," he shouted. "We're taking them to court. They stole our doorknobs!"

■ What happens if a buyer discovers that something has been removed from the house?

All things that are attached to the property — ceiling lights, awnings, window shades, doorknobs — are known as **fixtures**, and are automatically included in the sale unless specifically mentioned in the contract as going to the seller. You might be able to sue the seller if you did not discover the missing items until after the closing. But it would be *much* better if you inspect the house carefully before the closing (this is called a "walk-through") and demand that any missing items be returned before you pay for the property.

After a few weeks, Max and Beatrice were still trying to settle into their new home. The work seemed endless. Derek gave them a housewarming gift of five dozen tulip and iris bulbs, and they had been busily planting. That's when they first noticed the smell — a mixture of rotten eggs and horse manure. Then they discovered that on rainy days the odor permeated the kitchen and living room.

"It's absolutely vile," Beatrice complained to one of her neighbors, who informed her that that odor (which came from a sewage treatment pipe running under the house) was one of the main reasons the previous tenants had moved.

■ Does a buyer have any recourse if the seller has withheld information about problems?

Possibly. A seller's obligation to disclose problems varies from state to state. If the problem does not pose a health hazard, or if state law did not require the seller to disclose the problem, the buyer may be stuck. If state law did require disclosure, the buyer may have grounds for a lawsuit.

■ What if the buyer discovers that the seller withheld information about bad neighbors?

Some states have laws requiring disclosure about the "psychological impact" on a property — for instance, if a murder was committed there — but it is unlikely that noisy neighbors have to be disclosed. Your best protection is to become as familiar as possible with the property and spend a lot of time there before entering into a contract.

"Sweetheart, were these holes here before?" Beatrice asked, pointing to the kitchen cabinets.

"What holes?" Max innocently responded.

Two days later, the inspector from Pests Be Gone looked grim.

"Yeah, it's termites, ma'am," he said. "You've got 'em bad."

Beatrice was furious. She had had the house inspected before she went to contract.

"Someone's going to pay for this," she fumed.

■ What can the buyer do if a serious defect was undetected?

You may be stuck. If the house is brand-new, you are probably protected by the warranties imposed on the builder by the laws of your state. Typically, most warranties guarantee that new homes will be free from faulty materials, constructed according to sound engineering and workmanship standards, and in accordance with the local building codes. Most such state laws require the warranties to run for at least one year from purchase, and perhaps longer in the case of building code violations. In addition, buyers of new houses usually get manufacturers' warranties on their appliances (such as the stove or furnace), which typically run longer.

If you are buying an older home, you should assume that you are buying it "as is" and without any warranties. This is why it is so important to inspect the property for defects and other environmental problems. The buyer of an older home usually will have the house inspected for termites (if termites are common in the area) and other mechanical or structural problems. In addition, you are entitled to rely on information about the property from the seller or the seller's agent. If they misled you about the house and you have subsequent problems, that misinformation can provide the basis for a lawsuit against the seller or the agent. But defects in older homes discovered *after* the closing generally are the buyer's problem alone.

If you got a clean bill of inspection, you may also have a case against the inspection company. But many companies issue broad disclaimers, so unless they failed to detect what should have been an obvious problem, they may be protected from liability.

■ What if the oil burner or other major appliance gives out two months after you buy the house?

If the house is new, you should still be covered by the builder's and manufacturer's warranties. If the house is older, you will bear the expense unless you have received some specific assurance from the seller about the appliance (such as "It is only one year old," when in fact it was fifteen years old). Of course, since you have already paid the seller at closing, you may have to take legal action to recover anything.

FORECLOSURES

Derek was getting overly involved with salsa. He was working with a genetic engineer to try to develop a pest-resistant tomato that had the spicy hotness of a jalapeño pepper. Bea was worried that he was becoming obsessed. He wasn't answering his phone, and when she stopped by one night, she saw that he wasn't even opening his mail. This hot tomato was a great idea, but he was sinking all his money into the project and had fallen behind on his mortgage payments. In fact, he had just received notice that the bank was foreclosing on his new house.

"It's not fair!" he protested to Beatrice. "They can't do this to me. I'm just an innocent young man with a burning passion!"

■ When can a lender foreclose?

When a bank or other lender gives you a mortgage, it imposes some requirements on top of asking you to pay back the loan with interest. For example, you typically are expected to maintain the property, keep it insured, and pay taxes. The lender usually will foreclose only if you are more than one month behind in your payments and only after you have been given notice that you are in default in your payments. It is rare for a lender to foreclose on other grounds. If you owe delinquent taxes or are not maintaining the property, then the lender could initiate foreclosure proceedings even if your payments are current. That's an unlikely occurrence, however. More typically, the lender would just require that your taxes and insurance be paid up.

In most cases, you will receive a notice from the lender of any perceived problem, and you will have the opportunity to correct the problem in order to prevent the foreclosure.

Most mortgage notes (the document in which you promise to pay the money) give borrowers the right to correct any default on which foreclosure is based, up to five days before the foreclosure. If you are having difficulties making mortgage payments, your best bet is to inform the lender of the problem and see if it is possible to work out a plan to reduce the overdue debt. The lender, however, has no obligation to do so.

■ Does a declaration of bankruptcy end the foreclosure proceedings?

No. At most, you would delay the foreclosure. The foreclosure proceeding will be "stayed," or made inactive, possibly until the bankruptcy proceeding is concluded. However, once the bankruptcy stay is lifted, the lender is free to foreclose. (See "Bankruptcy," page 377.)

■ Can an owner sell a house during foreclosure proceedings?

Yes. Nothing prevents you from finding a buyer and entering into a contract. The property is still yours until the foreclosure judgment is entered. As long as you receive the sale proceeds more than five days before the scheduled date of the foreclosure, you should be able to "cure" your debt through a mortgage payoff and convey "good title" to your buyer.

If you do find a buyer, you should inform the lender of the impending sale. As a condition of releasing the mortgage, the lender will probably require you to repay the cost of bringing the foreclosure action. But with a pending sale in place, the lender may refrain from taking more actions for which you could be charged. If you are attempting to "cure" your debt, the best strategy is to communicate your intentions to the lender.

■ Can a person just give a home to the bank?

If the bank is going to institute foreclosure proceedings, you might be able to persuade it to accept a deed to the property instead and release you from liability. The advantage to doing so would be to avoid having a foreclosure on your credit record. On the other hand, if the bank does foreclose, you still may receive some money if anything is left after the bank sells the house and recoups the mortgage.

One thing you don't want to do is completely abandon the property without notifying the bank. In that case, the bank could foreclose and could also institute legal action for any deficit that still remains after the sale of the property (a right the bank has with any foreclosure). If you still owe the bank $100,000 on your mortgage agreement, and the condo is sold in foreclosure proceedings for only $90,000, then you will still owe $10,000. This type of transaction will definitely affect your credit rating. You would be better off trying to negotiate an agreement with the bank so that you do not appear irresponsible.

What Is the Procedure of a Foreclosure?

- The lender files action in court seeking to obtain "title transfer" (foreclosure).
- Notice of the pending foreclosure is served on the owner and any other interested parties, such as the holder of a second mortgage and anyone having a lien on the property.
- Notice of the pending foreclosure proceeding is recorded on the land records.
- The court establishes a timetable for the foreclosure, setting a deadline by which the owner can redeem the debt and "cure the default."
- If the money owed is not paid, the court enters an order transferring title from the owner to the lender.

THE GOVERNMENT'S RIGHT OF EMINENT DOMAIN

What luck! Derek inherited a sizable sum from his Aunt Gertie, who died at the ripe age of ninety-eight. Derek immediately "cured" his debt to the bank without having to sell the house.

Beatrice was thrilled that Derek could keep the house. And she was thrilled that he had abandoned his salsa project and his salsa fantasies.

"I think I took a wrong turn at the cilantro patch," he confessed. "I'm sticking to herbs from now on."

But Derek had a new worry. The town had decided to build a new highway linking the interstate to the sports arena, and Derek got a notice that one of the access roads was going to cut across his land, right where the garden was located.

Can the government take away property from individuals?

Yes. The government has what is known as the **right of eminent domain** — the right to acquire private property for public use. Since the government exercises this power on behalf of the "common good" and in the "public interest," the rights of individual property owners are subordinate. You can challenge the government's right to take your property, but the government will usually prevail. However, under the U.S. Constitution, the government may not take private property without fairly compensating the owner, which usually means you must be paid the market value of the property. If the government fails to compensate fairly, that is called an "**unjust taking**."

A "taking" does not always have to be the actual physical seizure of property. In some instances, where a government regulation has substantially devalued a property, the courts have found that to constitute an unjust taking. For example, say someone buys a beachfront lot intending to build a house on it. If the government rezones the land to prohibit building — which would essentially destroy the value of the property — that may be considered an unjust taking for which the owner could be compensated.

Just when Derek thought his garden was safe (he and others had convinced the town to relocate the new road), he was notified of a town sidewalk expansion project. "What about my roses?" he fumed. "Where will I replant them?"

Can a town widen the sidewalk without the owner's permission?

Yes, and you probably will not be compensated for land lost on account of the installation of a sidewalk. In fact, many towns *charge* property owners for curb and sidewalk repair and installation. If they are widening the *road,* however, you can expect to be compensated. That's because in a road widening, the government is taking a portion of your property and changing its boundaries. In a sidewalk extension, on the other hand, the boundaries of your property are not affected. Any compensation would be based on an appraiser's determination of the loss in value of your land. If you disagree with the estimate made by the government's appraiser, you can challenge it with your own appraisal estimates for your loss.

BUYING AN APARTMENT

Bradley and Peter had made a promise to buy an apartment together as soon as they could swing it financially. They were living in the place Peter had shared with his previous partner, and Bradley never felt at home there.

"Buying a new place will be fun," said Peter. "Especially shopping for it."

When the time came, they called Isabel, the broker Beatrice had used. She seemed to have a good handle on the real estate market, which was helpful since they didn't really know what they were looking for — a town house, a cottage, a co-op, a condo — and they didn't know how they would decide.

What is the difference between a co-op and a condo?

In a co-op (short for cooperative), the entire property is owned in the name of a corporation. Co-op owners don't actually own their unit (the apartment or town house); instead they own shares in the corporation, which is managed by a board of directors (elected share owners, usually living in the building). The board has the power to set all kinds of rules, governing such things as who is qualified to buy shares in the building, upkeep of apartments, and sublets.

Condominium owners, on the other hand, actually own their units. When you buy a condo, you have exclusive ownership of the interior of your unit. Though a condo may have an elected board of owners who make decisions about the common areas of the facility, condo boards typically have less power than co-op boards. In fact, some lenders are more reluctant to finance the purchase of co-ops than of condos, in part because the security for the loan is corporate shares, not actual real estate, and in part because co-ops tend to have more restrictive rules and financing arrangements than condos.

CASE IN POINT

Take That, and That . . . But Not That

The law clearly recognizes the government's right to take a person's private property for public purposes — known as the right of eminent domain. But the Fifth Amendment to the Constitution says owners must receive "just compensation" for such takings. While that sounds straightforward, the subject of "takings" is actually quite complex and has generated a good deal of litigation.

In a case from Hawaii, for example, a group of large landowners challenged the right of the Hawaiian government to take their large estates and break them up into small lots for resale to people who had been leasing the lots from the landowners. The landowners weren't complaining about compensation. Instead, they said the state's plan to resell the land to other individuals did not qualify as a taking for "public use" as required by the Fifth Amendment.

In a 1984 decision, a unanimous U.S. Supreme Court rejected this argument, ruling that the government itself does not have to use the property to make the purpose of a taking legitimate. In this case, the government had acted to redress a perceived economic and social problem that dated back hundreds of years to the days when Polynesian immigrants settled Hawaii, and land ownership had been concentrated in the hands of a tiny portion of the population. The Hawaiian government's attempt to remedy the inequity served a legitimate public purpose, the Court ruled, noting its intention to be extremely deferential when scrutinizing the legislative purpose for a taking.

In a California case decided three years later, the issue was whether something actually constituted a taking. The owners of a beachfront lot in Ventura County had sought a permit from the California Coastal Commission to demolish a small bungalow on the lot and replace it with a three-bedroom house. The commission said it would grant permission *if* the owners agreed to give the public an easement (access) to walk across their private beach, which was flanked on both sides by public beach area.

A series of Supreme Court decisions has held that various land-use regulations that place restrictions on property are *not* takings if two criteria are met:

- **the regulation must "substantially advance legitimate state interests"**
- **it must not deny an owner economically viable use of his land**

In a 1987 opinion in this case, the Court ruled that a taking had occurred and that the owners should be paid for an easement. The opinion reasoned that there was no connection between the government's objective behind regulating the size of the house (preserving public views of the ocean) and the property right to be taken (the easement). However, the decision noted, if California had conditioned the building permit on something that would have protected the public's view of the beach — a height or width restriction, for example — then it would not have constituted a taking.

■ **How do the tax liabilities differ?**

The only difference is in the billing. Co-op owners pay their share of the property tax through monthly co-op fees. Condo owners pay tax directly to the local government.

Isabel showed Brad and Peter dozens of apartments, and she finally won their hearts with a two-bedroom co-op with a fireplace and a terrace. It was the perfect size, had a great layout, and was dripping with charm. It needed a little work, but the price was right.

Their bid was accepted, and Peter and Bradley celebrateed when they signed the contract for the apartment. But then they realized that they still had to be accepted by the co-op board. This part of the process seemed mysterious to them.

"Will they reject us because we are a gay couple?" the two wondered.

■ **Does a co-op board have the right to reject a prospective buyer?**

Yes. A co-op board may choose to reject you on

- **financial grounds (your inability to pay the monthly fees)**
- **the number of people who will occupy the unit**
- **the nature of your proposed use (for example, rental rather than owner occupancy)**

The board pretty much has free rein to reject people, although it may not turn down a prospective buyer on any ground that is discriminatory under federal law, such as race, sex, religion, disability, or family relation (because you have children). Some states also protect against discrimination based on age or sexual orientation. If you are rejected by the board for a nondiscriminatory reason, such as your failure to show that you can pay the monthly fees, you usually are entitled to get your money back from the contract.

■ **What if a person suspects discrimination?**

You can take legal action. If you prove discrimination in court, you have the right to recover damages and attorneys' fees under the applicable civil rights or Fair Housing Act provisions.

The meeting with the board did not seem to go well. Brad was sure the three board members were snickering when they found out that Peter had once owned a florist shop. But their worries were unnecessary. Wally, the president of the board, called the next day to welcome them to the building.

Their move went pretty smoothly, except for one minor detail: one of the movers slipped in the lobby and wrenched his back. When the paramedics were carrying him away on a stretcher, he was mumbling something about "suing your aaaa . . ."

■ **Is a co-op shareholder or condo owner liable if someone is hurt in the building's lobby?**

Possibly. Both co-ops and condominiums maintain liability insurance for personal injury, but nothing prevents an injured person from naming you individually in a lawsuit. That's why it's a good idea for you to purchase personal liability coverage as a part of the insurance policy you buy for your co-op. The expense is not high. (See page 100.)

Six months after moving in, Brad and Peter started planning a kitchen renovation. They casually mentioned to Wally, the board president, that they were about to begin work.

"Whoa, slow down," he said. "We haven't approved your plans yet. Hand them over." Wally feigned a holdup.

"Why does the board care what we do in our apartment?" Bradley wondered.

■ **Why must a person submit renovation plans to the co-op board?**

When you live in a co-op, you have signed a written agreement to abide by the rules and regulations of the co-op board. You are free to do any basic interior decorating, but most boards require that plans for any renovation affecting the structure or mechanics of the building be subject to their approval.

If the co-op board rejects your renovation plans, you can try to prove that the board acted unreasonably, though it would rarely be worth your time or money to pursue a lawsuit. You would have little likelihood of winning, and you would surely increase any enmity with your neighbors. If the board had no valid reason for rejecting the plans, your best bet is to try to elect new, more flexible board members. That way you may be able to get the number of votes you need for approval of your plans.

Does a person need approval to renovate a condo?

As in the case of a co-op, the rules and regulations of the condominium association govern this issue. You are the owner of the interior spaces in your condominium and can decorate it in any manner you wish. It is likely, however, that you will need to obtain association approval for any significant electrical, mechanical, or structural change.

To increase the value of the property, Brad and Peter's co-op board voted to require all the owner/shareholders to install new thermal-pane windows. Peter thought it was a great idea, but the fact was that they were a little short of funds because of their renovation.

Can the board make a shareholder replace windows?

Each co-op's written rules determine this issue. If you cannot afford to replace your windows, and the board has the right to insist that you do so, presumably you would be in violation of the co-op's rules. You would then be subject to any enforcement process contained in the rules.

Co-op boards have a lot of power. If, for instance, a board wanted to, it could vote to paint a building's lobby Day-Glo orange and decorate it with black lights, so long as the decision was made in accordance with the co-op's own bylaws.

INSURANCE

8

Beatrice received a promotional letter from an insurance company, Prudential and Mutual Protection of All States Inc. In addition to the usual types of coverage — health, property, life, and automobile — the letter was pitching more exotic things like hand insurance ("For pianists and calligraphers") and foot insurance ("Especially for athletes").

"Is this an April Fool's joke?" Bea wondered.

■ Can anything be insured?

Basically, yes. If there's something you want to insure, you probably can find a company willing to provide coverage — for a price, of course. But most people don't have exotic needs. Instead, a typical person carries the basics: auto, property, liability, health, and life insurance, and in this section we try to provide an overview of the general legal issues surrounding all types of coverage. Details about the legal issues regarding specific types of coverage are outlined in other chapters (for auto insurance, see page 23; for health insurance, see page 317; for renter's insurance, see page 49). Since each person's requirements vary, depending on such circumstances as age, marital status, property owned, and number of children, we don't discuss what types of insurance you should have or what level of coverage would be appropriate.

■ Do insurers have guidelines they have to follow?

Yes. Most insurance issues are covered by state law. The main exception is employer-provided health insurance, which is governed by a federal law known as the Employee Retirement Income Security Act of 1974. If you have questions about your coverage or the actions of your insurer, the first thing you should check is your policy itself. It may be difficult to decipher because of its legalistic language. If you can't understand yours, ask your insurance agent or the company for clarification. If that doesn't help, you should contact an attorney or your state's department of insurance. (See page 103.)

An important note: If your insurance company acts in a way you think is tricky or unfair, there's a reasonable chance the law may think so, too. In almost all states, the law generally favors the policyholder over the insurer.

DEALING WITH AGENTS

An agent from the We Protect You Agency sent Beatrice a booklet describing a basic homeowner's plan. While the agent had said that all her possessions would be covered by the plan, Beatrice noticed a footnote stating that "precious valuables" had to be itemized separately. She asked the agent whether she needed to submit a list of things like her jewelry and antique silver. "No need to bother," he told her. "So long as your things fall within the limit of your coverage, which would be a maximum of $100,000, you're fine."

■ Is it okay to rely on an insurance agent's promises?

No. You should always get any clarifications in writing from the company, on company letterhead. Agents often don't work directly for the company, and when you have trouble submitting a claim, the agent may be long gone. An agent wants to sell you something and may be inclined, therefore, to tell you what you want to hear in order to convince you to buy the insurance. If you end up in a dispute with the company, you won't get very far arguing that "the agent told me so." (But sometimes an insurer is liable for what the agent told you no matter what the policy says, and sometimes agents carry "errors and omissions" insurance, which covers them if they make mistakes.)

How to Avoid Hassles with Your Insurer

- Read the policy carefully *before* signing.
- Ask for *written* clarification from the company if you are unsure about the scope of the coverage. Don't rely on an agent's declarations.
- If you are still confused, or if you're purchasing expensive coverage, consult a lawyer to make sure you are getting what you want.

WHEN ARE YOU INSURED?

Blossom decided to buy insurance that would cover her property in case of loss or theft. She filled out the application and mailed in a check. Two days later her apartment was robbed. The thief took her VCR, color TV, and a leather jacket. "Aren't I lucky I got that insurance," she said.

Is a person insured as soon as the first payment is sent?

Not necessarily. You are not insured until your application is approved and a policy is issued. Some companies require you to give them a check up front, before they will submit your application to the home office for approval. If you are not approved, your check will be refunded. Sometimes, however, an agent has the power to "bind," or initiate, coverage for the company even before the policy is issued. If your agent can do so, then you will be insured even before the formal policy is issued.

What happens when someone is late with an insurance payment?

Most insurance policies provide for a "grace period" during which you can make the overdue payment and keep your policy from lapsing. If your payment is sent before the end of the grace period, your losses will be covered if you are robbed. But you should read your policy to see whether it provides a grace period, and if so, how long it runs. Even if your policy does not include a grace period, the laws of your state may give you one. You can find out by contacting your state department of insurance.

CHECK'S IN THE MAIL

Beatrice dislocated her shoulder when she slipped off a chair while trying to dust-mop the ceiling. Her medical bills totaled more than $600, and she paid the fees directly to the doctor and then submitted a claim to her health insurer. Nine weeks and several phone calls later, she still had received no reimbursement.

Do insurance claims have to be paid within a certain amount of time?

Most states have laws requiring that insurance companies pay claims within a certain time period. (Some of these laws apply only to health, accident, and life insurance claims, while others cover every kind of insurance.) The general time frame for payment is thirty to sixty days, although it will vary from state to state. Usually, an insurer who delays or refuses to pay a claim without a good reason is violating the obligation to deal with you in "good faith." In such a situation the insurance company could be liable to you for the amount you were owed under the policy plus a penalty for emotional distress and possibly even punitive damages. Practically speaking, however, you would have to initiate a lawsuit to collect damages for late payment of a claim. That could consume a lot of time and involve considerable hassle (although some states do let you recover the costs of your lawyer if you have to sue your insurance company — so long as you win).

To determine what your state's regulations are, you can contact the state's department of insurance or an attorney.

Handling a Dispute with Your Insurer

If your insurer is refusing to pay a claim or is otherwise treating you in a way you believe is unfair, make every effort to resolve the conflict on your own before consulting a lawyer or adjuster. Document all communications with the company by

- **putting your requests for information in writing**
- **keeping a log of every phone call to the company, including the name of the person you spoke to and the date of the call. If someone at the company refuses to return your calls, note that, too.**

If you still can't get an adequate response from the company, you should consult a lawyer (see Chapter 30, FINDING AND USING A LAWYER). Most insurance disputes end up being settled rather than going to trial. That doesn't mean that you will always get what you think you're entitled to, but you probably will not have to endure a courtroom battle.

RATES

The company where Beatrice worked, Teddies and More, was undergoing reorganization and there were many rumors that the health care benefits were going to be slashed. She asked her brother Bradley to get her some quotes on rates from his agent. They were both surprised to learn that the rates for Beatrice were higher than those paid by Bradley.

Can men and women be charged different rates?

Yes, but the insurer must be able to show evidence that a person's gender is indeed a risk factor that justifies a higher rate. In other words, if an insurer charges more to a fifty-year-old man than to a fifty-year-old woman for major medical coverage, the insurer must be able to show (usually with statistics) that the man is more likely to get sick than the woman.

Auto insurance companies generally charge higher rates for coverage of male drivers, with the highest rates charged to males under thirty. This cost is based on the higher number of accidents involving young male drivers. Although this might be viewed as a form of discrimination, it is permissible since it is rationally based on a genuine statistical difference between the accident records of males and females and younger and older drivers. For similar reasons, insurance companies can legally adjust rates according to a driver's accident record, state of health, and even drinking and smoking habits, among other factors.

Five states have laws forbidding auto insurers to charge gender-based rates: Hawaii, Massachusetts, Michigan, North Carolina, and Pennsylvania. In addition, Montana forbids insurance companies from charging gender-based rates for *any* form of insurance.

You have the right to challenge a rate charge, but the courts have generally ruled in favor of insurers on these matters.

LIFE INSURANCE

Lying to the Insurer

Beatrice's friend Allen had been feeling ill for several weeks, and the doctor had just told him he had cancer and that it looked as if it was spreading quickly. It might be treatable, but the chances weren't great. Allen was only thirty-seven and married with two young children. He also had no life insurance. Now he was in a panic about what was going to happen.

If a person knows he has a terminal illness and fails to disclose that to a life insurer, can benefits be denied?

Yes, although in most states the insurance company first has to prove that you committed fraud. So if your illness had been diagnosed and you had been told of the diagnosis, and your insurer can prove it, the benefits could be withheld. Basically, whenever you misrepresent something about yourself, and the insurer relies on that misinformation when issuing the policy, you could have a problem. Some states specify that the misrepresentation has to be relevant to the risk the insurance company assumed in order for it to be considered fraud. Lying about a cataract problem, for example, would not be a significant factor in determining your risk of dying from a heart attack.

To protect people who make innocent misstatements on their applications, most life insurance policies include an "incontestability clause," which states that if an error on the application is not discovered within a certain time period — usually two years — the insurance company gives up its right to contest your coverage on the basis of the error. Thus, an innocent error cannot be used by the insurer to deny payment — if the time period has passed.

■ **What if a person simply lies about his or her age on an insurance application?**

In most states, an insurance company can collect the difference between the premium for your misrepresented age and that of your correct age. If your lie is discovered, the insurance company will usually deduct that amount from any benefits paid.

Suicide

Allen, it turned out, did have life insurance (his wife had handled the details when their first child was born). That didn't do much to ease his despair about dying. Nor his fear. He couldn't bear the thought of a slow, painful death, and he contemplated making it easier on everyone by killing himself.

■ **Can a person's life insurance benefits be canceled if he or she commits suicide?**

It depends on the policy. If the suicide occurs within two years of when the policy was issued, the insurer usually will have to pay back only the premiums. But if the suicide occurs after those two years, the insurer is obligated to pay out the full policy — unless the policy specifically states that benefits won't ever be paid in the case of suicide. However, few policies contain this provision.

If you believe a death was not a suicide and yet you fear it will be ruled to be one, you should contact a lawyer and arrange to have a pathologist hired by you present at the autopsy. Or your pathologist can examine the body before it is prepared for burial or cremation.

If the physical examination can't be done, you can call on mental health experts to perform what is called a "psychological autopsy," in which they try to determine whether the deceased fit the psychological profile of a suicide by examining medical records and interviewing friends, family, and co-workers.

If these experts determine that the death was not a suicide and the insurance company still refuses to pay the claim after being presented with the evidence, then you will probably have to bring a lawsuit against the insurer. Obviously, the amount of the insurance policy would have to be substantial to justify the expense of fighting an initial determination of suicide.

PROPERTY INSURANCE

What It Is

Beatrice had saved for months to take Vinny and Alena skiing for their winter vacation. They returned from the trip exhilarated, only to discover that the house had been ransacked and robbed. Everything of any possible value was gone: VCR, color TV, stereo equipment, Vinny's coin collection, Alena's costume jewelry, Beatrice's real jewelry. Even the microwave oven and food processor were missing.

The police told Beatrice to make a list of everything that was stolen and submit it to her insurance company. "You do have homeowner's insurance, don't you?" asked the young officer. Beatrice felt relieved that she had finally bought a policy.

■ **What is homeowner's insurance?**

Homeowner's insurance covers your house and its contents against loss from fire, storm, theft, and any other perils mentioned in the policy. These policies also typically include liability insurance, which means you are covered if someone is injured on your property. If, for instance, a guest trips in your living room and breaks an arm, you could be responsible for paying for the cost of his or her injury. If you have homeowner's insurance and someone is hurt on your property, your insurance company will pay the claim — up to the limits stated in the policy. Many people also purchase what is known as an "umbrella" or "excess" liability policy, which provides additional coverage if someone claims he was injured by some accident or harm you caused. Homeowner's insurance will also cover the costs of hiring a lawyer to defend you in court.

■ Who should have homeowner's insurance?

Anyone owning a residence, whether it's a house, a condominium, or a cooperative apartment. In fact, most mortgage companies require one if you are still paying on your house.

Even if you rent your home or apartment, you should carry similar coverage, typically called a renter's policy.

■ What is a "rider"?

A rider is an amendment, sometimes called an endorsement, added by the insurance company that changes your policy in some way. The rider may either expand coverage, take it away, or further define what is covered. Riders can also be added to health insurance policies, usually to exclude specific illnesses from coverage.

An insurer can add a rider without your consent if the state board of insurance has approved it. However, riders are usually added only at the time of the policy's renewal. Most riders limit coverage, rather than expand it.

A rider or endorsement also refers to coverage that you add to your policy. For instance, if you purchase expensive items like jewelry, fine art, or silver, you may want additional coverage. In fact, some insurers require that you itemize such objects separately.

Determining Replacement Value

Fortunately for Beatrice, the robbery occurred within the grace period, so she was covered. But then she was faced with making her claim. The insurance company told her to submit a list of everything that was stolen, so she had gone through the house with the kids trying to reconstruct a lifetime of accumulation. The TV and stereo were easy, but a lot of her clothing and all of her jewelry had been taken and she just couldn't remember every item. And the value of several items, such as some of her old lace tablecloths, was being disputed by the insurer. Beatrice collected them as a hobby and she knew they were worth a lot more than the company said it was going to pay.

■ Who determines the value of the stolen property?

The insurance company decides what it is going to pay you to replace your possessions, and you may not always agree with the company about what an item is worth. (You aren't actually required to replace every item that the insurer reimburses you for.) It helps if you have appraisals of valuable items (such as jewelry) to prove your claim. It also helps if you have photographs of all your valuables. That way there is less chance for debate over the characteristics that make an item valuable. It may also be useful to keep your original purchase receipts.

Make sure you know the rules of your policy. Most insurance companies offer special coverage for valuable items such as jewelry, and they often require that each individual item be described. Some companies may even require you to submit annual appraisals showing the item's value, although that doesn't happen too often. Getting such appraisals regularly is a good idea anyway, since it is the only way to be sure that your policy actually covers the value of your possessions.

If you can't agree with the insurer about how much your items are worth, you might be able to request that an independent appraiser make a determination. Or, if your loss is large, you can hire a "public adjuster" to help you. He or she typically will be experienced at negotiating and settling with insurance companies, but probably will charge you a percentage of your ultimate recovery.

If you still can't reach a settlement, you will probably have to sue the insurance company. (See the box on page 99.)

Recovering for Property That's Lost Away from Home

Three weeks after the break-in, Vinny confessed to Beatrice that his brand-new pocket watch had been lost on the ski slopes, not in the robbery. He thought it happened when he took a tumble on his last run down the mountain. But he wasn't sure. It might have been snagged from his pocket in the crush at the ski lift.

■ Is an item covered if it's lost, not stolen?

Valuables are usually covered whether they are lost or stolen, and most homeowner's policies pay even when the loss occurs away from the home. But while the insurer can't turn down your claim just because your forgetfulness caused you to lose something, it can decide not to renew your policy if it believes that your negligence is too great a risk.

When a Friend's Property Is Stolen from Your Home

Alena had borrowed her friend Janet's video camera for an art project, expecting to return it right after vacation. She left it sitting on her desk. Guess what? It was gone.

■ Does a homeowner's policy cover the theft of a friend's property?

No. Typically, a homeowner's policy covers only property owned by the insured. (That goes for a renter's policy as well.) But if Janet's parents are insured, their policy probably will cover the loss. If, however, Alena had negligently dropped and ruined the video camera, Beatrice's homeowner's insurance would likely pay for the loss.

When an Insurer Says No

Beatrice's movie-star friend Paolo had complained to her that he was having trouble buying homeowner's insurance. He lived in the mountains near Los Angeles, and the insurer told him there was too much risk of fire and earthquake.

■ Can an insurer turn someone down because he lives in a high-risk area?

In general, an insurance company can turn you down for any reason that is not prohibited by law. (Many, but not all, states prohibit insurers from using race, sex, sexual orientation, or marital status in determining insurability.) In certain high-risk areas, such as those along coastlines that are hit by hurricanes, states have created insurance "pools" where all companies that insure property are required to accept their share of the risks in that area. That way, coverage is available to any consumer in the area who wants it, with no single insurer bearing a disproportionate share of the risk.

■ What if a person lives in a high-crime area?

An insurer often can refuse to sell coverage. However, every state has laws against redlining — denying coverage to people based on the characteristics of their neighborhood or because they are considered poor economic risks. Some states, such as Texas, California, and Missouri, are considering regulations that would make it even harder for insurers to redline by requiring them to be more explicit about their reasons for denying coverage. The U.S. Congress is also considering anti-redlining legislation.

FOR FURTHER REFERENCE

Nationwide organizations:

National Insurance Consumers Organization (NICO)
P.O. Box 15492
Alexandria, VA 22309
703-549-8050

National Association of Insurance Commissioners
120 West 12 Street, Suite 1100
Kansas City, MO 64105
816-842-3600

State insurance departments:

Alabama
Insurance Commissioner
P.O. Box 303351
Montgomery, AL 36130-3351
205-269-3550

Alaska
Division of Insurance
P.O. Box 110805
Juneau, AK 99801-0805
907-465-2515

Arizona
Director of Insurance
2910 North 44 Street, Suite 210
Phoenix, AZ 85018
602-255-5400

Arkansas
Arkansas Insurance Department
1123 South University, Suite 400
Little Rock, AR 72204
501-686-2900

California
Department of Insurance
Consumer Communications Bureau
300 South Spring Street
Los Angeles, CA 90013
213-897-8921
800-927-4357 (toll-free in CA)

Colorado
Division of Insurance
1560 Broadway, Suite 850
Denver, CO 80202
303-894-7499

Connecticut
Connecticut Insurance Department
P.O. Box 816
Hartford, CT 06142
203-297-3900

Delaware
Insurance Commissioner
841 Silver Lake Boulevard
Dover, DE 19901
302-739-4251

District of Columbia
Superintendent of Insurance
1 Judiciary Square
441 Fourth Street NW
8th Floor North
Washington, DC 20001
202-727-8000

Florida
State Insurance Department
612 Larson Building
200 East Gaines Street
Tallahassee, FL 32399-0333
904-922-3110
800-342-2762 (toll-free in FL)

Georgia
Insurance Commissioner
2 Martin L. King Jr. Drive
Atlanta, GA 30334
404-656-2056

Hawaii
Insurance Commissioner
250 South King Street
Honolulu, HI 96813
808-586-2790

Idaho
Director of Insurance
700 West State Street, 3rd floor
Boise, ID 83720
208-334-2250

Illinois
Illinois Department of Insurance
320 West Washington Street
Springfield, IL 62767
217-782-4515

Indiana
Commissioner of Insurance
311 West Washington Street
Indianapolis, IN 46204-2787
317-232-2385
800-622-4461 (toll-free in IN)

Iowa
Iowa Insurance Division
Lucas State Office Building
Des Moines, IA 50319
515-281-5705

Kansas
Commissioner of Insurance
420 SW Ninth Street
Topeka, KS 66612
913-296-7801
800-432-2484 (toll-free in KS)

Kentucky
Insurance Commissioner
229 West Main Street
Frankfort, KY 40602
502-564-3630

Louisiana
Commissioner of Insurance
950 North Fifth Street
Baton Rouge, LA 70802-9214
504-342-5900

Maine
Superintendent of Insurance
State House Station 34
Augusta, ME 04333
207-582-8707

Maryland
Insurance Commissioner
501 St. Paul Place
Baltimore, MD 21202
410-333-6300
800-492-6116 (toll-free in MD)

Massachusetts
Commissioner of Insurance
470 Atlantic Avenue
Boston, MA 02210
617-521-7794

Michigan
Insurance Bureau
611 West Ottawa Street
Lansing, MI 48933
517-373-9273

Minnesota
Minnesota Department of Commerce
133 East Seventh Street
St. Paul, MN 55101
612-296-6848

Mississippi
Mississippi Department of Insurance
1804 Walter Sillers Building
Jackson, MS 39205
601-359-3569

Missouri
Director of Insurance
301 West High Street, Room 630
Jefferson City, MO 65101
314-751-4126

Montana
Commissioner of Insurance
126 North Sanders
Mitchell Building
Helena, MT 59620
406-444-2040
800-332-6148 (toll-free in MT)

Nebraska
Nebraska Department of Insurance
attention: Consumer Affairs
941 "O" Street, Suite 400
Lincoln, NE 68508
402-471-2201

Nevada
Director of Insurance
1665 Hot Springs Road
Carson City, NV 89710
702-687-7650
800-992-0900 (toll-free in NV)

New Hampshire
Insurance Commissioner
169 Manchester Street
Concord, NH 03301-5151
603-271-2261
800-852-3416 (toll-free in NH)

New Jersey
Commissioner
Department of Insurance
CN 329
Trenton, NJ 08625
609-292-5317

New Mexico
Superintendent of Insurance
PERA Building
P.O. Drawer 1269
Santa Fe, NM 87504-1269
505-827-4500

New York
for NYC and Long Island:
New York State Insurance Department
Consumer Affairs Bureau
160 West Broadway
New York, NY 10013
212-602-0434
800-342-3736 (toll-free in NY)

for rest of NY state:
Consumer Service Bureau
Empire State Plaza
Albany, NY 12257
518-474-6600
800-342-3736 (toll-free in NY)

North Carolina
Commissioner of Insurance
Dobbs Building
North Salisbury Street
Raleigh, NC 27611
919-733-7349

North Dakota
Commissioner of Insurance
Capitol Building
600 East Boulevard Avenue
Bismarck, ND 58505-0320
701-224-2440
800-247-0560 (toll-free in ND)

Ohio
Ohio Department of Insurance
Consumer Service Division
2100 Stella Court
Columbus, OH 43215-0167
614-644-2658
800-686-1526 (toll-free in OH)

Oklahoma
Insurance Commissioner
1901 North Walnut
Oklahoma City, OK 73105
405-521-2828
800-522-0071 (toll-free in OK)

Oregon
Oregon State Insurance Division
21 Labor and Industries Building
Salem, OR 97310
503-378-4271

Pennsylvania
Pennsylvania Insurance Department
attention: Consumer Services
1321 Strawberry Square
Harrisburg, PA 17120
717-787-2317

Rhode Island
State of Rhode Island
Department of Business Regulations/
Insurance Division
233 Richmond Street, Suite 233
Providence, RI 02903-4237
401-277-2223

South Carolina
Insurance Commissioner
1612 Marion Street
Columbia, SC 29201
803-737-6117

South Dakota
Director of Insurance
910 East Sioux Avenue
Pierre, SD 57501-3940
605-773-3563

Tennessee
Commissioner of Insurance
500 James Robertson Parkway
Nashville, TN 37243-0565
615-741-2241
800-342-4029 (toll-free in TN)

Texas
Texas Department of Insurance
Consumer Services
333 Guadalupe Street
P.O. Box 14904
Austin, TX 78714-9104
512-463-6169
800-252-3439 (toll-free in TX)

Utah
Commissioner of Insurance
3110 State Office Building
Salt Lake City, UT 84114-6901
801-538-3800

Vermont
Vermont Department of Banking, Insurance and Securities
89 Main Street
Drawer 20
Montpelier, VT 05620-3101
802-828-3301

Virginia
State Corporation Commission Bureau of Insurance
Life and Health Division
1300 East Main Street
Richmond, VA 23219
804-371-9691
800-552-7945 (toll-free in VA)

Washington
Office of the Insurance Commissioner
Consumer Protection Division
P.O. Box 470256
Olympia, WA 98504
206-753-7301
800-562-6900 (toll-free in WA)

West Virginia
Insurance Commissioner
2019 Washington Street, East
P.O. Box 50540
Charleston, WV 25305
304-558-3386
800-642-9004 (toll-free in WV)

Wisconsin
Commissioner of Insurance
P.O. Box 7873
Madison, WI 53707-7873
608-266-0102
800-862-1074 (toll-free in WI)

Wyoming
Wyoming Insurance Department
Herschler Building
122 West 25 Street
Cheyenne, WY 82002
307-777-7401

GETTING MARRIED 9

PRENUPTIAL AGREEMENTS

After dating for several years, Max proposed to Beatrice. ("Finally," sighed her mother.) Beatrice had waited patiently for Max to overcome his "commitment phobia," and she was now dreaming about their future. Max would move into the home she owned, but since she had a lot of money saved, she figured they could soon buy a bigger place. Of course, Max was still a starving musician, but that didn't matter to Beatrice. She loved him whether he made money or not, and as far as she was concerned, what was hers was his.

So Beatrice was quite dismissive when her father suggested that she and Max should have a prenuptial agreement — "Just in case things aren't always as happy as they are now."

"Don't be silly, Daddy," said Bea. "Max and I will be in love forever."

■ What exactly is a prenuptial agreement?

A prenuptial agreement (also called a premarital agreement) is a contract between two people who intend to marry. It can address how they will divide their property and responsibilities

- **during their marriage**
- **at the death of either spouse**
- **at their divorce**

Basically, you can use the prenuptial agreement to dictate everything from how the monthly bills will get paid to what religious institutions your children will attend. However, one of the main reasons that you might want a prenuptial agreement is to ensure that what is yours before the marriage remains yours if the marriage ends.

■ Who should have one?

Most often, a prenuptial agreement is used by people who are getting married for the second or third time *or* in a situation where one person has substantially more income or assets than the other person coming into the marriage. However, in light of the increased divorce rate in this country, many people are using prenuptial agreements as a way of decreasing the emotional and financial toll of divorce by specifying in advance how their marital property will be divided.

■ Do both parties need a lawyer?

Yes. It is certainly wise for both people to be represented by independent attorneys who can advise them about their rights and obligations. In fact, some states require it for the contract to be enforceable. They also require that both parties provide each other with full disclosure of their assets and income. You should both be aware of what you would be entitled to under the law of your state should the marriage break up. This helps prevent the possibility that one person will later challenge the prenuptial agreement as "unconscionable" — so unfair that it cannot be upheld.

MAKING THE MARRIAGE LEGAL

Licenses and Blood Tests

With just two weeks before the big day, Beatrice was deep into wedding preparation hysteria. The caterers needed to know how many guests were coming, and several invitees (mostly Max's friends) had not yet responded. Beatrice was on her way to the final fitting for her dress when she realized in a panic that she had no idea what, if anything, they needed to do to make the marriage legal.

■ What's the actual legal procedure for getting married?

Most states require a couple to obtain a license *prior* to the marriage ceremony. In fact, in several states, there is a waiting period of from twenty-four to seventy-two hours between the time you get the

When Is a Prenuptial Agreement Invalid?

A prenuptial agreement might be invalid if

- **one party withheld important financial information**
- **one party exerted force to get the other to sign**
- **the terms of the agreement would leave one of the parties destitute**

Both parties must enter into the agreement with **good faith**, that is, honestly and without deception. And both parties must have put all their cards on the table and made a full and accurate disclosure of the important and relevant facts — their income, assets, liabilities, and anything else that would be important to someone deciding whether to sign the agreement. Many states require this financial disclosure to be in writing.

license and when you can use it. In addition, most states require that the license be used within a specific period of time, usually from thirty days to one year.

Are blood tests required?

The rules vary from state to state. Many states no longer require blood tests or any other physical exams. In most states that do require a blood test, the purpose is to determine whether either party is infected with any venereal diseases. Some states also examine women for rubella (German measles), a disease that is highly dangerous to fetuses. Other diseases sometimes tested for are tuberculosis and sickle-cell anemia. With the recent increase in AIDS and HIV in the heterosexual population, many states now require that the parties be informed when they apply for a marriage license about the disease and the availability of testing. So far, however, no state requires an HIV test prior to marriage.

The Ceremony

Everything Beatrice and Max had planned for their wedding was traditional — except for the actual ceremony. Neither of them was particularly religious, so they asked Poppa Guru Phlaykee Krystalhead, a local spiritual leader, to lead the service. They also wrote their own vows. Bea's: "I will delight each day in the wonder of who you are and never stop working to keep our love growing and strong." Max's:

"You're the light of my life,
The love of my heart.
From this day hence
May we never part."

Are there guidelines as to who can perform the ceremony and what it must include?

Each state has laws that specify who may perform a marriage ceremony. Usually, judges, justices of the peace, and religious ministers are able to do so, though sometimes they must first be certified or licensed.

Most states do not require any specific language to be used by the presiding judge or minister, but some states do require that the parties must say that they take each other as husband and wife.

Changing Your Name

The name issue was a tough one for Beatrice. She liked the idea of being one "unit" with Max. She did not, however, like his last name: Beatty. She just wasn't sure she was prepared to spend the rest of her life as Beatrice Beatty.

Does a woman have to do anything special if she doesn't want to change her name?

No. In general, when you apply for the license, the clerk will ask you what name you intend to use after the marriage ceremony. Technically, the law permits you to use any name you like as long as you are consistent and are not doing it for a wrongful purpose.

If you do change your name, however, probably the most important thing you have to do is to contact the Social Security Administration (800-772-1213) and have your social security number converted to your new name. The Social Security Administration will need to see a certified copy of your marriage certificate, which you should receive within a few weeks after your marriage ceremony (duplicates will be available on request, generally for a fee). After you're married, you simply have to notify all your creditors, your state's Department of Motor Vehicles, your employer, and anyone else of the change.

If you won't be changing your name, there is nothing that you need to do. And if you later decide you want to change your name, every state has some kind of law that will allow you to bring a court action to do so. However, this will usually require that you pay a fee. Still, it may be worth it to avoid problems when you try to get a passport or deal with the Internal Revenue Service.

ax, a modern man, offered to change *his* last name in order to spare Beatrice any embarrassment.

Is there any reason a man can't change his last name?

Most states will permit a man to change his name after marriage in the same manner as a woman. While it is less common, there is generally no prohibition against doing so. And of course you have the right to use a name of your choice. If you both want to change your names and adopt a totally new

CASE IN POINT

I 'Vant' More

Even the most generous prenuptial agreements can be challenged as unfair. That's what Ivana Trump did when she and New York real estate developer husband Donald split up in 1990.

Donald and Ivana were married in April 1977. A month before the wedding, they signed a prenuptial agreement, which was revised three times after the marriage. The last revision, signed December 24, 1987, stipulated that in the event of divorce or separation, Donald would pay Ivana $650,000 per year for maintenance and child support until she remarried or cohabitated, plus a lump sum of $10 million. She would also get the couple's house in Greenwich, Connecticut, an apartment in Trump Tower (or $4 million), plus the use of the couple's 118-room Palm Beach mansion every March. The agreement also contained a provision prohibiting Ivana from publishing any diary, memoir, photograph, or account of her marriage or Donald's business affairs without his prior written consent. Doing so would cancel any financial obligations Donald had to her.

When their marriage hit the skids, Ivana challenged the agreement, arguing that it was unconscionable and a product of fraud. In a complaint filed with a New York state court, she asked for 50 percent of the $5 billion worth of property acquired during their marriage. Donald's lawyer countered that Ivana was just posturing and that she had given up her right to equitable distribution of the property when she signed the agreement.

In March 1991, Ivana withdrew her claims challenging the enforceability of the agreement and accepted its terms. The agreement was revised again in 1993, because Ivana was living with her boyfriend and Donald claimed she had violated the confidentiality clause during an interview with Barbara Walters. Ivana gave up the month at the Palm Beach mansion, the Trump Tower apartment, and $350,000 a year in support. Not to worry, though. She still got the $4 million housing allowance and $300,000 a year in child support. Plus she kept the lump sum of $10 million.

one, you could do that, although you should check with your state to find out what the procedures are.

MARITAL OBLIGATIONS

Financial Support

Max had a regular job with The Stuffed Shirts, a band that played weddings and retirement parties. He made decent money but hated the music, and he wanted to quit and spend more time composing and practicing with his own band, The Eardrum Busters. "You're earning plenty," he told Beatrice. "You can support both of us for a while."

■ **Are spouses obligated to support each other?**

Yes, to a limited extent. Spouses are each responsible for any "necessaries" that the other purchases, including food, shelter, clothing, and other basic necessities of life. Necessaries may also include more luxurious items, depending on the family's financial status and lifestyle. So if a spouse goes out and buys a fur coat, and a fur coat is within the normal and usual lifestyle of this couple, then that fur coat may be considered a necessary, even though to most people it would appear to be a luxury.

The difficulty, of course, is determining exactly what is a necessary, and certainly no spouse should go out and start spending money in the hopes that his or her spouse will be forced to pay.

■ **If one spouse does not want to work, must the other support him or her?**

Yes. Traditionally, according to English law that was adopted in this country, a husband had a duty to support his wife. Since women didn't usually work outside the home, there was no duty for a wife to support her husband. Now, theoretically, the duty goes both ways. If your spouse is unwilling or unable to support you, you can apply for public assistance such as welfare or Aid to Families with Dependent Children. Of course, an unsupportive spouse does not automatically make you qualified. There are other criteria you will have to meet. You can also file a lawsuit seeking support from your spouse (without also suing for divorce).

However, if you sue for support, it is quite possible that your spouse will turn around and sue for a divorce. Your spouse would still have to support you, but a divorce proceeding may be longer and more complicated than a support proceeding. If your spouse is withholding support, you may want to evaluate whether your marriage can be saved or whether you want to proceed with a divorce. (See Chapter 12, GETTING DIVORCED.)

Debts

Max didn't have much money, but that didn't keep him from buying things — especially expensive music equipment. When he and Beatrice got married, he was $4,000 in debt.

■ **Is one spouse liable for the debts the other incurred before the marriage?**

No. Each spouse remains responsible for his or her debts incurred prior to the marriage. However, if Beatrice had promised to pay off Max's debts, that promise might have constituted a contract (see page 51) that could be enforced by Max — if he gave something to Beatrice in return for her payment. (In some states, if the promise was not made in writing, it is not legally enforceable.) However, creditors won't care what promises Beatrice made to Max. They will just go after Max, because his name is on the bills.

Shortly after the wedding, Max bought a $5,000 synthesizer without Beatrice's knowledge or consent, signing a loan agreement with the store and putting $500 down. "It's great, sweetheart," he told his new bride. "Now I can really compose, and you only have to pay $150 a month."

"Forget it, Max," Beatrice shouted at him. "I did not agree to buy this frivolous thing."

■ **Is one spouse liable to a third party for the debts the other spouse incurs during the marriage?**

Not usually. Each individual is generally held responsible for his or her own debts. Since the purchase was made in Max's name, it's his debt.

Most purchases made by a married couple, however, are considered marital purchases, and both spouses could be held responsible for unpaid bills, especially when the purchase is made on a joint credit card. However, if one spouse independently signs a contract to buy something, the other does not become liable just because they are married. A creditor may still try to collect the debt of one spouse from the couple's joint assets but will probably fail if the purchase was not made on a joint credit card or checking account.

Having Children

Max was very eager to have children. Bea wanted them, but wasn't ready. Max tried to sway her by cutting out pictures of cute babies and leaving them around for her to see. "You've just got to give me more time," she insisted.

■ **Are spouses obligated to have children?**

There are no laws that require people to have children or to refrain from having children. Each individual has a constitutional right to decide whether or not to use contraception. Of course, if spouses cannot agree on the issue of children, this can be an extremely disruptive issue in their lives and could end the marriage. In addition, if the spouses had agreed prior to the marriage to have children (or not to), and if one of them continues to use contraception (or not use it), that action would be a violation of their original agreement and might be the basis for an annulment if promises were made with no intention to honor them. (See "Annulment" on page 193.) The disagreement might also be the basis for a divorce claim of cruelty or irreconcilable differences. (See Chapter 12, GETTING DIVORCED.)

MARITAL PROPERTY

Is What's Mine Really Yours?

Beatrice had lived on her own for several years before she and Max got married. She had bought a small house and furnished it. She also had a computer and car. Max owned mostly stereo and music equipment.

■ **What happens to property owned by each spouse before the marriage?**

The question of who owns what usually arises only if the couple is splitting up and trying to divide their property, or if one person is writing a will and wants to leave property to a person other than the spouse. Generally, property owned by each spouse prior to the marriage remains the separate, personal property of that person.

However, if the personal possessions are "commingled," they become **marital property**, assets that belong to both parties. So if Max regularly cooks with the pots and pans Beatrice owned before the marriage, and if she's always listening to CDs on the stereo he brought in with him, those things very well might be considered marital property.

Things that the couple acquires after they are married (including wedding gifts) are considered joint assets owned by both parties.

Real estate is somewhat different. The ownership of a piece of real estate depends on whose name is on the deed. Frequently, if parties are married, they buy property jointly as a married couple and thus each party is an owner of the property. (If they divorce, however, they don't necessarily split it fifty-fifty. It depends on how their state divides property. See Chapter 12, GETTING DIVORCED.) If only one party's name is on the deed as the owner of the property, only that person is the legal owner of the property.

However, even if only one spouse is named on a deed, the other spouse may have a right to share in the property if it was obtained with marital funds or if it would otherwise be unfair to exclude him or her from sharing in the value of the property or in the appreciation of the value. Such might be the

> **A General Overview of Marital Money**
>
> - Money and possessions you had before the marriage remain separate unless you commingle them. (Some jurisdictions may give you credit even when you commingle if you can clearly prove the money was yours.)
> - Things that you acquire together are joint property.
> - Most purchases made by a married couple are considered marital purchases, and both spouses could be held responsible for unpaid bills.
> - Even if a deed is in the name of one spouse only, the other may be entitled to a portion of the property if it was bought with marital funds, if it appreciated in value, or if it would be unfair not to permit the spouse to share.

case if they had lived together as a married couple in the property for several years.

Inheritances

A few years after she and Max were married, Beatrice inherited $15,000 from her Aunt Emily. By this time, their first child, Alena, had been born. Beatrice had taken several months off work, and the couple's income had dropped significantly. Max had gone back to work with The Stuffed Shirts and was excited about Beatrice's inheritance, because he wanted to quit.

■ Is a spouse required to use an inheritance to support the family?

As a general rule, inheritances are always separate property even if they are inherited during the time of the marriage. Thus, if Beatrice deposits the money in a separate account, it remains her personal asset. However, if she does not keep the inheritance money separate, it may be converted into **marital property**. For example, if she took the $15,000 and put it into the joint account she shares with Max, she would have commingled it with marital funds, thus converting it into marital property. In some states, like New York, she still might be able to claim it as hers even if it's in a joint account. That decision would depend on several factors, including whether there were frequent deposits and withdrawals from the joint account. It would be important to have detailed financial records to support any claim to money in a joint account.

If the inheritance is kept separate, she is free to use it to pay off the family's bills, but she doesn't have to do so. If she and Max separate or are divorced, the inheritance would be one of Beatrice's separate assets, and the court would not divide it between them. However, a court would take the inheritance into consideration when deciding whether she or Max is entitled to support.

BROKEN ENGAGEMENTS

During their courtship, Beatrice had grown impatient with Max and his ambivalence about making a commitment. She broke up with him and dated Paul, a doctor. After three months, Paul proposed and gave her an antique diamond ring. In a frenzy of excitement, Beatrice accepted and began planning the wedding. Two weeks before the event, she realized it was a mistake. Paul was a sweetheart, but he was a very dull sweetheart. It created utter chaos, but she called off the wedding.

■ Can she keep the engagement ring?

It depends on where she lives. Generally, gifts that are given in expectation or contemplation of a marriage are known as "conditional" gifts. If the condition (namely, the marriage) does not occur, the giver has the right to get the gift back. Thus, in many states, like New York and Georgia, a man can recover an engagement ring if the woman breaks off the engagement, though not necessarily if he breaks it off. In some states, however, the ring might be considered an outright gift, and the woman could keep it — although she would be a clod to do so.

And if he proposed on Christmas or her birthday, the ring might be considered an outright gift and could be more difficult to get back.

What about all the wedding gifts?

Gifts to the marrying couple are not usually considered to be conditional, because even though they are given with the expectation that the couple will indeed go through with the wedding, they are basically being given to wish the parties well. So long as the couple has not defrauded anyone into making the gifts, the giver has no legal right to get the gift back. However, if one of the gifts was a priceless family heirloom, like a great-grandmother's tiara or an uncle's pocket watch, there may be a legal obligation to return it, since such a gift clearly is given with the expectation that the couple will marry.

JUST LIVING TOGETHER

Contracts

Blossom moved in with her boyfriend, Jeremy. She was still in cooking school and working part-time at Chez Snooty, a fancy restaurant, so they agreed that Jeremy, a high school teacher, would pay two-thirds of the rent and other bills. Blossom agreed to do most of the cooking.

Should they have a living-together contract?

Most people who want to live together simply do so without making any explicit contractual arrangements. However, just as some people are now using prenuptial agreements to ward off potential problems when a marriage breaks up, some people are now entering into contracts to govern their cohabitation.

Even if you don't put your agreement in writing, you still may have an oral contract that arises out of the promises you have made to each other verbally. Even though these agreements may not be in writing, in many jurisdictions they are equally binding, though it may be harder to prove, since you'll just have one person's word against the other's. So when Jeremy says to Blossom, "Okay, I'll support you while you're in cooking school," and she replies, "Okay, I'll cook and make sure the house is clean," that's a contract.

The only restriction on such a contract is that it cannot be based on a promise to engage in sexual conduct or any illegal activity. Thus, it's illegal if a man says to a woman, "I'll support you so long as you will have sex with me," because basically what he is proposing is prostitution. However, if a couple agrees that one of them will work while the other will take care of the home, that's valid and

CASE IN POINT

With This Ring . . .

When Dennis Brown's engagement to Terry Thomas was called off in 1983, he did what any jilted fiancé might do: he asked her to return the ring. When Thomas refused, Brown took her to court in Wisconsin only to be rejected again. The trial judge ruled that Brown could not recover the ring because of a state law that prohibited lawsuits alleging emotional harm caused by the breach of a contract to marry. Translation: Don't bring your broken heart to the judicial altar.

Clearly not a man who liked taking no for an answer, Brown persisted, appealing to the Wisconsin Court of Appeals. There he found satisfaction. That court ruled in 1985 that Brown could get the ring back because it was a conditional gift given in contemplation of marriage. "A gift given by a man to a woman on condition that she embark on the sea of matrimony with him is no different from a gift based on the condition that the donee sail on any other sea," the opinion noted, quoting from the decision in a different case. "If, after receiving the provisional gift, the donee refuses to leave the harbor — if the anchor of contractual performance sticks in the sands of irresolution and procrastination — the gift must be restored to the donor."

Things to Include in a Living-Together Contract

Like a prenuptial agreement, a cohabitation agreement can include a discussion of

- **finances (how the bills will be split; whether there will be joint bank accounts)**
- **household responsibilities**
- **how property will be divided if the relationship breaks up**
- **whether a party will be supported after the relationship ends**

enforceable, and will entitle each person to certain rights, such as support or distribution of joint assets, if the relationship breaks up. You might have to file a lawsuit, however, to collect any money you believe is owed to you.

COMMON-LAW MARRIAGE

Blossom and Jeremy ended up living together for years without going through the formality of actual marriage. "Who needs a piece of paper?" Blossom liked to say.

■ **Do they have a common-law marriage?**
Maybe, but it depends on what state they live in. The idea of common-law marriage was brought to America by the English colonists, and its basic purpose was a practical one. In frontier days when there was a lot of settlement out West, there would often be hundreds of miles between towns where a couple could find a preacher or justice of the peace to marry them. So a common-law marriage protected people who wanted to be married but were unable to formalize their relationship right away.

In the modern world, cohabitation is no longer such a social stigma and is indeed widely accepted, so most states have phased out common-law marriage. In the states that do recognize common-law marriage, the effect is the same as though the parties had in fact been legally and formally married. The benefit of a common-law marriage is that it entitles you to all the rights and privileges you would have had you been actually married. Thus, if you split up or if your partner dies, you would be entitled to a share of certain assets.

You should check your state's law to see if common-law marriage is recognized and, if so, what the actual requirements are. Merely living together may not be enough. It is usually necessary that you and your companion:

- **live together for a specified length of time**
- **express an intent to be married**
- **hold yourselves out to the public as husband and wife.**

HOMOSEXUAL COUPLES

Bradley and Peter had been going out for two years and were talking about moving in together. One summer afternoon, Bradley packed a picnic lunch and drove Peter up into the mountains to a romantic spot where they had gone on one of their first dates. Brad poured champagne and presented Peter with a red velvet box. Inside was a diamond stud earring. "Will you spend the rest of your life with me?" Bradley asked.

The following states recognize common-law marriage:

Alabama	Ohio
Colorado	Oklahoma
District of Columbia	Pennsylvania
Georgia	Rhode Island
Idaho	South Carolina
Iowa	Texas
Kansas	Utah
Montana	

CASE IN POINT

Promises, Promises

The acceptability of "palimony" took hold in 1976 when the California Supreme Court ruled in a case brought against actor Lee Marvin.

Marvin's former live-in girlfriend, Michelle Marvin, had sued him for support after their six-year relationship broke up. She contended that they had entered an oral agreement to live together and "share equally any and all property accumulated," according to the complaint she filed against him. In addition, she asserted, they agreed "to hold themselves out to the general public as husband and wife." Thus, she had changed her last name from Triola to Marvin.

Ms. Marvin gave up what she said was a lucrative career as an entertainer in order to be a full-time companion and homemaker. In return, she said, Mr. Marvin agreed to provide financial support "for the rest of her life." Maybe so, but one year after they separated, Mr. Marvin stopped paying support and refused to divide with her any of the more than $1 million in property acquired during the time they lived together.

Mr. Marvin argued that he had no obligations to Ms. Marvin since they had not married. Any contract between them would be invalid because of their sexual relationship, he said.

The court rejected his arguments and ruled that an agreement between two parties is valid so long as it is not based on the performance of sexual services (because that would be prostitution), and that a party to a nonmarital relationship is entitled to receive a reasonable value for the household services rendered during the relationship.

Cohabitation had become so prevalent, noted the opinion, that it would no longer be useful for a court to impose a judgment that found live-in relationships to be morally undeserving and legally nonexistent. Nevertheless, some of the judges seemed uncomfortable giving judicial blessing to untraditional living arrangements. To make its own moral position clear, the court added that "the structure of society itself largely depends upon the institution of marriage, and nothing we have said in this opinion should be taken to derogate from that institution."

While the decision was a groundbreaker, it did not end happily for Michelle Marvin. The case went back to the trial court for a determination of the facts, and after hearing evidence from both sides, the judge awarded Michelle $104,000 for economic rehabilitation. However, the court found that Lee had never agreed to support Michelle for the rest of her life and that she had suffered no financial damage from her relationship with Lee and had, in fact, benefited economically and socially from the union. The $104,000 award was overturned by a California appeals court in 1981, which ruled that it was unwarranted given the trial court's finding that Michelle had suffered no damage and that Lee had never had any financial obligations to her.

Can homosexual couples get married legally?

No state in the United States recognizes the right of homosexual couples to marry, although some countries in Europe, particularly in Scandinavia, do permit such marriages. However, homosexual couples can and do live together, and they can enter into cohabitation agreements, which will settle most of the questions that might arise between them in the same manner as though they were married.

The major disadvantage that homosexual couples have in not being able to formally marry is that, in many cases, they do not qualify for certain benefits that spouses get. For example, since they are not legally married, they may not be able to cover each other on their medical insurance policies. However, the trend is moving to increase the rights of homosexual partners. Some cities, such as Atlanta, Boston, Minneapolis, New York, and San Francisco, have passed domestic partnership laws. Among other things, these laws extend health benefits to the partners of city employees.

FOREIGN MARRIAGES

Bartholomew, the intellectual member of Beatrice's family, won a scholarship to study medieval politics in Italy for six months. He came home bearing lots of little gifts — mostly very yummy Italian chocolates. He also had a big surprise: Allegra, his new wife, whom he had married two days before returning to America. "It was so romantic," he said, swooning.

"And probably illegal, too," shouted his dad, desperately hoping that he was right.

Is a foreign marriage invalid?

No. In general, as long as a marriage is valid in the country where it took place, it is valid everywhere. That's because a legal principle called **comity** governs the interactions between foreign countries. With comity, a sort of international code of etiquette, most countries agree to recognize and enforce the valid legal contracts and court orders of other countries. Because marriage is so universal, it would be unusual for one country to refuse to recognize a valid marriage that took place in another country. So while the United States may not agree politically with countries such as Libya or Cuba, it would still recognize as valid a marriage that took place in one of those countries as long as both parties entered into the marriage voluntarily.

VIOLENCE

Marital Rape

Beatrice was washing the dishes one evening when she heard a commotion from the next-door driveway. She looked out as her neighbor Gloria screeched her car into reverse and sped away. "You know I'm right," shouted Martin, Gloria's husband. "You're my wife. You have to sleep with me *whenever I say so.*" As he stormed back inside, Martin yelled, "And don't think you can pull that headache stuff again."

Are spouses obligated to have sex?

Traditionally, sex was considered a husband's right and a wife's duty. As women have achieved more equality and independence, such notions are rapidly disappearing and have been eliminated from the law.

Many states now legally acknowledge that a husband does not have a right to demand sex from his wife. In these states, a woman can charge her husband with marital rape if he forces her to have sex against her will. Some states, however, do not allow such prosecutions, and some states allow them only if the couple had been separated before the forced sexual contact occurred.

If your husband has forced you to have sex, you may be able to get a protective order to keep him away from you. Although there is no obligation to have sex, a persistent refusal to do so may constitute grounds for a divorce.

For Help If You're in Danger from Your Husband or Boyfriend:

- Check your local yellow pages under "Battered Women's Shelters" or "Crisis Help Lines."
- Call your state's coalition against domestic violence, if there is one.
- Call the National Coalition Against Domestic Violence at 202-638-6388 (hours are Tuesday–Thursday, 10 A.M. to 8 P.M., Eastern) or at 303-839-1852 (hours are Monday–Friday, 9 A.M. to 5 P.M., Mountain/Standard).
- Call the national office of the United Way at 703-836-7100, or call your local United Way chapter. The United Way is a private, nonprofit organization that runs crisis intervention centers and women's shelters.
- Call the National Battered Women's Law Project, which can direct you to the appropriate place for legal services. Its number is 212-674-8200. The project is part of the National Center on Women and Family Law, which provides information for policymakers and battered women's advocates.
- Most states also have local crisis help lines, or you can contact the Ingraham Volunteers, a nonprofit organization that runs a twenty-four hour telephone help service at 207-774-HELP.

Protective Orders

Gloria eventually came back, but Martin's anger had barely subsided. Almost as soon as she walked in the house, he slammed her up against the wall and snarled that if she ever tried to turn him away again he would lock her in the bedroom, chain her to the bed, stuff a rag down her throat, and let her die there. He slapped her face, kicked her in the stomach, and threw her favorite vase against the wall, shattering it. Gloria ran out the back door.

What can a woman do if she thinks she's in danger from her male partner?

Statistics show that domestic violence is far more common than most people think. As a result, many states and the federal government are passing laws and setting up programs aimed at preventing and stopping it. These programs vary from state to state, so the best course if you are in danger from your spouse is to contact your local police department to find out what needs to be done. The police will not be able to issue a protective order, but they can issue a report that will help a judge decide whether or not to grant such an order.

Could she change the locks?

She can, but it may not be effective without a protective order. Both spouses have an equal right to reside in their home, so changing the locks may not be advisable before you get a protective order, since doing so could result in getting your spouse even more angry. He or she would have every right to hire a locksmith to drill through the new locks. A protective order can make it illegal for the offending spouse to return to the marital residence or to your place of employment. Your spouse could be arrested for disobeying a protective order, so you should contact the police immediately if the order is violated.

How to Get a Protective Order

Call the police. They won't be able to issue the order (a judge has to do that), but they will be able to tell you exactly where to go and what to bring to get the order. You will have to appear before a judge and explain why you want the order. Usually the order can be granted immediately.

HAVING KIDS

10

PARENTAL OBLIGATIONS

A few weeks after the birth of their daughter, Alena, Beatrice and Max went to visit Milt and Sarah, a couple that had been in their prebirth class at the hospital. Milt and Sarah had a baby boy, Calvin, and Milt showed off his room, filled with toys, books, stuffed animals, and a custom-made crib. Sarah displayed their state-of-the-art stroller, instant bottle warmer, and musical swing. She also introduced Marie, their live-in nanny. "Have you signed up yet for nursery school?" Sarah asked as they sat down to eat dinner.

"Gee," said Max. "We've basically just been trying to decide whether cloth diapers are really better than disposables."

■ What obligations do parents have to support their children?

Every parent has a legal duty to provide basic financial support for his or her children. At a minimum, parents have to provide food, shelter, and clothing, and they may also have to provide other luxuries depending on the lifestyle they have led and can afford.

In many states, a parent's duty to support a child ends at the point when the child is **emancipated** (legally an adult) regardless of whether the child is actually capable of supporting himself or herself. (In most states, a child is considered to be an adult when he or she turns eighteen.) However, some states have modified this harsh rule to require parents to support their children beyond their eighteenth birthday; in fact, in some states, such as New Jersey, the parents may even be required to provide a college education. (For more on emancipation, see page 5.) Some states will also require a parent to continue supporting a child over eighteen if the child would otherwise have to go on welfare and become a "public charge."

You would have to consult a lawyer about the law in your state before making any decisions as to whether or not you can withhold financial support to one of your children. (See Chapter 30, Finding and Using a Lawyer.)

Beatrice's friend Renata was having trouble with her sixteen-year-old son, Gabe. He was skipping school, staying out all night, and stealing money from her purse. She suspected he was using drugs, but her attempts at discipline failed. When she tried to talk calmly to him, Gabe ignored her. When she shouted, he got up and left the room. Renata was divorced and her husband had little to do with the kids, so she couldn't turn to him for help. In a fit of anger one night (when Gabe stumbled in at 3:00 A.M., stinking of cigarettes) she told him he was going to be out on his own if he didn't shape up immediately.

■ Can a parent kick a child out of the house?

Not usually. A parent has certain obligations to support a child through emancipation. If you do not do so, or if you refuse to permit your child to reside with you, you could face accusations of abuse or neglect (see page 126) with very serious consequences. Before things get so bad, you should seek family counseling or other help to alleviate the situation.

Medical Care

Beatrice was beginning to wonder about the advice she was getting from her health maintenance organization's new pediatrician. In addition to the usual vaccinations and vitamin advice, the new doctor was suggesting that Vinny, age nine, ought to be seeing the HMO's orthodontist, and

that Alena, an attractive twelve-year-old, would look even nicer if she had a nose job. "Of course, it would also help her breathe better at night," the doctor added, scribbling down the name of the HMO's plastic surgery specialist. Beatrice thought plastic surgery and braces were needless.

What kind of medical care, if any, are parents required to provide their children?

In general, parents are legally responsible for the "reasonably necessary" medical expenses of their children. For the most part, a parent's consent to medical treatment is required, although many states allow for exceptions in the case of emergencies, pregnancy, venereal disease, or alcoholism. Parents are required to consent for two reasons:

- **They have the right, as well as the obligation, to determine what is best for their children.**
- **They are going to be responsible for paying the bill.**

If a child does not get adequate medical treatment, it could be considered neglect (see page 126). So could a mother's use of alcohol or drugs during pregnancy. While parents have the right to weigh the risks and benefits of a proposed procedure, if a child's life is in danger, a court might overrule a parent's refusal of treatment and let the government

Is It a Question of Faith or Murder?

If parents have valid religious beliefs that preclude giving medical treatment to their child, should they still be liable if the practice of those beliefs results in the death of the child? That was the question in a case involving young Robyn Twitchell, a two-and-a-half-year-old boy who developed a bowel obstruction. The problem, while serious, was treatable by surgery. However, Robyn's parents were Christian Scientists, and for them conventional medical treatment was out of the question. They believed that only prayer could cure their son, and they brought in a church-accredited practitioner who came to their home and prayed for the boy's recovery.

That, unfortunately, didn't work, and Robyn died in April 1986. His parents subsequently were charged with involuntary manslaughter and were convicted in July 1990. They appealed the conviction, arguing that the "spiritual treatment exemption" of the state's child neglect laws was meant to protect people like them from criminal prosecution if they were reasonably practicing their religion.

In August 1993, the Massachusetts Supreme Judicial Court overturned their convictions, but on a more technical point. The Twitchells had relied on a Christian Science publication that interpreted their legal rights and obligations as they had been outlined in a document issued by the state's attorney general. The document did not clearly assert that a parent could face criminal prosecution for failing to seek medical treatment for a child. The court ruled that evidence of the document and how the Twitchells relied on it had been withheld from the jury improperly.

However, the court clearly noted that the Twitchells' religious argument alone had not been persuasive, stating that the exemption law did not override a parent's duty to seek medical attention for a dangerously ill child, such as Robyn. Parents in similar situations, wrote Judge Herbert Wilkins, still could be charged with involuntary manslaughter if their conduct was deemed wanton or reckless.

Prompted by that decision, the Massachusetts Legislature repealed the religious exemption in December 1993 as part of a sweeping child-abuse bill. Massachusetts officials, however, decided not to prosecute the Twitchells any further.

intervene — even when the parent refuses treatment because of religious beliefs.

If a parent can't afford to pay for medical care, there are state and federal programs, such as Medicaid and Aid to Families with Dependent Children (AFDC), which may provide assistance.

If you find that you are unable to care for your child for any reason — physical, financial, or emotional — you can voluntarily surrender the child to the care of the state. If you do so, however, the state may begin the process to terminate your parental rights. For more, see pages 9 and 127.

■ What about immunizations? Are they required?

This is an area in which the government *can* dictate a parental medical decision. Because of the dangers to the population at large from a child with an infectious disease such as smallpox or measles, most states require children to be vaccinated against certain diseases before they can attend school.

If your child does not have the shots, he or she cannot attend school, and if he or she does not attend school, you are in violation of compulsory schooling laws. However, some states do allow a child to forgo the immunizations for religious reasons or if the vaccination would be medically dangerous or harmful to the child.

If you object to immunizations, you should find out the rules in your state. Your local school board can probably advise you whether your objection would be accepted and honored.

WHEN KIDS GET HURT, WHO'S LIABLE?

Four-year-old Alena pushed another child at the playground, causing him to fall and fracture two fingers. Beatrice and Max were in a quandary. Should they send flowers and an apology, or should they offer to pay for the medical bills?

■ Can parents be sued if their child hurts someone?

Yes, in certain cases. Almost every state has enacted laws that impose *limited* liability on parents for *intentional* harm caused by their children. Unintentional harm, such as the broken fingers that Alena caused, cannot be the subject of a suit against child or parent. But, say Alena had announced she was going to break the boy's finger. If she then bent it back, or used an instrument such as a hammer to do it, her parents could be liable for their own negligence in failing to exercise reasonable control over a child they know has vicious or violent tendencies. They might also be liable for negligently entrusting a dangerous item to a child.

Surprisingly, perhaps, it's possible in some cases for a child to be sued for his or her negligent acts. An act is generally considered negligent when a person fails to take "due care" and that failure causes harm to another person or their property. Typically, the due care expected of a minor is less than that demanded of an adult, and in most states, the minor must be sued through a parent or guardian.

Older minors, particularly when they perform adult actions, such as driving a car, are often liable to the same extent as an adult. The age of the child is key: very young children, including a four-year-old like Alena, cannot fully understand and appreciate the responsibility of due care, and so can't be held liable. Some states set a minimum age for liability, such as seven; but in most states, the cutoff will depend on the circumstances, including the maturity of the child and the nature of the activity.

It is rare that a child is sued personally, and the main reason for doing so is to collect from the family's insurance if the child is included in the coverage.

Parental Supervision and Liability

Vinny was playing in the backyard with his friend Roy. While pretending to be Robin Hood, Roy lost his footing on a tree limb and fell twenty feet to the ground, and suffered a concussion. His parents were hysterical and blamed Beatrice, who had known the kids were climbing the tree, but had been inside working and hadn't been watching.

■ **Is a parent liable if a child's friend is injured while climbing a tree in the backyard?**

Perhaps. A parent has a duty to warn a visitor of any hidden hazards that he or she knows about, so if you know that a tree is dead and scheduled to be cut down, you cannot idly stand by as a child climbs it. If on the other hand a tree is healthy, then your responsibility for the well-being of someone else's child depends upon the level of supervision that you accepted. The child's age is also an important factor; the younger the child, the more supervision he or she requires. It may be reasonable for a mother to assume two twelve-year-olds can play safely in a tree unattended. It may not be reasonable, however, if the children are only five years old.

Sporting Accidents

Alena was the first girl in her school to play on the Little League team. Beatrice and Max were enormously proud when she played her first game. She did well until the fifth inning, when she hit a ball that caught the shortstop short — in fact, it hit him on the head and knocked him out cold.

■ **Are parents liable when their child accidentally hits someone with a ball during a game?**

Probably not. A participant in a sport assumes the ordinary and expected risks that are inherent in the

CASE IN POINT

Boys Will Be Boys — and Parents Will Sue

How much legal responsibility do adults have for the children they're supposed to be watching? That was the issue in a painful Washington case involving two kids playing with matches.

Bert Ewing and Jeremy Reeve, two four-year-olds, were playing together at Jeremy's grandparents' house. They left, unnoticed, and went over to Bert's house. In Bert's backyard, they lit some matches and cigarettes, and suddenly Bert's shirt caught fire. Although Bert's mother was home, she didn't know the boys were there. Jeremy ran back and told his grandparents that his friend was hurt; by that time the fire was out, and an ambulance had been called.

Bert's mother sued, claiming that Jeremy's grandparents were supposed to have been supervising the boys, and were negligent in allowing them to stray. She charged that Jeremy was the greater firebug and had led her son astray.

In a 1989 decision, the Washington Court of Appeals disagreed, ruling adults in charge of minors are not required to watch them every minute. They have a duty to exercise reasonable care, but they have no duty to foresee and guard against every possible hazard. The court also found there was no evidence Jeremy had a special fondness of fire. Even if Jeremy's actions had been wrongful, the grandparents would not have been liable for his acts unless they had known he had a history of lighting dangerous fires.

Parents cannot always count on the law to protect them from the actions of their children, however. In a 1965 Connecticut case, for example, a troubled teenager was allowed to go home from a reform school and live with his father on a trial basis. He ran away, stole a car, and wrecked it. At the time, a Connecticut statute made parents liable for up to $750 damage caused by their child stealing a car. Even though the youthful culprit was still technically in the custody of the reform school when he stole the car, the father was held liable for the $750. That limit has since been raised to $5,000.

sport. Even professional ballplayers are occasionally hit by batted balls.

Bullies

Vinny was constantly coming home late from school, with his head hanging down and his shirt torn and dirty. He told his parents that a group of older boys was terrorizing him after he got off the school bus, beating him up for the fun of it. One day Vinny came home with a big grin and blood streaming down his forehead. He had struck back — but so had they, hitting him with a rock and cutting his head so it needed eight stitches. Max was apoplectic, and Beatrice was so upset she called the parents of each boy — though Vinny begged her not to — and gave them a piece of her mind, threatening to sue.

■ Are parents liable for the actions of their bully children?

Yes, they may be. If the offending child has a vicious or violent temperament, his parents probably were aware of it or *should* have been, and they may be liable for failing to exercise reasonable control over the child. Proof that a child has violent tendencies includes previous incidents of assault or cruelty that were made known to the parents. If the child has never been vicious before, then the parents have no way of predicting or preventing the first outbreak, so it would be very difficult to establish liability. However, nearly every state limits the amount of a parent's liability (see page 121).

PROPERTY DAMAGE

During the hot summer months, when school was out, Vinny used up three cans of green spray paint to write obscene words all over the front of a neighbor's house. The neighbor, an elderly widower, caught Vinny green-handed and demanded that Beatrice pay for repainting his entire house.

■ Are parents responsible for property damage by their child?

Usually. Nearly every state has laws that hold parents responsible for intentional or willful acts committed by minors, including vandalism. This is a type of "vicarious liability," which means it is not based on the fault of the parents. However, liability under these statutes is limited to relatively low amounts. For example, Texas limits a parent's liability to $5,000 for each act; Iowa's limit is $1,000 for each act. That means that if a kid burns down your entire house, all you can collect from the parents is the limit set by the state. Even if the child's parents are wealthy and the kid has a trust fund, it will likely be impossible to get any money from them.

If a child causes damage to your property, it's often best to try and meet with the parents to work out a deal.

SUING AND COLLECTING

Vinny's eye was badly injured by a baseball thrown by the father of one of his friends. Beatrice and Max sued and won a good-size recovery that paid all Vinny's medical and legal bills, and still left him with a large sum. Then they were unsure what to do with the money.

■ What happens when parents win a lawsuit on behalf of their child?

Parents receive the money, in their capacity as the natural guardians of their minor children. However, they can't spend it without court approval. They must manage the money by keeping it in a separate account earmarked for the child. Although the rules vary from state to state, the money or property usually must be made available to the child when he or she reaches the age of majority (in most states, age eighteen).

SCHOOL

Beatrice did not like what was going on in Alena's first-grade class. The students were learning to read, but Alena already knew how because Beatrice had taught her at home. So when the teacher, Mrs. Robertson, was pairing people up to practice reading exercises, she sent Alena to read by herself in the corner. ("You're already so good," she whispered in Alena's ear.) Mrs. Robertson also posted a set of rules for her students:

1. **Sharpen your pencils every morning.**
2. **Keep a sweater at your desk in case you get cold.**
3. **Go to bed at 8:30 P.M. so you won't be tired in class.**

Beatrice complained to the principal that Alena wasn't getting enough attention from Mrs. Robertson, and she also complained that Mrs. Robertson was setting up rules for things that were none of her business. The principal was not at all apologetic. "We like to give our teachers a lot of leeway," he told Beatrice. "If you hadn't taught Alena at home, she wouldn't be so far ahead of the others now."

■ Are parents required to send their children to school?

Every state has adopted laws that require attendance at school for some minimum period of a child's life, usually from age five or six to fourteen or sixteen. Parents, however, have the right to decide which schools their children go to, whether public or private, parochial or secular.

If you want to educate your child at home, for whatever reason, your state's law may require that you first get the approval of your local school board. Children who are taught at home are often required to take year-end examinations to evaluate their progress. If they fail to fulfill the state requirements for each grade level, the state law may require that they receive additional tutoring. You may also have to attend a hearing to determine whether it is appropriate for your children to be taught at home.

If you are interested in teaching your children at home, you should first contact your local public school board. You might also contact a lawyer to find out what the procedure is in your state.

Child Actors

Vinny was "discovered" in an ice cream parlor by a famous movie director. "Your son has exactly the look I've been trying to find for my new movie," he told Bea. "Can I give him a screen test?" Beatrice and Max agreed, and Vinny got the lead role in "Kombat King, Part 3."

■ Do child actors have to go to school?

Child actors and performers are not exempt from the requirement of education; their circumstances just make their learning process a bit different from that of the ordinary child. Generally, child performers receive private tutoring for several hours per day. Like any child, they must satisfy certain minimum requirements before they can advance to the next grade level.

CHILD CARE

Babysitting at Home

Beatrice's neighbor Paula had stopped working after her second child was born. The loss of income really hurt, so she decided to set up an informal child-care service for some of the other women in her neighborhood.

■ Can a mother charge money to take care of her own child and others without a license?

Not necessarily. The laws vary from state to state, and many states require a license if you accept payment to care for children not related to you by blood. However, if your own children are also present, the licensing rules are sometimes more lenient. Of course, many people rely on neighbors and friends who have children as a low-cost alternative to formal day-care programs. The laws of your state will dictate whether or not you need a license to supervise those other children.

Day-Care Centers

For several years, Max stayed home and took care of the kids. But the band he played with was getting some recognition and that meant traveling to out-of-town concerts. Their son, Vinny, was still too young for school, so they thought about sending him to a day-care center. Beatrice was nervous, though, because of all the horror stories she had heard about abused children and fatal fires. She wanted to pick the safest place.

■ Do all day-care centers have to be licensed?

The requirements vary from state to state, but most states require a day-care center that serves more than a certain number of children to be licensed, although centers that are operated by a church are usually exempt from licensing requirements. In reality, licensing generally just assures that a center has complied with certain minimum requirements (like having a fire extinguisher on the premises) that were set forth by the state; it does not necessarily mean that the center is particularly good or even better than average. All that a license will tell you is that the day-care center has passed some sort of inspection procedure.

Of course, because parents have the right to determine their child's care, many opt to send their kids to informal programs that are not licensed.

At-Home Care

Beatrice decided to hire a full-time babysitter, Josephine. She paid Josephine $200 a week, in cash (at Josephine's request). She also paid a neighborhood teenager $4 an hour to babysit every other Saturday night.

Paying Taxes on Your Babysitter's Income

If you pay a domestic worker (including babysitters, housekeepers, and gardeners) more than $1,000 in one year, you generally must pay Social Security and Medicare taxes. The total amount owed is 15.3 percent. You pay half and the worker pays half. (You deduct the worker's portion from his or her salary and forward the entire amount owed to the Internal Revenue Service.)

If you pay a household worker more than $1,000 in a three-month period, you also owe federal unemployment taxes.

You can get information on paying employment taxes for your household workers by calling your local Internal Revenue Service office. It will send you the necessary forms and will advise you how often you must make the payments.

You should also check with your state department of labor to find out if you have to also pay unemployment taxes or workers' compensation.

Be sure to notify the appropriate government offices if the babysitter stops working for you. Otherwise, it may continue to assume that you owe the money and try to bill you for it.

■ Does a parent have to pay taxes for a full-time babysitter?

Yes. If, like Beatrice, you hire a full-time babysitter you are considered an employer and are required to comply with employment laws, just as any company must do. Mostly this involves withholding money for Social Security and Medicare and forwarding that payment to the federal government. You may also owe money for federal and state unemployment taxes and for state workers' compensation. You are not required to withhold federal income taxes unless your babysitter asks you to and you agree.

■ What if the babysitter just works part-time?

If you pay him or her more than $1,000 in a one-year period, you must pay the Social Security, unless the babysitter is under age eighteen and lists "student" as his or her principal occupation. Because people generally hire babysitters on a very informal basis, most people don't realize that they have to pay taxes. But with the recent furor over people in public office not complying with this law, you should be aware that these requirements exist and that you could be subject to civil and criminal penalties if you fail to comply. In practice, the Internal Revenue Service rarely pursues people who don't pay, but it could.

CHILD ABUSE AND NEGLECT

Beatrice's neighbor Gloria was in the grocery store with her four-year-old son, Marty. Marty reached out from the shopping cart and grabbed for the Yummy Dummy cookies, causing a stack of boxes to tumble into the aisle. Gloria yanked the cookies from him, slapped his hands, and scolded him. When Marty started crying, Gloria shook him by the shoulders and warned him to behave.

■ Was this child abuse?

Abuse can be very hard to define. We all think we know it when we see it, but in actuality, whether a particular action constitutes abuse depends heavily on the circumstances and the social climate. Not so long ago, physical punishment and beatings were widely accepted as a method of discipline of even small children. Now, many parents are forgoing the physical aspect of punishment. In fact, in Sweden parents are forbidden by law to spank or slap a child for any reason.

Child abuse and neglect are generally defined by state statutes. **Abuse** usually occurs when a parent purposefully harms a child. **Neglect** usually arises from a parent's passive indifference to a child's well-being. Thus, physical actions that injure the child (such as hitting or kicking) would constitute abuse. In contrast, leaving the child alone or failing to feed him or her for a long period of time would constitute neglect. Placing the child in a dangerous situation might be both. You would have to check the statute in your state to find out exactly what the definitions of child abuse and child neglect are. In most cases, you can discipline your child with a slap or a spanking so long as you don't cause physical injury.

Whether an act constitutes abuse or neglect will also depend in large part on the particular child involved. A mature ten-year-old might be able to handle being alone for an hour, while an immature ten-year-old might not. The parents' right to bring up their children as they see fit has to be balanced with the state's obligation to protect children who cannot protect themselves. The movie "Home Alone," though a comedy, horrified many people because of the apparent negligence and uncaringness of the parents, who didn't notice that their child was not with them. Whether a parent's action is excusable will depend on the state statute and the specific circumstances of the case.

Reporting Suspicions of Abuse

Beatrice had observed several disturbing events involving her neighbors. Once Marty had shown up to play with Vinny with a puffy face, bruises on his arms, and an unwashed shirt. Beatrice asked how he had hurt himself, and Marty said he had slipped in the backyard. Beatrice decided to report her suspicions of abuse to the state's department of child welfare.

■ Are people required to report suspicions of abuse or neglect?

It depends on your relationship to the child. All states have mandatory reporting statutes, so if you have good reason to believe that a child is being abused, you may be required to report it to the appropriate authorities (the police or a child welfare or social services agency). In most states, the law specifies that certain people in positions of

What Happens When Parents Are Suspected of Abuse?

Once suspected abuse is reported, the state's investigation will begin, and it will not cease until a determination regarding the abuse has been made. The investigation may involve

- **physical examinations of the child**
- **visits to the home**
- **interviews with the parents, the child, and other individuals who may have been witnesses**
- **a psychological evaluation of the family**

If it is determined that the child is in physical danger from his or her parents, the state may remove the child from the home and place him or her in foster care. Because the system is primarily concerned with the protection of children, parents who are the subject of an investigation should seek the assistance of an attorney who can help them through all the steps in the procedure and protect their interests.

authority with regard to children, such as doctors, teachers, nurses, and day-care workers, must report suspicions of abuse. However, some states require *any* person who suspects abuse to report it. So if you believe that a child you know or work with is being abused or neglected, it is imperative that you find out the extent of your obligation to report your suspicions. You may be subject to penalties for not reporting it if there is genuine abuse. The penalties vary from state to state. However, if you report a suspicion and are wrong, it's possible that you could be sued for libel or slander (see page 287).

What gives the government the right to investigate?

The state has the power to pass and enforce laws for the protection of children (and adults, too). This is based on the idea that certain people, like children and the mentally ill, are unable to speak up for themselves and assert their own rights. Therefore, the government will do it for them. Thus, if a child is being abused by his or her parents, the state has the authority and the power to intervene. (When the government acts on behalf of a child or mentally ill person, it is asserting its role of **parens patriae,** Latin for "parent of his country." It refers to the "state" as the guardian of minors and incompetent people.)

Understandably, a parent may be terrified of an accusation of abuse — especially if it is untrue. But if a parent refuses to cooperate with an investigation, the child could be taken away — at least for the duration of the inquiry.

Who represents the child?

The judge supervising the process usually will appoint a **guardian ad litem,** or guardian at law. This person, typically a lawyer or government social service worker, represents the interests of the child (not the needs or desires of the parents) throughout the legal process of investigating whether or not to terminate the parents' rights. A guardian ad litem is different from a "legal guardian" (see page 129). The guardian ad litem represents the child throughout the legal process, while a "legal guardian" is assigned to take the place of a parent.

FOSTER CARE

A social worker determined that there were valid reasons to suspect Marty had been abused. Not only had Beatrice reported her concerns, but so had another neighbor as well as Marty's preschool teacher. The investigator also found that Marty had been treated by a doctor several times for suspicious "accidents." The social worker recommended that Marty be placed in a foster home, at least temporarily.

What is a foster parent?

Foster parents are individuals who volunteer and are approved to provide homes for children who are unable to remain with their parents for one reason or another. A child may be placed in foster care as a result of

- **child abuse or neglect**
- **a custodial parent's imprisonment**
- **extended illness of the custodial parent**
- **other family crises where there are no relatives or friends who can care for the child**

A child may also be placed in foster care voluntarily by his or her parents, if the parents feel that they are simply unable to care appropriately for the child. Unfortunately, in reality, once a parent places a child in the foster-care system voluntarily, it is often difficult to get the child back. That is why most parents do not do so.

Are foster parents paid?

Yes. They receive a small sum of money on a monthly basis to help defray the costs of caring for the child in their home. The child also receives medical benefits from the state, which retains legal custody of the child. In general, though, a foster parent acts with much of the same authority as a biological parent. A foster parent oversees the child on a day-to-day basis, providing a stable home, discipline, and affection. A foster parent often has the right to decide if the child needs medical care and take the child to the doctor, although sometimes decisions, such as ones about medical care or travel, will have to be made by the state agency in charge or even the biological parent.

What rights do the biological parents have when a child is in foster care?

It depends in great measure on the circumstances under which the child was placed in foster care. When a parent voluntarily surrenders a child to foster care, the state should (and by law often must) allow for reasonable visitation by the biological parent. On the other hand, if the child was physically or sexually abused, the situation is very different. The parent may be entitled to have minimal visitation in a supervised setting, but it is unlikely that an abusive parent would be able to take a child out unsupervised.

The amount and type of visitation will depend on the state's law and the particular circumstances of the individual case.

Does the child have any say in the situation?

The guiding principle in foster-care decisions will be to do what is in the best interests of the child. In reality, the child will have very little control over the process, although the judge will probably listen to his or her feelings, especially if the child is old enough to express them maturely.

Can the biological parent get his or her child back?

Yes, but it's not easy, and there's no guarantee you will be able to do so. The system often gives a parent a lot of leeway before taking away a child, but you will have to show evidence that you are a fit parent and that it's safe to return the child to your care. It's usually helpful to have a lawyer's help in such proceedings. If you can afford to pay a lawyer, it's best to find someone who has experience with this kind of case. You can try to get recommendations from the following sources:

- Local law schools. Ask a professor of family law for advice on who's good in your area.
- Legal aid lawyers. Ask for names of former lawyers who left to work in private practice.
- The court's guardian ad litem program administrators.
- Psychologists or other professionals who deal with custody issues.

If you cannot afford a lawyer to help you in a proceeding to get your child back, you are entitled to have one appointed.

APPOINTING A GUARDIAN

Beatrice's cousin Natalie, a young widow, had a suspicious lump in her breast that was going to require surgery. It might very well be benign, the doctor told her, but she would still need to be hospitalized for at least ten days. Recovery would probably take another two weeks after that. Natalie asked Beatrice and Max to care for her ten-year-old daughter while she was in the hospital and recuperating.

What exactly is a legal guardian?

A legal guardian is someone who is not the parent of the child, but who has the legal right and authority to act as a parent to that child. You should designate a legal guardian for your children if you believe that you will become unable to care for them and if there is no other parent to care for them. For example, if you become very ill and must be hospitalized for an extended period of time, your children would need adult supervision by someone who is legally responsible for them.

Generally, it is necessary for a court to approve a *permanent* appointment of guardianship. Your wishes will be given consideration, but they don't always have to be followed if the court believes it would not be in the best interests of the child. You usually can, however, authorize someone to care for your child on a *short-term* basis in a less formal manner. (See the box on page 130.)

What happens to a child if both her parents die?

As soon as a child is conceived, you should be thinking about the possibility that at some point while he or she is still a minor you and your spouse may both die. You should begin to consider who would be an appropriate guardian for the child in that event and speak to that person about whether or not he or she is willing to be the guardian. If the person agrees, both parents should draft a will that appoints that person as the legal guardian for the child in the event they both die. You should also consider selecting a **trustee** who can oversee any money the child inherits, since the child will not be able to take direct control of assets like bank accounts or a house. The legal guardian may be an appropriate person to appoint as trustee of the estate as well.

If both parents die without a will appointing a guardian, the situation becomes more complicated. Fortunately, the days of dreary orphanages and workhouses are gone, but most parents would probably prefer to avoid the possibility of their children being placed in foster care or a state-run institution. Also, if you die without a will, the state won't know your preferences and might appoint a relative as guardian for your child whom you would prefer not to have. For example, you may disagree with your sister's method of child rearing, or you may despise your wife's brother, but the state agency and court system making the determination about what happens to your child doesn't know those things.

CASE IN POINT

Who Decides What's Best for This Child?

Sadly, it's not unusual for courts and parents to fight over what is in the best interests of children, and happy endings do not always result. That, however, wasn't the case for Phillip Becker of San Jose, California. Institutionalized from birth, Phillip suffered from Down's syndrome as well as a congenital heart defect. Doctors said the heart problem would lead to Phillip's death by the time he was thirty if it was not corrected. Phillip's parents, who rarely visited him, refused the operation.

Their refusal prompted years of litigation and a custody battle between Phillip's parents and a couple named the Heaths. When Phillip was six, Patricia Heath, a volunteer at the nursing home, had taken a liking to him, and with the Beckers' permission, Phillip began spending weekends with Heath and her husband, Herbert. After the Beckers refused the operation, the Heaths sued to become Phillip's guardians, arguing that the boy was capable of leading a productive life. The Beckers disagreed and said he would forever be a burden, and so it was better to let him die.

The Heaths eventually won custody of Phillip, and in 1983 he had the heart operation. Not only did he survive, he also became a minor celebrity as well when NBC produced a television movie about his ordeal. Titled "Jonathan: The Boy Nobody Wanted," the drama aired in 1992.

> **How to Appoint a Legal Guardian**
>
> To avoid any confusion about your intentions, it's best to state your wishes for a legal guardian in writing. You should also specify the circumstances under which you want the person to act as a guardian (perhaps only while you are in the hospital for surgery, for instance) and the duration of the guardianship.
>
> For short-term situations, you may be able to fill out a simple form granting someone temporary authority to make decisions regarding your child. If you only want to grant authority to someone like a babysitter to make medical decisions in the event of an emergency, you could assign that person a limited power of attorney (see page 402).
>
> The rules on how to grant short-term or permanent guardianship vary from state to state, so if you have reason to believe that your appointment will be challenged, you should see a lawyer.

A state's preference is to place children with relatives who are willing and able to care for them. Don't leave these decisions of such paramount importance to be decided by a bureaucratic state process.

SURROGATE PARENTING

Beatrice and Max wanted to have more children, but after Vinny's birth Beatrice had had a series of miscarriages. They had tried fertility doctors, counseling, and even astrology. Nothing worked, and finally they had accepted that Beatrice was going to be unable to carry another baby to term. They decided to look for a woman who would agree to "fill in" for her.

■ How does surrogate parenting work?

In the typical surrogacy arrangement, a married couple makes a deal with a woman (the surrogate) who agrees to be impregnated with the husband's sperm, usually through artificial means. In a contract (usually written), the surrogate promises to surrender all her rights as the child's biological parent so that the wife can adopt the child. Typically, the couple pays for the surrogate's medical and living expenses during her pregnancy, which includes money for housing and food.

There are also cases where a surrogate agrees to be implanted with an embryo that was fertilized *in vitro* using the wife's egg and the husband's sperm. In such a situation, the surrogate essentially serves as a receptacle to carry the developing fetus.

■ Are these arrangements legal?

Yes, in most states. However, a few states, including New York, Michigan, and Florida, consider paid surrogacy the equivalent of selling babies and have outlawed it. Some other states will not enforce a surrogacy contract if a dispute arises, but they don't make the transaction illegal. In general, this is an area of the law that is still developing. The most important thing to know when contemplating a surrogacy arrangement is that most states consider it a crime to sell a baby. Thus, generally, if a contract says that the surrogate mother will bear a child to be adopted in exchange for a specified sum of money, that contract may not be valid. And, in fact, the parties could be subject to criminal prosecution. However, if the contract says that the surrogate mother will be paid a specified sum to cover the costs associated with her pregnancy, that is more likely to be valid.

Before making any surrogacy deals, you should discuss the issues with an attorney in your state who is experienced in family law.

Brokers

Max and Bea placed an ad in their local newspaper: "Loving, generous, healthy woman wanted to help married couple achieve their dream of having a big family." The first caller was a man who said he could introduce them to several women, including ones with physical traits similar to Bea's.

Is it legal to use a "broker"?

A "broker" or "intermediary" is a person who matches up a surrogate mother with an interested couple. If you're paying a broker just to introduce you to someone, you very well may be violating a criminal statute against baby selling. Often, however, the intermediary will be a lawyer who brings the parties together, oversees the negotiations, and drafts the agreement. So long as this lawyer charges a reasonable fee for itemized services, it probably won't be considered baby selling. But if, for instance, the bill includes an extra fee of $1,000 for the "administrative" cost of making the arrangement, that may be considered an illegal "brokering" fee.

If you're making a surrogacy contract, watch out for unspecified fees. If you later have a dispute over your contract, the entire thing could be invalidated and you could also be charged with a crime.

The Rights of the Surrogate Mother

Beatrice and Max met Darla. She was young, energetic, and even looked a little like Beatrice. She already had a three-year-old daughter, and her husband had recently lost his job. Quite frankly, she told them, they needed help paying the bills. She was less frank about the doubts she felt in her heart about being able to give up the baby.

What rights does a surrogate mother have if she changes her mind and wants to keep the baby?

There's no set answer to this question, since there is not a lot of established law on these issues. The Baby M case (see the Case in Point below) is considered the leading case in such matters, so many courts would probably be guided by that decision, in

CASE IN POINT

Surrogate Mother or Baby Seller?

The most famous case on surrogacy so far is the "Baby M" case, which was decided in New Jersey. In that case, the surrogate mother, Mary Beth Whitehead, was artificially inseminated with the sperm of William Stern, whose wife, Elizabeth, had medical problems that put her at risk if she were to carry a child to term. The child was thus biologically related to both the father and the surrogate mother.

When the baby was born in 1986, she went home from the hospital with the Sterns, although the adoption by Elizabeth had not yet been finalized. Whitehead then asked to see the baby and was permitted to. She refused to return the infant and took her into hiding.

Because the surrogacy contract had provided for a lump-sum payment of $10,000 to Whitehead, the New Jersey Supreme Court found that the contract was unenforceable because it was basically baby selling. However, the court did not completely rule out the possibility of legal surrogacy agreements. And though the court determined that it was in the best interests of "Baby M" to be raised by the Sterns, it would not terminate Whitehead's rights as mother of the baby, and Whitehead was permitted to continue visiting the child on a limited basis.

More recently, the California Supreme Court upheld a surrogate contract in 1993. Unlike Whitehead, whose own egg was artificially inseminated by William Stern's sperm, Anna Johnson was implanted with an already fertilized egg provided by Mark and Crispina Calvert. In a 1993 decision, the court ruled that surrogate contracts are valid regardless of whether the surrogate provides the egg, and it found that such contracts neither exploit poor women who often act as surrogates, nor infringe on their state and federal constitutional protections.

which the surrogate mother (who wanted to keep the baby) was given visitation rights, but was not allowed to have custody of the child.

If the surrogate mother changes her mind at any time before the adoption has been finalized, it is very possible that she will win, at the very least, the right to visit the child. Whether she would be able to win custody of the child is another question, since the biological father also has rights. If the baby has been living with the biological father and his wife for some time, the bonding that will have taken place is something that would be considered when determining custody and visitation arrangements.

If the biological mother does win custody, the biological father would still be entitled to visit the child. He would also be required to pay child support.

In the Event of Divorce

Darla liked Max and Beatrice and thought they seemed like nice people, but there was something about them that she worried about. It wasn't that she thought they'd be bad parents; it was more that their relationship just didn't seem quite right. They seemed eager to have another child, but there was a tension between them that troubled her.

■ What happens if the couple splits up before the surrogate gives birth?

The biological father has certain unavoidable obligations to the child, and if its biological mother (the surrogate) followed through on the agreement and surrendered her parental rights, the father would have to take the child himself. Since his wife is not the biological mother of the child, and since she did not have a caretaker relationship with the child during the marriage (they split before the child was born), it is highly unlikely that she would have any rights whatsoever where the child was concerned.

If the surrogate mother surrenders her parental rights, but the father is unable or unwilling to care for the child alone, he can always choose to give the child up for adoption.

Male "Surrogates"

Max, it turned out, had a very low sperm count. He and Bea had a friend, Spencer, who agreed to help out and be a sperm donor.

■ Does a sperm donor have any rights or obligations to "his" baby?

Yes. Technically, as the biological father of the child, he would have the right to visit the child as well as the obligation to support it. However, when a child is born to a married woman, it is automatically presumed in most states that the woman's husband is the child's biological father. Of course, a blood-typing test or DNA analysis could prove that he is not the father, but as long as no one challenged the assumption, Max would be considered the father of the child.

■ So should they have a contract?

Yes. A written contract would be helpful in preventing future misunderstandings. The contract should state the purposes of the agreement (why they are doing what they are doing), and it should explicitly state whether or not the biological father is to have any rights or obligations to the child. Both the mother and the father should be represented by separate attorneys to ensure that they both fully understand exactly what is happening.

Note: If you deal with a sperm bank, the donor, who typically is anonymous, will have no obligations to the child.

ADOPTING

The Process

Max sat Beatrice down one evening. "Look," he said. "We both want more children. I've got bum sperm, and whenever you get pregnant you miscarry. I think we should adopt." Bea knew Max was right, but the whole idea just seemed overwhelming.

How does adoption work?

Every state has agencies, either run by the state or licensed and monitored by the state, which arrange and supervise adoptions. An agency works with both the birth parents and the adoptive parents, offering counseling and advice and matching up adoptive parents with children. Typically, the adoptive parents will pay the birth mother's medical, living, and legal expenses associated with the pregnancy and adoption, and an agency will usually help each party complete the legal process of adoption.

You may also choose to adopt an older child. The issues are much the same, although if a child is in foster care, the biological parent's rights may already have been terminated. In some states, such as New Jersey, the foster-care family gets first choice on whether or not to adopt a child who has lived with them for more than two years.

The actual adoption procedure varies from state to state. You may adopt a child who lives in another state, but you must comply with the requirements of each state when you do so. All states, for instance, require adoptive parents to have a "home study" in which a social worker or other authorized official interviews them and inspects their home to determine if they are "fit" to adopt. An adoption is not finalized until the court approves it.

You can find adoption agencies listed in the phone book, although you may want to get a referral from a friend instead. That way you have a better idea of what to expect from the particular agency.

Private Adoptions

Signing up with an agency almost certainly meant a long wait. Max and Beatrice decided to look into alternative ways to adopt, but they weren't quite sure what the options were — or what was legal.

What is a private adoption?

A private, or independent, adoption occurs when there is no agency involvement. Instead, a connection is made between a woman who wants to surrender a child for adoption and a couple who seeks to adopt a child, often by an intermediary such as a friend, an attorney, a doctor, or other third party. This practice has become more and more frequent in the United States, and you may see advertisements in the classified sections of newspapers for private adoptions. Remember, however, that it is illegal to pay someone for a baby. So if the payments involved in a private adoption exceed the reasonable medical and legal expenses of the mother or if there is a "brokerage" fee to a third party, everyone involved runs the risk of being prosecuted for selling a baby.

Out-of-State and Foreign Adoptions

Beatrice contacted several agencies in her state. One had a three-year waiting list. Another had a disconnected phone number, and a third, she learned, was under investigation for fraud. Bea quickly began to think they were going to have to begin looking farther away from home.

Is it possible to adopt a baby from another state or even another country?

Yes, but if you want to adopt a child from somewhere other than your own state, you may need the assistance of a specialized agency. Adopting a child from another country is especially complicated. You will have to complete vast amounts of paperwork and deal extensively with the Immigration and Naturalization Service. (For more information on INS rules and regulations, call 202-514-5014.) Your best approach is to research the alternatives. Find other parents who have adopted from the country or area from which you wish to adopt. Find out the name of their adoption attorney and any agencies they used. Ask around for recommendations and look for support groups or other less formal organizations for people in your situation. It is certainly not something that you will want to tackle alone.

"Alternative" Adoptions

Beatrice and Max met several interesting people at an adoption seminar sponsored by two lawyers. There was Leah, a thirty-nine-year-old single woman who did not anticipate getting married before her biological time clock stopped ticking. There were Luis and his wife, Thelma, who was quadriplegic and confined to a wheelchair. And there were Chuck and Bob, a gay couple in their mid-thirties, who had been living together for seven years.

■ Can anyone adopt a child?

There was a time when only certain people who satisfied traditional notions of "normalcy" could adopt. Then, the civil rights and women's movements in the 1960s and 1970s promoted change, and today many factors that would have once been crucial, such as marital status, religious affiliations, and race, are barely considered. Instead, the focus is on what is best for the child and not what is "normal."

The rules still vary tremendously from state to state. Two states, Florida and New Hampshire, have outright bans against lesbian and gay adoptions (an appeal to Florida's law is pending), and in April 1994 a District of Columbia court ruled that two unmarried domestic partners may not adopt the same child, though either of them could do so as a single parent.

You should consult an agency or attorney to find out the specifics where you live.

When an Adopted Child Is Seriously Ill

Beatrice's neighbor told her a tragic story about an adopted baby that developed a degenerative brain disease and had to be hospitalized for several weeks. When he returned home, he required round-the-clock nursing. His adoptive parents couldn't afford to care for him.

A Misleading Adoption

Adoption agencies aren't usually expected to make any guarantees to adopting couples about the future healthiness of a child. They are, however, expected to fully disclose any *known* problems that would affect a prospective parent's willingness to adopt. That's the essence of a 1992 Minnesota Supreme Court decision.

The case arose after a couple, referred to in court documents as the H's, learned that their adopted child was the genetic son of a seventeen-year-old boy and his thirteen-year-old sister. The H's had adopted their son as an infant through Caritas, a Catholic adoption agency. The agency had informed them there was incest in the child's background and given them a description of the general physical health of both the baby's genetic parents.

During his childhood, the H's son developed serious behavioral and emotional problems. In response to a psychologist's request for more information about the child's background, Caritas produced a document that revealed that the boy was born of an incestuous relationship. The agency also disclosed that the genetic father was considered "borderline hyperactive" with a low-average range of intelligence.

The H's sued Caritas, alleging it had failed to disclose the relationship of the child's genetic parents in order to induce them to adopt. Because of that, they asserted, they had suffered mental anguish and had incurred considerable expense.

The court ruled that while in general an agency cannot be expected to guarantee a child's future health, it does have a duty to disclose enough information so as not to mislead prospective parents.

Can an adoption be rescinded if the child is not healthy?

It is always a terrible thing when a child falls ill, especially when the illness is permanent or fatal. Some parents do find that, emotionally and financially, they cannot deal with the child, especially if the couple has other, healthy children who also need support and love. However, most states will not permit parents to return a child they have adopted, although it may be possible to rescind an adoption if the adoptive parents were deceived or defrauded (if, for example, the agency knew the child was ill but never informed the adoptive parents). (See the Case in Point opposite.)

In either case, whether you are a biological or an adoptive parent, and you find that you are completely unable to care for the child (either physically, financially, or emotionally), you can voluntarily surrender the child to the care of the state, and the child will be placed in a foster home or in a state-run institution. The state will carry at least some of the financial costs of the child's treatment. However, by doing so, you probably will have to navigate through a morass of state bureaucracy, including court appearances, home investigations by social workers, and an almost total surrendering of your privacy as parents. The end result of such an action may very well be a termination of your parental rights.

Before it gets to that point, however, you should be sure that you have exhausted all your possible resources. You may be able to get state or federal assistance for the child's illness if you cannot afford to pay for the care yourself or if your insurance will not cover it. You should fully investigate your options before making a decision.

GIVING YOUR CHILD UP FOR ADOPTION

Blossom, a college junior, got some unwelcome news one morning when her home pregnancy test confirmed what she'd been suspecting for a couple of weeks. Even more unwelcome was the response of her boyfriend, Tony, the mostly indifferent senior captain of the hockey team, who immediately scrawled out a check for $300, shoved it in her hand, and grunted that she should "take care of it." Blossom had something altogether different in mind.

What happens when a woman chooses adoption?

Giving up a child for adoption traditionally meant totally surrendering all rights and responsibilities as that child's parent. However, some states now allow **open adoption,** in which the birth mother may retain some visitation privileges (see page 136).

If you choose a traditional adoption, it will at some point become irrevocable, and thus it is not a decision to be made lightly or quickly. The doctor or clinic where you go for your physical examination should be able to help you with the decision and give you information about your options. If you do decide to give the child up for adoption, you will be required to sign a legal document in which you agree to give up your parental rights.

Your state will have an agency or agencies that handle adoptions and can place your child in foster care until a family is found. There are private agencies as well, many of them run by churches or other religious organizations with which you might feel more comfortable. You may also arrange an adoption with a private couple, but remember that it is illegal for someone to pay you money for your child. The couple who wishes to adopt your baby may agree to pay your medical expenses and the hospitalization costs for you and the child at the time you give birth. You should consult a lawyer about your rights and responsibilities.

When the Mother Changes Her Mind

Blossom chose an agency run by a local church, where the people were extremely friendly. They had explained that her baby would be taken directly from the delivery room in the hospital and that she would never have contact with it. "It's better that way," one of the volunteers assured her. But as her pregnancy progressed, Blossom began to feel troubled about giving up the baby.

■ What happens if the birth mother changes her mind?

Most states have a waiting period after a mother gives a child up for adoption during which she can change her mind. If she does, the adoption will not go through, and she must take the child back and assume all the rights and responsibilities that go along with being a parent.

She may also be able to rescind the adoption, even if it is already complete, if she can show that she did not consent or that her consent was obtained by fraud or duress.

■ Does the birth mother (or father) have the right to visit the child once it's adopted?

Traditionally, parents who give up their children for adoption have surrendered all their rights and responsibilities toward the child. The adoptive parents become the adopted child's "real" parents for all purposes, as though the birth parents never existed. In such a situation, obviously, the birth parents have no rights of visitation or any other involvement in the child's life.

However, there is a growing trend toward what is known as **open adoption.** In such an adoption, the biological mother surrenders all her legal rights and responsibilities, as in a traditional adoption. However, the adoptive parents agree to let her visit the child on occasion and on a schedule that is acceptable to everyone involved. In this way, adopted children are not cut off from their biological heritage. And the knowledge that visitation is possible sometimes makes it easier for a pregnant woman to choose the option of adoption.

The Father's Rights

Tony was having a lot of misgivings about the callous way he'd reacted when Blossom told him she was pregnant. In fact, he was distraught over the idea of her giving the baby up for adoption. Like it or not, he had fathered that child, and he didn't want it to be raised by strangers.

■ Does the father have a say?

Yes. If the child is to be put up for adoption, most state statutes require that the father, if he is known, be notified. If he wants to raise the child, he generally will be allowed to do so unless there is a challenge to his fitness as a parent. If, however, he does not want the child to be adopted, but refuses to care for the child himself, he cannot force the mother to keep the child. The state will terminate his parental rights and release the child for adoption. He can't just stand in the way of an adoption without assuming full responsibility for the child.

■ Could he stop the mother from having an abortion?

No. While the father may intervene if the baby is being given up for adoption, he may not intervene if the mother decides to have an abortion. It is the biological mother's right to decide what to do when she becomes pregnant. Although it may seem unfair, the only "say" or choice a man has with regard to pregnancy occurs at the moment of intercourse — when he chooses whether or not to take precautions. (For more on abortion, see page 138.)

Adoption Records

Blossom had a bad dream. She was campaigning to be a senator, when a stranger came forward during a speech on the eve of the election. The stranger was shouting, "I'm your daughter. Why did you give me away? Why have you tried to hide the truth about me for all these years?"

Blossom awoke abruptly. She had no interest in politics, but she did wonder if her adopted child would be able to track her down years later.

■ Aren't adoption records supposed to be sealed permanently?

In order to protect the privacy of the birth parents and the adopted child, adoption records in most states automatically are sealed to prevent access by the public. In the 1970s and 1980s, there was a growing movement toward opening up these records so that adopted children and their birth parents could renew their relationships. At the same time, there was a very strong movement against this practice because of the loss of privacy and the potential emotional conflict and even embarrassment that might be caused. What if, for instance, a birth mother had gone on to marry and have a family without telling her spouse about the child she gave up for adoption, and the child one day showed up? Or what if adoptive parents had not told their child that he or she was adopted and the child's birth mother arrived on their front doorstep?

Due to these movements, many states have now instituted programs that attempt to balance the right to privacy with the right to know the truth. There are now **open adoptions**, in which the birth parent has a right to visitation with the child even after the adoption. There are also provisions that allow an adopted child who has reached the age of eighteen to learn the identity of his or her birth parents. Some states allow identities to be revealed only when both the birth mother and the adopted child give permission. In such cases, if either the birth mother or the adopted child refuses to allow the information to be released, then it won't be. The adoption will remain confidential. Also, in some instances, if the adopted child develops a serious health problem, the identity of the birth parents may be revealed if it is believed that genetic information would be helpful.

When the Adoptive Parents Are Unfit

Blossom was in her eighth month when she got a call from Mrs. Harriden, the mother of her best friend, Michele. Mrs. Harriden said she knew "a very nice couple" who had been waiting nearly two years with an agency for an adoption. She wondered if Blossom might want to let them adopt her baby. Blossom said okay, but told Mrs. Harriden she had no desire to meet the couple.

Two months after the birth (it was a boy), Michele called Blossom in tears. "I shouldn't tell you this," she whispered, "but that couple is terrible. The baby is always crying, and I thought maybe he's just colicky. Of course, it's so overwhelming in the beginning to be a parent, but yesterday when I went to the grocery store I saw the baby alone in the car in the parking lot. And you know how hot it is, and the poor thing was just wailing."

■ Can the biological mother do anything if she thinks the people who adopted her child are unfit?

It depends on whether a court order has been issued finalizing the adoption. (The process varies from state to state. Most states have a waiting period before an adoption is final during which it can be rescinded.) If a mother discovers something about the adoptive parents that would cause a threat to the child (such as drug or alcohol abuse or abuse of the child) before the adoption is final, she may be able to rescind the adoption. However, once the adoption is final, she has given up all her rights and responsibilities as a parent. This means that she has no decision-making power with respect to the child's upbringing. What school he or she goes to, what religion he or she is raised in, and whether or not spanking is an appropriate punishment are all decisions made by the adoptive parents. They have the same rights and control over the child's upbringing as the birth mother would have had if she kept the child.

Of course, if you suspect that your child is being abused or neglected, you have the same obligation to report the parents to the appropriate state agency as you would with any child (see page 126). However, even if the adoptive parents are later found to be unfit and their rights as the child's parents are terminated, your "standing" to get the child back may not be any greater than anyone else's, since you became like a stranger to the child when you gave him or her up for adoption. That is not to say that you cannot obtain custody of the child, but it will be difficult.

Fraudulent Adoptions

As her due date approached, Blossom was having second thoughts about her decision to give up the baby. But the couple that was going to adopt the child had promised she could visit the baby as often as she liked. "Our home will always be open to you," they said. But after the baby, a boy, was born and the adoption finalized, Blossom's efforts to visit were repeatedly rebuffed. Then, when the child was six months old, the couple informed her they were moving across the country. Blossom believed that they had known about this move all along. She felt they had tricked her into giving up the baby.

■ Can an adoption be rescinded?

Once an adoption is final, it is very difficult to rescind. You will need a lawyer who is experienced in adoption law and in this type of lawsuit. However, most states will permit a parent to rescind an adoption if it was obtained through force, fraud, or other improper means. There may be a time limit on when you can bring your lawsuit. Most likely, if you do bring a lawsuit to try to set aside the adoption, the judge's decision will depend very heavily on the individual facts in your case, and you will be faced with the very difficult task of proving that the adoptive parents not only acted in a way that deceived you but that they *intended* to deceive you.

ABORTION

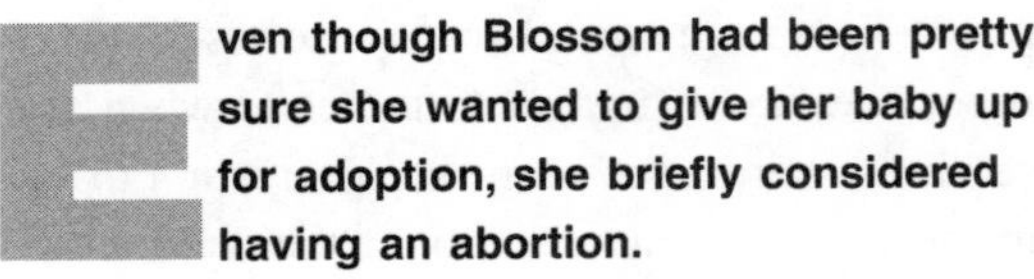

Even though Blossom had been pretty sure she wanted to give her baby up for adoption, she briefly considered having an abortion.

■ In what ways, if any, can the government limit a woman's right to an abortion?

In 1973, the Supreme Court issued its historic decision in *Roe v. Wade,* which established the constitutional right of a woman to choose to terminate her pregnancy. While the decision stated that the government may not restrict a woman's right to an abortion during the first three months of her pregnancy (known as the first trimester), it did allow states to impose regulations during the later stages.

According to the decision, a state could regulate abortion procedures during the second trimester in ways that were "reasonably related to maternal health." (The state could, for example, require that persons performing abortions meet certain qualifications and that the facilities where they were performed be licensed.) During the third trimester, the court ruled, the fetus was then "viable" — capable of surviving if it were born. Since the government has an interest in promoting life and the potential of life, the court ruled that during this trimester a state could regulate or even prohibit abortion, except when an abortion was necessary to protect the life or health of the mother.

In the years since *Roe v. Wade,* the Supreme Court has chipped away at the right to choose an abortion. In its 1992 decision *Planned Parenthood v. Casey,* the court reaffirmed the right of a woman to terminate her pregnancy but discarded Roe's trimester framework. This decision allows states to enact regulations on abortion during any trimester so long as the regulations do not impose an "undue burden" on a woman's ability to terminate her pregnancy. The following regulations were found to be permissible limitations on a woman's right to choose:

- **an informed consent provision requiring that physicians provide women seeking abortions with information about fetal development**
- **a twenty-four-hour waiting period**
- **a one-parent consent requirement for minors, with a "judicial bypass" procedure (see page 6)**
- **a requirement that abortion facilities file a confidential report on every abortion performed**

So while a state cannot deny a woman the right to have an abortion, it can impose the above requirements.

■ **If a woman wants an abortion, can her husband veto that decision?**

No. The U.S. Supreme Court's *Casey* decision found that a provision requiring a woman to get her husband's consent to an abortion was an undue burden on the right to choose, and thus was unconstitutional. A husband does not have a right to veto an abortion, nor does he have to give his consent before one can be performed.

Future litigation in the abortion arena will likely focus on what other types of state restrictions do or do not constitute undue burdens on a woman's right to choose to terminate her pregnancy.

CHILDREN BORN OUTSIDE A MARRIAGE

Blossom, who lived with her new boyfriend, Jeremy, was pregnant again. She and Jeremy were very committed to each other and had all intentions of staying together. Still, they weren't really interested in getting married, even with a baby on the way.

■ **Is a child born to an unmarried couple illegitimate?**

The concept of an "illegitimate child" is quickly becoming as outdated as the term "bastard." Such an expression generally serves to stigmatize a child who had absolutely no choice as to the circumstances of his or her birth. As more and more individuals choose to have children without being married, the concept of legitimacy is becoming less important.

In the past, a man had no legal obligations to support a child he fathered outside a marriage, and that child had no inheritance rights if the biological father died. Most states now require both parents to provide support for a child, so once a woman can prove that a man is the father (usually through a blood test) that man has a responsibility to support the child — no matter how fleeting his relationship with the child's mother was. And the child also has inheritance rights, although the rules vary from state to state. An unmarried father can also argue for custody or visitation rights. So the concept of "legitimacy" no longer has much legal significance, although it may still, of course, have moral or religious significance.

Getting Child Support

Beatrice's friend Elizabeth is splitting up with Charlie, the man she lived with for fifteen years. They have two children but were never married. Now Charlie has run off with another woman and is refusing to pay any child support to Elizabeth. "I'm not your husband," he told her. "So I have no obligations."

■ **Can an unmarried mother get support from the father of her child?**

Yes. She will have to bring a lawsuit (assuming the father does not want to cooperate), which asks the court to establish the legal obligation of the father to support the child and set an appropriate amount of support. Once you have such an order, it can be enforced like any other child-support order.

Elizabeth was able to prove Charlie was the father of her children, and the court ordered him to pay $400 a month in support. Charlie complied for two years, until he moved to another state. "Try and get it now," he wrote in a note to Elizabeth.

■ **Can she collect if he moves to another state?**

Yes. There is a statute that has been enacted in most states called **URESA, the Uniform Reciprocal Enforcement of Support Act**. Under URESA, an order of support issued in one state can be enforced in another state. You will have to go through some paperwork in order to do it. You can contact the court in your own state to start the process, or you can contact the court in the other state. If you are able to deal with the long-distance bureaucracy, it may be more efficient to contact the other court. However, the court in your own state can handle your claim; it just may take longer, because the court in your state essentially acts as a middleman.

For more details on collecting unpaid support, see Chapter 12, GETTING DIVORCED.

Grandparents' Rights

Charlie's parents were very upset that he ran off and refused to help Elizabeth. They loved their grandchildren and wanted to be able to visit them. Elizabeth, however, refused to let them see the children so long as Charlie was withholding support.

■ **Do grandparents have visitation rights?**
This is an area in which the law is evolving to expand grandparents' rights. Still, in most states grandparents have no independent visitation rights when the grandchildren's parents are happily married and living together. However, many states do permit a grandparent to sue for visitation in the event of a divorce or the death of their child.

How to Get Child Support

You will have to go through a legal process that has several steps:

- First, you file a complaint or petition. Often this is done in family court, and may be as easy as filling out a form.
- Next, you must establish that the other party is indeed the father or mother of your child, usually through a genetic test. If the other party does not consent to the test (or just concede that he or she is the parent), you will have to ask a court to order the test. (If you were married to the parent, it may not be necessary to go through this step.)
- Finally, if paternity or maternity is established, the court will set an appropriate amount of support. There will probably be a hearing during which both parties will be allowed to put on evidence. The judge will look at the income and assets of both parties and determine how much support should be paid.

Note: It is the obligation of *both* parents to support their child. A father who has custody can go after the biological mother for support.

Fathers' Rights

Blossom's friend Patty found out she's pregnant. She's been dating the father for a few months, but has no intention of marrying him. He's too much of a slob, for one thing, and he's never interested in anything other than sports. Patty decides, however, that she wants to have the baby. She's thirty-seven and tired of waiting around for Mr. Right. Since she doesn't want any long-term involvement (or meddling) from the Man of the Moment, she decides not to tell him she's going to have his baby.

■ **Are there any legal consequences if a woman fails to tell a man that she's having his baby?**
Yes. Regardless of whether a father knows about the existence of his child or not, he has an obligation and a duty to help support the child. Of course, if you never tell him about the child, he will never be in a position to pay you any support. In addition, if you do one day decide to bring a paternity action against the father seeking support retroactive to the child's birth, your delay may work against you. Say, for example, you wait until the child turns seventeen and then try to get tens of thousands of dollars of support for the years passed. It is highly likely that you will fail, because most states limit the amount of time you have to bring a claim for support. (These are known as statutes of limitations.)

In addition, your child's rights to inheritance may be affected if the biological father does not know of that child's existence, because then he could not place the child in his will. Your child might be able to challenge the will and seek to share in the father's estate, but the question of paternity will be more difficult to prove once the father is dead and is no longer available to testify or to provide blood samples for genetic tests.

You may also be depriving your child of other benefits, such as the right to collect social security in the event of the father's death. In all, unless you are absolutely committed to the idea that the biological father should have no involvement in the child's life whatsoever, the better course is to notify him of the existence of the child and get support and other benefits for your child. You should also consider the emotional impact on your child of growing up without knowing who his or her father is.

WILLS AND TRUSTS 11

WILLS: TO HAVE AND HAVE NOT

One December night Grace and Gordon faced each other across the kitchen table. In a few weeks they would be headed for a long-awaited vacation in the Florida Keys, but something two of their kids had said earlier that day had focused them on a more serious topic.

When Gordon was trying on his snorkeling mask and fins in the basement, sixteen-year-old Bradley jokingly asked if he would get his parents' new Jeep if they were both devoured by barracuda. Later that day, twenty-six-year-old Beatrice had brought in the mail, which included the plane tickets to Florida, and she also put in her bid for the Jeep "in case your plane disappears in the Bermuda Triangle."

Grace and Gordon had known for a long time that they should write their wills, but like many people had put it off. Now they were in their mid-fifties, and all of their four children except Bradley had left home. They had many questions to consider in thinking about a will, such as how to put together a plan that would satisfy everyone in the family (who gets the Jeep, for example), how to protect their own interests, how to minimize the tax burden, and how to create something that would stand up in court.

■ Who should make a will?

The vast majority of Americans die without wills, and the consequences vary greatly with individual circumstances. Every adult should think about making a will, and the need grows as your assets and family ties increase. Wills are especially crucial for parents with children who are **minors** (under eighteen in most states), since you can name a **guardian** in a will and make arrangements for financial support of children even past the age of eighteen. Gordon and Grace, for example, are nearing retirement but still have one son who is under age, and they could provide for such needs as college costs in any will they make.

Couples also have each other to think about. If your spouse dies without a will, state law might force you to split the assets of the **estate** (the deceased's property) with your children, leaving you without enough assets to support yourself. Also, any property going to a minor child in such a situation would be subject to an expensive court-appointed guardianship, which could eat up any inheritance.

When Beatrice heard that her parents were thinking of drafting wills, she wondered if she should have one, too. But then she couldn't think of anything she owned, other than some pots and pans, a less-than-stylish wardrobe of clothes, some beat-up furniture, and a car with 75,000 miles on it.

■ Aren't there some people who really don't need to worry about making a will?

Yes. If you are single, with few assets, you probably don't need one. And if you care about who would get something (such as a car) if you die, you could make the item **joint property** (see page 156) by naming a co-owner on the deed or title. That person would get full ownership of the item on your death. The potential downside of this is that you are giving the co-owner an interest in that property for life, and you may not be able to change your mind. Financial accounts can also be jointly held and will pass directly to anyone you name. Without this kind of planning, your possessions will go to your closest heirs, probably your parents or siblings — which may or may not suit you.

Steps in the Probate Process

- Someone dies.
- Someone, often the person named in the will as executor or personal representative, files the will with the probate court, usually in the county where the deceased lived.
- The executor inventories all assets and liabilities of the estate.
- The executor signs the **petition for probate,** a document summarizing the will's provisions and naming the **heirs** — relatives who would stand to inherit if there were no will.
- The executor may have to locate the witnesses and file sworn statements from them — or even have them testify — to affirm that they witnessed the signing of the will. This step can be avoided in some states if the witnesses sign a notarized affidavit at the time the will is signed. (See "self-proving wills" on page 165.)
- The executor sends a formal legal notice telling each heir and beneficiary that the will has been offered for probate. (The executor may hire an attorney, at the estate's expense, to file papers and represent the estate in court.)
- After this step, anyone wishing to challenge the will may appear in court to do it, either in person or through a lawyer (see page 164).
- Assuming no objections are made or upheld, the judge approves (**admits**) the will and formally appoints the executor. Once this happens, it is tough to upset a will, although some states do allow a late challenge under special circumstances.
- The executor settles all accounts by paying debts and taxes. The executor must provide details to certain beneficiaries — usually the **residuary legatees** (see page 146) — about what property the executor received; what was paid in expenses, taxes, and other costs; and what was given to each beneficiary.
- The executor pays out the remaining assets to beneficiaries and makes a final accounting of the estate to the court.
- The probate judge rules the estate formally closed, or, to save legal fees, the beneficiaries agree to release the executor by written agreement.

PROBATE

Gordon had a dream. At first he saw himself and his wife, Grace, flailing about in the choppy waters of the Bermuda Triangle, surrounded by voracious, man-eating fish. Grace was shouting, "I told you we should have done our wills!" But then the scene changed and he realized he was watching his kids in probate court, encircled by lawyers and court officials. The lawyers looked like barracudas. Gordon woke up in a sweat.

What is probate?

Probate is the legal process in which a court oversees the distribution of property left in a will (see the box above). The estates of people who die **intestate,** or without a will, also go through probate.

Time-consuming and often frustrating and costly, probate has gotten plenty of bad press, and it truly can eat away at the assets of an estate and the patience of those who may be heirs or beneficiaries under a will. A number of books on the market give advice on how to avoid probate, and it may be wise to do some planning of this sort. Also, many people, knowingly or not, already structure their finances so that significant assets will pass to others outside the probate process: a jointly owned house, for example, will pass directly to the survivor, and life insurance proceeds can go directly to a named beneficiary. Technically, the only property subject to probate is that for which there is no other legal mechanism for shifting title to a new owner.

Despite the possibilities of avoiding probate, it's still advisable to consider a will. As noted, a will lets you set up a guardian for your minor children and for their property (see page 150). You may also want to use a will as a kind of backstop to other estate planning. For example, even if you try to make sure that none of the property you own will pass through probate, a will can handle assets that you may not be able to plan for, such as an inheritance, lottery winnings, or a personal injury settlement (any of which could enter your estate *after* you die). Also, imagine a situation in which a husband dies and his wife gets all of his estate because they owned everything jointly. Nothing may pass through probate then, but when the wife dies, *she* may need a will if she wants to direct who gets her property.

How long does probate take?

When the will involves an estate that is small (generally less than $20,000, although it varies from state to state), it can be handled in a faster and less formal process known as "summary administration" or "small estates" procedure. To find out whether that route is an option, check with your local probate court clerk.

For most estates, however, the process can take many months, even when there are no objections to the will and the estate is uncomplicated. If the estate is large, or there are significant problems, such as estate tax controversies or an attempt to challenge the will, it can take years.

What happens if a person dies without a will?

If you die without a will — that is, **intestate** — state laws determine how your property will be distributed among your **heirs,** or closest relatives with the right to inherit. As a rule, the surviving spouse gets half the **estate** and any children divide the other half. Grandchildren would be next in line, followed by parents, siblings, and other relatives of the deceased. (See the box at right.) If a person dies without a will and without any traceable heirs, all property goes to the state.

What is the process if there is no will?

The estate is legally in limbo until the state appoints an **administrator** (usually an heir), who must make sure there is no will and notify all heirs they are in line to inherit. The administrator performs many of the functions of an executor (see page 148) — he or she pays debts and taxes, and accounts for and distributes the money to the heirs. If there is no family member who is able to act, a state will appoint a public trustee or administrator to do the job.

Dying Without a Will: Who Gets What?

Assume that Frank and Fiona have three children, Albert, Alexis, and Andrew. Andrew has two kids of his own, Zoe and Zachary, and then dies. In most states, when Frank dies, his wife, Fiona, would get half his estate. The other half would be divided equally among Frank and Fiona's kids. But since one of those kids — Andrew — died before Frank, Andrew's two kids would split Andrew's share equally. To express it in fractions, the estate would be divided as follows:

Fiona — 1/2
Albert — 1/6
Alexis — 1/6
Zoe — 1/12
Zachary — 1/12

DO YOU NEED A LAWYER?

As they talked about what to do with their property, Grace said that in the morning she would call their neighbor, a real estate lawyer, to see if she could recommend another lawyer who did wills. But Gordon mentioned that he'd been in one of the warehouse bookstores that had opened in town and noticed at least a half-dozen books on drafting your own will. Most of them even had form wills you could copy. He'd also seen some computer software that provided guidance in drafting a will.

Grace was surprised that Gordon — who always seemed to change the subject when death came up — had browsed through books on

Will Essentials

A few basic requirements must be met for any will to be valid:

- The will must be in written form. A videotape recording of your wishes *won't* do.
- It must be signed by the person making the will.
- It must be signed by two (or, in a few states, three) competent witnesses (see page 164).
- The will maker, or **testator,** must be competent — not insane, senile, or mentally disabled — and not acting under duress or under the controlling influence of another person.

Other things, while not vital, would be wise to have in almost any will:

- A clause revoking all previous wills.
- Names of all **beneficiaries** (people to whom you wish to leave property), along with what you wish to leave them, and who gets the property if that beneficiary dies before you. Another term for beneficiary is **legatee.**
- If you have minor children, the name of a **guardian** for them if your spouse does not survive you, and, if need be, a guardian or a person to manage the child's assets (see page 150).

- The name of an **executor** (sometimes called a **personal representative**) and, if needed, **trustees** for any **trusts** created by the will (see page 160).
- A statement naming a **residuary legatee** for the **residue of the estate**. The residue is the portion of the estate left after bequests of specific items of property are made. In fact, the **residuary estate** is often the largest portion of the estate, and the person or people who get it are those the deceased intended to get the most. The executor may also use the residuary estate to pay fees and taxes.
- A statement eliminating **bonds.** Many states require executors and trustees to post a bond (usually paid out of estate funds) to guarantee that they complete the job properly. You can save them this expense by stating that no bond is needed.

wills. But she also wondered if, even with a book or a computer program, this could be a do-it-yourself project. While they were far from rich, Grace pointed out that they had accumulated some substantial assets, including their big four-bedroom house they bought twenty-five years ago, and their beach house, which all the kids loved. Then there were questions of what to do with life insurance proceeds, and how to name a guardian for Bradley. And how could they arrange for Bradley's expenses to be covered until he was through with college, without Bradley getting his hands on the money himself? (She pictured him buying a fleet of Jeeps in a rainbow of colors.)

■ **Is a lawyer necessary for drafting a will?** The simple answer is that wills made without lawyers can be legally sound if the proper procedures — especially those governing witnesses — are followed (see the box above). The books and computer software on the market can guide you on issues you might want to address and on proper procedures. For people with relatively simple estates, a do-it-yourself will may work fine.

That said, we don't recommend doing without a lawyer. Just making a valid will won't ensure that your exact intentions will be carried out. This area of the law — called estate law — has many wrinkles and complexities, often arising from variations in state law. There are many potential pitfalls, particularly when jointly owned property (see page 156) or spouse's inheritance rights (see page 150) are involved. Even with small estates, you can best make sure that your property will be disposed of according to your wishes by consulting an attorney.

OF SOUND MIND AND BODY

As Gordon was flipping through a book on wills, he got a call from his ninety-two-year-old Uncle Hubert. A few years ago, Hubert's senility had gotten so bad that the family decided to place him in a nursing home. Ever since, he had taken to placing calls to Gordon at all times of the day and night. Sometimes Hubert would be quite funny, but often the calls made Gordon sad, because Hubert didn't even seem to know whom he was calling. I bet Hubert's never done a will, Gordon said to himself.

Can someone who is senile or incapacitated write a will?

As a general rule, a valid will can't be made by a person whose mind has deteriorated to the point of not knowing who his or her family is or what property he or she owns. The same is true for a person who is physically incapable of communicating. The best way to protect such a person's assets is to have him or her declared "incompetent" in a special proceeding (see page 322).

CASE IN POINT

Undue Influence

Lily Glickstein was an elderly woman who lived out her last years in Florida while suffering from an organic brain illness and Alzheimer's disease. Robert Grayson, the son of her late brother-in-law, was in charge of her finances as manager of a trust that his father established with Lily's money to provide for her care. In 1977, during her illness, she amended her will to leave everything to Grayson and his sister, Peggy Bonamo. In doing so, two previous beneficiaries, Herbert Gladstone and Helen Newman, were excluded.

After Glickstein's death, the new will went through probate, and Grayson and Bonamo — who had been named as the sole beneficiaries — withdrew $338,000 from the trust. Gladstone, Newman, and two others challenged the revised will. In the course of their challenge it was discovered that Grayson and Bonamo had not acted in a completely upfront manner. In fact, Grayson and his sister had not bothered to tell Glickstein's family or her lawyers about the new will — or about their withdrawal of the trust money.

Under Florida law, if someone has a confidential relationship with a person making a will, and is active in procuring the will, as Grayson was — he called in his own lawyers to handle the new will, for example — it is automatically presumed that "undue influence" existed. Therefore, the court set aside the second will in 1988 and affirmed the first one, finding that Grayson had acted improperly in several ways:

- He was the wrong person to arrange for a revision of the will because he was in a confidential relationship with Glickstein, as her financial manager and trustee.
- He shouldn't have recommended the lawyers or allowed his own lawyers to do the rewriting.
- He shouldn't have hidden the revision from the family and Glickstein's original lawyers.

Most suspicious of all, he was the prime beneficiary of the new will and the prime mover behind its creation.

PRELIMINARIES: GATHERING YOUR PAPERS AND YOUR THOUGHTS

Persuaded that seeing a lawyer was a good idea, Gordon joined Grace in an initial visit to the law office of Maria Heritage. Maria began by saying she wanted to go over some general issues for Gordon and Grace to think about before she could draft their wills. Who, for example, would they want to name as an executor? How did they want to handle disposition of assets vis-à-vis each other, assuming, as is usually the case, one died before the other? What did they want each of the four kids to get, and who would they name as a guardian for sixteen-year-old Bradley?

Also, Maria said, Gordon and Grace needed to put together a list of their assets, which would include real estate, bank accounts, insurance policies, retirement accounts, and significant personal property, be it a painting, a pendant, or a piano. "Don't forget the Jeep," Gordon muttered.

Once this information was gathered, Maria said, she would draft wills that reflected Gordon's and Grace's wishes, and Maria would tell them what, if any, estate-planning issues — mostly involving taxes — might be involved.

"What's this all going to cost?" Gordon asked warily.

"Well, it depends how complex the will and any related trusts get," Maria replied, "but based on what you've told me so far, this seems pretty straightforward, so my charge would be $350 per will."

"Can't we save by doing a joint will?" Gordon asked.

"No way," said Maria.

■ Can spouses do a joint will?

Joint wills — where a single document is signed by both husband and wife — are a bad idea. A surviving spouse, for example, may not be able to change his or her mind about things. And some states might let the surviving spouse take only income from the deceased spouse's estate, preserving the principal for future beneficiaries.

Choosing an Executor

After meeting with Maria, Gordon and Grace immediately began to gather their financial information. After a brief discussion, they decided to name their oldest child, Beatrice, as executor of both wills.

■ What exactly is an executor?

An executor compiles a list of the assets of the deceased and seeks to carry out the directives of the will. The job involves a mixture of legal, administrative, accounting, and, often, personal mediation skills. (See the box opposite.)

■ What kind of person does it make sense to choose as an executor?

A good executor can prevent delays, mediate conflicts, and reduce costs. If you can, try to pick someone who is organized and can deal with numbers. But people skills, in particular a sense of fairness, may end up being what's most important. An executor can always turn to professionals for help with complex legal and accounting issues — a cost that is borne by the estate.

The executor may be a beneficiary or may not be mentioned in the will at all. Often spouses name each other and an alternative as well. A couple may choose different executors for their wills, or they may choose the same person.

It's courteous and sensible to inform the person you want to name as executor. He or she may decline, and you may have to find another person willing and able to do the job, which can be a big one, depending on the estate.

■ Do executors get paid?

If the will is silent on this subject, state laws provide for payment of commissions to executors, often based on the size of the estate or on the court's assessment of reasonable compensation. If you be-

What Does an Executor Do?

The typical duties of an executor include

- **presenting the will to the court, with a petition to obtain authority over the estate**
- **finding the witnesses and getting sworn statements from them, unless the will is self-proving (see page 165)**
- **listing and determining the value of all the property in the estate**
- **deciding which debts are valid and paying them**
- **paying all estate, property, and income taxes**
- **managing the property of the estate and investing certain funds**
- **paying the expenses of the estate, such as the maintenance of houses or other property**
- **selling property or investments when necessary to preserve the estate or pay taxes and other expenses**
- **distributing assets to beneficiaries — the recipients named by the will**
- **preparing a final accounting of the estate**

lieve that your chosen executor will serve without compensation, you can state this in your will.

■ What happens if the executor named is dead or refuses to serve when the will goes to probate?

The court will appoint one. Beneficiaries of the will can file a petition with the court suggesting a particular person.

Naming Beneficiaries

As they watched the news one evening, Gordon and Grace talked more about their wills and decided that, like many couples, they would leave everything they owned to each other. They also agreed that the next in line to inherit would be their four kids — though Gordon, a bit peeved at Bradley and Beatrice for starting them down this road, groused that the kids should make it in life on their own, and he'd just as soon leave everything to charity. The news then cut to a live report from the local airport, where a plane had crashed. What if Grace and I both die at the same time, Gordon wondered.

■ Can anyone be named as a beneficiary?

Yes, but there are some important restrictions. Spouses, for example, have certain automatic rights to portions of an estate that may not be overridden by a will (see below). And property for minor children must be administered by a guardian or a trustee (see below).

■ What if the named beneficiary of a will is dead?

It's always a good idea to name alternative beneficiaries of bequests you make in a will. Thus, a clause in Grace's will might read as follows:

> I give all of my residuary estate to my husband if he survives me for thirty days, and if he does not so survive me, then I give all of my residuary estate to my children who survive me for thirty days, in equal shares.

The above clause does two things: (1) it instructs the executor about Grace's alternate choice; (2) it specifies that both her first and her alternate choice be alive for thirty days after Grace dies. So if Gordon and Grace's flight to Florida does crash, and Grace is killed, and Gordon survives a week in the hospital and then dies, Gordon never inherits from Grace. Grace's property then gets distributed according to the instructions in *her* will. If Gordon had survived the crash, lived three months, and then been hit by a truck, he would have inherited from Grace, and her property would have passed under *his* will. If Gordon and Grace both die instantly, neither inherits from the other, and the alternate choices of each are followed.

Since it's impossible to cover all contingencies, some wills also name an **ultimate beneficiary,** who receives the **residuary estate** in the event all other beneficiaries are dead. This is sometimes referred to, rather indelicately, as a "wipeout clause."

Is it possible to leave money to charitable organizations, such as hospitals, schools, or churches?

It's not only possible, it's quite common. If you are unmarried, most states allow you to leave all your money to whomever you choose. But again, spouses have certain rights to an estate that can't be circumvented by a bequest to charity. And a few states specifically prohibit a person who has a spouse or children from leaving more than a certain percentage of any assets to charity. Bequests to charitable organizations are generally deductible for federal estate tax purposes (see page 160). However, because many estates won't need this deduction, it may be better for tax purposes to ask the survivors to make memorial gifts, and they can take the deduction on *their* tax returns.

A SPOUSE'S RIGHTS: FOR BETTER OR FOR WORSE

A few days after meeting with their lawyer, Gordon and Grace went to a neighborhood Christmas party. They eventually found themselves seated in a corner, sipping eggnog with their longtime friends Trevor and Tina. When the subject of wills came up, Trevor rolled his eyes and told a story from his first marriage, which had lasted only five years. During the final two years of the marriage, Trevor recounted, the only time he and his wife talked was to fight. After one particularly nasty argument, Trevor stalked out, drove right to his lawyer's office, and insisted that his will be redrafted to cut his wife out of everything. "I don't want her romping around our dream house if I die. I want her homeless!" he fumed to his lawyer. It turns out, Trevor recalled with a chuckle, that his wife had gone to *her* lawyer to do the same thing.

Can one spouse completely disinherit another by cutting him or her out of a will?

Not usually. Most states give your spouse the right to your assets under **elective share** or **community property** laws, which make it very difficult to prevent your spouse from claiming a share of the estate, no matter what you write in your will. The box opposite offers a general overview of how each state handles spousal rights to a deceased's estate. The most important factor has to do with the rules governing a couple's ownership of property during their lifetime — whether they live in a community property or a common law state. However, in a number of states there are additional wrinkles to consider, and some states may be modifying their laws. Things also get more complex if a couple moves from a community property state to a common law state or vice versa. So if you need to know specifically what spousal rights exist in a given situation, you should consult a lawyer in the relevant state.

Does being legally separated or filing for divorce end a spouse's rights to a share of the estate?

Neither filing for divorce nor getting a legal separation automatically cuts off spousal rights. However, in a number of states a legal separation agreement and financial settlement end all rights to an elective share. A final divorce decree does cut off spousal rights.

KID STUFF: LEAVING PROPERTY TO A MINOR AND APPOINTING A GUARDIAN

Bradley was a great kid, but like many sixteen-year-olds, he was going through a difficult period. Gordon and Grace had a hard time figuring out who could step in as surrogate parents in the event of their deaths. Eventually they decided that Grace's brother Ted and his wife might be the best choice. Brad had always seemed to enjoy the fishing trips with his uncle, and they didn't live far away, which meant that Brad would be close to his siblings. Grace suggested that they discuss the choice with Brad, and then with Ted.

While Ted and his wife were reasonably well off, Gordon and Grace didn't want Brad to be a financial burden to them. And Gordon and

Disinheritance Protection: Spousal Rights by State

Spouses may try to cut each other out of their wills. But, depending on where you live, two very different sets of rules operate to give a surviving spouse rights to a certain amount of property — regardless of what the will says. One set of rules is followed by the nine community property states: Arizona, California, Idaho, Louisiana, Nevada, New Mexico, Texas, Washington, and Wisconsin. (Wisconsin is technically not in this group, but its marital property laws function much the same as those in community property states.) The remaining states and the District of Columbia follow common law property rules, which are more varied. The two approaches are summarized below.

Community property states: In these states the protections for a surviving spouse are built in to the laws governing marital property while both members of a couple are alive: Each spouse has rights to half of all income earned by either spouse during the marriage, as well as all property acquired with community property funds, no matter whose name is on the title. Unearned income — inherited property, for example — is not community property. In a will, each spouse can bequeath only his or her half share, as well as assets not deemed to be community property. The will may or may not designate the surviving spouse as a beneficiary. In either case, the surviving spouse automatically gets the other half share of the community property.

Common law states: Nothing in these states prevents a husband or wife from being the sole owner of all, or substantially all, of the assets acquired during a marriage. The spouse who earns money or acquires property owns it, unless it is transferred to joint ownership. This means that one spouse could use his or her will to leave the surviving spouse quite literally standing out in the cold. To prevent this, common law states have come up with a variety of means to assure that a surviving spouse gets some minimal share of an ungenerous mate's estate. The surviving spouse may elect to take what is left in the will or what he or she is entitled to under law — what is sometimes known as the "elective share." As noted, the approaches vary:

- Georgia simply allows a spouse to receive one year's support, which obviously varies with circumstances.
- Connecticut, Kentucky, Rhode Island, South Carolina, Vermont, and West Virginia give a spouse the right to use a deceased spouse's real estate for life.
- All the other common law states give the surviving spouse the right to choose a fixed portion of the deceased spouse's estate, most typically one-third. A number of these states factor all the property of a deceased spouse into this calculation, not just the property left in the will. That's because a significant amount of property can pass outside of probate (see page 162). A few also consider the assets owned by the surviving spouse.

Grace fervently hoped Brad would go to college, as their other three children had. So although they basically wanted to divide their estates equally among their four children, they wanted to provide Brad with extra funds to see him through his education. But Gordon wanted to make sure any money they left Brad wouldn't be splurged on a fleet of Jeeps.

■ What's the best way to choose a guardian?

Two concerns arise in providing for minor children after your death. The first is who will take custody of the children and provide for their care and upbringing — what is known as a **personal guardian.** The second issue involves the best method for providing and administering financial support for your children and is discussed below.

In the event of the death of a biological or adoptive parent, it is almost certain that the surviving parent will retain sole custody of minor children, unless that parent is proved to be unfit or incompetent — because of problems with alcohol or crime, for example. The real issue when thinking about selecting a child's **personal guardian** is whom to name in the event both parents die. In selecting a personal guardian, you should choose the person you think will do the best job, of course, but it should be someone the court will find capable of taking proper care of the child. Courts usually give most weight to the selections made by the last surviving parent in his or her will, but a judge's duty is to serve "the best interests of the child," not the desires of the deceased parents.

If two parents have been involved in raising a child, a court may look to the guardian named in each parent's will, and it's best if that is the same person. Other things a court would consider include how much contact the person has had with the child, what kind of resources he or she has to take care of the child, and what his or her ideas are about such things as education and upbringing. A stepparent has no special rights to custody, though he or she might be named guardian if both natural parents die.

You should ask the person you're thinking of in advance whether he or she agrees to take on such a responsibility. It's also important to name an alternate personal guardian, in case your first choice is unable or unwilling to serve. And finally, even if you think of having another couple serve as guardians, it's best to name only one member of the couple, to avoid problems in the event that couple splits up.

■ What's the best way to leave property to a minor?

You and your spouse can leave property to a minor directly by a bequest in your wills — but if you die before the child is grown, he or she will not be able to take the money directly. The law would require the creation of a court-supervised guardianship. While the judge will likely appoint a competent adult family member as **property guardian,** the judge may also have the power to appoint an outside lawyer to administer it. That could cost your child a lot of money, because a court-supervised guardian is entitled to fees from the minor's estate. Even a family member who doesn't take fees would have to file frequent accountings with the court and be subject to strict supervision over how funds are spent — which may require the assistance of a lawyer and an accountant. When the child turns eighteen, the guardian must give him or her the remaining money.

If you name a property guardian, it's a good idea if it's the same person who is your child's personal guardian, and your alternate choices should match as well. Having separate people handle these functions is fraught with potential for conflict.

Given the many drawbacks of using a property guardian, there are two other ways of leaving property to children that should be considered. One is to leave property to a child under the Uniform Transfers to Minors Act. This act, which has been adopted in most, though not all, states, lets you appoint a **custodian** who has broad authority to manage and dispense funds for your child without constricting court supervision and accounting requirements. A child receives the balance of the funds at anywhere from age eighteen to twenty-five, depending on the version of the UTMA adopted by your state.

A UTMA custodianship works particularly well for relatively small amounts of money — $50,000 or less. Amounts above that leave open the possibility that a child could end up receiving a large chunk of money at a relatively young age. That may not sit well with you if you want to assure that someone will oversee your child's finances through the time he or she is in college, or if your child needs special care of some kind.

In this case, the option you may turn to is a trust, which in this case would be called a **children's trust.** You select a trustee and give him or her broad authority to use both income and, if necessary, principal from the trust assets to provide for your child's living expenses, health care, and education. You also specify the age at which the child gets control of the trust property. As with a UTMA transfer, there is no court supervision. However, trust income may be taxed at a significantly higher rate than income in a UTMA account. A children's trust can be set up as part of your will or outside it.

"AFTERBORN" AND ADOPTED CHILDREN

As they were driving home from the holiday party where they had discussed wills, it dawned on Trevor and Tina that two of their three children — including one they'd adopted just four months earlier — hadn't been born when they wrote their wills.

What happens to a child who is born after a will is made?

Most states have "afterborn child" laws that permit children to receive bequests if they were born *after* a will was signed, as long as the will makes pro-

CASE IN POINT

Stronger Than Probate: A Grandmother's Love

Sometimes a grandchild is still a grandchild, even after being adopted by a new family.

After her daughter became ill in 1956, Irene Lippincott, a New York resident, took in two of her three granddaughters. The third, Dyann, who was about two and a half at the time, went to live with Eugene Woodard and his wife. Dyann's mother died in 1964.

Dyann continued to maintain a close relationship with her grandmother but grew up considering the Woodards as her parents. They legally adopted her in 1975, when she turned twenty-one.

Grandmother Irene died in 1987. Her will, drafted in 1969, named Dyann as her granddaughter and bequeathed her some antiques. She also set up a trust for "each granddaughter" to be paid over to them at the age of twenty-five. Even though Dyann was not legally adopted by the Woodards at the time the will was drawn, the executors sought instructions as to whether Dyann should be counted as a "granddaughter."

The issue was crucial because in most cases adoption completely cuts off the right to inherit. This is the case for two reasons — the goal of the law is to ensure that the status of an adopted child in his or her new family should essentially be that of a natural child. Moreover, allowing adopted children to inherit would disrupt family life by breaching the confidentiality of adoption records. It might also delay distribution of estates, since executors would have to search for missing heirs.

On the other hand, a person making a will has the right to leave money to any specific person he or she wishes. In the case of Irene Lippincott, the Surrogate's Court of Erie County, New York, in Buffalo, said that there was no confidentiality issue — the adoption was not secret, and Dyann was an adult at the time. Furthermore, the wording of the will itself — in which Irene referred to "my granddaughter Dyann" — showed that Irene intended to include her in the trust arrangements. So in the end, Dyann got her share of the trust money.

visions for the children who had been born at the time it was executed. The afterborn child typically gets the same portion of the estate as his or her siblings.

A good way to get around this potential problem is to avoid using specific names of children when dividing up the residuary estate. Instead, you can leave it to "all my children, in equal parts." (An old-fashioned term for children used in some wills is "issue.")

What inheritance rights do adopted children have?

Most states have passed laws giving adopted children the same inheritance rights as natural children, with minor exceptions. Usually, adopted children have no right to inherit from their natural parents, though of course the natural parents might decide to leave them something in their will.

LEAVING MONEY TO PETS

Grace looked out the window one morning and saw three French poodles being led down the street by Felicity, who had once described herself to Grace as a "professional" dog walker. Felicity had told Grace that an elderly woman in the neighborhood had died and left a significant amount of money to have her dogs boarded, walked, groomed, and otherwise pampered until the ends of their natural lives.

Can a person leave money to a pet?

An animal lover cannot make a bequest to a pet or set up a trust in its name. But he or she can set up a trust for someone who will care for the pet, or bequeath money to the animal's caretaker in a will.

CONDITIONAL BEQUESTS: "YOU GET THE MONEY IF . . ."

Gordon and Grace's daughter Beatrice had been dating a guy at college who was a member of a religious cult that worshiped mushrooms. Gordon was not pleased. "What if," he mused aloud, "we don't let Beatrice have anything under our will unless she marries a Catholic?"

"Oh, please," said Grace.

Can bequests be conditional on a person doing — or not doing — something?

Yes, but courts look at bequests such as these and decide whether following them would violate "public policy" — things the court thinks the state wants to foster or discourage. It's likely that a requirement that someone marry a Catholic would be up-

CASE IN POINT

"Honey, I Left Out the Kid!"

Under "afterborn child" statutes effective in many states, a child who is left out of a will *unintentionally* is entitled to the share he or she would get if the deceased had died without a will. This is true unless other survivors can prove that the child was omitted on purpose.

Even when a parent has seemingly abandoned a child, Minnesota courts have ruled that the legal right to inherit still holds. Virgil Israelson found this out after a lifetime of estrangement. His father, Valley Ervin, had tried to disown him, and Israelson's mother had to pursue a paternity suit, which she won. Nonetheless, Ervin never visited his son, never paid support, and never talked to or wrote to him.

Ervin died in 1984, leaving an estate of approximately $60,000 but no surviving spouse and no children other than Israelson. His will left all his money to two nieces, but didn't mention Israelson, who sued. He won at trial and on appeal, with the court finding that despite the lack of contact between Ervin and Israelson, there was no evidence that he intended to disinherit his son. Israelson got the whole estate in 1987.

held, since that probably wouldn't be seen as a significant restraint on the ability to marry (marriage tends to be seen as good public policy)—though you never know until the court decides. But a will provision that requires someone to divorce a present spouse or remain unmarried would probably be deemed unenforceable.

FIGURING OUT WHAT YOU OWN

As their lawyer had warned them, gathering information about their assets proved to be a big job for Gordon and Grace, not because they had so many of them, but because the records they needed were in so many places. Bank records were in a flimsy cardboard box in the attic, and Grace found the deed to their vacation house in an old wooden filing cabinet in the basement. When she read the fine print on the deed — as Maria advised — she was shocked. It turned out the deed was made out in the names of her husband Gordon *and* his estranged brother Jim.

When she showed it to Gordon, he looked sheepish and admitted that he had forgotten all about it. The brothers had bought the house for almost nothing in the early 1960s. Then a few years later, after Gordon and Jim had their big falling-out, Jim and his family never used the house again.

Grace wanted to know whether that meant that Jim's two kids, whom she hadn't seen for over a decade, had a right to part of the property. After all, she and Gordon wanted to leave the house to *their* children, free and clear, to share among themselves. Now they weren't sure whether Gordon could leave his share to anyone.

CASE IN POINT

Some Things Can't Be Controlled from the Grave

In 1911, a United States Senator from Georgia, Augustus O. Bacon, bequeathed a park to the city of Macon. His will stated that the park was to be used by white people only. It also stated Bacon's opinion that "in their social relations, the two races should be forever separate."

The will set up an all-white board of managers to run the park, and for a number of years the city kept it segregated. In 1960, however, a group of black Macon residents sued for desegregation of the city's public parks and publicly owned and operated recreational facilities. That case went all the way to the U.S. Supreme Court, which in 1963 ruled there was no justification for the city's continued segregation of the parks.

Despite that ruling, some members of the park's board of managers sued, arguing that the desegregation had violated the terms of the trust and that the title should be transferred from the city to a new group of trustees. Other heirs of Senator Bacon argued that they should get the land for themselves.

Several black Maconians filed a separate suit, arguing that segregation of a city park was illegal and asking that the court not transfer trusteeship to private individuals. The case went up before the U.S. Supreme Court, which in 1966 agreed that segregation of the park was unconstitutional whether it was held by trustees or by the city. Even if a park is privately owned, the court ruled, it takes on a public character over time.

The city of Macon had cared for the park for years, and the court found that where the tradition of municipal control had become so firmly established, private ownership of the park could not justify its segregation.

What are the different forms of property ownership, and how do they affect rights to leave property in a will?

Anyone, married or unmarried, may be a co-owner of certain possessions, and this co-ownership can limit your right to give something away in your will. Read the fine print on your deeds and titles. When two or more co-owners are named on the document, and it states that the property is held in **joint tenancy,** then the asset — whether it's money in a bank account, a car, or a house — will go directly to the surviving owner or owners upon your death — even if you have tried to give your interest to someone else in your will. That's because a joint tenancy automatically carries what is known as a **right of survivorship.** If the property is held this way by spouses, it will usually pass to the survivor free of gift or estate tax. (Joint tenancy has been abolished or restricted in Alaska, Pennsylvania, Tennessee, and Texas, and anyone thinking of using a joint tenancy in one of these states should consult a lawyer.)

Tenancy in common, on the other hand, allows you to sell your share or leave it in a will without the consent of the others. If you die without a will, your share goes not to the other owners, but to your heirs.

It's important to remember that either form of ownership can sometimes be overridden by community property laws and other forms of spousal rights (see page 151). In other words, when Gordon's brother Jim dies, Jim's widow might be able

CASE IN POINT

The "Mom Always Liked You Best" Suit

Some of the most painful will contests are those in which siblings who never got along when a parent was alive lock horns after the parent's death. In the case of Joan West, fifty, and her brother David, fifty-one, the groundwork for a battle royal was laid long before their mother Margaret, a Delaware widow, died in April 1974 at the age of seventy-eight. To Joan's shock, her mother's will left everything to her brother. She sued to set aside the will, feeling especially incensed because David had been adopted, while she, her mother's only natural child, had been cut out completely.

The terms of the will came as no surprise to David, who had cared for his mother until her death from cancer. Margaret had decided to change her will during the final week of her life, which she spent at the home of David and his wife. At her request, David found a lawyer who drafted a new will, which his mother signed two days before she died. A second lawyer came for the signing, and both lawyers later testified she was of sound mind.

By most measures, David was the more stable and responsible of the two children. He was married and had been employed for nineteen years as a refinery mechanic-welder in Delaware. In contrast Joan, a college dropout who had struggled with mental health problems, worked as an office cleaner in Florida and had difficulty supporting herself. Her relationship with her mother was distant, and her contacts with her brother were stormy at best.

Joan claimed that David had exercised "undue influence" to get their mother to change her will. In a 1987 decision, the Supreme Court of Delaware disagreed, and Joan found out to her dismay that there was no law against a parent's cutting out a child (natural or adopted) from a will.

The court ruled that it was evident from testimony that Mrs. West had remained clear-minded until her death. Furthermore, David had brought in an independent lawyer, rather than his regular attorney, to handle the matter, which indicated he hadn't exerted improper pressure. The court also found, to Joan's chagrin, that Mrs. West had other rational considerations that might have led her to decide her daughter didn't deserve her money.

to claim an interest in the beach house although she's not named in the will or on any deed.

■ **If two brothers own a vacation house together, like Gordon and Jim, can one of them leave his share to his children?**

Yes, if the deed shows they are "tenants in common," but not if they are "joint tenants with rights of survivorship." In Gordon's case, the deed showed that he and his brother held the house as tenants in common, so Gordon could leave his share of the house to his children. (In certain states, Gordon's executor might have to get the consent of Gordon's wife's before the deed is transferred.)

■ **If one brother leaves his share to his children, what options does the surviving brother have if he doesn't want to share the house with his nieces and nephews? Could they force him out of the house?**

If Gordon and his estranged brother did not come to terms before one of them died, the surviving brother would have little choice but to try and buy out his nieces and nephews — or be bought out by them. If they can't agree on a price, the matter could end up in court as an action for **partition**: if the property can't be physically divided, it is sold to the highest bidder and the proceeds are divided among the owners. In this sense, the nieces and nephews can force the remaining brother out of the house, and vice versa.

This sticky family situation could have been avoided by some advance planning by the two brothers when they bought the house. They could have chosen to set up a **buy-sell agreement,** under which the surviving brother gets the right to buy the other's half-interest at either a preset price or a price determined by an appraiser. Or the two brothers could have worked out a time-share arrangement, or similar plan, allowing the surviving brother's family to use the house.

CASH AND PRECIOUS OBJECTS

Although she was well aware that settling an estate could be an ugly, rancorous affair, Grace couldn't imagine her own family being driven apart and fighting in court over their parents' wills. She could predict a great deal of sorrow and confusion, though, about closing down the house and dividing up their things, and she wanted to know whether she could do anything to minimize the emotional toll.

■ **What's the best way for a parent to divide possessions among children?**

There are several ways to divide your **tangible personal property,** which is anything other than real estate or money, and includes such things as furniture, cars, jewelry, china, and so on. You can

- Itemize your bequests in your will, naming who gets each item.
- Leave your personal possessions outright and in equal shares to your children. File a memorandum with your will with instructions on how your possessions should be divided. Many states will recognize it as legally binding; in the states that don't, the memo will still (you hope) carry moral weight with your children. Such a memo can also contain information useful for finding or using your assets, such as the location of car keys or other small items. The advantage of such a memo is that you can change it without all the formality necessary when modifying your will.
- If you think your children may not see eye to eye on the value of your things, or on what makes an equal share, you can give your executor authority to decide which child gets which item. (With this method, don't name one of your children your executor!)
- Direct your children in your will to choose items in sequence. If you think they might argue over who gets first choice, direct them to draw lots to decide who chooses first, second, and so on.

As she mentally sorted through the many items in the house and beach house that she wanted to leave to people in her will, Grace pictured a number of the items that had been left to her by other people, including her Aunt Nell.

Aunt Nell had led a rather wild and eccentric life. As a flapper in the twenties she frequented speakeasies in New York and bistros in Paris. In the thirties she married the heir to a tobacco fortune, divorced him, and then parlayed her rather meager divorce settlement into millions in the stock market. For all Nell's financial savvy, though, Grace recalled that her will had been a mess. In some of her bequests of personal property, for example, Nell had been excruciatingly specific, detailing who got each of dozens of pairs of earrings. But she also neglected to mention the contents of her summer home in Newport, which contained a great deal of precious art and antiques.

■ What happens if a person forgets to designate certain assets?

Typically, a will contains a clause saying something like, "I give my car to Henry, my boat to Ellen, and the *balance of* my tangible personal property to George." In that case, George gets any items that haven't been given away under more specific provisions. If the will doesn't have such a general clause, the items go to the person named as **residuary legatee.** (See page 146.)

Aunt Nell left Grace a beautiful pair of earrings, but she left Grace's sister a diamond ring that was worth far more. At first Grace had been offended, but then she learned that Nell had also left her a cash bequest specifically to make up the difference in value.

■ What's the best way to leave items of different value to children or others without offending anyone?

Aunt Nell had a good solution: Leave additional cash to the person getting the item of lesser value. (You probably need to think about this only if there is a significant difference in value.)

One clause in Aunt Nell's will left $100,000 to Grace's father, but both Grace's father and mother died before Aunt Nell. Four little words in the will meant Grace and her siblings never saw a penny of that $100,000.

■ What happens to bequests to people who die before the person who writes the will?

It depends on what the will says. As noted, it's always a good idea when writing a will to name alternative beneficiaries (see page 149). This and other key phrases can guide an executor to, in effect, fulfill a deceased's plan B if plan A doesn't work. In the case of Aunt Nell's will, she had left $100,000 to Grace's father "*if he survives me.*" Without those words, the bequest would have passed to Gordon's heirs, assuming that there was an applicable "anti-lapse" statute. Not all states have such statutes, and their provisions vary. Basically, though, they direct that a bequest to a predeceasing beneficiary pass to his or her heirs. But in the case of Aunt Nell's will, the requirement of survivorship meant that the $100,000 passed to an alternate-named beneficiary or to the residuary legatee (see page 146).

Aunt Nell's will left her house in Newport to the Stamp Out Smoking Society. Shortly before she died, however, the house burned to the ground, and it was not insured.

■ What happens if property left in a will no longer exists?

That's probably tough luck for the person named as the beneficiary. In most cases, he or she would get nothing.

Grace and Gordon had $60,000 saved in various mutual fund accounts. They decided that, in the event they both died, $30,000 should go into a trust fund to help pay for Bradley's college, and

the other $30,000 should be split equally by Beatrice, Blossom, and Bartholomew. Grace worried that a dive in the stock market could cause the funds to lose much of their value.

■ **What happens if there is less (or more) money to be divided among heirs than at the time a will was written?**

It is almost certain that the value of financial accounts will change over time, and thus can't be specified in a will. You can deal with this two ways. First, you can have a specific amount set aside for one person (such as the $30,000 for Bradley) and have the balance go into the residuary estate, to be divided according to other directions you leave (in this case, equally between Brad's siblings). If Grace's and Gordon's accounts did lose half their value, Brad's trust would still get $30,000, but his siblings would get nothing. Or you can specify how much each person will get. In that case, the funds will be distributed proportionately. So if the value of Gordon's and Grace's accounts dropped by half, each beneficiary would get half of what was designated ($15,000 for Brad's trust, $5,000 each for his siblings). If the value of the accounts doubled, each would get twice as much.

DEATH AND TAXES

There were few things Gordon hated more than paying taxes. And he certainly didn't want to leave a penny more than necessary to Uncle Sam rather than to his family. So when their lawyer mentioned that part of her job was to do some estate planning so that they could greatly reduce taxes, he was all ears. Maybe it was worth shelling out some money to a lawyer after all, he thought.

■ **What kind of taxes must be paid on an estate?**

There are several kinds:

- **federal estate tax**
- **federal gift tax**
- **state estate tax**
- **state inheritance tax**

The biggest potential bite is the federal estate tax, but that applies only to estates larger than $600,000. Any estate that is smaller does not pay federal estate tax. This tax is levied before the property is distributed to the beneficiaries. Its base rate is 37 percent on amounts over $600,000 and rises to 55 percent on amounts over $3 million.

Many people try to avoid taxes — and bring their total estate to under $600,000 — by giving away assets before their death. This is made possible by a lenient provision in the federal gift tax laws, which allows anyone to make gifts of $10,000 to a single person per year without paying any tax (married couples can give a person up to $20,000 per year). Because you can make an unlimited number of gifts to different people, and because the recipients don't generally pay taxes on the gifts, the law can operate as a significant loophole (for more on gift taxes, see page 282).

But if you're giving away money to try to keep your estate under $600,000, be careful. Any amount in excess of the $10,000 ($20,000 if from a couple) to one person in any year is considered a **taxable gift** and must be reported to the IRS by the *giver* (in this case, you). Once the total amount of your taxable gifts exceeds $600,000, you will have to pay taxes on them.

More important, for those of us who will never be rich enough to give away this much money, any taxable gifts also count against your $600,000 federal estate tax exemption. So if you and your spouse give your daughter $30,000 in one year ($10,000 over the limit), your exemption drops by the same amount — to $590,000. By eating away at your exemption, such taxable gifts may end up working at cross-purposes with your efforts to reduce the value of your estate.

On the state level, estate and inheritance taxes vary widely, but all rates are far below federal rates.

■ **Who pays these taxes: the estate, the beneficiaries, or both?**

That depends on the type of tax. Many states require each beneficiary to ante up his or her share of inheritance tax, determined by the size of the bequest. All other taxes are paid from the estate by the executor, who gets the money either from beneficiaries or from the **residuary estate,** depending on state law and whether the will contains specific provisions on who should bear the tax burden. Allocating tax to the residuary estate can save time, and saves the executor the chore of trying to collect tax money from each beneficiary. Of course, if the residuary estate is too small to pay the tax, each beneficiary may have to pay a share, and the executor may be able to demand money from people who didn't get anything through the will but received property through such things as trusts or joint accounts. Sizable estate taxes could wipe out the residuary estate, which may actually pass to the person the deceased most intended to benefit. The tax payment process is governed by arcane laws, and has been known to foster lawsuits about who has to pay for what.

■ Is it possible to avoid taxes altogether?

It may be possible to avoid certain taxes, depending on how much money you have, how old you are, and what you want to do with it. For large estates, tax planning can be quite difficult; myriads of lawyers and accountants spend their entire careers working in these fields. But even for smaller estates, a lawyer can help you take the best advantage of complicated tax laws and make certain that your plan will divide the tax burden equitably. An error on this point could result in your inadvertently disinheriting a beneficiary by forcing him or her to pay most of the taxes.

■ Can leaving money and assets to a charitable organization help reduce taxes?

Bequests to charitable organizations are generally deductible for federal estate tax purposes. However, the bequest must be made to a bona fide charitable organization, recognized by the IRS. If you are unsure of an organization's status, ask the charity for a copy of its IRS exemption letter, or check the "Cumulative List of Organizations" published by the IRS. And remember that state laws may limit the amount you can leave to a charity, especially if you have a spouse or children (see page 150).

THE TRUST OPTION

Maria Heritage, Grace's and Gordon's lawyer, had told them that one of her goals would be to come up with an estate plan that would shield as much of their assets as possible from transfer taxes. One way to do that, she said, would be for Gordon and Grace to put some of their money into trusts for their four children. Gordon snorted at this. Having risen up the ranks to become a regional manager at Tech Security, Gordon was proud that his family was comfortable, but he was bemused at the idea of setting up trust funds. "We're not the Kennedys, after all," he said.

"You don't have to be super-rich for trusts to be a good idea," Marie explained. "Besides," Grace chimed in, "don't we need to find out about a trust for Brad's college expenses?"

■ What is a trust?

A trust is property given to a trustee to manage for the benefit of a third person. Generally, the beneficiary gets a "trust income," the interest and dividends on the trust assets, for a period of years. After a certain time specified in the trust (say, the beneficiary's turning twenty-five) the trust "terminates." At this point the beneficiary gets the remainder of the principal (whatever hasn't been paid out during the life of the trust).

There are two main kinds of trust: those created by provisions in wills, called **testamentary trusts** (as in last will and *testament*), and those created during the maker's lifetime, called **living trusts**. Some living trusts are set up so that they can be changed during the grantor's lifetime, but others are set up so that they can't be touched. The first kind of living trust is called **revocable,** the second is called **irrevocable.** There are major tax-law differences between the types, and people setting up trusts should be sure they understand the tax consequences, which can be very complicated.

How can a couple use a trust to save on estate taxes?

Couples with combined estates of more than $600,000 may want to consider a **bypass trust,** also known as a **marital life estate** or an **A-B trust.** A spouse can leave any amount of property to a surviving spouse totally free of estate tax. But when the surviving spouse dies, if his or her estate is worth more than $600,000, significant estate taxes will be due. A bypass trust is designed to let the $600,000 exemption be used by each spouse, thus shielding up to $1.2 million from taxes. But bypass trusts aren't for everyone, particularly for younger couples. And setting up and administering these trusts can be tricky, so anyone considering it should discuss it in detail with a lawyer.

Can a trust protect assets from a child's creditors?

Generally, yes. If you think your child could have problems with creditors, you should give the trustee broad discretion to withhold income and principal from the child.

Let's say your twenty-five-year-old son goes into default, after your death, for $40,000 in college and law school loans, and you have left him a trust worth $50,000. You could have set up the trust as a **spendthrift trust,** which is designed to keep the money out of the hands of creditors. The sum in the trust will generally be safe from the banks, although creditors can collect from any money paid directly to your son from the trust. To be fully effective, a spendthrift trust must be irrevocable, it must last for the entire lifetime of the beneficiary, and it must give the trustee full discretion over the assets of the trust.

Is a lawyer needed to set up a trust?

Most trusts should be drawn up with the help of a lawyer or financial manager. Because there are so many issues to consider, with so many weighty consequences if things go wrong, it is a situation in which expertise is really needed.

The only exception is the **totten trust,** which allows you to go to a bank and open an account yourself, while naming a beneficiary. A totten trust is best for amounts of about $20,000 or less — larger amounts could present problems in payment of estate tax at your death, since the assets in these accounts are added to your taxable estate. A totten trust can be paid out quickly after your death with a minimum of formalities. Because the money transfers directly, there's no need for choosing a third-party trustee, and the advantages are the same as with any other trust — you keep those assets out of probate. You can revoke a totten trust at any time during your life, and the beneficiary can't take out the money until you die.

How to Avoid or Reduce Federal Estate and Gift Tax

If your estate is less than $600,000 when you die and you've made no taxable gifts that reduce your exemption (see page 159), you pay no federal estate tax.

If your estate exceeds $600,000, you can:

- Bequeath all your estate to your spouse. The federal estate tax laws allow you to make unlimited transfers to your spouse, free of tax. This merely defers the tax, however, until his or her death. If the surviving spouse spends it all before his or her death, there's no estate and no estate tax to pay. But there's nothing to leave to anyone, either.
- Set up a **bypass trust** to allow each member of a couple to use the $600,000 estate tax exemption.
- Bequeath anything in your estate over $600,000 to charities.
- Give away enough assets during your lifetime to keep your estate below $600,000, the taxable level. But be careful: taxable gifts, gifts of more than $10,000 to a person in a year ($20,000 if you are married), end up reducing your $600,000 exemption — and subject you to gift tax during your lifetime if such gifts exceed $600,000.

Why Set Up a Trust?

There are many reasons, but some of the more common are as follows:

- **to manage assets during the lifetime of the person creating the trust, and to pass them on to chosen beneficiaries without probate (often done through revocable living trusts)**
- **to manage assets for a child until he or she reaches a certain age. The trustee can use the income or principal as he or she sees fit to pay for the child's needs, such as college (see page 153)**
- **to manage assets for an adult who is incapable of handling them**
- **to attempt to shield assets from creditors through irrevocable and spendthrift trusts (see pages 160 and 161 and Chapter 25, Owing Money)**
- **to manage assets for a surviving spouse while holding property for the children of a prior marriage**
- **as a way to reduce estate taxes for couples with estates of over $600,000 (see page 159)**

Who should be selected as a trustee?

Many people choose relatives or close friends, although institutions — banks or trust companies — also provide this service. Often a person selected as a minor child's guardian is also named a trustee of any trusts established for the child — but there is no requirement that these be the same people.

State law often sets commissions for trustees, but different rates can be specified in a trust, and institutions usually get paid commissions under their regularly published fee schedules. Friends and relatives often waive commissions.

AVOIDING PROBATE

Gordon's head was spinning from all the thinking he had to do about trusts, and who owned what, and who should get what. And when Beatrice told him what she'd learned about the probate process, which sounded neither simple nor fast, it threw him into a crisis of doubt: couldn't they just get around doing wills, and avoid the whole probate mess?

Is there any way to bypass probate?

Yes, there are several methods. Some (especially the totten trust described on page 161) are simple because they usually involve comparatively small amounts and can be set up without lawyers. Others, involving larger sums, may have unexpected costs and consequences. You may want to see a lawyer to determine which of these methods are appropriate.

Avoiding probate has its limitations. It doesn't fill the urgent need to provide for minor children by naming guardians, which generally can be done only through a will or other formal document recognized by the state. Moreover, some methods for bypassing probate such as irrevocable trusts may deny you access to your property while you are alive and bar you from changing your mind, as you always can with a will. They may also prove to be more expensive than going through probate.

Another warning: *Avoiding probate won't automatically make you exempt from creditors or from taxes.* The popular trust form called the revocable living trust (see box opposite) allows you to change or cancel it, but has the disadvantage of leaving your beneficiary open to creditors. Depending on the size of your estate, federal and state taxes will still be levied on most assets. A bereaved spouse can keep *some* of your assets out of the hands of creditors, but you'll stand a chance of protecting all your assets from creditors only if they are placed in the right kind of airtight, irrevocable trust.

Do retirement and insurance accounts go through probate?

It depends. When you set up these accounts or buy the insurance, the financial institution will ask you to name a beneficiary, which could include your estate, in which case the assets would go through probate. If you don't name your estate as beneficiary, the named beneficiary would get the funds directly — outside of probate — upon your death.

If you are single, you are free to name whomever you want as a beneficiary. Married people, in contrast, are required to name their surviving spouse as beneficiary of any pension or profit-sharing plan. Under the Retirement Equity Act of 1984, the spouse must receive the funds unless he or she has signed a statement consenting to the designation of someone else. These funds also do not pass through probate.

If a couple with minor children name each other as the principal beneficiaries, they may want to name their estates as secondary beneficiaries. This is because they may have set up trusts in their wills to hold assets for their children, and in the event that they both die, they would want proceeds of life insurance or retirement accounts to pass into those trusts. But a smarter solution in this case — one that would avoid having the funds pass through probate — would be for the couple to set up children's trusts outside their wills and direct that life insurance proceeds be paid directly to those trusts.

Ways to Bypass Probate

- You can give all your property away before you die, but you may have to pay a stiff gift tax (see page 159). And once you give something away, you can't be assured that you'll get it back if you change your mind.
- You can hold your property jointly with another person so it goes to him or her automatically upon your death. If you are married, joint property transferred to persons other than your spouse could be affected by state laws governing inheritance between marriage partners, referred to as **spousal rights** (see explanation, page 150). As with gifts, once you make property jointly owned, you may not be able to get your share back if you change your mind.
- You can set up trusts that will be paid upon your death to any person you name. A **trust** is property given to a **trustee** — a friend, relative, or business adviser chosen by the person setting up the trust — to manage for the benefit of someone else. A popular form is the revocable living trust, which the person who sets it up (called the **grantor**) can change or revoke while still living. At death, the trustee pays the deceased's debts, taxes, and expenses, including the trustee's fee and the costs of maintaining trust property, and then turns over the balance of the property to the beneficiary.

  The revocable living trust was popularized in the best-selling book *How to Avoid Probate!* by the late Norman Dacey. However, this kind of trust is not a panacea. In order to avoid probate, title to all the property in the trust must be held by the trustee, which can be cumbersome and time-consuming to achieve.

  In general, trusts are not simple or foolproof. They often require a lawyer to set up, and are subject to estate taxes if the assets exceed $600,000. Since they can be costly, they are best for larger estates — with the exception of trusts established for minor children.
- For moderate amounts, you can set up a special bank account that requires no trustees, and transfers to the designated person upon your death. Called a totten trust, it is a simple and inexpensive way for those with smaller estates to bypass probate.

Challenging a Will

A challenge to a will can make the probate process protracted — and nasty. Often people who bring challenges are hurt and angry because they have been left little or nothing in someone's will.

Any of your heirs — your relatives who would receive a portion of your estate under intestacy laws (see page 145) — can challenge your will by filing objections in probate court. In many states a person (or organization) can also make a challenge if a codicil has reduced or eliminated their bequest.

Objections typically allege that the testator lacked the legal capacity to make a valid will or was unduly influenced by someone to make a will provision in that person's favor. They might also claim that a will is a forgery or was executed under duress. Any of these allegations would have to be proved in court.

CHANGING A WILL

When Gordon and Grace got a draft of their wills from their lawyer, they read them over and decided there were a few things they wanted to change. Grace decided that Beatrice instead of Blossom should get Grace's mother's engagement ring. And they decided that the trust they set up for Bradley should terminate when he reached twenty-four, not twenty-six. That made Gordon wonder about how they could change their will in the future, once it was signed. What if they changed their minds again, he pointed out, or what if they win the lottery? "Yeah, and what if we start growing younger, not older," said Grace, but she thought he raised a good question.

■ Why might people want to change their wills?

There are many reasons for changing a will — the birth or death of beneficiaries, the death of the named executor or guardian, or changes in the property you own. Some people have petty or vindictive reasons for changing a will, or may want to cut someone out of a will after a falling-out. And sometimes people simply change their minds.

■ What's the best way to change a will?

The best way is to make a new will, even if changes are slight, and to make sure it clearly states that all previous wills are invalid. While you can change just one part of a will with a document called a **codicil** — an amendment that must be signed and witnessed just like a will — this kind of shortcut can pose problems. If a person has his will bequest reduced or eliminated by a codicil, he usually gets court notice of this, which can lead to hurt feelings and, sometimes, a will contest. (See box at left.)

■ Is it advisable to have a lawyer to make a change in a will?

Yes, because the changes made by a codicil have to be carefully integrated with the will. Also, you might want advice about whether an entirely new will is needed.

WITNESSING WILLS

The great moment had arrived: Gordon had gotten over his crisis of confidence in the probate process and been persuaded that a will was a good idea; Maria had drafted wills (each setting up some trusts), and Gordon and Grace had reviewed them, made some changes, and gotten a few last-minute questions answered by Maria; now all that remained was for the wills to be signed. "Come by the office at two o'clock tomorrow," said Maria. "Both my secretaries will be here then, and they can be witnesses." Perfect, thought Gordon and Grace, whose Florida vacation would begin the day after. "Now we can get eaten by barracudas without worrying,"

Gordon laughed. "Or crash in the Bermuda Triangle," Grace offered.

How many witnesses are necessary?

Nearly all states require that there be at least two witnesses, but some states require three, so, if in doubt, use three. Though a witness must be an adult, it's best to choose ones who are young enough that they are likely to be alive when the will goes through probate. Many states require all witnesses to be present when the will is signed. Even in states where this is not required, it is safer to do it this way to prevent problems in probate. Also, it's best to choose disinterested witnesses — people who won't get anything under the will. Using an interested witness won't invalidate the will, but the witness won't be allowed to take anything under it.

Do wills have to be notarized?

Usually not. Proper witnessing is the important thing. However, in order to avoid the cumbersome process of requiring the executor to track down the witnesses, many states, including New York and New Jersey, allow **self-proving wills:** wills accompanied by a sworn statement from witnesses, signed before a notary public. Acceptance of these sworn statements — or affidavits — is not automatic, and the probate court is more likely to respect them if the will execution was supervised by an attorney.

If the will is challenged, witnesses may be called into court to testify as to whether the **testator** (the person who wrote the will) signed the will voluntarily, understood what was being signed, declared the document to be his or her will, and asked the witnesses to sign. Recently people have been videotaping themselves as they sign their wills, which may provide additional evidence of their competence. However, this is not a legal requirement — *nor is it a legal substitute for witnesses.* If a will is made with no witnesses (even if you videotape it), it will be declared invalid in almost every case.

A few states allow unwitnessed handwritten documents, called **holographic wills,** to be admitted to probate, but this is a very risky course, since almost all courts will be very reluctant to accept them.

WHERE TO KEEP YOUR WILL

With visions of palm trees dancing in their heads, Gordon and Grace got up from their seats in their lawyer's office and told her they were going to celebrate with piña coladas. "Wait one sec," Maria said. "I want you to be sober when you tell me where you want the originals of your wills kept." Gordon and Grace looked at each other, shrugged, and asked Maria, "What do you recommend?"

Where should original wills be kept?

You can leave your original will on file in your lawyer's office, with the clear understanding that you are free to remove it at any time. Law offices often have vaults for safe document storage. Some lawyers may urge keeping the will in their office to further the chance that they will be selected when it comes time to submit the will to probate. But even after the testator's death, the executor, and not the attorney who drafted the will, is in control, and can pick whomever he or she wishes to act as counsel for the estate.

If you don't leave your will with your attorney, the original should be kept in a safe place, though not in your safe deposit box, because these are sometimes sealed when a person dies.

Is it okay to have photocopies of wills?

It may be useful to have a photocopy of your will, so you don't have to go to the trouble of getting the original out of safe storage. It's best to write *"Copy"* clearly on any photocopy and to leave copies unsigned, so there's no confusion with the original.

GETTING DIVORCED 12

After fifteen years of marriage, Beatrice and Max were having serious problems. From the outside all looked well enough. They had a big house, two good cars, two great kids, Vinny, seven, and Alena, ten. On the inside, however, old resentments had built to a crescendo. Beatrice had supported Max for years until his band, The Eardrum Busters, finally got some recognition. Now that it had, he was on the road all the time, playing to sellout crowds. Beatrice suspected he was earning more than what he deposited in their joint account. She also suspected he was having an affair with the band's lead singer.

Max was fed up, too. He'd taken care of the kids for years while Beatrice developed her computer consulting business. She'd never recognized how much work he did for the family, and now that his career was taking off all she did was complain.

Their efforts to work things out had sputtered with no significant changes or compromise. The best option seemed to be the dreaded "D" word.

■ How does a couple go about getting divorced?

Traditionally, since divorce was not as socially acceptable as it is today, the only way you could get a divorce was by proving that your spouse had done something so horrible, such as commit adultery or physically abuse you, that you should no longer be required to live with him or her. Even if your breakup was mutual and amicable, one spouse had to accuse the other of failing to live up to the marriage contract — and then prove it.

Divorce is easier today, but that doesn't mean you can just walk into a courtroom and say "I want to end my marriage." Even if you and your spouse are in total agreement about how you will divide your assets (see page 172), you must still show the judge, who has the final power to grant the divorce, that both parties are being treated fairly in the division of property and settlement of custody and support. As important, you must also show the judge that there is a *reason* why the divorce should be granted. These reasons are commonly referred to as **grounds for divorce,** and there are two kinds: **fault** and **no-fault.**

In most states, a divorce will be granted if you can show that your spouse was at **fault** for the failure of your marriage. The most common fault grounds for granting a divorce are

- **adultery**
- **physical or mental abuse**
- **imprisonment for a crime**
- **drug or alcohol abuse**
- **willful and deliberate desertion**
- **incest**
- **mental incapacity or insanity**
- **fraud**
- **impotence**

Today, most states also have laws that provide for **no-fault** divorce. The concept of a no-fault divorce is that it doesn't matter who did what to whom that caused the marriage to break down; all that matters is that there is no reasonable prospect of reconciliation. You still have to show the court that you are no longer able to live together as a couple. The most common grounds for a no-fault divorce are

- **separation**
- **irreconcilable differences**
- **irretrievable breakdown**

So if you file for divorce on no-fault grounds, you are in essence saying that you should no longer be married because: (1) you no longer live together or (2) you are no longer compatible and have very different goals, needs, and expectations of life or (3) your marriage has deteriorated beyond the point of repair.

Again, the essence of these no-fault grounds is that it doesn't matter what caused the breakdown of the marriage. No-fault divorce recognizes that, in many cases, neither individual is solely to blame. However, a no-fault divorce is not necessarily quick and easy, since you still have to agree on the issues of child support, custody, and division of property.

■ Which is the better way to proceed — fault or no-fault?

It really depends on several factors, including the laws of your state and the circumstances of your breakup. All states allow you to include both fault and no-fault grounds in your petition for a divorce. Sometimes you will be able to speed up the process by including fault grounds, like an accusation of abandonment. And in some states, you may also be entitled to more alimony or child support if you can prove your spouse is at fault. Other states, however, don't consider fault an issue, so there may be nothing to gain. An attorney can advise you on the best strategy based on the laws of your state. (See Chapter 30, FINDING AND USING A LAWYER.)

Also, if you file for a no-fault divorce, it does not necessarily mean that your spouse agrees with you about ending the marriage. The distinction between a divorce on no-fault grounds and a divorce on fault grounds lies in the nature of the proofs

CASE IN POINT

Grounds for Divorce

The development of no-fault divorce has made it much easier to end an unhappy marriage than it once was. In the past, one of the parties typically had to claim the other was guilty of something and then provide evidence to prove the claim. The result? A lot of dirty laundry got aired. Consider a few cases where divorces were granted:

- In 1966, an Iowa court found that a wife was guilty of cruel and inhuman treatment and granted her husband a divorce. She had, among other things, constantly berated him, sometimes in a high, screaming voice; purchased a piano, a $1,500 organ, and a $300 accordion at a time when important bills were unpaid and the house was in serious disrepair; prevented her husband from watching the Iowa football team on television — even going so far as to lend the set to the garbage man.
- In 1968, a Maine court granted a wife a divorce on the grounds of cruel and abusive treatment. During their two years of marriage, her husband had deceived her about his use of their money and subjected her to frequent physical and mental abuse. After one argument, "he forced her to get down on her hands and knees and kiss his feet telling her that she would never leave the bedroom until she did this," noted a court opinion.
- In 1946, a Texas court granted a teenager a divorce, finding that her husband's excessive demands for sex were cruel and abusive because of his wife's delicate physical health. The wife was fourteen years old and seven months pregnant when she married her husband, who was sixty. He insisted on sex at frequent intervals, day and night, despite her protestations of pain and discomfort. She left him after less than a week.

Such attempts to end a marriage don't always succeed. In one case, a wife's request for divorce based on cruel and unusual treatment was rejected by the Supreme Court of Iowa in 1953. Her claim? She asserted that her husband caused her mental torment because he regularly woke her up for sex in the middle of the night and pouted and sulked — sometimes for days — when she refused. The court ruled that the husband's actions did not rise to the level of cruel and inhuman treatment and denied the divorce with reasoning that would likely be unacceptable today: "While we may not compel husband and wife to live together," the opinion noted, quoting from an earlier case, "we can at least make it so difficult to obtain a divorce as to encourage another effort at observance of the matrimonial vows."

required to get the divorce and not in whether both parties have agreed that a divorce is the best course.

■ What happens if one spouse does not consent to a divorce?

Even if your spouse doesn't want a divorce, it's still going to move forward. However, your spouse may contest your claims and force you to prove they are true. What's key is that as long as you can prove grounds for divorce (that your spouse committed adultery, for instance), your spouse cannot force you to remain married. If you can't prove it's true, then your divorce won't be granted unless you have some additional grounds that you can prove. That is one reason why it may be good to file for divorce on more than one ground.

THE DIVORCE PROCEDURE

When they finally discussed getting a divorce, Max was surprised that Beatrice was hesitant to go through with it. They had both been so miserable, he thought she'd be relieved by the idea. She was in a way, but she was none too thrilled with the idea of telling all the dirty laundry of her marriage to some lawyer she had never met before. And she was concerned that splitting up would be a drawn-out process that would rack up hundreds, if not thousands, of dollars in legal fees, and devolve into a bitter fight over custody of the children, support, and splitting up of their property.

■ How long does the whole process take?

It can be as little as several months or as much as several years. The amount of time depends in great part upon how much you and your spouse can agree on; the more you are able to determine between you, the less will be in dispute for a judge to decide. If you both are employed and have minimal income other than what is shown on your W-2 forms every year, financial issues will be fairly easy to work out. On the other hand, if one or both of you owns a small business or is working in a family business, sorting out the financial issues can be incredibly complex and may take years to investigate properly.

The time that a divorce takes also depends in great measure on the judicial system in your state, and maybe even the one in your county. Some court systems move more efficiently than others, and each case is unique. So there really is no way to tell how long it will take to get divorced. Even apparently simple cases can blow up suddenly into complex ones. (See also "quickie divorces" on page 191.)

■ Is there always a trial?

Only if you and your spouse cannot reach a settlement. If you do go to trial, the decisions on custody, support, and dividing property will be left to the judge, so it's often best if you and your spouse can negotiate a **settlement agreement** outside of court. This agreement spells out the terms of your divorce.

If your case does proceed to a trial, it will probably be heard by a judge. Juries rarely hear divorce cases.

■ Is a lawyer necessary?

No, but it's always best to be fully aware of all your legal rights. You may feel willing to give up your rights to property or pay more support in order to get out of your marriage as quickly as possible, but it's still advisable to have at least one consultation with a lawyer. When your emotions settle later, you may regret not having done so, especially if you didn't end up with your fair share.

Do-it-yourself forms are available, so if you and your spouse agree on most of the details, have few assets to divide, and no custody issues to negotiate, then your divorce may be relatively easy to handle alone. However, if you have children or a significant amount of property to divide, you likely will need a lawyer.

Also, if you are contemplating a divorce, it may be in your interest to speak to a lawyer before taking any action, such as moving out or withholding support to your spouse, because doing so can have negative consequences further down the line. For instance, if you move out of the house, your spouse could accuse you of abandonment. You could

The Procedure for Getting a Divorce

Even if you and your spouse agree on all the terms of your breakup, divorce is still an adversarial process, in which one party must sue the other. You can't just both say we agree and get divorced, since our laws reflect society's belief that it shouldn't be easy to end a marriage. Of course, the specifics vary from state to state, but in general

- You establish that you have **grounds** for a divorce.
- One spouse files a **petition** or **complaint.** It asks for a divorce and explains all the reasons why one should be granted. You may list both fault and no-fault grounds at the same time.
- A **summons** will be served, notifying the other spouse that the petition has been filed. If the spouse cannot be located, each state has different rules about how to proceed. Some, for instance, require that a notice be published in the newspaper.
- The other spouse must respond within a certain time limit. Otherwise it is assumed that the spouse does not contest the petition.
- The other spouse may countersue if he or she has grounds for divorce. (One reason this might be done is so that both parties "win." It's more psychological than anything else.)

- Both sides may engage in **discovery,** in which the lawyers will request relevant information and documents.
- An attempt is made to reach a settlement.
- If a settlement is reached, then the settlement agreement is submitted to the court, and a hearing is held. The judge will ask a number of questions to determine that both parties entered into the agreement freely and understand what they are doing. The judge basically cares that you've entered into the agreement freely, not whether you should or shouldn't get the house. If the judge approves the settlement agreement, he or she will issue a divorce decree. (A judge can refuse to grant a divorce if he or she finds that there are no grounds to do so, or if neither of the parties is a resident of the state.)
- If no settlement can be reached, then there will be a trial. The judge will decide the outcome and issue a divorce decree. Juries rarely hear divorce cases.

lose your share of the house, and you might also lose your right to custody of the children.

You and your spouse should always have separate lawyers, since one lawyer cannot fairly represent the interests of both of you.

What is divorce mediation?

An increasing number of people are using mediation as an alternative to the traditional route of litigation. In mediation, one person works with both spouses. The mediator knows the law and is often a practicing attorney or a retired judge. The mediator will listen to both sides, make suggestions, and attempt to lead the two of you to a consensus, instead of imposing a decision on you as a judge would.

An advantage of mediation is that consensual agreements are more likely to be complied with in the future, and they usually leave the parties feeling more satisfied with the outcomes. It is also usually much cheaper to mediate than to litigate.

Unfortunately, because you still must go through the court system to get divorced, you may not be able to avoid lawyers altogether. The mediator can help you work out the settlement agreement, but he or she can't file it for you in court. (That's because it would be an ethical conflict for the mediator to represent both of you in a court proceeding.) Even if your mediator is a lawyer, you should each have a separate attorney review your agreement.

Of course, mediation does not always result in an agreement and, therefore, litigation may become necessary. Also, mediation may not suit every situation. If you and your spouse have difficulty communicating, or harbor strong feelings of anger and hostility toward each other, or if there are allegations of abuse, or if one of you is extremely resistant to the idea of a divorce, mediation may be doomed from the start. On the other hand, if you have a relatively simple case and you and your spouse already agree on many issues, mediation may be beneficial.

DIVORCE RECORDS

The expense of a divorce was only one of Bea's concerns. Publicity was another. While Max was hardly as famous as Mick Jagger, he had become very popular with the media. (*People* magazine ran his photograph with a caption that read "Who's This Sexy New Musician?") On several occasions fans had called or come by the house trying to snap his photo and get an autograph. Beatrice was worried that the media would play up their divorce, especially if reporters learned that she accused him of hiding his money and committing adultery.

Are divorce records public?

Yes. Anything that is filed with the court is part of the public record, and any interested individual can go to the court clerk's office and request to see a divorce file. Similarly, anyone who is interested can come and sit in the courtroom while a divorce case is being presented.

However, due to the sometimes sensitive nature of allegations in divorce cases, it may be possible under your state's laws to have your file sealed and the courtroom closed during proceedings. Such a request might be granted, for example, if there are allegations of sexual abuse of children. In other situations where the file contains information, such as intimate financial details, that could be damaging to the business of one of the spouses, it may be possible to obtain a **protective order.** That order would prevent the disclosure of the sensitive information (except to certain individuals under certain conditions). Whether or not your case can be sealed will depend upon the particular case and the law in your state.

What Should Someone Look For in a Divorce Lawyer?

Depending on the complexity of your case, you may not need a specialist in matrimonial law, although you may want one. Most general practitioners have enough knowledge of matrimonial law to handle a relatively simple case, or even a fairly difficult one, but you should make sure they've had some previous experience handling a divorce.

The most important thing that you need to look for in your attorney is someone you can trust and someone you respect. Your lawyer will be privy to the most intimate personal and financial details of your married life. He or she will also be advising you as to what results to expect and how to proceed. You must trust his or her judgment and you must respect his or her knowledge and ability if the relationship is to work. You should also bear in mind that a divorce lawyer is not a marriage counselor or a psychologist, and your emotional problems should be handled by an appropriate professional. (See also Chapter 30, FINDING AND USING A LAWYER.)

SEPARATION AGREEMENTS

Beatrice wanted to hold off on a divorce, so she suggested to Max that they try counseling once more. But they'd already been to couples therapy, group therapy, individual therapy, and a weekend "Learn to Love Your Partner Again" retreat. "Why put off what's inevitable?" asked Max. Beatrice proposed that they just separate for a while, and Max agreed to move out.

How Do Lawyers' Fees Work in a Divorce?

You will generally be charged at an hourly rate, although some attorneys do have flat fees for simple divorces where there is no property distribution. The hourly rate of an individual attorney, as well as the overall cost of a divorce, will vary due to the location of the case and the experience of the practitioner. In general, a family law "specialist" will charge more than a general practitioner, and an experienced attorney will charge more than a newer attorney.

Some courts will require the spouse with the greater means to pay at least part of the counsel fees of the other spouse, but you should not count on that happening.

Most attorneys will require a specified sum up front as a minimum **retainer** to start the action or begin negotiations on your behalf. The attorney's hourly rate will typically be charged against the retainer. Once the hours worked on your case exceed the retainer, you will be required to pay the balance when billed.

Unlike other types of cases, most states do not allow lawyers to use a contingency-fee arrangement in a divorce. (For more on lawyers' fees, see page 440.)

■ Should they have a written agreement?

If they agree that a separation is the best thing for them, they could simply live apart without any formal agreement for as long as they want. However, they may wish to have a **separation agreement** in order to protect them in case things do not remain harmonious. A separation agreement is especially advisable if one of the spouses does not work and will be caring for children on a full-time basis. The risks are simply too great that a spouse may change his or her mind about the amount of money paid for child support. Also, an agreement is helpful if disputes arise about personal property and bills on the marital residence.

As with any other agreement, you can write it yourself, but at some point you should consult a lawyer to make sure you have covered all the contingencies and that you are getting an appropriate amount of support based on the laws of your state. Whether or not you consult with a lawyer, it is always best to put any agreement in writing and make sure both of you sign and date the agreement. You may even want to have witnesses or a notary so that there will be no question at a later time about the circumstances surrounding the signing of the agreement.

You are not required to file the separation agreement with a court.

PROPERTY

How It Gets Distributed

Beatrice and Max decided to make a list of all their assets. They divided it three ways: "Max's Stuff," "Bea's Stuff," and "Couple Stuff." They started with the house. "That's Couple," said Max.

"No way," said Beatrice. "My name is on the deed."

"But I help pay the mortgage," said Max.

"Yeah, only since your band's been working. How about all those years before?"

"Bea, this was our dream house. We picked it out together. I made renovations. So what if you made the down payment. It's ours."

"Forget it, Max. I'm keeping the house."

■ How is property divided in a separation or divorce?

If the couple has no prenuptial agreement (see page 107), it depends on the laws of each state. Three basic systems govern how property is divided in a divorce. They are known as:

- **title**
- **community property**
- **equitable distribution**

The **title** system of distribution is not used anymore, because it is considered unfair. Under this

Issues a Separation Agreement Should Address

- the right of each spouse to live apart
- child custody
- child support
- visitation rights
- spousal support
- medical and dental expenses
- children's education expenses
- children's recreational expenses, such as camp or afterschool music and dance lessons
- division of property, with a complete listing of the income and assets of both spouses
- life insurance
- income tax
- divorce
- any other issues that are of importance to you

A separation agreement may be declared invalid if either of the parties failed to make a full disclosure of his or her assets. Also, there are certain rights that cannot be given away, such as the right to receive child support if you have custody of the children.

system, each asset was divided based on whose name it was held in. Traditionally, since the husband was almost always the breadwinner, all assets such as cars, bank accounts, stocks, bonds, and even houses were bought by him and held in his name. Thus, he would end up with most of the assets in a divorce.

The unfairness of this system has led to its replacement in most states by **equitable distribution.** Here, the basic idea is that the property acquired during a marriage is *jointly* owned by both spouses. But equitable distribution does not necessarily mean *equal* distribution, and ownership does not automatically split fifty-fifty between the two. At the time of the divorce, a judge must decide how the property should be distributed. The distribution must be fair and just (equitable) and the judge must consider several factors, including

- **the length of the marriage**
- **the age and health of the parties**
- **their respective ability to earn in the future**
- **any responsibility to minor children**
- **any other circumstances that are particular to their marriage**

Forty-one states and the District of Columbia divide property in this manner. The specific details vary from state to state, but the general concept is the same. (See the box on page 174.)

While equitable distribution is the system used in the majority of states, there are nine **community property** states. The idea of community property is that everything a husband and wife acquire once they are married is owned equally (fifty-fifty) by both of them, regardless of who provided the money to purchase the asset or whose name the asset is held in. If the couple divorces, their property is divided evenly under this system.

What about property each spouse owned before the marriage?

Under both equitable distribution and community property systems, that property remains separate and does not get split during the divorce. The same is true of any personal gifts or inheritances a spouse receives during the marriage. However, if you don't keep your personal assets separate, they may be converted into marital property. Then your spouse may be entitled to a share. For example, if you receive a $10,000 inheritance and keep it in your own personal account, that is your separate property. However, if you deposit the money into the joint account you share with your spouse, it would probably be considered marital property.

You can sometimes convert a separate asset into joint property even if you don't commingle it with marital property. For example, say you inherit 10,000 shares of IBM stock from your parents during the marriage, and you keep those shares in your name only, and you never do anything with that stock. It remains yours, and if you get divorced your spouse will not get any of it.

But perhaps you decide that this is your big opportunity to start playing in the stock market, and you begin to devote several hours a week to

How States Divide Property

Community Property States

Arizona	New Mexico
California	Texas
Idaho	Washington
Louisiana	Wisconsin
Nevada	

Equitable Distribution States

The remaining forty-one states and the District of Columbia

Important note: If you are married and acquire property in an equitable distribution state, your property could be converted if you move to a community property state.

trading, buying and selling shares, and reviewing financial and business journals. You do well and the value of that inheritance has increased by $50,000 due to your own efforts. Even if you keep this money in a separate account in your name and you never use any of the money to benefit your family, the $50,000 increase in the value of your stock portfolio, which resulted from your personal effort (as opposed to any appreciation in its value earned while it sat there), may be considered marital property that can be distributed.

In another example, say that several years before your marriage you bought a house. It's in your name and is considered a nonmarital asset. After your marriage, you continue to live in the house and pay the mortgage from your employment income, which is considered a marital asset. Thus you are mixing a marital asset with a nonmarital asset. In some states, that mixture will cause your house to become marital property that can be divided between the parties. In other states, the part of the house that you had paid for before the marriage will remain a nonmarital asset, while the other part will be a marital asset that can be divided between you and your spouse.

It turned out that Beatrice had put Max's name on the deed for the house as a present for his thirty-fifth birthday. So it was, indeed, his to share. But she didn't want to move. In fact, it was the thing she felt strongest about.

Does she have to buy out his share if she stays?

Yes. When you and your spouse are both owners of the property, then part of the value is yours and part of the value is your spouse's. Therefore, if you want to keep the house for yourself, you will have to trade off certain other assets in order to equal the balance.

What if the house was owned by one spouse before the marriage?

Things that you owned prior to the marriage do remain separate property. However, in an equitable distribution state, it may not be fair to exclude your spouse from sharing in the value of the house, especially if your spouse has helped pay the mortgage or has made improvements in the house. Also, if you bought the house specifically in contemplation of the marriage and the title just never got transferred into joint names, a court will usually find that it was intended to be a marital asset and will probably give your spouse a fair share.

Figuring Out What You Have to Divide

Beatrice and Max decided to list all their assets first and figure out how to divide them later. "It's easy," said Max. "We've got the house, the cars, and our bank accounts. That's basically it."

"Max, you oaf. We have a lot more than that." To herself, Beatrice muttered, "How could I have ever married a musician?"

How does a couple identify their assets?

The easiest assets (items of value) to identify are the tangible things that you own. These include

- **your home**
- **furniture, including lamps and rugs**
- **appliances**
- **works of art**
- **vehicles, including cars, bicycles, boats, and snowmobiles**
- **money (cash in the bank)**
- **stocks, bonds, and other investments**
- **pensions and retirement accounts**
- **personally owned businesses and partnerships**

There are also assets that do not have a physical existence. These are known as intangible assets. An example of an intangible asset would be the patent on an invention or something known as "celebrity goodwill," which is a person's ability to sell his or her image. This typically applies to famous people who can make a lot of money because of their fame. See the Case in Point on the next page.

Usually one of the most significant assets to divide is your **real property.** Real property is essentially land and all the things that are attached to it. If you own your own home, you own real property. Anything that is not real property is personal property, and personal property is anything that isn't nailed down, dug into, or built onto the land. Thus, your house is part of your real property, but your dining room set is not. (Note to those who own cooperative apartments: They are actually considered personal property.)

Would a professional degree be considered an asset?

Not usually. Very few states would consider professional degrees and licenses as marital property, although if you have supported your spouse and put him or her through school, you may be entitled to some form of reimbursement that will give you back the investment that you made in your spouse's future. The reason that these degrees and licenses are generally not considered marital assets is because they are nearly impossible to value. There is no way to predict what your spouse's future income will be, nor could your spouse sell his or her degree or license on the open market.

What about life insurance and pension plans?

A life insurance plan is an asset to which the parties have contributed during the marriage, but it is an asset which, again, is difficult to value because it will not be received until the insured person dies. Typically, there are two kinds of life insurance policies: term insurance that pays death benefits and has no present value, and a policy with a cash surrender value. A state may consider the cash surrender value of any life insurance policy to be marital property that can be divided (your policy will state whether it has a cash surrender value).

A pension plan is also an asset of the marriage. Depending on the law in your state, even if you are not vested in your pension and cannot collect from it or borrow against it for many years, the court may still consider it an asset of the marriage.

Miscellaneous Assets

Beatrice showed Max her list of assets. It included every piece of furniture, music equipment, computer, money they had invested in mutual funds, and the copyrights to all of Max's songs. "Hey," he said. "If you can include those, I get a share of your MBA."

Valuing a Business

Contrary to what Beatrice may have thought, Max did have a brain, and it was trying to calculate the value of Beatrice's computer consulting business. She'd started it seven years earlier as a one-woman operation. Now she employed ten workers and earned a healthy six-figure income. Of course, she did keep that income in a separate account, but Max thought that he should get a cut.

■ **Is one spouse entitled to a share of the business of the other spouse?**

Yes. If your spouse owns his or her own business, you are entitled to some share in the *value* of that business, although it is unlikely that you will get a piece of the business itself. If the business existed prior to the marriage, you will be entitled to share only in the increase in the value of the business since the marriage. If the business was set up during the marriage, you will be entitled to share in the entire value of the business.

■ **How is the value determined?**

It's an extremely complex procedure that usually requires the help of an expert whose services will probably cost several thousand dollars. Don't expect that you will receive pieces of machinery or inventory, or that you will be given a controlling share of the stocks of the corporation. Instead, since it is really your spouse's business (and presumably he or she wants to run it without your input), you probably will receive a cash buyout or the equivalent amount in marital assets. Even if you want a piece of the business, it is unlikely that a judge would give it to you, since that would be very disruptive to the flow of the business.

CASE IN POINT

Your Fame Is *Our* Fame

People who support their spouses through graduate school are often entitled to a share of the spouse's future earnings. So, too, are spouses who help nurture their mates on the path to celebrity status.

Such was the ruling in a 1989 New Jersey case involving comedian Joe Piscopo, who was splitting up with Nancy, his wife of twelve years. The two had met in college and then married. The focus of their life together: advancing Joe's rise to stardom. To that end, Nancy took care of all their personal needs, kept house, raised one child, and provided a sounding board for Joe's artistic ideas. "It took them ten years to move Mr. Piscopo from penury to celebrity," notes one court opinion.

In their divorce proceedings, Nancy argued that Joe's celebrity status was marital property that was subject to equitable distribution. Joe countered that his celebrity reputation was not an asset with monetary value and that his future earnings were subject to all sorts of variables — including illness, politics, reputation, and connections. A New Jersey appeals court disagreed, finding that Nancy had played a significant role in Joe's success and was entitled to share in its financial rewards. An accountant was hired to estimate the value of Piscopo's show business personality. According to the opinion, the value was found to be $98,708.60.

A similar finding was reached in a case involving opera singer Frederica Von Stade, who was divorced in 1990 after seventeen years of marriage. Von Stade's husband, Peter Elkus, argued successfully that his contributions and efforts had led to an increase in the value of his wife's career. During the course of their marriage, Elkus had been actively involved in teaching, coaching, and critiquing Von Stade, as well as caring for their two children. In the first year of their marriage, she earned $2,250. In the last, she earned $621,878.

Von Stade argued that her career and celebrity status were not licensed or owned like a business and thus were not marital property. A New York state appeals court disagreed, finding that while it was true that Von Stade had gained professional success even before meeting Elkus, he had actively contributed to her career's increase in value. Even though it wasn't marital property in the traditional form, the court ruled, her success was an asset that could be distributed.

CHILD CUSTODY

Who Gets It?

Beatrice and Max were still arguing over how they would divide their property, when Beatrice flippantly said, "Of course, I'll get custody of the kids."

"What are you talking about, Beatrice?" Max said. "I'm as responsible for them as you are, if not more. Who did everything for them during those years when your business was getting off the ground? I want them living with me at least half-time, and if you fight me, I'll argue that I should have full custody."

"Yeah, right," scoffed Beatrice. "Mr. On The Road now wants to be a family man. How can you even argue for partial custody if you're never home? And how do you think you can make decisions about the kids' daily lives if you're always out of town?"

"Well, Ms. Computer Consultant, if you haven't noticed, technology makes it pretty easy to keep in touch. You have, I presume, heard of the telephone? I have a lot of control over my schedule, and I know when I'm going to be away. In fact, shared custody would work out well. If we did one month at your place and one month at mine, then I can schedule my tours for the month when they're with you."

■ What are the basic forms of child custody?

There are two different kinds: **legal custody** and **physical custody.** A parent who has **legal custody** has the right to be involved in all the decision making typically involved with being a parent, such as

- **religious upbringing**
- **schooling**
- **health and medical decisions**
- **moral development**

A parent who has **physical custody** simply lives most of the time with the child.

The guiding principle in custody decisions is this question: What is in the best interests of the child? There is no single definition of what is meant by this very broad concept. It is tied to the facts of each specific situation and allows a judge to do what he or she thinks is best for a child based on the particular circumstances.

Custody can be either **sole** or **joint.** In the past, it was common for a mother to receive sole legal and physical custody, thereby pretty much shutting fathers out of the parenting process once a divorce occurred. However, the recent trend is toward **joint legal custody,** so that both parents have an equal involvement in the major life decisions affecting their children, regardless of who has physical custody. Sole legal custody is becoming less common, and most courts prefer to keep both parents actively involved in their children's lives unless there is a very good reason why they should not be. One such good reason would be abuse or neglect.

Since joint legal custody doesn't usually mean that the children live half the time with one parent and half with the other, it is necessary to work out a schedule of **visitation** that will be incorporated into the final divorce order. Everyone should work out a schedule that meets their own particular needs. Typically, the nonresidential parent will have the children every other weekend (Friday to Sunday) throughout the year and will visit one night or two during the week. Major holidays and birthdays alternate.

The guiding principle in working out a schedule should be what is in the best interests of the child. If one parent often travels during the week, it may be more feasible for the children to live with that parent during the weekends. Also, when making a schedule it is important that both parents have quality time with the children. Thus, it would be unfair to a working mother with physical custody if the children spent every weekend with their father.

As joint legal custody becomes more prevalent, it is also becoming more common for a father to have **joint physical custody** of the children. In fact, there is an active and growing "fathers' movement" that is seeking to refute some of the assumptions on which custody decisions have typically been made, namely that children of a very young age are best off with their mother. Joint physical custody doesn't necessarily mean that the children live exactly one-half of the time with one parent and one-half with the other. It does mean that both parents spend a substantial amount of time with the children.

It is important that your divorce not become a battle over custody if that is not genuinely an issue; custody should not be used as a threat or a weapon. However, if you genuinely feel that sole legal custody is appropriate or that you are the more appropriate residential parent, you should certainly make your feelings known.

■ Is the preference of the children considered in custody decisions?

Very possibly. Generally, when judges have to make a custody decision, they will interview the children in private. The age of the child will determine how much weight the judge gives to his or her preferences. For example, a three-year-old really can't make a choice about custody because he or she is too young to understand the ramifications of that decision. In contrast, a teenager may have some very clear preferences and some very strong reasons to back them up. The older the child gets, the harder it is to compel him or her to obey a custody and visitation order, so an older child's wishes will carry more weight.

Judges will listen very closely to what the children have to say. If the judge determines that the child has been coached or bribed or convinced in some way to choose one parent over the other, the judge will generally disregard those statements and may penalize the parent who influenced the child.

Making Decisions About How to Raise the Children

A downturn in her business had led Beatrice to strange behavior. She had become increasingly involved with the Crystal Worshippers, a spiritual group that held daily meditation meetings and weekend retreats lead by Guru Chad. Beatrice had been bringing Vinny and Alena to the meditation meetings, and they had also been attending "Sunday Spirituals," where, among other things, the guru condemned all organized religions. Now she was planning to send them to a summer program where they would learn to hear their "inner voices." Max strongly objected. Although he had a couple of crystals stashed away in a drawer, he was not especially religious and this inner spirit stuff was too much for him. He wanted the kids to go to a regular Catholic Sunday school.

■ Can one parent decide what religious upbringing the children will have?

Not if the parents have joint custody, and certainly not if their divorce settlement stated that the children were to be raised as Catholics. If it did, then raising them in any kind of religious institution against the wishes of the other spouse would be a violation of the settlement agreement. The other spouse could apply to the court for a restraining order. If no previous decision was made and they have joint decision-making power, a court would hear both positions and determine what is in the best interests of the children under the circumstances.

Spouses in this type of situation may need to seek counseling together in order to resolve this issue. The religious upbringing of children, just like their education, is typically a decision for both parents, if they have joint custody, and you should not hesitate to seek court intervention if your former spouse is disregarding your wishes on such an important issue.

■ Can one parent stop paying child support to protest how the children are being raised or because visitation is being denied?

No. Generally, child support is a court-ordered financial obligation. One parent's displeasure with an aspect of custody or even a denial of visitation does not allow for a unilateral termination of the child-support obligation. The remedy is to go to court.

Giving Custody to a Nonparent

Max's mother was distressed about the divorce. She was old-fashioned and didn't like the idea of the children being in a home without two parents. She also was worried that Beatrice was not going to let her visit the kids. She told her husband she'd like to try to get custody of the children. He told her to stop meddling in other people's business.

■ Can custody go to somebody other than the parents?

In very rare cases where it would be inappropriate to award physical custody to *either* of the biological parents, the child may be placed with someone else. Generally, however, the rights of biological and adoptive parents are superior to the claims of any other relative by blood or marriage. If the biological parents feel that a grandparent or stepparent would be a better custodian for their child, they can certainly agree to that arrangement.

Giving Custody to a Homosexual Parent

Bea's friend Sarah had surprised her friends with the announcement that she was involved in a serious relationship with another woman. Her marriage was breaking up, and her husband vowed to keep her from getting custody of their two kids. He had never been especially interested in parenting, but he was determined "not to let that broad raise my sons to be fairies."

■ Can a parent be denied custody because he or she is gay?

The rights of homosexual parents are only recently being recognized. For a long time, a gay parent could not obtain custody of his or her child, because it was felt that such a person's lifestyle was wrong or immoral. However, as with many other lifestyle choices, such as interracial marriage or single parenthood, the laws in most states have recognized that the simple fact that a parent is gay should have no bearing on whether he or she is unfit to raise a child. As with all custody decisions, the important question is what is best for the child and what bearing the parent's lifestyle — be it gay or heterosexual — will have on the child.

Altering the Custody Arrangement

Beatrice and Max agreed to joint physical custody. She had the kids one week, and he had them the other. Max sometimes took them on some short road trips (when it didn't conflict with school), and even though a reliable babysitter went along, Beatrice worried that there was drinking and drug use on the trips. She also didn't like the fact that Max's new girlfriend had moved in with him.

■ Under what circumstances can the custody be changed?

The reasons for a change in custody will vary from state to state. In general, however, if it becomes inappropriate for one reason or another for a parent to have physical or legal custody, the other parent can attempt to have custody changed. For instance, if the parent with custody becomes involved with drugs or other illegal activities, thus exposing the children to immoral and unlawful behavior and to physical danger, it would likely merit a change. (Of course, the court would require proof of this.) On the other hand, if the parent with physical custody chooses to live with someone without being married, few courts are likely to interfere.

You should contact a lawyer to determine what the law is in your state regarding change of custody.

If a Custodial Parent Dies

The Eardrum Busters were traveling in a chartered jet for a five-city tour. The band was heading home after the last concert when the jet got caught in a sudden thunderstorm and crashed. Two band members were killed. Max was seriously injured, but he survived. His near-death experience led him to contemplate disastrous events.

■ **What happens if the parent who has custody dies?**

Custody would generally revert to the other parent. If that parent would not be an appropriate caretaker, a third party could intervene on behalf of the child.

Denying Visitation

Both Alena and Vinny complained every week when they were supposed to go to Max's. "I don't like it there," Alena cried one Friday morning. "We just sit around all day. Daddy plays music loud and yells when we bother him, and then he leaves us with a babysitter at night." Beatrice wondered if the kids should stop seeing Max for a while.

■ **Can a parent be denied visitation rights after a divorce?**

Yes, but only under extremely limited circumstances. In general, it is presumed that it is in a child's best interests to have contact with both parents. It is only if the parent (or the parent's behavior) is a threat to the child in some manner that visitation will be denied. For example, if it is demonstrated that the parent abused the child in some way, a judge may determine that it is best not to permit the parent and child to be alone together. The person seeking to prevent visitation will have a very heavy burden to prove that circumstances justify a total denial of contact.

An alternative to no visitation is supervised visitation, where the parent sees the child in the presence of a third party who will be able to prevent any harmful action. The person who supervises can be a family member, close friend, counselor, or clergyman. Some communities have court-supervised visitation programs, in which a government worker or volunteer oversees the visit.

Relocating with the Children

Beatrice realized that she'd have much better luck with her business if she relocated to another state. She also wanted to live near her sister, Blossom, and she thought it would be good to have some distance from Max (although she didn't tell him that). Max threatened to charge her with kidnapping if she left the state with the children.

■ **Can an ex-spouse who has custody move with the children to another state?**

Not unless the court gives permission or the other parent consents. The rules vary from state to state, and you should consult an attorney to find out what your local laws are. The obvious problem with moving out of state with the children is that it will usually interfere with your former spouse's visitation with the children. (A parent who does not have physical custody can move anywhere he or she wants.)

You will be asked about the reasons for your move. The questions might include

- **What impact will the move have on the children?**
- **Will you find opportunities there that are unavailable here?**
- **How far away are you moving?**
- **What will the impact be on your former spouse's visitation rights?**
- **Are you doing this just to thwart your spouse's visitation?**

Everything depends on the specific circumstances of your case, as well as the law in your state. It may be, for instance, that by moving out of state, you only add a few minutes or half an hour onto the drive, and the visitation times can be adjusted to account for that time. Or, if you have enough money and an airport is convenient to both of you, your ex-spouse may agree to see the children for several longer visitations each year instead of every other weekend.

If you move without the consent of your former spouse or court permission, you may be arrested for kidnapping, so you really should consult an attorney if this problem arises for you.

Note: In some states, like New Jersey, you may be restricted from moving even one mile if it means you'll cross state lines, though there are no limitations on your freedom to move within the same state — even if it's 200 miles away — unless your divorce agreement specifically restricts your ability to relocate.

Visitation Rights of Other Relatives

Max's mother, Goldie, was very upset with her son, because he never brought the kids to visit. She tried, with no luck, to talk to Beatrice about it, but since she had once suggested that Beatrice was a selfish mother, Beatrice had turned cold toward her. Goldie was heartbroken that she hadn't seen her grandchildren for months.

■ Does a grandparent have the right to visit the children after a divorce?

In general, no one other than the children's biological or adoptive parents and, in some states, siblings have an automatic right to visit. Grandparents and other relatives may see the children when the custodial parent permits it or when the noncustodial parent has visitation. Many states provide for grandparent visitation if it is demonstrated that such visitation would be in the children's best interests.

As with all issues in a divorce, the parties involved may agree to whatever terms and provisions they want. Thus, if you and your spouse want to allow grandparents to visit, you can negotiate to include such a provision in your divorce settlement.

■ Do stepparents have a right to visit?

Not usually, unless it is demonstrated that visitations would be in the best interests of a child. This is especially true when a stepparent has assumed the role of parent. And again, you and your spouse could agree to include a visitation arrangement in your divorce settlement.

CHILD SUPPORT

How It's Figured

Beatrice's business was foundering. She had laid off all her workers and was barely able to make her mortgage payments. Max, meanwhile, was thriving. His band was touring the country and had even been invited to appear on David Letterman's show. Braced for a fight, she told him she needed child support. To her surprise, Max didn't put up an argument.

■ How is child support determined?

Child support, like alimony, is intended to support the children in a style to which they became accustomed during the marriage. Obviously, child support should be sufficient to provide food, clothing, and shelter, but it should also cover the kinds of expenses that the children can expect with the sort of lifestyle that their parents' income made possible for them. This may involve private school, summer camps, vacations, and automobiles when they get their driver's licenses.

Each state has guidelines that help determine how much child support should be. The amount of child support will depend on the incomes of both parents. Usually, child support can be increased when the paying parent achieves an increase in income through a raise or promotion. It can also be increased as the cost of living rises. Often a divorce decree includes a provision for an automatic cost-of-living increase each year. If it doesn't, the spouse receiving child support can ask the court for an increase.

In addition, federal laws require child support to be reviewed *automatically* every three years in a proceeding led by an administrative officer, usually from the state's probation department. Questions have been raised about the legality of such a constant invasion of the privacy of individuals and the propriety of putting such reviews in the hands of administrative officials instead of the state courts. But so far no challenges have succeeded in overturning the law.

■ **Can child support ever be reduced or increased?**

Yes. Child support will generally be reduced if the paying parent suffers an economic loss or downturn that is relatively permanent in nature. For example, if the parent loses his or her job, child support may be reduced for the time in which the parent is not working. When the parent hits retirement, support can then be adjusted as well. Likewise, if the paying parent receives a substantial increase in income, it may be possible to modify the support.

■ **Can one parent get child support when the parents share physical custody of the children?**

Probably, if the parent can show a financial need for it. In general, though, child support is payable from the parent who does not have full-time residential custody to the parent who does. The reason for this is that the parent who cares for the children on a day-to-day basis will incur the bulk of the costs for the children's care and well-being.

Doctors' Bills

Even though Max had more free time during the day before the divorce, Beatrice was generally the one who took the kids to their doctor and dentist appointments. Now, after the divorce, Alena was going to get braces, and Beatrice didn't want to get stuck paying all the bills.

■ **Should child support include money for health care bills?**

Depending on the family's financial circumstances, either one or both of you will be required to maintain health insurance, and someone will have to pay for the deductibles and whatever unreimbursed expenses there are. If you are both working, you will probably share the unreimbursed expenses in proportion to your incomes, or fifty-fifty. If you are not working, and you were not working during the marriage, your former spouse will probably be responsible for 100 percent of the health expenses.

For More Information on Child Support

Contact your state's child support enforcement agency. Or, the U.S. Department of Health and Human Services has an information booklet. You can receive a copy by calling or writing to:

Office of Child Support Enforcement
Administration for Children and Families
370 L'Enfant Promenade SW
Washington, DC 20447
202-401-9382

Private School and College

Alena was an exceptionally bright child, and Beatrice wanted to send her to private school. She also wanted to start saving money for both kids' college tuition. Max was balking. He didn't think private school was necessary, and he thought the kids should work their way through college just like he did. "That was only because your parents didn't have the money to pay for it," said Beatrice. "You do have the money to pay for this."

■ **Does child support include college and private school expenses?**

The question of schooling will depend primarily on the lifestyle the couple enjoyed while they were married and any intentions that were expressed during the marriage. If they were financially secure and had planned for their children to go to college or to private school, that should not change because they have divorced. If one spouse was and is the sole financial provider, he or she will probably have to pay all the education expenses. If the other spouse is also employed outside the home, he or she will most likely have to contribute something toward the schooling.

The law varies from state to state as to whether parents who are divorced are required to pay for their children to attend college. In a few states there is no such obligation.

If your state requires you to pay for college, your contribution will be determined by

- **your income and assets**
- **the income and assets of your former spouse**
- **your child's ability to contribute**

Of course, if any funds were set aside during the marriage for the child's college education, those funds should be used first and the child should take advantage of any financial aid or scholarships that are offered.

Collecting Unpaid Support

Max turned out to be less enthralled about paying child support than his original enthusiasm had indicated he would be. For six months every check arrived late. With Beatrice's cash flow at a standstill, these lapses made a crucial difference. Then the checks stopped coming altogether.

How can a spouse collect the support if it's delinquent?

One of the biggest issues with child support is the difficulty in collecting it. Most states have set up programs for payment of child support (and alimony) through the court system so that if your former spouse is consistently late or fails to pay at all, the state knows immediately and can act to collect the money or issue a warrant for your spouse's arrest. There are also private agencies that will seek out a nonpaying parent for a share of the amount collected. If you are owed a substantial amount of money, this may be a good alternative for you.

If you know where your former spouse works, you can apply to the court (usually it's family court) to order a **wage execution** or **garnishment,** which would deduct your support payment directly from your spouse's paycheck on a weekly basis. There are strict federal guidelines as to how much of your spouse's income can be taken, so it is possible that you may not get the entire amount of your support payment this way.

You can also have your spouse's income tax refunds and certain other federal government benefits withheld or frozen if support is delinquent.

Is it possible to collect if the nonpaying spouse has moved to another state?

Yes. There is a procedure for collecting support if the payor lives in a state other than where the order to pay was entered. The law is called **URESA,** the Uniform Reciprocal Enforcement of Support Act (sometimes RURESA for its revised version), and it has been adopted by all fifty states and United States territories. Under URESA, an order of support issued in one state can be enforced in another state. To enforce an order under URESA, you have two options:

Registration:

- You register the court order that says your former spouse has to pay support in the state where he or she now lives. You can call the family court in the appropriate county to find out what its local procedure is.
- Your ex-spouse's state moves to "enforce" your order, which means it acts to make your ex-spouse pay.

This approach has a downside: Your ex-spouse can go to court in the new state and argue that he or she is being required to pay too much. The court is free to adjust the amount of support, which could result in your getting less money. If your ex-spouse's state does this, your state has to accept the modification.

Enforcement Application:

- You go to the family court in your state and start an enforcement action. You should bring your original order for support with you, and you will probably have to fill out some forms.
- Your state's child support enforcement agency then contacts the state where your former spouse now lives.
- Your ex-spouse's state cannot adjust the amount of support *owed,* but it can determine that the amount is too high and thus order that only a portion of it has to be *paid.*

Dealing with Bureaucracies

Collecting unpaid support can be a bureaucratic nightmare involving lots of paperwork and requiring lots of patience, and you should do all you can to make the system work *for* you, not against you. Basically, anything you can do to get someone within a bureaucracy to care about you and your case will help make the process easier.

Some pointers to help move things along:

- If you're dealing with the court system, check in regularly to see where your case stands. Always have your case or docket number available.
- When dealing with people on the phone or in person, get their names so you can ask for them directly if you need to call to check or follow up.
- Notify the appropriate person or agency immediately if a problem arises. Don't put it off.
- Be aggressive about asking for help and checking on the status of your case, but don't be obnoxious or rude — even though you may be frustrated and angry.

With this option, your state does not have to accept the modification. So if your former spouse pays you the amount ordered by *his* (or her) state, he will still owe you money *in your state.* If the amount owed piles up, your state may issue a warrant for his arrest. The failure to pay would show up on his credit report, and he could run into problems if he tried to buy property in your state. (Note: A new interstate law, the Uniform Interstate Family Support Act, UIFSA, would not allow another state to alter a support order. Most states are expected to adopt the law.)

You should consider both options carefully before you file. Unfortunately, the process tends to be slow and bureaucratic, but eventually you should be able to collect your support. If you can't, you should consult a lawyer to find out what other remedies may be available to you.

ALIMONY

Who's Entitled to It?

Rick, a drummer friend of Max's, was also going through a divorce. But unlike Max, Rick was out of work, waiting around for that career break to finally come his way. He was also tending to the household duties and taking care of his two young children, ages three and five, while his wife, a lawyer, worked. In fact, he probably could have done more with his career if it hadn't been for the kids, but he felt it was important that they have a parent home with them during the day, and his wife had not wanted to sacrifice her lucrative job.

When is a spouse entitled to alimony?

When a couple marries, they essentially are pledging to support each other for the duration of their lives. This financial obligation does not end if they divorce. **Alimony,** also known as maintenance or spousal support, is the money paid by one spouse to the other in order to fulfill that obligation. In the traditional marriage, a husband had to pay alimony to his wife upon their divorce, because he had the career and she was the full-time homemaker.

These notions and biases, however, have become outdated and are being eliminated from the law. Today, in most states either a husband or a wife may be awarded alimony. It is also no longer a given that a spouse will receive alimony for the rest of his or her life after a divorce. Instead, temporary or "rehabilitative" alimony, which gives a spouse alimony for a limited period of time so that he or she may establish a career and become self-supporting, is becoming far more common.

Say, for example, that you and your spouse were married after high school. You both worked for a few years, then you stayed home to raise your children. You are now both twenty-eight, you have two children, ages two and five, and you have been out of the work force for five and a half years. During that time, your spouse has been advancing rapidly in his or her chosen field and is doing fairly well. Since you are still young, and since your marriage was of fairly short duration, you are unlikely to be awarded lifetime alimony. But since you have sacrificed your own career in order to devote yourself to your spouse and your family, you should not be penalized for that decision.

In this case a judge may order rehabilitative alimony for the period of time it takes you to reestablish yourself in your field. This could be as little as one year or as long as ten years, depending on what further education you need, what kind of salaries you could hope for in the first few years, the job market, and your responsibilities to any minor children. If you are unable to find a job, you could apply to the court for a modification that will extend the alimony period. However, you will need to have a good reason why you were unable to find a job.

Rehabilitative alimony is a flexible concept, which has been very helpful to people who are not entitled to lifelong alimony but who need assistance in the short term.

The obligation to pay alimony usually ends if the supported spouse remarries, since he or she presumably will no longer need to be supported. The obligation may also end if the supported spouse lives together with someone in a relationship tantamount to marriage.

Ways to Collect Delinquent Payments

- **have money withheld from paychecks**
- **have probation department monitor payments**
- **have tax refunds withheld**
- **URESA**
- **seize real estate or personal property**
- **require a cash bond be put down as a security deposit**

Calculating Alimony

The factors on which alimony is based depend on state law. Generally, they include

- **the age and health of the parties**
- **the length of the marriage**
- **the ability of both spouses to be self-supporting**
- **responsibilities to minor children**
- **the income of the breadwinner**
- **the lifestyle the parties enjoyed during the marriage**

Alimony is intended to support the spouse at the level to which he or she became accustomed during the marriage, so if you have no means to support yourself, or if your income is inadequate to maintain you at the level to which you were accustomed during the marriage, you will generally be entitled to some amount of support, although it may be for only a limited duration.

Medical and Life Insurance

Beatrice's Aunt Mildred was getting divorced after thirty-five years of marriage. She had never worked while raising her four children, and now at age fifty-five, she was not about to start. Clearly, her husband was going to have to pay alimony. Mildred was just worried about what it would cover.

■ Can alimony include payments for medical and life insurance?

Yes. Medical and life insurance are both usually taken into account these days in divorce settlements. If you did not work during the marriage and you relied on your spouse to provide medical insurance for you, he or she may be required to maintain you on the policy while the case is proceeding and may have to buy an alternate policy for you after the divorce. Alternatively, if you receive alimony on a monthly basis, the amount you receive may include a sum for health insurance costs, but you would then be responsible for maintaining your own policy.

How to Collect Your Share of Pension Fund Benefits

You can file what is known as a Qualified Domestic Relations Order (QDRO or DRO). This is a court order that tells the pension plan administrator how to distribute the fund when your spouse does, in fact, retire. The order is usually granted after a couple is divorced. It's advisable to consult a lawyer to help you because the process is very complicated. You may also need to hire an accountant.

Once you get the QDRO, what generally will happen is that you will receive a check from the pension fund at the same time that your former spouse does, and the amount that your former spouse receives will be less than it would have been without the QDRO. Depending on the plan, you may be able to elect how and when you will receive your benefits, regardless of what your former spouse does. If the plan can set aside the amount you are entitled to, you would receive a monthly check directly from the plan. Remember, though, every plan is different!

You would continue to receive that money until you hit the maximum amount to which you are entitled, after which all payments to you would cease. If your ex-spouse's plan cannot set aside a lump sum for you, you would simply receive a fixed percentage of his or her monthly pension benefit for as long as he or she received it. If he or she never collected, neither would you.

If you are receiving permanent alimony (as opposed to temporary alimony), it is likely that your former spouse may be required to maintain life insurance as a protection against his or her untimely death. However, if you want to maintain insurance on your own life, your former spouse probably will not be required to pay for that life insurance (since your former spouse is probably not going to be the beneficiary).

Note: If you participate in the health insurance plan offered by your spouse's employer, you are entitled by federal law to remain in the plan for thirty-six months after your divorce. Either you or your ex-spouse will have to pay for the coverage.

Pension Plans

Mildred's soon-to-be ex-husband was planning to retire in the next few years (which was what precipitated the divorce). They had been saving a lot of money through his company's pension plan, and Mildred thought she was entitled to part of that money, especially since they had had some very specific plans about how they were going to spend it together.

What happens to pension plan money in a divorce?

The theory is that, while you were married, part of your spouse's compensation was in the form of deferred benefits, which you expected to share in at retirement. In general, you will be entitled only to that portion of the pension or retirement fund that had accumulated during the marriage. And then you will get only your share, not the whole thing.

You should be aware that money that is to be received in the future has a lower value in the present. So, if Mildred has $100 in the bank today, that $100 will be worth more in ten years because it will earn interest. At the same time, if her husband says he is going to give her $100 in ten years, the value of that money today will be less since it has not yet earned the interest.

To determine the reasonable value of pension and other retirement benefits, most people hire a professional known as an actuary. Then, if your spouse can afford to buy you out at that present value, you can get your money up front. If that is not possible, you will have to wait to receive this money until your spouse retires.

Does a divorced spouse have a right to share an ex-mate's Social Security benefits?

Probably. If you were married for at least ten years, you would be entitled to a portion of the Social Security benefits your spouse receives after retiring — even if he or she wasn't supporting you during the marriage. Also, if you receive child support from your spouse, the children will usually be able to receive Social Security payments if your ex-spouse becomes disabled and collects Social Security benefits.

Finding Hidden Assets

Beatrice was pretty sure Max had been making more money than his financial documents showed. In addition to the income he earned playing with the band, he'd been negotiating several deals to manufacture Eardrum Busters products, including caps, T-shirts, and coffee mugs. Beatrice was pretty sure Max had been paid a lot of money to use the band's logo, but it didn't show up anywhere in his bank records. She thought he had either invested the money, stashed it in a secret account, or actually bought things that he was keeping hidden somewhere else.

What can a spouse do if he or she thinks the other is lying about finances?

Perhaps one of the most difficult financial aspects of divorce is making sure that everything is "on the table" when you sit down to negotiate a settlement or to present your case to the court. It is difficult, time-consuming work to trace the movement of money, stocks, and similar assets, and it is nearly impossible to trace items of personal property, such as jewelry, Krugerrands, clothing, and other similar items. Even cars and boats that are registered with the state can be disposed of fairly easily if your spouse knows the right people.

It is very difficult to prove that assets have been hidden, especially if you have only a suspicion that it has been done. For example, if you knew for a fact that your spouse had a bank account in a certain bank that was in only his or her name, you could get a court order to see the records of that bank and find out information about the account. But if all you have is a suspicion that your spouse was stashing money somewhere, it's generally not cost-effective to search every single bank in the United States hoping that you'll find something. The services of a private detective or investigator may be useful in finding misappropriated assets, but again, there is no guarantee. If your spouse is clever, and if he or she contemplated the divorce

> **Finding Hidden Assets**
>
> If you suspect your spouse is hiding assets, you can search for them through a legal process known as **discovery** (in which you are trying to "discover" relevant information). Through discovery your attorney can ask your spouse to turn over applicable financial records, such as
>
> - **tax returns**
> - **bank account statements**
> - **brokerage house statements**
> - **real estate records**
> - **loan applications**
>
> Your spouse and others, such as employers, business associates, or bank officials, can also be questioned under oath in a **deposition.**
>
> An analysis of the records, together with the information from the depositions, should help you put together an accurate picture of your spouse's finances.
>
> If you find out after your divorce that your spouse had some assets that were concealed from you and from the court, you can ask the court to modify the order or rescind the entire agreement since it was based on fraud. However, most states have time limits during which the agreement can be "attacked." If you discover the fraud after the time limit has passed, you may, unfortunately, be stuck with the agreement.

long before you knew about it, the money may be long gone and even out of the country.

How Alimony Gets Paid

Beatrice's friend Renata was getting divorced. She didn't trust her husband, a wealthy car dealer, to pay her alimony regularly. She also wanted to avoid contact with him as much as possible.

Can alimony be paid in one lump sum instead of spread out over time?

Yes. Alimony is usually paid on a regular schedule out of the income of the paying spouse. However, if both parties desire, and the paying spouse has the financial ability, they can certainly arrange to have alimony paid in one lump sum. Remember, almost anything is possible if you and your spouse agree to it. One advantage of getting a lump sum would be psychological; both of you would be able to get on with your lives as individuals without ties to your past. Another advantage would be the fact that you would have all your money to spend or invest as you wish and you would not have to rely upon someone sending you a check every week or every two weeks or every month.

What are the disadvantages of a lump-sum payment?

The main disadvantage is that you would not have a guaranteed, steady income in the future. So if you were not good at budgeting yourself and investing so that you got steady income from the lump sum, you could find yourself in dire financial circumstances.

CASE IN POINT

The Man Could Not Be Trusted

Judges don't look too kindly on people who secrete assets during divorce proceedings. When Stavros and Dea Economou split up after thirteen years, the dissolution of their marriage "involved a truly staggering amount" of property, noted one California appeals court judge.

In their initial agreements, Dea was to receive $2,250 a month in child support for the couple's two sons, plus $1.5 million in cash. In addition, both she and her husband were to cooperate in sharing and exchanging financial records. After Stavros failed to comply with court orders to disclose financial information, Dea asked for a modification of the child support and received an increase to $6,200 per month in child support and $10,000 a month in spousal support.

It was subsequently discovered that Stavros had fled to Greece and misappropriated more than $6 million of the couple's community property, according to a 1990 opinion. In addition to the monthly support payments, Dea was ultimately awarded $3,762,314 in liquid assets. In addition, Stavros's visitation rights were severely restricted, for fear he would abscond with the children.

At trial, Dea had "painstakingly reconstructed the couple's assets and debts," calling several experts, including an accountant who testified that Stavros had kept secret foreign accounts and a private investigator who tracked Stavros down in Greece and took photographs of real estate and personal property he had purchased there. Dea's lawyer stated that tracking the assets was "like an anthropologist constructing a dinosaur out of a jaw bone or an archaeologist that can construct an Inca temple out of a couple of stones."

Stavros contested the amount of money awarded to Dea, arguing that he was being unfairly sanctioned for having secreted assets. The panel of appeals judges rejected his argument, noting that he had failed to comply with any court orders to produce financial records. Quoting the lower court's assessment of Stavros, the opinion notes that he "cannot be trusted; his word is worthless. He is more than a cad and a bounder, he is a con and a thief."

You might arrange for the lump sum to be paid in several installments over the course of a few years. If so, you might lose some of the future installments if you remarry. Also, you may face a high tax bill if you get all the money at once, since the recipient must pay taxes on alimony. An accountant or tax adviser can advise you whether a lump sum would result in a heavy tax burden. (Taxwise, a lump-sum payment might be good for the spouse who pays it, because the alimony payments are tax-deductible.)

Collecting Unpaid Alimony

Renata's husband (as she suspected) was not making his alimony payments on time. In fact, he had paid her nothing for over a year, forcing Renata and her three children to move in with Renata's parents.

How does a person collect delinquent alimony?

Unfortunately, this problem arises very frequently. It has always been a difficult task to collect alimony from an unwilling former spouse, but state and federal laws are making it a bit easier to do so now. The remedies for collecting unpaid alimony are similar to those for collecting unpaid child support. (See page 183.)

Increasing Alimony

Max's friend Rick was seriously injured in the plane crash that killed two of the band members. His arm and leg were broken and his back was dislocated. The doctor told him he would not be able to play drums for at least a year (two of his fingers had nearly been cut off, and it was going to take that long for them to heal). In the meantime, Rick had physical therapy bills, and he had joined a health club so he could work out regularly. He also had to eat out a lot since he really couldn't cook. His monthly alimony payments weren't covering all these expenses. He wanted more.

Under what circumstances can alimony be increased?

If your judgment of divorce provides for payments of alimony over a long period of time without taking into account inflation and other increases in the cost of living, there will undoubtedly come a time when the alimony payment you receive is simply inadequate to meet your needs.

Other changes that would justify an increase in alimony include

- **an injury that renders you incapable of ever working again (if you were working to contribute to your own support)**
- **a long-term illness**
- **termination from your job**
- **illness of a child that requires your full-time, long-term care**

Any of these (and others) are possible foundations for a request to increase alimony payments. You should consult an attorney who can tell you specifically under the laws of your state whether or not an increase is warranted.

Decreasing Alimony

Even though Rick's wife felt bad about the accident, she got a good chuckle out of his sob story. "He's probably meeting women at the gym, then wooing them over dinner," she thought. But whatever his reasons were for needing more money, they didn't really matter, since her law firm had lost a lot of clients and was on the verge of bankruptcy. As it was, she was barely keeping up with her own bills.

When can alimony be decreased?

When circumstances change such that it is no longer fair or reasonable for you to pay the same amount. One of the most frequent changes is retirement. If your final judgment of divorce does not take into account this event, you may need to make a motion to the court to modify your alimony obligation. Many courts distinguish between voluntary early retirement and mandatory retirement. If a person retires at age fifty-five, the court might deem that to be a voluntary retirement that does not justify a change in alimony.

Some of the other changed circumstances that may justify a downward modification of alimony include

- **an illness or disability that prevents you from working**
- **the loss of your job and an inability to find a similar position at a similar salary despite a diligent search**
- **a downward turn in the economy that results in bad times for your privately held business, partnership, or a corporation**

You will need to consult an attorney as to the specifics of the law in your state. Regardless of whether you are seeking an increase or a decrease, you will need to show a significant change in circumstances affecting your ability to pay.

Invalid Settlements

Bea's friend Trisha was getting divorced. She had negotiated an agreement that her husband, a wealthy stockbroker, would pay her 50 percent of his income for ten years. The day after their divorce was approved, he quit his job. "Guess you're on your own," he told Trisha with a smirk.

■ Was this fraud?

Probably. The fact that he quit his job the day after the divorce was granted is a pretty clear indication that he never intended to live up to the terms of the settlement and that he acted in **bad faith** when he was negotiating. As with any contract, a divorce settlement can be set aside for fraud, which is essentially what he had committed. No court will condone such an act.

Which is not to say that you can never change your job or career path once you are obligated to pay support. What it means is that you may not enter into negotiations knowing that you do not intend to live up to the terms of the agreement. Even if Trisha's husband could show that he did not intend to deceive anyone and that he had had a sudden inspiration that motivated him to quit his job and do something else with his life, his spouse does not have to suffer because of that decision. Most courts would require him to continue to pay the alimony at the same level (or a close approximation) that was set in the agreement.

Starting New Relationships: Will You Lose Your Alimony?

Max was dating Maggie, a vivacious woman he met at his health club. She was divorced, had two daughters, aged seven and ten, and was receiving monthly alimony from her ex-husband. Max composed a ballad to play in a local concert:

> **The gym that day was humid and dank.**
> **The guys, as usual, were sweaty. They stank.**
> **But there you stood lifting weight after weight**
> **And all I thought was, Gee, man, she's great.**
> **Maggie, oh Maggie, so pretty and free.**
> **Maggie, oh Maggie, will you please marry me?**

■ Does a person who remarries lose his or her alimony?

Very possibly. The original concept of alimony assumed that a spouse (generally female) was simply incapable of taking care of herself and needed to be looked after (first by her father, then by her husband). Therefore, it made sense that alimony would end when she remarried, because now she had another caretaker who was able to support her.

The general principle remains that once a recipient of alimony remarries, the need for alimony disappears. If you could talk your spouse into it, you might be able to reach a settlement that provided for alimony to continue past your remarriage. It is doubtful, however, that anyone would agree to such an arrangement, and judges can't generally impose such a requirement.

The only possible exception to this "marry and lose it" concept arises if you are receiving rehabilitative alimony (see page 184). Since the concept of rehabilitative alimony is to get you reestablished in a career, it is not so heavily tied to the idea that you need someone supporting you because you can't

How to Get an Increase in Your Support Payments

If your payments are being made through the probation department, as many are, there is probably a form you can fill out to request an increase. You will most likely be required to show exactly why you need an increase. If, for instance, your settlement did not include a cost-of-living increase, or if you can prove your former spouse is making more money, you may be able to get an increase.

If your payments are not being made through the probation department, you will have to start a lawsuit by filing a motion to increase the payments. There may be forms available, but it would probably be helpful to consult an attorney.

take care of yourself. Thus, it's possible that your divorce settlement could state that your rehabilitative alimony would continue (probably at a reduced rate) if you remarry.

Maggie was flattered by Max's proposal — and by its presentation. But she wasn't ready to get married. She suggested that they just live together for a while to see how things felt.

■ **If an ex-spouse is living with someone, is that grounds to stop paying alimony?**

Maybe. If your ex-spouse is living with someone in a relationship that is akin to a marriage, where they both contribute to expenses, or where his or her companion is providing full financial support, you should have a good argument for termination of alimony. It helps if your divorce decree listed cohabitation as a reason to terminate the alimony. If it doesn't, you will have to check the law in your state to see under what circumstances a living-together relationship can be used to terminate alimony. If your ex-spouse is simply sharing quarters with a person in order to save money, he or she can't be punished for that. The nature of the relationship and its similarity to marriage are what counts when deciding whether alimony should be terminated.

■ **Can a person just stop paying?**

It's not advisable to do so. You may find yourself sued for nonpayment and you would have to defend your actions. If you are arrested for nonpayment of support, your arguments about why you don't have to pay won't mean much to the police.

REMARRIAGE

Max met Jenny after he and Beatrice first separated. She was a bartender in a local nightclub, and he was attracted by her assertiveness (he didn't mind her long, blond hair, either). He asked her out, but she told Max she wanted nothing to do with a married man. (She'd read about him in *People* and knew he had a family.) She didn't care a hoot about his separation, she said. "Call me when the divorce is final," she said. Max didn't want to let her slip away.

■ **Is it possible to get a "quickie" divorce?**

A so-called quickie divorce may not in fact be valid, and you should be very careful about getting one. All states require that you reside there for some period of time before a divorce petition can be filed, with the time periods ranging six weeks up to one year. The only benefit to this type of divorce is that it may free you quickly to remarry. However, if you want to get alimony or child support, or contest any issues of property settlement, this is not the route to go.

If you do want to obtain a quick divorce, you (or your spouse) would have to move to the other state and establish a bona fide residence there for the minimum time required. States impose these time limits to assure that marriage as an institution is not trivialized and that people do not act rashly and without thinking their decisions through.

Can a person go to a foreign country for a quick divorce?

There are countries that do not have stringent requirements in order to get a divorce. One of the best known is Mexico. However, many states will refuse to recognize a foreign divorce if the parties legally resided in the state and went to the foreign country only for the purpose of obtaining the divorce. Again, you would have to check your state's law to determine whether or not a foreign, quick divorce would be valid in your state. If your divorce is not considered valid in your state, you could someday run into a problem with bigamy if you remarry.

Beatrice was dating George, a really romantic guy who adored her. She told him her divorce would be final in two weeks and that she wanted to take him out to dinner to celebrate. "Just dinner?" smiled George. "How 'bout you and I get married?" Beatrice was surprised that she found the offer somewhat tempting.

How long after a divorce must a person wait before getting remarried?

In most states, you can get married the day your divorce decree is made final if you want. In the few states that do set a time limit, the period is not very long, except in Oklahoma and Wisconsin, where the parties must wait six months after a divorce is final to remarry. You would have to check the laws in your state to determine whether or not there is any restriction on your remarriage.

STEPCHILDREN

Maggie finally agreed to marry Max. She and her two daughters had already been living with him for nearly a year. He loved the girls, but with the new formalities, he was a little worried about how his responsibilities would change.

What are a person's obligations to stepchildren?

Every parent has a legal responsibility to support his or her own biological children. Thus, stepparents have no independent obligation toward their stepchildren. Of course, if the children are living with you, you will probably end up providing for some of their support, since you will be paying rent or a mortgage, and you will undoubtedly drive them around in a car that you bought for yourself. However, this does not mean that you are legally obligated to provide these things, and if you and your new spouse separate or divorce, you will have no obligation to pay support directly.

The only exception to this is when you essentially "step into the shoes" of the child's other parent and become the sole provider of support. Say, for example, that your new wife was deserted by her ex-husband several years ago. She marries you, and you essentially become her ten-year-old son's parent. You may be obligated to support him if this marriage fails. Generally, the determination will depend on several factors, including

- **whether her first husband provides financial support to the child**
- **the length of your second marriage**
- **the intentions you and your second spouse have about the new family's relationships**

Can a stepparent adopt the children?

Typically, you will not be able to adopt your stepchildren without the consent of their other biological parent. Divorced parents do not surrender their parental rights. However, if your new spouse is a widow or widower, or if the stepchild was abandoned or, in some states, born out of wedlock and without any substantial ties to the other parent, then you probably can adopt. If you choose to do so, you would need to see a lawyer about getting the legal process started. You will have to appear in court before a judge; it is not the kind of thing that you can simply do on your own. (For more on adoption, see page 132.)

ANNULMENT

On a Club Med vacation in Mexico, Bartholomew met Janet. They spent every minute of the week there together, sailing, windsurfing, and dancing under the stars. They were giddy in love, and at the end of the week, Bart proposed. Janet accepted, and they flew directly to Las Vegas and got married. "Nothing like seizing your opportunities," Bart laughed as a group of well-wishers tossed rice at them.

Two months later, Janet was tossing out old newspapers and magazines. She was flipping through the alumni magazine from Bart's college, when she saw the headline: "Bart Goodfriend Back From Italy With New Bride." The woman in the picture was, needless to say, not Janet.

"New bride?" she shouted, shoving the magazine at Bart.

To her great dismay, Janet learned that Bart had indeed been married and that he had never bothered to get a divorce. She immediately began packing her bags.

When can a marriage be annulled?

An annulment is a legal decree, like a divorce, but it states that the marriage was never valid. It has the *legal* effect of wiping out a marriage as though it never existed. It is not the same as religious annulment, which will have its own requirements, and a religious annulment will have no bearing on the legal status of your marriage.

There are two different types of marriages that can be annulled: **void** and **voidable.** A void marriage is one that is void and invalid from its beginning. It is as though the marriage never existed, and it requires no formality to terminate it. Some of the reasons why a marriage would be considered void from its inception include:

- **incest**
- **bigamy**
- **fraud or duress**
- **one party was incapable of consenting because of his or her mental state**
- **impotence at the time of the marriage**

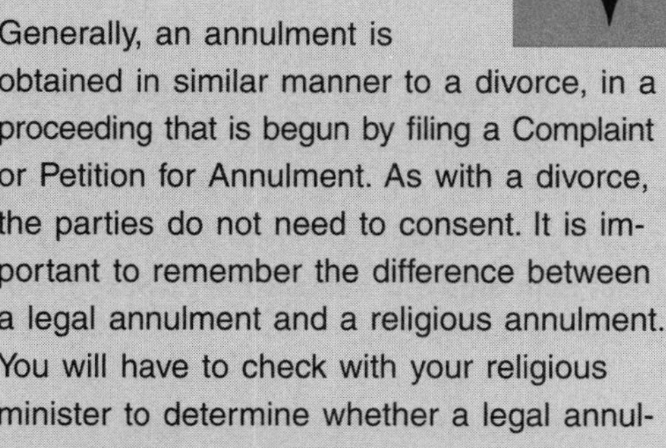

How to Obtain an Annulment

Generally, an annulment is obtained in similar manner to a divorce, in a proceeding that is begun by filing a Complaint or Petition for Annulment. As with a divorce, the parties do not need to consent. It is important to remember the difference between a legal annulment and a religious annulment. You will have to check with your religious minister to determine whether a legal annulment obtained will dissolve your marriage for purposes of being able to remarry in accordance with the laws of your religion.

A voidable marriage, by contrast, is a valid marriage with an inherent flaw. Say, for instance, one of the parties was not yet of legal age to marry. If they never challenge the marriage, it remains a valid marriage. If, however, one or both of them decides to challenge the marriage, and the challenge is found to be valid, then it will be as though the marriage had never taken place. (However, despite the annulment, children will not be made illegitimate.) So, if two minors get married and have children and then twelve years later decide to split up, they can probably have their marriage annulled.

Can a spouse collect alimony when a marriage is annulled?

When a marriage is annulled, it is the same as if it never existed, and therefore alimony traditionally was not available. Most states have changed that harsh rule. Also, your state will determine how property should be distributed after an annulment. Since the obligation to pay child support arises out of being a parent, not out of being married, the noncustodial parent will still owe child support. (For more on child support, see page 181.)

SPLITTING UP IF YOU'RE NOT ACTUALLY MARRIED

Beatrice's friend Elizabeth has lived with Charlie, her "significant other," for fifteen years. Though they never formalized their relationship by getting married, they are in all respects living as a married couple. They have two children, and Elizabeth, an amateur calligrapher, doesn't work. Now they're splitting up.

■ Can a person collect child support and alimony from someone if they were not married?

You certainly will be entitled to receive child support if you are the parent with primary physical custody of the children, since the obligation of child support arises from the biological or adoptive relationship between parent and child and not on any social construct such as marriage. The rules about alimony or distribution of any property, however, vary from state to state. For instance, if you live in one of the few states that still recognize **common-law marriage** (see page 114), then the dissolution of your relationship would probably be treated the same as the dissolution of any other marriage. You might also have prepared for a possible breakup by writing a **living-together contract** (page 113; also see the Case in Point on page 115).

GETTING ARRESTED 13

YOUR BASIC RIGHTS

Max and Beatrice were reminiscing about old times. "D'ya remember the time I got busted by an undercover cop at that Grateful Dead concert? It seems like a different lifetime," said Max, musing over lost youth.

It had been an outdoor concert on a beautiful Sunday afternoon years before, with the mellow crowd swaying in the park as one to Jerry Garcia's voice. Max was so high he hadn't suspected a thing. He lit up another joint, and the next thing he knew, a big man put a big hand on his shoulder and said, "Police. Follow me."

■ What rights do people have when they're accused of a crime?

Several amendments to the U.S. Constitution protect your rights within our country if you are arrested and tried on a criminal charge. These amendments were developed in reaction to abuses by the British government before and during the American Revolution, and the people who wrote our state and federal constitutions included many procedural safeguards to ensure the fairness of criminal prosecutions.

In the U.S. Constitution, the safeguards are part of the amendments that make up the **Bill of Rights,** and they include:

- The Fourth Amendment. It protects you against unwarranted search and seizure of your property or person, and from being arrested without **probable cause** (for a fuller explanation, see page 196).
- The Fifth Amendment. It gives you the right to remain silent during questioning, protecting you against **self-incrimination.** It forbids **double jeopardy** (being tried twice for the same offense; see 196), and it requires the government to provide **due process** — to obey its own laws and apply them fairly to all people within our nation.
- The Sixth Amendment. It gives the accused in criminal cases the right to counsel and to a speedy trial and the right to call witnesses and cross-examine the government's witnesses.
- The Eighth Amendment. It protects citizens against "cruel and unusual" punishment.
- The Fourteenth Amendment. It gives citizens the right to **equal protection under the law,** meaning that the government may not discriminate against any citizen in applying laws.

Defining and fine-tuning the meaning of these amendments has occupied the U.S. Supreme Court since its inception.

■ How are criminal cases different from civil ones?

There are a few major differences. A criminal case is always brought by the local, state, or federal government, represented by the **prosecutor** (sometimes known as the district attorney, state's attorney, or United States attorney) seeking punishment — a fine or imprisonment or both. Civil cases, on the other hand, are usually brought by private parties or corporations seeking to collect money damages.

Second, in a criminal trial, the **defendant,** the person accused of the crime, has a right to testify in his or her own defense, but also, under the Fifth Amendment, a right *not* to testify (see page 215). The decision made by the defendant and his or her attorney about whether or not to testify may be one of the most crucial decisions in a criminal case. However, in a civil case, the defendant can be compelled to testify against his or her will.

The third major difference involves the **burden of proof.** In a civil case, the plaintiff (the person who brings the lawsuit) only has to show by "a preponderance of the evidence" that the facts alleged are true (see page 424). In a criminal case, the prosecution has the much heavier burden of proving that the defendant is guilty "beyond a reasonable doubt" (see page 214).

What Is a Crime?

When a law is violated, a **crime** has been committed. There are different types of crimes, but the main classifications are

- **Petty offenses.** These are minor crimes, generally punishable by a fine or a short jail term. Traffic offenses, disturbing the peace, and minor trespass are some examples.
- **Misdemeanors.** Generally, these are crimes that are punishable by less than one year in jail, such as minor thefts and simple assaults that do not result in substantial bodily injury.
- **Felonies.** These are serious crimes that are punishable by incarceration in a prison rather than a jail. These include rape, murder, robbery, burglary, and arson. (The main difference between a jail and a prison is in the population of inmates in each facility.)

You can't generally claim ignorance of the law as a defense if you are accused of a crime. That's because in order to have a workable criminal justice system it is presumed that everyone knows the law. So if you're driving in a state that requires four-year-olds to be in car seats, you could be charged with a crime (probably a petty offense) if your child was not in one, even if you didn't know the law (although a judge might let you off with just a small fine the first time).

To be convicted of most crimes, it is required that you have had the "intent" to commit the act or bring about the result for which you are accused. That doesn't necessarily mean you had to know the act was illegal. If you intend to shoot a deer, for instance, then you had the intent to poach even if you didn't know that it was not yet hunting season. You are required to know when deer hunting is permitted.

Routine traffic offenses are considered "strict liability" crimes that do not require "intent." A person commits these minor crimes simply by doing that which is forbidden, such as driving seventy miles per hour in a fifty-five-mile-per-hour zone.

Fourth, and perhaps most important: In a criminal trial, once you are acquitted, you can never be tried again for the same crime. The prosecution can't try to overturn your acquittal and can't charge you again for the same crime because the Constitution protects against **double jeopardy.** However, the rule against double jeopardy has one important loophole: If the same set of actions violates both state and federal laws, you can be prosecuted twice — once by state prosecutors and once by federal prosecutors. Say, for example, someone commits a bank robbery. Under state law, that person can be charged with robbery. Whether acquitted or convicted, the same person can also be charged with the federal crime of robbing a federally insured bank. Still, while such double prosecutions are possible, they are extremely rare.

(For more on civil cases, see Chapter 29, SUING AND BEING SUED.)

PROBABLE CAUSE

Max wasn't the only guy pulled in from the concert. But he was one of the few who actually had a joint hanging from his mouth. Many of the others had just been standing peacefully swaying to the music when they were herded away by the police.

Can the police just arrest anyone?

No. The state must be able to demonstrate that the police knew enough at the time of arrest to believe that an offense had been committed and that the defendant likely committed it. In other words, police or prosecutors must show **probable cause** to make an arrest without a **warrant,** which is a judicial authorization for the police to arrest someone. (For more on warrants, see page 210.)

While the law favors arrests made on the basis of a warrant issued by a judge, there are circumstances when it excuses the lack of a warrant. This happens most often when the situation does not give the police time to get a warrant. Thus, a police officer without a warrant can still find probable cause to believe a crime has been committed. If the officer sees the crime committed, or if the officer can later prove that his (or her) observations gave him probable cause to act as he did, then a warrantless arrest can be justified. A hunch that someone is a bad guy is not enough to establish probable cause; the officer must be able to cite concrete details, such as a marijuana cigarette hanging from the suspect's mouth.

If the defendant chooses later to challenge the right of the police officer to arrest him or her, the officer will have to explain (usually at a hearing) how he or she determined that probable cause existed. The judge will decide if there was probable cause to detain and charge the suspect. For serious felonies in most states, this may involve a **preliminary hearing** (see page 208). For a misdemeanor, this may involve only a judge's examination of the police report.

If time and circumstances allow it, the police should obtain a warrant before an arrest. A prosecutor or an officer can go to a judge with evidence that there is probable cause to believe a defendant committed a crime and ask for an arrest **warrant.** For instance, if a witness says she saw Max stash a load of pot in the trunk of his car, the prosecutor (or sometimes the police) could ask a judge to authorize a warrant for Max's arrest. The judge must grant the request if it is shown that it is based on facts showing probable cause rather than on a hunch without any evidence.

CASE IN POINT

Who Was This Guy Miranda?

While the Miranda warnings (see page 199) are considered a cornerstone of our civil liberties, the person after whom they were named was hardly someone most people would consider a hero.

In 1963, Ernesto Miranda, an eighth-grade dropout with a criminal record, had been picked up by Phoenix police and accused of raping and kidnapping a mildly retarded eighteen-year-old woman. After two hours in a police interrogation room Miranda signed a written confession, but he apparently never was told that he had the right to remain silent, to have a lawyer, and to be protected against self-incrimination.

Despite his lawyer's objections, the confession was presented as evidence at Miranda's trial, and he was convicted and sentenced to twenty years. His appeal went all the way to the Supreme Court, where it was joined with three other similar cases. In a landmark ruling issued in 1966, the court established that the accused have the right to remain silent and that prosecutors may not use statements made by defendants while in police custody unless the police have advised them of their rights.

That ruling offered only temporary reprieve to Miranda. He was retried. The second time around, the prosecutors couldn't use the confession, but they did have additional evidence from a former girlfriend of Miranda's who testified that he had told her about the kidnapping and rape. He was convicted again and served eleven years before being paroled in 1972. He was arrested and returned to prison several times after.

Miranda died in 1976 at age thirty-four after being stabbed during an argument in a bar. The police arrested a suspect who chose to remain silent after being read his rights. The suspect was released and no one was ever charged with the killing.

What Is the Basic Procedure in a Criminal Case?

There are several steps, and the time of day and time of week and location and circumstances of the arrest will all affect how long the process takes. And, of course, the procedures vary from state to state, but generally the procedure is as follows:

- A crime is committed.
- A **grand jury** issues an indictment, or a judge issues an arrest **warrant,** or an arrest takes place without a warrant.
- A suspect is arrested and taken to jail for **booking.** A suspect may be arrested and jailed without a warrant, usually for having committed a crime in the presence of an officer, or if an officer has probable cause to believe the person committed a crime.
- Many suspects may be offered immediate release if they pay **stationhouse bail.** People with strong ties to the community (a home, job, family, clean criminal record) may be released without bail (on a judge's order) if they promise to appear later as ordered.
- A suspect is **arraigned,** or formally charged by a judge. Suspect enters a plea of guilty or not guilty.
- If **bail** has not been set yet and if the suspect has not previously been released, bail is now set. The judge also schedules a court date for trial or preliminary hearings.
- In some cases, preliminary hearings or hearings on pretrial motions follow.
- The defendant chooses to be tried by a jury or to be tried before a judge alone, in a **bench or court trial.**
- If the defendant opts for a jury, the selection of jurors follows. Jurors are called from a pool and questioned by both sides — the state and the defense — in a process called **voir dire** (see page 422).
- The trial officially begins with opening arguments by both sides, summarizing the strong points of their cases.

- The prosecution presents its evidence, calling witnesses to the stand and asking them questions. (Asking questions of a witness friendly to your side is called **direct examination.**) The defense may choose to question the witnesses afterward, a process called **cross-examination.** The prosecution may then question on new matters brought up during cross-examination during what is called **redirect examination.** And if the defense follows up, that is **recross-examination.**
- The defense presents its evidence and witnesses. The prosecution cross-examines. The defense asks additional questions on matters brought up during cross-examination, and the prosecution can cross-examine once more on newly raised issues.
- Both sides present their **summations,** or closing arguments.
- The judge gives the **jury charge,** instructions on the law in the case and definitions of the relevant legal concepts. These instructions are often pivotal in the jury's discussions (see page 424).
- The jurors gather privately to deliberate. Most states and the federal government require the jury to be unanimous in its decision. If the jurors cannot reach a verdict, they are declared a **hung jury.** If this happens, the prosecutor may be allowed to retry the case.
- When the jurors do reach a verdict, the jury foreperson will send a note to the judge, and the court will reassemble for the reading of the verdict.
- The verdict is read. If the jury finds the defendant guilty, the judge will set the sentence (except in a few states in which juries set sentences).
- In more serious cases, a judge will often hold **sentencing hearings** and ask for a **presentencing report** from the probation department before setting a sentence.
- The convicted person may appeal the verdict to a higher court (see page 425).

MIRANDA AND SELF-INCRIMINATION

Max had thought the cop was just some joker until he grabbed the joint out of Max's mouth. He never said a word about any rights, but grabbed Max roughly by the hair (it was long in those days), handcuffed him, and pulled him through the crowd. On the way to the station, the officer kept asking questions. "Aren't you supposed to read me my rights?" Max asked.

What is the Miranda warning?

You've probably heard it lots of times on TV crime shows: "You have the right to remain silent. Anything you say can and will be used against you in a court of law. You have the right to speak to an attorney, and to have an attorney present during any questioning. If you cannot afford a lawyer, one will be provided for you at government expense."

That is the Miranda warning, named after a famous case involving a suspect named (what else?) Miranda (see the Case in Point on page 197).

All the statements in the warning are true; however, *it is not necessary for a police officer to recite the magic words in order to arrest you.*

In most situations, the police will give the warning only if you are going to be asked questions; if they interrogate you outside the presence of your lawyer without giving the warning, any answers you give probably cannot be introduced in court as evidence against you. However, the police are allowed to ask routine booking questions such as your name, address, date of birth, and social security number in order to establish your identity, without reading you the Miranda warning. You can also be given a Breathalyzer test without the warning. (See page 30.)

Is an arrest illegal if the police neglect to read the Miranda rights to the suspect?

No. These rights are your protection against *self-incrimination* only, not against being arrested. The only thing the police need before making an arrest is "probable cause" (see page 196) — a sufficient reason, based on facts and observations, to believe you have committed a crime. Police must recite the Miranda rights only when they are about to interrogate a suspect. If they do not, then a judge might later throw out any statements made, although the arrest may still be valid.

THE POLICE INTERROGATION

At the station, another officer did read Max his rights. Then he started quizzing Max about who sold him the pot. "It'll go a lot easier if you cooperate with us. We can make you a good deal here," he said.

Is it wise to cooperate with the police?

If you are arrested, the safest policy is to treat the police with courtesy, *but do not answer any questions unless your lawyer tells you to.* In every case, it's better (from your point of view) to remain silent. Remember that Miranda is a *warning that you have a right not to speak;* it is not a formula that absolves the police from trying to pressure you. However, Miranda was designed to stop police misconduct by allowing suspects to have their representatives — lawyers — present to stop police coercion.

What if the officer tells a person that talking will make things go better?

Don't fall for it. Officers may try to cajole you into talking, or tell you things will go easier for you if you talk, but many people have been convicted by their own mouths in such situations. The police may even offer a deal — promising that if you talk, your punishment will be lighter — but this is generally a ploy, since only the prosecutor has the authority to make such a deal stick. Besides, your lawyer is better trained to negotiate for you.

The Difference Between State and Federal Cases

Although the federal government's reach has extended greatly in the last sixty years, states prosecute the vast majority of crimes, from the most petty to the most heinous. So how is it decided whether a crime is to be tried in state or federal court?

The question is trickier than it looks. It's not just a simple matter of the seriousness of the crime; anyone can be prosecuted in a federal court for littering in a national park, for example. The distinction between federal and state prosecution is important for the defendant. Procedures differ on several points:

- After a federal arrest, you will have a quick initial appearance before a federal magistrate — a court official who is not a full judge — to set bail. In state systems, bail decisions wait until arraignment.
- In federal court, the judge does **voir dire,** or the interviewing of prospective jurors, instead of the lawyers for each side.
- In federal court, judges are allowed to comment on the evidence to the jury just before they go in for deliberation; in most state courts, they are not.
- Unlike most state judges, who have broad discretion in sentencing, federal judges must follow strict sentencing guidelines for felonies.

Officials take a number of factors into consideration in deciding whether a case is state, federal, or both, including:

- Where was the crime committed? If it was in areas under federal control, such as offshore waters, an Indian reservation, a military base, or a national park, the federal government has clear jurisdiction. In many places, however, federal and state powers will have overlapping jurisdictions.
- Is the crime prohibited by a federal statute or administrative rule regulating interstate commerce, foreign commerce, currency, or other activities regulated primarily by the federal government, such as the stock market? Did a suspected criminal flee across state lines? Did the crime interfere with a constitutional right? Were the mails or interstate phone lines used to commit the crime? If yes, there is a strong likelihood that the federal government may take jurisdiction.
- Prosecutorial discretion: What do the federal and state prosecutors want to do? When federal and state criminal jurisdictions overlap, it is up to the prosecutors in each jurisdiction to decide to bring a case. While both may decide to bring separate cases simultaneously, this almost never happens.

■ What does it mean when someone waives Miranda rights?

After a suspect has been read his rights, the police often go on to try to obtain information and a confession, if possible. If the suspect decides to cooperate, he must do so voluntarily. Because he has the right to remain silent, the act of speaking about the case is considered a waiver, or a conscious decision to speak despite those rights.

■ What if a suspect starts talking even when the police have asked no questions?

A suspect who talks freely without being asked any questions has given up his or her Miranda rights — even if the warning wasn't given. Anything you say to the police is "on the record" as soon as you open your mouth. Only when the police ask questions after you are arrested and in custody are they required by law to inform you of your right against self-incrimination.

Again, it all comes down to a pretty simple rule: No matter what happens in the course of being stopped and questioned or arrested, don't answer questions by police without an attorney present. In fact, you probably shouldn't talk to anyone else about the case before consulting with a lawyer.

Can people incriminate themselves after being arrested by talking to others out of earshot of the police?

Yes. Let's say you are thrown into a police van with other suspects and you boast that you did what you're being arrested for. Those people can be called to testify against you, and their evidence can be used to convict you. The same thing applies to any statements you make to a friend or bystander, and it holds true whether or not you've been given the Miranda warning.

Isn't there anyone a person can confide in once he or she has been arrested?

Yes. You may talk to your lawyer and to his or her assistants. In fact, it is crucial that you tell your attorney the full truth in order for him or her to formulate the best defense. Don't try and keep bad news from your lawyer.

There was a time when you could also speak frankly to your spouse, religious adviser, personal doctor, or therapist. Such conversations were considered "privileged," and these people usually could not be compelled to testify against you. Recent changes in the law have restricted these privileges, so the best rule is to discuss your case only with your attorney and follow his or her guidelines before discussing the details with any other people.

GETTING BOOKED

Finally, a guard called Max's name and took him to the booking area of the jail, where other guards asked him a lot of questions about who he was. Then they fingerprinted him.

What is booking?

It's the process in which the details of who you are and why you were arrested are entered into the police records. If this ever happens to you, you'll find it something like registering at a hotel, only much slower and less pleasant. You'll be asked a lot of questions about your identity — it may remind you of movie scenes in which prisoners of war are asked for "name, rank, and serial number" — and you may be fingerprinted.

The police don't need to read you the Miranda warnings before asking questions about your identity, and you should comply with the booking procedures. The questions are not designed to incriminate you, and establishing your identity will be necessary in order to be released on bail. Your personal property, including your money, will be inventoried, put into a locker or other storage, and returned when you are released. If you need medical attention, or if you have prescription medication that you must take, such as an asthma inhaler, you should tell the jailers during the booking procedure. They don't have to let you keep any medication, but they may send you to a doctor or nurse to administer what you need.

After booking, you'll probably be put into a cell, awaiting an appearance before a judge or magistrate, and you'll probably be given the opportunity to make a phone call. If you are arrested late at night or on a weekend, the process is likely to move more slowly.

YOUR RIGHT TO A PHONE CALL

After his arrest Max sat in a holding cell for two hours with a bunch of scary-looking guys. Guards passed the cell frequently, but no one would stop and tell him what was going on. From the moment he'd been taken into custody, Max was telling everyone that he had the "constitutional right to a phone call." The other guys in his cell just looked at him like he was crazy.

Doesn't the Constitution give people the right to make a phone call after being arrested?

No. There is no stated constitutional right to make a phone call from jail. In every state, you have the basic constitutional right to an attorney, which means a right to an attorney before questioning by police (if you wish) and before and at every court appearance; it doesn't mean you have a right to call an attorney from jail as soon as you want to do so. Generally speaking, most places will eventually allow you to make a phone call to a lawyer after you are arrested. If you don't know any lawyers to call, yet you want a private lawyer to represent you, call a friend or relative and ask him or her to find one for you. (For more on finding a lawyer, see Chapter 30, FINDING AND USING A LAWYER.)

Rules about phone access vary from state to state. California law, for example, requires that a person be given the opportunity to make three completed phone calls within three hours of an arrest. In the absence of state laws, authorities have no obligation to let you make calls to your friends or family, but they generally will, though usually only after they are done with the booking process. With whatever call you are given, let family or friends know where you are so that they can arrange bail and contact an attorney. Remember, if you cannot afford an attorney, one will be appointed for you but only after you get to court (see next page).

Once bail is set, police departments usually allow well-behaved prisoners to make several phone calls to arrange bail. Often permission hinges on the prisoner's attitude and actions while in custody. Act violently, irrationally, or rudely, and you may not get to make any phone calls to arrange bail. The best advice is to remain quiet and, once the booking is over, politely ask if you can make a phone call in order to contact a friend or family member.

Also, you'll probably have to call collect, which can make it difficult to leave a message on an answering machine. And jail telephones often don't accept telephone credit card numbers because of possible misuse by prisoners.

Are phone conversations in jail completely private?

No. It is possible that any calls you make from jail are being taped. It is important to remember that once you are arrested you have few privacy rights. The authorities frequently — and legally — listen in on conversations held over jail telephones. The only type of conversation that is "privileged," meaning that it cannot be used against you, is one between you and your attorney. Unless you are talking to your attorney, bugging is legal even without a beep to tell you the conversation is being recorded. Even if you are talking to your attorney, the call may be recorded unless you specifically inform a guard that you are making a "legal call" that should not be recorded. In general, you should be very careful what you say over the jail telephone even if you're talking to your lawyer. If possible, ask that your lawyer come to the jail to speak to you, rather than do so over the phone. Also remember: If you call from a phone that lacks privacy, whatever is overheard can be used against you. Don't talk about your case — just get the word out where you are and the amount of bail you need to get out of jail and work on your defense.

Does the State Have to Get Me a Lawyer?

It depends. You have the right to an appointed counsel only if:

- **you are charged with a felony — a serious crime for which the penalty may be more than a year in state prison, and**
- **you can show you are too poor to afford one.**

In most states, you may be required to make a financial disclosure in order to prove your **indigence** (lack of funds).

If you are indigent and charged with a **misdemeanor** — a crime for which the maximum sentence is less than a year or a crime for which you may be sentenced only to jail, not prison — you will be assigned a free lawyer *only* if the prosecutor is seeking a jail term. If the prosecutor or the judge declares beforehand that you will receive only a fine and not be imprisoned, you lose the federal constitutional right to appointed counsel.

APPEARING IN COURT

To his dismay, Max spent the night in jail. "There were a lot of drunks. I'll never forget that smell," he later told Beatrice, who had lost him in the crowd at the concert and then worried all night about where he was. Finally, the guard came in and told him it was his turn to go to court.

■ What happens at an arraignment?

You appear in court before a judge, the charges against you are read, if you cannot afford a lawyer one is appointed, and your plea is entered. Generally, you must be brought before a judge for arraignment within twenty-four to forty-eight hours after arrest. The exact time limit varies from state to state, although the U.S. Supreme Court now requires that if you were arrested without a previously issued warrant, you must be brought before a judge within forty-eight hours so that a judge may determine whether there was **probable cause** to arrest you (see page 196).

GETTING COUNSEL

At the arraignment, the judge, Solomon Wiseman, told a haggard-looking Max that he was charged with marijuana possession, a misdemeanor. The judge said he had read the police report and found that there was probable cause to hold Max on the charge. He then asked if Max had a lawyer or any money to hire one. "No," sighed Max.

■ Does a person accused of a crime have the right to a lawyer?

Yes, but that doesn't mean the government always has to pick up the tab. If, like Max, you can't afford an attorney, the judge may appoint one to represent you — either a **public defender,** who works for a state or local agency, or a private attorney paid a minimal fee by the state. To qualify for court-appointed counsel you must be too poor to hire your own *and* the charges against you must carry a potential jail term (see the box opposite). There is no federal constitutional right to counsel for **infractions** (sometimes called "violations"), minor offenses (often traffic tickets) that are punishable only by a fine.

When Max heard that the judge was about to assign him a public defender, he asked to know if he had any say in the matter. What if he didn't trust the person?

■ Can a person object to the choice of a public defender?

You generally have no right to choose what lawyer the court will appoint for you. Public defenders are often excellent attorneys, with a tremendous breadth of experience and expertise in criminal law. However, they may have much heavier caseloads, and consequently may have less time to spend on your case than a private attorney.

If the public defender is already representing another defendant in the same case, or if there is no public defender office in your locality, the judge may need to appoint a private attorney paid by the state. However, such attorneys are paid much less for appointed cases than for their private clients. While some extraordinarily dedicated attorneys try to devote as much time to their appointed clients as to their private clients, in many localities the state pays so little that it is impossible for lawyers to spend as much time on appointed cases as they would like. In criminal cases, the money defendants pay for private counsel pays for a variety of services, including time put into it by the lawyer's investigative staff and legal assistants, and any expert witnesses that might be hired.

Max, feeling out of control, decided to take action. "Look," he asked the judge, "how about I just represent myself?" Wiseman gave him a weary look.

■ Does a person have the right to represent himself in a criminal case?

Yes. Anyone may represent himself in court; doing so is known as **pro se** representation. But it is

CASE IN POINT

How Competent Does a Lawyer Have to Be?

An issue that often comes up during the appeal of a criminal conviction is whether or not the defendant received "effective assistance" from his or her lawyer. If the defendant can show that the trial's undesired outcome — a conviction — probably resulted from the attorney's incompetence, the conviction can be overturned. To make such a showing can be a big hurdle, however. Consider the excerpts from the following cases in which appellate courts *refused* to reverse convictions:

- "Although a defense counsel's sleeping during the course of a trial is reprehensible . . . the defendant was provided with meaningful representation." In addition, the court-appointed lawyer had solicited and accepted $5,000 from the defendant's mother to "help him work harder on the case." Nevertheless, the court ruled that "proof of defense counsel's fraudulent, criminal, and unethical conduct does not, per se, establish violation of constitutional right to counsel." *People v. Tippins,* 1991, New York.
- In a case where the defense lawyer had admitted using heroin and cocaine throughout the trial, the court rejected the defendant's appeal, noting that proof of a defense counsel's drug addiction does not in itself amount to a violation of constitutional right to effective counsel. *People v. Badia,* 1990, New York.
- In the appeal of a death-penalty conviction, a court ruled that the "murder defendant was not deprived of effective assistance of counsel, though counsel was alcoholic." The court-appointed lawyer in this case was found to have consumed large amounts of alcohol each day of the trial — in the morning, during court recesses, and throughout the evening. He also was arrested during jury selection for driving to the courthouse with a .27 blood alcohol content, and he ultimately died of alcohol-related diseases. The defendant's conviction was upheld, though the death penalty sentence was overturned for other reasons. *People v. Garrison,* 1989, California.
- "Counsel's . . . seeming indifference to defendant's attire . . . [though] defendant was wearing same sweatshirt and footwear in court which he wore on day of crime, did not constitute ineffective assistance." *People v. Murphy,* 1983, New York.

The following are excerpts from cases in which appellate courts decided that the defense counsel *was* incompetent enough to require a reversal:

- A defense counsel's closing argument that admitted a client's guilt without the client's consent and argued that "permissive society in general, and television and rock music in particular, produced a nihilistic attitude in young people so that society should be held responsible" for defendant's conduct, constituted prejudicial ineffective assistance of counsel. *People v. Diggs,* 1986, California.
- A defendant in a narcotics case was found to have received ineffective assistance of counsel because the "counsel was himself under indictment on unrelated cocaine charges and repeatedly informed prospective jurors of this fact." *People v. Barret,* 1988, New York.

almost impossible for a nonlawyer to master the complexities of the criminal justice system. The old saying that "he who represents himself has a fool for a lawyer and an ass for a client" is often true. Many people brashly hope they will be able to save money and beat the odds, only to find that they are hopelessly lost amid the proceedings of the court. All in all, it's far better to rely on a court-appointed lawyer if you qualify for one.

■ If a person can afford a lawyer, are there any restrictions on whom he or she may choose?

No. You have the right to hire any licensed attorney that you choose for any crime with which you may be charged. Any lawyer can take a criminal case — but most shouldn't. Try to screen names you are considering and search for someone with experience in criminal defense.

GUILTY OR NOT GUILTY? A CRUCIAL CHOICE

Max decided not to represent himself, and he was appointed a public defender, Mary Goodheart. She took him aside during the arraignment and asked a lot of questions about the circumstances of the arrest, his job, and past criminal history (of which there was none). "Okay," she said. "I'll enter a not guilty plea and try to get your bail reduced."

"The joint was hanging out of my mouth," said Max. "Don't I have to plead guilty?"

■ How does a person decide which way to plead?

That's a crucial decision you and your attorney make. At the arraignment, the judge will ask you (or your lawyer) to enter a plea. If you plead not guilty, then the judge will set your next court date. If you refuse to enter a plea or ask for more time to consult a lawyer, the judge will enter a not guilty plea on your behalf.

If you plead guilty, you are admitting that you committed the crime. A guilty plea, even to a small crime, is an extremely serious matter. If you plead guilty, you are convicted without a trial, and you may be sentenced and sent to jail on the spot. Generally, you should plead guilty only if your lawyer advises you to do so as the condition of a **plea bargain,** in which you agree to plead guilty in exchange for an oral promise of a lower sentence or other concession (see page 212).

If you plead guilty, the judge will question you carefully to be certain that you understand the consequences of the decision and that you're doing it voluntarily. If you don't consult an attorney before this important step, you probably will be passing up the opportunity to plea-bargain, and you may receive a significantly heavier sentence.

■ Can a person change a not guilty plea to guilty?

Yes. A guilty plea is an admission of the crime, and you are allowed to admit your guilt at any stage of a criminal case, so long as your plea is voluntary. One of the chief reasons lawyers advise clients to enter not guilty pleas is to gain time to study the facts and engage in plea negotiations with the prosecutor. There are many reasons defense lawyers can use to convince a prosecutor to plea-bargain. For example, if the evidence in the hands of the prosecution is weak, the defense lawyer may be able to convince the prosecutor to lessen the charges or sentence. Whether to accept a plea bargain or go to trial is a decision that depends on the facts of each particular case. Generally, the more a defense attorney can exploit weaknesses in the prosecution's case, the more opportunity there will be to seek a better bargain.

■ Can a person change a guilty plea to not guilty?

Generally not. A guilty plea amounts to a confession. There are rare cases when a guilty plea may be set aside because it was not made voluntarily, and therefore the defendant's constitutional rights were violated. (See also "Plea Bargains" on page 212.) The judge is required to closely question a defendant to be sure she knows all her rights and understands that she is waiving them by pleading guilty. Also, the judge must be convinced that the

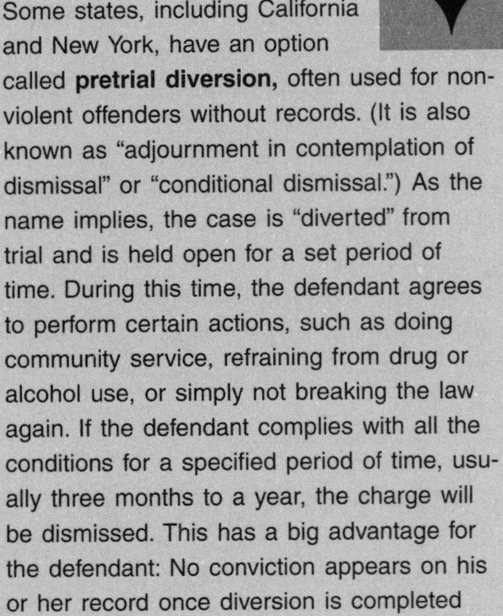
Pretrial Diversion

Some states, including California and New York, have an option called **pretrial diversion,** often used for non-violent offenders without records. (It is also known as "adjournment in contemplation of dismissal" or "conditional dismissal.") As the name implies, the case is "diverted" from trial and is held open for a set period of time. During this time, the defendant agrees to perform certain actions, such as doing community service, refraining from drug or alcohol use, or simply not breaking the law again. If the defendant complies with all the conditions for a specified period of time, usually three months to a year, the charge will be dismissed. This has a big advantage for the defendant: No conviction appears on his or her record once diversion is completed successfully.

defendant is voluntarily entering the plea and is not doing so because of coercion or extortion.

What is a plea of nolo contendere, or "no contest"?

That means you don't intend to fight the charges, but you don't admit them, either — so it is not quite the same as a confession. Some states and the federal government allow for no-contest pleas only under certain circumstances. *Such a plea is the same as a guilty plea,* in that it will result in conviction and sentencing. The only advantage of such a plea comes further down the road: If a defendant gets sued later for damages in a civil court by a victim, a nolo plea cannot be used as evidence in a civil suit. If there is a guilty plea, on the other hand, a victim may introduce it as evidence that a defendant committed the crime. The advantages of a no-contest plea are mostly mythical. You will be treated as if you pleaded guilty.

BAIL

Max wasn't the only person close to Beatrice with a crime story. When her brother Bart was nineteen, he had been picked up for driving the getaway car during the armed robbery of a convenience store. The police had called his parents in the middle of the night. At the station, they found a grim sergeant who told them that Bart had played a key role in helping his friend Ted rob a Handy Dandy store of $300. While Bart waited in the car, Ted had held a gun to the head of the clerk's girlfriend and threatened to kill her. The clerk pulled a silent alarm, and the police caught Bart and Ted less than a mile from the store.

"I didn't know what Ted was going to do, Mom, I swear on the Bible," said a pale-faced Bart. "I didn't even know he had a gun. You've got to believe me."

Gordon and Grace were livid, but said nothing. Bart's tongue-lashing would come later. Instead, they went to talk to the officer on duty to see if they could take Bart home.

Is it possible to get out on bail before seeing a judge?

Sometimes. Bail is money a defendant pays as a guarantee that he or she will show up in court at a later date. Many defendants are allowed to pay bail before they ever see a judge, obtaining release much sooner, sometimes within hours of being arrested. This kind of arrangement is known as **stationhouse bail,** and in most places it's offered for misdemeanors and most felonies. If the defendant can pay the amount set by a **bail schedule** for the charge, then he or she can leave before appearing before a judge. If he or she fails to show up for a court appearance, the stationhouse bail is forfeited — which means the state gets to keep the money.

Note: Most large metropolitan areas have a bail schedule that sets the amount of bail based on what a person is charged with. For instance, if you're charged with armed robbery, the schedule might set the bail at $25,000. If you are able to pay the set amount, you could then be released even before seeing a judge. However, it may be in your interest to wait to appear before a judge (usually it shouldn't take more than twenty-four hours), because a judge may reduce the amount of bail you have to pay.

How does a judge set bail?

There are no set rules. Sometimes, especially in large cities, a defendant may be interviewed before arraignment by a representative of a pretrial release project — an agency that will try to verify your ties to the community and advise the court whether you are a good risk to be released on **personal recognizance,** or PR (sometimes called OR, or own recognizance). If you qualify for PR, you will be released on your signed promise to appear, without having to pay any money to the court.

Both the defense and the prosecution (and perhaps the pretrial release project) may make recommendations as to how high your bail should be. Generally, the prosecution will try to get the judge to set the highest bail commensurate with the crime. Sometimes, the court may attach conditions to your release on bail or PR, such as requiring you to remain in the state until trial.

When can a judge deny bail?

Certain offenses, like murder, are so serious that the court may deny bail, though even in some murder cases a suspect will be granted bail. In addition, many states and the federal courts allow the judge to deny bail to a person charged with a violent crime or a crime that carries a severe penalty if the judge believes there is a serious risk that the person will flee or be a threat to the safety of the community.

The right to obtain a reasonable bail, and thereby be released from jail pending a trial, is an important one. Defense lawyers will fight hard to obtain bail because it is much easier to defend a criminal case if you are out of jail and more able to assist in preparing your defense.

Jumping Bail

Bart pleaded not guilty, and the judge set bail at $5,000, which his parents promptly paid (seriously draining their savings account). Given the crime, the bail was fairly low, because Bart's lawyer showed he had strong ties to his family, school, and job and was highly unlikely to skip town.

What happens if a person doesn't come back to court after paying bail?

If you pay bail, you will be released and given a court date for your next appearance. If you fail to show up, the amount you posted for bail will be forfeited and a warrant will be issued for your arrest. If you skip out on bail and are rearrested, it will be harder, perhaps even impossible, to get out on bail a second time. If you're offered a second chance at bail, it will be for a much higher amount.

If a person pays bail, is the money ever returned?

Yes, the court will refund the money at the end of the case *as long as you made each required court appearance.* If you owe money for a fine and you yourself posted the bail, courts in some states may take the fine and court costs out of your bail money. However, if someone else posted the bail, he is generally entitled to a full refund upon completion of the case if you made your appearances, even if you owe a fine or are given a sentence to serve. Of course, if you don't show up for court, the money will not be returned, no matter who paid it.

What happens if a person can't afford bail?

Many states allow bail to be posted by a bail bondsman, which can be an expensive way to get out of jail. Bondsmen charge a *nonrefundable* premium of 10 to 15 percent of the amount of the bond, which they will keep as payment for the service. If your bail is $5,000, your bail premium will be $500 to $750, and no matter how the case turns out, you will never get this bail premium back. You may also have to put up property, such as your house, car, or bank account, as a guarantee in case you skip bail. If you do skip out, the bail bondsmen may pay bounty hunters to find you and return you to the court to make good their financial loss. They may be even more persistent in trying to find you than the police would be.

Many jails post the numbers of local bondsmen by the phones. If a bondsman decides that you are likely to show up at the appointed court date, he or she will post the bond for you, promising to pay the full amount of your bail to the court if you don't show up.

PRELIMINARY HEARINGS AND GRAND JURIES

Son, you are in big trouble," Gordon told Bart when they finally got home.

"Gee thanks, Dad. I didn't notice."

"Cut it out, you two," ordered Christine, the family's lawyer and next-door neighbor, who was representing Bart. "We've got serious business to tend to."

"Yeah," said Bart. "When does the trial start?"

"We've got a long way to go before that," said Christine. "If we're lucky, there may never be a trial."

■ What's the next step after the arraignment?

The procedure varies from state to state and also depends on whether you're charged with a misdemeanor or a felony (see page 196). If you are accused of a misdemeanor, the prosecution just has to file a sworn statement with the court charging you with the crime. If you are accused of a felony, the prosecution has to convince either a judge or a **grand jury** that there is probable cause that a crime was committed and that you committed it.

■ What is a grand jury?

It's a group of from sixteen to twenty-three citizens, chosen from voter registration lists, driver's license applications, and other lists used to call smaller trial juries. The main purpose of a grand jury in a criminal case is to determine whether probable cause exists to prosecute a suspect. The prosecutor will present evidence and witnesses, and if the grand jury finds there is probable cause that a felony was committed by the defendant, it will issue an **indictment,** a formal accusation.

A grand jury is a secret and one-sided proceeding. A defendant has no right to be present, has no right to testify, and has no right to have his or her side of the story explained to the grand jurors. If a suspect is called as a witness, which sometimes happens, he or she has no right to counsel. Any witness or defendant does have the right to have a lawyer present during testimony (or waiting outside the grand jury room), but only as an observer, not as an advocate who can make objections to the proceeding.

If you receive a **subpoena,** a judicial order compelling you to testify or produce documents, you must comply or face being jailed or fined for **contempt of court.** If you are served with a subpoena, you should consult an attorney immediately. If the subpoena is defective in some way (you aren't the party named in it, for example) or if it is not sufficiently relevant to the grand jury's investigation, the attorney may be able to get it **quashed,** or made invalid, and prevent you from testifying. An attorney can also explain your Fifth Amendment rights not to answer questions before the grand jury that might incriminate you.

You might still be forced to testify if the prosecutor offers you **immunity** — a promise to partially or fully protect you from prosecution if you testify. This is an extremely complicated and technical area of law, and you shouldn't make any such deal to testify without the assistance of a qualified criminal defense attorney.

■ What is a preliminary hearing?

Some states don't bother with grand juries, substituting a **preliminary hearing,** in which the prosecutor presents evidence to the judge in an attempt to show that there is probable cause that you committed a crime. If the judge is convinced there is probable cause to charge you with a crime, the prosecution proceeds to the next phase. If the judge is not convinced that probable cause exists, the charges will be dropped.

You do have the right to present evidence at a preliminary hearing, but the strict rules of evidence used at trials don't apply at these hearings. So either side can introduce police reports and statements made out of court that would be inadmissible during a trial. (See "Evidence" on page 423.) At this stage, the prosecution needs to convince the judge only that there is probable cause to believe a suspect committed the crime charged in order to justify the continued prosecution. If the judge dismisses the case at this point, many states allow the prosecutor to go to a grand jury and seek an indictment. In some states, like New York, all felonies are presented to a grand jury for indictment. The preliminary hearing is not held. In other states, like Colorado, the grand jury is seldom used and almost all cases go through preliminary hearings.

If you are charged with a *federal* felony, the case *must* go to a grand jury.

CASE IN POINT

The Knock on the Door (or Tent Flap)

The law generally grants people a higher level of protection from searches and seizures in their homes than in their cars, and courts tend to insist that police get a warrant before searching a home. For example, in a 1993 Wisconsin case, a police unit targeted Dean Johnston's house because they'd heard he was having illegal beer parties for college students. Without obtaining a warrant, an undercover team attended a party at Johnston's home, bought beer with marked bills, and then made arrests. Johnston was convicted of selling and giving away alcoholic beverages to underage persons.

In his appeal Johnston argued that the warrantless search of his home violated his Fourth Amendment right to privacy. A Wisconsin state appeals court agreed, ruling that the officers had ample time to telephone or radio in a request for a warrant during the course of the party and should have done so.

Of course, if the courts are going to give more protection to homes because people have the greatest expectation of privacy there, the courts have to define what constitutes "a home." This isn't as easy as it sounds, especially when the home is made of nylon. In a case heard by the U.S. Court of Appeals for the Ninth Circuit, campers at a state campground called police in the middle of the night to complain about noise and threats made by camper Kenneth Gooch. One man said that Gooch had fired a shot at him and tried to stick his head into the fire.

Without an arrest warrant, the cops woke Gooch, ordered him out of the tent, and arrested him. They then searched the tent and found a loaded gun. Because Gooch had a previous felony conviction, he was convicted of being a felon with a gun.

Gooch appealed, arguing that the search was illegal because the tent was his home, and his home had been invaded without a warrant. He asserted that at the time of the arrest he had no other residence and had been living in his tent. The appeals court agreed and overturned his conviction in 1993, ruling that a tent at a campsite was like a residence and that officers should have obtained a warrant before searching it.

On the other hand, in a case decided just four months before *Gooch,* the U.S. Court of Appeals for the Tenth Circuit upheld the warrantless arrest of a drug dealer in a motel room, ruling that the police had probable cause to believe the defendant had committed a crime and to fear he might skip town. The court ruled that a motel room is not a home, and thus the same standard of privacy does not apply.

PRETRIAL MOTIONS

Bart was pleading with his lawyer, Christine: "You say you've got a lot of pretrial emotions to deal with? How do you think I feel?"

"Slow down, Bart," she insisted. "*Motions.* Not emotions. Pretrial motions — to help us win the case."

"Oh," murmured Bart, confused and a little embarrassed.

■ What is a pretrial motion?

Whenever a lawyer wants a judge to issue a ruling or order on a legal matter, that request is made through a **motion.** Motions may be brought by either side. One of the most important motions a defense lawyer makes is a motion to suppress evidence. Say you made a statement to the police or they found a weapon in the back of your closet. Your lawyer may argue that there is some legal reason why that evidence cannot be presented at the trial. The prosecutor, of course, will argue that the evidence should be admitted. Other typical pretrial motions include

- **requests that the prosecution disclose additional evidence (the defense has a right to any evidence controlled by the prosecution that might tend to help the defense case)**
- **requests to separate one person's trial from that of any co-defendants**
- **requests to learn the names and statements of the witnesses against you**
- **requests to move the location of the trial**

WARRANTS, SEARCHES, AND SEIZURES

Bart should have known better than to hang around with Ted. Only a week before the Handy Dandy escapade, they'd been hanging out at Ted's apartment when two detectives knocked on the door. "We'd like to talk to you about some jewelry that's missing from your girlfriend's apartment," one of the cops told Ted.

"You got a warrant?" asked Ted.

"We can get one easily enough," said the detective.

"Buzz off," sneered Ted, slamming the door.

"Hey," said Bart. "Why'd you do that?"

■ What is a warrant?

A police search — particularly of your home — is generally valid only if the police have first obtained judicial permission, known as a **warrant.** They usually get this by telephoning a judge or appearing before him and giving a sworn statement explaining what facts have led them to believe that evidence of a crime may be found in your home (or other place they want to search). The judge may issue the warrant only if he or she is convinced that the facts offered by the police amount to **probable cause** — a reasonable belief that you have committed a crime or that the search will turn up evidence of a crime (see the box opposite).

■ Do the police always need a warrant to conduct a search?

No. There are many exceptions to the warrant requirement, and this is currently one of the most confused and unsettled areas of American law, so it is important to see a criminal lawyer if you get searched and charged with a crime (see Chapter 30, FINDING AND USING A LAWYER).

■ What happens if the police get a warrant to search a person's boat, but instead they come and search her house?

The search is illegal. The warrant gives the police the right to search only the place or places it specifies and for the items it specifies. If you can prove that a search was illegal, any evidence it yielded cannot be used against you in court. Your attorney will bring this to the attention of the judge through a **motion to suppress evidence.** You may also be able to sue the police for damages for trespassing, but that is very time-consuming, expensive, and seldom worth the effort.

Do the Police Have to Have a Warrant?

Not always. There are many situations in which a warrant may not be required. Here are some of them:

- A person voluntarily **consents** to a search.
- The evidence is in **plain view.** If the officers have a legal right to be where they are (standing on the roadside looking in your car window, for instance) and they see an illegal item (drugs or a weapon) in plain view, they may seize the item and you can be charged.
- There are **exigent circumstances,** or emergency conditions. The police may search without a warrant when evidence is in danger of being destroyed (for instance, when they believe people inside a house are flushing drugs down the toilet). They may also search and seize when they are in **hot pursuit.** For example, an officer chasing a suspect may barge into a home if he just saw the suspect enter it.
- The search is limited to the interior of a vehicle. This is called **vehicle exception.** Generally, you have fewer rights while driving your automobile than you do in your home, and the Supreme Court has begun to widen rules to legalize many searches of autos. Some situations require the permission of the driver, but not all (see page 27). As is true of other search situations, if the officer lacks a warrant but requests your permission to search, you are within your rights to refuse. Your refusal cannot be used as the grounds to get a search warrant.
- You are being arrested. The police can search your person and any areas more or less within your reach if you are being legally arrested. But remember: The police need probable cause *before* they arrest you, and can't search you until they have it. Even then, the search is supposed to be related to the type of crime being investigated. So if you're arrested for shoplifting, the police can't search your car for drugs. They can, however, do a "body search" for security purposes, and if that search reveals drugs, then it's a legitimate seizure.

Are there limits to where the police can look in a house even if they have a warrant?

Yes. They are allowed to search only areas that might contain the evidence they are looking for and that are specified in the warrant. For example, if the police suspect you have hidden in your house a rifle that was used in a crime, they will attempt to get a warrant to search those areas where a rifle can be hidden. That usually means that they can look under beds, in closets, or behind doors. It will not authorize them to look into your bedroom drawers or kitchen cabinets for the rifle, unless there is the possibility it would fit into one of those areas.

Can the police break down a door to enter an apartment or house?

Generally, no. The police cannot simply break down the door to gain entrance into your home. Every person has a constitutionally protected right to privacy in his or her home. If the police have a warrant, they are supposed to knock and announce themselves first. However, there are many exceptions to this rule; for example, if they have a reasonable fear for their own safety, or if evidence, such as drugs or gambling records, might be destroyed if they announced themselves, they can break down the door and come in without warning.

If the police come to your home just to ask questions, you can simply close the door and refuse to talk, or refer them to your lawyer. This is your right in every state. If they want to enter, they have to get a warrant. If they already have a warrant and you shut the door on them, they can legally break in. So long as the police have a search warrant, they do not need your permission to enter or search your premises. Usually, they must read the warrant to you and leave you a copy. They must also leave you with a copy of the list of items they have seized during the search.

For more on getting stopped by the police when you are driving, see page 27.

Your Rights at the Airport

Blossom and her friend Carlos decided to go on a super-bargain package trip to Cozumel. When they walked through the airport on the way to the gate, an airport policeman stopped Carlos and frisked him, asked him how much money he was carrying, and released him, telling him he was free to go.

They were both outraged. Blossom ran after the officer and demanded to know why only Carlos was searched. She was stunned to hear that her friend, a dark young Argentinian dressed in jeans and sandals, fit the profile of a drug courier.

■ Can a person be singled out from a crowd at an airport and searched?

Yes, but only under certain circumstances. You can't arbitrarily be stopped and *searched.* So even at an airport, a police officer can't just pull you aside and ask you to empty your pockets. But at airports and other places, a police officer can stop and *question* you, though it's your choice whether or not to answer. You should, however, provide your name and, if asked, appropriate identification, such as a driver's license.

Most stops at airports involve people suspected of drug crimes. Law enforcement agencies have developed profiles of suspected drug dealers. For example, police are suspicious of people who buy one-way tickets with cash and travel with little luggage. An officer who stops you for questioning may do a gentle "pat-down" if he or she has good reason to suspect you are about to commit a crime and can justify the belief that you are carrying a weapon. The pat-down is not considered an actual search, but if it reveals something that feels like a weapon, the officer may then have probable cause to proceed with a more in-depth search. In some limited situations, the officer may proceed to search you if the pat-down reveals something that feels like drugs.

Note: When you are entering or leaving the country, customs and immigration officials have much wider powers of inspection than do the domestic police, and they may search you or your possessions even without probable cause. Also, when traveling via air, you and your bags usually will pass through machines screening for concealed weapons. You have consented to these searches by going through the security checkpoint. If you do not want to have your bags searched, do not go through the checkpoint. Of course, that would mean forgoing your flight.

PLEA BARGAINS

"I've got good news," the public defender told Max. The prosecutor had agreed that Max could plead guilty to disorderly conduct, a less severe misdemeanor than marijuana possession. That meant Max wouldn't have a drug crime on his record and his punishment would be much less severe. If Max rejected the deal, the public defender said, the case would go on to trial and the outcome could very well be less desirable.

■ Do all cases get resolved through a plea bargain?

No, but the vast majority do. A plea bargain is an agreement in which the defendant pleads guilty, and in return the charge or sentence is usually reduced. In state cases, plea bargains are often oral agreements only, not written, but it is very rare that they are not honored. Federal cases usually require agreements to be in writing. Over 90 percent of criminal cases are settled through plea bargaining, saving the need for many expensive and time-consuming jury trials.

One of a defense lawyer's jobs is to get the best possible deal. He or she may have several things to offer to convince the prosecutor to give you a reduced sentence. For example, your lawyer can argue that

- **"justice requires" that you be allowed to plead to a lesser charge if, for example, the results would be too harsh or inequitable with the greater charge**
- **the prosecution will have trouble proving its case**
- **the case is not worth the trouble of taking to trial on a crowded court calendar**
- **you are willing to cooperate as a witness**

Judges, faced with the need to move cases as fast as possible through overcrowded courtrooms, will often encourage the two sides to come to terms.

THE TRIAL

Compared to Max, Bart had a far more serious set of choices to make. He faced a felony charge and jail time, not a misdemeanor and a fine. Bart met with his lawyer, Christine, to discuss the options: He could go to trial and take his chances, or he could plea-bargain for a lighter sentence. But that meant admitting guilt, and Bart didn't like that. Besides, he thought he had a good defense: He didn't know the car was stolen, since Ted had told him it was borrowed from his uncle.

Still, the thought of leaving his fate to a jury scared him.

Are all criminal cases tried before a jury?

No. There are two forms of trials: those before a jury and those before a judge, known as "bench trials" or "court trials." In a trial without a jury, a judge hears the case alone and rules from his or her raised desk, known as the bench. The process is usually faster and cheaper than a jury trial. In general, defendants are better off with a trial by a jury than a judge. Some defendants waive a jury trial because the main issue in their case may be very technical and best understood by a judge. Or a defendant may fear that jurors would be too prejudiced because of the type of crime or adverse publicity surrounding it. The right to a jury trial is an important constitutional right and should not be waived without a very good reason.

A trial with a jury is still held before a judge, but it's up to the jury to make a ruling about the facts of the case.

CASE IN POINT

Search and Seizure Law: The "Stop and Frisk"

Terry v. Ohio is an important Supreme Court decision, issued in 1968, upholding the right of police, acting with no warrant, to stop and "pat down" a suspect — without going into his pockets or searching his car. They may then either arrest or release him.

In the criminal case that led to this ruling, Ohio police saw a suspicious man who looked as though he was "casing" a store. The police seized the man, patted him down, and found illegal guns on him. He was charged with possession of illegal weapons and convicted.

The conviction was appealed on the grounds that the police did not have a warrant or probable cause (see page 210) to search him, just suspicion. It went all the way to the U.S. Supreme Court, which ruled in 1968 that an officer can pat you down if he has a "reasonably articulable suspicion" that you might be carrying drugs or weapons. This means that the officer has to be able to explain clearly to a court why he thought you might be carrying drugs or weapons.

Remember, though, that the police would still need probable cause to search your clothing, pockets, or car. In other words, *Terry* allows an officer to do *only* a "stop and frisk."

Who determines whether a trial will be before a judge alone, or a jury and judge?

Generally, the choice is up to the criminal defendant, though some jurisdictions require the prosecutor's consent as well. While the defendant always has the right to a jury trial for all felonies and for misdemeanors carrying a sentence of six months or more, he or she may choose the quicker route of a bench trial, especially with minor crimes.

A bench trial is faster because jurors don't have to be picked, and the judge's deliberations are usually shorter. That makes it much cheaper both for the state and for the defendant, whose lawyer will spend far less time in court on the case.

A word of caution: All in all, opting for a bench trial is not a good idea, because social science research has shown that a jury is more than twice as likely to acquit as a judge. A few states allow anyone convicted by a judge to get a second chance before a jury, called a "trial de novo." This is rare, however. So don't waive a jury on the assumption that you can get a second trial if you don't like the results of the first one.

For more details about trials (including jury selection, trial procedures, evidence, and jury deliberations), see "The Trial" on page 421.

Reasonable Doubt and the Presumption of Innocence

Bart opted for a jury trial, and his entire family came to show support. Bart was feeling confident about his case until the prosecutor, Terry Tough, addressed the jury with a grim face, denouncing him as a thoughtless, dangerous, thrill-seeking young thug. "Ladies and gentlemen," Tough intoned, "the evidence will convince you, beyond a reasonable doubt, that this sweet-looking defendant is actually a reckless criminal."

What is reasonable doubt?

It's one of the most important safeguards in the criminal justice system. Because our system tries to do all it can to ensure that no innocent person is wrongfully convicted, a defendant cannot be convicted at trial without "proof beyond a reasonable doubt." Contrary to other justice systems, a person who is charged with a crime in America *is presumed to be innocent and must be acquitted* unless the government offers evidence to prove the contrary beyond a reasonable doubt.

A good description of the term "reasonable doubt" is elusive. In essence, jurors are instructed to look at all the evidence presented in a case and to weigh the strength of the evidence on both sides. If, after doing so, a juror does not have a strong feeling that the defendant is guilty, then reasonable doubt exists and the verdict must be not guilty. If a juror is sitting in the deliberation room and says, "I'm just not sure" or "Maybe he didn't do it, but the evidence looks like he might have," that might be considered reasonable doubt upon which to vote not guilty. On the other hand, it would not be reasonable doubt if a juror feels sympathetic for the defendant or is concerned about the possible sentence.

The "burden" of proving a defendant is guilty lies with the prosecution, which must prove that a defendant's conduct violated each and every element of the crimes charged. These elements are defined by the wording of criminal statutes. To prove a crime, a prosecutor generally has to show:

- **that the defendant committed an act prohibited by law**
- **that the defendant had the level of evil intent prescribed by the statute**

Say a person is charged with vandalism, which is defined by the state's statute as the "willful and malicious destruction of property over $50 in value." The prosecution must prove beyond a reasonable doubt that

- **the property was destroyed by the defendant**
- **the defendant intended to cause the property destruction (that's the willful part)**
- **the property destroyed was worth more than $50**

If the prosecution misses any element, the jury should acquit. If the prosecution case is so obviously deficient that no reasonable person could find the defendant guilty, the judge, at the request of the defense, may dismiss the charges.

Prosecution of Capital Cases

A capital crime is defined as one for which a defendant may be punished by death. In 1994, thirty-seven states allowed the death penalty for a range of crimes, including

- **premeditated murder**
- **murder committed in the course of a felony such as armed robbery**
- **murder with depraved indifference and cruelty**
- **murder of a police officer**

To get a death sentence in a case, the prosecutor usually must announce an intention to ask for death at the start of a case, long before the trial opens. In some states, a single jury tries the case, and the judge sentences. Other states have a two-trial system, known as **bifurcation,** for capital cases. In these states, a defendant must first be tried before a jury on the issue of guilt or innocence. This is known as the **criminal liability phase.** In the second part, called the **penalty phase,** the jury hears more evidence and decides whether or not to impose the death penalty. This is done either by a new jury (in some states) or the same jury. Either way, the same judge will handle the entire trial.

After being convicted and sentenced, a person has the right to appeal. Death-row appeals can be complex, protracted, and expensive, and may be argued in both state and federal courts. Most states provide lawyers for a condemned person's initial appeal. However, if that appeal is not successful, it may be necessary for death-row inmates to find other legal counsel for subsequent appeals. There are networks of lawyers who oppose the death penalty or who donate their time to such cases. The following organizations can help you locate counsel for a death-penalty case:

National Coalition to Abolish the Death Penalty
1325 G Street NW
Washington, DC 20005
202-347-2411

NAACP Legal Defense & Educational Fund Inc.
99 Hudson Street, Sixteenth Floor
New York, NY 10013
212-219-1900 or 800-221-7822

Your Best and Worst Witness: Should the Defendant Testify?

The prosecution had presented its case, and Bart now faced another critical decision: he had to decide whether or not to testify. He wanted to do so, because he was convinced his sincerity would show to the jurors. He also wanted to tell his own story in his own words and have the chance to make direct contact with the jury. The downside, Christine warned him, was that he would be exposing himself to cross-examination by the prosecution.

Should a defendant take the stand?

That's a decision that every defendant must make with his or her lawyer. The price of telling your own story is that you have to undergo cross-examination and take the chance that you'll expose something you didn't want to reveal, or say something against your best interests. If you and your lawyer don't think you will come across believably and sympathetically, getting up on the stand may well work against you.

If you decide not to testify, the prosecution may not comment on this fact to the jury, because your refusal to testify is a constitutional right and is not to be considered evidence of guilt.

Lesser Included Offenses

After consulting with his lawyer, Christine, Bart decided to take the stand. It was a disaster. His good looks and confident manner made him seem cocky and without remorse. He felt terrible when he smiled at the jurors and none smiled back. He felt even worse later when the prosecutor gave her closing argument and told the jurors that if they didn't think Bart was guilty of armed robbery (because he didn't have a weapon on him), they could still find him guilty of robbery.

■ What are lesser included offenses?

At the end of a trial, after the lawyers from each side have given their closing arguments, the judge will instruct the jurors on what they are to consider in their deliberations. This is known as the **jury charge.** In it the judge explains the law and the specifics of the charge. Sometimes there will be **lesser included offenses** that the jury can vote on. These are charges that contain elements of the most serious charge against the defendant. For instance, a person who is charged with first-degree murder (which requires premeditation) could be convicted of second-degree murder (a killing done without premeditation) or even manslaughter (a killing done in the heat of passion). The jury may find that all the elements to convict for the most severe crime (first-degree murder, in this example) weren't present, but that all the elements of the lesser crime of second-degree murder or manslaughter were.

SENTENCING

As Bart and his family and lawyer sweated, the jury stayed out deliberating for three hours. They came back and announced to Bart's shock that he had been found guilty. His mother, Grace, wept, while his father, Gordon, looked on stunned, clutching his wife's hand.

■ What happens after a defendant is found guilty?

The next phase is sentencing. Usually it is the judge who passes sentence, though in a few states, such as Texas, juries determine the sentence. Generally, the most important factors in sentencing are the seriousness of the offense and the defendant's prior criminal record.

Before sentencing, the defense will have the chance to present any **mitigating factors,** information about the defendant that might tend to lessen the sentence. Such information could include evidence of the defendant's

- **feelings of remorse**
- **efforts to apologize and make restitution to any victims**
- **responsibilities toward family and employers**
- **health problems**
- **participation in alcohol, drug treatment, or psychiatric counseling programs**

It is up to the judge to decide in what manner the mitigating factors will be presented. Some judges will ask the defense to prepare a written report; others will hold hearings with the prosecutor present, allowing the state to object to assertions the defense makes. In some jurisdictions the probation department may also investigate and produce a **presentencing report** with recommendations. The defense may try to attack the findings of that report.

The judge may also listen to recommendations from the victim. (See page 219.)

For more on appeals, see page 425.

At Bart's sentencing hearing, Christine tried to present him in the best light possible. She told the judge that Bart had been an upstanding citizen before his arrest. "This young man volunteered at a nursing home on weekends," she told the judge. "He's a responsible guy who has never had any legal troubles, not even a traffic ticket." She presented letters from his parents, his teachers, bosses, and neighbors, all pleading for the judge to go easy on Bart.

■ How much freedom do judges have to set sentences?

Much less than they once did. Judges used to have discretion to sentence anything from probation to the maximum time for the charge. But today, in the federal courts and in many state courts, judges must follow sentencing guidelines, which give them a fixed range of years that varies depending on the type of crime and the defendant's criminal history.

Convicted defendants may be given fines, sentenced to imprisonment, or both. Probation is another option. So is a suspended sentence, which means that a person doesn't do jail time, but if he or she is arrested again during probation, the sentence then has to be served, in addition to whatever sentence the person gets for the second offense. (If the person is not convicted of the second offense, he or she can remain on probation.)

If a person is convicted of more than one charge, there will be a sentence for each charge. The judge may impose them either **consecutively** (one after the other) or **concurrently** (at the same time). The distinction is extremely important: the first term means more prison time and far less leniency. If a convicted felon gets sentences of one, five, and seven years "to be served consecutively," he faces thirteen years in jail. If the judge says they may be "served concurrently," it means that the convict may be released after the longest sentence is served — seven years.

■ What is a mandatory sentence?

Recently there has been a movement to restrict further judges' freedom to set sentences. While the stated reason is to ensure greater uniformity regardless of which judge a defendant gets, some critics have charged that the reformers' real agenda is to increase punishments. One method followed by many state legislatures is to introduce **mandatory sentences** for specified crimes. In Massachusetts, for example, there is a mandatory minimum sentence of one year for possession of an illegal handgun. Other states have mandatory sentences for child abuse, domestic violence, and driving under the influence of alcohol.

The changes in the federal system have been even more sweeping. Congress has abolished parole for felonies and has established the United States Sentencing Commission, which sets minimum, intermediate, and maximum sentences for each federal crime. Many judges, particularly in the federal system, have been severely critical of the trend toward mandatory minimum or fixed sentences, because they feel it has led to unduly harsh punishments for some people who have the potential for rehabilitation and deserve shorter sentences.

PROBATION

The judge in Bart's case, after making it clear he despised crimes involving guns, announced the sentence: two years in jail, with all but six months suspended. He also ordered Bart to two years of supervised probation and fifty hours of community service. On hearing this latest blow, Christine looked pale. It had not been a good day for the defense.

■ What is probation?

Probation is the release of a defendant into the community, often under certain conditions. These may include

- **paying a fine**
- **doing community service (such as working for a state road crew or helping out in a nursing home or charitable agency)**
- **accepting a suspended jail sentence (which must be served if probation is violated)**
- **pledging to attend a drug treatment program**
- **consenting to be searched at random without a warrant**

Defendants on probation are often required to report periodically to a probation officer. If those conditions are violated, a hearing is held, and the defendant may be sent to jail or have stricter conditions imposed.

Probation conditions are a flexible tool of social control. They may be as restrictive as house arrest (confinement to a private residence) or frequent meetings with a probation officer. In some places, probationers must wear electronic ankle bracelets so that their movements can be tracked. For minor crimes, probation may be unsupervised.

EARLY RELEASE AND PAROLE

While he was in prison, Bart shared a cell with two other guys, Duke and Bruno. One day a guard brought in a three-piece suit for Bruno, who had been convicted of robbing a popular pizza parlor and shooting three of its workers. "Here's your party dress," the guard said.

"You bet it's gonna be a party," said Bruno. "I'm going for my parole board hearing, and I'm getting out of this stinkin' joint."

What is parole?

Parole is a system for the supervised release of prisoners before their terms are over. Although Congress has abolished parole for people convicted of federal crimes, most states still have parole boards. Most prisoners may petition the board for release after serving a part of their sentences; in many places prisoners have the right to an annual hearing after a certain percentage of a sentence has been served. At the hearing the prisoner will try to convince the board that he or she is capable of living lawfully in the outside world.

Parolees who win their restricted freedom must visit their parole officers frequently, and many conditions may be attached to their parole. If they break the law again or otherwise violate the conditions of their parole, the parole can be revoked. Plus, they may face time for the additional crime.

CASE IN POINT

An Unusual Condition for Parole

John Walrath was convicted in Illinois in 1970 of kidnapping and sexually molesting a six-year-old boy. He was released on parole in 1992 under the special condition that he participate in a mental health program at a facility that specialized in treatment for pedophilia and other deviant sexual practices.

As part of the program's initial evaluation, the facility required Walrath to take a penile plethysmograph exam, a test designed to measure a person's patterns of sexual arousal. To take this test, a man places a "circumference gauge" around his penis. This gauge, hooked up to an electronic meter, records the circumference of the penis while the man is presented with various audio and visual material. The man wears a hospital gown during the test.

Walrath sued to stop the parole commission from requiring the test, claiming it would violate his Fifth Amendment right against self-incrimination and his Fourth Amendment right against unreasonable searches and seizures. In a July 1993 decision, a federal district court judge in Illinois ruled that the test did not violate Walrath's constitutional rights.

Why not? For two reasons, according to the opinion by Judge Marvin Aspen. First, because the plethysmograph is a physical test of a person's sexual reactions, it does not gather information used to incriminate. Rather, wrote Aspen, "the test is designed to determine how best to help [Walrath] overcome any sexual deviance he might still harbor, so that he may be returned, safely, to society."

On the search and seizure question, Aspen ruled that the government is authorized to impose certain conditions on a parolee's release in order to rehabilitate him and ensure he doesn't jeopardize public safety. In addition, he noted that the plethysmograph was not really any more intrusive than other ordinary procedures such as physical exams involving full nudity and internal probes as well as some psychological exams that could invade a person's mental privacy.

Due to overcrowded conditions in jails and prisons, in some states a few prisoners, especially those convicted of nonviolent crimes, are being released before their sentences are up. Early release is not parole; it has no strings attached.

LISTENING TO THE VICTIM

Bruno may have had his hopes up too high. When he arrived at the parole board hearing, he saw a dozen picketers carrying signs: "Bruno is a Brute-O." Several of them were chanting: "Justice for the victim. Do the crime. Do the time." Two of the men he shot in the robbery were there — dressed just as nicely as he was.

Do victims have a say during criminal proceedings?

Yes. In the last few years, several states have enacted legislation to define and recognize the rights of crime victims. States have tried to improve communications between courts and victims, especially about the availability of police protection for victims who plan to testify. These states also have required prosecutors to notify a victim, or a victim's family, about the status of a case. That is, they must tell the family or the victim when the defendant has been released on bail, what sentence has been imposed, and when the prisoner has won an early release.

In some states, the prosecutor is required to contact and consult with the victim or the family on sentencing and parole matters. In a few states, the victim has the right to testify at sentencing and parole hearings. At sentencing the victim generally is asked to talk about the crime and its severity, the impact on his or her daily life, and its emotional and physical toll. Generally, the testimony is offered as a reason to increase the punishment, but in rare cases the victim has asked for leniency. In some states, the victim is allowed to say what sentence he or she would desire for the criminal. The judge can weigh the request in deliberations, but is not required to follow it.

Courts have also been extending more services to victims — such as ensuring that they have parking at the courthouse, giving them separate waiting areas where they can sit out of sight of defendants, offering free translation services, referrals to counseling, and other services.

Victim's Compensation

If you are the victim of a crime and you are injured or lose property, you may be eligible for two kinds of compensation:

- Restitution. The courts may require a criminal defendant to pay you back as part of his or her sentence. Some states also give the victim the right to testify at a criminal defendant's sentencing.
- Many states also maintain funds to repay crime victims. For more information about what is available in your state, contact your local district attorney's office.

Can you sue the criminal?
Yes, but the truth is that most criminals who are going to jail have few assets and are not worth suing. There are some exceptions, as in the case of white-collar crimes, such as embezzlement. Also, you can seek to attach any profits the criminal may have made from publicizing or selling his story.

HABEAS CORPUS

After Bruno struck out with the parole board, he met with Victor "Two Brains" Stallman, the prison's resident legal know-it-all. "It just doesn't seem fair," Bruno told Two Brains. "I've got all this evidence my lawyer never presented at the trial."

"I think you should file a habeas petition," Two Brains said.

"A what?"

"A habeas petition. I'll write it out for you. But it'll cost you four cartons of cigarettes."

What is habeas corpus?

Prisoners have few legal rights, but the most important is probably the right to seek release through a **petition for a writ of habeas corpus**, or a review by a judge of the legality of their imprisonment. Any prisoner with certain complaints — for example, that prison conditions are so bad as to be unconstitutional, that he was illegally denied a lawyer, or that he was jailed because of improper procedures — can ask a judge to review the legality of his imprisonment.

The petition itself is a document that can be filed by a prisoner or his or her lawyer in any state court. The prisoner may also file for habeas in any federal court when alleging that the case has constitutional flaws; to do so, a prisoner must file a special form with the federal court. Prisoners are generally barred from rearguing the facts of their case except when gross injustice has occurred.

Thousands of prisoners send in such petitions every month. Many of them do the legal work themselves, often submitting multiple petitions to state and federal courts. In former years, a judge granted a petition by issuing a **writ** (an order) requiring an official to "bring forth the body" of the prisoner from jail to appear before him. These days, however, a prisoner's appearance is usually not required when a judge grants an order setting into motion the review process. Extremely few of these *pro se* (self-represented) petitions succeed; the chances are much better for a prisoner who uses a lawyer to file a petition, but even then habeas corpus petitions are very seldom granted.

CASE IN POINT

"She Kept, Kept, Kept Pushing Me"

Some cases seem to cry out for the use of an entrapment defense. Consider, for example, the situation of Marion Barry, the former mayor of Washington, D.C. After federal investigators had gathered evidence that Barry was a regular user of cocaine, they set up a "sting" operation to catch him.

Their ruse? Hazel Dian "Rasheeda" Moore, a former girlfriend and drug partner of Barry's, invited the then-mayor up to her room in Washington's Vista Hotel on January 18, 1990. Barry initially refused Moore's offer of crack cocaine. After serving him cognac and tempting his sexual appetite, she persistently asked him to partake of the drug. Barry finally gave in. While a videotape documented the event, he took a deep drag from the crack pipe.

Agents crashed into the room to arrest Barry, pinning him up against the wall. "Bitch set me up," he mutters on the tape. "She kept, kept, kept pushing me." Barry was subsequently indicted on fourteen charges, including eleven misdemeanor charges relating to cocaine possession and three felony perjury charges for allegedly lying to the grand jury during the initial investigation before his arrest.

At his 1990 trial, Barry's defense focused on the sting operation. His lawyers argued that it amounted to entrapment. Of all the charges, Barry was convicted of only a single cocaine possession misdemeanor. He was acquitted of another drug misdemeanor, and the jurors deadlocked on the rest of the counts, including the Vista drug possession charge. While the entrapment defense was legally relevant only to that one count, many of the jurors felt a distaste for what seemed to them as lawless behavior by the government. And that distaste colored their deliberations. "It left a bitter taste in my mouth," one juror said, referring to the tape of police agents storming the Vista room.

Barry was up for reelection, but chose not to seek another term before he was sentenced to six months in prison. Prosecutors chose not to retry him on the deadlocked counts.

Washington residents were quick to forgive a contrite Barry. In 1992, he was elected to the City Council in a resounding victory. In 1994, he ran for mayor again and won.

One of the most hotly contested battles in Congress in recent years has been over limiting the right to file habeas corpus petitions. Originally part of the English system of civil liberties developed during the seventeenth and eighteenth centuries, habeas limited the power of kings to arbitrarily imprison people. Now because of the strain that processing habeas petitions puts on crowded courts, the assertion has been made that too many petitions are frivolous, and Congress has moved to limit the right to file them. Opponents see the effort as clashing with guarantees written into the Constitution, arguing that in many cases prisoner petitions have brought fundamental injustices to the attention of the courts.

DEFENSES

Entrapment

Bart's other cellmate, Duke, had an interesting story. He was just a regular guy, he told Bart, minding his own business, taking tourist groups out fishing on his boat, when a guy approached him and offered him a couple of thousand dollars if he would pick up some boxes from a cruise ship in the middle of the night and transport them back to the marina. "I was pretty sure it was cocaine," said Duke. "I wanted nothing to do with it, but the guy kept coming back and saying how easy it would be. I needed that money, so finally I said I'd do it. Soon as I arrived back in the marina, I got busted. The whole thing was a setup by the cops."

■ What is entrapment?

Entrapment is a term used to describe a criminal defense that can be raised by a defendant. The definition of entrapment varies from state to state, but in general a person accused of a crime was "entrapped" if he was not predisposed to commit the crime until government agents induced him to do so. In some states, the key question in an entrapment case will be "Would the defendant have committed the crime without the inducement by the government?" In other states, the focus is on the government, and the key question is "Was the conduct of the government agents overzealous or outrageous?"

Entrapment is a difficult defense, and the burden is on the accused to prove he was entrapped.

Self-Defense

Beatrice's neighbor shot and killed her husband. "He was abusing me," she told the police. "He was about to attack me again, and I wasn't going to let him." She was charged with murder. Her lawyer insisted she had acted in self-defense.

■ What is self-defense?

This is a defense an accused person can use in a criminal case. What this defense basically says is that "I used force against a person, and either injured or killed him, because he was the aggressor and I was simply protecting myself from bodily harm."

If you believe that some other person is about to harm or attempt to kill you, you may be justified in using enough force to thwart the attack. However, you must generally be in *imminent* danger of an attack, and in some states you must first do all you can to retreat from the attacker. Courts will generally look at all the surrounding circumstances, including your background and experience, the aggressor's intent, and the amount of force threatened by the aggressor and the amount of force you used.

Insanity

During a break in Bart's armed robbery trial, Blossom sat in on a murder case down the hall. The defendant, a young man in his twenties, had been drinking coffee and muttering to himself at a local luncheonette one afternoon, when he jumped up abruptly and began choking the elderly woman seated next to him, while shouting "Die, you ugly alien." As the other patrons pulled him away, the woman collapsed on the floor, suffered a heart attack, and died.

Blossom caught the last bit of the defendant's testimony. "She was staring at me," he

said, describing the dead woman. "She was giving me the evil eye, and then she was laughing hysterically. Flashes of light were coming out of her head. She was about to put a rat's head in my coffee when the voices told me to stop her. I couldn't help it. I knew it was wrong afterward, but I had no control. I thought she was from another planet."

■ What is an insanity defense?

In the eyes of the law, a defendant is legally insane if he or she is unable, because of a mental problem, to form a *mens rea,* a Latin term meaning a guilty mind. Because the law punishes only people who are mentally responsible for their actions, most states allow juries to find a defendant not guilty if he or she was insane at the time a crime was committed. At the heart of an insanity defense is the notion that because of mental illness, either the defendant could not understand the difference between right and wrong or could not keep from doing the wrong act.

Each state has its own definition of insanity, but most states follow the M'Naghten Rules, which come from a famous English case decided in 1843. Under this rule, a defendant may be found not guilty by reason of insanity if, at the time of committing the act, he or she suffered from such a diseased mind or defective reasoning that it was not possible for him to know the nature and quality of the act. That would be the case if a person thought he was stabbing a log rather than a human being.

A person also can be found not guilty by reason of insanity if he or she did know what was happening but did not understand that it was wrong. This would be the excuse of a woman who shot her dentist, for example, if she had suffered from a psychotic delusion that her dentist was trying to kill her rather than clean her teeth.

Since this rule requires a disease or defect of the mind, the lowering of a person's inhibitions by drugs, alcohol, blind hatred, extreme anger, or some neurotic behavior would not provide an insanity defense.

While an insanity defense could be raised in almost any criminal case, it usually is reserved only for the most serious crimes carrying harsh punishment, such as the death penalty or life in prison.

■ What happens when a person is found not guilty by reason of insanity?

Most states require that such a person be housed in a maximum security mental institution that is virtually indistinguishable from a prison. That person must stay there for as long as it is determined that he is a danger to himself or to others. This time period is not fixed (though there may be a minimum required) and can last, in theory, for the rest of that person's life. As a result, it does not make much sense for a person charged with less serious felonies or misdemeanors to use the insanity defense.

■ How does a person get out of the mental institution?

Usually, a release hearing or trial is required, and it is very difficult to get a release if the institution believes the person is still a potential danger. Release does not require that the person be "cured." It requires only that he or she no longer pose a danger.

■ What is incompetence?

A person is deemed "incompetent to proceed" in a criminal case if he or she is not capable of understanding the nature and purpose of the proceedings, or is not aware of what's going on during the trial, or is incapable of cooperating with counsel in conducting a defense. Generally, this means that the defendant must be able to understand the basic functioning of a criminal trial and assist his or her attorney by answering the attorney's questions about the charges. The defendant basically must understand

- **the crime with which he or she is charged**
- **that the prosecutor is seeking to convict**
- **that the judge or jury will decide his or her guilt or innocence**

If a defendant is found to be actively psychotic, with no contact with reality, he or she will not be competent to stand trial.

When a lawyer asserts that a client is incompetent to proceed, the entire criminal case is put on hold while the person is examined. If he or she is indeed found to be incompetent, the case remains on hold until he or she is "restored to competency."

This doesn't mean that the defendant is cured or made healthy. Rather it means that he or she can now understand the charges and cooperate with the defense attorney.

When and if a person regains competency (which can take months or even years), the case begins again. None of the time spent in a mental institution counts as incarceration, and the incompetency cannot be used as a defense to the crime.

MISCELLANEOUS ILLEGAL ACTIVITIES

Poker Games

Gordon loved his weekly poker games with the boys. One day a new friend of an old friend showed up and threw the group into an argument by announcing that they could all be arrested and had better keep it quiet! "What the hell are you talking about?" Gordon demanded to know. "Gambling at home, even among friends, is illegal in this state," the stranger said smugly.

■ Is a friendly poker game illegal?

It depends on where you live. The regulation of gambling varies greatly from state to state. A weekly poker game in some states may be allowable, while in other states, it is criminal. Police seldom bother with "friendly" games, though large-stakes games are sometimes the subject of a "bust."

In states that do allow friendly gambling, it is not illegal to play poker for money as long as no person is taking a percentage of the pot or a fee for setting up the game.

Sexually Transmitted Diseases

Blossom was in a rage. Her last boyfriend had taken a new job and moved away from town, leaving her lonely and angry. Now, she had just discovered, he had also left her with a nasty and incurable case of herpes. The breakup had been messy — but not half as messy as the lawsuit against him that Blossom vowed to bring. She thought she had a criminal case against him as well, and wondered whether she could get him hauled off to jail.

■ Is it a crime to infect someone with herpes?

Generally not, though many states, including Arkansas, California, Georgia, Illinois, Michigan, Nevada, Oklahoma, Texas, and Washington, have instituted criminal penalties for knowingly transmitting or exposing another person to the HIV virus that causes AIDS. (Some laws only punish people who knowingly donate HIV-inflected blood; others punish those who knowingly expose others through sexual activity.) However, since herpes is not considered a deadly disease, it does not receive the same consideration.

Finders Keepers?

Bradley went to see a movie that turned out to be a dud, but he didn't mind a bit. That's because he found a paper bag under the sink in the theater's bathroom with $5,000 in it! He took it home but didn't spend it, because he was nagged by doubts about whether what he had done was immoral, or worse, illegal.

■ Is it a crime to keep money if it is found in a public place?

It's not illegal to do so, but the money is not rightfully yours. The proper procedure is to turn the money over to the police, who will hold it for a specific period, determined by each state. If after this time the money goes unclaimed, you may then be entitled to it. The rule behind this is similar to a situation where the bank machine malfunctioned and you received $1,000 instead of $100. It is not your money and you should not be able to simply claim it as a bonus. The rightful owner should be given the opportunity to reclaim his property. In fact, if a bank machine or teller (or even your employer's accounting department) gives you too much money, you could face criminal charges for keeping it.

Being in the Wrong Place at the Wrong Time

One night Grace got a call from the police to come bail out her daughter Beatrice. "What's she in for?" the bewildered mother asked. "She was at a party we raided. The kids were using drugs. You'd better get down here," she was told. Grace couldn't speak for a minute, she was so stunned. Beatrice was such a health nut that she didn't smoke cigarettes and never took a drink! Grace was sure she hadn't taken anything, so how could she be held responsible?

■ If some people at a party are using illegal drugs, are the others who aren't using the drugs guilty of a crime?

Not necessarily. Each state's laws differ in this area, but mere presence at a crime generally is not enough to create guilt. If a person had no drugs actually on or near her at the time of an arrest, that might make a conviction less likely. If she was in control of a box or bag from which the drugs were distributed, or if she was in control of the premises where the drugs were found, a conviction for possession is more likely. Basically, mere presence is not enough, but presence and other evidence may be enough to obtain a conviction.

WORKING

14

Beatrice wanted to change jobs. After three years as a computer programmer and technology specialist for Teddies and More, a family-owned stuffed animal manufacturer, she was ready for more responsibility. And she was ready for better working conditions. Teddies had been taken over by Bearco Inc., an international toy distributor, and the transition was a disaster. Several people, some of them near retirement age, had been fired and replaced with younger workers at lower wages. The company had stopped contributing to the pension plan and group health insurance. Phone calls were being monitored, and employees who took sick days were now required to verify their illness with a note from the doctor.

■ Don't employers have some guidelines they have to follow?

Absolutely. From the first interview to the last paycheck, employee-employer relations are governed by a morass of state and federal laws. They include

- **laws that apply to every employer — whether it's a private company, government agency, religious institution, or nonprofit enterprise**
- **laws that apply to private companies but *not* government employers**
- **laws that exempt small businesses (usually those with fewer than fifteen employees)**

In addition, private businesses that do work for the government often have to follow specific guidelines that other companies do not. And, in addition to all the federal laws, each state has its own rules regulating the workplace.

■ How do people know which laws apply to *their* employers?

We'll try to explain as much as we can below. But for specific information about your job, you can call a federal agency like the Equal Employment Opportunity Commission (EEOC) at 800-669-4000 or the Department of Labor at 202-219-6666. Your state's department of labor or antidiscrimination agency can also provide helpful information about your rights and the laws that govern your particular work situation. And if you have an individual contract with your employer or if you are a member of a union, you may be entitled to additional rights that are spelled out in your contract.

■ When should an employee consult a lawyer?

If you've had a problem at work and are unhappy with the way it's been resolved (or are unhappy because it hasn't been resolved), then you may want to consult an attorney. A lawyer can tell you whether your rights appear to have been violated, and if they have been, advise you on what to do. For many workplace problems, such as discrimination or sexual harassment, you may not even need a lawyer — at least not in the initial stages, since you can often get good guidance from the EEOC. The staff there can help you determine what your rights and options are and whether you have a valid claim. For more about the EEOC, see page 240.

If you need the name of a lawyer, ask your friends and acquaintances. If you are a member of a union or other professional organization, legal services may be available to you, or the union may be able to give you a reference. You can also try your local bar association (see listings on page 449). Most will have names of lawyers who specialize in different areas. You can also try the National Employment Lawyers Association (415-397-6335), a group that represents employees who have problems at work. There are also local organizations of employment lawyers. Many lawyers will take employment cases on a contingent basis, which means you may not have to pay any money up front (see page 440 for information about fees).

Always keep in mind that if you want to file a claim with an enforcement agency like the EEOC, you should first make every effort to use procedures set up by your employer (if there are any) to deal internally with employee grievances. Go up the chain of command and report your problem and try to resolve the situation. If your immediate supervisor is the person with whom you have a problem, then report the problem to that person's supervisor.

Trying to resolve the situation internally demonstrates what lawyers call "good faith," that you honestly believe there is a problem, not that you are being prompted by some less sincere motivation to "get" your employer. Dealing with the situation internally also lets your employer know you have a grievance and gives him or her the opportunity to try to find a solution. The law doesn't require you to handle your grievance this way. It just makes good sense.

The "No-No" Questions

The specific topics you cannot be asked about in a job interview include

- **your age**
- **your sexual preference**
- **your national origin**
- **your race**
- **your religion**
- **your medical history**

GETTING HIRED

Applications and Interviews: What Can an Employer Ask You?

Beatrice sent her résumé to several companies, and many invited her in for an interview. Most of them followed a predictable course: some small talk, then a lot of questions about her responsibilities as a programmer, the courses she took in college, how she liked working with people, how she would handle different kinds of problems. One interviewer, however, peppered her with more personal queries: "Do you have a boyfriend? Planning to get married soon? Any children? Do you smoke? Ever been arrested?" Beatrice wasn't quite sure what the point was — or whether she had to answer.

Are certain questions off-limits during a job interview?

Yes. According to state and federal laws, prospective employers generally must limit their inquiries to topics that explore your qualifications for the job. Any questions that probe for personal information that can be used to discriminate against you are no-nos. Not that it stops some prospective employers from trying to decipher the information more indirectly. A seemingly friendly question about your name ("Gee, Kotzamani, that's interesting. Where's your family from?") is not so friendly if the interviewer is really trying to scope out your race or nationality.

Which is not to say that every friendly question is a veiled attempt at discrimination. Potential employers are allowed to inquire whether you're married and the ages of your children — so long as they ask every potential employee the same thing — and don't base their hiring decisions on the answer. If, however, only female job candidates are being asked their marital status, and if the company is not hiring any candidates with children under age five, then what is a totally legal question may be suspect. (Once you are hired, an employer may have a legitimate business reason for asking your marital status, since it may be relevant to the tax deductions taken from your paycheck or to your health insurance coverage.)

You can often judge whether a potential employer is prying improperly by the manner in which the questions are stated. If, for instance, you mention you are divorced and then the interviewer asks you to elaborate on the details of when and why it occurred, those questions may suggest a discriminatory motive.

If you believe you have been discriminated against, you can register a complaint with the company's human resource department or you can pursue a lawsuit (see page 236).

Checking Your References

Beatrice applied for a job in the computer department of Frozen and Fabulous, a company that manufactures and distributes low-fat gourmet dessert products. She interviewed with several people, including Arthur, the head of the company. He liked Beatrice and was prepared to offer her a job — until he checked her references. He called one of her former employers, a bank where she had worked after graduating from college, and talked to Jeanine, who had been her supervisor there.

Jeanine told Arthur there had been nothing unusual about Beatrice's departure. She simply had found a better job. But, Jeanine added (with no prodding from Arthur), it wasn't as if anyone was sorry to see Beatrice go. She had missed a lot of days because she was sick and the outfits she wore to work were a little bit too "funky" — bell-bottoms and platform shoes — the kind of clothes, Jeanine said, you'd expect to see in a nightclub, not in a bank. She also wore too much perfume.

■ What information is a former (or current) employer allowed to provide?

Potential employers are free to ask for and check your references, but your previous employers can't say just anything. The laws vary from state to state, but the same issues (such as age, race, medical condition, credit history, and sexual preference) that are off-limits in a job interview are off-limits in a discussion with your former employer. The purpose for this restriction is to prevent an employer (or potential employer) from snooping out information that can be used to discriminate against you.

Generally, an employer or former employer can release information about your

- **position**
- **dates of employment**
- **salary**
- **the circumstances under which you left the job**

Which is not to say that your former (or current) boss can't give a candid assessment of your performance. If, for instance, you were fired because you stole money from the company, your former boss is free to disclose this information. If you were difficult to work with, your former boss can say so. He or she just better be able to back it up.

Many companies now ask departing workers to sign a release allowing them to provide personal information to potential employers. However, an employer is not required to have a release before giving out information about you. Also, your signature on such a form (no matter how it's worded) does not give your former boss carte blanche to say just anything about you. If a former employer gives out damaging or untruthful information about you, you may still have the grounds for a lawsuit even if you signed a release form.

An employer who is giving out false information about you can be sued for defamation or invasion of privacy. (See Chapter 18, BEING A CITIZEN.) To prevent getting entangled in such lawsuits, some companies now will respond only to written inquiries, and the only information they will provide are your dates of employment and job title. However, an employer who fails to disclose completely the reasons why a job candidate should *not* be hired could be sued by the new employer for giving a false or incomplete reference.

Note: in some instances where an employer fires a worker for a reason that cannot be substantiated, the worker may be able to succeed in a defamation suit if he or she was forced to tell prospective employers the presumably false reason for leaving the previous job. For example, several insurance company workers were fired for "gross insubordination" when their expense forms were challenged after a business trip. The employees refused to change the forms, claiming they were accurate. When they interviewed for new jobs, they had to repeat the former employer's allegations, and they claimed this constituted defamation. A jury agreed and awarded them roughly $450,000, which was upheld on appeal.

Background Checks

Having received one less-than-stellar recommendation about Beatrice, Arthur decided he needed to know more. After all, Beatrice would have access to top secret company recipes. So he hired a private detective to investigate her.

Can a prospective employer do a background check?

Yes. However, the courts in all states have recognized that people have a right to privacy, so a prospective employer probably shouldn't be snooping into your personal life and asking about things that don't have to do with the position. Also, according to the federal Fair Credit Reporting Act, the employer can seek out records of your credit history. However, some states, such as California, have laws that require an employer to notify a job applicant before doing so. If you are denied a job because of information received from a credit reporting agency, the employer must give you the name and address of the agency that made the report.

Pre-employment Tests

Beatrice got a call from Arthur at Frozen and Fabulous. The background check was fine, but he wanted her to take an IQ test, an "integrity" test, and a personality test.

Are pre-employment tests allowed?

Yes, so long as the employer has a legitimate business reason to give them and so long as all applicants for a similar position are required to take them. (See the Case in Point on page 230.)

There are limits, however. The Americans with Disabilities Act prohibits pre-employment medical examinations, and some states have restricted the use of **psychological tests.** (The Americans with Disabilities Act also prohibits psychological tests if they are being given for medical purposes.) And many states allow an employer to take fingerprints

CASE IN POINT

Heathens Need Not Apply

As "born-again" Christians, the owners of the Sports and Health Club, Inc., which operated seven clubs in Minnesota's Twin Cities area, wanted to hire people with a "teachable spirit," and they worked to avoid bringing "fornicators" or homosexuals into the club.

During most job interviews, applicants were asked many personal questions, including whether they attended church, read the Bible, were married or divorced, prayed, engaged in premarital or extramarital sexual relations, believed in God, heaven, or hell.

The Supreme Court of Minnesota ruled in 1985 that such questions violated the state's Human Rights Act by probing into the religious beliefs and marital status of prospective employees. The court ruled that because the sports club was a business and not a religious corporation, it had to abide by the laws which the state established for the purpose of eliminating discrimination in the workplace. The club's questions served no legitimate business purpose and therefore were impermissible.

Such was not the ruling in a 1981 opinion by the same court, which dismissed a case brought by a gay man who claimed he was rejected for a job because of his sexual preference.

Timothy Campbell had applied for a position with the Minnesota Chemical Dependency Association. During the interview, Campbell was asked about his participation in several activist organizations, including various gay rights groups. While Campbell believed the line of questioning was discriminatory, the court ruled the questions were relevant and aimed at determining if his involvement in outside activities would interfere with how he performed his job.

or photographs only if the applicant will be working in the following positions:

- **safety officer (such as a policeman or security guard)**
- **the driver of a vehicle**
- **child-care employee**
- **school employee**
- **operator of dangerous equipment**

You usually must be offered the job before the photographs and fingerprints can be taken.

The use of **lie detector tests** is also limited by the Federal Polygraph Protection Act of 1988 to people who will be working in the following positions:

- **security guards**
- **armored car personnel**
- **security alarm design, installation, or maintenance**
- **manufacture, distribution, or dispensing of controlled substances**

Beatrice did well on the tests. She especially impressed Arthur on the integrity test when he left her alone for twenty minutes with a trayful of cookies and chocolate cake and she didn't eat any. He offered her the job. But there was one more hoop — she had to take and pass a physical.

Can a prospective employer make a person take a physical?

Yes, but not until you've been offered the job. That's a requirement of the Americans with Disabilities Act. The employer can reject you after getting the result of the physical exam if they show that you have a health problem or disability that will seriously affect your ability to perform the job.

The nurse who conducted the exam told Beatrice she was going to draw blood and do some routine tests for cholesterol and blood-sugar levels. Beatrice was uncomfortable because she was afraid they might secretly be testing for drug use or AIDS. (She was also terrified of needles.)

Can a prospective employer conduct a test without the applicant's knowledge?

The law on testing varies from state to state, but generally it's a good business practice for an employer to inform you of a test's purpose. Most states allow prospective employers to test for drug use, and some require that you be informed beforehand. An employer can reject an applicant who tests positive for current drug use.

Federal law does allow an employer to ask you to take an AIDS test, but only *after* you have been offered a job. And then the employer is restricted in what he or she can do with the information. The job offer cannot be rescinded unless the employer can prove that there is a legitimate basis for requiring you to be HIV-negative. And in some states, you must give written permission before the test can be given.

YOUR RIGHTS ON THE JOB

Inspecting Your Personnel Files

Beatrice got the job! After all the runaround she was pretty curious about what kind of information they had gathered about her.

Do employees have the right to inspect their personnel files?

Yes. In some states there are laws permitting employees to inspect their own files. To do so, laws state that the employee must give "reasonable" notice to the employer, and the employer must provide access to the file at a "reasonable" time and place. (The definition of what's "reasonable" varies from case to case, and it's often left for a judge or jury to decide based on the particular facts of each situation.) You usually will not be allowed to copy any of the documents in the file, though in some states you can copy documents that you have signed, such as an employment application or a performance appraisal. If your employer has a file with your medical records, you are also permitted to inspect that file.

Noncompete Agreements

On Beatrice's first day of work, she had to fill out a lot of forms. One was a "noncompete agreement," which stated that if she left Frozen and Fabulous, she would not go to work for one of its competitors for at least a year.

Can an employee be prevented from going to work for a competing company?

It depends. Most states have laws governing noncompete agreements. In general, if you're already an employee with an existing work contract for a defined term and your boss requires you to sign such an agreement, it's not enforceable unless your boss compensates you for not taking a job with another company (see also page 276).

AIDS and the Workplace

Beatrice shared an office with Warren and Cynthia. Warren, a gay man, tested positive for the HIV virus that causes AIDS. He wanted to keep the information secret from his co-workers, but he did tell Beatrice and Cynthia. Cynthia had never liked Warren — not because he was gay but because he was always getting positive attention from the boss and because he had the aggravating habit of "borrowing" pens and pencils from her desk without returning them. So she revealed his health problem to Arthur and demanded that Warren be moved to another office.

What are an employee's rights if he or she has AIDS?

The employee is protected from discrimination under the Americans with Disabilities Act. That means the supervisor can't switch Warren to another position (or office) so long as he is able to continue working. And it also means that an employer must reasonably accommodate a worker like Warren who has AIDS or is HIV-positive. Such accommodations might include

- **transferring the employee to a position within the company that the employee can perform with the "disability"**
- **providing a flexible work schedule if necessary to accommodate the disability**

Also, under the Family and Medical Leave Act, the employee may be entitled to take extended unpaid leave.

CASE IN POINT

Some Topics Are Off Limits

It may be okay to ask job applicants to take a psychological test, but there's a limit to how deep a potential employer can probe.

Applicants for security officer positions with Target Stores in California were required to take a 704-question psychological test that included the following statements (to be "answered" true or false):

- **"I have never indulged in unusual sex practices."**
- **"I feel sure there is only one religion."**
- **"I am very strongly attracted by members of my own sex."**
- **"I have had no difficulty starting or holding my urine."**

Several applicants filed a class action suit against the store, charging that the test violated state privacy and antidiscrimination laws. Target argued that the test was necessary in order to screen out emotionally unstable applicants who might put customers in jeopardy or who would fail to take direction and follow Target procedures.

A settlement was reached in 1993. It prohibits Target from giving the test to most applicants for at least five years and requires that the store destroy records of all previous test results within a specified amount of time. Also, Target agreed to establish a settlement fund of $1.3 million to be divided among the estimated 2,500 persons who took the test.

Drug Testing

One day, a few months into the job, Arthur tromped into Beatrice's office. "Time for the pee test," he announced, handing Beatrice a paper cup and a memo stating the company's policy that every employee would be checked periodically for drug use.

■ Can employees be required to take drug tests?

Yes, but there are restrictions. Federal laws allow people in certain jobs, such as airline pilots, long-distance drivers, and transit workers, to be tested at random as a condition of their employment. That means the boss can walk in at any time and demand a specimen, and the worker can be fired for insubordination if he or she refuses.

In many jurisdictions, people in other jobs where safety is a factor, including firefighters and prison guards, can be tested only if the employer has a "reasonable basis" to believe the worker's performance has been impaired by drugs — they are involved in a workplace accident or are exhibiting violent behavior, for example.

Beyond the people in these jobs, an employer who requires a drug test runs the risk in some states of violating a worker's right to privacy. And there are strict guidelines in some states as to when and how people can be tested. For instance, an employer must give reasonable notice to the worker before the test is administered, although if the employee was involved in an accident, the test can be administered right away. The employer must also have an established procedure that ensures that each specimen is handled properly. The employer must have a written policy that outlines the guidelines.

An employer should use caution when asking an employee to take a drug test, because in many jurisdictions the employee can turn around and sue for invasion of privacy or wrongful discharge if the testing isn't handled properly.

Lie Detector Tests

Crisis! Someone had stolen the Frozen and Fabulous recipe for No-Fat Nuggets, its best-selling ice cream candy, and sold it to Healthy Treats, its biggest competitor. Arthur called in a private investigator to rout out the double-crosser. Because the people in the computer programming department had access to the recipes, the investigator demanded that all the staff there take a polygraph test. Many of them, including Beatrice, refused.

■ Can any employee be required to take a lie detector test?

No. Under the federal Employee Polygraph Protection Act of 1988, only an employee who is reasonably suspected of involvement in an incident at work that resulted in economic loss or other harm to the employer's business can be tested. In this case, the investigator must narrow down the suspects. He can't just test everyone who has access to the recipes because they work on the computer system. He must have some other evidence that causes him to believe a particular person may have stolen the recipes. He had no such evidence implicating Beatrice, so she was right to refuse.

Your Right to Privacy at Work

Beatrice and her friends at work sent each other E-mail messages throughout the day. Many were work-related. Many more were personal — a recap of the weekend's social events or some office gossip. One morning they all signed onto their computers and got the same message: "Big Brother Is Watching You! No Gossiping Allowed During Work Hours."

■ Is an employer allowed to monitor an employee's conduct?

It depends on the type of surveillance used and where it's being used. Some states prohibit employers from venturing into what are considered "personal" areas, and some courts have restricted an employer's freedom to intercept your personal mail, monitor electronic mail, or set up a hidden camera or microphone in a nonwork area, such as a rest room or office cafeteria. But in many states, an employer is free to plant cameras and microphones in work areas (although some states also require that workers be notified when the boss does so).

Telephone conversations, however, are a different matter. The federal Omnibus Crime Control and Safe Streets Act of 1968 allows employers to tap into your workday phone conversations by listening in on an extension. Still, some courts have limited how freely an employer can eavesdrop on these calls. And some courts have ruled that you must be informed beforehand that your employer has a policy of listening in.

Dress Codes, Dating, and Discipline

Beatrice was attracted to David, the company whiz kid who had concocted more than twenty exotic (and very popular) frozen yogurt flavors. So when he invited her to the movies, she was thrilled. They had gone out only a few times, but the office rumor mill was buzzing after one of the ice cream tasters spotted them holding hands in the company parking lot. Word reached Arthur, who informed Beatrice that she and David were violating the company's anti-dating policy. He warned her that they both could be fired unless they called off the romance.

CASE IN POINT

"Sex, Lies, and Audiotapes"

Malicious gossip was the subject of a 1991 case in which an Arkansas federal court ruled that an employer is not allowed to tape the private telephone conversations of its employees, even when the conversation takes place during working hours on a company phone.

Newell Spears, the owner of an Arkansas liquor store, began to record all incoming and outgoing phone conversations from the shop after $16,000 was stolen in what Spears suspected was an "inside job." Spears recorded several conversations between an employee, Sibbie Deal, and Calvin Lucas, a man with whom she was having an extramarital affair. Many of their conversations were sexually provocative in nature.

Spears's wife later divulged the nature of the calls to the spouses of the clandestine lovers, according to an opinion by Judge Oren Harris. As a result, Deal's husband contemplated killing Lucas.

Judge Harris dubbed this "a case of sex, lies, and audiotapes" and ruled that there was no legitimate business purpose to the taping and disclosure of the sexually provocative calls. The Spears were found liable for intentionally intercepting and recording the telephone conversations. Deal and Lucas were awarded $10,000 each.

Larry Voss was not so lucky as Deal and Lucas. In a 1989 case, the Indiana state appeals court ruled that his employer *could* use phone-monitoring techniques in the workplace.

Voss was fired from his job at the Manville Building Materials Group in 1987 after making 190 unauthorized phone calls over a four-week period, including several to a Texas business that gave out gambling information.

Manville had posted notices warning employees that personal calls were prohibited and that phones would be monitored. When Manville investigators discovered Voss's personal calls, he was fired. The court ruled that Voss's unauthorized and excessive calls represented a breach of his duty as an employee and were grounds for dismissal.

Can an employer prohibit employees from dating each other?

Yes, but the employer must make sure that employees know there is an anti-dating policy and are warned about possible violations before imposing discipline. In other words, the boss can't fire you without giving you ample warning.

Beatrice had initially noticed David because he wore two hoop earrings in his left ear. David, in turn, was fond of Bea's short skirts and funky hats — which she typically wore in the office. Arthur, the boss, decided some decorum was needed. He issued a memo instructing all employees to follow a strict dress code:

- **no earrings on men**
- **no nose rings on either sex**
- **no skirts shorter than one inch above the knee**
- **no platform shoes**
- **men's hair must be cut above the collar**
- **no hats worn inside (except for the people who prepared the food products)**

Can employers set dress codes?

Yes, so long as they are not discriminatory or do not significantly burden an individual employee. Rules that set different standards for men and women without any legitimate business reason for doing so may be discriminatory. For instance, if all the female ticket takers at a movie theater were required to wear short skirts, while the male ticket takers could wear whatever they wanted, that rule very likely would be struck down as unfair. If an employer can show that a dress code is job-related, it will likely be left intact. And if the rules are found to be reasonable, an employer generally can fire an employee who refuses to follow them.

CASE IN POINT

Not So Pretty in Pastel

In 1976, a Michigan hospital was sued by a female employee who had refused to comply with the hospital's dress code. The dress code required female lab technologists to wear a white or pastel-colored uniform, complete with white or pastel shoes, socks, and underwear. Female technologists were also told to wear skirts of "respectable length" and accessories "appropriate for the occasion." However, male technologists were allowed to wear white laboratory coats over their ordinary street clothing.

Starrla Cornell, a histotechnologist, showed up at work twice in clothing that was against the dress code for females but appropriate for males. She was sent home the second time and ordered to change.

"The codes were intentionally designed to reinforce sexual stereotypes," wrote Judge G. Mennen Williams in a 1985 decision by the Michigan Supreme Court that found the dress code was discriminatory. "Men were dressed to look like doctors, and women were dressed to look like nurses." Cornell was awarded back pay.

In contrast, the Oregon Court of Appeals found in 1990 that a rule prohibiting male employees from wearing facial jewelry while allowing female employees to wear jewelry that was not "unusual or overly-large" was *not* discriminatory. The court upheld an employer's right to impose grooming standards in order to further a company's public image.

In a similar decision in 1976, the Supreme Court of Kentucky ruled that a waitress who refused to return to work after her employer forbade her from wearing a pantsuit did not prove sexual discrimination. That court ruled that an employer has the right to set reasonable standards of dress for employees.

Dorothy, Arthur's secretary, had trouble spelling. (Beatrice had wanted to get her a spell-checking program, but Arthur had nixed the request.) Arthur tolerated the problem for a long time, but when she typed this letter to a disgruntled customer: "Sorry to hear that you found our new desert dry and uninteresting. We are sending you a free sample of our chocolate mouse. We hope you'll enjoy its creamy, smooth texture," he'd had enough. He told Dorothy that from then on, he was going to withhold five dollars from her paycheck for every word misspelled.

■ Can the boss dock a worker's pay like that?

Probably not. Most states prohibit employers from withholding a person's salary for disciplinary reasons. In addition, employers must pay workers the minimum wage set by federal law. If a dock in pay dropped a person's wages below that level, it would be illegal.

Smoking

Business was booming for Frozen and Fabulous, and the company was hiring a lot of new employees. Beatrice was asked to share her office with Megan, a label designer. Megan, it turned out, smoked two packs of cigarettes a day — and insisted that she do so in the office despite numerous pleas not to from Beatrice. "I can't create without a cigarette," huffed Megan. Beatrice demanded that Arthur move one of them to another office.

■ Are employees entitled to work in a smoke-free environment?

Generally, yes, depending on state and local law. Employers have a duty to provide a reasonably safe workplace, and second-hand smoke has been designated unsafe by the Environmental Protection Agency (the designation has been challenged by the major cigarette manufacturers). If you have a health complaint about smoking in your workplace, you should

Fighting Harassment

What should you do if you think you're being harassed?

- First, keep a record of any incidents you believe constitute harassment.
- Try to deal with the problem internally. Notify your employer by filing an oral or written complaint with your company's human resources (personnel) department or reporting it to your supervisor. If your supervisor is the person you are accusing of harassment, then report the complaint to the next person up the chain of command.
- If you are not satisfied with how your company has handled the problem, you can file a complaint with your state's antidiscrimination agency or with the United States Equal Employment Opportunity Commission (EEOC), a federal agency. Although you don't need a lawyer to do this, it's probably a good idea to consult one.
- You can also file a lawsuit, but you will probably have to wait until the EEOC has investigated and issued a "right-to-sue" letter. This document verifies that your case has completed its course with the agency. After receiving a right-to-sue letter, you have a limited amount of time to initiate a lawsuit — usually no more than ninety days.
- If there is a finding of harassment, you may be entitled to
  - **payment for your lost wages**
  - **payment for your pain and suffering**
  - **punitive damages**
  - **a restraining order to prevent the person from continuing to bother you**
  - **payment for your attorney's fees**
- *Remember:* watch the clock. You have a limited time to make a claim after an incident occurs.

direct it to the nearest regional office of the Occupational Safety and Health Administration, rather than the EPA. You can find out the number by looking in the government pages of the phone book, or you can call the OSHA office in Washington at 202-219-8148.

Employers are free to restrict smoking in the officeplace. They can ban it outright or restrict it to designated areas. In fact, some states ban smoking from all common areas, such as

- **cafeterias**
- **office reception areas**
- **kitchens and rest rooms**

Some employers allow people to smoke in their individual offices. Some employers forbid smoking anywhere in the office.

While an employer can restrict smoking in the workplace, some states have laws that protect smokers from discrimination. That means that an employer can't reject an applicant because he or she is a smoker. It doesn't mean that employees get to smoke anytime or anywhere they want during work hours.

In some states, such as Georgia, however, an employer can reject smokers *and* insist that they refrain from lighting up on and off the job. That policy may be difficult to enforce, but it's legal so long as workers are adequately informed when they take the job.

Sexual Harassment

As the technological troubleshooter, Beatrice was Ms. Popular around the office. She dealt with people at all levels of the company — from the mailroom to the chief executive's suite, and while she enjoyed being helpful, there were some problems. For instance, Beatrice often spent several hours a day working on the computer system in the shipping department, a lounge-like area where truck drivers milled about before leaving to make their deliveries. They had decorated their "space" with body-building posters and pinups of scantily clad women, and they pestered Beatrice incessantly with suggestive comments about how she might spend her time after work with them.

And then there was Arthur, her boss. One day he had requested her help on a complex programming problem. They were working alone in his office, when he got up and shut the door. "You know, Beatrice, you're a very attractive woman," he said. "I'd like to take you to dinner sometime." Beatrice demurred and reminded him of the no-dating policy.

"Oh, you don't have to worry about that," he said softly, leaning over and touching her leg. "Join my team, babe, and I'll get you places. Don't join my team, and well, I can't make any promises. You know it's a pretty tough market out there. A gal can use all the help she can get. Especially a pretty gal like you. So how about dinner tomorrow night?"

■ Was all of this sexual harassment?

Probably. There are two kinds of sexual harassment. The first is **quid pro quo** harassment, where an employee is threatened with a demotion (or promised a promotion) in exchange for "sexual favors." It usually comes from a supervisor or other person in a position of authority (such as Arthur). Conduct that would be considered harassment consists of

- **unwelcome sexual advances**
- **requests for sexual favors**
- **verbal or physical conduct of a sexual nature, such as lewd comments or inappropriate touching**

When a superior threatens to fire a worker who fails to comply with sexual advances, that's usually quid pro quo harassment, just as it is when a superior promises that a worker will be promoted for complying with a sexual proposition. However, if your boss says, "Gee, you look great today," that's probably not harassment. But if he tells you that every day, and then one day suggests that you have a drink with him because his wife is out of town, then that is beginning to cross the line.

Hostile environment harassment is slightly different. Here there can be harassment even if the "offender" is not your superior. Hostile environment harassment exists when

- **a person is subjected to sexual advances, requests for sexual favors, or other verbal or physical conduct of a sexual nature**
- **the conduct was unwelcome**
- **the conduct was sufficiently severe or pervasive to alter the conditions of the victim's employment and create an abusive working environment**

So the constantly lewd comments and offensive posters of the truck drivers very well might be considered hostile environment harassment. (See the Case in Point below.)

In both types of harassment the frequency of the conduct and the intent of the person (or persons) who acted objectionably will be taken into consideration. You should keep track of any offensive behavior, recording the date and time and place it occurred. In some circumstances your employer can be held liable for sexual harassment even if he or she is unaware of it, because it is the employer's duty to provide a "hostile-free" work environment. Still, you should report sexual harassment when it occurs.

Discrimination on the Job

Beatrice got a call from Risa, another Frozen and Fabulous computer specialist. "We have to talk," said Risa. When they met after work, Risa, who is Hispanic, told Beatrice that she'd been keeping track of all the company's promotions during the last year. Twelve of the fifteen people who had been promoted were men, she said. And, of the ten new hires, all were white. Five people had been laid off. They were all over forty, and their replacements were all under thirty. "There seems to be a pattern," Risa said. "And I don't like it."

Risa said she had applied for several promotions — and had been passed over for every one, while less productive males had shot ahead rapidly. When she asked Arthur why she regularly received positive performance evalu-

CASE IN POINT

Unwelcome Transactions

The U.S. Supreme Court addressed the issue of sexual harassment for the first time in 1986, when it ruled in favor of a female bank employee who had sued her supervisor and the bank where she worked.

Mechelle Vinson claimed that she had been subjected to constant sexual harassment by her supervisor, Sidney Taylor, during the four years she worked at the Meritor Savings Bank. Vinson asserted that Taylor made repeated demands on her for sexual favors, and she estimated they had sex forty or fifty times during her tenure at the bank. In addition, she testified that Taylor had fondled her in front of employees and that he raped her on several occasions.

The Supreme Court ruled an employee could have a claim for sexual harassment even when the harassment had no economic effect on the employee. Moreover, the court ruled, the fact that Vinson and Taylor had a sexual relationship would not shield Taylor from a claim of sexual harassment. "The correct inquiry is whether [Vinson] by her conduct indicated that the alleged sexual advances were unwelcome, not whether her actual participation in sexual intercourse was voluntary," wrote Justice William Rehnquist.

The court also ruled that Vinson's employer, the bank, was not protected from liability simply because it had a grievance procedure for unhappy employees. The bank's grievance procedure "apparently required an employee to complain first to her supervisor, in this case Taylor," wrote Rehnquist. "Since Taylor was the alleged perpetrator, it is not altogether surprising that [Vinson] failed to invoke the procedure and report her grievance to him."

ations but failed to move ahead, he mumbled something about her "attitude" problem — a problem no one had ever mentioned. "Some people just aren't comfortable working with you," he told her.

■ What "categories" of people are protected against discrimination?

Many federal and state laws have been passed to protect workers (see box on page 238). Under these laws, employers must not discriminate against people based upon their

- **race**
- **sex**
- **age (if forty or older)**
- **gender**
- **religious beliefs**
- **national origin**
- **skin color**
- **physical handicap**

In addition, many state laws prohibit discrimination on the basis of a person's marital status or sexual preference.

Antidiscrimination laws cover a wide range of workplace activities. For instance, under Title VII of the Civil Rights Act of 1964, it is illegal to discriminate in such areas as

- **hiring and firing**
- **compensation, assignment, or classification of employees**
- **transfers**
- **recruitment**
- **testing**
- **use of company facilities**
- **training programs**
- **fringe benefits**
- **retirement plans and disability leave**

In addition, a person who files a charge of discrimination is protected against retaliation by the employer while the case is pending. Even if you lose your discrimination case, so long as you made your claim in **good faith,** it will be difficult for your employer to retaliate against you. If, however, your employer can show that you made the claim in **bad faith,** knowing that there was no substance to the accusation, you could be fired.

■ What should people do if they think they've been the victim of discrimination?

You should call the EEOC or talk to a lawyer who will help you assess whether or not you have a claim and how you should proceed. If you're accusing your employer of discrimination, it's very important that you have facts to support your charge. The EEOC or a lawyer should tell you exactly what you need to prove in order to win. (Of course, that doesn't mean you *will* win.) You should not file a claim against your employer if you do not have the evidence to support the claim.

What you will need to prove your case depends on several factors, including the type of claim you are making (such as age discrimination or equal pay violation) and the type of employer you work for (such as a private company or government agency). Antidiscrimination law is complex and constantly evolving, and the kind of proof you may be required to present to support a claim this year is not necessarily the kind of proof you will be required to present next year. In most cases, you will have the obligation to show ("burden of proof") that your employer intended to discriminate. In other cases, it will be the employer's burden to prove that the employment decisions were made for legitimate business reasons.

If you decide to proceed with your claim and if you are still working, you should first file an internal complaint with the company — although you are not required to do so by law. A responsible employer should then conduct a thorough investigation to determine whether or not your discrimination charge can be substantiated by the facts.

If you are dissatisfied with the results of your internal complaint, you can file a charge with either your state's antidiscrimination agency or the federal agency (EEOC). (See the box on page 240.) The decision on where to file the complaint depends on what state you live in. Some states require that you first file with the EEOC. Other states require that you first file with the state. And while your harassment claim must be filed with the EEOC within a specified time limit, some states give you a longer period in which to file. (Note: employees who work in a securities industry job must first go

Your Rights in the Workplace

These are the main federal laws governing employment discrimination:

• *Title VII of the Civil Rights Act of 1964*

What does it prohibit?

Discrimination based on race, color, religion, sex, or national origin.

Which employers are subject to the law?

All employers with fifteen or more employees.

When must charges be filed?

Within 180 days of the alleged discriminatory act.

Do charges have to be filed with the EEOC before pursuing a private lawsuit?

Yes.

• *Americans with Disabilities Act*

What does it prohibit?

Discrimination against qualified individuals with disabilities.

Which employers are subject to the law?

All public sector employers; all private employers that have fifteen or more employees.

Who is protected?

A qualified person who has a physical or mental impairment that substantially limits one or more major life activities. A person who has a relationship with a disabled individual is also protected.

Impairment includes

- **epilepsy**
- **paralysis**
- **HIV infection**
- **AIDS**
- **substantial loss of hearing or vision**
- **mental retardation**
- **learning disability**

Impairment does not include

- **minor illnesses of short duration**
- **sprains or broken limbs**
- **flu**

Life activities include

- **seeing**
- **hearing**
- **speaking**
- **walking**
- **breathing**
- **performing manual tasks**
- **learning**
- **caring for oneself**

Also protected are people who have recovered from cancer, alcoholism or drug abuse, and mental illness.

How must an employer "reasonably accommodate" a qualified person with disabilities?

- **By making the work facility readily accessible**
- **By restructuring the job or modifying the work schedule**
- **By acquiring or modifying equipment**
- **By adjusting or modifying training materials**
- **By providing readers or interpreters**

When must charges be filed?

Within 180 days of the alleged discriminatory act.

Do charges have to be filed with the EEOC before pursuing a private lawsuit?

Yes.

• *Equal Pay Act*

What does it prohibit?

Discriminating between men and women on the basis of sex in the payment of wages where

- **they perform substantially equal work**
- **the working conditions are similar**
- **they work in the same establishment**

Which employers are subject to the law?

All private employers and most government employers.

When must charges be filed?

Within two years of the discriminatory act (in some cases, the filing period is three years).

Do charges have to be filed with the EEOC before pursuing a private lawsuit?
No.

• ***Age Discrimination in Employment Act of 1967***

What does it prohibit?
Age discrimination in hiring, discharge, pay, promotions, and other conditions of employment.

Who is protected?
All persons forty years of age or older.

What employers are subject to the law?
All private employers with twenty or more workers, and all government employers, employment agencies, and labor unions with twenty-five or more employees. However, governments are permitted to make age-based hiring and retirement decisions for firefighters and law enforcement officers.

When must charges be filed?
Within 180 days of the discriminatory act.

Do charges have to be filed with the EEOC before pursuing a private lawsuit?
Yes.

through arbitration before filing a discrimination claim. In addition, some employers require that employees sign an agreement that they will go through an arbitrator when there is a workplace dispute rather than through the court system.)

You can contact the agencies (or a lawyer) to find out the guidelines for filing a complaint in your state.

Risa decided to pursue a discrimination claim. She convinced the other minorities and women in her department to join her.

■ What evidence does a person need to prove discrimination?

When you make a complaint, it's not enough to say "I was discriminated against." It's not even enough to say "I was the only black sales representative and they fired me, and therefore it was discrimination."

Proving discrimination can be very difficult, because an employer rarely says something blatant like "I'm not promoting you because you're a woman." Though you may feel that you're not being promoted because of your sex (or your race or your religion or any other reason), you must have more than your gut feeling to make a case for discrimination. You've got to establish that you were treated differently, and you've got to show that people of a different race, sex, or age were treated more favorably.

Basically, there are two kinds of evidence: **direct** and **circumstantial.** Direct evidence is harder to come by, and it includes actual comments or actions that are clearly discriminatory. For instance, if your supervisor says, "You're fifty-nine. We have a very young workforce. I think it's time you retire," or if your co-workers or former superiors provide statements that they heard the supervisor say she wanted "to sack the old guy," that would be pretty strong direct evidence of age discrimination.

Proving discrimination with circumstantial evidence is more complex. Say the fifty-nine-year-old man has worked for the company for fifteen years and always received positive reviews. Then a new, younger supervisor gives him a bad review and warns that his job is in jeopardy because he doesn't know how to use a computer. In the meantime, this supervisor hasn't even bothered to give reviews to the other employees she oversees (they're all in their thirties). Also, a thirty-nine-year-old man who worked in a different part of the company but who had the exact same qualifications as the fifty-nine-year-old (also unable to use a computer) got a positive review from his supervisor. All this adds up to circumstantial evidence of age discrimination.

How to File a Charge with the EEOC

- Call the EEOC at 800-669-4000. An assistant there will tell you which local office you should contact to make your charge.
- You will probably have to submit your charge in writing (EEOC will send you a form). If your state has an antidiscrimination agency, it may have to investigate the charges before they are passed on to the EEOC. In some states, the EEOC automatically sends the case to the state office. In other states, you may be required to do so yourself.
- You will be interviewed about the alleged discrimination and a charge will be drafted.
- Your employer will be notified of the charge, and an investigation will begin. The EEOC will request documents from your employer and interview witnesses, if there are any.
- If the EEOC does not find evidence to believe there is a "reasonable cause" that discrimination occurred, you will be notified and given a "right-to-sue" letter, which allows you to pursue a private lawsuit.
- If the EEOC does believe discrimination occurred, the agency will try to work out a settlement with the employer. The settlement could include reinstating you to your job and awarding you back pay and punitive damages.
- If the EEOC cannot reach a settlement, it may bring a lawsuit on your behalf.

Affirmative Action

Risa went to Arthur with a plan to hire and promote minorities more equitably: 10 percent of new jobs would be set aside for minority applicants and a certain number of promotions would go to minorities already in the company. "This is what you have to do to rectify the unfair system that has been in place here for so long," Risa told Arthur. He shrugged her off. "Filling spaces with a number system is not the way to correct the problem, but I will make the effort to promote qualified people," he said.

Are employers required to have affirmative action programs?

It depends. Title VII, the federal antidiscrimination law, *allows* private employers to establish programs in order to remedy imbalances in the workforce or to cure the effects of past illegal discrimination, but it does not *require* that they do so. Usually, an employer voluntarily creates an affirmative action program. However, if an employer is sued and is found to have discriminated illegally, a court may order the employer to implement an affirmative action program. Also, companies that contract to do work for the government may be required to make an effort to hire women and minorities in order to receive federal funding, and government employers are required to have affirmative action programs.

Arthur actively tried to hire and promote minorities in order to balance the workforce more equitably. Risa finally got promoted. So did Lyla, another Hispanic woman who had been with the company only for a year as a junior accountant. Lyla's promotion really upset Carl, a white junior accountant, who had been with Frozen and Fabulous for two years. He had always assumed that the next promotion would be his. Not only had he been at the company longer, but he was sure his work was much better than Lyla's.

Is there such a thing as reverse discrimination?

Yes. Reverse discrimination is discrimination against whites or males, and it exists when people in a "protected class" (such as minorities, women, or disabled workers) are given favorable treatment (such as a promotion) solely because of who they are. To make a case for reverse discrimination, you would generally have to show that the person who was promoted was not qualified — and that you were qualified.

However, an employer that has an established affirmative action program can argue that the promotion of a less-qualified minority was justified in order to serve the ends of that program. But you may be able to show that the employer had less discriminatory options. For example, if the employer could have promoted the less-qualified "protected" person to another open position, and thus still have promoted you, then you might have a claim of reverse discrimination.

IT'S PAYDAY

Getting Your Paycheck

Beatrice and everyone else at Frozen and Fabulous had been working overtime for a month to get a new macadamia nut ice cream sandwich ready for shipping. More than three weeks had lapsed since their last payroll distribution, and they were usually paid every two weeks. Tempers were rising, but Arthur only shrugged and promised that the checks were on the way.

■ Can employers just wait until the mood strikes them to hand out the paychecks?

No. Every state has wage and hour laws that regulate when and how employees are paid. The rules, of course, vary from state to state, but the majority of states require that wages be paid at least twice a month. How much you get paid is also regulated. Every worker, with the exception of some minors, must be paid at least the minimum wage set by the federal government, and some states have set an even higher minimum wage. You can find out what the minimum in your state is by calling the local department of labor.

Note: If you earn tips, your employer can pay you less than the minimum wage. Federal law allows your employer to pay you half the minimum wage per hour if you earn at least $20 a month in tips. Some states, however, require the employer to pay you more than half the minimum wage. And you must be allowed to keep your tips.

CASE IN POINT

Redress for Success

Ann Hopkins, a senior manager at Price Waterhouse, was considered a highly competent worker who had a winning way with clients and expertly managed her staff. She worked in the firm's Washington, D.C., office and was responsible for helping to win lucrative contracts with federal agencies.

But her situation changed after she was proposed for partnership in 1982. Suddenly, Hopkins was faced with criticisms by other partners in the firm who said she was sometimes overbearing and abrasive and acted in a "macho" manner. They advised her to "walk more femininely, talk more femininely, dress more femininely, wear make-up, have her hair styled, and wear jewelry." She ultimately was rejected as a partner.

That didn't seem fair to Hopkins, who sued, charging sex discrimination. Her case traveled to the U.S. Supreme Court, which in 1989 upheld the finding that she was denied partnership at Price Waterhouse in part because of sexual stereotyping, which is a form of sex discrimination. It sent the case back to the district court for reconsideration of Price Waterhouse's nondiscriminatory reasons for rejecting Hopkins. The district court found Price Waterhouse failed to present enough evidence to support its position, and it ordered Price Waterhouse to make Hopkins a partner and awarded her $371,000 in back pay. The case ended in 1990 when the U.S. Court of Appeals for the District of Columbia Circuit upheld that finding.

Can You Claim Overtime?

To determine whether you are entitled to overtime for your work, you have to look at your overall responsibilities. People are usually exempt from overtime if they are paid a salary and if they have a lot of individual discretion about how to do their job. Also, people who are supervisors are often exempt from overtime.

People who are entitled to overtime are usually paid by the hour, have fairly prescribed tasks, which don't require individual judgment, and are under the strict control of other people.

Overtime

Finally Beatrice got her check. But, she immediately noticed, there was no compensation for the thirty extra hours she had worked, which included many late nights — and the Fourth of July. Arthur shrugged again and told her she wasn't entitled to overtime pay.

■ Doesn't everybody who works more than forty hours a week get paid for the overtime?

No. Certain workers, known as **exempt** employees, are not entitled to overtime. They include white-collar workers who are in executive, administrative, or professional positions. (Beatrice was in an administrative job.) In addition, apprentices, trainees, and independent contractors (see page 248) are also not entitled to overtime. (See the box above.)

Nonexempt employees include secretaries, factory workers, clerical workers, and typically anyone who is paid by the hour. A nonexempt employee who works more than forty hours in a five-day workweek is entitled to overtime pay. At a minimum, overtime must be paid at your normal rate plus half (time and a half).

Police officers, firefighters, and people who work in hospitals and other health care facilities are entitled to overtime, but the calculations are made on a different basis. For instance, a hospital worker does not get overtime unless he or she works more than eighty hours during a two-week period. (See the Case in Point opposite.)

Also, some states limit the number of hours certain employees (like hospital workers) may work in one shift without a break.

"Comp" Time

Bob, one of the Frozen and Fabulous cake bakers, had also worked thirty hours of overtime, and unlike Beatrice, he was entitled to be paid for the time. When there was no sign of extra wages on his paycheck, he confronted Arthur. "No problem," said the boss. "Just take thirty hours off whenever you want to during the next six months."

■ Can an employer make an employee take compensatory ("comp") time instead of money?

No. If you want the money, your employer has to give you the money, unless you work for a state or local government. In some cases, the boss *has* to give you cash even if you would prefer to receive compensatory time. Generally, however, an employer can legally offer you the choice of taking your overtime in cash or in time. The comp time must be awarded at a rate equal to at least one and a half times the overtime worked, and the employer can insist that you take the time off during the same pay period in which the overtime hours were worked.

Equal Pay

Beatrice was friendly with Marcel, a programmer who had started work at Frozen and Fabulous a month after she did. One week when he was sick with the flu, Marcel called and asked Beatrice to finish a quick project for him. The information she'd need, he said, was in his top desk drawer.

That's not all that was there. Beatrice would never have looked for it, but right on top in the drawer sat Marcel's paycheck stub proving what she had always suspected: he was making more money — and their jobs were exactly the same.

Are women entitled to equal pay for equal work?

Basically, yes. When a man and a woman perform the same job, the federal Equal Pay Act of 1963 (as well as some state laws) requires employers to pay them the same salaries. (See the box on page 238.) The definition of "equal work" is complex and evolving, but in general it means that

- **men and women perform equal work**
- **the work is performed under similar working conditions**
- **the jobs require equal skill, effort, and responsibility**

Equal pay laws, however, don't guarantee that salaries won't differ. What an employer has to ensure is that salaries are determined by a system that is fair and not based on a person's sex. If your employer determines your salary according to seniority, merit, or the quantity or quality of your work, then your employer will probably be justified in paying different salaries to men and women, because the basis for the difference is something other than gender. (See the Case in Point on page 244.)

If you are a woman and you think you are being paid less than a man for the same work, you should first file an internal complaint with your employer. If that does not resolve the problem, then you can file a claim with the EEOC or with your state's antidiscrimination agency. (See the box on page 240.)

Deductions

Arthur announced that all employees who worked in Frozen and Fabulous dessert "shoppes" would be required to get new uniforms (white shirts with an F & F logo and white chef hats) and that the cost would be deducted from their paychecks. In addition, kitchen workers would now be docked for broken dishes, and the professional staff would be charged for their traveling expenses that exceeded a daily limit of $50.

CASE IN POINT

This Time Clock Never Stopped Running

In 1991, a federal district court in Washington State awarded ninety-one mechanics at an ITT-Rayonier pulp mill $58 million in overtime. For several years, the workers had been "on call" and required to respond within ten minutes if paged. Because the mechanics handled dangerous equipment, they had to remain sober and mentally alert at all times, day and night, in case they were paged. Workers had to remain continuously available or face penalties, formal discipline, and the threat of discharge.

Some of the mechanics had spent more than 16,000 uncompensated hours on call. The court ruled that the workers were entitled to overtime pay plus damages, for a total of $57,680,829.45. Unfortunately for the workers, that judgment was reversed by the Ninth Circuit Court of Appeals in 1992, which ruled that they were not actually working while on call. Indeed, the court found the employees could do what they wanted with their free time.

■ **What deductions can an employer take?** It varies from state to state. Employers in all states must deduct for taxes and social security. In addition, some states allow employers to deduct for

- **cash shortages (sometimes the employer can deduct for this only if you were dishonest or very negligent)**
- **breakage (by you)**
- **an advance payment of your wages**
- **tools and equipment**
- **meals and lodging**
- **uniforms**

An employer usually can't charge you for breakage or theft by customers, and no employer can deduct for the cost of your uniform if doing so makes your salary drop below minimum wage. And, in some states, the employer must provide and maintain your uniform regardless of how high or low your salary is.

CASE IN POINT

"I Ain't Going to Give You No Raise"

In 1985, six women employed by an Alabama construction company angrily confronted their boss, complaining that they were doing the same work as their male colleagues, but were being paid less money.

The women worked at White and Son Enterprises, a company that built trusses used in the construction of chicken houses. Their jobs — sanding, staining, building beams, and sawing lumber — all required the same skill and level of responsibility as the jobs held by men in the company. However, women at the company were paid less than the men, regardless of their experience or ability. Even one woman who trained male employees for various jobs received a lower salary than they did.

The case went to trial, and owner Orvis White testified that when the women confronted him about the pay disparity, he responded, "I ain't going to give you no raise." He then told his secretary to draw up their paychecks, in effect, dismissing them.

Soon after, the women filed charges with the Equal Employment Opportunity Commission. In 1989, the U.S. Court of Appeals for the Eleventh Circuit ruled that White had violated Title VII and the Equal Pay Act by discriminating against the employees based on sex. The judge awarded the women back pay as well as the pay they would have earned on the job had they been men.

In contrast, the U.S. Court of Appeals for the Seventh Circuit ruled in 1987 that Southern Illinois University did not discriminate against a female assistant professor who was paid less than her male predecessor.

In 1974, Patricia Covington was hired by the university to work as an adviser in SIU's School of Art. She later learned that the man she had replaced, Donald Lemasters, was paid substantially more when he held the position, and Covington sued the school for discrimination based on sex.

The court ruled that the difference in salaries was not a result of discrimination. Rather, it found that Covington was not paid less because of her sex and that there were several legitimate reasons to justify her lower salary. Most notably, she had less experience than her male counterpart. She had taught high school for one year and had worked as a teaching assistant at SIU for two years. Lemasters, on the other hand, had already worked at SIU for five years as a full-time instructor when he was transferred to the adviser position and had other professional experience that warranted a higher salary.

BENEFITS

The Basics: What You Do and Don't Get

Beatrice had missed a week of work because she was sick. She felt even sicker when she got her next paycheck and saw that it was half her usual salary. "Sorry, hon," said Arthur. "We don't pay for sick days."

"So count it as vacation time," Beatrice argued.

"Nope, we don't pay for that either."

"What do you mean?" Beatrice, now incredulous, insisted. "When you hired me, you said I was entitled to two weeks off a year."

"That's right," grinned Arthur. "But two weeks *off* doesn't mean two weeks *paid.*"

■ Do employers have to offer paid vacations and other benefits?

No. A few states do require employers to provide health care insurance (and the requirement may be extended under proposals to change the federal law), but beyond that nothing is mandatory. Paid time off, life insurance, disability insurance, pension and retirement plans are all offered at the employer's discretion. (For more on pension plans, see Chapter 26.)

However, once an employer does offer benefits — as most do — there are some rules. For instance, most benefits must be offered to every employee in a given "class" of employees. A class is any group of similar employees. All executives in a company would be a class, for instance, and all hourly workers in the same company would be a different class. So if you are one of four secretaries in a small company, and your boss decides to offer a retirement plan, he or she must offer it to all four of you.

Certain things, however, are considered extras that don't have to be offered to everyone. For instance, you may negotiate for the boss to pay your parking fees or provide you with an additional week of paid vacation. Such perquisites do not have to be offered to everyone.

■ What about health insurance?

Most employers aren't required to offer health insurance, but if your boss does offer this benefit, you generally can be required to pay for all or part of it. Employer-sponsored health plans are governed by the federal Employee Retirement Income Security Act of 1974 (ERISA), which pretty much prevents states from imposing regulations in this area. However, as with other benefits, your boss can't selectively pick and choose who gets to participate in the health insurance plan. All employees in a similar job classification must have the same opportunity to participate.

Disability

Beatrice and her friend Renata went hiking one weekend. Renata, never known as a graceful person, slipped on a wet rock and fell down a ravine, breaking her arm and hip. She was in a body cast in the hospital for three weeks, then at home and unable to work for six more. Luckily, the graphic design company she worked for offered better benefits than Frozen and Fabulous, so she received nearly all her salary during that time.

■ What is disability pay?

It's a benefit that compensates employees for some or most of their lost earnings when illness prevents them from working full-time. Employers may offer both short-term and long-term disability insurance coverage, but they are not required to do so. In addition, some states offer disability insurance.

■ When is someone entitled to collect disability?

It depends on the insurance plan and the particular problem. Many disability plans have a waiting period (usually ninety days) before an employee is entitled to collect long-term benefits. If your employer also offers short-term coverage, then payments may begin immediately or as soon as you have used up any available sick leave.

Family Leave

What Is Family Leave?
The Family and Medical Leave Act of 1993 allows employees to take up to twelve workweeks of unpaid leave during a one-year period for

- **the birth of a child**
- **the adoption of a child**
- **placement of a child with the employee for foster care**
- **care for a spouse, child, or parent with a serious health condition**
- **care of a serious health condition that makes the employee unable to work**

Who has to offer it?

Family leave must be offered by most public agencies and by any business that has employed fifty workers or more for twenty weeks of the current or preceding calendar year.

Who gets it?

To qualify for leave, a worker must have been employed for at least 12 months and worked at least 1,250 hours.

What job guarantees are there?

Most employees who take leave are entitled to return to their same position or to an equivalent position with the same benefits and pay. Seniority and other benefits do not accrue during the leave. In some cases, a company's highest-paid employees may be denied their former jobs if it would be an undue hardship for the employer to make do without them. These tend to be jobs that involve a lot of responsibility, say a chief financial officer or head of human resources.

Leaves of Absence

Elly, one of Frozen and Fabulous's best salespeople (and Beatrice's best friend at work), was pregnant with her first child. She was very excited — and very confused. She had been saving up vacation time so she could spend as much time with her newborn as possible. But she didn't want to jeopardize her job or lose any seniority. The company had instituted a plan that offered pregnant women paid "disability leave," but Elly couldn't figure out whether she would qualify if her pregnancy and delivery went forward with no complications.

What kind of maternity leave are women entitled to?

It varies. No laws require employers to offer paid maternity leave, but many do. In addition, pregnancy, childbirth, and related medical conditions are technically considered to be disabilities, so if your employer offers paid disability leave, you are entitled to take that leave when you are pregnant or when you give birth.

Unpaid leave, however, is a different matter. Most employers have to offer unpaid leave under the Family and Medical Leave Act of 1993 (see the box). Women who are eligible to take leave under this law are entitled to take up to twelve weeks off.

In addition, some states require that a woman be given up to four months of unpaid leave after the birth of a child.

Often a woman who plans to take a disability leave for pregnancy, childbirth, or related medical conditions must give her employer reasonable notice of the date she will leave and the date she will return. And, under the Family and Medical Leave Act, a woman who adopts a baby is also entitled to take up to twelve weeks of unpaid leave.

What about new fathers? Are they entitled to paternity leave?

Yes, under the Family and Medical Leave Act, new fathers can take up to twelve weeks of unpaid leave.

Also, some employers now offer new fathers *paid* paternity leave.

Arthur was hardly thrilled with the news that Elly was pregnant. She was one of his best salespeople, and he did not like the idea of having to do without her for several weeks. He also worried that her growing belly would detract from her ability to sell desserts, and he knew the pregnancy might limit her ability to travel. So he promoted her to the marketing department, where it would be her job to devise methods for grocery stores to draw more attention to the Frozen and Fabulous desserts. To Elly this was hardly a step up, since she would no longer be earning commissions.

Can an employer force a woman to change jobs because she's pregnant?

No. A woman can't be penalized for being pregnant. Expectant employees (and new mothers) are protected by the federal Pregnancy Discrimination Act, which requires that employers treat pregnant workers the same as other employees. Even if a woman works in an industry where she might come into contact with chemicals or be required to exert herself physically in ways that could be hazardous to her pregnancy, an employer would have to show considerable evidence that she is at risk before she could be forced to move from her job.

If a woman's ability to do her job is truly diminished by her pregnancy, then her employer may be able to move her. For example, if a woman works in a construction job where she is required to do a lot of heavy lifting, but will be unable to do so during the later stages of pregnancy, the employer may be able to move her — though every effort must be made to find a comparable job for her with comparable pay.

That doesn't mean that the employer has to create a new job for her. If, for instance, a woman works as an elevator mechanic and her doctor tells her she can't work past a certain point in her pregnancy, her boss should try to move her to another position in the company with comparable pay. That may be difficult though, since she earns $40 an hour and the only other positions in the company are for a secretary and a bookkeeper. She may, however, be entitled to collect disability pay for the time she is unable to work before her baby is born.

CASE IN POINT

Occupational Hazards

In 1982, Johnson Controls Inc., a battery maker, instituted a fetal-protection policy that barred all fertile women from jobs that involved actual or potential exposure to lead. Only women who could show medical documents stating that they were infertile were allowed to work at these jobs.

A group of employees brought a class action suit charging Johnson Controls with sexual discrimination. The plaintiffs included a woman who chose to be sterilized in order to save her job; a fertile woman who had been transferred into a lower-paying job; and a man who had been denied a request for a leave of absence in order to lower his lead level before he became a father.

The company argued that its policy was necessary to promote industrial safety. The U.S. Supreme Court rejected the notion that discrimination was justified in order to protect women. In 1991, the court ruled that the fetal protection policy was discriminatory and in violation of the Pregnancy Discrimination Act.

Among its findings, the court noted that despite evidence about the debilitating effect of lead exposure on the male reproductive system, the battery maker did not try to protect the offspring of its male employees. "The bias in Johnson Controls' policy is obvious," wrote Justice Harry Blackmun. "Fertile men, but not fertile women, are given a choice as to whether they wish to risk their reproductive health for a particular job."

Injuries Not Covered by Workers' Compensation

A worker may not be entitled to benefits when

- he or she is injured in an activity that was solely for the benefit of the worker or someone other than the employer. For example, if the employee was playing catch in the hallways and was injured, or had an attack of appendicitis, these have nothing to do with work and wouldn't be covered.
- the injury occurred while the worker was traveling to or from work. There are exceptions: if an injury occurs while you are just driving your regular route to work, it wouldn't be covered, but if you were supposed to stop and pick up office supplies on the way, it might be. Injuries you sustain while out of town on a business trip *are* covered.
- the injury was due to the employee's intoxication or willful failure to use safety equipment. This varies from state to state, however.
- the injuries were suffered in an activity that was forbidden by the employer.
- in addition, there are some injuries, for example some occupational diseases, for which the statute does not provide benefits.

Does an employer have to guarantee a woman's job when she goes on maternity leave?

Yes, for the most part. Employees who return from maternity leave are entitled to return to their previous position *or* to an equivalent position with equivalent benefits, pay, and conditions of employment. Fathers who take time off to care for a newborn under the Family and Medical Leave Act are entitled to the same benefits. (See page 246.)

If you think you've been discriminated against because of your pregnancy, you can file a complaint with the EEOC (see the box on page 240).

PART-TIMERS AND FREELANCERS

Independent Contractors

Beatrice, tired of the 9-to-5 grind, thought about going out on her own as a computer/technology consultant. That way, she figured, she could set her own hours and determine how to accomplish a project without Arthur breathing down her neck. And she could work at home in comfortable clothes.

What makes a worker an "independent contractor"?

A person who offers his or her services to several companies and then performs the work autonomously is considered an independent contractor. Generally, a person is considered an independent contractor when he or she — and not the company for whom the work is being done — has complete control over any given project.

Usually, any kind of outside consultants who come into a company to work on a specific project are considered independent contractors. So, too, are outside professionals, such as accountants, architects, and lawyers.

Independent contractors are not considered "employees," and they are not covered by wage and hour laws. They typically negotiate their fees with the company, and they are responsible for making their own tax and social security payments. An independent contractor may negotiate for certain benefits, but the employer is under no obligation to provide them.

The Internal Revenue Service has begun taking a closer look at employers who hire independent contractors to make sure they aren't classifying their workers as independents just to avoid making the social security payments. As a result, many employers now require independent contractors to fill out lengthy questionnaires. So long as the questions are limited to the nature of the work relationship, there is nothing illegal about them.

When You Get Hurt on the Job

If you've been injured and think you're entitled to workers' compensation, you should notify your employer as soon as possible. Your employer should give you a claim form to complete and should then submit your form (along with related documents) to the insurance carrier and to the workers' compensation agency in the state in which you live.

You will then be notified (usually by the insurance carrier) how much compensation you are to receive. If you think you are not getting enough money to cover your medical costs and lost wages, or if you are unhappy with any aspect of how your claim is handled, you may request a hearing before a workers' compensation judge.

You have up to one year to report a workers' compensation injury. If you wait one year and one day, you will be unable to collect anything.

Part-Timers

Beatrice knew it would take a while to establish herself as a freelancer, so she asked Arthur if she could work part-time. That way, she figured, she'd at least have some income she could rely on.

■ Are part-timers entitled to benefits?

It depends. A part-timer who works more than 1,000 hours in a calendar year ordinarily is entitled by federal law to participate in the pension plan if the employer also offers it to full-time workers in the same category. (For more on pension plans, see page 387.) Health insurance and other benefits, on the other hand, are offered at the employer's discretion.

ACCIDENTS AND SAFETY

Workers' Compensation

Beatrice's sister Blossom was the assistant pastry chef at La Chi-Chi, a fancy four-star restaurant. She was lugging a bushel of apples to her cutting board when a deliveryman from the restaurant's produce vendor slid a crate of broccoli across the floor in front of her. Blossom tripped, dumping the apples and crashing onto her elbow. She broke her arm and was unable to work for two months.

■ Does an employer have to pay a worker who's injured on the job?

Yes. Most likely she's entitled to **workers' compensation**, a benefit paid to employees who suffer a work-related injury or illness. (The money is paid by the employer or by the employer's insurance company.) No matter how serious the injury, if you are hurt on the job, you are probably entitled to reimbursement for the cost of your related medical expenses. And if you're going to be out of work for a limited time, you would probably be eligible for temporary disability pay. If you are more seriously injured and unable to return to work, you may be able to receive permanent disability pay.

And if injury prevents you from returning to your old job, but does not prevent you from working altogether, you may be able to receive vocational rehabilitation.

Most employees are entitled to receive workers' compensation. However, some states exempt smaller companies (usually those with five employees or fewer) from providing coverage. Some states also exclude domestic workers, farmworkers, and independent contractors. If injured, these employees may sue their employers. They will have to prove they were hurt because of the employer's negligence.

Blossom didn't get a very good workers' compensation settlement. It covered most of her lost pay and some of her medical bills, but it did not cover her twice-a-week physical therapy or the expensive, custom-made arm brace she had to wear.

■ **Can a person bring a suit against her employer if she's getting workers' compensation?**

No. The point of workers' compensation is to redress workers' injuries without forcing them to go through the court system. Thus, it is supposed to be a relatively routine process for an injured worker to receive compensation, and the only time the worker can go to court (instead of through a state workers' compensation agency) is when a third party who is not the employer may have been responsible for the injury. If, for instance, Blossom could show that the deliveryman had acted negligently when he pushed the crate in front of her, she might be able to collect money from him or his employer (see "Personal Injury," on page 335).

If an accident occurs at work because of the employer's negligence, you may be able to get an additional penalty award.

Unsafe Working Conditions

The hazards in the kitchen of La Chi-Chi seemed small-time compared to the hazards in the industrial kitchens of Frozen and Fabulous. Workers were frequently complaining to Arthur about the state of things there: a frayed electrical cord on a food processor; a blade guard missing on the slicer; no fire extinguishers; an oven that heated too hot, too quick; and suspicious animal droppings. The kitchen seemed to be a disaster waiting to happen.

■ **Are employers required to meet safety standards?**

Yes, the Federal Occupational Safety and Health Act requires all employers to take all reasonable steps possible to ensure that a workplace is free of dangers. In addition, employers in certain industries (such as chemical manufacturers or hospitals) must follow very specific safety guidelines.

Whistle-Blowing

Beatrice spent a lot of time in the kitchens of Frozen and Fabulous working on the computer where the recipes were stored. She didn't need anyone to tell her conditions were unsafe and unsanitary. When none of the supervisors responded to the complaints of the kitchen staff, Beatrice decided to report the problems to the local board of health.

■ **What is whistle-blowing?**

Whistle-blowing occurs when an employee complains about an employer's illegal activities or about safety and health hazards in the workplace. The complaint can be made to the employer or to an "outside authority," usually an agency, such as OSHA, that monitors workplace activities.

■ **Does a whistle-blower have job protection?**

Yes. Employers are prohibited by federal law and by laws in all states from retaliating against a whistle-blowing employee. For example, if you contacted the Securities and Exchange Commission to report that your boss had committed a white-collar crime (such as insider trading), your boss cannot turn around and fire you. And, in some states, your boss cannot fire you if you refuse to break the law or lie on his or her behalf. However, if your report turns out to be false, and if your boss can show that you made the report out of maliciousness, then you can be fired for misconduct. If, however, you had a reasonable basis to make the report, in some states, then your boss cannot fire you, because that would be retaliation.

■ **If a person has damaging information to reveal about an employer, what precautions should be taken?**

You should do all you can to learn whether what is being done is truly inappropriate or illegal by contacting the government agency that regulates your business (such as OSHA). You should also make every effort to inform your employer of the problems and make as much evidence available as possible for the problem to be taken care of internally.

What you are basically trying to do is protect yourself in the event that you are fired for whistleblowing. If you get fired after complaining about something that is indeed illegal, in some states you will have been wrongfully discharged, and in those states you would probably be able to collect lost pay and be reinstated to your job. However, if you accuse your employer of illegal activity and you are wrong, then you most likely would not win a wrongful discharge case.

So even if you truly believe that the employer is violating the law somehow, you should do all you can to get an outside opinion and to solve the problem within the company. Such measures will help to protect you.

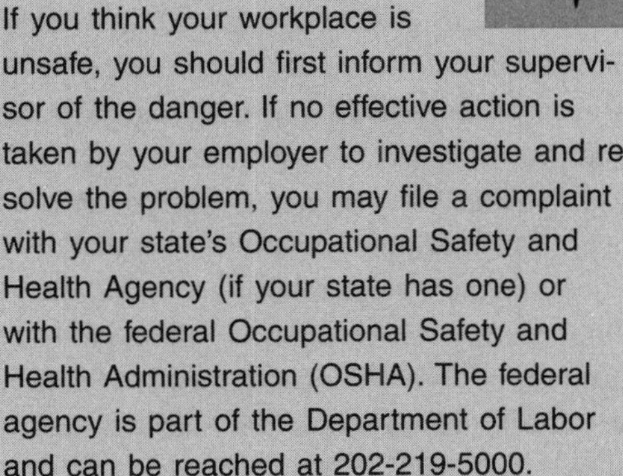

Reporting Unsafe Conditions

If you think your workplace is unsafe, you should first inform your supervisor of the danger. If no effective action is taken by your employer to investigate and resolve the problem, you may file a complaint with your state's Occupational Safety and Health Agency (if your state has one) or with the federal Occupational Safety and Health Administration (OSHA). The federal agency is part of the Department of Labor and can be reached at 202-219-5000.

PARTING COMPANY: GETTING FIRED AND QUITTING

"At-Will" and "Just-Cause" Employment

Arthur asked Beatrice to order him a laptop computer. He wanted it with the works — modem, built-in fax, color monitor, lots of memory. Beatrice was miffed. Arthur did absolutely nothing on his computer except store addresses and write an occasional memo. She knew he wanted the fancy getup only to impress his friends. In the meantime, she had been trying for months to persuade him to upgrade the office systems, which were hopelessly outdated. He refused, saying it was a waste of money. So when he made the request for his own new plaything, Beatrice told him she thought he was being frivolous and that the money would be better spent improving a system that someone was actually going to use.

To which Arthur responded, "That's it, Beatrice. You're out of here. I am sick and tired of your attitude. You're fired."

■ Can the boss just up and fire someone?

Yes, because most people's jobs are considered **at-will.** In an at-will employment relationship, the employer has the right to fire a worker for any cause at any time — usually without any notice. That gives a boss a lot of leeway to get rid of people, but it doesn't put the company beyond the reach of employment laws. For example, if an employee thinks he or she was fired for discriminatory reasons (such as being too old), the employee has the right to pursue a claim. (See page 236.)

Not all employees can be fired at-will, however. It depends on the policies of your employer and the laws of your state. Many employers must have **just cause** (a good reason) to fire someone. An employee is not at-will if

- **the employer specifically has a policy that there must be a "just cause" for discharge**
- **there is a contract between the employee and the employer with such a provision**
- **the state prohibits at-will firings (Montana law, for instance, requires that an employer have "good cause" for firing a worker)**

■ Can you be fired for telling the boss he's a terrible manager?

Only if you are an at-will employee. If the boss must have "just cause" to fire someone, then he would need to have a good reason to fire you. In that case, if you're only occasionally sassy, but your job performance is adequate, then he probably can't fire you. However, if you are constantly grumbling about work assignments and making the work environment difficult for others around so that they can't perform adequately, and if you have failed to improve your behavior after several warnings, he may have just cause to say that your attitude is interfering with your job performance.

Many companies require new employees to go through a **probation** period. No law prohibits the practice, and there generally is no limit to how long an employer can set the period — although the typical time is between 60 and 120 days. During this time period, the employer has more leeway. So even in a company where regular employees can be fired only with just cause, a probationary employee can be fired at will.

If you are a member of a labor union (see page 255), it is likely that your employer cannot fire you at will unless you are still in the probationary period.

Taking Sick Days

Unfortunately, Beatrice had more than an attitude problem working against her. She had had a bad winter — two bouts of the flu, a case of food poisoning, an emergency appendectomy, and numerous painful dental problems. She had missed several weeks of work, and Arthur was planning to fire her.

■ Can a person be fired for being sick too often?

Yes, but if you are legitimately ill, your employer has to make a reasonable effort to accommodate you. That doesn't mean the employer has to pay you for the sick days you miss, but if your work can be assigned to another employee or a temporary worker, then the employer should try to do so. If the employer can show that accommodating your illness is causing an "undue hardship," then you might lose your job.

If you're missing work but are not really sick, your absence would be considered an attendance problem, and you could be fired.

Drug and Alcohol Abuse

David, the ice cream taster, asked Arthur if he could take an extra half hour at lunchtime two days a week in order to attend meetings of Alcoholics Anonymous. David had always been a reliable employee, and he had not had a drink for five years. But when Arthur learned that he had once had a problem, he fired him immediately.

■ Can an employee be fired because of alcoholism?

It depends. A *recovering* alcoholic (or a recovering drug abuser) is protected from discrimination by the Americans with Disabilities Act (see the box on page 238), and many states also have laws protecting employees from discrimination because of their alcoholism or drug use. So an employee usually can't be fired for alcoholism if the drinking does not affect his or her job performance.

However, an employee can be dismissed for drinking on the job, *or* for poor performance that is affected by the drinking. However, some states require the employer to provide counseling or other rehabilitative therapy before firing the worker, and some states allow an employer to require that an alcoholic worker seek treatment as a condition of keeping his or her job. A worker who fails to do so could be fired.

When an employee volunteers to seek treatment, some states require that the employer make reasonable accommodations. So unless it would be an undue hardship on the company, the employer would have to allow the worker time off to participate in the rehabilitation program. Most state laws, however, do not require the employer to pay for any time the worker misses while in rehab.

Religion

Sam works full-time as a Frozen and Fabulous truck driver. When he was hired, the company made no deliveries on weekends, so his hours were seven to four, Monday through Friday. But business began picking up, and delivery hours ex-

panded. Drivers were told they'd have to rotate working on weekends. Sam observes the Jewish sabbath on Saturdays and told his supervisor he could not drive that shift.

Can an employee be fired if a religious practice interferes with work?

Probably not. Most companies must reasonably accommodate the religious interests of their workers — so long as it doesn't place an "undue burden" on the business of the employer. Thus, an employer could not force you to work on Saturday — especially if you were not originally hired to work that day. However, if Saturday is a key business day for your employer, and you knew that when you were hired but failed to speak up about your inability to work, then the employer probably could fire you.

WRONGFUL DISCHARGE

The Frozen and Fabulous pastry chefs were each required to bake fifteen cakes a day and they all usually met the quota. For an inexplicable reason, Arthur ordered Sandra, one of the top chefs, to bake twenty-five cakes a day. She protested that it was impossible, but he refused to listen. For a week straight she baked twenty cakes a day, while everyone else baked fifteen. At the end of the week Arthur fired her.

Was this wrongful discharge?

Probably. When an employee is fired for reasons that are not legitimate, it usually is wrongful discharge. Remember, though, that at-will employees can usually be fired for any reason, legitimate or not. So, it is very rare for an at-will employee to win a wrongful discharge claim.

Wrongful discharge occurs in several ways:

- A person with performance problems is fired before being given the opportunity to correct the problems.
- A person (like Sandra) is held to a standard different than other workers doing the same job — and then fired for not meeting that standard.
- A person whose performance is satisfactory is given a poor, undeserved evaluation (and fired because of it).
- A person is fired in retaliation for complaining about health and safety issues in the workplace.

If you believe you have been wrongfully discharged, you should first notify your employer, in writing, explaining why you think your firing was unfair. This gives the employer the opportunity to correct a misunderstanding, if there was one. It also makes it difficult for your employer to later say, "Gee, he didn't complain that we did anything unfair when we fired him. Funny how he's doing so now that we're in court."

After notifying your employer, you should see a lawyer who can advise you if you have a case. A lawyer may be able to negotiate a reasonable settlement for you with the employer, or the case may proceed into litigation and possibly a trial. Your employer is likely to argue that the reason you were fired is because your performance was inadequate, and your employer will probably be able to delve into your entire life history. This could be a very protracted and emotionally draining experience.

Severance Pay and Unemployment Insurance

Arthur fired Beatrice in the morning and ordered her to clear out her desk and be gone from the office by that afternoon.

Doesn't an employer have to give at least two weeks' severance pay?

No law requires a company to do so. If an employer has no formal policy that's stated in an employee handbook or promised verbally to an employee, then the boss is free to give (or not give) severance pay. However, according to federal law, when a company does have a set policy to offer employees severance pay, it can't be withheld unless the plan is amended. However, if a person has been fired because of misconduct, the severance pay can be denied.

How to Collect Unemployment Insurance

- Find out which agency in your state handles unemployment. You can usually find this in the section of your phone book with government listings.
- You will need to go to that office and file a claim. Bring along any evidence, such as a termination notice, to show that you did not voluntarily leave your job. You should also bring your social security card or your alien registration card.
- Depending on your case, you should start receiving payments anytime within three weeks or three months.
- If you are denied unemployment payments, you can appeal to your local unemployment office, which will be the same office that denied your claim. In most states you have twenty days to file an appeal.

■ Can a person who is fired collect unemployment insurance?

Probably, so long as she has worked at her job for the minimum length of time required by her state. Generally, people are eligible to collect unemployment after they have been fired — so long as they weren't fired for gross misconduct. A person who voluntarily leaves a job usually cannot collect unemployment unless the employee can show that he or she was forced to leave the job because the employer had done something to make continuing in the work environment intolerable.

Unemployment compensation benefits usually last for twenty-six weeks. However, there have recently been some special circumstances in which the President of the United States has ordered that the benefits be extended.

■ Does a person who is fired lose his or her health insurance?

No. Under the Consolidated Omnibus Budget Reconciliation Act, when a company employs twenty or more people, you must be given the option to continue on the health insurance plan for a period of up to eighteen months (unless you were fired for gross misconduct). You have to pay the premiums (but you get the benefit of a group rate), and you may also have to pay the company an administrative fee of as much as 2 percent. Even if you quit, your employer has to make the health insurance available to you for eighteen months. Note: this law does not apply if you are employed by the federal government or by certain church-related organizations.

Mass Layoffs

After a customer found a dead mouse in a quart of Exotic Tangerine frozen yogurt (it wasn't supposed to be *that* exotic), grocery stores stopped ordering F & F desserts. The company went on a massive campaign to regain consumer confidence, but Arthur was afraid it could take months, if not years, for business to pick up again. With practically no cash coming in, Arthur fired 70 of the 120 members of the staff. On a Monday morning employees on the hit list were handed a check for two weeks' pay and ordered to pack up their belongings and leave by the end of the day. A note was posted on office bulletin boards thanking them for their years of service.

■ Can an employer fire a large group of workers at one time without warning?

Not always. Under the federal Worker Adjustment and Retraining Notification Act, a company that employs 100 or more workers usually must give at least 60 days' notice when it plans to lay off 50 workers or more. Even if the company does not give 60 days' notice, it must give the workers 60 days' worth of pay.

LABOR UNIONS

Your Right to Form a Union

Beatrice and many other employees had become exasperated with the working conditions at Frozen and Fabulous. One of the cake icers from Mega Foods had been stopping by regularly and encouraging the unhappy crew to join the International Personhood of Gourmet Food Preparers, a well-organized union that formed in the mid-1980s.

What is a labor union?

A labor union is an organization that negotiates with employers on behalf of employees. Its major role is to negotiate group employment contracts for its members and to represent members who have grievances at work.

Not everyone in every profession has the right to form a union. Certain categories of workers are excluded, such as managers and supervisors, some government employees, domestic workers, and some agricultural workers.

Your right to join a union and the activities of a union are governed by the Labor Management Relations Act (also called the Taft-Hartley Act).

Unfair Labor Practices

The Frozen and Fabulous workers decided they didn't really want to join the union or form their own. They just wanted to be able to meet to air their grievances and discuss possible ways of dealing with Arthur and other members of company management.

Are employers required to allow workers to meet — even if they don't want to form a union?

Generally, employers must allow workers to meet as a group to air common grievances. In addition, there are other "protected activities" that your employer cannot interfere with. They include your right to create, join, and participate in a labor union. An employer is prohibited from unfairly disciplining, intimidating, or otherwise punishing employees for their union activities.

What constitutes an unfair labor practice?

Employers are prohibited from interfering with your right to organize or form a union. "Unfair labor practices" are violations of the National Labor Relations Act. They include situations where an employer

- **treats a worker unfairly because of the worker's support for unionization**
- **provides benefits to employees (to which they otherwise would not be entitled) in order to dissuade them from promoting a unionization effort**

Unions may also be accused of engaging in unfair labor practices when they

- **threaten employees who refuse to cooperate with efforts to develop or maintain a union**
- **encourage an employer to harass employees**

Eric, a cake decorator, jumped ship to join Mega Foods. When he was hired, he was told that all nonmanagement employees had to pay union dues, like it or not.

Can an employee be forced to join a union?

Sort of. Your employer may have an agreement with a union that all employees will be required to pay dues as if they were members. So if you accept a job with that employer, the equivalent of dues will automatically be deducted from your paycheck and paid to the union even if you decide not to join.

Several states have enacted right-to-work laws that allow employees to work at a job without having to join the union or pay dues.

Strikes and Lockouts

Union leaders had been negotiating for months with the management of Mega Foods over the terms of a new employment contract. A lot was at stake. The workers wanted an 8 percent salary increase, better health care benefits, improved safety precautions in the kitchens, and a guarantee there would be no layoffs. Management was offering a 3 percent pay raise and nothing else. Neither side was showing any sign of changing its position, and the workers were growing restless and debating whether or not they should go on strike.

Under what circumstances are union workers allowed to strike?

Union workers may strike (stop working in order to force the employer to change a bargaining position) under two conditions:

- **if the employer has committed what the union believes to be unfair labor practices**
- **when the employer and union are in dispute over the terms and conditions of a collective bargaining agreement, the contract that spells out the terms of employment**

The union must generally give notice to the employer of its "intent to strike" (the amount of notice is usually specified in the labor contract). A failure to give notice could be a violation of the National Labor Relations Act, and the employer would probably be able to stop the union from striking.

If the union does decide to strike, the members are allowed to picket so long as they don't interfere with the employer's property. Even if the members don't go on strike, they may picket as a way of bringing the public's attention to the grievances.

While the Mega Food workers strategized about a strike, the management negotiators debated their own game plan. To force the union to make concessions, they decided to shut the doors for a week — and thus withhold every worker's pay.

If You Have a Complaint

If you think your employer or your union has engaged in an unfair labor practice, you can file a complaint with the National Labor Relations Board. Claims forms should be available from your union or from the local office of the NLRB. For more information, call the NLRB at 202-273-1991.

Can an employer lock out the workers?

Yes. An employer has the right to lock out workers to try to force the union to support the company's bargaining position. Workers don't get paid during a lockout.

Replacement Workers

The Mega Foods workers finally did go on strike, and negotiations continued with little progress. The strike had lasted for three months when the company announced that unless something changed within a week, it was going to bring in outsiders to do the job.

Is an employer allowed to hire replacement workers?

The conditions for hiring replacement workers are usually outlined in the agreement between the union and the company, but usually an employer can hire temporary replacement workers. However, the company may not always hire *permanent* replacement workers. If the union workers are striking for economic reasons (they're unhappy about the pay or benefits), the employer will often be able to hire permanent replacement workers. If, however, union members are striking because the employer engaged in unfair labor practices (the work areas were unsafe, for instance), the employer will probably not be allowed to hire permanent replacements.

RUNNING YOUR OWN BUSINESS

15

SOLE PROPRIETORSHIPS

Blossom, the head chef at Chez Snooty, was tired of the rigorous insistence of Pierre, the owner, that all ingredients (including salt and pepper) must actually come from France. So she decided to start her own restaurant, Made in America. She met with a lawyer to explore how she should set up the business. "What are you thinking," he asked, "sole proprietorship? Or do you have backers? A partner?"

Blossom was silently perplexed.

■ What is a sole proprietorship?

It's the most common form of business organization. A sole proprietor is fully and *personally* liable for all the obligations (including debts) of the business. Of course, the sole proprietor is also entitled to all the business's profits and exercises complete managerial control. Generally, the earnings of the sole proprietorship itself are not subject to income tax, although some state and local governments do impose an unincorporated business tax on profits. Income and losses, however, must be included in the owner's personal tax returns. The sole proprietorship terminates on its owner's death or retirement.

A sole proprietor is not ordinarily required to file any documents with the state unless he or she is doing business under an "assumed" or "fictitious" name — that is, a name other than the real name of its owner. In that case, the owner must usually file a "doing business as" or "d/b/a" certificate. This typically gets filed in the county or with the secretary of state of the state in which the business is located, and a filing fee is often required. (For more on picking a name for your business, see page 269.)

PARTNERSHIPS

Blossom opened Made in America as a sole proprietor, and business was booming at the all-American, all-natural restaurant. Every day, people were begging for her coleslaw recipe, and travelers called from out of town weeks in advance to make reservations. "The best chicken potpie in America," one man gushed.

One night after closing, Made in America's night manager, Hannah, approached Blossom. "You know, business is so strong, I think we should open another branch across town," Hannah tentatively explored.

"We?" Blossom perked up her ears.

"Well, you know, I invested my *Jeopardy!* winnings in the stock market and did pretty well. So I was thinking we could become partners," Hannah said in one breath.

■ What is a partnership?

In its most basic form, a partnership is an association of two or more people who agree to share in the profits and losses of a business venture. A partnership can usually be formed without paying any fees or filing any papers, except for the "d/b/a" certificate discussed above. In fact, you're not legally required to put a partnership agreement in writing, although it is highly recommended, especially if you're starting a venture with several partners who are investing different amounts of money. Typically, when you form a partnership, it is done in the spirit of optimism and success. Unfortunately, conflicts often arise. By putting your agreement in writing, you can help avoid potential conflicts at the outset. Some of the topics that your partnership agreement might include are

- **partners' voting rights and management responsibilities**
- **the allocation of profits and losses among the partners**

- **partners' rights to transfer or sell their interests in the partnership**
- **the circumstances under which the partnership may terminate**
- **means for settling disputes among the partners**

In the absence of a partnership agreement, your state's partnership law will determine how these matters are resolved — and you may not like the result.

If there is a significant amount of money involved in your partnership venture, you should consult a lawyer to help you work out the terms of your agreement.

What are the advantages and disadvantages of a partnership?

A key advantage of a partnership is that no taxes are paid by the partnership itself. Although a federal income tax return must be filed by the partnership, it is for informational purposes only. Profits or losses are "passed through" directly to the partners, who report them on their individual returns. Also, because filing requirements are minimal, partnerships can be created relatively inexpensively.

One of the main disadvantages of a partnership involves liability — each partner is personally liable for the obligations of the business. This means that someone who sues the partnership can also sue and recover from each individual partner. If the partnership owes money, each partner can be held liable for the amount of the entire debt.

So when you enter into a partnership agreement, not only is your investment in the business at stake, but all your other personal assets may be at risk as well. In addition, any one partner can enter into a contract for which that partner *and all the other partners* will be responsible. If your partner in That's the Way the Cookie Crumbles makes a deal to buy $100,000 worth of chocolate chips, you, your partner, and your partnership's business will be liable for paying the $100,000 — even if the partnership had already decided to discontinue the chocolate chip cookie line.

Another disadvantage of a partnership is that partners aren't always free to come and go. If you want to sell your interest in a partnership, you usually need the consent of all the other partners. If you leave without their approval, you may forfeit your partnership investment.

You should remember, though, that many of these disadvantages can be anticipated and addressed in a partnership agreement. That's a good reason for having one.

LIMITED PARTNERSHIPS

From the night it first opened, Made in America, Too was a roaring success. The restaurant was booked solid. Hannah's idea to "Celebrate Diversity" by featuring a different ethnic cuisine every weekend was a stroke of brilliance. Customers were begging for the addition of callaloo and coconut sticky rice to the regular menu.

A group of investors — Women Backing Women — approached Blossom and asked whether she wanted to expand and open branches around the state — maybe even create franchises all over the country. "Made in America is made for America," the group's leader exclaimed enthusiastically. "The sky's the limit! You can write your own ticket."

Blossom took their excitement with a grain of salt (American salt). The idea of expanding without having to take a lot of financial risk herself was appealing. But she didn't want to grow too fast, and she wanted to stay in charge.

Blossom and Hannah laid out their terms. "Let's start with a limited partnership for now," said Blossom. "And let's put franchising on the back burner."

What is a limited partnership?

A limited partnership has two kinds of partners: **general** and **limited.** The rights and obligations of a general partner are very similar to those of a partner in a regular partnership. A general partner has the right to participate in the management of the partnership and has unlimited personal liability for its debts. A limited partner, on the other hand, is personally liable for the debts of the partnership only to the extent of his or her investment in it and has little, if any, voice in its management. You might want to form a limited partnership if you have financial backers for your partnership venture who do not want to be involved in running it. As a matter of fact, limited partners who become actively involved in the management of the partnership run the risk of losing their limited personal liability.

While a regular partnership can be entered into rather informally, a limited partnership is created only when it is formally registered with the state in which the partnership proposes to do business. To register you must file a "certificate of limited partnership," which provides certain information required by law regarding the partners and the partnership.

If you are thinking about forming a limited partnership, you should consult an attorney. Not only should you have help preparing your written agreement, but you also may have to comply with certain federal and state securities laws intended to protect investors from fraud. When you sell interests in a limited partnership — or even offer to sell them — you may be required to file certain documents, such as a financial statement or a prospectus. These documents generally should be prepared with the assistance of an attorney. A failure to make the required disclosures could result in steep fines and even criminal penalties.

CORPORATIONS

Blossom and Hannah were exhausted from the big push to open six new restaurants. After getting the kinks out — no, Canadian cheddar does not qualify as made in America — the business was humming along, and its backers were already looking forward to a nice return on their investment.

After retreating to the mountains for a week (with fax machine and cellular phones) to do some R & R and soul-searching about their booming business, Blossom and Hannah returned and called a meeting with Women Backing Women.

"Made in America is on the move," Blossom announced. "We are going to package prepared food, like our coleslaw dressing, and market it around the country. We've decided to incorporate. Maybe later we'll even go public."

What is a corporation?

A corporation is an independent entity that is usually created to conduct a business. A corporation is like an individual. It can

- **sue or be sued**
- **borrow money**
- **pay taxes**
- **apply for business licenses in its own name**
- **enter into contracts**
- **assume liabilities**

A corporation can do all these things under its own name, without making the individual owners and investors, known as **shareholders,** liable. The shareholders must *always* keep in mind, however, that they and the corporation are *separate* entities, and that they must treat the corporation as such in order to take advantages of its benefits. This rule applies even when the corporation has only one shareholder.

What are the advantages and disadvantages of a corporation?

One significant advantage of the corporate structure is that the shareholders are usually protected from personal liability. Of course, any shares you own are vulnerable if the corporation has excessive debt or goes bankrupt. Still, you will be liable only to the extent of your investment in the corporation; your assets beyond that ordinarily will be shielded. Another advantage is that, unlike with a partnership, you are free to sell your interest (shares) in a corporation. In addition, unlike a sole proprietorship or a partnership, a corporation's life span is usually perpetual, even when there is only one shareholder. Particularly if you intend that your corporation grow beyond your lifetime, the fact that it can "outlive" you and that your shares are transferable can be very helpful in getting long-term financing as your business grows.

The major disadvantages of a corporation are the expenses of start-up and the meticulous record-

The Board of Directors

A corporation can have as many or as few directors as its shareholders choose, so long as it has at least one. While large corporations routinely include on their boards individuals who possess complementary skills that will be relevant and helpful to the business (lawyers and accountants, for example), small businesses usually limit seats on their boards to those active in its management and any investors. If you are incorporating a small business, you and your fellow shareholders would ordinarily elect yourselves to the board, along with individuals who will support your respective positions and whose judgment you trust.

Board members have a duty to represent the interests of the shareholders, and they are expected to use their best business judgment when making decisions for the corporation. For example, a director who proposes that the corporation enter into a contract with another company in which that director has a financial stake must disclose the potential conflict of interest to the other board members. In addition, the transaction must ordinarily be approved by a majority of directors who do not have a conflict.

keeping that is required to comply with the many formalities of state laws. A failure to make filings and payments on time carries penalties. In addition, all important corporate decisions must be approved by the board of directors and sometimes may require the involvement of an attorney.

■ Are there different types of corporations?

Yes, there are several types. These include charitable (not-for-profit) corporations and professional (P.C.) corporations. Professional corporations are formed by certain professionals who are required to be licensed in order to render their services. This structure is typically used by attorneys and physicians, for example.

For most small businesses, though, there are basically two types of corporations: the "C" corporation and the "S" corporation. A "C" corporation may have an unlimited number of shareholders. An "S" corporation, on the other hand, can have no more than thirty-five shareholders, all of whom must be U.S. citizens or residents.

The key difference, though, lies in the way the two types of corporations are taxed: "C" corporation shareholders are taxed *twice* at the federal level. First, the corporation pays tax on its earnings, and then the shareholders pay tax on any dividends they received.

"S" corporation shareholders, on the other hand, are taxed only *once,* because the corporation pays no tax on earnings. As with a partnership, profits or losses of an "S" corporation are passed through to the shareholders, to be reported on their personal tax returns in proportion to their ownership interests in the corporation. You should note, however, that the "S" corporation shareholders are taxed on the corporation's earnings whether or not a dividend actually is paid.

To qualify as an "S" corporation, a corporation with thirty-five or fewer shareholders must file a special form with the IRS requesting to be treated as an "S" corporation. In addition, about two-thirds of all states recognize "S" corporations for state tax purposes. You must file a form with your state's tax authority to qualify.

You should consult with your tax adviser to determine your corporation's eligibility for treatment as an "S" corporation and to ensure that you comply with IRS and state law requirements once your corporation qualifies.

■ What is the difference between a publicly held and closely held corporation?

There is a key distinction between types of corporations. A "publicly held" company is one that typically either

- **has shares that trade on a recognized exchange (for example, the New York Stock Exchange) or**

- **has assets of more than $5 million and has a class of stock held by 500 or more people**

A "closely held" or "privately held" corporation usually has

- **a relatively small number of shareholders**
- **no shares of stock available for public purchase**
- **active participation by many of the shareholders in the management of the corporation**

Publicly held corporations are regulated by both state agencies and the federal Securities and Exchange Commission (SEC), which require that they make regular "disclosures" to shareholders regarding the corporation's assets and liabilities. The purpose of these disclosures is to enable the investing public to make informed decisions when considering the purchase of the corporation's securities.

Small businesses are closely held companies and are not required to make the same types of disclosures. As a small business owner, however, you must keep in mind that you and your corporation must still comply with the relevant antifraud provisions of both the laws of your state and the SEC. You should consult with an attorney about your responsibilities — and potential liability — under these laws, particularly if you intend to offer or sell interests in your business to the investing public.

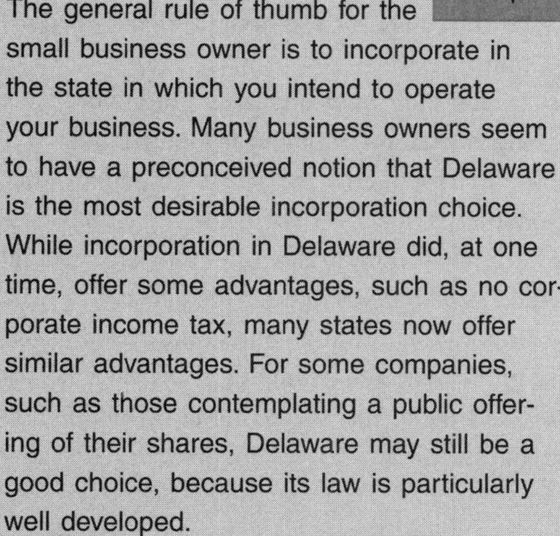

Where Should You Incorporate?

The general rule of thumb for the small business owner is to incorporate in the state in which you intend to operate your business. Many business owners seem to have a preconceived notion that Delaware is the most desirable incorporation choice. While incorporation in Delaware did, at one time, offer some advantages, such as no corporate income tax, many states now offer similar advantages. For some companies, such as those contemplating a public offering of their shares, Delaware may still be a good choice, because its law is particularly well developed.

Because individual business circumstances vary, you should carefully consider which state to incorporate in. In making your decision, you should bear in mind that states generally impose a tax (commonly known as a franchise tax) on corporations that are either incorporated under their laws or do business within their borders. So if your business is incorporated in one state, but headquartered in another, it will probably be subject to tax in both states.

How is a corporation run?

Major business decisions for a corporation are made by its **board of directors** (see the box opposite), which is elected by the shareholders. The day-to-day responsibility for running the corporation is typically handled by its **officers.** The corporation's **bylaws** (its rules and regulations), which are written at the time of incorporation (when the company is formed), specify the number and respective duties of directors and officers. Traditionally, state statutes have required all corporations to have certain officers, including

- **a president**
- **at least one vice president**
- **a secretary (the officer who keeps the corporate minutes and records)**
- **a treasurer**

In this traditional corporate form, one person can hold any two offices — except for the offices of secretary and president — unless the corporation has only one shareholder.

A corporation's officers are usually elected by the board of directors. The directors have the power to elect anyone they wish, including themselves or family members. The board also has the power to fire corporate officers.

Members of the board of directors as well as corporate officers have what is known as a **fiduciary duty** to the corporation. This means that they have an obligation to protect the shareholders' interests rather than their own personal interests. (This is true even when the board member or officer is a shareholder.) This fiduciary duty requires all board members and officers

- **to act with honesty, good faith, and diligence**
- **to act solely for the benefit of the corporation**
- **to use their best business judgment in making decisions affecting the corporation**

These are essentially the same guidelines that a reasonable person uses when running a business.

Corporate officers and directors are generally not held personally liable for the success or failure of a corporation's actions unless they have violated these guidelines. For example, an officer who commits fraud using the corporation's assets could be held liable for any losses incurred by the shareholders.

What are the rights of the shareholders?

Although the shareholders are the owners of a corporation, their role in management is usually limited unless the business venture is relatively small. Shareholders of large or small companies can, however, influence the conduct of business in a number of ways. For example, shareholders have the power to

- **elect and remove directors**
- **influence the allocation of power by making changes to the corporation's "articles of incorporation" (the document under which the corporation is formed)**
- **approve or disapprove such fundamental changes as a merger, a sale of substantial assets, or the dissolution of the corporation**

The more shares a person holds, of course, the more influential his or her vote will be, since each share ordinarily gets one vote.

Shareholder Agreements

Blossom met with her attorney to go over the paperwork involved with incorporating the restaurant. "You really should have a written shareholder agreement," he advised.

"What for?" asked Blossom. "We have only five partners, and we're all good friends."

"That's the point," he said. "You may not always be on such cheery terms."

When is it advisable to have a shareholder agreement?

Anytime your small business has more than one shareholder, you should enter into a shareholder agreement and consult an attorney for help in preparing it. A key reason for having such an agreement is to provide for the handling of the shares of a shareholder who "departs" (whether by death, disability, retirement, or simply a desire to sell out). Obviously, what happens to a departing shareholder's shares will have great consequences — and potentially adverse ones — to the shareholders left behind.

Entering into a shareholder agreement can help avoid adverse consequences. The agreement typically includes restrictions on a departing shareholder's right (and that of his or her estate) to transfer shares or, for example, to pledge them as collateral, without first offering them for purchase by the corporation or the remaining shareholders. The agreement should also include a method for arriving at a value for the shares, because there is no ready market or "handy" reference guide for pricing the shares of small corporations.

Because state corporation laws do not, by and large, address the contents of shareholder agreements — or require them at all — the agreements are very flexible documents. You should view them — and may use them — as a type of "pre-incorporation blueprint" for putting into writing what you and your fellow shareholders have agreed to regarding the formation and management of your corporation.

How Do You Incorporate?

The rules for incorporating vary from state to state. Generally, however, you must file **articles of incorporation** with the secretary of state of the state in which you are incorporating and pay a filing fee. The information in the articles of incorporation usually includes

- **the name of the corporation and its principal address**
- **the general purpose of the corporation — for example, "to conduct lawful business" or "to make a lawful profit"**
- **the number and types of shares of stock authorized to be issued and the rights of each type (for example, voting and any dividend rights)**
- **how long the corporation will exist (it can be perpetual)**
- **the names and addresses of the members of the initial board of directors**
- **the names and addresses of the "incorporators" who prepared the articles**

Your filing will be dated on its receipt in the secretary's office, and if it is approved, your corporation will be considered to have been formed on that date.

Is a lawyer necessary?

No, but it is advisable to consult one. If there is any problem with your filing, the corporate structure could be jeopardized, and you could end up with a liability that you did not expect (see Chapter 30, FINDING AND USING A LAWYER).

Are there other steps necessary to complete the incorporation process?

Yes. Although your business is officially incorporated on the date of acceptance of your filing in the secretary of state's office, several additional steps must be taken to get your corporation up and running. First, the initial board of directors or the incorporators (depending on the laws of your state) must adopt **bylaws** — the procedural rules and regulations that govern how the corporation is run. The bylaws generally cover the following considerations:

- **meetings of officers, directors, and shareholders (including requirements on the number of members who must be present at a meeting in order to conduct business and the process of notifying people of meetings and other important developments)**
- **number, tenure, and qualifications of officers and directors**
- **procedural rules relating to the approval of contracts, loans, checks, and deposits**
- **formalities regarding share certificates, share transfers, and the corporate seal, which is used to authenticate the corporation's legal documents**
- **procedures for amending the bylaws**

Unlike the articles of incorporation, the corporation's bylaws do not have to be filed with the secretary of state. After the bylaws have been adopted, the following actions are taken by the board:

- **the officers of the corporation are elected**
- **the corporate seal and form of share certificate are adopted**
- **shares are issued, provided that proper payment has been received**
- **certain officers are authorized to open the corporation's bank accounts and to sign checks on its behalf**
- **if appropriate, the "election" of "S" corporation status is authorized**

On the adoption of these resolutions, the corporation is usually in business. Some states may require you to file additional documents, such as your employee identification numbers, before the corporation is considered up and running.

In addition to provisions regarding share transfer restrictions, which you should include in any event, your agreement may address a number of other topics as well:

- **the structure of the corporation (including, for example, the "classes" of stock (that is, common or preferred) and the number of shares that the corporation will be authorized to issue**
- **arrangements regarding the initial financing of the corporation**
- **the allocation of ownership interests among the shareholders**
- **the initial composition of the corporation's board of directors**
- **any understandings regarding employment agreements between the corporation and shareholders who will be managing its business on a day-to-day basis**
- **means for the settlement of shareholder disputes**

Many small business owners are reluctant to enter into shareholder agreements for two reasons: cost and "trust." Shareholders in start-up situations, in particular, are usually eager to cut costs. They do not see the need to use funds that they believe can be more usefully allocated elsewhere to prepare an agreement with fellow shareholders, often close friends or relatives, whom they trust and who might be alienated by the suggestion.

While this reasoning is certainly understandable, a shareholder agreement can help resolve disputes or even avoid the substantial costs that go hand in hand with small business litigation.

In addition, in the absence of a shareholder agreement, you may find yourself the business "partner" of a complete stranger — an estate or an heir — who has no interest in the business, but who can be bought out only at an inflated price.

A shareholder agreement — or any business agreement discussed in this chapter — can be as simple or as complicated as your particular circumstances require and your funds allow. Rather than have no agreement at all, you might initially consider a simple document that addresses the basic scenarios most likely to occur. This may be all that you will ever need. You can revisit the agreement with your attorney if and when your business circumstances change.

LIMITED-LIABILITY COMPANIES

Daunted by all the paperwork involved with incorporating, Blossom asked her lawyer whether there was any alternative. "I need the liability protection," she told him. "But I don't really want to be bothered with all these reporting and minute-taking details. I'm also not too happy about paying taxes for both the corporation and my dividends."

He pulled out the latest copy of *Small Business Owners Monthly.* There on the cover was his grinning face, under the headline "The Limited-Liability Company: Friend of Small Business."

"You obviously didn't see this magazine," he said, handing the copy over to Blossom.

What is a limited-liability company?

A limited-liability company is a business structure best described as a hybrid between a partnership and a corporation that gives its owners the best of both worlds — a pass-through of all profits and losses to the owners without taxation of the entity itself, as in a partnership, and a shield from personal liability, as in a corporation.

An "S" corporation and a limited partnership also offer these advantages. But unlike an "S" corporation, a limited-liability "company" is actually a noncorporate entity. State laws, which would require a board of directors and officers and dictate adoption of bylaws, do not apply.

Also, unlike the limited partner in a limited partnership, a member of a limited-liability company may participate actively in its management without risking loss of the limitation on personal liability.

The limited-liability company, then, offers a great deal of flexibility. It is preferred primarily by owners of small, relatively risky ventures who seek an active management role and limited liability.

Which Business Structure Is Best for You?

While the advantages and disadvantages of each type of business structure are readily identified, choosing the most appropriate for your business may be a somewhat thorny issue. Many small business owners reflexively — and often wrongfully — assume that the corporate form is best for them simply because of the liability protection it offers.

Before incurring incorporation and other expenses, though, you should consider several factors. First, forming a corporation does not necessarily guarantee protection from personal liability. For example, you may be asked to give a personal guarantee on a commercial lease entered into by your corporation.

Also, there is a legal concept known as **piercing the corporate veil.** If your corporation is substantially undercapitalized, or if you consistently fail to observe corporate formalities (such as keeping your personal assets separate from those of the corporation), a creditor may ask a court to rule that you and the corporation are essentially one and the same. The court could pierce the corporate veil, and your personal assets could be used to satisfy the creditor's claim.

Certain state law provisions may also result in personal liability even if your business is incorporated. In New York, for example, the top ten shareholders of a closely held corporation are *automatically* personally responsible for the wages and certain other benefits owed to employees.

Finally, you should investigate whether insurance can adequately cover your risk of personal liability. Depending on the nature of your business, reasonably priced insurance — rather than incorporation — may offer enough protection and save you from additional expense and administrative burdens.

In choosing a corporate structure, you should also take tax considerations into account. If you are like most small business owners, chances are that you will lose money during your first few years of operation. From the tax standpoint alone, then, there may be no advantage to incorporating — at least during the years in which you are posting losses.

For the startup small business in particular, the driving consideration for determining the appropriate business structure probably remains the question of liability. If your business puts human life at risk (for example, you run a bike touring company), or you have substantial contracts with outside vendors, you probably should incorporate to make sure that you run a "tight corporate ship" even if you are adequately insured.

■ **How is a limited-liability company formed?** Although a limited-liability company is free from the restrictions of the corporate form, its formation and general manner of operation are governed by state law. The entity may be formed by two or more persons who must pay a fee and file its "articles of organization" with the secretary of state of the state in which the enterprise is to be established. Because the powers of the limited-liability company are very similar to those of a corporation, the provisions of its articles of organization, which are also prescribed by law, are quite similar to those of the articles of incorporation of a corporation. The limited-liability company comes into existence when the secretary of state issues a "certificate of organization." The duration of a limited-liability company ordinarily is limited to a fixed number of years.

Unlike a corporation, the limited-liability company has no bylaws. The consensus of its members regarding managerial and related issues is set forth in an "operating agreement," which is analogous to the "shareholder agreement" among the owners of a corporation. In fact, state laws typically re-

Business Structures

Type of Business	Number of owners	How to form	Level of personal liability	Tax consequences	Ability to transfer ownership
Sole Proprietorship	one	just do it	unlimited	owner pays	totally transferable
Partnership	two or more	verbal or written agreement	unlimited for general partners; limited partners can lose up to the amount they've invested	individual partners must pay	may need consent of other partners
"C" Corporation	unlimited	follow rules set by state law	only the amount you've invested	corporation pays on earnings; shareholders pay on dividends	totally transferable
"S" Corporation	up to thirty-five, must be U.S. citizens or residents	follow rules set by state law and the Internal Revenue Service	only the amount you've invested	individual shareholders pay	may be limited in order to preserve "S" status
Limited-Liability Corporation	two or more	follow rules set by state law	only the amount you've invested	individual owners pay	generally need consent of all owners

quire that the limited-liability company have an operating agreement.

FRANCHISING

Blossom was an empire builder. She wouldn't deny it. Her business had kept growing even through the recession. After she took the final step and offered franchises of the Made in America restaurant — an offer that was met with an overwhelming response — her picture was on the cover of all the national business magazines.

What is a franchise?

A franchise is a business relationship in which an owner (the **franchisor**) licenses others (the **franchisees**) to operate outlets using business concepts, property, trademarks, and trade names owned by the franchisor. Your local McDonald's may be operated as a franchise. Franchise relationships are regulated by each state and by the Federal Trade Commission and are often quite complex.

A contract known as a **franchise agreement** should spell out the details of each particular venture. The franchisor often provides the initial capital for the franchise and, in turn, typically takes in a larger share of future profits. In addition, a franchisor usually provides

- **a proven business concept**
- **name recognition**
- **business know-how**
- **experience**
- **advertising support**

The franchisee provides

- **supplemental capital**
- **the effort to make the business concept work**

The franchisor and the franchisee both share in the risks and returns of the business, although each agreement is structured differently. Typically, the franchisee is his or her own boss on a daily basis. The franchisor also has a say in the business. For instance, the franchisor is usually responsible for quality control and for maintaining a uniform image among all franchisees. If the quality is not up to par, the franchisor may direct the franchisee to make changes.

Is a lawyer necessary?

It is highly advisable to consult one. A franchise agreement is a highly technical business document that can have serious financial consequences. The laws regarding franchising vary from state to state, and you do not want to end up with an invalid agreement or unintended liabilities.

TRADEMARKS

Blossom knew that she was onto something big after she began selling pints of her coleslaw dressing at her restaurant, Made in America. But she hadn't realized just how big until she had a logo and packaging designed and started shipping the dressing to gourmet food stores around the country. People were giving it as Christmas presents! One of Blossom's investors offered a valuable piece of advice: "Register your name and logo." And a good thing too, because imitation is the highest — and the sliest — form of flattery.

Are You Thinking of Opening a Franchise?

Before entering into a franchise agreement, you should consult a lawyer to be sure that you understand what your responsibilities are. As a potential franchisee, you, along with your lawyer, should

- **thoroughly review the financial disclosure and other documents relating to the franchisor and the business**
- **understand the franchise fee that you will have to pay and the payment schedule**
- **review state law requirements, if any, regarding franchise advertising**
- **familiarize yourself with federal and any state law regulations governing the franchise relationship**
- **learn about your competition and the legal issues dealing with the handling of competitive activities**

Before signing the franchise agreement, you should know what it says regarding certain key issues, including

- **your right to have the only franchise within a certain territory**
- **its term, termination, and renewal**
- **any limitations on your right to sell the franchise**
- **costs and procedures for terminating the agreement**
- **any restrictions on your right to operate a competing business when the franchise agreement terminates**
- **your liability, if any, if the franchise does not make its projected profits**

What is a trademark?

A trademark is a word, name, or symbol that is used to identify products sold or services provided by a business. A trademark distinguishes the products or services of one business from those of others in the same field.

A trademark lets consumers know precisely what they are buying. For example, when consumers purchase cotton swabs bearing the trademark Q-tips® Cotton Swabs, they know — or are entitled to assume — that those swabs came from one source: Chesebrough-Pond's USA Co. They also know — or are entitled to assume — that the Q-tips® swabs are not swabs from some other source.

A business using a trademark has a **trademark right,** which means that it can prevent other businesses from using the trademark and can get money to compensate for the infringement of the trademark right. Trademark protection is intended to protect consumers from confusion about what they are buying and help manufacturers guard the value of trademarks in which they have invested.

A trademark right can be acquired simply by using a trademark to identify your products or services. However, you should pick a trademark with care and make sure you are not choosing one that belongs to another business. Otherwise you could spend several months and much money promoting a new product line only to find that your advertising dollars are lost and that you have ended up assisting your competitor. You could also face a lawsuit if you fail to stop using someone else's trademark. Before deciding on a new trademark, you should have a lawyer conduct a search to locate any similar trademarks that may already be in use.

If someone is using *your* trademark, you should call the infringer and ask him or her to stop. If that fails — as it often does — you can threaten court action. If that fails — as it often does — you can commence an action and seek an order prohibiting further use of the trademark by the infringer. Courts often issue these orders. This process can be ex-

CASE IN POINT

Serving Big Macs in a Pigpen

When Raymond Dayan decided he wanted to open a McDonald's in Paris in 1971, the Illinois-based company gave him several franchise options. If he accepted the company's basic agreement, McDonald's would provide extensive services in all areas of restaurant operations, including marketing and training, to ensure Dayan kept the quality standards at the high level required. With this arrangement, McDonald's would collect three percent of Dayan's gross receipts.

But Dayan rejected the conventional arrangement and instead opted for one where he paid McDonald's only one percent of his receipts and received help from the company only when he requested and paid for it. McDonald's subsequently issued Dayan licenses to operate fourteen establishments.

Under these agreements, Dayan promised to keep his French McDonald's restaurants clean, neat, and in good condition. Unfortunately, Dayan broke that promise. Witnesses used a range of terms to describe the uncleanliness: "filthy, grimy, cruddy," "contaminated," "disgusting," and "pigpens." The problems included grease dripping from the ceiling, dogs defecating where food was stored, and insecticide blending with chicken breading. "The only likeness I could see to McDonald's was the signs," noted one witness.

Even though his employees encouraged him to do so, Dayan never requested any operational assistance from McDonald's. When the hamburger giant finally decided to pull the plug on its franchise agreement with Dayan, however, *he* sued in Illinois state court, arguing that McDonald's did not have good cause to end the contract. He also argued that the company should have helped him more and that it did not act in "good faith" by terminating the agreement.

During a sixty-five-day trial before a judge, McDonald's presented considerable evidence that Dayan had failed to meet the fast-food company's high standards for quality, service, and cleanliness. And, the company argued, he had rejected most attempts to help him.

At the conclusion of the trial, the judge agreed that McDonald's could terminate the contracts with Dayan because he had failed to meet the company's standards. He was allowed to continue operating his French restaurants but was prohibited from using McDonald's trademarks. In 1984, an Illinois state appeals court upheld Dayan's disenfranchisement.

Registering Your Trademark

Although you obtain the right to a trademark simply by using it, your right will be strongest if you register the trademark. You can register by filing an application with one or more state agencies, with the United States Patent and Trademark Office, or with both. Federal registration is preferable, because the benefits of state registration are available only in the state of registration. The benefits of federal registration are available *nationwide.* Federal registration lasts initially for ten years if the registration requirements are met and the trademark is used in connection with the product for which it is registered. The registration is renewable for consecutive ten-year periods. State registration and renewal periods vary from state to state.

A registration application typically asks for

- **a description of the trademark**
- **an explanation of how you are using it or plan to use it in the future**
- **a statement that you believe no one else has a right to use it**

If you are applying for federal registration, you also will have to show that you are involved in interstate commerce. You can apply for registration if you have actually used the mark or if you have an intention of using it.

There are restrictions on federal registration of a person's last name or a geographic location as a trademark. For example, if you want to register trademarks like "NEW YORK" Cream Soda or "MR. SMITH'S" Cough Remedy, you will have to show that these common names have come to be associated with your products. You probably will have to prove that you have a consumer base that identifies "NEW YORK" with your cream soda and "MR. SMITH" with your cough syrup.

The federal registration process can take a year or more. The filing fee, at present, is $245. You can prepare and file the necessary papers on your own, but it is advisable to consult a trademark lawyer for at least some initial guidance. The legal fees involved in registering a trademark are typically less than those involved in obtaining a patent.

To signify your claim to a particular trademark, you can use the ™ symbol if the trademark is unregistered. If it is registered, you can use the R inside a circle symbol: ®.

pensive. But it can be vital to the prosperity and future of a business. Imagine how Ford would fare if GM, Chrysler, Toyota, and BMW were all free to call their automobiles Fords.

Trade Names

After opening shop as a sole proprietor, Max held an informal contest among his friends to name the business. (He promised the winner a lifetime supply of hats.) He got some good submissions — Rocks in Your Head, Head Trips, and Hat Tricks — but Max, a slightly biased judge, picked an entry from his kids, Vinny and Alena, that he thought was brilliant: The Mad Hatter.

■ Can a person choose any name for a company?

No. While most states have only minimum requirements regarding the choice of a company name, known in legal lingo as a **trade name,** you will have trouble if you pick the exact name or one that too closely resembles that of a competitor. In general, state laws

- **require that a company that is incorporated include a designation such as "Inc." or "Company" in the name**

Use It or Lose It

To preserve the rights to a trademark, its owner must use it and must police how others use it. (That's why ads for a product often state that its name "is the registered trademark of XYZ Corporation.") Many words that have become part of our everyday vocabulary were once registered trademarks whose use became so widespread that their owners could no longer rightfully claim them. Some of the most well-known **lost trademarks,** as they are called, include aspirin, cellophane, escalator, thermos, and nylon.

- **prohibit the use in the name of such words as "insurance" or "mortgage," for example, unless the corporation is going to engage in that particular business**
- **prohibit the use of a name under which a business is already incorporated in that state**

If you are incorporating, you should first check with the secretary of state of the state in which you plan to incorporate to determine whether the name you have chosen is available for your use. In many states this can be done simply by telephone, at a nominal cost.

If the name that you have chosen appears to be available, you may incorporate under it. It is important that you understand, however, that your right to incorporate under that name does not automatically give you exclusive rights to the name itself. There may be, for example, an already existing *unincorporated* enterprise doing business under the identical or *similar* name, and that business might have rights that are superior to yours. In fact, the use of a name could, under such circumstances, put you at risk of a lawsuit by that enterprise for "infringing" ("trespassing") on its rights to the name.

The outcome of such a lawsuit would depend on a number of factors, including, in particular, whether you were both engaged in similar lines of business and served roughly the same geographic markets. If so, the other corporation might be able to prevent you from using the name and, possibly, even recover damages from you. This would be a particularly undesirable outcome if you had invested substantial time and money developing marketing materials, for example, in which you used the name.

Before choosing a corporate name, then, you should check not only its availability with the appropriate secretary of state's office, but also its use within the general area in which you intend to do business. You can begin with telephone directories and trade directories, which should be available at your public library or local chamber of commerce. You should also check for "d/b/a certificates" that may have been filed with the secretary of state or the county clerk's office (see page 257).

If your preliminary searches do not turn up a similarly named business, or if they do, and your respective businesses are in unrelated fields or nonoverlapping markets, the chances that you will be able to incorporate and do business under that name, undisturbed, are improved.

Quite often, though, circumstances are not particularly clear-cut. You should consult an attorney, particularly if you intend to produce expensive marketing materials, before you incorporate.

CREATING 16

PATENTS

After experimenting for months in his basement workshop, Beatrice's friend Derek made a major breakthrough, finally perfecting "The Salsa Stop" — a pill that brings an abrupt halt to the burning sensation people get on their tongues when eating hot peppers. Derek was sure there was a huge market for his tablet, and he found a manufacturer who was willing to produce it for him. He even thought that he could distribute "The Salsa Stop" in partnership with a salsa maker.

He was about to send off his business plan to Hot To Trot Inc. when Beatrice gave him a warning. "Don't you think you'd better patent it first?" she asked. "After all, you could have something really hot on your hands. What if they steal your idea?"

■ What is a patent?

A patent is a document that is issued to an inventor by the United States Patent and Trademark Office in Washington, D.C. It contains a detailed description of what the invention is and how to make or use it. In addition, each patent has at least one "claim," which summarizes what the inventor asserts to be his or her protectible invention. Patents can have lots of claims, ranging from the general to the specific, if the invention warrants them.

If someone other than the inventor starts making, using, or selling what is described in any claim of a patent, the patent is **infringed.** An inventor has the right to stop such an infringement and may be able to obtain money to compensate for any damage or injury caused by the infringement. This is called the **patent right.** An inventor has this right for seventeen years after a patent is issued by the Patent Office.

The basic idea behind patents is to encourage inventors to make their creations known to others so that everyone working in a particular field can develop further inventions based on the most up-to-date technology — or get a license to use the creations. The seventeen-year patent right is granted as a fair exchange for full disclosure of the invention by the inventor. It also is meant to give inventors incentive to invest in development of new products by rewarding them with an exclusive right (for seventeen years).

■ What makes an invention patentable?

In deciding whether or not to grant a patent, the Patent Office considers a number of issues. These same issues may be reconsidered in court if a patent is later challenged in litigation. In general, to qualify for a patent, these conditions must be met:

- The invention must be *new.* If it was invented before and was not concealed by the previous inventor, it usually cannot be patented now, even if the prior inventor did not patent it.
- The invention must *not be on sale or in public use* more than a year before the application is filed. This is true even if the inventor has put it on sale or in public use. The aim here is to get the application on file as quickly as possible.
- The invention must *not be obvious.* Even if the exact invention was not made before, a creation cannot be patented if others have made similar inventions that render the new one obvious to other people in the same field.
- The invention must be fully *disclosed* in the application. If an inventor knows of a particularly good way to produce the creation, but keeps it secret, the patent may be invalid. If the creator tries to fool the Patent Office and a court later finds out, the creator will probably lose the patent.
- The prior inventions of others that an inventor knows about must be *disclosed* to the Patent Office — if not in the application, then in a separate paper. If an inventor hides prior inventions from the Patent Office, and a court later finds out about it, the patent will probably be lost.

How to Obtain a Patent

The first step is to prepare an application, which is then filed with the Patent Office. Your application should give a very detailed description about how best to make and use the invention. Sometimes, if a patent application is well written and describes a functional and reproducible invention, the application itself may be sufficient. If it is unclear from your description that the invention will actually do what you say it will do, you may be asked to prove that your idea is workable by developing a prototype.

The application will be examined by government patent examiners whose job it is to decide whether the application describes and claims something that is patentable. If an examiner decides that it does, a patent will be issued. If the examiner decides that it does not, your application will be rejected. You may try to change the examiner's mind, or you can try to modify your application so that the examiner finds it acceptable.

This process can take considerable time — well over a year. If an examiner cannot be persuaded to issue a patent, you can either give up or appeal the rejection to a special board in the Patent Office.

This takes more time.

Is a lawyer necessary?

No, but if you can afford one, it's advisable. However, it's not cheap. The going rate for a simple application that sails through the Patent Office is several thousand dollars. More complicated applications may cost even more. And there are also filing fees in the Patent Office ($355 minimum, at present). The cost of an attorney may be worth it, though. Patent Office procedures can be obscure and complex, and a seasoned patent attorney will know how to usher your application through as quickly as possible. If you seriously think you've reinvented the wheel (and if you think your idea is likely to be infringed on and thus the subject of court actions), it is usually best to hire an attorney. (See Chapter 30, FINDING AND USING A LAWYER.)

Mountains of paper have been written on the requirements for patentability — by judges, lawyers, professors, and others. If you plan to try getting a patent on your own, you should have at least a passing familiarity with these requirements.

- The invention must be *more than a mere idea.* It must relate to a process, machine, manufacture, or composition of matter, such as the recipe for "The Salsa Stop" pill.

Note: special patents are also available for ornamental designs that are new and original. For instance, if Derek designed a distinctive bottle in the shape of a chili pepper for "The Salsa Stop," he could apply for a design patent. These are granted for only fourteen years, rather than seventeen, and the procedures for applying are pretty much the same as for other patents (see the box), although a design patent application is usually shorter and simpler to prepare, since it is largely made up of drawings of the design.

What if someone else comes up with a slightly different creation?

A rival invention that improves on your idea does not diminish your patent right, and you may be able to stop your competitor and collect money damages. You cannot, however, sell your invention with your rival's patented improvements. They are your rival's property, not yours. You are entitled only to continue selling your invention in its original form. You also are free, of course, to dream up and patent your own improvements. Or you and your rival could reach an agreement in which one of you creates the improved product and the other is justly compensated.

What should a person do if someone is infringing on a patent?

You most likely will need a lawyer, since it is rarely a problem to be solved by calling up the infringer and declaring: "I have a patent that covers what you are doing. Please stop and pay me for the harm you've caused." In most cases, you will have to go to court, or at least threaten to do so. And if a court case is filed, you can usually expect a long, hard — and expensive — battle. The alleged infringer might claim not to be infringing or that your patent is not good.

The more valuable your invention, the more likely it is that people will try to copy it and then fight you in court. Patent lawyers often take cases on a contingency basis, which means you don't have to pay up front. Still, if you don't have significant financial resources, you may want to recruit a partner (or partners) in advance to help you defend the patent in exchange for a share of profits. The company that is going to manufacture your invention may be interested in such a deal.

Is a patent always the best way to protect an invention?

Not necessarily. Some inventions, like recipes, may be better off kept as **trade secrets.** That's what the Coca-Cola Company has done for years with its soft drink formula, which remains a cherished trade secret that has never been patented.

The choice of whether or not to patent an invention or keep it as a trade secret is often dictated

CASE IN POINT

Instant Infringement

Infringing on someone else's patent can be an expensive mistake. That's the lesson Kodak learned when it entered the instant camera market in the 1970s. Polaroid, which had held the exclusive domain in that market, sued Kodak for patent infringement in 1976 — starting a lawsuit that took fifteen years to resolve.

What took so long? First, both companies, with around two dozen lawyers between them, spent more than five years preparing for trial. The trial took place in late 1981 and early 1982 before federal district court judge Rya Zobel in Boston, who then spent three years sorting through the reams of technical testimony. Her ruling, issued in September 1985, found that Kodak had indeed infringed seven Polaroid patents. She issued an injunction banning the company from continuing to use the patents, thus effectively kicking Kodak out of the instant photography business.

Obviously displeased, Kodak appealed, arguing that Zobel's verdict should be thrown out because her mother-in-law had bequeathed Zobel some shares of Kodak stock, thus making her less than impartial. (No matter to Kodak, apparently, that Zobel's ruling would not help the value of her stock.) But the U.S. Court of Appeals rejected the motion, noting that Zobel had disclosed her holdings of stock at the start of the trial and Kodak should have objected then.

So Kodak had to pay damages to Polaroid for its infringement, and it also had to compensate the customers who had bought more than 16 million Kodak instant cameras — and who would no longer be able to buy film. To customers, Kodak offered refunds and rebate coupons good for Kodak products. Compensation for Polaroid was a more complicated issue, and a second judge, A. David Mazzone, presided over a separate hearing on the question of damages.

In 1991, fifteen years after the suit had been filed, Mazzone issued his final judgment, assessing damages against Kodak for $873 million. In a surprise move, Kodak settled with Polaroid six months later, agreeing to pay $873 million plus $52 million in interest for a total of $925 million. While that's a far cry less than the $4 billion in damages Polaroid had sought, it's still believed to be the largest settlement ever in a patent infringement case.

How to Register a Copyright

Registering a copyright is relatively easy. The Library of Congress has a copyright office, which provides a simple form. You can get one by calling 202-707-3000. In addition to filling out and submitting the form, you have to send a copy of your work and pay a nominal fee.

You don't need a lawyer to register a copyright, though if it's your first time, you may want help. If you have any concerns about the ownership of the copyright (say you worked on the project with another author, for example, or you're not sure whether it's owned by you or your employer) or the extent to which you have the right to use material that was copyrighted by others, then you should consult a lawyer.

by commercial issues. So long as your potential competitors can't study your creation and figure out how to make — and possibly patent — it themselves, you may be fine keeping it as a trade secret.

Trade secrets do have legal protection against disclosure. For example, if a manufacturer is using a secret process, he or she can require that any employees keep the process secret — even after they leave the company. And if an employee leaves to work elsewhere, the manufacturer can ask that the new employer not encourage disclosure of the secret process. It's also possible to file suit in court to prevent disclosure.

COPYRIGHTS

Beatrice was excited when Blossom hired her to develop software for Made in America. She worked nights and weekends writing custom-made programs for Blossom's products, and she realized that, with only a few modifications, she could sell the programs to other restaurant chains and prepared food packagers. Blossom, who had been wrangling with a competitor over her trademark, urged Bea to copyright her programs.

What is a copyright?

A copyright is very much what it sounds like: a right to prevent others from copying works that you have written, designed, or otherwise created on your own. The works that a copyright protects include

- **writings**
- **software**
- **photographs**
- **films**
- **videotapes**
- **recordings**
- **artworks**

Ideas by themselves cannot be copyrighted. But the expression of ideas in your own way is what copyright protection is all about.

Your work is protected by copyright — or **copyrighted** — as soon as you create it. No application is required. Indeed, no application is permitted on the state level. The only registration available is on the federal level with the Library of Congress in Washington, D.C. You will need this registration if you want to be able to enforce your copyright in federal court, which is the only place you can sue for copyright infringement.

Whether or not it's registered, a copyright lasts for the life of the author or artist, plus fifty years. If the owner of the copyright is an employer or corporation (a newspaper publisher, for example), the copyright lasts for 100 years from the creation of the work or 75 years from its publication, whichever is earlier.

Because it may be impossible to prove that something has been copied, copyright infringement is often determined by evaluating whether or not there is a *substantial* similarity between two works. There are no hard rules about what constitutes a substantial similarity. It is generally determined by the courts on a case-by-case basis.

A copyright does not completely prevent someone from using your work. Portions of a copyrighted work can be used without infringing the owner's rights if the use is considered a **fair use.**

Fair use may include uses for

- **educational purposes**
- **literary or social criticism**
- **activities like news reporting, which is protected by the First Amendment right to free speech**

Whether a use is fair or not depends on the answers to four questions:

- What is the purpose and character of the use of the material? The more for a public purpose and the less for a commercial purpose, the more likely the use is fair.
- What is the nature of the copyrighted work? The more it is a compilation of facts rather than a work of literature, the more leeway you will have to use a portion of it.
- What proportion of the copyrighted work is being used, both qualitatively and quantitatively? The less the better.
- What is the economic impact of the use of the work? The less profit the copyright owner loses, the more acceptable the use.

The question of whether the use of copyrighted material is fair depends on the facts of each specific use. Say, for example, that a high school social studies teacher wants to use information from three separate publications: a history textbook, a magazine, and a government booklet. She can probably copy the government publication as many times as she wants.

The magazine article is more problematic. While the teacher can probably make a copy for herself,

CASE IN POINT

It's a Bird, It's a Plane, It's . . . Ralph!

As superheros go, Ralph Hinkley was a bit of a klutz. Instead of leaping tall buildings in a single bound, he would often crash into them. Hinkley, who was the main character in the ABC-TV series *The Greatest American Hero,* was clearly no Superman. But Warner Brothers, owner of the copyrights in various works embodying the character of Superman, was not amused. They felt Hinkley was too similar to the Man of Steel and sued ABC and several of its producers alleging copyright infringement and unfair competition.

This was one time when it did not take Kryptonite to defeat Superman. All it took was the U.S. Court of Appeals for the Second Circuit, which ruled for ABC in a 1983 decision, finding that the two characters were not sufficiently similar to constitute infringement. "Superman performs his superhuman feat with skill, verve, and dash, clearly the master of his own destiny," notes the opinion, written by Judge Jon Newman. "Hinkley is perplexed by the superhuman powers his costume confers and uses them in a bumbling, comical fashion. In the genre of superheros, Hinkley follows Superman as, in the genre of detectives, Inspector Clouseau follows Sherlock Holmes."

The court ruled that merely stirring the memory of a character is not the same as being substantially similar to that character, which would trigger an infringement claim.

Warner had claimed that Hinkley conjured up the Superman image because he wore a cape and tights and was able to fly. But the court said that was not enough similarity to be an infringement. In fact, the court noted, the paths of the two heroes diverged in significant ways: Where Superman deflected bullets, Ralph cringed and covered his face to dodge them. Where Superman could find his way around using X-ray vision, Ralph needed a lantern to fly at night. "Superman looks and acts like a brave, proud hero, who has dedicated his life to combating the forces of evil," notes Newman. "Hinkley looks and acts like a timid, reluctant hero, who accepts his missions grudgingly and prefers to get on with his normal life."

Small wonder then that Hinkley never quite became a household name.

she begins to move beyond the zone of fair use if she makes copies for all the students in her class, even if it's for educational purposes. The magazine's publishers would want and expect her to buy a copy for each student (or ask them to buy it for themselves). Or they might be willing to let her make copies — for a reasonable reprint fee.

Copying from the textbook is pretty clearly a violation of the copyright — especially if it was written for teaching at the level of the teacher's class. By copying and distributing portions of the book to her students, the teacher effectively is depriving the textbook writer of royalties on a work intended precisely for the commercial purpose the teacher is putting it to — education of students.

CREATIONS AT WORK

Beatrice had started her consulting company to serve small businesses that needed computer support but couldn't afford to hire a full-time person to do the work. Her business was booming, and Ethan, one of her best programmers, was developing software for the local public library. Bea could see that the product had tremendous potential . . . and a tremendous market. As dollar signs danced in her head, Beatrice started calling around to see if other libraries might be interested in buying the software.

Ethan overheard her making a sales pitch, and he was furious. "You think you can start marketing my work just like that?" he yelled.

"Sure can," said Beatrice. "What you make for me is mine. I can sell it any way I want."

■ Does an employer own what an employee creates while at work?

Usually. Copyright laws generally give employers ownership of the work created by employees that falls within the scope of employment. That means that if an employee created a work as part of his defined job responsibilities and used the employer's resources to create it, then it is likely that the employer will own the copyright in the work. On the other hand, if the employee created the work outside the office during time off, using her own resources, and if the creation falls outside the scope of her normal work responsibilities, then she very well may be awarded ownership.

Beatrice and Ethan were at loggerheads. On his own time, Ethan had been doing some work for the public schools. After his success with the library project, he had been approached directly by the superintendent of schools to write a program that would help kids develop imaginary languages for animals. Ethan was calling the program "MooNeigh Speak" and was generating a lot of excitement as he demonstrated his prototype around town.

Bea was not happy. After all, she was the one who had given Ethan all those great opportunities and her most interesting projects to work on. She thought that she should get a piece of this "MooNeigh" thing.

"Sorry, Bea," Ethan said quietly. "You've proven that you own me from nine to five, but after that, I'm a free man."

■ Can an employer prevent an employee from doing related freelance work during off-hours?

Maybe. If an employee freely signs a reasonable employment agreement that gives the employer the copyrights in freelance work or specifies that the employer owns the copyrights to any of the employee's work, regardless of when or where it is performed, then the employee would be restricted in the outside work he or she could do. Without such a written agreement, however, an employer would probably have no right to work done by an employee on his or her own time. However, the person or company that commissioned the freelance work might have an ownership right in the work. (See also "Noncompete Agreements" on page 230.)

PAYING TAXES

17

Alena came home from her summer vacation in high spirits. She had spent two months living with a family at the beach and helping to take care of their kids — basically building sandcastles, playing in the water, and making macaroni and cheese . . . and flirting with the lifeguard. Plus, she had made great money, and barely spent any of it, since room and board were included.

Alena and Beatrice had made a deal: if Alena could earn half the money, she could go to Europe during spring break with her French class. "Paris, here I come," dreamed Alena.

"I wonder if you have to pay taxes?" asked Beatrice.

"Taxes? No way! I'm not even old enough to vote!" protested Alena.

Who has to pay income tax?

Everyone who earns over a certain minimum amount has to file an income tax return, minors included. That minimum amount is listed in the instruction booklet accompanying your tax return form, and it varies according to your age, marital status, and whether or not you have any dependents. (If you don't automatically receive a tax return form and booklet in the mail, you can usually pick one up from a bank or your local post office.)

All employers are required by law to withhold income tax. The amount withheld is determined in part when you (the employee) complete a Form W-4 claiming exemptions (for yourself, your spouse, and your dependents) that can reduce the amount of withholding.

Even if you have taxes withheld from your paycheck by your employer, and even if you don't owe any tax, you still *have* to file a return if you have earned the specified minimum amount of income. And even if your income is below the minimum amount, you usually *should* file a return to claim a refund for any taxes that were withheld. It is a misdemeanor not to file a return when one is required. You could be prosecuted and charged penalties for failing to file.

Do married couples have to file jointly?

No, but you will generally save taxes if you do so. The exception is if one spouse has a much lower income than the other. Filing separately in that case may result in lower taxes.

Note: our focus here is on income taxes, which are paid to the federal government and to most state and local governments. Besides income taxes, most state and local governments raise money by charging a variety of other taxes such as property, utility, and sales tax. These will vary from state to state.

WHEN YOU ARE SELF-EMPLOYED

Bradley's private investigation business was finally getting off the ground, and he had a steady stream of clients who wanted to pay for his detective services.

"I never realized you were such a spy," his boyfriend, Peter, teased him. "My guy the spy. What are your secrets?"

Brad did have a secret, and as April approached it began to worry him. After nine months of working for himself, he hadn't paid any taxes.

If a person is self-employed, what are his or her tax obligations?

Your income (and any deductions) from self-employment should be reported on Schedule C of Form 1040. In addition, you are responsible for paying your own Self-Employment Tax, which goes toward social security and medicare benefits. You probably also need to make quarterly estimated tax payments.

What are estimated tax payments?

The federal tax system is a pay-as-you-go system, meaning that you have to pay taxes throughout the year, not just when you file your return. These "prepayments" are made either through withholding by an employer or by estimated tax payments. Estimated tax payments are quarterly payments toward the tax you will report when you file your return. They are "estimated" because you may not know exactly what your income for the year will be.

The IRS imposes a penalty for failure to make adequate prepayments of tax, either through withholding or estimated tax. To avoid the penalty, you must generally prepay either 90 percent of the tax you owe in the current year, or 100 percent of the amount you paid in the previous year. (Some higher-income taxpayers have to pay 110 percent of their previous year's taxes.)

Who should make estimated payments?

Generally, self-employed people do not have taxes withheld from their paychecks, so they pay estimated taxes. In addition, some employed people may also have freelance income that is not subject to withholding. If you have any significant investment (dividends or interest) or freelance income from which there is no withholding, then you probably should pay estimated taxes.

Estimated taxes are reported on Form 1040ES, which is filed quarterly.

KEEPING FINANCIAL RECORDS

After three rainy days of being cooped up in the house, Beatrice decided to tackle the attic. During the first two hours she was engrossed in a box of letters that she had received over the years — some from Max, some from other men. She clumsily descended the attic ladder clutching a big dusty box and nearly fell on top of Vinny.

"What's in that box?" he asked, brushing dust off his shirt.

"Just old financial papers. I'm tossing them," Bea answered.

"I know you're supposed to be the grown-up here," said Vinny. "But don't you think you should look at them first?"

How long should a person keep financial records?

To be safe, six years. In general, the Internal Revenue Service, the agency that oversees federal tax collection, has three years from the filing date to review your return and assess any additional tax. However, in some cases the IRS may be able to review up to six years of your old records. If your return is being audited, or if you believe it may be audited, you should keep all your records until the matter is resolved. If necessary, you may obtain a copy of old tax returns going back three years by paying a small fee to the IRS. You should call or visit your local IRS office to find out which forms you need to fill out. Returns that are older than three years are sent to a central record center and may be more difficult to obtain.

AUDITS

Max couldn't believe his bad luck. Just when his hat business, The Mad Hatter, was getting off the ground, he got a letter from the IRS that he was being audited. And not for the current year, which would have been relatively easy. They were going to examine his financial records going back two years!

What happens in an audit?

In an audit, the IRS examines whether you correctly reported your income, deductions, and credits on your return. Being audited doesn't always mean that you'll have to turn over every piece of documentation and financial record for the period in question. Since some audits focus only on specific return items, such as deductions, you may be asked to provide documentation only for a particular item. Sometimes you'll be able to handle the matter through the mail, but sometimes you'll have to go to an IRS field office. If the audit includes an extensive examination of records, as in the case of a business audit, an IRS agent may go to the

Challenging an Audit

If you don't agree with an auditor's findings, you have the right to a conference with an IRS appeals officer, whose job is to help resolve cases. If you can't settle with the appeals officer, you have two options.

- You can pay the disputed amount and file a claim for a refund with the IRS. The IRS will likely reject your claim. If it does, you may file a suit in federal district court or the U.S. Court of Federal Claims, which hears cases against the federal government. Federal district courts are located throughout the country. The Court of Federal Claims is headquartered in Washington, D.C. You can get information about that court by calling 202-219-9657.

If you pay the disputed amount, your case proceeds like most other lawsuits and you can take it to a jury if you choose. This is a route sometimes used by corporations or individuals when large sums of money are in dispute and the tax issues are complex. This route is likely to be expensive, and you should not choose this option without consulting a lawyer.

- You can decline to pay the disputed amount and file a petition with the U.S. Tax Court in Washington, D.C., within ninety days of the date the IRS issues a Notice of Deficiency. If you file a petition with the Tax Court, the IRS cannot charge you for the tax or attempt to collect it until the case is resolved. However, interest will accrue on any additional tax that the court ultimately determines that you owe. (The interest rate is set by the IRS and fluctuates with changes in market interest rates.)

You can file the petition by writing to the

U.S. Tax Court
400 2d Street NW
Washington, DC 20217

You should send a copy of your Notice of Deficiency with your petition. For cases under $10,000, a general statement that you are disputing the amount is usually sufficient. If the IRS says you owe more than $10,000, you must follow a complex procedure and should have the help of an experienced accountant or attorney.

Which option is better?

It depends on your situation. When you appeal to the Tax Court, you don't have to pay anything up front, and the system is generally pretty user-friendly. Disputes are heard by well-informed judges who specialize in tax cases. In addition, Tax Court has the equivalent of a small-claims section for amounts under $10,000. The process is expedited, and you can represent yourself.

If the amount in dispute is over $10,000 or if you paid someone to prepare your taxes, it is probably a good idea to have representation. The Tax Court permits nonlawyers who have passed an exam and been admitted to practice with the court to present cases, so it's possible your accountant could represent you if he or she is registered.

For more information on Tax Court, you can write or call 202-606-8754.

taxpayer's office or to the office of the accountant, if the records are located there.

During an audit, you have the burden of proving that your return is correct. So if you don't have documentation, some deductions may not be allowed. However, an examiner sometimes may accept a reasonably estimated amount for expenses that were obviously paid, even without the documentation. Many audits result in no changes to the tax return, and some audits actually result in a refund.

Should a person have a lawyer during an audit?

It's not necessary, but if your situation is complicated, you may want one. Also, if an accountant helped you prepare your return, you probably should consult that person about the audit. Whether or not you will have to pay extra depends on your original fee arrangement. If you paid by the hour, you will probably have to pay extra for the time involved on the audit. If you paid a fixed fee for your return, the audit preparation may be included.

If you are challenging the audit (see the box), you probably should consult a lawyer. It's not mandatory, and you are free to represent yourself in court, but it is recommended that you have an attorney with you.

MONEY EARNED ILLEGALLY

Nervously preparing for his audit, Max was deep into his financial papers and refused to let his friend Betsy, an accountant, help him.

"What are you so worried about?" she asked.

"Well," he mumbled. "Let's just say that my Mad Hatter business never really saw the light of day."

"What do you mean," she cajoled. "I thought you were selling hats with your band's logo on them. What *were* you doing?"

"Do you promise that this information won't leave this room?" Max asked. Betsy nodded yes. "I sold pot."

"You sold pots?" Betsy asked, wide-eyed. "Cookware? What's the big deal? Did you smuggle it in from somewhere?"

Max shook his head in amazement. "Have you been off the planet for the past twenty years? Pot. Reefer. Grass. Marijuana . . . What can I say? It kept the kids in shoes."

If a person makes money illegally, does it have to be declared?

Yes. Illegal income is taxable just the same as legally earned income, and in theory it should be reported on Schedule C of Form 1040, as would any other self-employed income. Rather than identify a business in a way that's incriminating, some people might identify it in general terms. For instance, in the early 1980s the convicted mob leader John Gotti received income from a plumbing company and identified himself on his tax returns as a salesman for a plumbing company. A person is not permitted to claim any deductions from the business of selling drugs other than the wholesale cost of the goods sold (that is, the amount paid for the drugs that were sold).

Why would anyone who is running an illegal business bother to file a tax return? For one reason, a failure to do so could tip off the government to investigate how you earn a living and could also subject you to monetary penalties and criminal prosecution for nonpayment of taxes. Also, historically, many people who engaged in illegal activities — Al Capone, for instance — have gone to jail for failing to pay their taxes, rather than for their income-producing illegalities.

TAX OVERPAYMENTS

When Betsy offered to review Max's old tax returns, she made a surprising discovery. Through pure sloppiness, Max had overpaid his federal tax during the previous year. He had started the "hat business" in his basement and was so nervous about all the improprieties that he hadn't made the appropriate deductions.

What happens if a person overpays his or her taxes?

If you simply made a calculation error, the IRS computers may catch the mistake and issue a refund. If they don't, you may still be able to get a refund — depending on how much time has elapsed. You can file an amended tax return (Form 1040X) within three years of when your return was due, or you can file a claim for a refund (Form 843) within two years from the date your taxes were paid.

What if the error was the accountant's fault?

That won't make a difference to the IRS. If your accountant is responsible for your overpayment, you could sue him or her for failing to prepare your return in a professional manner. However, if you have been able to collect a refund on your overpayment, there may not be much point to doing so, since your damages will be minimal.

UNDERPAYING YOUR TAXES

Bart was worried. He was being audited, and apparently there was a problem with his return. A $3,000 problem. He had wondered why he got a big refund for the last year, but since he and his wife needed the money for their kitchen renovation, he hadn't wondered for too long. Now the auditor told Bart that since he had failed to report all his income from speeches and lectures, he was going to have to pay $3,000 pronto. Bart had given all the information to his accountant, Ludwig, and left the details of the tax return up to him. Now Bart intended to make Ludwig pay for this costly mistake.

Can an accountant be held responsible for a person's underpayment of taxes?

Maybe. But first of all, you have to deal with the government. Even if your accountant made an error, you are ultimately responsible for paying the taxes you owe. Generally, the IRS does not impose penalties if an accountant made the mistake and if you did not contribute to the error. But interest on the tax owed is charged regardless of whose fault it is.

If an accountant's error was based on misinformation that you provided, then you don't really have any recourse against him or her. If, however, the accountant failed to prepare your return in a professional manner, you could, as mentioned above, sue. But a better course of action might be to negotiate directly with the accountant to recover the amount of any penalties or interest you had to pay because of the error. Even if you went to court you

What Is Earned Income Tax Credit?

The earned income credit is a tax credit available to low-income workers who maintain a household with dependent children. To be eligible for the credit, you must earn income, have a qualifying child, and meet the low-income requirements. A qualifying child is

- **your own child**
- **a grandchild**
- **a stepchild**
- **an adopted child**
- **a foster child**

The child must have lived with you for at least half the year (unless he or she was absent because of education or illness). The child must be either

- **under age nineteen**
- **under age twenty-four and a full-time student**
- **permanently and totally disabled**

The earned income credit reduces your taxes, and is claimed on Schedule EIC. The amount of the credit is based on your earned income and is calculated by using a table provided by the IRS. Even if you didn't earn enough money to owe income tax, you must still file a return if you want to receive a refund for the earned income credit. Married taxpayers must file a joint return to receive the credit.

might not get much more than that, and you would have to endure the time, hassle, and expense of a lawsuit.

INCOME FROM TIPS

Ever since Blossom received the liquor license for her restaurant chain Made in America — California wine only, no imports — the waiters and waitresses had been a lot happier, because the tips were so much better. And tips were what Talia wanted to discuss with Blossom.

"A lot of the other waitresses have been asking me about this," Talia said. "We don't have to pay taxes on our tips, do we? I've got a kid to support, and I'm not the only one who does."

■ Does a person have to pay taxes on tips?

Yes. Income from tips is taxable just like any other income and is also subject to social security tax. The law requires you to report your tip income to your employer, who is required to include it on your W-2 Form and to withhold taxes from your paycheck based on your tips. If your tip income is so large that your employer cannot make the necessary withholdings from your salary, you should make quarterly estimated tax payments on Form 1040ES to avoid a penalty.

If you fail to declare your tip income, you could be charged a penalty and interest as well as the actual tax owed. In extreme cases, you could face a criminal prosecution.

GIFTS

Bradley, the private eye, was feeling very proud as he watched the father and son embrace in his office. He had brought the two together, having tracked down the son, who had disappeared without a trace six years earlier after a lot of anger and mutual recriminations. All three men had tears in their eyes.

"How can we ever thank you?" the older man asked. "I would really like to give you something in addition to your fee. How about a laptop computer?"

Bradley was taken aback. "Uh, great, sure, thanks," he said.

■ Do gifts (like a car or a computer or cash) have to be declared on a person's tax return?

Maybe. A true gift is not subject to income tax, and you do not have to report it on your income tax return. However, the *giver* may have to pay a gift tax if he or she gives more than $10,000 to any one person in one year. Generally, cash or property received from your employer is presumed to be compensation and not a gift, so you would be expected to declare it. The same is true if a client gives you a gift, unless there is a strong indication that the client is displaying what one judge has called "detached and disinterested generosity." The less time there is between the performance of your services to the client and the giving of the "gift," the more difficult it is to call it an untaxable present. So Bradley would probably have to declare the value of the computer as income.

■ What if a person gets lucky and wins the lottery?

Uncle Sam gets a piece of it. Prizes won in lotteries, on game shows, or in sweepstakes are taxable at the same rate as other income. You may deduct the costs of winning the prize (such as the price of the lottery ticket or any expenses you had traveling to a game show), but you do have to declare the value of the prize as income.

HOUSEHOLD EMPLOYEES

See page 125 for details on paying taxes for household workers.

BEING A CITIZEN

18

PERSONAL EXPRESSION

Right to Protest

Beatrice learned that an "adult" bookstore, Kinky Is Us, was planning to open across the street from the junior high school that her two children attended. Outraged that her kids would be exposed to smut (and to the people who purchase it, whom Beatrice called "perverts"), she organized a group of parents to march in protest, starting at the school and ending up with a rally in the park across from City Hall. They had gone only two blocks (and created a major traffic jam) when a police officer asked to see their permit. "Hey pal," shouted one of the protesters. "This is America. We've got the freedom of speech. We don't need a permit."

"I don't care what freedom you think you've got," said the cop. "You can't march without a permit, and if you don't get out of the road, I'm going to have to arrest you."

■ Can the government place limits on a person's freedom of expression?

Yes. While the First Amendment gives Americans a right to speak openly and without fear that is unparalleled anywhere else in the world, our courts have never interpreted the freedom of speech to be an *absolute* right that allows people to say anything they want anytime they want anywhere they want. There are, in fact, a number of ways in which the government can and does limit people's freedom of speech.

For example, the government may control *when, where,* and *how* you can engage in some forms of expression such as protest marches, rallies, and parades. These controls are known as "reasonable time, place, and manner restrictions." So while you have a right to organize such an event, the government may require that you hold it in a "public forum" such as a street, park, or other place where people traditionally gather to express themselves. (Public places that are not "public forums" include prisons, post offices, and military bases.) The government may also require that you obtain a permit and that your event be held during certain times of the day.

But while the government can create regulations that limit speech, the U.S. Supreme Court has imposed many "constitutional checks" intended to keep such regulations from intruding too far upon free speech. For instance:

- Government officials can't pick and choose who gets a permit. All applicants must be treated the same, no matter how offensive their views may be.
- Regulations must not be based on the *content* of the message.
- Regulations must serve a significant governmental interest (such as keeping traffic moving during rush hour).
- Regulations must leave open ample alternatives for communication. (For instance, the government could restrict marchers from Main Street but allow them to protest on Center Street.)

Picketing

Beatrice and the other angry parents were pretty riled up about the lack of response from the mayor and town council about Kinky Is Us. They formed a group, Parents Against Porn, and planned to picket in front of the home of I. M. Pigg, the bookstore owner.

■ Are there any restrictions on a person's right to picket?

Yes. Picketers have the right to assemble in public to communicate their message without the fear of unwarranted government interference, but there are some restrictions that do not run afoul of the Constitution. For instance, the government may

- **restrain picketers from blocking the entrances and exits of an establishment**

What Is Obscene?

True obscenity is not protected by the Constitution. However, defining exactly what is obscene has confounded the courts for decades. "I know it when I see it," the late Supreme Court Justice Potter Stewart once noted in a case. Generally, something will be considered obscene (and thus not protected as free speech) if it meets all the following criteria:

- **an average person finds that it appeals to a prurient interest (that is, a crude or unwholesome or unusual sexual interest)**
- **it offensively depicts sexual conduct**
- **the work taken as a whole lacks serious literary, artistic, political, or scientific value**

Different Kinds of Speech

Not all speech is shielded from government regulation by the First Amendment. The government has more freedom to regulate "commercial" speech (advertising or other communications that are intended to promote business), for instance, than it does to regulate "political" speech (criticisms of the government and debates about issues of importance to society).

The classic example of speech that's not protected by the First Amendment is when someone falsely shouts "Fire!" in a crowded theater. The government can limit a person's right to that expression, because the government has an interest in keeping things orderly and preventing a panic that could cause injuries.

Certain other types of speech also get no protection from the First Amendment. These include obscenity, libel, and "fighting words," which would incite people to commit immediate acts of violence. These include such taunts as "Kill him!" or "Burn It Down!" right in the presence of the target. They also include face-to-face epithets that invite retaliation, such as shouting "You ugly, prickly-faced jerk!" at one of your archrivals.

- **limit them to a maximum number**
- **require them to remain a specific distance from such places as consulates and courthouses if necessary to maintain security or good relations with a foreign country**

While residential streets are traditional "public forums" in which picketers may rightfully express their views, local governments may pass laws against picketing that singles out one individual's home — so long as the law gives the protestors ample alternatives to be heard. That means Beatrice's group could march down Mr. Pigg's street, but they might not be able to gather in front of his house if their town has a law prohibiting such picketing. Thus they would have the right to express their views, but the individual's privacy would also be protected.

■ Are there limits to where people can leaflet or solicit signatures?

Yes. Like all other forms of protected speech, both the passing out of leaflets and the solicitation of signatures are subject to time, place, and manner restrictions. Still, so long as the leafleting or solicitation is relatively unobtrusive, it will be difficult to prohibit it. For instance, in 1992, the Supreme Court struck down a regulation that would have prohibited distribution of leaflets anywhere within an airport.

The Rights of Pornographers

A topless dancing club, Wiggles, announced its plans to open down the block from Kinky Is Us. Parents Against Porn demanded that the town council intervene and stop both places from opening.

Can the government regulate a pornographic bookstore or nude dancing club?

Yes. While "adult" bookstores and theaters and nude dancing clubs do have the right to conduct their business, local governments can restrict where they are located. However, the government must do so in a "content-neutral" way. That means a law can't say, "Pornography is immoral and offensive, and so pornographic bookshops are prohibited in this neighborhood." Such a law would be attempting to regulate based on the content of the books. The government can, however, say that the bookshop is prohibited in this neighborhood because it will attract transients and increase the crime rate.

Thus a city may pass a zoning ordinance that prohibits an adult theater or nude club from locating within a certain distance of residential areas, schools, and churches so long as the law is specifically intended to combat the undesirable "secondary effects" of such businesses, while not specifically targeting the explicit content.

While the government can restrict the location of nude dancing clubs and pornographic bookstores, it is much more difficult to restrict the *activities* that take place inside these places. Nevertheless, the Supreme Court has ruled that a statute that bans *any* form of public nudity does not violate the First Amendment — even though such a law has the added effect of restricting the "free expression" of nude dancing in clubs.

CASE IN POINT

When Hate Speech Meets the Constitution

When American Nazis wanted to hold a march in Skokie, Illinois, in 1978, the village was no random target for their message of hate. Skokie is a heavily Jewish suburb of Chicago that is also home to thousands of Holocaust survivors. Having Nazis march through their downtown was something village leaders could not stomach. It did not matter that the Nazis proposed to bring in no more than fifty demonstrators and march single file down a sidewalk without making speeches or distributing handbills.

After Skokie leaders tried unsuccessfully to get an injunction stopping the demonstration, they instituted several rules specifically intended to stop the march. Among other things, the rules required demonstrators to obtain a permit. In order to grant the permit, the appropriate officials had to find that the assembled group would not "incite violence, hatred, abuse, or hostility" toward a person or group because of their religious, racial, ethnic, national, or regional affiliation.

The Nazis sued to stop the village from enforcing the ordinances and ultimately won following a series of hearings. The final decision was issued by the federal appeals court in Chicago. While the court was mindful of the anger and painful memories that a Nazi march would conjure up, it ruled that the First Amendment guarantees freedom of expression, and thus the town could not censor the Nazis, no matter how repugnant their message.

Of course, in some instances speech is subject to reasonable regulations, and a law that prohibited an intentional incitement to riot might be allowed. But Skokie officials had conceded that the fear of violence by the marchers did not weigh in their passing of the laws in question. So under the First Amendment, the court ruled, it was not possible for the village to reasonably prevent the march because the effort to do so was aimed at the content of the Nazi message. No matter how false or disgusting the Nazi dogma may be, it and other kinds of hate speech cannot be suppressed. In his opinion, Judge Wilbur Pell Jr. quoted a previous Supreme Court case: "However pernicious an opinion may seem, we depend for its correction not on the conscience of judges and juries, but on the competition of other ideas."

Flag Burning

At an anti-porn rally, several hundred parents and neighborhood supporters chanted and carried signs ("It's just like the sixties," exclaimed one woman). Speakers took turns at the microphone, offering encouragement. Bea's brother Bradley got up to speak. "I can't believe the mess this city is in," he shouted. "I can't believe our town council cannot and will not act to stop this madness. Here's what I think of our government's failure to listen to our demands." As everyone watched in horror, he lit a match to an American flag.

■ Does a person have a right to burn the American flag?

Yes. While the First Amendment generally safeguards only speech, not conduct, certain acts that are expressive in nature are protected. Things like burning the flag or making a hostile hand gesture at a cop during a rally are typically protected.

Usually, the courts will focus on the context in which the conduct occurred. Thus the Supreme Court has held that a demonstrator who burned an American flag at a rally in protest against policies of the government could not be punished, even though a state law forbade "desecration of a venerated object." The Court has also determined that a law passed by Congress that banned flag desecration violated the First Amendment.

While a local government may not outlaw flag burning as a means of expression, it may pass a law that forbids the burning of *any* object in the city streets in order to protect public safety. So a flag burner could be punished because the act of burning anything is dangerous, but not because the act of flag burning is seen as offensive.

CASE IN POINT

Constitutional Protection for a Pithy Profanity

Even Supreme Court justices use four-letter words, at least when such words are the focal point of the case before them.

In 1968, Paul Robert Cohen was arrested in Los Angeles for wearing a jacket that said "Fuck the Draft" across the back. Charged with disturbing the peace by engaging in "offensive conduct," Cohen testified at his trial that he had worn the jacket to inform the public of his opposition to the Vietnam War and the draft.

Nevertheless, Cohen was convicted, and in 1969 a California state appeals court upheld his conviction. "Offensive conduct," that court noted, includes "behavior which has a tendency to provoke others to acts of violence. . . . It was certainly reasonably foreseeable that [Cohen's] conduct might cause others to rise up to commit a violent act against [Cohen] or attempt to forcibly remove his jacket."

Cohen appealed, and his case went to the U.S. Supreme Court, which overturned the conviction in 1971, finding it an unconstitutional restriction of his freedom of speech. In a 5-4 decision written by Justice John Harlan, the court rejected the notion that the statement on Cohen's jacket was obscene. For an expression to be obscene, it "must be, in some significant way, erotic," wrote Harlan, and the four-letter word in question was unlikely to "conjure up such psychic stimulation in anyone."

The court also rejected the argument that the government was justified in arresting Cohen because it was attempting to regulate the violence that his jacket could have provoked in others. Such reasoning, Harlan wrote, "amounts to little more than the self-defeating proposition that to avoid physical censorship of one who has not sought to provoke such a response by a hypothetical coterie of the violent and lawless, the States may more appropriately effectuate that censorship themselves."

Begging

Beatrice's wacky Great-aunt Agnes, once a famous ballerina, died in her home in New York City. Beatrice went there for the memorial service and was awed by the excitement of urban life. What she didn't like was the number of homeless people she encountered. On the streets and in the subways, someone was always begging for spare change. Even outside the funeral home a shameless man shaking a cup asked her, "Hey lady, could you pay your respects to the living?"

■ Are there restrictions on where a homeless person can ask for spare change?

Yes, but they are limited, since begging is generally considered a form of "protected speech." So while a complete prohibition on begging in public places "offends" the First Amendment, some restrictions, such as a New York City law that prohibits panhandling on subway cars and other areas of the transit system, have been found constitutional. The reason? Some studies showed that begging generates a high level of fear in transit passengers, especially because they are constricted from moving away from beggars they fear and thus are discouraged from using the system.

■ Are the rules different if it's an organized charity making the solicitation?

Not really. Generally, fund solicitation by charities is a protected activity. But government can make reasonable time, place, and manner regulations and can forbid solicitations in places like post offices and airports. The reason is because the solicitation impedes the orderly use of the facility by causing people to stop, make a decision, and search for change or write a check. (Handing out leaflets, which is permitted in airports and post offices, is not considered disruptive, because it generally does not require people to stop.) The U.S. Supreme Court has struck down laws that impose blanket bans on door-to-door charitable appeals, finding that such requests involve the communication of information, the dissemination of ideas, and the advocacy of causes — all of which are considered protected speech.

How Does a Court Decide When Speech Can Be Limited?

While the government can restrict where and when you express yourself, it is limited in its ability to restrain the expression itself. When the government does pass restrictions on free speech that are aimed at suppressing information or ideas (in other words, the *content* is the target of the restriction), such laws are given what is called "strict scrutiny" by the courts. To be considered a permissible restriction on free speech, a content-based regulation must pass two hurdles. It must

- **be necessary to achieve a "compelling government interest" (like preserving the peace)**
- **be no broader than necessary to satisfy that interest**

Very few content-based restrictions pass the "strict scrutiny" test.

DEFAMATION

Libel and Slander

Blossom, the head chef at Chez Snooty, was tired of the rigorous insistence of Pierre, the owner, that all ingredients (including salt and pepper) must actually come from France. She left, planning to start her own restaurant, Made in America. Shortly after her departure, a friend told Blossom that Pierre was spreading rumors that she had stolen most of her recipes from him. Blossom was certain Pierre had fabricated the story to retaliate for her defection.

■ Is this defamation?

Very possibly, if Blossom can prove that it's not true. The law of defamation, which protects people against false statements about them that injure their reputations, has traditionally been broken down into two categories: **libel** and **slander.** Libel refers to defamatory (false and injurious) written statements or materials, such as movies or photographs, while slander refers to defamatory oral statements or gestures. Generally, statements are defamatory only if they contain facts that are false. Expressions of opinion are considered constitutionally protected speech.

Historically, libel was treated as a more serious offense than slander because of the power of the written word and the likelihood that it would reach a larger audience. Broadcasting has blurred that distinction, however, because of its potential to reach a large audience, and courts have disagreed on how to categorize it. Some have ruled that defamatory broadcasts are slanderous because they are spoken, while others have decided that broadcasts are libelous because they are based on a script or because of their great capacity for harm.

Defamation is a **tort** — an injury to a person that the law considers wrongful. For more information on how to pursue a claim against someone you think has injured you through defamation, see Chapter 29, SUING AND BEING SUED. See also related material on negligence, page 337.

CASE IN POINT

How Public Is the Public Library?

The Joint Free Public Library of Morristown, New Jersey, found itself in the middle of a constitutional battle when it passed a series of rules aimed largely at keeping a homeless man from entering the library.

Library officials were concerned about the offensive and disruptive behavior of Richard Kreimer, which included staring at patrons, following them around, and talking loudly to himself and others. Also, Kreimer apparently had such bad body odor that certain areas of the library became unusable.

To help curb the problem, the library issued written rules prohibiting certain behavior and authorizing the expulsion of violators. Poor bodily hygiene was considered grounds for ejection, and Kreimer was kicked out of the library.

With the help of lawyers from the American Civil Liberties Union and elsewhere, Kreimer sued, arguing that the library was violating his First Amendment rights. In a 1991 decision, a federal district court judge agreed. He threw out the library rules on a number of grounds, including that library personnel seemed to have "unfettered discretion" to decide who could get evicted. "The greatness of our country lies in tolerating speech with which we do not agree," wrote the judge, H. Lee Sarokin. "That same toleration must extend to people, particularly where the cause of revulsion may be of our own making. If we wish to shield our eyes and noses from the homeless, we should revoke their condition, not their library cards."

The library appealed that ruling, and in 1992 Kreimer was handed a defeat by the U.S. Court of Appeals for the Third Circuit. That court agreed that First Amendment rights were at issue in the case, noting that a long line of Supreme Court opinions makes it clear that the First Amendment protects the right not only to *convey* information, but also to *receive* it. The appeals court then undertook a highly formalistic analysis of the different types of places in which people receive information, from "quintessential" public forums (such as parks and streets) at one end of the spectrum, to "limited" public forums, such as the public library. Based on this analysis, the court ruled that library officials have great leeway to set guidelines for conduct without violating the First Amendment.

Kreimer had also filed a suit alleging police misconduct, and in 1992 — before the 3d Circuit issued its opinion — he accepted $150,000 to settle his cases against the library and the city.

Public Figures

Bartholomew is running for town mayor. His opponent accused him of failing to pay taxes for three years, and the newspapers have printed the allegations. Bart, however, has always paid taxes, and he has proof.

Can public figures bring libel suits?

Yes, but they will have a far more difficult time winning than an ordinary private citizen. Even if Bart can prove he paid the taxes, it might not be enough for him to win a lawsuit because, as a candidate for mayor, he is considered a public figure. The U.S. Supreme Court has ruled that in order to win a defamation suit, public officials or prominent people, such as political candidates or movie stars, must prove that the offender made the false statement with what is called **actual malice.** This is a legal term that means the statement was made with knowledge that it was false or with serious doubts about whether it was true. This rule allows the press and members of the public to speak and publish freely on matters of public concern without fear that an *honest* mistake will result in a defamation judgment against them. Although this might seem unfair, it's vitally important in order to en-

CASE IN POINT

Sending Panhandlers Packing

When a beggar rattles a cup of coins at you and asks for spare change, is it a shakedown that can be prohibited by law, or is it a form of expression protected by the First Amendment?

That was the question raised by a case that started in 1989, when the New York City Transit Authority issued regulations prohibiting begging and panhandling in the city's subway system. The regulations grew out of a study examining "quality of life problems" experienced by riders of the subways. A survey found that two-thirds of subway riders had been intimidated into giving money to beggars, and that the presence of beggars contributed to the public's perception that the subways are fraught with danger.

An advocacy organization filed a class action suit on behalf of homeless and needy people, claiming that the regulations violated First Amendment rights to free speech. They argued that "whenever a homeless and needy person is extending his hand, he is communicating and, therefore, the action enjoys full First Amendment protection."

In a May 1990 decision, the U.S. Court of Appeals for the Second Circuit rejected that argument and upheld the Transit Authority's regulations. The court expressed doubt that begging is "speech" fully protected by the First Amendment. The real issue, Judge Frank Altimari wrote, is whether begging is "expressive conduct" that is entitled to less protection. Given the "special surrounding circumstances" of the subway, Altimari continued, whatever message beggars and panhandlers might be communicating gets overshadowed by the harassment and intimidation felt by passengers. The simple message of "give me money" is not protected by the First Amendment. Even if it were, Altimari concluded, the government had shown sufficient justification for issuing its regulations.

While individual beggars were restricted, the Transit Authority *did* permit solicitation by organized charities, a distinction Altimari upheld. "While organized charities serve community interests by enhancing communication and disseminating ideas," he wrote, "the conduct of begging and panhandling in the subway amounts to nothing less than a menace to the common good."

Dissenting Judge Thomas Meskill found such a distinction impossible to justify and argued that solicitation by both individuals and organizations should be entitled to First Amendment protection.

courage free and open debate about important issues, such as the qualifications of political candidates. Also, candidates and other well-known people, such as movie stars, can more easily command the attention of the press and correct an error if one is made, and thus do not need as much protection as a private individual would.

Opinions

A newspaper reporter called to ask Blossom why she had left her job at Chez Snooty. "Well," she said, "in my opinion, Pierre wasn't complying with the proper health and safety regulations." The reporter asked her to cite specific violations, but Blossom was unable to provide any examples.

■ Does a person have a right to say anything if it's an opinion?

No. If a statement contains an assertion of "objective fact," which can be proven to be false, you can be sued for defamation — even if the statement is your opinion. Therefore, saying "*In my opinion* Pierre's place is teeming with roaches" is no different from saying "Pierre's place is teeming with roaches," because both statements contain a factual assertion that could be proven to be false. In short, prefacing your statement with "In my opinion" or "I think" won't save you from a lawsuit.

A restaurant critic, Sara Tastebud, came to eat at Made in America. Her review, which was printed in the local paper, was very negative. "The food was bland," she wrote. "The service was slow. I waited so long for my soup, it was lukewarm when I finally got it. I'm not sure that head chef/owner Blossom is ready for prime time." Business dropped immediately at the restaurant.

■ Can a person (or a business) sue when his or her reputation is damaged?

Blossom certainly can sue on behalf of herself and her business; anyone can. But it's highly unlikely she would win. First, restaurant reviews are classic "opinion" pieces with very few provable facts. Even saying that the soup was "lukewarm" is likely to be held more opinion than fact because someone else might disagree. Furthermore, restaurants are generally treated by the courts as "public figures," so even if the reviewer actually wrote false statements, Blossom would have to prove it was done with "actual malice" (see page 289).

It's as difficult to sue for a bad movie or theater review. Although a negative review by a theater critic could cause a play to close, the reviewer cannot be held liable because he or she is merely expressing an opinion as to the quality of the production.

■ Does that mean that anything that reporters write or broadcast is protected by the First Amendment?

No. It means that *critics* have a lot of freedom (although not *absolute* freedom) to express their *opinions.* But the press in general is subject to the same laws that limit the expression of individuals. If a newspaper prints a story that is false and if a person or business is hurt by that story, the newspaper could be liable for defamation.

Insults

Beatrice's son Vinny did not get along with his history teacher, Ms. Birdseye. She scolded him about everything from the crumpled homework papers he turned in to his talking during class. One day she told him to spit out his gum. Vinny strode casually up to the garbage can. "Did anyone ever tell you you're really ugly?" he asked her. The class burst out laughing.

■ Does a person have the right to just say anything he or she feels like?

The answer to this question — like a lot of questions asked of lawyers — is yes and no. As a general rule, insults and epithets are not considered defamatory. The victim cannot recover damages because courts see insults as having no real meaning, except to indicate that the speaker dislikes the

God Knows. Maybe.

The first words of the First Amendment, known as the Establishment Clause, state: "Congress shall make no law respecting an establishment of religion, or prohibiting the free exercise thereof . . ." Applying those words to particular facts, though, might at times benefit from divine guidance. Consider a 1989 case that tied the Supreme Court in knots.

It all started when the county of Allegheny and the city of Pittsburgh decided to decorate some downtown landmarks with holiday adornments. Each year since 1981, the Holy Name Society, a Roman Catholic group, had been permitted to display a creche in the county courthouse during the Christmas season. Like other creches, it contained a visual representation of the scene in the manger in Bethlehem shortly after the birth of Jesus. Attached to the manger was a crest with an angel bearing a banner. The banner proclaimed: "Gloria in Excelsis Deo!", a Latin phrase that means "Glory to God in the Highest."

A block from the manger scene was a second holiday display. There, outside a government office building, the city of Pittsburgh had put up — as it did every year — an enormous Christmas tree. In 1986, the 45-foot-high tree was joined by an 18-foot-high menorah, a branched candlestick that holds the lights for the Jewish holiday of Hanukkah. The Pittsburgh menorah was owned by Chabad, a Jewish group, but was stored, erected, and removed by the city. Next to the tree and menorah, the city placed a sign with the title "Salute to Liberty," which stated that the holiday lights "remind us that we are the keepers of the flame of liberty and our legacy of freedom."

In December 1986, the Pittsburgh chapter of the American Civil Liberties Union and seven Pittsburgh residents sued, seeking removal of both the creche and the menorah (but not the tree), arguing that each violated the Establishment Clause.

To decide such questions, the U.S. Supreme Court has developed something known as the *Lemon* analysis (first set forth in a 1971 case by that name). Under that analysis, a statute or government practice that touches upon religion is permissible only if it meets the following three-part test:

- It must have a secular purpose.
- It must neither advance nor inhibit religion in its primary effect.
- It must not foster excessive entanglement with religion.

In applying this test to the situation in Pittsburgh, a divided Supreme Court issued a tangle of opinions in which the justices openly bickered with each other, with some supporting and some explaining away a decision the court had issued just five years earlier. In that case, the court had upheld the right of a city to include a creche in a holiday display at a private park.

The upshot of the Pittsburgh case was somewhat different. The ruling decided that:

- The creche had the effect of endorsing a patently Christian message, and thus impermissibly violated the Establishment Clause.
- The twin display of the Christmas tree and Hanukkah menorah under a sign saluting liberty did not endorse both the Christian and Jewish faiths (which would have been impermissible), but was a secular celebration of Christmas coupled with an acknowledgement of Hanukkah as a contemporaneous alternative tradition.

Much of the decision's analysis was devoted to considering the overall physical settings of the creche and the tree and menorah and whether these traditionally religious symbols could be infused with secular meaning. What was most clear from the court's decision was how befuddling the justices find this area of the law. Indeed, they were unable to settle on a single rule to provide clear guidance to any government officials who might be planning the trimmings for next holiday season.

other person. In addition, insults are usually not intended or understood as statements of fact.

Vinny, therefore, probably may insult his teacher without being held liable for defamation. That does not mean, however, that he can't be punished. Schools have broad discretion to punish student speech that interferes with or disrupts school activities. Thus if your son (or daughter) stands up in class and insults the teacher, he might not end up in court, but he very well may end up in detention or on suspension. (And if it were the other way around and the teacher was insulting Vinny, it still probably would not be defamation.)

The same is true if you insult your boss. He or she may not be able to sue you, but it's very possible you could be fired for insubordination.

There are times when a verbal assault can be defamation. If, for instance, a man storms angrily into a bank and shouts at the manager, "You lying, cheating so-and-so. You defrauded my wife," and if his comments are false, then it may be defamation. At least one other person besides the bank manager has to hear him make the statement (the law requires a defamatory statement to be "published" to a third party).

RELIGION

Separating Church and State

As Bartholomew pulled into his "Reserved For Mayor" parking spot at City Hall, a crowd of picketers marched over to his car, carrying signs that said "Keep Your Religion Off Public Property," and barking "If there's a manger, that's a danger."

"What's going on?" asked Bart.

"We object to the manger scene set up in front of City Hall," said one of the protesters.

"Oh come on," said Bart. "Where's your holiday spirit?"

■ Can the government put up Christmas decorations on public property?

It depends on what they are, but under the Supreme Court's current interpretation of the Constitution, a city council cannot erect a manger scene standing alone on the lawn of the town hall or any other government property. That's in part because a city council's actions are restricted by the Establishment Clause of the First Amendment, which prohibits government from "establishing" a religion. In order to preserve the freedom of religion, the Supreme Court has held that the government, in general, is barred from getting involved in matters of religion, particularly by taking actions that appear to "endorse" a specific religion or religious belief. Thus it is said that there is a separation of church and state.

The Supreme Court has, however, upheld a government display of a Hanukkah menorah next to a Christmas tree, finding that in that case the overall symbolic message did not endorse or convey a preference for one particular religion. (See the Case in Point on the previous page.)

■ Can a church erect a manger scene on its property?

Absolutely. A church has every right to erect a manger scene on its private property during any time of the year. The prohibitions in the First Amendment against "establishment" of religion do not apply to the use by private individuals or organizations of their own property.

Religious Practices

Bradley and his college friends formed a secret religion called the Disciples of Faith. They held daily "prayer" meetings in which they smoked marijuana from a "spirit pipe" and philosophized about the meaning of life. "Isn't freedom of religion great?" Brad asked the others.

■ Can the government restrict a practice that is part of someone's religion?

Yes. While the "free exercise of religion" clause of the First Amendment to the Constitution guarantees your freedom to believe in any religion, it does not give you the right to perform every act that might be part of, or even essential to, your religious worship. Therefore, you are not free to engage in a religious practice (like smoking marijuana) if it is prohibited by law.

However, if a law is specifically intended to limit a religious practice, it probably is unconstitutional.

RIGHT TO PRIVACY

General Rights

Several members of the town council were fed up with the problem of teenage pregnancy. Two of them proposed a law that would require all unmarried teenage mothers to receive the contraceptive

CASE IN POINT

Is Fund-raising a Religious Activity?

The broad religious freedoms offered by U.S. constitutional law extend even to unpopular and unorthodox religious groups. Consider, for instance, the practices of the International Society for Krishna Consciousness, which took root in this country in the 1960s. Devotees of the Krishna movement typically shave their heads and wear long robes and face paint. They also engage in a practice known as Sankirtan, which involves going to public places to inform nonbelievers about the Krishna faith. While proselytizing, they attempt to fund-raise, which, in the past, has involved handing a person a small gift and then trying to sell the person religious literature or phonograph records.

In the late 1970s, officials of the New York State Fair received a number of complaints about the activities of roving Krishna devotees who wandered throughout the fairgrounds. Some people accused Krishna members of trying to pin flowers on them and thus touching them without permission. Others complained of outright fraud by Krishna members who lied about the purpose of their collection efforts or were deceptive when making change.

State fair officials attempted to restrict the Krishna fund-raising activity to a booth, rather than having it take place throughout the fairgrounds. Many other organizations had booths, including such diverse groups as Right-to-Life, Planned Parenthood, and the Seventh Day Adventists. Nevertheless, the Krishnas sued to overturn the "booth rule," arguing that Sankirtan was an essential part of their religious practice that could not be limited.

The two federal courts that considered the case agreed that Sankirtan — including the solicitation of funds — was a genuine religious rite. At the same time, both courts recognized that government (acting through state fair officials) had a strong interest in combating fraud.

Where the two courts differed, however, was in balancing the Krishna's First Amendment rights with the government's interest in fighting fraud. In a 1980 decision, a federal district court judge found that the booth rule was reasonable since less confining options, such as setting up a liaison to mediate complaints, or using criminal law to prosecute particular instances of fraud, had not worked.

The U.S. Court of Appeals for the Second Circuit disagreed and struck down the rule in 1981. The court found, in essence, that the government simply hadn't tried hard enough to make less restrictive measures work.

Interestingly, the Krishnas have not fared as well in a number of other cases where the issue was congestion rather than potential fraud. Courts have limited the Krishnas' ability to practice Sankirtan in several places, including the United Nations Plaza and World Trade Center, both in New York. And at the Atlanta airport, a court permitted Krishna activities to be confined to a booth.

Norplant, which is implanted under the skin of a woman's forearm. They also proposed that all single mothers with two or more children must receive Norplant in order to continue receiving welfare benefits. They sent their proposals to Bartholomew, the town's mayor.

Are there limits to how much the government can interfere in a person's private life?

Yes. In the 1965 landmark case of *Griswold v. Connecticut,* the U.S. Supreme Court ruled that the Constitution grants people a right to privacy — even though there is no specific mention of "privacy" in the Constitution. (See the Case in Point below.) The Supreme Court has found that a right to privacy exists in several areas, including

- **the use of contraception**
- **procreation**
- **abortion rights**
- **child rearing and education**
- **viewing obscene material in one's own home**

Not all judges agree that the Constitution gives people a right to privacy. Conservative judges who believe that courts are empowered only to enforce the "original" meaning of the Constitution denounce the right to privacy as a judicial usurpation of the democratic process. These judges believe that if a right is not explicitly granted by the text of the Constitution, then the matter should be resolved by the legislative branches of the government.

On the other hand, liberal judges who favor a broad, evolving interpretation of the Constitution praise the court decisions that give people privacy rights. These judges view the Constitution as a set of principles that creates a number of protected

CASE IN POINT

Some Privacies Weren't Always Taken for Granted

In 1965 the U.S. Supreme Court found that the intimacies of the marital bedroom are protected from the reach of the government — at least when it comes to the use of contraception.

The case stemmed from the prosecution of the executive director and medical director of the Planned Parenthood League of Connecticut, who were fined $100 each because they had given married couples advice on using contraception. A Connecticut law made it illegal for any person to use "any drug, medicinal article or instrument for the purpose of preventing conception," and also made it illegal to counsel anyone on how to do so.

Even though there is no specific reference to a "right of privacy" in the Constitution, Justice William O. Douglas noted in the 1965 decision striking down the Connecticut law that a number of provisions of the Bill of Rights relate to things of importance to individuals. These things, like the freedom of speech, protection against illegal searches, and the right against self-incrimination, Douglas wrote, all have "penumbras" — or shadows — that create "zones of privacy" for individuals. He noted that Connecticut's law forbidding the use of contraceptives "concerns a relationship lying within the zone of privacy created by several fundamental constitutional guarantees." In effect, he ruled that a generalized right to privacy could indeed be found in the Constitution.

Not all of Douglas's colleagues agreed with his reasoning. "I think [the Connecticut statute] is an uncommonly silly law," wrote Justice Potter Stewart, one of two dissenters. Nevertheless, Stewart found nothing in the Constitution (either a right of privacy or anything else) that would allow the court to strike down the law. Even those justices who sided with Douglas based their decisions on other reasoning.

Nonetheless, the extension of the privacy concept to the area of procreation would have far-reaching consequences, most notably in the court's later decisions ruling on abortion. (See page 138.)

liberties, even if the liberties aren't listed item by item.

Rights of Homosexuals

Bradley and his boyfriend, Peter, were planning a two-week vacation. They had several destinations in mind, but weren't quite sure where to go. They were swayed, however, by a mailing they received from a gay rights organization. It listed all the states that should be boycotted to protest their laws banning homosexual behavior.

■ Don't homosexuals have the right to do what they want in private?

No. In the 1986 case *Bowers v. Hardwick,* the U.S. Supreme Court ruled that the Constitution does not protect the right of individuals to engage in homosexual acts even if they are done in private with the consent of both parties. A few states, including Montana, Kansas, and Arkansas, have laws that declare oral or anal intercourse between consenting adults of the same sex illegal. Thus these states could arrest homosexuals for engaging in such acts, though they rarely do. However, there have been instances where the courts in some of these states have found that such laws violate the *state's* constitutional protections of individual liberty (which can be broader than the U.S. Constitution, but never narrower).

■ Are there any laws that prohibit sexual acts between heterosexuals?

Yes. Many states, including Georgia, Florida, Maryland, Oklahoma, and Arizona, have laws on their books forbidding sodomy between consenting heterosexuals. The constitutionality of such laws, at least as applied to married couples, is doubtful. However, there have been few legal challenges to them, and they are rarely enforced.

Invasion of Privacy

Bart thought he was seeing things. Actually he *was* seeing things: his face plastered ten feet high on billboards across the city advertising a local restaurant, Country Joe's. "The favorite of our mayor, Bartholomew Smith, who eats breakfast here every morning," boasted the signs.

It was true that Bart usually ate breakfast at Joe's place, but no one had ever asked if it was okay to advertise that fact.

■ Was this an invasion of privacy?

Probably. Although the law varies from state to state, people generally have the "right to be let alone" even when they're public officials. There are four basic types of behavior that may constitute an invasion of privacy, which is a **tort.** (See Chapter 21, GETTING HURT.) They are

- **appropriating a person's name or likeness for purely commercial use (such as printing Bart's picture in the advertisements without his permission)**
- **making an unreasonable and highly offensive intrusion into a person's privacy (such as electronically eavesdropping on a private conversation or peering through the windows of a home)**
- **publicly disclosing private facts in a manner highly offensive and objectionable to a reasonable person of ordinary sensibilities (such as publishing the details of a person's sex life, especially if that person is not a public figure)**
- **putting a person in a "false light in the public eye" (such as publishing a fictionalized account of the person's life)**

■ Can famous people sue for invasion of privacy?

Yes, but it's much harder for them to succeed, since famous people generally receive less protection than private individuals with respect to "public disclosure of private facts."

Taping Telephone Conversations

Blossom wanted to sue Pierre, but she needed to gather some evidence against him. She had a friend, Bernadette, a former pastry chef at Chez Snooty, call several of the waiters and waitresses there, trying to get information that would show that Pierre had plotted to sabotage her new restaurant. Blossom figured she'd have a stronger case if Bernadette tape-recorded the conversations. Of course, Blossom didn't want Bernadette to tell Pierre that she was doing so.

■ **Can one person tape-record a telephone conversation without telling the other?**

It varies from state to state. Some states, such as New York, Kentucky, and Oregon, allow telephone conversations to be taped so long as *one* of the parties consents. In these states, you are free to tape your conversation because you are considered one of the parties. However, in other states, such as Illinois, conversations may be recorded only if consent is obtained from *both* parties, unless a court order is granted.

THE RIGHT TO VOTE

Beatrice's daughter Alena was on her way to vote for the first time! She had turned eighteen a month before the presidential primary, and she was excited to be casting her ballot and having a say in who should lead the country. At the poll, however, she was turned away because she had failed to register. "What do you mean?" she asked angrily. "I'm eighteen. You have to let me vote. It's my right."

■ **Does every American citizen age eighteen and over have the right to vote?**

Yes, but states may regulate this right in ways that are reasonable and nondiscriminatory, such as by requiring voters to register. Also, in a few circumstances, a state may restrict a citizen from voting. For example, a state may deny the vote to all persons who have been convicted of felonies. A state may not, however, take away that right from people who have simply been arrested and are in jail awaiting trial.

Time Off from Work

Beatrice was encouraging all her friends to vote for her brother Bartholomew, who was running for a seat on the city council. Her neighbor Mary complained that voting was a real hassle for her because she had to leave home very early for an hour-and-a-half commute, and didn't usually get back until after the polls were closed.

■ **Does an employer have to give workers time off to vote?**

It varies from state to state. Even in states that do give time off, you aren't necessarily entitled to take

CASE IN POINT

Life, Liberty, and the Pursuit of Clean Telephones

In 1982, a group of Virginia prison inmates filed a lawsuit against American Telephone & Telegraph Affiliates, alleging that their constitutional rights had been violated because the telephone receivers installed by AT&T in the prison were not germ-free. In rejecting the case, the decision by a federal district court judge in Richmond, Virginia, noted that "even if every detail in the complaint be accepted as true, no constitutional deprivation exists. The Constitution has absolutely nothing to say about chance germs found on a prison telephone. The telephone company's alleged failure to provide antiseptic telephones in the prison is a matter on which the Constitution, no matter how vibrant, flexible, living or expansive it might be considered, is simply silent."

more than a couple of hours. In California, for example, employees are allowed to take up to two hours off for voting in a public election. But if you are able to vote during nonworking hours, your employer might be able to require that you do so.

THE RIGHT TO OWN A GUN

A serial rapist was attacking women in Beatrice's neighborhood. Terrified of becoming victims, Beatrice and several of her friends decided to arm themselves for protection. Bea went to the local gun shop, picked out a classy handgun, The Lady's Friend, and asked the clerk to wrap up five of them. "Hold on a minute, little woman," he said. "You've got to show me five permits to buy five guns. And you'll have to wait three days for processing before I can let you take these. That's the law."

■ Can the government place controls on gun ownership?

Yes. The Second Amendment states that "[a] well regulated militia, being necessary to the security of a free State, the right of the people to keep and bear arms, shall not be infringed." While there is much debate between advocates for gun control and those for gun ownership about whether or not the words of the amendment give individuals the right to own weapons, most federal courts and legal scholars typically agree that the Founding Fathers who wrote the Constitution intended to give only *state militias* (not individuals) the right to bear arms in defense of their communities. No federal court has ever ruled that an individual has a constitutional right to own a gun. In fact, the Supreme Court has rejected that interpretation of the Second Amendment.

Therefore, federal and state governments are free to regulate the possession of guns by individuals. In fact, they could outlaw civilian gun ownership entirely if they wanted to — so long as the state's constitution did not guarantee individuals the right to own a gun. No states have an outright ban on gun ownership, and it is probably unlikely that a broad ban would ever pass. More typical regulations include

- **laws that bar the possession of concealed or unregistered weapons**
- **laws that impose purchase restrictions such as mandatory waiting periods**
- **laws that ban interstate transport of guns or the sale of particular types of firearms such as automatic weapons and machine guns**

In 1993, Congress passed the Brady Handgun Violence Prevention Act (known as the Brady Bill), which imposes a five-day waiting period on the sale of handguns through licensed dealers. During that time, local law enforcement officials are required to do a background check on prospective purchasers to see whether the sale would violate state or federal law. (Convicted felons, for instance, are not allowed to own guns.) In states that already have a checking system in place, the waiting period may not apply. Also, in some cases where a person needs to buy a handgun because of a threat to his or her life, the waiting period may be waived.

GETTING INFORMATION FROM THE GOVERNMENT

For several years Beatrice had been actively lobbying to get the government more involved in the fight against breast cancer, and she had, in fact, been arrested a few times. (Once she had managed to break into a television studio during the broadcast of the evening news. Her face was seen in millions of homes before security guards hauled her off the set.) Beatrice was sure the FBI and other law enforcement agencies had been investigating her, and she was pretty certain they had sent undercover agents to some of her group's strategy meetings. She was very curious about what kind of personal information the government had collected about her. She also wanted to know what kind of research the government had done on new methods of treating breast cancer.

How to File a Request for Government Records

In order to obtain records, you must file a written request with the federal agency that has the information you want to see. If you are asking for records about yourself, you should mention both the Privacy Act and FOIA in your request because some information may be exempt under one act but not under the other. If you are asking for information about a particular subject, you need to mention only the FOIA.

No matter what kind of documents you are asking for, it's best to make your request as specific as possible because it will save the federal agency time and result in a faster response. That's in your interest, since the Privacy Act and FOIA allow agencies to charge you fees for their copying costs. FOIA also allows them to charge you for the search.

If the records you ask for are exempt from disclosure under both the Privacy Act and FOIA the government can reject your request. If that happens, you can appeal within the agency from which you requested the records as well as to the federal courts.

If you're looking for records about other people, you may have some trouble. Individuals have only limited access to records about other people, since both the Privacy Act and FOIA are designed to prevent disclosure of private information about people to third parties. If what you are requesting is private information, access usually will be denied.

If you're seeking general information from the government on a particular subject, a request under FOIA alone is sufficient because no one's privacy is at stake. As long as the information requested is in an agency record that is not exempt from disclosure, access should be granted. An agency is not required to answer questions or compile information for a request; it need only search for and provide access to records already in existence.

Although the Privacy Act and FOIA are federal laws that apply only to federal agencies, all states and some localities have passed laws like FOIA that allow access to their records.

To request FBI records, you can write or call:
FOI/PA
FBI Headquarters
J. Edgar Hoover Building
Washington, DC 20535
202-324-5520

Or, you can call the local FBI field office listed in your phone book. For records held by other agencies, contact the agency directly for information on where to mail your request.

■ Do individuals have a right to request information from the government?

Yes. You can request several types of information from the government, including

- **information about yourself**
- **information about other people**
- **information about specific subjects**

Two federal laws, the Privacy Act and the Freedom of Information Act (FOIA), allow individuals to see records kept by the federal government about themselves, with certain exceptions. These exceptions, called "exemptions," include some records that are used by law enforcement agencies (such as the FBI) and also records that are vital to national security. However, if an agency like the FBI has a file on you, you probably will be able to see it, although some of the information (such as the name of a confidential informant or details of an ongoing investigation) may be blacked out if the government decides it would be a security risk to release it.

MILITARY SERVICE

Registering for the Draft

Many of Vinny's friends were planning to enlist in the military when they graduated from high school. But Vinny had other plans. He really wanted to go to college and become a marine biologist. His best friend, Wyatt, planned to sign up with the marines and urged Vinny to join him.

"Hey man, if you can't become a marine biologist in the marines, where can you do it?" Wyatt asked.

"No way," Vinny responded. "I'm going to the bottom of the deep blue sea . . . my way."

Wyatt laughed. "Well, you have to register for the draft anyway. At least if you enlist, you get to choose which branch you'll be in."

"I don't have to register, there's no draft," asserted Vinny. "Besides, I'm going to college."

"Wanna bet, buddy?"

■ Who is required to register for the draft?

There is currently no draft in our country. Nevertheless, all males between the ages of eighteen and twenty-six are required by federal law to register with the Selective Service System, a federal agency, in case a draft is needed. This includes male citizens of the United States as well as every other male residing in the United States, including most aliens (even those without green cards). There are some exceptions, including

- **lawfully admitted aliens with nonimmigrant status, such as visitors, students, and members of diplomatic or trade missions and their families (for more on nonimmigrant aliens, see page 304).**
- **foreign diplomats and their families**
- **people already enlisted in the military**
- **people on active duty in the reserves**
- **students in officer procurement programs at approved military colleges**
- **commissioned officers of the Public Health Service**
- **active duty members of the reserve of the Public Health Service**

Ministers and other people with pacifist beliefs must register, but they can apply for conscientious objector status.

■ What is the process for registering?

You can register at any U.S. post office by completing a registration form. You must submit evidence of your identity, such as a driver's license or birth certificate. If you are out of the country, you must go to a U.S. embassy or consulate to register.

If you are a citizen, you must register within thirty days of your eighteenth birthday — either before or after. Aliens must register within thirty days of their eighteenth birthday or within thirty days of arriving in the United States.

Once registered, you must notify the Selective Service System if you change your name or address. You can contact the agency by writing or calling:

Selective Service System
Registration Information Office
P.O. Box 94638
Palatine, IL 60094-4638
708-688-6888

Refusing to Register

A few days after he turned eighteen, Vinny sat with Beatrice in the kitchen.

"Mom, I really don't want to register for the draft," Vinny confessed. "I don't want to be drafted."

"I've never thought of you as a pacifist, sweetheart," answered Beatrice. "Are you one?"

Silence.

"Well, it's your decision, but it's pretty serious," Beatrice told him. "If you don't register, you might have to go to jail, you know."

"No way, mom." Vinny looked disbelieving.

"Way."

■ What happens if a person refuses to register?

If you refuse to register for the draft, you could face federal criminal charges. If convicted, you could be imprisoned for up to five years, fined up to

$250,000, or both. In addition to criminal penalties, if you don't register, you won't be eligible for certain benefits, including federal student aid, job training, and federal employment. In addition, some states may deny you state student aid, entrance to a state college or university, state employment, and permission to practice law.

Your Job and the Draft

Tensions between the United States and France were heating up because the French president had called Americans "unsophisticated oafs who can't tell the difference between a croissant and a jelly doughnut." All men between the ages of eighteen and twenty-five were ordered to register for military service in case the baked-goods gaffe escalated into an all-out food fight.

■ Does a worker lose his job if he gets drafted?

No. A drafted worker is considered to be on a leave of absence, and he has a right to be rehired without losing any seniority. He also has the right to receive any other benefits normally offered by the employer when people take a leave of absence, such as continued health care coverage or membership in the company pension plan.

■ What happens if he voluntarily enlists?

He may request a leave of absence. If the employee is just signing up for the reserves and will miss only a minimal amount of work, the employer must make every effort to accommodate him. However, if the worker is shipping off for a three-year tour of duty, his employer must do all that is possible to reinstate him on his return, but he obviously does not have to hold the job open while he is gone.

JURY DUTY

Beatrice was having a particularly busy period at work and was overwhelmed at home as well, where her two children were raging with teenage hormones. And her favorite aunt, Belinda, had just had surgery and was home recuperating. Beatrice had promised to stop by each day for a cup of tea and a game of cribbage.

"This is the last thing I need right now," Beatrice said with disgust when she opened the notice calling her for jury duty.

■ Does a person have to go when called for jury duty?

You may not be required to appear in person in your jurisdiction, but if you are summoned for jury duty, you must respond in some manner. Your options will usually be specified in the summons. If you ignore a summons, you could be held in contempt of court and fined, although the punishment depends on the jurisdiction. Some jurisdictions, like New York City, allow you to defer several times. Still, you must notify the official in charge by mail before the date you are to appear.

Each state also has its own exemptions, so if you want to be excused, you usually should show up. The judge and the lawyers (or perhaps even the clerk in charge of jurors) will decide if you have a legitimate reason to be excused.

Even if you're fearful of the defendants in a criminal case, you are not automatically entitled to an exemption. Serving on a jury is considered a duty for everyone who enjoys the privileges of our judicial system. However, if a judge is convinced that you will not be able to consider the facts in a fair and impartial way, then you may be excused from that case. If you have concerns or fears about jury service, you may ask to speak to the judge in private if you would rather not state your reasons before the other potential jurors.

Beatrice had hoped to be excused immediately, but instead she was put on a panel of potential jurors in a murder case. She realized she'd get out early enough to stop at Belinda's and then get home to the kids. What made her nervous, however, was the possibility of losing her job if she got stuck on this case for a long time.

■ **Can a person be fired for going on jury duty?**

Not usually. Most states prohibit employers from firing or discriminating against an employee who takes time off for jury duty, although the employer will sometimes be able to require the employee to work in the evenings or on days when the court's not in session. However, most states do not require employers to pay workers who are gone on jury duty.

Note: if your employer does pay for your time on jury duty, you may be required to give your employer the money you are paid by the government for your service.

Being Sequestered

This jury experience was turning out to be fascinating. Beatrice wasn't supposed to discuss the trial with anyone, but it had been getting a lot of publicity because the accused killer was a well-known novelist who lived in town. Beatrice had heard some rumors that the jury would be sequestered. She hoped not. What about poor Aunt Belinda?

■ **When are jurors sequestered?**

Jurors are sequestered when there is a serious possibility of outside influences affecting their deliberations. In some states, jurors are automatically sequestered in death-penalty murder cases; in other states it is up to the judge. The point of sequestering is to keep the jurors from having any contact with anyone or anything that might influence them about the case, so usually they are not allowed to see or talk to anyone, including immediate family members. Sometimes, however, sequestered jurors are allowed brief phone calls or in person visit.

FOR FURTHER REFERENCE

When you have questions that can be answered by someone in the federal government, you can call the Federal Information Center. If staff members there can't answer your questions, they will direct you to the appropriate government office.

To call the center, dial the toll-free number listed below for your area, or call 301-722-9000. Users of telecommunications devices for the deaf (TDD/TTY) may call 800-326-2996 from anywhere in the United States.

Alabama	800-366-2998
Alaska	800-729-8003
Arizona	800-359-3997
Arkansas	800-366-2998
California	800-726-4995
Colorado	800-359-3997
Connecticut	800-347-1997
Florida	800-347-1997
Georgia	800-347-1997
Hawaii	800-733-5996
Illinois	800-366-2998
Indiana	Gary 800-366-2998
	Indianapolis 800-347-1997
Iowa	800-735-8004
Kansas	800-735-8004
Kentucky	800-347-1997
Louisiana	800-366-2998
Maryland	800-347-1997
Massachusetts	800-347-1997
Michigan	800-347-1997
Minnesota	800-366-2998
Missouri	St. Louis 800-366-2998
	All other locations 800-735-8004
Nebraska	Omaha 800-366-2998
	All other locations 800-735-8004
New Jersey	800-347-1997
New Mexico	800-359-3997
New York	800-735-8004
North Carolina	800-347-1997
Ohio	800-347-1997
Oklahoma	800-366-2998
Oregon	800-726-4995
Pennsylvania	800-347-1997
Rhode Island	800-347-1997
Tennessee	Chattanooga 800-347-1997
	Memphis, Nashville 800-366-2998
Texas	800-366-2998
Utah	800-359-3997
Virginia	800-347-1997
Washington	800-726-4995
Wisconsin	800-366-2998

COMING TO AMERICA

19

WHO CAN COME TO AMERICA?

The summer before their senior year of college, Beatrice and her roommate, Renata, embarked on a European adventure. They visited England, France, Italy, and Greece, staying at bed-and-breakfasts and making new friends, most of them rather bohemian. At a London coffeehouse they met Martin, an actor with a wicked sense of humor, and John, a graphic artist and avowed Communist. In a French art gallery they met Penelope, a student from New Zealand who was traveling around the world. And in an Athens disco they met Nikos, an up-and-coming pop star whom both girls had a crush on (even though he was dating a famous English supermodel).

Bea and Renata invited their foreign friends to visit in America, and they all promised to come. The first to plan a trip was Nikos. But right away he ran into a snag: because he'd been dating that supermodel, he'd been in the headlines of the Greek and English papers, which were making a big fuss about his conviction, years ago, for drug possession.

■ Can anybody come to America?

No. Even though Nikos just wants to visit as a tourist, he's still considered an "alien" — someone who is not a citizen of the United States. So he's subject to the rules and regulations of the Immigration and Naturalization Service (INS), one of the U.S. agencies in charge of determining who can come here to visit or stay.

A person can be denied entry to the U.S. on several grounds, including the following:

Criminal History

This includes people who have been convicted of certain crimes (such as assault with a deadly weapon, murder, rape, arson, forgery, robbery, burglary, tax evasion, welfare fraud, and drug-related crimes) or who admit to an INS officer or State Department consular official that they have committed a crime. (Most people probably don't do this.)

Health

This includes aliens who suffer from

- **certain physical or mental disorders (such as pedophilia, kleptomania, pyromania, or schizophrenia) that may lead to harmful behavior**
- **drug abuse or addiction**
- **communicable diseases of public health significance (such as AIDS)**

If an INS officer suspects a tourist might have AIDS or another illness, the tourist may be detained and sent for a medical examination at the airport. The exam could include an AIDS test, and the tourist would either be detained in an INS detention center or released pending the results of the exam.

Poverty

This includes aliens who are likely to be unable to support themselves financially. The INS and State Department consular officials look at a variety of factors, including a person's age, income, work history, capacity to earn a living, and whether he or she has ever received public assistance.

Morality

This includes aliens who have been involved in prostitution in the last ten years or who are coming to the U.S. to practice polygamy. Because aliens outside the U.S. are not protected by the U.S. Constitution, the INS can exclude suspected prostitutes even if they've never been convicted or arrested.

National Security

This includes aliens who

- **have been, or are likely to be, involved in terrorist activities**
- **want to spy or get involved in sabotage**
- **belong to the Communist Party and want to immigrate permanently (although Communist *tourists* are welcome)**
- **would be involved in activities in the U.S. that could have adverse foreign policy consequences (such as a controversial foreigner whose government threatens trade sanctions against the U.S. if it permits him in to give a lecture)**

Improper Documentation

This includes aliens who

- **have been excluded or deported previously**
- **people without valid visas**
- **people the INS suspects are lying about their reasons for visiting. For instance, if someone with a tourist visa is discovered at the airport to have a large stash of cash and several relatives in the U.S., the INS officer might doubt that the alien is truly a tourist who intends to return to his or her country. A very common reason for exclusion is an alien's inability to satisfy a consulate officer or INS inspector that the alien has sufficient family, job, and financial ties to his or her home country and thus is not likely to overstay in the U.S.**

VISAS

Penelope, a carefree New Zealander, decided to head for an extended stay in the U.S. She knew Beatrice and Renata would put her up for a while. After that, she figured she'd play it by ear — probably tour the country, then get a job — though she'd heard she might need something called a green card.

■ Can a foreigner (alien) stay in America for an extended period of time?

It depends on the kind of visa the foreigner is issued. There are two main kinds of visas: **immigrant** and **nonimmigrant.**

Nonimmigrant Visas

These are granted to foreigners who do not intend to stay in this country permanently. They go to

- **tourists**
- **fiancés of American citizens**
- **businesspeople sent by their companies**
- **students**
- **temporary workers in certain occupations, including fashion models, nurses, athletes, entertainers, physicians, professionals, and farm workers.**

The length of stay depends on which category a person is in, but the typical range is six months to one year. However, tourists from many countries, including Canada, New Zealand, Japan, and most European countries, are allowed to enter without obtaining a visa, though of course they still must have a valid passport. Under this visa waiver program, a visitor may enter for a maximum of ninety days without any possibility of an extension.

Visa applications are made by a foreigner at the U.S. Embassy or consulate in his or her home country. The visa is only a preliminary "ticket" to come into the U.S. The INS inspector at the U.S. airport or point of entry determines whether the alien may enter and for how long. If, for instance, Penelope says she's coming only for a short vacation, the INS officer will normally stamp her entry card valid for six months. Sometimes the INS will approve an extension of a nonimmigrant visa.

Immigrant Visas

More commonly known as a "green card," this visa allows an alien to

- **remain permanently in the U.S. with no expiration date**
- **work in the U.S.**
- **travel abroad and reenter the U.S.**

- **become eligible for citizenship**
- **bring in a spouse and children (who are also granted green cards)**

Aliens who are granted green cards are known as "lawful permanent residents."

In most cases, an individual does not apply for a green card. A petition must be filed on the individual's behalf with the INS by a potential U.S. employer, a U.S. citizen, or another lawful permanent resident. (There are some exceptions. Aliens with very extraordinary talents in the arts and sciences may apply on their own behalf as may certain businesspeople who have invested at least $1 million in an enterprise that employs at least ten U.S. workers.)

Once the petition is approved, and an immigrant visa is granted, the alien will receive a stamp in his or her passport and will be able to enter the U.S. The "green card" will come in the mail a couple of months later. An alien who has already entered the U.S. with a nonimmigrant visa may also apply for permanent status.

Most applicants for permanent residence must

- **have a medical examination by an INS-approved doctor**
- **provide any police records from every country lived in since the age of sixteen, unless they are already living in the U.S.**
- **provide evidence of income and assets**

The two most common ways that people get green cards are through their relatives or through their employers (see below). For some categories, the number issued annually is limited, and there can be a wait of several years.

GETTING A GREEN CARD THROUGH FAMILY TIES

Martin, the English actor, was sure his career would flourish in America, and if he lived there, he'd have a chance to visit his mother more often. She had divorced Martin's father years earlier, moved to the U.S., married an American, and eventually became a U.S. citizen.

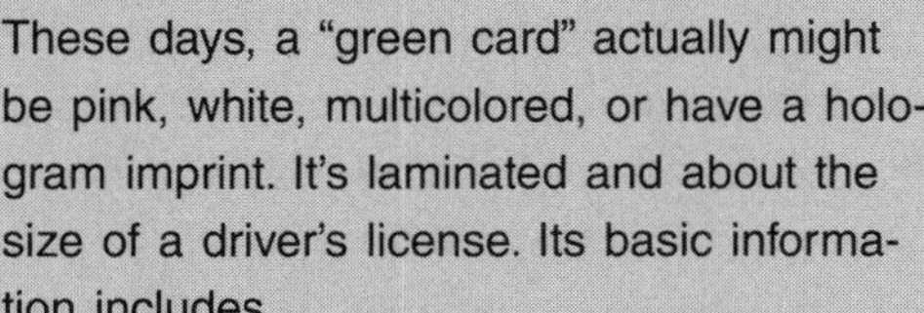

Not So Green Card

Before 1978 immigrant visa cards were indeed green in color. These days, a "green card" actually might be pink, white, multicolored, or have a hologram imprint. It's laminated and about the size of a driver's license. Its basic information includes

- **the cardholder's name and date of birth**
- **the date the card was issued**
- **the date it expires**
- **the cardholder's photo**
- **coded security data**

■ Can anybody related to a U.S. citizen get a green card?

Not anybody, but if you're a U.S. citizen it's possible to get a green card for your

- **spouse**
- **unmarried children under twenty-one**
- **parents (if you are twenty-one or older)**

Petitions should be filed at the Regional Service Center nearest you; the processing normally takes at least a couple of months. Unless your immediate relative has a criminal history or falls under one of the other categories of exclusion, there should be no problem getting a green card.

The wait is usually longer for other relatives, who are given different orders of "preference." Married sons and daughters of citizens, for instance, have to wait about two to three years. For brothers and sisters, it's even longer — at least nine years or more. Other relatives are basically out of luck, since U.S. citizens may not sponsor aunts, uncles, cousins, or grandparents for a green card. Citizens can petition for stepchildren and adopted children, but certain age and custody requirements may apply.

The waiting period also varies depending on what country the immigrant is from. Nationals of Mexico, India, and the Philippines face the longest waits, because they have "oversubscribed" in years past.

When Is a Lawyer Necessary?

Generally, if you wish to come to the U.S. to work or if you want to obtain a permanent immigrant status, you probably should seek at least preliminary advice from a lawyer experienced with immigration issues. If you're being threatened with deportation or are seeking asylum, you should also consult a lawyer.

In Texas, California, and Florida, immigration lawyers are specially certified. You can get a list of names by calling or writing the

American Immigration Lawyers Association
1400 Eye Street NW
Suite 1200
Washington, DC 20005
202-371-9377

Can the relatives of lawful permanent residents (green card holders) get a green card?

Yes, but only spouses and unmarried children are eligible, and there's usually a wait of two to three years. Lawful permanent residents may not sponsor their parents, siblings, or married children. (But a lawful permanent resident who becomes a U.S. citizen may petition for such relatives.) (See "Becoming a Citizen," on page 310.)

GETTING A GREEN CARD THROUGH EMPLOYMENT

Nikos, the Greek pop star, was the black sheep of his academic, middle-class family. His older sister Zoe, on the other hand, had become a renowned historian, authoring several books on twentieth-century Greek-American political and social relations. She had visited the U.S. many times to do research and had completely fallen in love with America. She wanted to find a way to work and live there permanently.

Can a person get a green card through his or her employer?

Yes, but this visa is harder to get than a temporary, nonimmigrant employment visa (see page 307). Only 140,000 are available each year, and due to processing time and possible backlogs, it may take a year or longer to get one.

Employment-based green cards are divided into "preferences," each with its own requirements and waiting periods. First preference goes to people deemed truly extraordinary in their field, such as Nobel Prize winners. These people may file a petition for a visa on their own behalf, without the need of an employer to "sponsor" them.

There's also no current wait for professionals and skilled workers who have a sponsoring employer in the U.S. However, the employer generally must get a certification from the U.S. Department of Labor that no U.S. citizen or lawful permanent resident is able or willing to do the job, and that hiring the alien won't hurt similar workers in the U.S. This can be a difficult, time-consuming process.

Workers who are not professionals and have less than two years of training or experience for a particular job have a long wait — at least six years — since only 10,000 visas a year are allocated to them. On the other hand, religious workers, such as ministers and monks, have no wait (unless they are from the Philippines, in which case they must wait about a year, because of the high number of applications from that country).

One of the most welcome groups are entrepreneurial aliens who establish new commercial enterprises, hire at least ten U.S. workers full-time, and invest a minimum of $1 million in the business (or $500,000 if the business is in a specially targeted rural or high unemployment area). They presently get their green cards with no backlog or waiting period.

FORFEITING A GREEN CARD

Beatrice had an Australian friend, Harry, who moved to the U.S., married an American, and got a green card. Harry also was an aspiring actor who wasn't having much luck finding work. To pay

the rent and make contacts, he started selling cocaine. He didn't land any roles, but he did make a fortune — until he got busted by an undercover cop, who told him he was as good as shipped back to Sydney.

■ **Can the INS take away a person's green card?**

Yes. Under certain circumstances, the INS may confiscate the green card and deport the alien, who may be banned permanently from the U.S. or who may have to wait at least five years before applying for another green card or nonimmigrant visa.

An alien can forfeit a green card in the following ways:

- By engaging in activities that are grounds for deportation. These include convictions for many felonies, terrorist activities, drug abuse, firearms violations, and smuggling aliens.
- By falling under one of the other grounds for exclusion when returning to the U.S. after a trip abroad (see page 303).
- By becoming a public charge.
- By engaging in marriage fraud (see page 312).
- More typically, by staying abroad too long — usually more than a year. The INS assumes that such a person has abandoned permanent residency in the U.S.

If Deportation Proceedings Are Brought Against You

All aliens placed in deportation proceedings have a right to a hearing before an immigration judge (who works for the Department of Justice). At this hearing the alien has the right

- **to bring a lawyer at his or her own expense**
- **to have an interpreter provided by the court**
- **to present evidence**
- **to cross-examine any government witnesses**

If the judge orders deportation, the alien can appeal to the Board of Immigration Appeals (also part of the Department of Justice). If the alien loses there, he or she can appeal to the Federal Circuit Court and eventually even to the U.S. Supreme Court. Note, though, that the U.S. Supreme Court rarely hears a deportation appeal.

GETTING WORK WITHOUT A GREEN CARD

Penelope, the easygoing New Zealander, had been camping out in Beatrice and Renata's dorm room for nearly a month. Beatrice's grades were slipping, so she finally told Penelope it was time to move on. The problem was that Penelope couldn't really afford a hotel because she had spent most of her money partying in clubs, so she thought she'd look for a job.

■ **Can people with nonimmigrant visas work in the U.S. legally?**

Not tourists, like Penelope, and not foreigners with student visas, unless they are working as part of the practical training in their field of study and the INS has given them permission to do so. Other nonimmigrants, such as fiancés of American citizens or temporary workers (see page 304), may be issued a document by the INS authorizing them to work if they meet certain qualifications.

Employers may sponsor aliens for nonimmigrant working visas. While these visas are only temporary, they may still be valid for several years and can often be extended. They also are easier to get than a green card.

Sometimes even undocumented aliens — people with no visa at all who are here illegally — may obtain permission to work if they've applied for asylum and their claim has been judged not "frivolous" (see page 313). Even aliens in deportation or exclusion proceedings may be granted permission to work by the INS.

CHANGING JOBS

Zoe got a job teaching history at Brainmore College, a prestigious university in the U.S., which sponsored her application for a green card. But after numerous run-ins with the head of the department (who believed that students learn only when they are publicly humiliated before their peers), she decided to look for a job elsewhere in the U.S. academic community.

Can an alien change jobs?

It depends on the type of visa a worker has. If (like Zoe) you were granted a green card on the basis of an employer's petition, you are free to change jobs — so long as you can show that when the petition was filed you *intended* to work for the sponsoring employer on a permanent basis. In other words, you have to show that your original application was not made frivolously just to get a green card. On the other hand, if the green card was granted on the basis of a relative's petition, you can freely change jobs.

Nonimmigrant visas, on the other hand, are employer-specific. If an employee stops working for the company that sponsored the visa petition, he or she will not be authorized to work for another company until the new employer petitions for a new visa petition.

HIRING ALIENS TO WORK IN THE HOME

Shortly after Beatrice and Renata finally kicked Penelope out of their dorm room, her tourist visa expired. That didn't stop her from looking for work, and she found a job as a live-in nanny for an affluent professional couple, Adam and Jennifer, parents of a two-year-old daughter. They were so desperate to find someone nice to care for their child that they chose to believe Penelope when she falsely assured them she had a green card.

CASE IN POINT

To Love, Honor, and Get a Green Card

Mordchai Bashan, a citizen of Israel, wanted to live the American dream, and he appeared to get off to the right start when he married his wife, Kathryn, a U.S. citizen, in New York City in 1975. After the marriage, the Bashans had a daughter and started a business, and Mordchai became a naturalized citizen five years later. Unfortunately, all was not quiet on the home front. The reason? Mordchai, like many other hopeful immigrants, seems to have loved his green card more than his spouse.

In 1981, Kathryn reported to the Immigration and Naturalization Service that she and Mordchai had been living apart since she sued for divorce in May 1980. There would generally be nothing wrong with that, except that in order to become a citizen, Mordchai had sworn in his naturalization application that he had been living with his wife the previous three years. That statement was made in October, five months *after* he moved out of his house.

Their marriage, it turned out, had never been a match made in heaven. Two months after they exchanged vows, Mordchai told Kathryn he had married her solely to get a green card and become a legal alien. And, at one point, Kathryn had considered filing a harassment complaint against her husband but then declined to do so because he threatened to take their daughter out of the country.

While being a lousy husband is not enough to get naturalization papers revoked, lying on those papers is. Thus, in 1982 a federal district court in New York revoked Mordchai's naturalization order, setting the grounds for deportation.

Verifying Work Status

To prove that he or she is authorized to work in the U.S., a prospective employee must establish two things:

- **identity**
- **authorization to work**

The employee can choose which document or documents to show. Any one of the following is sufficient to establish *both* identity and authorization to work:

- **U.S. passport**
- **certificate of U.S. citizenship (issued to individuals who were born abroad and adopted by U.S. citizens, or were born abroad to U.S. citizens, or who derived their citizenship through naturalized parents)**
- **certificate of naturalization (issued by the INS to naturalized aliens)**
- **foreign passport with visa indicating the alien is authorized to work in the U.S.**
- **permanent or conditional green card**
- **temporary resident card (issued by the INS during a period of amnesty for undocumented aliens)**
- **employment authorization card with photo (issued by the INS)**
- **refugee travel document (issued by the INS to aliens who have been granted asylum or refugee status)**

An employee may also satisfy the verification requirements by submitting one document from Group 1 (for employment authorization) and one document from Group 2 (for establishing identity):

Group 1:

- **Social Security card (unless the card states "Not Authorized For Employment")**
- **original or certified copy of U.S. birth certificate**
- **Native American tribal document**
- **U.S. citizen identification card**
- **certification of birth abroad for U.S. citizens**
- **employment authorization card without a photo**

Group 2:

- **driver's license**
- **photo ID card issued by state**
- **school ID card with photo**
- **military ID**
- **voter's registration card**
- **U.S. Coast Guard Merchant Marine card**
- **Canadian driver's license**

Is it illegal to hire an undocumented alien?

Yes — if the employer knows (or has reason to know) that the alien isn't authorized to work. Since November 6, 1986, employers have had the responsibility to verify a person's work authorization, and both the employer and employee must fill out an INS I-9 form confirming that the employee is authorized to work. This rule applies to employers of domestic help unless the worker is a "casual hire" (see below).

Certain types of workers are not considered "employees," and so the person who hires them does not have to verify their immigration status. The workers in this group include

- **independent contractors (see page 248)**
- **"casual hires" — people who perform sporadic domestic jobs, such as a babysitter who comes every few months. A once-a-month gardener, on the other hand, would not qualify as sporadic (though he might be exempt as an independent contractor)**

In addition, some workers are exempted from the verification process if they have been employed continuously by the same employer since November 6, 1986.

Penelope quit the nanny job, and Adam and Jennifer hired Maria, a bona fide green card holder. They decided they should pay the appropriate taxes for their employee.

■ Does an employer have to pay taxes for an alien employee?

Yes. People who hire household employees must pay social security and medicare taxes (and sometimes federal unemployment tax and state tax, as well). The IRS does not exempt an employer from paying the appropriate taxes on *any* employee — regardless of whether the worker is a U.S. citizen *or* an undocumented alien without permission to work legally. The IRS is concerned only with how much an employee is paid per quarter. (See page 125 about paying taxes for household employees.)

■ Does an alien employee have to pay taxes?

Yes. Aliens, regardless of their immigration status, are supposed to pay taxes on any taxable income earned in the U.S. If the alien is undocumented but hopes to legalize his or her status, this issue may well come up. (Paying taxes to the IRS usually does not alert the INS of an immigration status problem.)

WHAT RIGHTS DO ALIENS HAVE?

Zoe's colleague Irena, a physics professor, was also from Greece and had lived in the states for several years with a green card. Now, Irena's young son was ready to enter kindergarten.

■ What rights do lawful permanent residents (green card holders) have?

They are entitled to many things. Some are granted by federal or state statutes, and some have been granted by court rulings or the U.S. Constitution. Among other things, lawful permanent residents are entitled to

- **freely seek employment (with the exception of a few jobs set aside exclusively for U.S. citizens for national security reasons)**
- **attend public school**
- **legal representation if prosecuted for a crime**
- **food stamps**
- **unemployment insurance**
- **Medicaid**
- **federal housing**

In times of a draft, green card holders may be called to service just as any U.S. citizen, and all alien males eighteen and older are required to register for the Selective Service — even undocumented aliens.

■ What rights do undocumented aliens have?

Their rights are more limited. Court rulings and federal law have granted undocumented aliens the right to

- **receive medicaid in case of emergency**
- **attend public school**
- **some welfare benefits**
- **legal representation if prosecuted for a crime**

Schools are not allowed to ask a person's immigration status. Neither are hospitals in the case of an emergency.

■ So what sets U.S. citizens apart?

U.S. citizens enjoy a number of rights that aliens, no matter what their status, do not. For one thing, only a citizen can vote in national or state elections. And only citizens can rest assured that they'll never be deported or excluded from the U.S., a risk that aliens always run. Also, aliens may not generally hold political office or become law enforcement officers.

BECOMING A CITIZEN

Martin, the English actor, arrived in America with an immigrant visa (thanks to his mother), and right away he was "discovered" by an eager talent agent he met in New York. He appeared in several commercials and TV movies before landing a role in a feature film. America was good to Martin, and he became interested

in U.S. politics. In fact, before long Martin began to feel more American than British and wondered if he ought to try to become a U.S. citizen, like his mother.

■ Can a green card holder become a U.S. citizen?

Yes, through a process called "naturalization." Generally, you need a green card before you can naturalize, and you must have lived in the U.S. for a specified number of years — usually three years for those married to U.S. citizens and five years for other lawful permanent residents.

In addition:

- You must be a person of good moral character, not a subversive, and not a member of the Communist Party.
- You must pass an English literacy test (though some exceptions are made for elderly people and people with disabilities).
- You must pass a test that shows you have a knowledge and understanding of the fundamentals of U.S. history and government.

FOREIGN SPOUSES

Bartholomew, a U.S. citizen, landed a Fulbright scholarship in Italy, where he met Allegra, a beautiful Italian economist. After only a two-month courtship, Bart had to return home. Since he couldn't bear to leave Allegra, he proposed to her. She said yes, and they married in Florence, two nights before leaving for the States.

■ Does the spouse of a U.S. citizen automatically become a U.S. citizen?

No. You can't become a U.S. citizen without first being a lawful permanent resident (green card holder) for three years, except in rare circumstances. You must also have been married at least three years, and must have lived in the U.S. for eighteen months of those three years.

If you are a U.S. citizen, getting a green card for your foreign spouse is relatively easy, although it may take three to six months to complete the

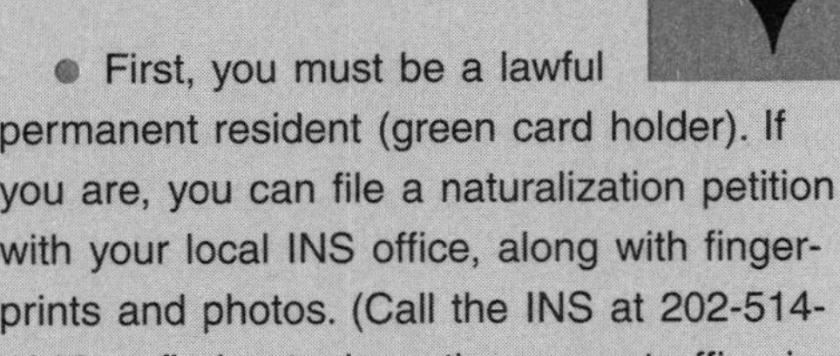

- First, you must be a lawful permanent resident (green card holder). If you are, you can file a naturalization petition with your local INS office, along with fingerprints and photos. (Call the INS at 202-514-4316 to find out where the nearest office is located.)
- Once your application is processed, you'll be asked to come into the INS office for an interview. This is to determine if you are eligible for citizenship and to test your knowledge of English and U.S. history and government.

The interviewer will test your language skills by speaking with you. Basic knowledge is all that is required. You will also have to write a simple sentence or two in English. To test your familiarity with history and government, the interviewer will ask you a couple of questions from a list of about 100. These questions are available to the public if you want to study in advance.

- If you fail any portion of the test, you may try again at a later date. If your naturalization petition is denied, you may file an appeal in federal court.
- If you pass the test, you're not a citizen until you take an oath of allegiance and renounce your foreign citizenship. Some countries, like the United Kingdom, don't recognize the renunciation, so you legitimately may be a citizen of both countries. You may take the oath in a formal swearing-in ceremony with other new citizens, which could mean waiting as long as six months. Or, in certain INS districts, you may take the oath at an INS office. You won't get the formal ceremony, but you also won't have to wait as long.

procedure. Also, it doesn't matter if your spouse is already in the U.S. (legally or illegally) or is living overseas. However, your foreign spouse will be granted only "conditional residence" if you have been married less than two years.

Conditional residence lasts for two years, during which an immigrant has the same rights, privileges, and obligations as any lawful permanent resident, including the freedom to travel abroad, work, and receive public benefits such as welfare.

To convert conditional residence into a permanent one, the couple must *jointly* file an application (Form I-751) during the last ninety days before the visa expires.

■ Can conditional residence be revoked?

Yes. The purpose of conditional residency for foreign spouses is to prevent "sham marriages" that are entered into solely for the purpose of getting a green card. Any payment of a fee to the American spouse is considered evidence of "bad faith" and fraud. If the INS suspects your marriage is a sham, it may investigate and call you in for an interview. (The INS also investigates couples at random.) The key question will be whether you live together as husband and wife as it is traditionally defined in our culture.

Conditional residence can be revoked if the marriage is found to be a sham. The couple may also be subject to criminal prosecution and could be imprisoned for up to five years and fined as much as $250,000.

■ What if the marriage ends (or is on the rocks) before the two-year period is over?

Conditional residence might be revoked, but certain waivers are available

- **if the couple divorces and the alien spouse can convince the INS that the marriage was entered in "good faith," even though it didn't last long**
- **if the alien spouse has evidence of mental or physical abuse**
- **if the INS determines that deportation would cause extreme hardship (If, for instance, Allegra developed a serious health problem that couldn't be treated in her native country, the INS might allow her to stay in the U.S. even if she and Bart broke up.)**

REFUGEES AND ASYLUM SEEKERS

Peter Wong, originally from China, was tired of living life in the U.S. "underground," and he decided he'd rather become legal so he could find a decent job. He'd heard that people who face persecution in their native countries might qualify for refugee status, and since he was a dissident from China he wondered if he was eligible.

■ What are refugees and "asylum seekers"?

The distinction is mostly semantic. A refugee applies to enter the U.S. from outside the country, while an asylum seeker is already in the U.S. or at the border. It doesn't matter what an asylum seeker's immigration status is; undocumented aliens may apply for asylum even if deportation proceedings have been started.

Refugees and asylum seekers must prove the same thing: an inability or unwillingness to return to (or remain in) the home country because of a well-founded fear of persecution. It's not enough to come from a country where violence affects the entire population. Instead, the asylum seeker must show that the fear of persecution is on account of his or her

- **race**
- **religion**
- **nationality**
- **membership in a social group**
- **political opinion**

"Persecution" generally includes the threat of death, torture, or imprisonment by the government or by guerrillas or paramilitary death squads. Economic deprivation, simple discrimination, and forced military service are not generally considered persecution.

Refugees and asylum seekers have the burden of proving their case. Evidence, such as expert witness testimony about the human rights situation in their country, articles, or letters from relatives or friends, can be very helpful in meeting that goal. Sometimes, if the applicant has fled with nothing more than the clothes on his back, his credible testimony alone may be sufficient to prove a well-founded fear of persecution.

Even when there's a well-founded fear of persecution, asylum and refugee status may be denied if the alien

- **has committed certain crimes**
- **is living safely in a third country**
- **poses a security danger to the U.S.**
- **has persecuted others**

Peter applied for asylum and immediately hit the streets looking for a job. He wanted something full-time, with a decent wage and benefits.

■ Can applicants for political asylum work legally in the U.S.?

Yes, if the application is not deemed to be "frivolous." Generally, applications from citizens of countries with no human rights problems are considered frivolous; the INS figures they're just trying to get a work permit. While an asylum request is pending (which can be many months or years), the "non-frivolous" applicant will be authorized to work.

It's a lot easier, however, to convince the INS that an application is not frivolous than it is to be granted asylum. More than 100,000 aliens apply each year. In 1992 only about 4,000 requests were granted.

Asylum or refugee status can be granted to the applicant *and* to his or her spouse and children if they are included in the application. People granted asylum or refugee status may work here legally and receive public benefits. After a year they may qualify for permanent residence status.

DUAL CITIZENS

Beatrice's friend Denise was born in the U.S., but her mother was a French citizen. Denise traveled to Paris regularly (and came back with the clothes to show for it). To Beatrice's surprise, Denise announced that she was going to work full-time in France after graduation. "Can you do that?" asked Bea. "Sure," said Denise. "I'm a French citizen."

■ Can a U.S. citizen also be a citizen of another country?

Yes, under certain circumstances. Babies born in the U.S. are automatically U.S. citizens even if their parents are undocumented aliens or green card holders. (The one exception is children of certain foreign diplomats. They don't become citizens.) If one or both of a baby's parents are from a country (like France) that bestows citizenship based on "blood" (nationality of your parents) and not "soil" (where you were born), then the baby can be a citizen of both countries. (The U.S. bestows citizenship based on either blood or soil.)

A foreigner who has become a naturalized U.S. citizen may retain his or her native citizenship *if* that other country does not require that it be relinquished.

Similarly, U.S. citizens may become citizens of another country and keep their U.S. citizenship *if* the other country doesn't require the American to renounce U.S. citizenship.

■ If a baby is born to a U.S. citizen while she is out of the country, is the baby automatically a U.S. citizen?

Maybe. A foreign-born child will be a U.S. citizen if both parents are U.S. citizens and if at least one of them once resided in the U.S. The child will also be a U.S. citizen if one parent is a U.S. citizen and lived in the U.S. for at least five years prior to the child's birth (and was fourteen or older for at least two of those years).

Blossom went to France to attend a famous cooking school. She was such a great success that a high-powered Parisian chef offered her a post in his popular Left Bank bistro.

Can a U.S. citizen lose citizenship by living and working in a foreign country?

No. Living and working abroad — even marrying somebody from a foreign country — are not considered acts of "expatriation," and citizenship is not lost as a result.

A citizen of the U.S. — whether born here or naturalized — may lose his or her citizenship only by *voluntarily* performing any of the following acts, *with the intention* of relinquishing U.S. citizenship:

- **becoming a citizen of another country**
- **making a formal declaration of allegiance to a foreign country after turning eighteen**
- **serving in the armed forces of a country engaged in hostilities against the U.S., or serving as an officer in another country's armed forces**
- **being employed by the government of the other country while being a citizen of that country**
- **formally renouncing U.S. citizenship to a U.S. diplomatic or consular officer while living abroad**
- **formally renouncing U.S. citizenship when the U.S. is in a state of war and when the renunciation is found contrary to the interests of national defense**
- **committing an act of treason or trying to overthrow the U.S. government by force**

CASE IN POINT

The Politics of Birth

Babies born in the U.S. automatically become citizens — even if their parents are here illegally. However, just because the *child* is entitled to the rights and privileges of citizenship doesn't mean the Immigration and Naturalization Service won't still try to deport the parents.

So learned Joaquin and Maria Ramos, who came to the U.S. from the Philippines on a tourist visa in July 1967. Despite the fact they had permission to stay only until the following April, Ramos and his wife both found good jobs in Chicago and later had two children.

But the INS eventually caught up to the Ramoses and ordered them deported. They appealed, arguing that it would be an extreme hardship on them and their children to return to the Philippines, especially because the children would have trouble adjusting to life in a totally foreign culture. In 1981 an immigration judge rejected their plea and gave his own answer to the dilemma: the children could stay with an aunt who was a legal resident, but the parents had to go. That decision was overturned in 1983 by the U.S. Court of Appeals for the Fifth Circuit, which ruled that the lower court judge should have fully considered the emotional toll on the children if they had to be transplanted to a culture where they had no ties.

Carlos and Beatriz Acosta had a similar problem, but were not as lucky. They had overstayed their visa in 1974, but it took the INS less than a year to catch up to them. By then, Beatriz was pregnant, and she gave birth soon after.

The Acostas tried to prevent their deportation, claiming it would impose hardship on the family and deprive their infant daughter, Lina, of the equal protection of laws she was entitled to as a citizen.

While a federal district judge found those arguments compelling, a panel of judges on the U.S. Court of Appeals for the Third Circuit in Philadelphia was not as convinced. In 1977 they ordered that the deportation order was valid and that Lina's constitutional rights were not violated by it. The court's reasoning? While the privilege of citizenship allows someone, in this case little Lina, to live wherever he or she wants, it does not extend that privilege to alien parents. When Lina reached decision-making age, the court noted, she would be free to choose to return to the U.S. if she wanted.

DENATURALIZATION

Bartholomew's wife, Allegra, eventually became a U.S. citizen, but their marriage was in trouble. They fought most bitterly about politics. Bart was civic-minded (in fact he was running for town mayor). Allegra, on the other hand, had declared herself an anarchist. During one fight, Bart threatened to ship her back to Italy.

■ Can a naturalized citizen be deported from the U.S.?

Yes, but only after the person is "denaturalized" — stripped of U.S. citizenship. Denaturalization proceedings are initiated if a person

- **obtained citizenship illegally, by concealing or misrepresenting a material fact**
- **takes up residence in a foreign country within one year of naturalization**
- **becomes affiliated with a subversive, Communist, or anarchist organization within five years of naturalization (Merely expressing anarchist views, however, is not cause for denaturalization.)**

GETTING SICK

20

HEALTH INSURANCE

(For general insurance information, see Chapter 8, INSURANCE)

When You Leave Your Job

Bradley was taking a huge step and going into business for himself as a landscape designer. One of his main concerns about leaving his employer was losing his group health insurance.

■ Can you stay on a company health plan after you leave your job?

Yes. Under the Consolidated Omnibus Budget Reconciliation Act (COBRA), a company that employs twenty or more people must give you the option of staying on the health insurance plan for a period of up to eighteen months — unless you were fired for gross misconduct. Whether you quit or were laid off, your employer has to make the health insurance available to you for eighteen months. You have to pay the premiums, but you get the benefit of a group rate. You may, however, have to pay the company an administrative fee of as much as 2 percent. Note: this law does not apply if you are employed by the federal government or by certain church-related organizations.

When You're Denied Coverage

Bradley stayed on his former employer's health plan for eighteen months. When it was about to run out, he shopped around and found a company he liked. However, his first application was rejected. Brad was furious.

■ Under what circumstances can an insurer refuse an applicant?

Basically, an insurer can refuse to insure anyone it wants, as long as the reason for doing so is not against the law. An insurer can refuse to cover a person who is currently experiencing health problems or who might be at risk for future problems. For example, a cancer survivor would probably have difficulty getting coverage. Many, but not all, states prohibit insurers from using race, sex, sexual orientation, or marital status in determining insurability. Also, many states prohibit or sharply limit companies from basing insurance decisions on a person's physical disabilities.

To find out exactly what your state prohibits, you can call your state department of insurance. If you think you have been turned down illegally, your state's department of insurance may decide to take action on your behalf. You can also hire a private attorney.

■ What about "preexisting conditions"?

Typically, many insurers refuse to insure a "preexisting condition." This is usually defined as a health condition for which medical advice or treatment was given or recommended within five years (sometimes less) of the effective date of the policy. If you had symptoms but failed to seek treatment, your condition could still be excluded. If you disclose the condition on the insurance application and the insurer does not exclude it, then it will be covered.

Some policies will provide coverage for preexisting conditions so long as you have had no treatment for two years. An insurer must notify you in advance that preexisting conditions will not be covered.

If You Are Turned Down for Health Insurance

If an insurance company refuses to insure you, it may be because it received erroneous information from the Medical Information Bureau, a clearinghouse used by most major insurers that maintains a database with files on more than 15 million people. You can request a copy of your file from MIB, which is obligated to send you a report within thirty days if it has a file on you. To obtain a copy, write to:

Medical Information Bureau
P.O. Box 105
Essex Station
Boston, MA 02112
617-426-3660.

If you find an error in your report, you must notify MIB in writing. Since it may take some time to get an error corrected, you may want to request your file from the bureau *before* you apply for health insurance, in order to reduce the chances that you will be turned down because of an inaccuracy. Virtually all applications for health insurance will ask whether you have ever been turned down for coverage. The whole process will be a lot easier if you can avoid being rejected in the first place.

Tests

Bradley found out that the insurance company had rejected him because he was being confused with another Bradley Goodfriend, who was much older and in ill health. Once he cleared up the misunderstanding, the insurance company told him he'd need to take a few tests, including one for the AIDS virus. Brad was getting worried about the continued delay.

■ Can an insurer require that an applicant take tests?

Yes. Typically, insurers require only blood and urine tests and electrocardiograms (a heart test), but more recently insurers have begun to require that applicants take AIDS tests. There are no prohibitions against doing so, but many states require that you first sign a form authorizing the test. Some states also prohibit insurers from using the results of an AIDS test to deny you insurance or raise your rates *unless* the test was conducted according to a medically accepted procedure designed to reduce the chances of a false positive result.

Canceled Coverage

Bradley took the AIDS test and was relieved when it came back negative. Nevertheless, he had a bad year healthwise. A sinus infection dogged him for weeks until the doctor prescribed a controversial (and costly) horseradish sniffing treatment. Then Brad broke his arm skiing. That took four months, three specialists, and two operations to heal. And he learned that his Uncle Paul was a carrier for a rare genetic disease, and that it was likely that he was too. This information went into his medical records, and Brad was worried how the insurance company would respond.

■ Under what circumstances can an insurer cancel coverage?

In most cases, an insurer can cancel only under two circumstances:

- **you fail to pay for the policy**
- **you misrepresent yourself on your application**

If you were unaware of having an illness at the time you applied for a policy, the insurer has no right to cancel. However, some policies are "cancelable," and in those cases, the insurance company can revoke them. These policies must clearly state that they are cancelable. Still, most policies state that they are "guaranteed renewable."

Can an insurer refuse to renew a policy?
Yes, so long as the policy doesn't have a provision for automatic renewal. Also, some states require that an insurer have a reasonable basis for canceling or failing to renew a policy.

Refusal to Reimburse

After Brad submitted the bill for his $200 sinus treatment to the insurance company, he received notice from the company that the "prevailing rate" for horseradish sniffing was only $150. "What's the deal," thought Brad. "I'm not going to some fancy, big-time doctor. This isn't fair."

Can an insurer refuse to reimburse someone because the fee is above the "prevailing rate"?
Yes, but if you think the decision is unfair you should contact your doctor and tell him or her what the insurance company has said. If the doctor agrees that the company is wrong, ask him or her to write a letter explaining why the charges are acceptable and requesting reconsideration of the decision to deny full reimbursement.

Your insurance company may also have an established procedure for appealing a claim.

"Minor" Ailments

Bradley was feeling great and had no signs that he had inherited the genetic disease. Still, he wanted to be checked by his doctor once a year to make sure everything was in order. But when Brad reviewed his policy, he discovered that his insurance doesn't cover routine physicals. However, the doctor said he simply would diagnose some minor ailment so that Bradley could be reimbursed after the exam.

Is it a crime for a doctor to diagnose something minor in order for the patient to get insurance reimbursement?
Yes, if the diagnosis is fraudulent. Both you and the doctor may be violating your state's criminal laws. On the other hand, if the diagnosis, though "minor," is genuine, no law has been broken. However, a danger of this practice is that your medical records may become laden with so many "diseases" that a future insurer may decline to insure you.

When You Have Problems with Your Health Insurer

In general, how you handle a problem with a health insurer depends on whether you have an employer-sponsored plan or your own private plan. Private health insurance plans are governed by state laws, which require insurers to handle claims fairly and in good faith. If there is no reasonable basis for an insurer's refusal to pay a claim, you can sue for

- **the amount of the benefits wrongfully withheld**
- **damages for your pain and suffering**
- **punitive damages**
- **your attorney's fees**

To determine just what your rights are in any given case, you should consult a lawyer or your state's department of insurance.

Employer-provided health plans are governed by a federal statute called ERISA, the Employee Retirement Income Security Act. Your right to sue is limited under ERISA, which requires that you first go through an administrative appeal procedure. You should consult your plan booklet and talk to the person at work who deals with insurance matters to determine how to make an appeal. If you do end up suing, you will be able to collect only your actual damages and attorney's fees. You cannot collect money for pain and suffering or for punitive damages, nor do you have the right to a jury trial. (Because of these limits, many lawyers don't like to take health insurance disputes that fall under ERISA.)

What Information Must a Physician Tell a Patient?

You always have the right to ask your doctor questions about your medical care. In fact, before your doctor can treat you, he or she must obtain your **informed consent.** That means your doctor must tell you enough information for you to decide whether or not you want the treatment.

Generally you must be told

- **the nature and purpose of the treatment**
- **the risks and consequences**
- **the alternative courses of treatment, including the consequences of no treatment**

Before giving you something other than routine treatment, such as performing an invasive procedure, your physician may ask you to sign an informed consent form. Often such a form notes that you have been told of the risks of the procedure and agree to undergo it. But no matter what the form says, your doctor always has the obligation to exercise due care when treating you, regardless of what you have signed. And you always have the right to sue if your doctor is negligent, so long as you initiate your suit before the statute of limitations has expired. (See "Medical Malpractice" on page 330, and "Statutes of Limitations" on page 340.)

Note: except in a few instances, nothing in the law requires that consent be given in writing. However, if a patient sues a doctor for failing to provide informed consent, it may be difficult for the physician to prove that proper consent was obtained if there is no supporting document. That is a key reason why patients are asked to sign consent forms.

YOUR MEDICAL RECORDS

Because of her constant headaches and back pains, Beatrice had been seeing a lot of doctors. They all poked and prodded, stopping occasionally to jot something down on a chart. So far none of them had helped much, and Bea usually felt too intimidated to ask what they were doing or why. But the pain finally was getting the better of her, and she decided to give herself a crash course in medicine. One weekend she came home from the library with textbooks on neurology, orthopedics, osteoporosis, arthritis, migraine headaches, and even psychosomatic illness. The jargon and detail were all pretty confusing, and Beatrice decided that what she really needed to do was gather all her medical records and examine them herself.

Do patients have a right to see their medical records?

Generally, yes. Recent trends permit patients greater accessibility to their records, and some states, including New York, have laws that allow patients to review their charts. Some states require physicians to furnish a patient with at least a summary of the patient's office records, if not with a copy of the complete record.

Even if there is no state law granting you automatic access to your records, you often may see them. It's usually up to the health care practitioner to decide whether or not to show you the records. That person must weigh your right to know what's in the records against the possibility of unnecessarily alarming you. It's important for doctors to feel uninhibited when they make notations in your records, and they may be less honest and direct if they think all their comments may be shown to their patients.

Even in states that do have laws granting you access to your medical charts, it is within your doctor's discretion to withhold certain records, such as psychiatric reports or other information that the doctor thinks would be likely to harm you. For instance, if your records indicate that you have a fatal disease, a psychiatrist may withhold them if he thinks knowledge of the illness would drive you to commit suicide. Generally, the law gives psychiatrists wide discretion to withhold information that may alarm or agitate the patient and cause his or her condition to deteriorate.

Still, these records concern you, and if you want to know what's in them, don't be afraid to ask. You can also request that your doctor review them with you and explain any distressing or confusing information.

Who besides the patient and doctor is allowed to see a person's medical records?

Generally — but not always — only the people giving you medical care are allowed to see your records. Most of the time, medical information will be released to someone else only with your consent or the consent of a person who has been legally designated to make medical decisions for you. (See "Health Care Proxies" on page 328.)

Some information receives extra protection because it is so sensitive. For example, federal law imposes strict constraints on the disclosure of records concerning treatment for drug and alcohol abuse. Some state laws limit disclosure of sex-related treatment, and some restrict the release of HIV and AIDS information.

Still, while your medical records are generally regarded as private, there are times when they may be examined by people other than your doctor. If the information in them is important to a criminal case, for instance, a judge may order that the records be released. Also, your doctor may be allowed to reveal confidential information about you if it is necessary to protect another person. If, for exam-

CASE IN POINT

A Therapist's Duty to Warn

In October 1969, Prosanjit Poddar killed his ex-girlfriend, Tatiana Tarasoff, in Berkeley, California. Though he was tried for murder, his crime also prompted a civil case by Tarasoff's parents after it came to light that police officers and two psychologists knew Poddar had threatened to kill Tarasoff but had done nothing to warn her.

The summer before the murder, Poddar had told his therapist, Dr. Lawrence Moore, a psychologist at Cowell Memorial Hospital at the University of California at Berkeley, that he was going to kill a girl, whom Moore determined was Tarasoff. After consulting other doctors, Moore decided that Poddar should be committed to the hospital, and he talked to the campus police about the matter.

While Tarasoff was on a trip out of the country, Poddar was taken into custody. At that point, Moore's supervisor stepped in and ordered that Poddar be released. The supervisor asked the police to turn over the warning letter Moore had written, and he ordered Moore to destroy the notes from his sessions with Poddar.

Tarasoff returned to Berkeley but was told nothing of the threats. After Poddar killed her, Tarasoff's parents sued the two therapists, the police, and the University of California for negligently causing her death. A state appeals court ruled in 1976 that the therapists could be held liable for not warning Tarasoff or her parents of the danger posed by Poddar. The case against the police was dismissed.

The therapists argued that their conversations with patients are privileged and that a warning would have been a breach of confidentiality. But the court held that a therapist has an obligation to use reasonable care to protect an intended victim against violence once the therapist determines a patient poses a real danger. "The protective privilege ends where the public peril begins," the opinion written by Justice Matthew Tobriner noted.

The Tarasoff family subsequently settled the case out of court.

How Can a Person Be Declared Incompetent?

Every state has laws that allow the courts to step in when a person becomes unable to take care of him- or herself. There must be a court hearing at which the person may be represented by a lawyer. (If the individual has no legal representation, the judge will usually appoint a lawyer.) If the court finds that a person is incompetent, a guardian or surrogate may be appointed to manage his or her affairs and make medical and other important decisions.

To avoid such a major loss of control, you can name someone to be your conservator in the event that you become unable to care for yourself (see page 400).

ple, a psychiatrist's patient expresses an intention to kill someone, or if a physician's patient with AIDS refuses to inform his or her sexual partners, those doctors may be permitted by state law in some instances and obligated in others to inform the proper authorities.

Many states also have laws requiring disclosure of medical information when the public interest is at stake. These laws vary from state to state, but doctors are commonly required to report things like births and deaths. Some states also require doctors to report industrial accidents, abortions, cancer, contagious diseases such as smallpox, gunshot wounds, Legionnaires' disease, and AIDS. Usually the patient's name does not have to be disclosed. Also, in every state it is mandatory for doctors to report cases of suspected child abuse.

YOUR RIGHT TO KNOW YOUR MEDICAL CONDITION

The family internist, Dr. Komfort, told Beatrice that her elderly aunt had developed a very serious — and possibly terminal — disease. Beatrice was convinced that it would be kinder not to tell her aunt the news, and she begged Komfort to keep it to himself.

Can a doctor withhold a diagnosis from a patient?

Not usually. However, if a doctor reasonably believes that the patient's mental or physical well-being would suffer from learning a diagnosis, something known as the "therapeutic privilege" may permit the physician to withhold that information. Still, this privilege is narrow, and the fact that a patient could be upset by certain facts does not usually permit a doctor not to tell the patient. Knowing the facts must pose a serious threat to a patient's physical or mental health to justify a physician's withholding the facts.

A mentally competent patient may, however, ask the doctor to withhold bad news. In that case, the doctor has no legal obligation to disclose information that the patient makes clear he or she does not wish to know.

When a patient is not mentally competent, a doctor must always disclose information about the patient's condition to a person who has authority to make medical decisions for the patient. (See "Health Care Proxies" on page 328.)

YOUR RIGHT TO TREATMENT

Any timidness Beatrice had about dealing with doctors evaporated when she became pregnant with her first child, Alena. A combination of hormones and maternal instincts turned her into what the obstetrician, Dr. Neuborne, privately called a "terrorist patient." Beatrice second-guessed every recommendation and phoned several times a week with annoyingly mundane questions. After Beatrice had Neuborne paged during the opera to ask whether it was okay to eat spicy food for dinner, the doctor considered referring Beatrice to someone else.

Can a doctor refuse to treat a patient?

It depends. While some states have Good Samaritan laws that obligate doctors to help out in certain life-threatening situations, doctors generally have no legal obligation to assume the care of a patient. However, once a doctor-patient relationship has been established, the physician usually cannot refuse to treat you. Doing so could be considered "abandonment." If a doctor wants to terminate the relationship with a patient, adequate notice must be given so the patient has a reasonable opportunity to find alternative care.

It is standard practice for a doctor to have a covering doctor on call when he or she is unavailable for patients. Also, if a doctor's office is not equipped to handle an emergency, the doctor must advise you to seek care at an emergency room. If the doctor does this in good faith (and not just because he or she doesn't feel like treating you), then it probably does not constitute abandonment. (See also "Medical Malpractice" on page 330.)

Can hospitals turn patients away?

Not if it's an emergency. Federal law requires most public and private hospitals that accept medicare patients to stabilize any patient who needs emergency care. In addition, statutes and court decisions in most states require hospitals to treat any patient who requires emergency care. These "anti-dumping" laws developed out of concern that private hospitals were denying emergency care to financially undesirable patients by transferring them to public institutions.

Nonemergency treatment is different. Private hospitals are not required to provide such care to people who cannot pay, but federal law requires most public hospitals to offer charity treatment in order to qualify for federal loans or grants.

Once any hospital, public or private, accepts a patient for treatment, it cannot unreasonably stop treating that patient without risking liability for "abandonment." Even if the patient has failed to pay his or her bills, the hospital cannot discontinue treatment without giving the patient sufficient notice and enabling the patient to arrange for care elsewhere. If the patient is still hospitalized, the facility may be required to arrange for transfer to another facility. If that can't be done, the hospital may have no alternative but to continue to provide care. Even if a patient no longer requires hospitalization, a hospital could be liable for abandonment if it fails to make reasonable arrangements for a patient's postdischarge needs.

A hospital may sometimes be able to discontinue treatment if a patient is disruptive or noncompliant. A disruptive patient is someone whose behavior interferes with the facility's ability to provide quality care and ensure the safety of other patients, visitors, and employees. A noncompliant patient is

When Can a Person Be Held in a Mental Institution Involuntarily?

A person can be admitted to a mental institution against his or her will through a process called "commitment," and every state has laws that control this procedure. Most states limit such admissions to people whose mental illness makes them dangerous to themselves or others, and all states give the patient the right to request a review by a court at some point in the commitment process. No state permits a facility to retain a patient forever without regular review of the patient's need for continuing hospitalization.

The standards for civil commitment vary from state to state, but every person who has been committed against his or her will has the right to a hearing and an attorney before being committed indefinitely. (Some states require that the hearing occur before commitment. Others require that it occur if a person is committed involuntarily for more than a certain number of days.) In most states, an individual must be found mentally ill and posing a danger to himself or to others. The person's judgment must be so impaired that he or she does not understand the need for psychiatric treatment, and there must be no less-restrictive method of care available.

All states will provide legal representation for psychiatric patients who are unable to afford it.

someone whose failure to cooperate with the treatment makes it impossible to provide appropriate care.

Of course, a hospital has no legal obligation to keep a patient who no longer requires hospitalization. If you remain in the hospital past the date set for your discharge, the hospital may either remove you physically or bring an action for trespass.

YOUR RIGHT TO REFUSE TREATMENT

Bea had been pestering Max to have an unsightly birthmark removed. The doctor had assured him it could be done with minor surgery right in the office. Max, however, turned white at the thought and fled the building, the doctor's consent form still clutched in his clammy hand. Beatrice joked to a friend that if she thought she could get away with it, she'd sign the form herself.

■ When a spouse refuses to consent to medical treatment, can the other spouse give it?

Not usually. If your spouse is a mentally competent adult, he or she has an almost absolute right to refuse treatment — including necessary treatment for a serious illness.

There are a few circumstances, however, in which a patient's right to refuse treatment is limited, especially when the person suffers from a contagious disease that threatens public health. In these instances, the patient may not be permitted to refuse treatment. Vaccinations, for example, are routinely required for everyone — even people who object on religious grounds.

But if a person lacks the mental capacity to make an informed choice, consent is usually obtained from the patient's next of kin or legal guardian. In some cases where a mentally incompetent patient refuses treatment, it may also be necessary to get a court order.

■ Can a person in the hospital be forced to take medication?

Not usually. A patient cannot be forced to take medication unless it is an emergency or a court has ordered that treatment be administered. Hospitals generally are reluctant to force treatment on someone who is refusing even if the patient "lacks capacity" and does not understand the nature of the proposed care or the consequences of refusing it. Even a patient who has been committed involuntarily to a psychiatric facility has the right to refuse medical treatment — unless a judge overrides the patient's objection.

For more on refusing treatment, see "Living Wills" on page 327.

DOCTORS' FEES

Beatrice went to a highly regarded specialist, Dr. Coughman, about a sore throat. The doctor provided her with some cough drops and a bill for $250. The only thing that stopped her from suing him was the expense of hiring a lawyer.

■ Are doctors allowed to charge anything they want?

Yes. There generally are no legal limitations on what a doctor may charge. However, marketplace forces will often determine how high fees will go. In addition, private insurance as well as Medicare and Medicaid usually cover only charges that are reasonable and necessary. Sometimes, too, a doctor may arrange with insurers to keep fees within a certain range, in which case the fees cannot exceed the agreed-on limit.

■ Can a doctor charge for a missed appointment?

Yes, though most doctors don't. No law prevents them from doing so, but since it's standard practice for physicians not to bill for missed appointments, a doctor who did so might lose patients.

However, it is accepted practice, for instance, for psychiatrists and psychologists to bill their patients for sessions they miss. If your psychiatrist tells you the ground rules up front and you accept them, then you have a contract and must abide by it. Of course, if you refuse to pay a bill, the doctor probably wouldn't take you to court, but he or she probably would not continue to treat you, either.

Challenging a Fee

When you think a doctor or hospital has charged an unreasonable fee, there are steps you can take, depending on how badly you have been overcharged and who ultimately pays your bill.

If you have health insurance and your carrier declines coverage, ask your physician to explain to the insurer why the services rendered were reasonable and necessary. You can also ask your state's department of insurance how to appeal excessive medical bills.

If you are on Medicare, a doctor cannot charge you more than 15 percent over the limit Medicare has established for a given service. (That's set by federal law; some states have even stricter limits and do not allow doctors to bill you for the balance that is not covered by Medicare.) Thus if Medicare allots $100 for a service, your physician cannot charge you more than $115 for that service. If your doctor's bill exceeds the 15 percent allowed, you have been either overcharged by the doctor or underpaid by Medicare. If the doctor won't adjust your account, you can ask Medicare to reexamine your claim. If Medicare finds the doctor overcharged you, the physician must adjust your account within fifteen days of receiving Medicare's decision. If your physician does not comply, you can report him or her to Medicare or to the Health Care Financing Administration (HCFA). The number for the Medicare hotline is 800-638-6833. The number of the HCFA is 410-966-3000. (See also "Medicare" on page 394.)

If you are a Medicaid patient, a participating Medicaid physician should not charge you anything. If you are billed for medical services, you don't have to pay the bill. You can also report your physician to Medicaid. (Nonparticipating physicians will likely refuse to treat you at all.)

If you think you have been overcharged, you should contact the licensing board in your state or the local medical society in your area, both of which may have a procedure for investigating excessive medical charges. If an overcharge is exorbitant, you may also consider consulting a lawyer, since you may be able to sue your doctor for fraud.

ORGAN DONATION

Max finally agreed to have his birthmark removed, but it turned out he would require hospitalization. Ever the skeptic, Max was convinced terrible things would happen to him there. "If I die," he told Beatrice, "don't forget that my driver's license approves giving away my organs." Beatrice pretended not to be listening.

What is the procedure for organ donations?

The Uniform Anatomical Gift Act, which has been enacted with slight variations in all fifty states, and the National Organ Transplant Act provide guidelines explaining how you may donate specific organs, tissues, or even your entire body. Generally, any individual who has mental capacity and is at least eighteen years old may arrange to give away all or part of his or her body. A donation cannot be made until all efforts have been exhausted to save your life, and for most organ donations (other than eyes) a doctor must also determine that you no longer have brain activity. Then, most hospitals are required to get the permission from your next of kin — even if you have signified your desire to donate on your driver's license or on a donor card.

If you did not specifically state a wish to donate an organ, a gift can be authorized by your family, a legal guardian (if you are still alive), or by the person in charge of disposing of your body after death. However, if you specifically stated a wish *not to* donate an organ, neither your family nor

Resources

For further information about dealing with AIDS or HIV-related legal problems, contact one of these organizations:

AIDS Action Council
1875 Connecticut Avenue NW, Suite 700
Washington, DC 20009
202-986-1300
An umbrella organization of AIDS service providers

AIDS Legal Referral Panel
114 Sansome Street, Suite 1129
San Francisco, CA 94104
415-291-5454

AIDS Policy Center of the Intergovernmental Health Policy Project
2021 K Street NW
Washington, DC 20052
202-872-1445
Keeps track of federal and state legislation on AIDS

Gay Men's Health Crisis
129 West 20th Street
New York, NY 10011
212-807-6655 (AIDS hotline)
212-807-6664 (reception)

Lambda Legal Defense and Education Fund
666 Broadway, 12th Floor
New York, NY 10012-9996
212-995-8585

Lesbian/Gay Rights and AIDS Project of the American Civil Liberties Union
132 West 43d Street
New York, NY 10036
212-944-9800

National AIDS Hotline: 800-342-AIDS
Provides information and referrals to advocacy organizations in individual states

National Association of People with AIDS
1413 K Street NW, 8th Floor
Washington, DC 20005
202-898-0414

anyone else can override that wish. In fact, health care institutions generally are forbidden to accept an organ if it has been informed that the deceased did not wish for the anatomical gift to be made.

If you want to donate your entire body, you generally should contact a medical school in advance of your death to make arrangements.

AIDS

When Beatrice went in for her checkup every year, her doctor drew what seemed like gallons of blood to send out for tests. The doctor always told her that the results of these tests were "normal," which reassured Beatrice without really telling her anything. She wondered what she was being tested for. Specifically, she wondered — with more than a hint of nervousness — whether she was being tested for HIV.

Can a doctor test a person for HIV without his or her consent?

Generally, no.

Blood tests are low-risk procedures, which usually don't require signed consent forms. Instead, "implied consent" is all that is needed. Usually, your doctor will tell you what tests he or she plans to perform, and you give consent simply by holding out your arm. However, due to the potentially devastating personal and social consequences of a positive HIV test, many states, like New York, have passed laws stating that "implied consent" is not sufficient, even though the blood test itself is low risk. In most instances, informed consent must be obtained before you can be tested for HIV infection. Some states also require that you be counseled about dealing with HIV infection and AIDS before and after the test.

The law regarding consent for HIV testing is still evolving, however, and there are circumstances in some states where you could be required to submit to an HIV test without your consent. If, for example, a health care worker is stuck with a needle while drawing your blood and wants to know if you're infected, you might be ordered to take the test.

If you donate blood, it will be tested for the HIV virus. If your blood is found to be HIV-positive, it will be thrown out and you will be informed. The blood bank is not permitted to inform anyone else of your HIV status.

■ Can a doctor or dentist refuse to treat a person who has AIDS or is HIV-infected?

Hospitals have a clear obligation to admit and treat patients with AIDS or the HIV virus if the facility's staff has the appropriate training and resources. The law relating to individual physicians and dentists is less clear and is evolving. Traditionally, physicians have been free to choose which patients they treat. Now, however, the American Medical Association Council on Ethical and Judicial Affairs has ruled that a doctor has an ethical obligation to care for AIDS and HIV-infected patients, and some state professional licensing agencies may adopt similar policies. In addition, the Americans With Disabilities Act may also provide some protection for people who have AIDS or are HIV-positive, and some state and local governments have made it a violation of antidiscrimination laws to refuse medical treatment to a person who is HIV-infected.

■ Is a doctor or dentist with AIDS or the HIV virus obligated to inform his or her patients?

No. Your doctor has no legal obligation to tell you. Even if your doctor were HIV-infected and performed surgery on you, the likelihood of transmission would be extremely remote.

Of course, you are free to ask if your doctor is HIV-positive. If he or she refuses to answer, you can go to another doctor.

LIVING WILLS

Though Beatrice's grandfather Carl looked as though he would live forever, he gave a prudent amount of thought to the fact that he would not. He was content to go on being old indefinitely, but he was determined not to linger for a long time if he should become sick. If anything disastrous befell him, he did not want to be hooked up to a respirator or some other device if there was no hope of recovery.

■ What is a living will?

A living will (also known as a medical directive or advance directive) is a written document that states your wish to decline life support or other medical treatment in certain circumstances, usually when death is imminent. Generally, a living will takes effect when you become terminally ill, permanently unconscious, or are conscious with irreversible brain damage.

A living will also allows you to state with particularity the forms of treatment you want and do not want. For example, if you do not want artificial life support, you can sign a living will stating that desire.

Living wills are recognized in every state, but each state has different requirements. If you are interested in making a living will, you can contact an expert in your state, such as a hospital, local agency on aging, or local bar association. Or you can get a free copy of a living will form that will be valid in your state from Choice in Dying, a nonprofit organization. You can call it at 800-989-WILL.

To help ensure that your living will is honored, you may want to give copies to your family members, physicians, lawyer, and others involved in your care. Federal law now requires most health care facilities (hospitals, nursing homes, HMOs, and home health agencies) to ask patients on admission if they have a living will or would like to complete one.

■ Can medical care legally be stopped if there is no living will?

When there is no written document, a spouse or close family member may still request that treatment be withheld if you cannot do so, but the request could be denied. The way states and health care providers handle such cases varies widely. Typically, a doctor or hospital representative will meet with a person's family to discuss what that person's wishes were. In some cases a health care facility may want to withhold or provide life support against a family's wishes. In such cases a formal hearing may be held to determine how to proceed.

How to Make a Living Will

The rules for preparing a living will vary from state to state. Some states require that the document be signed with the same formalities required for execution of a will (see Chapter 11, WILLS AND TRUSTS), but many states recognize the effectiveness of more informal declarations.

Generally a living will

- **should be in writing**
- **should be signed and dated before two adult witnesses who are neither related to you, directly responsible for your medical care, or entitled to any portion of your estate**
- **should contain a statement that you have the capacity to understand your action and are signing the will voluntarily**
- **should contain a statement that you wish no extraordinary measures be taken to keep you alive if you become permanently unconscious or terminally ill**

In addition, you may want to state the specific kinds of treatment, such as artificial nutrition and hydration, that you do not want to receive. You may also want to describe the kind of treatment you do want to receive.

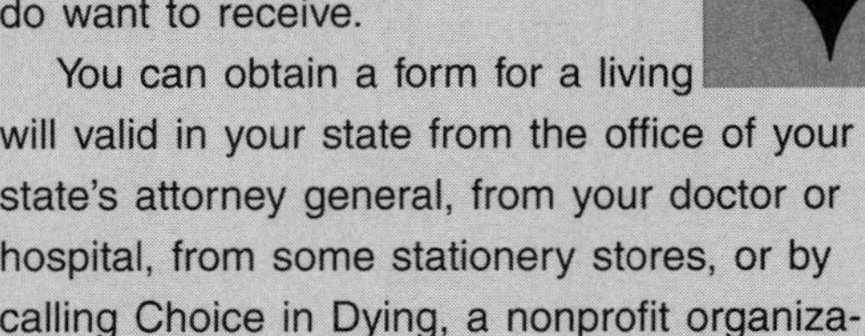

You can obtain a form for a living will valid in your state from the office of your state's attorney general, from your doctor or hospital, from some stationery stores, or by calling Choice in Dying, a nonprofit organization, at 800-989-WILL. It can supply living will forms for each state. You can also write to

Choice in Dying
200 Varick Street
New York, NY 10014-4810

You can cancel your living will at any time, but the procedure for doing so varies from state to state and depends on the means by which you distributed copies of the living will. If the only copy is in your home or with your lawyer, you can usually just tear it up. If you passed out multiple copies, it may be in your interest to formally revoke it in writing.

Note: In many states, a pregnant woman's living will won't be honored because of a concern for the life of the fetus.

HEALTH CARE PROXIES

While Carl was thinking about when and where he wanted to be allowed to die, he also thought about the kinds of medical care he'd be willing to receive. He decided that if he was going to trust Gordon with his checkbook and Social Security benefits, he might as well go the whole nine yards and let him make medical decisions, too, if that ever became necessary.

What is a health care proxy?

A **health care proxy** is someone designated to make a broad range of decisions for you when you are not personally able to give informed consent (see page 330). You don't need a lawyer to appoint a "proxy" or "agent," but your designation should be in writing, should be witnessed by at least two adults (neither of which should be the appointed proxy), and should meet any other requirements established by your state. Your doctor, hospital, local agency on aging, or local bar association may be able to tell you these requirements. Or you can contact Choice in Dying, a nonprofit organization that provides free forms that are valid for each state. Its number is 800-989-WILL.

In addition to designating who your proxy is, the document should include any specific desires you have about the medical procedures you will and will not allow to be performed. You may want to consult someone knowledgeable about medical technology to learn about the kinds of extraordinary services you might receive when incapacitated so you can make the proxy form as clear as possible.

Because some states, such as Alaska, do not allow a health care proxy to make decisions about life-sustaining treatment, you should still have a

CASE IN POINT

When Is a Life Over?

Black's Law Dictionary defines death as "the cessation of life; the ceasing to exist; defined by physicians as a total stoppage of the circulation of the blood, and a cessation of the animal and vital functions consequent thereon, such as respiration, pulsation, etc." In 1976, the Karen Ann Quinlan case showed just how inadequate that definition had become in a world of advanced medical technology, in which machines can make dying bodies breathe and blood pulsate long after death's deadline.

In April 1975, at the age of twenty, Karen Quinlan went into a coma. Her breathing stopped twice, for at least fifteen minutes at a time. She sustained brain damage but survived, although she never regained consciousness. Given 24-hour intensive care, she lived on in a vegetative state with no cognitive functions, curled in a fetal position, her limbs and body stiffly shrunken. She was not brain dead, however; her noncognitive functions showed that there was brain activity. She could blink and make nonverbal sounds, but doctors could not say whether she suffered pain or perceived anything of the world. They agreed there was almost no chance her condition would ever improve and predicted she would die within a year.

The court appointed a lawyer as her personal guardian, but Quinlan's father sued to be named guardian instead. His aim was to gain the power to have his daughter — whom all agreed was in a shocking and pitiful state — taken off the respirator, allowing her to die. His attorney argued that her right to privacy included the right to choose death and that, because she was incompetent, her guardian had the right to decide the issue for her. State prosecutors and hospital authorities opposed him, citing their constitutional duties to protect life.

In 1976, the Supreme Court of New Jersey granted her father's plea, and Karen Ann Quinlan was freed from her respirator. A medical mystery ensued: she continued to breathe unassisted, and lived on years past anyone's prediction, a small and troubling shape whose fate had brought to national attention the concept we now call "the right to die." She died on June 11, 1985.

Courts have been far more resistant to the idea of "pulling the plug" on unconscious brain-damaged people who (unlike Karen Quinlan) can still breathe on their own, but cannot eat, so are being fed by tubes. Disconnecting the tube causes the patient to starve to death, and authorities are far more reluctant to take this step.

After a car accident in which her brain was deprived of oxygen, Nancy Cruzan was kept alive in a vegetative state for several years, fed via a tube. Her parents received a court order to disconnect the tube after Nancy's housemate testified that Nancy had told her that if she was ever irreparably comatose, she wouldn't want to live like a "vegetable."

Nevertheless, the state of Missouri kept fighting the Cruzans, and the case went to the U.S. Supreme Court, which upheld a Missouri law requiring "clear and convincing evidence" that a patient would have wanted to be disconnected. The family subsequently presented further evidence — testimony from more friends who recalled specific conversations about Nancy's wishes — and a Missouri court ruled that the tube could be removed. Despite much protesting by anti-euthanasia activists, the tube was removed in December 1990. Cruzan died less than two weeks later.

living will that specifically addresses your desires about treatment during life-and-death situations. Give copies of the written documents to the designated proxy as well as to your doctor, attorney, relatives, and other loved ones. If you become unable to express your views, the health care proxy must follow your instructions.

As with living wills, federal law now requires most health care facilities to ask patients upon admission whether they have a health care proxy or if they would like to appoint one.

Even if you haven't designated a health care proxy or written a living will, some states are passing laws that give relatives decision-making power over your health care when you are not competent to make decisions.

MEDICAL MALPRACTICE

(See also Chapter 21, Getting Hurt, and Chapter 29, Suing and Being Sued.)

Blossom had severe pains in her abdomen. Her doctor, Len Bazzara, tested her for a number of ailments, then recommended that she have her gall bladder removed. He explained the situation and referred Blossom to a surgeon, Dr. Mildare. The operation seemed to be a success, but after Blossom woke up in the recovery room she felt a sharp stabbing in her stomach, much worse than the pain from the gall bladder. A young resident, Dr. Riscus, told her that pain was normal after surgery.

Blossom's agony persisted for several days, and then she came down with a high fever. Finally, an x-ray was taken. It revealed that Dr. Mildare had left a pair of forceps inside the incision, and Blossom was rushed into surgery to have them removed.

What is medical malpractice?

Medical malpractice is behavior by a doctor or other health care provider that is **negligent.** A doctor's behavior is considered negligent when he or she fails to follow accepted professional **standards of care,** and that substandard care causes harm to the patient.

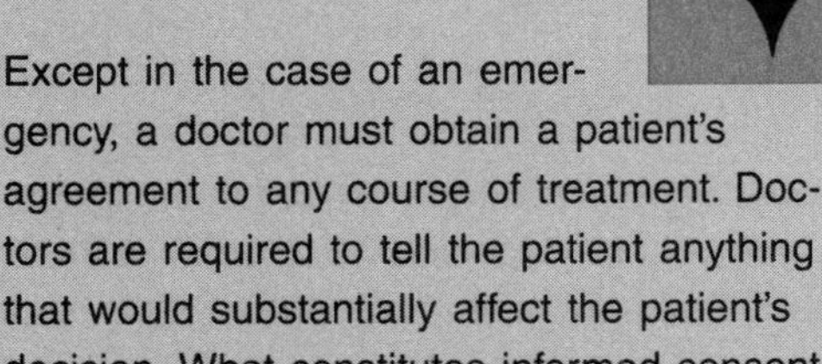

What Is Informed Consent?

Except in the case of an emergency, a doctor must obtain a patient's agreement to any course of treatment. Doctors are required to tell the patient anything that would substantially affect the patient's decision. What constitutes informed consent varies from state to state, but doctors are generally required to explain

- **the nature of the treatment**
- **its foreseeable risks, side effects, and results**
- **reasonable alternative courses of action**

If a person is senile or otherwise incapable of making an informed decision, consent must be obtained from the person's legal guardian. Some states allow older minors to give consent to certain procedures, from the setting of a broken bone to an abortion. Again, informed consent does not apply to emergency treatment; in fact, doctors can be sued for not giving emergency treatment when it is called for.

Failure to obtain informed consent may make the doctor liable for damages if the treatment results in harm of which the patient should have been made aware, and the information would have changed the mind of a reasonable patient.

That doesn't mean that a doctor (or hospital) is required to guarantee successful treatment. Generally, a doctor is required to have the knowledge and use the skill and care that any reasonably well qualified physician would use under similar circumstances. If, for example, it is not customary for doctors to administer a CAT scan after someone gets a slight blow to the head, a doctor or a hospital would not be liable for failing to perform that test, even though it would have revealed internal injury that resulted in brain damage.

In order to determine what the "reasonable doctor" should have done in any given case, it is usually necessary to hire medical experts to evaluate a patient's charts. In Blossom's case, it probably would not require an expert to conclude that leaving a surgical instrument in the patient isn't up to the practices generally accepted by surgeons. The success of a case against the resident is less clear. He did misdiagnose the cause of Blossom's pain, but doctors aren't required to be right all the time. They also aren't required to guarantee that their treatments will be successful. She would have to show that, given the information the resident had at the time, he should have suspected that there was something other than normal postoperative pain. Other doctors would have to look at the medical chart and determine whether the resident acted appropriately.

What Surgery Is "Unnecessary"?

Beatrice was only thirty-five when her doctor told her she needed a hysterectomy. He'd used a lot of jargon and told her it would be risky to "wait and see" if her "condition" improved. Beatrice's friend Renata was livid when she heard about the upcoming surgery. "You're the fourth friend of mine to have this operation in the last six months. What's going on? There can't be so many young women who really need a hysterectomy. I think you should get a second opinion."

Is it malpractice if a doctor performs unnecessary surgery?

Not always, because it's hard to define "unnecessary." The choice of treatment is a matter of professional judgment, and doctors will disagree on the necessity of many operations. If the surgery performed meets accepted standards of practice and informed consent was obtained, the fact that another surgeon may have chosen a nonoperative treatment does not mean the operating surgeon was negligent.

But if there is *no legitimate medical need* for the operation, for example, or a doctor operates on the basis of a negligent misdiagnosis or for purposes of financial gain, the doctor may be held liable.

Experimental Drugs

Beatrice had been suffering from constant headaches. Her new doctor offered to treat her with an experimental drug intended to alleviate the kind

CASE IN POINT

Surgery: Know Before You Go

Dolly Rogers was having trouble getting pregnant. She'd had a child by her first husband, but couldn't seem to get pregnant again with her second husband. Looking for help, she had visited Dr. L. Keith Mason and his partner, Dr. Fleater Palmer Jr., in 1952. Several years later she still hadn't conceived, but she kept seeing Dr. Palmer, who clearly knew of her concern.

In 1958, Rogers went into the hospital for what was supposed to be a simple appendectomy. Without telling her in advance, Mason and Palmer also removed her reproductive organs. Although the surgeons might have been justified in performing a hysterectomy if there had been an emergency, Mason admitted that it had merely been a preventive measure, and that he'd made no attempt to get the consent of her relatives who were right outside the operating room.

Rogers sued. She had consented only to having her appendix removed; at no time before the operation did the doctors discuss a hysterectomy, and she argued they had a duty to obtain her informed consent to the specific operation, consent Mrs. Rogers said she never would have given. She won a judgment for $3,500 plus interest from the two doctors, almost a year's salary in those days. (A similar case these days would probably result in a far larger award.)

of pain she was having. He told her it was likely to do wonders for the headaches and would probably have few side effects. Beatrice agreed to try, but after two weeks on the medication she'd broken out in an awful rash and was constantly nauseous. She'd also developed a blood clot in her leg and had to be hospitalized for a week.

■ **Is it malpractice for a doctor to prescribe an experimental drug that has been undergoing testing on humans but is not yet approved by the Food and Drug Administration?**

It is not automatically malpractice. All new drugs must be tested to determine whether they are safe for humans and then submitted to the FDA for further testing and approval. Sometimes doctors will suggest that a patient take such an experimental drug, having obtained it from colleagues who are developing it, or from foreign sources. That in itself does not constitute malpractice: if a doctor is accused of being negligent in ordering a drug, experimental or not, the question of liability will focus on whether he or she used professional judgment, not on whether the drug had government approval.

If a drug hasn't been government approved, the doctor will have to supply it himself, since it won't be available for prescription. A doctor must inform a patient if a drug is experimental, or if it has not been approved for the particular ailment for which it is intended. The wise physician should inform the patient fully of a drug's potential risks.

FDA approval indicates only that a drug has been tested and found reasonably safe and effective for certain purposes, subject to various limitations. If a drug harms a patient, the fact that it was not approved for a particular use by the FDA may indicate that the doctor failed to use due care in prescribing the drug. However, if the doctor chose the drug based on knowledge of the patient's condition and assessment of the risks and benefits, the doctor may not be liable for harm.

Negative Side Effects

Grace had a bad case of rheumatoid arthritis. The pain was so terrible that her doctor, trying to alleviate the suffering, put her on strong painkillers, and she became addicted.

■ **Is it malpractice if a patient becomes addicted to painkillers?**

It does not automatically signal the possibility of malpractice if a patient develops an addiction to a prescribed drug. If the drug is an appropriate treatment, the doctor is not liable for its adverse side effects, like addiction. However, a prescribing physician must always warn a patient about the side effects of any new medicine. Therefore, the case of Grace's mother depends on whether the doctor warned her of the possible addicting effects of the painkiller. If he did tell her, she probably would not have a case. If he neglected to mention it, she might have a case. She would have an even stronger case if he had known she was susceptible to such a side effect and did nothing to minimize that risk.

When the Diagnosis Is Wrong

Bartholomew suffered for years with a bad stomach. Suspecting an ulcer, he went to the doctor, who told him not to worry — it was only chronic heartburn. The medicine he prescribed didn't change a thing, and the pain steadily got worse. Finally, one rainy night, Bart had to be rushed to the hospital emergency room with a perforated ulcer.

■ **Is a doctor liable for a misdiagnosis?**

Not necessarily. The law does not require the doctor to be right every time. Nevertheless, a doctor may be liable if his misdiagnosis is the result of a failure to take an adequate medical history, perform the right tests, or recognize the symptoms of a particular illness. However, if a doctor only misdiagnoses an ailment, and there has been no harmful treatment, you're not significantly worse off than before the incorrect diagnosis. Thus, you have not suffered an injury that would warrant filing a claim.

But if a doctor's misdiagnosis means that you fail to seek the treatment you do need and subsequently develop a worse problem, then you may have a case.

Failure to Detect Impending Illness

Bart was put in a hospital room with sixty-year-old Carl, who was recovering from a heart attack. Carl's doctor had given him a clean bill of health only days before his attack, so he'd gone about his daily routine, playing tennis in the morning, eating a big lunch, and then speed walking in the mall with his wife in the evening.

Can a doctor be found liable for failing to detect an impending illness?

A medical negligence claim must show that the doctor's negligence caused the patient's harm. If a patient like Carl had signs of an impending heart attack that a competent physician should have detected, and if prompt treatment would have prevented the heart attack, then a causal connection can be shown. Certainly, if the doctor approved or recommended vigorous exercise that brought on the heart attack, there might be a causal connection. These are questions another physician, an expert, must consider based on his or her review of the records. Only another doctor familiar with the standard of care in a particular field can testify about the examining doctor's possible negligence.

Unsuccessful Treatments

Troubled by chronic back pain, Beatrice tried everything from a custom-made mattress to acupuncture. She finally went to a specialist recommended by a friend, and he charged hundreds of dollars for a series of painful and prolonged treatments in his office. But Beatrice's back stayed the same, locked and aching.

Is it malpractice when a treatment is unsuccessful?

Probably not. The doctor did not cause the back pain. And even though he or she did not cure it, the law does not require doctors to guarantee that their treatment will be successful. Even if the doctor's treatment did not meet with the appropriate

CASE IN POINT

Paying Through the Nose

Doctors must use their skills competently, but they don't have to guarantee results. This is a lesson Clarence Folse Jr. learned the hard way. He brought a malpractice suit for $36,000 against Dr. Jack Anderson, a Louisiana plastic surgeon, claiming the doctor gave him a botched nose job in 1960.

Folse argued he'd asked the doctor to operate merely to correct "a slight thickening of the skin on the end of [his] nose." In Folse's view, Dr. Anderson had exceeded his authority by giving him a complete nose job — and a bad one at that. Folse claimed he looked worse than before and that the new nose hampered his breathing. The doctor countered that he'd met with Folse four times before the operation and informed him fully about what he would do.

Folse fought tenaciously, going through several lawyers and ultimately deciding to represent himself. He wasn't too good at it — he even hired an expert doctor who testified that Folse's new nose was "nice-looking" anatomically and that his problems amounted to no more than a mild infection and allergies. All the witnesses agreed that Folse's nasal troubles had *nothing* to do with the operation by Anderson.

Not surprisingly, Folse lost at the trial. Undeterred, he appealed, only to be thoroughly rejected by the Louisiana Court of Appeal, which found nothing in the record to support his malpractice claim.

So Folse had to live with his hated nose — as well as with the bills it engendered.

standard of care, there must still be evidence that the continuing pain was caused by the doctor's negligence. If there is no negligence, the money spent for treatment is not an "injury" that would warrant filing a claim.

Disappointing Face-lifts

Grace, who was in her late sixties, decided after much scrimping and saving to get a face-lift. She was terribly disappointed when she looked in the mirror after her bandages were removed. She had spent almost $15,000, and she still looked her age!

■ Is it malpractice if a plastic surgery patient still has wrinkles after a face-lift?

Probably not. If you are disappointed with the results of a treatment, that's not an injury under medical negligence law. If, however, the physician made a promise to you that the wrinkles would disappear, he or she may be liable for breaching that promise. (For more on contracts, see Chapter 6, BUYING AND SELLING.)

GETTING HURT

21

PERSONAL INJURY CASES

Who Pays for Grace's Ankle?

Grace, a sixty-five-year-old substitute teacher, needed a prescription filled, so she drove to a twenty-four-hour pharmacy. It was a cold winter night, but there had been no snow for two weeks. As Grace got out of her car, she slipped on a patch of ice in the unlighted pharmacy parking lot. She broke her ankle, which required a pin and screw to set correctly, and because she could not walk up and down stairs, she also lost out on most teaching jobs for an entire school year. Moreover, the doctor told her she would never be able to walk as well as she had before the accident.

Is the pharmacy responsible for her injuries?

Quite possibly. This is a classic **slip-and-fall** case, a very common one in our court system. This type of case is known as a **tort** — a civil (not criminal) "wrong" that results in injury to a person or to property. There are many kinds of tort claims a person can bring. Several, such as medical malpractice cases (see page 330), involve actual physical injury. But some, like slander and libel (see page 287), involve damage to a person's reputation or feelings. Many also involve damage to a person's property. What you need to prove to win each different kind of case may differ from state to state.

Life, obviously, is full of situations where a person can get hurt. Unfortunately, some injuries are just tough luck. You can't go to court for everything. But for some injuries you can seek redress in the courts. The key question in most cases like Grace's is who, if anyone, is legally responsible for the injuries? That is, who is obligated to *pay* for her injury as a result of her accident? Someone can be held liable only if it can be proved that there was some **negligence** — the failure to fulfill a legal duty to be careful toward someone else. An injured person who initiates a lawsuit is known as the **plaintiff.** The person or company that is being sued is known as the **defendant.** The procedure of a tort lawsuit follows that of the typical civil case. (See Chapter 29, SUING AND BEING SUED.)

Personal injury law has become a much-criticized area of the law. Defense lawyers and others critical of our legal system claim that plaintiffs' lawyers bring unmeritorious suits in an effort to extract money from "deep pockets" — insurance companies, cities, and large corporations — that can afford to pay big settlements. Defense lawyers, on the other hand, come under attack for using spare-no-expense litigation tactics designed to wear down opponents with limited resources.

There's some truth to both positions, and proponents of tort reform often focus on personal injury litigation. That said, in any individual case what matters legally is whether a defendant has breached a duty, which then caused a plaintiff's injury. Of course, a defendant's resources will be a factor in deciding whether or not to bring a suit, and a plaintiff may decide that it is not worth the time and effort to seek redress from a party who will be unable to pay a settlement or judgment.

When a person is injured, the amount of **damages** he or she is entitled to depends on many factors, including

- **the extent of the injuries**
- **the economic losses sustained as a result of the injury, such as loss of wages**
- **proof of the defendant's negligence**
- **whether the plaintiff's own negligence may have contributed to the injury.**

Damages may be awarded by a judge or a jury. But 90 percent of cases are settled by negotiation, as plaintiff and defense lawyers haggle about the amount of money that they estimate a jury *would* award if the case went to trial.

Do You Have a Personal Injury Case?

If you're injured and believe someone else is at fault, answer these questions to help you begin to assess your case. If you consult a lawyer, be sure that all these points are covered.

- WHO could be held **liable?** Did any **negligence** contribute to your injury, and whose was it?
- WHAT is the extent of your injury? Is it permanent or temporary? How much time did you lose from work? How much money did you spend on medical bills; how much do you owe?
- WHERE did the injury occur? This affects who can be found liable. For example, did it happen at work, in a store, or on a public street? If you were injured on the job, you probably qualify for **workers' compensation** (see page 249). If you fell in a store, you may have a case against the owner (see page 337). If you stumbled on a crack in a public street, you may have a case against a local government.
- WHEN did it happen? If you wait too long to file a claim, you may be out of luck because of rules, called **statutes of limitations,** setting deadlines for filing (see page 340).

Finding Counsel

Grace decided she'd better find a lawyer, and she went to Bob "Break-A-Leg" Bulldog, a local attorney who was always in the news. She had assumed she couldn't afford to pay someone as well known as Bulldog, but when she called his office to ask if they could recommend someone cheaper, the receptionist suggested Grace come in for a visit.

Does a person have to have a lawyer in a personal injury case?

No, but it is often advisable. In the case of a minor injury, you might want to try a preliminary do-it-yourself approach. Many people and businesses carry liability insurance, so you should send a letter via certified mail to the party you believe is responsible for your injury. You should inform them that you were hurt, describe your injuries, and ask for their insurance company to contact you. Often the insurer will assign an "adjuster" (whose loyalty is to the insurance company, not to you) to try to settle the claim without the involvement of lawyers. If you have any questions about whether you are getting a fair or proper settlement, you should consult a lawyer before finalizing an agreement.

In the case of a serious injury, you should consult a lawyer as soon as possible if you believe the injury was caused by somebody else's negligence. Most likely, the insurance company for that other party will investigate immediately, but it helps keep the playing field level if you have a lawyer to represent your interests and protect any important evidence.

How do fees work in a personal injury case?

Usually, you will not have to advance any money, because most personal injury lawyers take cases on a **contingency basis.** That means that the lawyer takes his or her fee out of any damages that you are awarded. Typically lawyers take one-third, although it may vary from state to state. If you win no damages, the attorney gets no fee.

The first consultation will usually be free, and if the attorney thinks you have a case, he or she will probably ask you to sign a written fee agreement. Even though the lawyer gets a fee only if you win damages, you will probably be responsible, win or lose, for expenses such as court filing fees and the costs of investigators and expert witnesses. Some lawyers may ask a new client to put up some money — a couple of hundred dollars, perhaps — to cover these expenses.

If you are unhappy with your lawyer, you can fire him or her at any time. However, if you do, your lawyer may be able to charge for the hours he or she has worked on the case.

Proving Negligence

Grace was pretty excited. The big-time Bulldog was taking her case! Visions of a six-figure settlement (and what she would spend it on) were flitting through her head. "Is it legal for my husband and me to spend our settlement money on a vacation?" she asked Bulldog.

"Let's slow down a minute," he said. "First we've got to see if you've got a good case."

What does it take to win a personal injury suit?

A person is entitled to damages only if someone else's **negligence** caused his or her injuries. That means the defendant failed to act the way a hypothetical "reasonable person" would act under the same or similar circumstances to prevent harm.

To prevail and collect in a negligence suit, you have to prove several things:

- **that the person or business that injured you had a duty to be careful toward someone in your position (such as a customer or visitor)**
- **that the person or business failed to meet the duty**
- **that the failure to meet the duty was the cause of your injuries**
- **that as a result of all of the above, you had an injury, which can include expenses, financial losses, or pain and suffering as a result of the accident**

Assume, like Grace, you slip and fall on a patch of ice in a store's unlit parking lot. You first have to prove that the store had a duty to keep its parking lot safe. Unless your city has a specific ordinance requiring stores to clear away natural obstacles like snow and ice, their presence, alone, is probably not enough to win a negligence case. The store's failure to install adequate lighting, on the other hand, may indeed have been negligent.

When Negligence Is Obvious

Sometimes there is no question that a person's injury would not have occurred were it not for the negligence of another party. If, for instance, you are walking by a store and a barrel comes crashing out of the second-story window and lands on your foot, or if you take your car to a repair shop for a new transmission and on the way home the transmission falls out, a judge or jury may infer that somebody was negligent. Even though you may be unable to prove precisely what happened, you are entitled to argue that such things do not ordinarily happen in the absence of some negligence. The legal term for such obvious negligence is **res ipsa loquitur,** a Latin phrase, which loosely means "the thing speaks for itself."

A key issue in negligence cases is whether the defendant could reasonably have **foreseen** that someone might be hurt. If a store is open twenty-four hours a day, for instance, its owner or operator has a duty to make its parking lot safe at night by lighting it, because it's foreseeable that patrons could be hurt by things they can't observe in the darkness. But if the light had burned out only minutes before Grace pulled into the parking lot, a court might find that the resulting injury was not foreseeable. It would be a different story, of course, if the light had been out for several days. If people have previously complained about the dark parking lot, then the store would be "on notice" that there was a problem. It would be difficult for the store then to claim that an injury was "unforeseeable."

Determining a Property Owner's Duty

Bulldog asked Grace a lot of questions related to the legal issues in her case: Why was she in that particular parking lot where she fell? Was she there to do business with the pharmacy, or was she

really parking there because it was convenient to the restaurant on the other side of street? Or, he challenged, was she really going in to visit her friend who worked as a cashier at the pharmacy?

Grace was getting a little miffed (and confused) by all the questions.

■ If a person is hurt on someone's property, does it matter what the purpose of the visit was?

In some states, yes. Property owners may have different obligations to visitors depending on why the person is on the premises. There are three basic categories of visitors:

- **Business invitee.** This is someone, such as a customer, who comes onto the property for the benefit of the owner. The owner has a duty to do everything within reason to protect business invitees from being hurt.
- **Licensee.** This is a person, such as a social guest or door-to-door salesman, who did not enter the property for the benefit of the owner. In most states, a property owner's duty to protect a licensee from harm is not as great as the owner's duty to protect a business invitee. In most states, a licensee will have to prove that the property owner failed to warn or protect him or her from a danger that the owner knew existed.

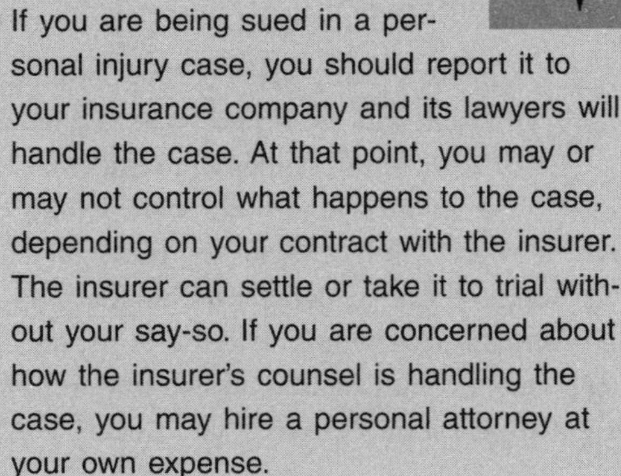

What to Do If You Are Sued

If you are being sued in a personal injury case, you should report it to your insurance company and its lawyers will handle the case. At that point, you may or may not control what happens to the case, depending on your contract with the insurer. The insurer can settle or take it to trial without your say-so. If you are concerned about how the insurer's counsel is handling the case, you may hire a personal attorney at your own expense.

- **Trespasser.** This is someone on the property illegally, without the permission of the owner. In most states, the property owner has no duty to protect a trespasser from unintentional harms. Thus a trespasser is likely to lose a suit. If Grace was parking in the pharmacy lot but was going to the restaurant across the street, she may be a trespasser.

Note: in a minority of states, including California, New York, and Illinois, owners have the same obligation to protect *any person,* from business invitee to trespasser, who enters the property. A few other states, including Massachusetts and Minne-

CASE IN POINT

Things Go Better (in Court) with Coke

It would seem on the face of it to be a once-in-a-blue-moon accident: a Coke bottle explodes for no apparent reason, injuring an innocent bystander. Yet a lucrative new area of personal injury law was born when famed (some would say notorious) San Francisco attorney Melvin Belli joined forces with injured waitress Gladys Escola in the early 1940s and sued the Coca-Cola Bottling Company of Fresno for negligence. Belli won a judgment from Coca-Cola, one of the richest companies, and therefore one of the deepest pockets, around.

Escola had suffered a deep cut when a Coke bottle exploded as she was placing it in a refrigerator. Belli had argued that the bottle had burst either because it had been overpressurized or because the glass had a defect, or both. Using the principle of *res ipsa loquitur* ("the thing speaks for itself") Belli claimed that his client need only prove that the bottle exploded, not why it did. If it exploded, he reasoned, there must have been negligence by the bottler. A jury agreed, ignoring Coca-Cola's claim that Escola might have mishandled the bottle.

CASE IN POINT

Criminals Who Cry Tort

Bertha Briney and her husband, Edward, were mad as hell, and they were not going to take it anymore. After Bertha Briney had inherited her parents' Iowa farm in 1957, the old house had stood empty for years on its eighty acres of land. The Brineys lived elsewhere, and it was proving impossible to defend the place from vandals who continually tore off planks covering the doors, broke windows, and trashed the place.

So the Brineys came up with a plan. Edward rigged a loaded shotgun to a bedstead in the bedroom, setting it with a spring to shoot anyone who came into the door uninvited. In 1967 the trap caught a local gas-station attendant, Marvin Katko, as he was poking around the old house with a friend one night. The shotgun blew a good part of Katko's leg away, and he was in a cast for a year. His doctor had even considered amputation, and he testified later that the injury was serious and would be permanent.

Katko had confessed to having stolen a few glass jars from the house for his collection, and he pleaded guilty to petty larceny. Still, Katko sued the Brineys for negligence and battery, and at the trial he and his friend both testified they'd thought the place was abandoned. In a surprising jury verdict, Katko won $20,000 in compensatory and an additional $10,000 in punitive damages, which was upheld on appeal in 1971 by the Supreme Court of Iowa, which ruled that the jury had a reasonable basis for finding that the Brineys had acted with malice and reckless disregard.

Thirty thousand dollars in 1971 was a huge verdict — especially considering that Katko was a thief and a trespasser and, in a sense, had brought it all on himself. An even more lucrative result was achieved by a mugger who was shot in the back by a New York transit cop as he fled the scene of a crime in 1984. The mugger, Bernard McCummings, did not deny his involvement in the attempted robbery of an elderly man in a New York City subway station. In fact, he pleaded guilty and served nearly three years in prison.

But McCummings, who was paralyzed by the bullet, sued the Transit Authority, alleging that the officer who shot him had negligently used more force than was reasonable in the situation. The key question was whether the transit officer actually saw McCummings commit a violent crime, which would have given him justification for shooting. The jury believed the use of force was excessive and awarded McCummings $4.3 million. Their verdict was upheld on appeal to New York's highest court, which ruled that while deadly force may be appropriate sometimes to prevent a felon from fleeing, this case did not establish that fact.

Two judges dissented from the opinion. One, Judge Joseph Bellacosa, argued that the decision was an "inversion of justice" that "approaches the surreal zone." Analyzing the split-second decisions that a police officer has to make in a dangerous and volatile situation, he noted, was not something to leave to a jury.

The mugger, Bellacosa noted, should be prevented from receiving a windfall because he assumed the risk of his injuries by engaging in his "predatory pursuits."

sota, have abolished the distinction between licensee and invitee, but still protect landowners from most liability to trespassers.

Sharing Responsibility for the Injury

Bulldog was asking Grace a lot of questions: What kind of shoes was she wearing when she slipped? Had she been drinking? How old was she? How was her health? Was she a clumsy person? Grace was beginning to feel offended. "I run two miles a day," she said. "I was wearing sneakers. I'm a careful person. That accident was not my fault."

"Well, the store is going to try to prove that it was," said Bulldog.

■ What happens if a person is partly responsible for an accident?

In some states, the defendant wins hands down and will owe nothing. In those states, for instance, if you slip and fall in a puddle in a grocery store, and the store can show that you fell because you were drunk or somehow careless, that could be seen as **contributory negligence** — negligence on your part that contributed to the accident. Such a finding protects the defendant from liability.

But it's rather harsh to deny a person any recovery when he or she is only partly responsible for an accident. So, most states have adopted a rule of **comparative negligence,** which leaves it to the jury to decide how negligent each party was. Some states block a plaintiff from collecting any money for damages if he or she is found to bear more than 50 percent of the fault. Other states proportion the money damages based on how much the plaintiff was at fault. In that case, if a plaintiff was 60 percent at fault for an accident, while the defendant was only 40 percent at fault, the plaintiff could still recover partial damages.

Sometimes, defendants are also able to raise the defense of **assumption of risk** — that the plaintiff knew that a particular activity was dangerous but decided to do it anyway. This is a defense that cigarette manufacturers have relied on very successfully in cases where smokers sued.

Statutes of Limitations

Each state has laws, known as **statutes of limitations,** that require you to bring suit within a certain period after an injury. The time limits vary from state to state and for different types of cases. Some limits may be as short as thirty days, and they are seldom greater than six years. In cases where the injury is not immediately apparent (for example, a person has been exposed to a substance that causes cancer many years later), the time period in which a person can bring a lawsuit usually starts when the person knew or should have known of the wrongful injury.

In medical malpractice cases, some states have absolute time limits on how long after an injury a person may sue, no matter how long it took the patient to realize the injury may have been wrongfully caused. (For more on medical malpractice, see page 330.)

For more on the procedure of a lawsuit, see Chapter 29, SUING AND BEING SUED.

Sporting Accidents

Beatrice broke her leg while skiing. She had gone down a trail that was steeper than she had thought it would be, and she fell while taking a sharp curve.

■ Can a person sue the operator of a ski slope?

Sure, but many states have laws protecting ski slope operators from liability. Even without such laws, it would be a tough case, because the slope operator could argue that a skier assumed all the ordinary risks of the sport — including falling and breaking a leg. This would also apply to activities like rollerblading, ice hockey, waterskiing, and other sports where an element of danger is assumed.

After a skiing accident, some people attempt to sue makers of equipment on the basis of product liability. Such suits are sometimes successful, but it all depends heavily on the individual circumstances of the case. If there was something defective about Beatrice's skis that may have caused her accident, she might have a claim against the manufacturer of the skis. If her injury was related not to a simple fall but to ski-lift equipment malfunction, she might consider suing the ski-lift manufacturer.

Dog Bites

As Vinny, age eight, was wheeling his skateboard down the sidewalk, a large rottweiler jumped out from behind a bush and attacked him. Vinny's wound needed stitches, and he had to have painful tetanus and rabies shots. As soon as he was taken care of, Max canvassed the neighborhood, asking about the dog's reputation.

■ **Is the owner responsible when a dog bites someone?**

Under changes in the law that have occurred in recent years, the dog owner is generally responsible. An owner used to be liable only if he or she knew the dog had a tendency to bite, and an injured person would have to show proof that the dog had previously bitten someone.

Now many states have adopted laws holding owners **strictly liable** for bite injuries, meaning they are responsible whether or not the dog had bitten anyone before. However, an owner may have no liability if he or she can show the victim provoked the dog.

Drowning Accidents

Mr. Drucker was known as the meanest old man in the neighborhood because he wouldn't let any children swim in his expensive new pool. On hot summer days the kids would sneak into the bushes to watch him sitting alone by the water, sipping a beer and glaring at them.

One late night, Alena and several friends decided to take a sneak dip. (They had easy access to the pool, since there was no fence or wall.) One boy, a ten-year-old, drowned by accident. In the chaos that followed, Mr. Drucker told the police that it couldn't be blamed on him. After all, he'd put up a sign — "No Trespassers Allowed. Danger. Owner Not Responsible for Violators' Safety."

CASE IN POINT

A Jockey's Last Ride

A jockey who shot to fame as the rider of one of the greatest thoroughbreds of all time tragically found himself at the center of one of the saddest and most famous personal injury cases in sporting history. Ronald Turcotte, the jockey who rode Secretariat to his Triple Crown, was crippled in 1978 by a fall from a horse named Flag of Leyte Gulf at Belmont Park in New York. Jockey Jeffrey Fell was next to him, riding Small Raja. Seconds after the race began, claimed Turcotte, Fell cut in front of Turcotte's horse, causing Turcotte to fall. He sustained severe injuries that left him a paraplegic.

Turcotte sued, claiming that Fell was negligent because he broke racing rules by cutting in front of other horses before he was clear. He also sued the track owner for grooming the track improperly. Turcotte lost, with the New York Court of Appeals ruling in 1986 that a professional athlete should be well aware of the dangers inherent in his sport, thus assuming the risk of injury.

■ **Is a homeowner responsible if someone drowns in his swimming pool?**

Not automatically. An injured person, or a bereaved parent, must still prove the pool owner was negligent. Most states have statutes regarding pools on private property, and some require the owner to erect a fence if it is foreseeable that children will come near the pool. Statutes concerning public pools are generally stricter. Some states require every public facility to erect a fence around every pool, period. Violation of a state's statutes could leave the pool owner liable in case of an accident. If you're going to buy or build a pool, be sure you find out what these statutes are in your state. Some states hold owners liable in an accident if their pool or related equipment, such as a diving board, are found defective; others rule that pool owners must put up signs spelling out pool depths, for example.

■ **Does a posted disclaimer protect the pool's owner?**

Probably not. A sign disclaiming responsibility is frequently useless as a shield from liability. Pool owners can still be held responsible, whether or not they post a sign, for failing to put up a fence to keep small children out. A warning of hidden dangers — such as a warning against diving because the water is too shallow — is more effective than a general disclaimer.

In the investigation that followed the drowning tragedy, the police found beer cans littering Drucker's front yard. Alena and the other kids admitted that they'd all been drinking that night to get up the nerve to trespass into the pool.

■ **If the person who drowned was drunk, is the pool owner still liable?**

Possibly. Drunkenness alone may not exonerate the owner from liability. A suit may still be brought, but the judge or jury will weigh any findings about drinking when deciding how much blame to assign the owner. At that point, the information that the person had been drinking may reduce or even bar recovery for the drowning victim or his or her survivors.

Grace and Gordon were staying at a hotel in Key West with a swimming pool. Their vacation was jarred by a terrible accident that happened to a young couple down the hall. After dinner, when the sun was still hot, their two preschool children had climbed over the locked fence around the pool; a lifeguard was on duty during daytime hours, but not after 6 P.M. One of them playfully pushed the other, who fell into the pool. The toddler didn't know how to swim and drowned.

■ **Is a hotel liable for a drowning death in an unsupervised but fenced-in pool?**

It is doubtful that the parents could succeed in a lawsuit against the hotel in a case like this. A hotel has a duty to take reasonable steps to maintain its premises in safe condition for the guests. Obviously, a swimming pool presents some danger to children. Placing a fence, with a locked entry, around the pool might be all that is reasonably required. It would not be reasonable to require that the hotel provide lifeguards around the clock.

■ **What if there is no fence?**

Without the fence, there is a greater likelihood that the hotel may be liable. Even though the pool was closed when it happened, it was predictable that people, especially children, might try to enter it. A lot depends on the circumstances and the age of the children. The danger of drowning is greatest with small children, who can easily be kept away from the pool by a fence. On the other hand, a judge might rule that an older child (who can appreciate the fact that he does not know how to swim) knowingly assumed the risk when entering a pool after hours.

The drowning tragedy made Grace worry about the small lake on their country property. They had no fence of any kind around it and no signs, either.

■ Are lake and pond owners liable if someone drowns?

Lakes and ponds are generally considered to be so obvious a danger that owners will rarely be found negligent (and therefore liable) if someone, even a child, drowns on their property. The assumption is that any child who is old enough to be allowed to walk alone through the countryside without adult supervision is old enough to know the danger.

There are some exceptions to this rule. Is there some special danger in this lake that should be pointed out to a child or which could have been removed? Are there any conditions that might attract a child out onto the water — such as a covering over the water or a barrel frozen in a pond? If so, and if it was foreseeable that a child would be curious to explore, the owner may be liable.

PRODUCT LIABILITY

Max and Beatrice bought some lakeside property out in the country. Max was a great admirer of Abe Lincoln and wanted to imitate the Old Railsplitter by clearing the trees off the land himself and hauling them up to the top of a steep hill to build a log cabin for a summer home. So he went to the local hardware store and bought a new chainsaw. He stashed it in the back of his Blazer and headed home to read the instructions. As he fired up the chainsaw, though, he forgot the sentence on page 40 of the how-to booklet, which recommended wearing safety glasses. Shortly after Max started cutting trees, a chip of wood hit his eye. In the emergency room, the doctors said they could save the eye, but he'd probably have to wear thick glasses for the rest of his life.

CASE IN POINT

A Smell of Burning

Many consumers may not realize that many warning labels that feature a cautionary alert about a product's potential harms are often there to protect the manufacturer as well as the consumer. The warning on cigarette packs, for example, is used by tobacco companies in arguing that they are not liable when blamed for a smoker's cancer death. (See the next Case in Point.)

Labels have proliferated as more product liability and personal injury cases win awards in court. Even something as seemingly inoffensive as perfume can be shown to be dangerous, as the Fabergé company found out. In 1969, a teenaged girl named Nancy Moran and her friend Randy Williams were listening to music and hanging out on a warm summer night. Nancy and Randy idly speculated on whether a candle in the room was scented. When they decided it wasn't, Randy said, "Well, let's make it scented," and grabbed a bottle of Fabergé cologne. She poured some onto a portion of the candle. There was a whoosh, and a burst of flame sprang out, burning Nancy's neck and breasts.

Far-fetched as her case might seem, Nancy Moran sued Fabergé for damages and won on appeal. (She also sued Williams and the owner of the home, but both were exonerated by the jury.) In 1975, an appeals court upheld the jury's award of $27,000 to Moran, and held that Fabergé should have put a warning on the bottle that the contents were flammable, because it was reasonably foreseeable that in household use the contents might come into contact with open flame.

What's a Defect?

In a product liability case, the plaintiff usually argues that a product was defective. There are two general kinds of product defects: manufacturing and design. Manufacturing defects are usually fairly easy to prove. If a new camp stove explodes when it's first lit, or if the brakes in a car fail a week after you've bought it, it is reasonably clear that the product was not manufactured properly. Proving that a product has a design defect is more difficult, since it involves passing judgment on technical choices. For instance, if a truck bursts into flame upon impact, a plaintiff might claim that the design was faulty because the gas tank was too exposed. Experts would be asked to testify for each side, and the jury would have to weigh their credibility and make a decision.

■ What is "product liability"?

As the marketplace for consumer goods has expanded since World War II, courts have made it increasingly easier to hold manufacturers responsible for injuries caused by their products. This shift in the law was as much a policy decision as it was a legal one. If injured by a defective product, a consumer no longer has to prove a manufacturer *knew or should have known* that the product was designed or made poorly. Instead, manufacturers now have what is known as **strict liability.** That means that manufacturers are legally responsible for injuries caused by **defects** in their product, even if they were not negligent.

One of the ideas underlying this change in **product liability law** is that companies are in the best position to prevent defective products from reaching the market in the first place. So by shifting responsibility to manufacturers, courts have tried to assure a higher level of quality control.

In a product liability case, an injured person has to prove three things:

- **that there was a defect in the design or manufacture of the product, or that the manufacturer didn't do enough to warn consumers of possible dangers of the product**
- **that the product caused an injury**
- **that the consumer was using the product the way the manufacturer intended it to be used**

It's up to the manufacturer to prove that the plaintiff misused the product. However, if the manufacturer could have predicted that a consumer might "misuse" the product in the way that he did, then the maker still might be held liable.

Manufacturers have a **duty to warn** customers of a product's potential dangers — and to advise users of any precautions they should take. To be adequate, the warning must be conspicuous, to grab the attention of the reasonable user. It must clearly explain the nature and gravity of the risk so that the user has an accurate appreciation of the danger. Burying a key safety notice on page 40 of an instruction manual, where it could easily be overlooked, may be tantamount to a failure to warn. On the other hand, the chainsaw manufacturer could accuse Max of **comparative negligence** (see page 340) — arguing that he assumed the risk by failing to wear safety glasses he should have known were necessary when sawing down trees. The manufacturer might say that Max's assumption of the risk, not its failure to warn, contributed to the accident. And if Max had been carving ice sculptures with the chainsaw instead of cutting wood, the manufacturer might not be liable since he was not utilizing the product for its intended use.

CASE IN POINT

Where There's Smoke, There's Litigation

Should cigarette makers share some responsibility for a cancer death? That was the far-reaching issue in one of the most bitterly fought lawsuits of the eighties. On August 1, 1983, lung cancer patient Rose Cipollone and her husband sued three tobacco manufacturers in New Jersey federal court alleging that she had contracted cancer as a result of smoking the defendants' cigarettes.

The Cipollones argued, among other things, that the design of the cigarettes was defective; that the companies had failed to warn of the hazards of smoking before 1966, when the federal government instituted the rule that warnings must go on all packages; that certain cigarette ads effectively functioned as warranties that the product was not harmful; and that the cigarette makers had fraudulently conspired to represent that their product was not a health hazard.

The tobacco companies argued that smoking had been Cipollone's personal choice and that she had persisted to smoke long after the warnings and hazards were well known. They also argued that it was not clear that her cancer was caused by cigarettes.

Rose Cipollone died in 1984 before the case went to trial, but her husband Antonio continued. At the trial, the jury rejected several of the claims, but did find defendant Liggett Group Inc., maker of Chesterfields, one of Mrs. Cipollone's favorite brands, liable for failure to warn of the hazards before 1966 and for breach of express warranty because its pre-1966 ads implied that cigarettes were not harmful. They awarded $400,000 to Antonio — the first damages ever awarded to a plaintiff in a cigarette product liability suit.

The case was appealed, and the U.S. Court of Appeals for the Third Circuit overturned the verdict in 1990 and ordered a new trial. Antonio Cipollone died less than two weeks later, and his son Thomas took over as a representative of Rose's estate. Arguments were heard by the U.S. Supreme Court in 1991. There, Liggett argued that the federal laws requiring the warnings on cigarette packages made the companies exempt from state failure-to-warn claims. In a divided opinion, the Supreme Court ruled, among other things, that even though the federal government had enacted legislation in 1965 and 1969 requiring warnings on cigarette packages, some legal claims could still be brought under state law.

The case was sent back for a retrial, but was voluntarily dropped on the family's behalf in 1992, thus effectively sustaining the industry's record of total victory in cigarette liability suits.

LOST AND DAMAGED GOODS

22

WHEN BAD STUFF HAPPENS TO GOOD THINGS

Natural Catastrophes: One Crushed Porsche

Beatrice's car was crushed by a tree limb during a thunderstorm. She was visiting her friend Susan, and had parked out front under the tree, which was struck by lightning. "Geez," said Susan, surveying the damage. "That darn tree's been dead for a long time. I'm sorry we didn't cut it down."

■ **Is a homeowner responsible when lightning strikes a tree and causes damage to someone's property?**

No. Lightning is an unforeseeable act of nature, sometimes called an act of God. A property owner is not liable for damage caused by this type of natural event. Even if the tree were dead and could be easily knocked down, the lightning was the cause of the damage to the car.

■ **What if the struck limb fell because it was dead, and the tree it fell from was city property?**

In most jurisdictions, a municipality is liable for damage caused by a tree that falls on a public street *if* the city knew or should have known it was damaged or dead. But a court might also rule that the lightning, not the city's negligence, was the real culprit.

The Stolen Coat: Whose Fault?

Grace took Beatrice to lunch to celebrate Beatrice's upcoming wedding. On the way out of the restaurant, Beatrice discovered that her suede jacket, which she'd hung on a coatrack near the register, was gone. She rushed over to the manager to complain. "That coat was an engagement present from my fiancé's parents," she cried.

"Sorry, lady," shrugged the manager, pointing to a sign near the coatrack that stated, "We are not responsible for your personal belongings."

■ **Can a restaurant be held liable when a patron's coat is stolen?**

It depends on exactly where the coat was when it was stolen. There's a big difference between a coatrack that is open and unguarded and a coatroom that is supervised by an attendant. When you give property to someone else for safekeeping, you create a legal relationship known as a bailment. To create a bailment, a restaurant (or other business establishment) must *knowingly* have exclusive control over the property. There are many types of bailments, but generally the receiver must use **reasonable care** to protect the property — that is, the same care any typical person would have used if they were in possession of the object. If the item is lost or stolen because the attendant was absent or careless, then the restaurant would be liable.

In other words, if Beatrice had given the coat to a coat-check attendant, it would have created a bailment and the restaurant would have been responsible. Because the restaurant merely provided a convenient place for customers to hang their coats, there was no bailment, because a patron is understood to use the rack at his or her own risk. The same is true if a patron's purse is stolen from the table. Since the purse was not in the exclusive control of the restaurant, the restaurant would not be liable. If the restaurant owners know there's been a problem with theft, they may have a duty to warn patrons to watch their belongings.

■ **Is a restaurant or club protected if it posts a disclaimer about property stolen from its coatroom?**

No. If the restaurant has control of your property, the disclaimer is meaningless. It does not erase the restaurant's responsibility to exercise care with your belongings.

Who Pays the Cleaning Bill?

Beatrice, who loved classical music (to the dismay of her rock-and-roller fiancé), had gone to an opening night performance of Mozart's *Magic Flute.* She loved it, but on the way out her friend noticed a big wad of gum stuck to the seat of her wool pants.

■ Does the concert hall have to pay the cleaning bill?

No. An operator of a concert hall, theater, or similar establishment is required to take reasonable steps to provide safe seating. That means the proprietors have a duty to inspect seats for hazards that may result in physical injury, but they don't have to guarantee that a patron's property and clothing will be unharmed.

Employers' Responsibility

Beatrice was having a bad week. First her coat was stolen, then she sat on a piece of gum, and now she discovered that her purse was stolen from her office. Even worse, it contained the nonrefundable tickets to Europe, where she and Max were going for their honeymoon.

■ Is an employer liable for the theft of an employee's property?

Not usually. Employers (and other people) are not generally responsible for the criminal act of a third party, especially when the owner of the stolen property (in this case, Beatrice) had control of the property and was able to guard it more carefully than the employer could have.

If, however, there had been other robberies in the office, and the boss knew about them yet did nothing to warn employees, then a jury *might* find that the employer failed to exercise due care to warn of the danger and prevent it from happening again.

Bad Hair Days

Wanting to look good for Beatrice's wedding, Grace had gone to a highly recommended hairdresser. (He was rumored to have cut Hillary Rodham Clinton's hair!) Grace asked for a new cut and some highlights in her graying light brown hair. What she got instead was a platinum bob that looked a few shades whiter than Madonna's hair. She was so embarrassed that she'd worn her hair in a turban for the wedding (prompting her husband to tease her for looking like Gloria Swanson in *Sunset Boulevard*).

■ Can a person sue a hairdresser for causing humiliation?

If humiliation is the only damage, probably not. A hairdresser is required to possess the knowledge and apply the skill that would be used by other hairdressers. Even if you get an unwanted result, you must determine whether that result was bad enough to constitute an injury, rather than mere dissatisfaction with your hair's appearance. You probably would not prevail in a lawsuit unless the hairdresser's ineptitude actually caused your hair to fall out. That's considered real injury, and in such a case you might be able to collect additional damages for the embarrassment and humiliation you suffered.

Taking the Cleaners to the Cleaners

Max was having a problem with the dry cleaner. For his wedding to Beatrice, he had bought his first good suit — an Armani that actually made him look suave. Everyone had oohed and ahhed at his transformation, and he felt for one afternoon that the thousand dollars he'd paid for the suit was worth it. While he and Beatrice were off on their honeymoon, however, the dry cleaner managed to ruin the suit, leaving grayish blue chemical stains on the jacket and pants. Max was livid. He was also worried about the small print on his pink receipt that said "We

try very hard to please you but will not be responsible for damages."

■ **Is a dry cleaner liable if it ruins a piece of clothing?**

Probably. Leaving your suit at the dry cleaner creates a bailment, and because the dry cleaner profits from the transaction, it is expected to be careful with your clothes. In legal terms, the dry cleaner is expected to exercise the degree of care of those knowledgeable in the field. That means the cleaner should be up-to-date on what the best dry cleaning procedures are, and should follow the same procedures that the average dry cleaner would follow. When a good suit is ruined, a court will presume that the dry cleaner was negligent — unless the cleaner can prove otherwise.

■ **What about the disclaimer?**

The disclaimer is an attempt to create a contract that limits the dry cleaner's responsibility. This is called an "exculpatory contract," and courts usually rule that such blanket attempts by businesses to evade responsibility are invalid.

Even when a disclaimer is found to be valid, you must be aware that it exists. If the disclaimer was printed on the back of the ticket in very small type, as they usually are, and if you can truthfully state that you were not aware of it, then a court may rule that it had no effect.

■ **What if the disclaimer limits the dollar amount of the dry cleaner's liability to a low figure, such as $30, and the damaged item is worth $500?**

You have two options. You could go to court — the expensive route — and argue that the disclaimer was invalid or too tiny to read, which may work. Or you could write a letter to the cleaner threatening action and hope to get a settlement offer you can live with.

The Car Wash Blues

The side-view mirror on Max's new Blazer broke off at the car wash. Max was positive that the operator had put the car in the track incorrectly, and his face reddened the moment he saw the mangled dent in the door. "You'll pay for this," he shouted. The attendants just shrugged and pointed to a sign that read "We Are Absolutely and Positively Not Responsible For Any Harm That Comes To Your Car While It Is In Our Possession."

■ **Does a disclaimer protect a car wash from liability when a vehicle is damaged?**

Sometimes. A prominent disclaimer, seen and understood by the driver, may serve to limit the car wash's liability for *accidental* harm. However, a disclaimer of responsibility rarely cuts much ice with judges and juries when the harm is a result of the operator's negligence. If the damage at the car wash resulted from the careless operation of equipment, you could argue that the disclaimer did not relieve the car wash of responsibility for its own negligence. Even if the store tried to be clever and explicitly proclaim in its signs that it is "not responsible for any of our own negligence," the disclaimer would still be a weak defense and could be attacked.

Although the damages in these cases can be highly annoying, the monetary value is usually not large, so most people do not go to the time and expense of taking proprietors to court. Some people use small-claims courts for cases involving small sums; the cutoff for small claims varies from state to state, but usually a case cannot involve more than a few hundred dollars. (For more on small-claims court, see page 431.)

The best tactic is to try to negotiate with the proprietor, seeking to obtain either a payment or a credit for services, and threatening legal action if there is no relief. Often just writing a letter stating that you are considering a suit is enough to bring results.

Moving

Beatrice and Max moved into their dream house. But what should have been a joyous event was one nightmare after another. The plumbing in one of the new bathrooms wasn't working. Their mail was being forwarded to the wrong address. Several boxes of clothes were missing, and when Beatrice went to unpack the dishes, she found that half the crystal they'd gotten as wedding presents was shattered.

■ Is a moving company responsible for goods that are lost or damaged during a move?

Generally, yes. The chance you will recover is greater if federal regulations apply to your move. These rules apply whenever a move is interstate, or when the movers travel on an interstate permit within a state — as is the case with many large moving companies. These companies are highly regulated by the Interstate Commerce Commission, and they must give you a booklet approved by the ICC before the move, whether or not your move is within one state or from one to another. If they don't, they are liable for damages.

If, however, you hire two college kids with a van to move your apartment from one side of town to another, most likely they won't give you any booklet, nor are they required to. Such freelance movers are unregulated and usually uninsured, so their liability is reduced (as well as the chance you have of recovering damages from them personally).

A professional mover is supposed to exercise a high degree of care with the items in its possession. Your biggest challenge (if your things are damaged or lost in a move) will be to establish that the damage occurred *while the goods were in the mover's possession.* If you can, keep an accurate inventory of the goods, including photographs of particularly expensive or valued items.

TRAVELING

23

AIR TRAVEL

Lost Luggage

Beatrice was going on her first business trip for Teddies and More: the annual Plush and Rubber Toy Fair. She was representing Teddies at a press conference where she was to announce their new product, Hairy Beary, with hair that grows.

Beatrice had agonized about what to wear for the press conference and ended up buying a new suit. After all, she might be on national television! As the baggage carousel emptied out with no sign of her plaid garment bag, Beatrice had a sinking feeling. Her bag had been lost. What could she do? What could she wear? The press conference was that evening.

■ What is an airline's responsibility when it loses a person's luggage?

An airline is responsible for your damages for lost luggage, but there are limits on the amount of liability, and these limits may vary depending on the type of flight. In most cases, airlines are required to print their liability limits on the ticket. In general, the limits are

- **domestic flights: $1,250 per passenger for most interstate flights**
- **international flights: $9.07 per pound of checked baggage (plus $400 for unchecked items)**
- **commuter, charter, and in-state flights: the limit of liability can be lower; you can request a printed statement of the limits if it doesn't appear on your ticket**

Beatrice took a taxi straight to the nearest shopping mall and bought another suit. Considering her nervousness, the press conference went well. Much to Beatrice's relief, her suitcase was returned to her the next morning. Still, she had shelled out the money for the suit — not to mention a new toothbrush and dental floss.

■ Does an airline have to reimburse a passenger who replaces lost items?

Yes. Even if the luggage is later found and returned to you, the airline is responsible for any reasonable expenses you incurred as a result of their delay in delivering your luggage. These expenses include the cost of purchasing any needed substitute clothes. Make sure to keep receipts for any substitute items that you buy.

Damaged Luggage

Bradley and Peter's great Florida flyaway was not getting off to a riproaring start. They had been in Florida for five hours already and still had gotten no sight of the beach. After checking into their room at the Breakfree Inn, Brad discovered that his suitcase had been pried open. Not only had his portable tape player, extra batteries, and shave kit (with electric razor) been stolen, but his brand-new bathing suit was gone too.

■ Is an airline responsible if items are stolen from a person's luggage during travel?

Yes. Airlines are responsible for returning your luggage to you in the same condition it was in when you checked it. That means the airline is responsible for items stolen while the luggage is in its possession, as well as any damage to the bag itself. As noted, though, there are limits to their liability.

Limit Your Losses

Travelers can limit lost luggage expenses in several ways:

- Most airlines offer additional lost or damaged luggage coverage for an extra fee.
- Some homeowner's insurance policies provide protection during travel.
- Document the items you pack.
- Avoid losing essential items by placing them in your carry-on luggage.

Getting Bumped

In spite of the rocky start, Brad and Peter were heading home happy. They had accomplished their vacation goals of getting tan and relaxing. When they arrived at the gate to board their flight, however, they found chaos. Their flight was oversold, and people were being bumped.

Does an airline have any obligations when passengers are bumped from a flight?

Yes. Federal regulations require airlines to compensate any bumped passenger who has a valid ticket or reservation on an oversold flight. The amount of compensation depends upon the length of the delay. Under current rules, if the passenger is placed on another flight that arrives within one hour of the original flight's scheduled arrival, no compensation is required. On domestic flights, if the delay is one to two hours (on international flights, one to four hours), the airline must pay the value of a one-way regular coach fare, up to a maximum of $200. If the delay is longer, the airline must pay twice the amount of a one-way regular coach fare up to $400.

Often, airlines will ask for volunteers to give up their seats in exchange for a free ticket and a seat on a later flight. If you accept a free ticket under these circumstances, you do so with the explicit understanding that the ticket will be your sole compensation.

Although they are not required to do so, many airlines voluntarily provide additional compensation, such as hotel accommodations and meals. To be eligible for compensation, the passenger must have checked in within the minimum time specified by the airline on the ticket or boarding pass. Being in line does not count. Chartered flights are not covered by these federal rules.

Federal law limits the traveler to the above-described compensation, but this law is not completely settled because of recent changes in airline regulation. As it currently stands, if you refuse the compensation offered by the airline, you may be able to sue under state law for damages caused by your being bumped from the flight.

Is there any way a passenger can ensure he or she won't be bumped?

No, but you can reduce the chances of it happening. The most important thing is to check in well before departure time. In addition, you must obtain a boarding assignment, which means checking in at the boarding gate or ticket counter. Having a boarding pass without checking in may not be sufficient. If first class or business class is an option, keep in mind that those passengers are usually the last to be bumped.

What happens if a plane is delayed several hours because of weather or a mechanical problem?

Federal regulations require airlines to provide you with compensation only if you are bumped because of an oversold flight. No compensation is required for other interruptions of service caused by such things as weather or mechanical problems.

Ticket Refunds

Beatrice was asked to stay at the toy convention for an extra day and sit on a panel discussing the future of stuffed bears. After getting approval from her boss, she called the airline to change her reservation. All the flights for the next three days were booked, so she asked about getting a refund so she could fly another airline.

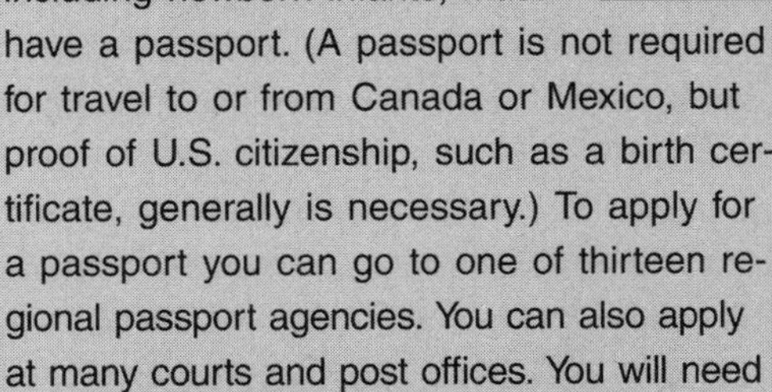

Passports

To travel abroad, every person, including newborn infants, must have a passport. (A passport is not required for travel to or from Canada or Mexico, but proof of U.S. citizenship, such as a birth certificate, generally is necessary.) To apply for a passport you can go to one of thirteen regional passport agencies. You can also apply at many courts and post offices. You will need

- **proof of citizenship (such as a previous U.S. passport or a certified copy of your birth certificate) or naturalization**
- **two photographs taken within the past six months, 2 by 2 inches, showing your full face from the front**
- **proof of identity (such as a driver's license)**
- **a fee ($65 for a ten-year passport)**
- **a social security number**

If you lose your passport while abroad, you should contact the nearest U.S. embassy or consulate.

"Sorry," said the agent. "Your ticket is nonrefundable."

■ Under what circumstances can a person get a refund on a nonrefundable ticket?

If your ticket is nonrefundable, the airline is not required to provide refunds or transfers. Federal regulations require the airlines to print any refund prohibitions or penalties on tickets for most flights. Likewise, airlines are not required to replace or refund lost tickets, though most airlines will do so voluntarily, depending on the circumstances. Most charge a fee for the service, and some issue the refund only after several weeks.

Many airlines also voluntarily provide a voucher or refund if a death or serious illness in the family disrupts travel plans, but there is no legal requirement to do so.

DEALING WITH A TRAVEL AGENCY

Blossom and Jeremy thought of themselves as adventurers, but they admittedly found it hard to live without their creature comforts. They booked a three-week tour of India with a local travel agency, which promised quiet camel rides in the deserts of Rajasthan, swimming in solitude on the beaches of Poona, a meditative dawn at the Taj Mahal . . . and sleeping in four-star hotels every night.

Instead, the camels got into traffic jams; they couldn't find room to spread their towels on the beach; and they had to wait in line for two hours to enter the Taj Mahal. And, the hotels were vermin-infested dives. Blossom wanted a refund.

■ Under what circumstances can a person get a refund from a travel agency for a trip that goes awry?

Travel agents usually are not liable for the failure of unrelated companies to properly provide services. Thus an airline's flight delay or a hotel's poor service is not the agent's responsibility unless the agent knew or should have known about the problems in advance.

When the travel agency offers a "package trip" that it organized and sponsored, it becomes a seller of services, not just an agent securing the services on your behalf. A seller is usually responsible for goods or services that fail to meet the promised quality. When goods or services are totally unacceptable, you should be able to collect a full refund. If the trip was merely less than promised, the agency may be liable for the difference in monetary value between the tour as promised and the tour as provided.

As with other goods, if you paid for the trip with a credit card, you may have an easier time securing your refund. Many credit card companies automatically delete charges from a bill when there is a dispute. (See pages 62 and 370.)

Travel Agent Gaffes

Allegra had been promising to visit her cousins in Italy for years. When Sylvester announced his engagement, Allegra knew it would be an easy and fun way to see everyone at once. As soon as she received the wedding invitation, she asked her travel agent to book a flight, but a week before the big event, she still hadn't received the ticket. Her travel agent had completely forgotten about it. He promised to take care of it right away. Of course, as Allegra feared, the discount fare was not available anymore.

■ Do travel agents have to pay for their own mistakes?

Yes. Travel agents, like other providers of services, are required to perform in a competent manner. If your agent has breached his duty, you are entitled to recover the difference in price between the two fares. In this case, where the agent simply forgot to book the tickets, the liability is clear. In other cases, there may be a dispute about what the instructions were and when they were given. A confirming letter or fax from the traveler (at the time of making the arrangements) documents the situation, but the traveler should be sure to keep a copy.

HOTELS

Beatrice desperately needed a vacation. Between pressure at work, the winter weather, and constant arguments with the kids, she just wanted a break. She decided to book a package at a resort — Surf 'N Turf, a happy holiday half in the mountains and half on the beach. After she sent in her deposit, she received an invitation to a conference on "Tomorrow's Teddy Technology," which she desperately wanted to attend. But it was the same week as her vacation.

■ Under what circumstances can a person get a deposit (or full payment) back on hotel rooms or a group tour?

As a general rule, the seller of goods or services is not required to provide a refund just because the buyer no longer wants or needs the reserved items. Recovering a deposit or full payment hinges more on the seller's rights than on the buyer's reasons for cancellation. The seller is probably entitled to keep your deposit and may also be able to charge you for other expenses and lost profit, although the hotel or tour agency should make reasonable efforts to mitigate the damages by trying to fill your spot. If that can be done, you would pay little or no damages (though you still may lose your deposit if that's what your written agreement specified). If your spot cannot be filled, you probably will owe all or most of the full price.

Price Hikes

Beatrice couldn't afford to lose her deposit, so she skipped the conference. When she arrived at Surf 'N Turf, the desk clerk informed her that there had been a change in management, resulting in higher rates. Her room, therefore, was going to cost $100 per night instead of $50. But they had good news, too: she was invited to have a complimentary cocktail in the bar.

■ Can a hotel raise the rate after a room is booked?

Not usually. Most courts have ruled that unless a hotel explicitly tells you verbally or in writing that it reserves the right to change its price, it must honor the price quoted when the reservation is made. Furthermore, the hotel must honor the reservation for the type of room reserved. If the hotel has only more expensive rooms available, you can insist on paying the price of the cheaper, reserved room. In turn, the hotel may make the customer meet certain requirements in order to honor a reservation, such as asking you to check in or confirm by credit card by a certain specified time.

When You're Dissatisfied

Beatrice worked out the room rate problem (she got the lower price). Still, Surf 'N Turf wasn't everything she had hoped for (no interesting men, for instance). And there was one especially unpleasant surprise: at the end of the week, she was presented with a bill for drinks and snacks. She paid it, but then had second thoughts as she recalled something in the resort's advertisements about "One price includes everything."

■ Can a person be reimbursed for unexpected costs?

It depends. Can a guest reasonably expect the items in question to be provided free? If the agreement you signed when you checked in states (or other readily available hotel literature states explicitly) that these items will cost extra, then the hotel may charge for them. In the absence of any explicit agreement or disclosure, the hotel's right to charge for services depends on whether a person would reasonably expect the items to be free. Usually, when hotel guests order items, they expect to pay for them. But if drinks, snacks, and flowers are provided without being requested, the expectation is that the items are complimentary.

Hotel Thefts

Beatrice bought a coral necklace for Alena and a replica of a sunken ship for Vinny. As she was packing to leave, she couldn't find the gifts. She knew she stored them with her winter coat and was sure the presents had been stolen.

■ Is a hotel liable for property that is stolen from a patron's room?

Usually not. Normally, a company (other than a "common carrier" — like a train, bus, or airline company) is not liable for the intentional wrongful acts (theft in this case) of its employees or others. A company is liable if it knew or should have known that an employee was a thief or that the room was unreasonably vulnerable to theft — perhaps because it had a faulty lock or a broken window.

RENTING A CAR

Rates

Bradley and Peter had just stepped off the plane in Florida for their winter vacation. They were ready to pick up their rental car and drive straight to the beach and start soaking up the rays. But when the agent at the Rara Car Rental desk punched up their reservation on the computer, she quoted a weekly rate that was much higher than what they had been told when they reserved the car by phone.

■ If a car is booked at a specific price, can the renter be charged more?

Not usually, but additional charges can add greatly to the advertised rate. Collision damage waivers, model upgrades, excess mileage charges, fuel refilling, pick up charges, premium time surcharges, as well as taxes, can even double the basic rate. When reserving or comparison shopping for a rental car, you should ask for the total costs for the specific time, model, and services you will be using.

The rental car company is required to honor a reservation at the stated price unless it disclosed the right to change the price. Sometimes the reservation will require you to guarantee it on your credit card or arrive to pick it up before a specified time of day. If you fail to comply with those terms, the company has the right to change the rate. If you complied with all the conditions of your reservation, and if the company claims it is out of the size or model of car you reserved and only has more expensive models available, you can insist that the more expensive model be provided at the promised reservation price.

Collision Damage Waivers

Brad and Peter were trying to limit their vacation expenses. That's why they shopped around so carefully for the cheapest car rental. They decided not to take any of the extras offered on the car that seemed to do little more than jack up the price.

■ What is a collision damage waiver?

Rental car contracts almost always make the renter liable for any damage to the car. The damage waiver is an agreement by the company to waive your liability for any damage if you pay an additional fee. If you have an accident and have not bought the collision damage waiver, you will be responsible for the damage. You may get reimbursement from the other driver — if that driver caused the accident and has car insurance. You also may be covered for rental cars by your regular car insurance company, assuming you have one. Many regular car insurance policies either provide this coverage in their basic policy or will add the coverage for a modest fee. The regular schedule of deductibles will apply.

Obtaining coverage through your regular policy is usually much cheaper than buying a collision damage waiver from the car rental company. Check with your insurance agent before taking a trip that includes a car rental. Also, some credit card companies include collision damage coverage at no charge for car rentals charged on the card.

Parking Tickets

As soon as they left the airport parking lot, Peter realized that he had left his sunglasses on the airplane. At the first opportunity, Bradley pulled over, and they ran into a store to buy some shades. They returned to the car just in time to encounter a meter maid writing out a parking ticket.

"Welcome to Florida," she smiled. "Have a great vacation."

■ Do people have to pay parking tickets they get on a rental car?

Yes. If you read the fine print of your rental car agreements, you will see that you are responsible for the ticket. If you don't pay it on your own, the rental car company will bill the credit card account you used for the amount of the ticket as well as any penalties.

Accidents

Just as they were pulling into the parking lot of the Breakfree Inn, a taxi swerved into their car, smashing the left headlight. Bradley and Peter were shaken, but fortunately, no one was hurt.

■ What happens when a person has an accident in a rental car?

After first attending to anyone who was injured, contact the rental company. If you have purchased the collision damage waiver, the rental company will handle the paperwork for payment of the repairs. If you have not purchased the waiver, the rental company will probably use the cash or credit card deposit you left and bill you for any remaining repair expenses. You then can recover the damages from your car insurance policy (if it covers you while driving a rental car) and from the other driver's insurance, if he is at fault. You should also follow the general instructions set out elsewhere in this book for steps to take in any car accident (see page 24).

Additional Drivers

Am I wearing a big sign that says 'Kick Me?'" Brad wondered aloud to Peter. Their vacation was really starting off with a bang — a ticket and an accident. Bradley just could not get behind the wheel again, but they still were determined to get to the beach. They agreed that Peter should drive, at least for the rest of the day.

■ Is it okay to let a friend drive a rental car?

You should be very careful about allowing others to drive your rental car. Rental agreements usually require you to list all persons who will drive the car. Often the company will charge an extra fee for additional drivers.

Typically, the collision damage waiver covers only listed drivers. Similarly, only you and any other drivers specifically named on your personal car insurance policy would be covered when driving a rental car. If there is an accident, you will be responsible for paying the rental company for damages, even if the accident was the fault of the driver of the other car. You would have the right to be reimbursed by the person at fault (or by the person's insurance carrier, or your own carrier in a no-fault insurance state), but you would also have the burden of recovering it. (For more on insurance, see page 23).

HAVING MONEY 24

DEALING WITH BANKS

Opening an Account

Beatrice was pregnant! Although she was only in her fifth month, she was already busy buying itty-bitty clothes and decorating the nursery in a green ivy motif. Naturally, she and Max were still arguing about names, but that was part of the fun. One thing they did agree on was that they wanted their child to be financially secure and responsible. They planned to give him or her a weekly allowance as soon as he/she was born and put it in a savings account. In her pre-birth efficiency, Beatrice even went to the bank to see if she could open the account.

"You're getting ahead of yourself," the bank manager told her. "After all, your baby doesn't even have a name yet."

■ Can anyone open a bank account?

Yes. Even a minor can open a bank account, although state laws generally require that such accounts be "custodial accounts." That means that a parent or guardian can transfer the money in and out of the account on the minor's behalf, although the money is considered to be the property of the minor. Once the minor is able to sign her name, she is free to make withdrawals and deposits on her own. However, if it's a custodial account, the parent will be held responsible if the minor bounces a check.

If parents receive checks for their child before opening an account in the child's name, some bank branches may allow them to cash or deposit the check in their own account by signing the child's name and indicating that the check is being cashed or deposited "On behalf of (child's name)" by "(parent's name)." Generally, however, parents must open an account on behalf of the minor.

■ Are there any limits on the fees a bank can charge?

Not usually. Banks are generally free to charge fees and place conditions on accounts as they see fit. As a result, many banks have raised their minimum balance requirements (some are as high as $5,000 or $6,000), increased service charges and fees, and instituted fees for services that previously were free. Some banks even charge for using live tellers. However, a few states, such as New Jersey, have passed laws requiring banks to offer basic "no-frills" accounts to low-income people.

■ Do interest rates vary from bank to bank?

Yes, the rates may vary, but when you open an account, the federal Truth in Savings Act requires banks to make up-front disclosures about interest rates, fees, and any other terms and conditions. The Truth in Savings Act also requires banks to pay interest on the entire balance of a savings account for each day. In addition, banks are required to disclose an account's annual percentage yield (APY), which is the percentage of interest that would be earned on a deposit during one year.

Transactions with the Bank Machine

Every month when Beatrice sat down to balance their checkbook, she plowed through the pile of printed receipts from the bank machine. One month she discovered a discrepancy. She had been on her way to lunch with her mother-in-law — to plan the baby shower — and she had stopped to deposit a $100 check. She still had the machine's printed receipt, but there was no indication of her deposit on the bank statement. When she called the bank, the customer service representative told her the bank never received the $100 and that her receipt was not proof.

If You Have a Complaint

Different federal agencies have jurisdiction over financial institutions. You can always ask someone at the institution for the name and address of the appropriate agency, or you can consult this list:

- Nationally chartered banks (with National or NA in their names):
  Comptroller of the Currency
  Compliance Division
  250 E Street SW
  Washington, DC 20219
  202-874-4820
  (You must direct your complaints to one of the six local district offices of the Comptroller of the Currency. You can call the above number to find out which district office you should notify.)
- State-chartered banks that are FDIC-insured and are members of the Federal Reserve System:
  Federal Reserve Board
  Division of Consumer and Community Affairs
  20th and C Streets NW
  Washington, DC 20551
  202-452-3000
- State-chartered banks that are FDIC-insured but are not members of the Federal Reserve System:
  Federal Deposit Insurance Corporation
  Office of Consumer Affairs
  550 17th Street NW
  Washington, DC 20429
  800-934-3342
- Federally chartered or insured savings and loan associations:
  Office of Thrift Supervision
  Consumer Programs
  1700 G Street NW
  Sixth Floor
  Washington, DC 20552
  202-906-6237
- Federally chartered credit unions (will say "federal credit union" in name):
  National Credit Union Administration
  1775 Duke Street
  Alexandria, VA 22314-3428
  703-518-6300
- State-chartered credit unions, government lending programs, state-chartered banks or savings institutions without FDIC insurance, finance companies, charge card companies, retail stores, credit reporting agencies, debt collectors, independent mortgage companies (that aren't part of a bank):
  Federal Trade Commission
  Bureau of Consumer Protection
  Division of Credit Practices
  Sixth Street and Pennsylvania Avenue NW
  Washington, DC 20580
  202-326-3758

Additionally, state-chartered institutions may also be governed by state banking departments and regulatory agencies.

Isn't a receipt from the bank machine proof of a transaction?

No. A receipt from an automated teller machine is evidence that a transaction took place but is not considered to be proof of how much you deposited. That's because you might have "told" the machine you were depositing $100 when you really were depositing only $50. If you have a problem, you should notify the bank within sixty days after receiving the first statement with an error, otherwise the bank may have no legal obligation to respond. If you have given proper notification, the bank is required by federal law to investigate and report its findings to you within a set period of time. Often, a bank will acknowledge there was an error.

If you are not satisfied with the outcome, you can report the problem in writing to

- **the federal banking regulator with jurisdiction over your bank**
- **the government agency in your state that regulates banks**
- **your state's Better Business Bureau**
- **your state's department of consumer affairs, usually part of the office of attorney general**

You might also sue the bank, although the amount in dispute may be too small to merit the effort.

Stolen Checks and Credit Cards

Beatrice was concerned about her state of mind. She had become so spacey and distracted with her pregnancy that she left her checkbook and driver's license in the cart at the grocery store. Someone had stolen them and successfully forged her name.

■ Is a person responsible if someone writes checks on her account and forges her name?

Usually not. It's the bank's responsibility to compare the signature on the check with the signature card on file. You should report the theft promptly to the bank so that it is alerted to the problem and can close the account as quickly as possible. If someone does forge a check, the bank usually will be liable and you won't have to pay. However, failure to report a lost or stolen checkbook in a timely fashion could result in your being held liable for any loss. But thefts typically are detected early, because checks start bouncing or an ATM refuses to give money.

Beatrice couldn't believe it. Only a few days later she left her purse dangling on the back of her chair (where she usually didn't leave it) as she sat in a restaurant waiting for her friend Shaneequa. Surprise, surprise. Someone stole it. Fortunately, Shaneequa had been able to loan her some cash.

■ Is a person responsible for the use of her stolen credit cards?

Under the federal Truth in Lending Law, you cannot be held responsible for any charges made on your card *after* you reported it lost or stolen. You are, however, liable for the first $50 of unauthorized charges made before you reported the loss. Therefore, you should report a loss or theft immediately.

> **Insurance for Bank Accounts**
>
> The Federal Deposit Insurance Corporation (FDIC) is a federal agency that guarantees deposits in most of the country's banks and savings institutions. The FDIC insures up to $100,000 in an account in any particular institution. If you have accounts in separate institutions, each is covered up to $100,000. Accounts in different branches of the same bank are not considered accounts in separate institutions. A bank that has FDIC coverage will display an official FDIC sign at each teller window.
>
> The type of accounts that are insured include
>
> - **checking accounts (including NOW accounts)**
> - **savings accounts**
> - **money market deposit accounts**
> - **certificates of deposit**
>
> Banks may also offer other "products" that are not insured. These include
>
> - **mutual funds**
> - **life insurance**
> - **stocks and bonds**
> - **Treasury bills and bonds**
>
> Note: Accounts in federal credit unions get similar protection from the National Credit Union Administration.

You should follow the same procedure if your automated teller machine card or telephone credit card is stolen — especially because you face greater liability for unauthorized use of those cards if you fail to report their loss. Under the federal Electronic Funds Transfer Act, you can't be held responsible for any charges made after you've reported that an ATM or telephone credit card is missing. If you report the missing card within two days of realizing it is gone, you are only liable for up to $50. If you wait more than two days, your liability jumps to $500. If you fail to report an ATM card missing within sixty days of receiving

Checks and Balances

If the recipient's name is misspelled on a check, is it still valid?
Yes. However the bank may first require you to endorse the check using the misspelled version of your name and then spelling it correctly before cashing or depositing it.

Do checks have to be cashed within a certain period of time?
Check expiration dates vary from state to state, but the typical time is six months. Federal government checks usually are valid for up to one year from the date of issue. Sometimes checks state that they are void after a specific date. In that case, you must cash or deposit the check within that time period.

Do checks have to clear within a certain period of time?
Yes. The federal Expedited Funds Availability Act sets deadlines for when deposited checks must be made available. Generally, government checks must clear the next day, local checks must clear within two business days, and out-of-state checks must clear within five business days. The deadlines may not apply if you deposit checks totaling more than $5,000 in one day, if you deposit a check that had bounced previously, or if you have frequently overdrawn your account.

What happens if the bank mistakenly pays a check that a customer asked to be stopped?
The law varies from state to state, but the bank typically will not charge the customer so long as there is some proof that the request was actually made. (Usually the proof would be the bank's assessment of stop-payment charges against your account.) To avoid such a problem, you should confirm your oral request in writing within three days.

a bank statement that shows unauthorized use, you could lose up to the total balance of your account.

BROKERAGE HOUSES

You and Your Broker

Blossom's successful business, Made in America, left her with lots of profit. For the first couple of years, she rolled the money back into the business, but eventually she opened an account with a brokerage house. And that's where her trouble started. When she analyzed her monthly statements, she realized that her assets were shrinking, not growing. She called Jim, her broker at Miller, Jones, Jones and Miller to discuss the situation.

"That's the way the cookie crumbles, Blossom," Jim said coolly. "The stock market is a high-risk operation."

"There's risk and there's risk," snapped back Blossom. "I told you I wanted to invest conservatively, and that I wanted to make money, not lose it. You're in trouble, buster. I'm calling my lawyer."

■ Is a broker responsible for a client's losses?

Not usually, so long as the trading and management were handled professionally. However, financial advisers have an ethical responsibility to their clients, and they are obligated to disclose the risks of your investments and to make investments that are in line with the personal financial goals that you've communicated to them. Your relationship with a broker is governed by the Securities Investor Protection Act of 1970, the National Association of Securities Dealers' Rules of Fair Practice, federal securities laws, and possibly state law.

Customers are typically asked to sign a statement that indicates the degree of risk they are willing to assume. A broker's failure to act in an ethical fashion can result in restitution paid to the client, fines and penalties against the broker and brokerage firm, suspension of the broker's license, and in rare instances, revocation of the license. If the financial adviser acted with fraudulent or criminal intent, then criminal liability can also result.

Generally, a broker can buy and sell only with your authorization. Usually, that authorization is given verbally, for both convenience and timing. Because of the verbal nature of the broker-client relationship, any after-the-fact disagreement about transactions are governed by general contract law. If you can prove that the broker misled you or violated an understanding you had, your broker may be liable for your losses.

If you have a complaint against a broker, complain in writing first to the broker, then to the branch manager of the brokerage house. If you are not satisfied with how they handle the problem, you can contact your state's securities regulator as well as the federal Securities and Exchange Commission. To contact the SEC, write or call:

Securities and Exchange Commission
Office of Consumer Affairs/Investor Services
450 Fifth Street NW
Washington, DC 20549
202-942-7040

In an effort to avoid litigation, many brokerage houses require their clients to sign agreements stating that they will consent to arbitration of disputes by a neutral third party, rather than sue in a court of law. If no such arbitration clause exists, you might consider suing the broker and the firm, although it may be difficult to find an attorney to take the case if the disputed amount is small. (See page 428 for more on arbitration.)

There are some instances in which the broker does not need your authorization for a transaction. In what's called a "discretionary" account, brokers are essentially given free rein to manage the account. However, the creation of a discretionary account must be authorized in writing. If there are certain precautions you want the broker to follow, such as investing only in blue-chip (low-risk and well-established) stocks, you should specify that in writing.

How Secure Are Your Securities?

Blossom was fuming. She just got off the phone with her broker's assistant. His assistant! He didn't even have the courage to call her himself to tell her that Miller, Jones, Jones and Miller was going under. And the assistant was too flustered to give a straight answer about her money.

"I want a certified check for my account on my desk by the end of the day," she had warned him.

"I really don't know if that will be possible, ma'am," he had waffled. "But I'll pass on your message."

■ Is an account with a brokerage house insured?

Yes, up to a point. The Securities Investor Protection Corporation (SIPC) protects up to $500,000 of your securities in a brokerage house. Of this $500,000, only $100,000 can be applied toward any cash in your brokerage account. That means that if you have $500,000 invested — $300,000 in securities and $200,000 in cash — your securities are fully covered, but only $100,000 of your cash is.

An important thing to know is that the SIPC does not insulate you from market losses. Rather, it protects you if the brokerage house goes out of business, declares bankruptcy, or becomes insolvent. Many brokerage houses also sell additional insurance on top of what the SIPC offers. Your broker can give you details.

Note: even though your money with a brokerage (or a bank, for that matter) may be insured, you won't be able to get it instantly if the institution runs into trouble.

Minors and Their Money

Blossom thought it was time that her niece and nephew, Alena and Vinny, started thinking about high finance. She gave them each $500, along with an explicit directive to invest the money in the stock market. She advised them to study the

business pages of the paper and then buy stock in whatever companies they wanted.

■ Can a minor buy stocks and bonds?

Not usually. In most states, minors lack the ability to enter legally into a contract until they reach age eighteen. "Minor" transactions can usually be conducted by the minor's parent or guardian on behalf of the minor. Stocks or bonds would be purchased by the parent or guardian as "custodian for" the minor.

LENDING MONEY

With Blossom's business success came an unexpected, and unwelcome, influx of requests for money. She gave a lot to charity, but then so-called friends started to approach her with all sorts of cockamamie business ideas. She had a standard response to these requests, asking these "friends" to send their business plans to Women Backing Women, an investment group that funded women's businesses.

But Blossom had a different reaction when her friend Marco told her about his idea to open a chain of cappuccino bars around the state.

"Not just in the obvious places, like big cities," Marco waxed enthusiastically. "A cappuccino machine in every gas station . . . a chicken in every pot."

Now this was a business Blossom could get behind. She decided to help Marco get it off the ground.

■ Should a person document a loan to a friend in writing?

Yes. When you loan a significant amount of money to a friend, you should write up what is called a **promissory note,** which is basically a statement in which your friend agrees to pay you back according to the terms of the agreement. Also, if your friend is offering something as **collateral** (an asset that you can take if he or she fails to repay the loan), then you should have a written **security agreement.** The security agreement should state that you can take possession of the collateral if your friend defaults (fails to pay you back).

Both the promissory note and the security agreement should include the following information:

- **your name and address**
- **your friend's name and address**
- **the amount of the loan**
- **the purpose of the loan**
- **the duration of the loan and a promise to pay according to a set schedule**
- **the amount of interest to be charged and how it will be assessed**
- **a description of any collateral securing the loan**
- **the actions you can take to collect the debt in the event of a default**

If the offered collateral is personal property, you may want to make what is known as a UCC filing, usually with the office of your state's secretary of state. There may be a fee (generally between $5 and $50), but the filing can help make it easier for you to claim the collateral in the event of a default. It will also notify any other lenders that you have first dibs on that property. If the offered collateral is an automobile, you should check whether you need to file anything with your state's department of motor vehicles. And if the collateral is real estate, you can file a lien against the property. (For more on liens, see pages 54 and 87.) In fact, before you accept property or real estate as collateral, you may want to check whether anyone else has filed a lien or claim that would supersede yours.

■ So it's okay to charge interest on the loan to a friend?

Yes, though many states set "usury ceiling limits" for interest rates on loans. The limits vary, but the average is around 20 to 30 percent. You can find out the limit in your state by calling the state agency that regulates banking and commerce.

To avoid confusion, the interest rate should be spelled out in the promissory note.

■ Does the recipient of an interest-free loan have to declare it to the IRS?

No. In general, loans of any sort, whether they are made with interest or not, do not qualify as income that has to be declared because the loan will have to be paid back. That's another reason why it's important to have written documentation of the loan.

■ **Is it possible for an individual to do a credit check on a friend?**

No. Since individuals are not in the normal business of granting credit, they do not have the authority to request credit reports. To get around this, you can ask your friend to request a copy of his or her report so you can examine it before deciding whether or not to lend the money.

Unpaid Loans

Bea, I am really in a bind and need to borrow $500," her friend Kate began. "I'm sure that if I can just fly to Paris to be with Jay during his business trip, he will leave his wife and marry me. Goodness knows he's been talking about it for long enough."

Bea nodded cynically. "Sure he'll leave his wife. Sure he will. Why would you want to marry a man who leaves his wife for another woman?"

"I'm in love," Kate shrugged. "But if you don't want to help me . . ."

Beatrice took out her checkbook. "No, it's okay. If it's what you really want . . ."

Beatrice was not surprised when Kate reported back on her trip. Jay may have been planning to leave his wife, but it wasn't for Kate. When she arrived at his Paris hotel, she found him there with *another* woman. Kate took a taxi right back to the airport and flew home immediately.

A few months later, the loan was still unpaid, and Kate's interior decorating business was failing. "I guess there just aren't that many people who want to turn their garages into rec rooms in the 1990s," she complained.

■ **What can a person do if a loan is unpaid?**

It depends on how much the loan was for and what kind of documentation you have. Your first step is to make a formal demand in writing and send it to your debtor (the person who owes you money) via certified mail, return receipt requested. Your letter should refer to any relevant documents (like a promissory note), indicate your understanding of the agreement, and request a response by a certain date. Note that you are serious about the matter and plan to pursue all available remedies to get your money back. (Of course at this point you are almost certainly dealing with an ex-friend.)

Your collection task will be much easier if you have a signed promissory note and/or a security agreement. To enforce either one, you first will need a court judgment that orders your debtor to pay you. If the amount owed falls within the limit of the small-claims court in your jurisdiction, you can bring your case there (for more on small-claims court, see page 431). Otherwise, you will have to sue in the regular trial court (usually state court unless your friend is a resident of a different state and more than $10,000 is at issue).

If your friend has some financial resources, the court may order payment in full or payment according to a regular schedule. If he or she has money in a bank account or is currently employed, the court may grant you authority to seize property (up to the value of your claim) or take a percentage of the debtor's wages until you've been repaid.

If your friend is unable to pay you because he or she doesn't have the money, you will probably have a hard time. If your friend files for bankruptcy (see page 377), then you could file a "proof of claim" with the bankruptcy court in order to make sure that you get on the official list of that person's creditors. You can get "proof of claim" forms from the clerk of the bankruptcy court; you don't need a lawyer to complete them.

You might also be able to deduct the unpaid loan from your taxes. An unpaid personal loan is known as a **capital loss,** or "nonbusiness bad debt." You can use that loss to offset any **capital gains** you may have. Capital gains are profits you have made from the sale of "capital" assets such as stocks or real estate. (Capital gains are limited to the money you make through sales as a private individual, not as part of your business.)

Co-signing a Loan

Because Bradley was self-employed, when he and his boyfriend, Peter, bought their co-op apartment, they had difficulties getting a mortgage. With great reluctance, Brad asked Blossom (his sibling with the highest income) to co-sign the loan, assuring her that they would have no problems making their mortgage payments.

Blossom agreed to co-sign, but she wasn't happy about it. After all, there were no guarantees that Brad's private-eye business would continue to be successful.

■ If a person co-signs a loan, is he or she liable if the other signers fail to pay?

Yes. The point of having a co-signer on a loan is so the lender can collect the full amount (usually with interest, late fees, and collection costs) from the co-signer if the original borrower cannot pay. Thus if you co-sign for your brother and he fails to pay, you are liable for the loan *just as if it were your own,* and the creditor is free to collect from you or to sue you for the balance due. In most states, the creditor can look to you for payment as soon as the original debtor misses or is late on one payment. If the original borrower has the money and refuses to pay, you can sue him for repayment.

If you are considering co-signing a loan, the creditor is required by rules adopted by federal regulatory agencies to disclose to you information about the terms of the loan and about your obligation to repay it before you sign.

OWING MONEY

25

CREDIT

Max wanted to surprise Beatrice for their anniversary. He had noticed her admiring a diamond watch in the window of Bedecked, Bedazzled and Bejeweled, and he decided to buy it. Max himself got a surprise when he went in and asked the price.

"But I know how it is when you just have to have something," the salesman sympathized. "Fill out a credit application, and you can pay it off over a couple of years."

When Max returned to the store the next week to pick up the watch, the salesman told him that his credit application had been denied.

■ What are the valid reasons that a person can be denied credit?

You can be denied credit only if the creditor (the entity that is considering loaning you the money) believes that you will be unable to repay the loan. Buying something on credit is essentially a good-faith transaction in which the creditor is saying, "I trust you will pay me back according to the terms we have agreed on." If you don't have a steady income, if you have too many other financial obligations, or if you have not made payments to other creditors in a timely fashion, a creditor may decide it's not worth the risk of lending to you.

Under the federal Equal Credit Opportunity Act, sex, marital status, age, color, race, religion, and national origin are *not* legal reasons to deny credit. In addition, your prospective creditor must act on your application within thirty days.

If your application for credit is rejected or approved for a lower amount than you requested, you are entitled to know why. If the rejection notice does not explain the reasons for the adverse action and you request this information in writing within sixty days, the creditor then has thirty days in which to respond.

If you believe that you have been discriminated against, you should first complain directly to the lender. If this doesn't produce the desired result, contact the federal agency that oversees the financial institution, company, or store that denied you credit (see page 360 for a listing of agencies and their jurisdictions). If you have a strong case, you might consider suing in federal court, but this often won't be worth it, particularly since the statutes limit the amount of damages that can be collected.

Credit Reports

Max was pretty surprised when he received a notice in the mail that the store was rejecting his credit application. He'd bought many things on credit before and had never once been turned down. Of course he wasn't too timely about paying some of the bills, but he didn't think the store would know about that. He was wrong.

"According to your credit report, you have some bad debts," the letter stated.

"Credit report?" wondered Max.

■ What information appears on a credit report?

A credit report contains information regarding your credit history. This includes accounts you currently have, your past repayment activities on loans, charge accounts, credit cards, and other extensions of credit. It also includes information about whether you have ever filed for bankruptcy or been sued for a bad debt. Typically, any companies with which you have (or have had) credit will be listed along with the status of your debt. Since some lenders do not disclose their accounts to credit reporting agencies (also known as credit bureaus), all your accounts may not be reflected in your credit report.

Any stores or organizations that have requested a copy of your credit report in response to your

If You Are Turned Down for Credit

If you believe your credit application should not have been rejected, you might want to appeal to the person (or committee) in charge of making the final decision.

- Write a letter outlining why your application should be reevaluated.
- Provide any additional positive credit information that might be helpful, including accounts under previous names or addresses, recent bank statements that show you have substantial assets, a copy of your tax return, the deed to your house, or your pay stub.
- If you think you were rejected for reasons prohibited by the Equal Credit Opportunity Act, mention that you understand your rights under that law forbid such discrimination.
- Be polite and respectful. If you're hostile, they'll be less likely to reconsider.
- If you can't reach a satisfactory resolution and you believe the law has been violated, see the box on page 373.

application for credit must be listed on your report for at least six months. The purpose is to allow creditors to see how much credit you're requesting. They may think you're overextending and thus deny you.

Credit reporting agencies are prohibited from disclosing adverse information about your accounts that is more than seven years old, so such activity should automatically be deleted from your file seven years after the date of last activity. A bankruptcy filing remains on your credit report for ten years from the date judgment was rendered. (For more on bankruptcy, see page 377.) Favorable credit information can remain on your report indefinitely, as can any current accounts you maintain.

There are four major private companies that offer credit reporting services: TRW Credit Data, Trans Union National Consumer Disclosure Center, Equifax, and CSC Credit Services, Inc. Under federal law they are required to provide you with a copy of your credit report if you make an appropriate written request (see the box at right). If you've been denied credit recently, you're entitled to a free copy of your report. Some agencies will also give you one free copy each year, although the law doesn't require them to do so. If you have not recently been turned down for credit, you may have to pay a fee of $5 to $30, depending on the state in which you live.

Your credit report can be obtained (without your permission) to determine your eligibility for insurance or employment. If you are turned down for a job, insurance, or credit because of information in your report, the federal Fair Credit Reporting Act requires that you be told that information contained in your credit report was used in making the decision.

Finance Charges

Bradley and Peter had to get new furniture after their poodle, Butch, did irreparable damage to the couch and the rug. (It was revenge, no doubt, for their leaving him alone during the day while they were at work.) They bought a great new leather couch and a beautiful oriental rug. Peter generally took care of paying their bills, but shortly after the furniture arrived, he'd gotten swamped with a new project at work. In addition, his mother was in the hospital, so he'd spent a lot of time visiting her and helping to take care of his father. So he'd neglected some of the finer details of domestic life, such as paying the bills, for a few weeks. When he opened the second bill from Fly Me To The Moon Carpets, he was alarmed to see that the store was already charging interest. He had had no intention of paying finance charges and thought it was unfair. After all, he meant to pay his bill, and he had the money to do so.

■ When can finance charges be assessed? Finance charges accrue on a bill that is not paid in full by the creditor's due date. Some stores and credit card companies provide a grace period (usu-

Obtaining Your Credit Record

Check your yellow pages under "Credit Reporting Agencies" for the companies that serve your area. You might also ask local merchants for this information. You can also contact directly one of these credit reporting agencies to see if they have a file on you:

TRW Credit Data
for a free annual report, write to:
P.O. Box 2350
Chatsworth, CA 91313-2350
to purchase an additional report, write to:
P.O. Box 2104
Allen, TX 75002
800-262-7432

Equifax
P.O. Box 740241
Atlanta, GA 30374-0241
800-685-1111

Trans Union National Consumer Disclosure Center
P.O. Box 390
Springfield, PA 19064
312-408-1050

CSC Credit Services, Inc.
652 East North Belt, Suite 133
Houston, TX 77060
713-878-4840

Each agency will have its own procedure, but typically you must make a written request, providing your:

- **name**
- **date of birth**
- **address (and previous addresses if you've been at your current one for less than three years)**
- **Social Security number**

A copy of your report must be sent to you within thirty days of the agency's receipt of your request.

If you discover that something in your record is either inaccurate or incomplete, you should immediately contact the credit reporting agency *in writing.* (Often a consumer dispute form will be provided by the agency.) The agency will contact your creditor to confirm or deny the information you dispute. If your creditor stands behind the information as reported, you're entitled to make a brief statement (usually not more than 100 words) giving your side of the story. The statement, or a summary of it, will be provided to prospective creditors who request your report.

If the creditor is willing to revise the information that appears in the report, you should ask the credit reporting agency to notify any parties that received the misinformation. You should also ask the creditor that provided the erroneous information to correct it. If the creditor agrees to change the status of your account, both you and the creditor should inform the agency so it can correct your record.

Do all of this in writing and keep records of your correspondence. Clearing up a credit report error can be a bureaucratic nightmare, especially if your records have been mixed up with those of someone who has your same name but not your credit history.

Note: If you find an error on a report from one credit bureau, you may want to check with the others to see if they contain the same error. You will have to go through separate procedures with each agency.

ally five or ten days beyond the due date) during which no finance charge is calculated. No federal law requires them to do so, but some state laws do. The federal Truth in Lending Act does require that prior to your opening a charge account, the store or credit card company must disclose in writing information about the rate of interest charged on the account, when finance charges accrue, and how they are calculated. This information also must be included in each billing statement.

■ Are there limits on how high finance charges can go?

Generally, there are, but different rules apply to different types of credit. For example, retail cards from merchants are bound by the law in the state in which you live. Bank cards, on the other hand, are governed by the state in which the bank card's operations are located. State usury laws limit the amount of interest that can be charged on all types of credit. During recent years, however, these ceilings have been raised. Thus, they provide less and less protection against high interest rates.

If you're buying something on an installment plan, which essentially is buying it on credit, you should know that while the monthly payment may seem low, you may actually be spending much more for the product than it is worth, because you could be paying a high amount of interest.

Credit Card Errors

"Mama mia!" Beatrice exclaimed when she opened her monthly credit card statement. She'd been fantasizing about a trip to Italy ever since The Rialto had run an Italian film festival. She'd even signed up for an Italian conversation class. But she definitely had not spent $220 on an espresso machine and $95 on a pasta maker. So how come, she wondered, they were there on her bill? And how was she going to get them off of it?

Your Spouse and Your Credit Report

A good credit history is usually necessary to obtain credit. Many married women do not have credit histories in their own names either because they changed their name when they married or because their creditors report their accounts only in the husband's name. If you and your spouse share accounts or credit cards, these accounts should appear on both your credit reports, since you are both equally responsible for the accounts. In addition, the Equal Credit Opportunity Act entitles you to have any existing account opened after June 1, 1977, listed on your credit report if you use it or are liable for it even if it is in your spouse's name only. Thus, if such an account is listed on your spouse's credit report but not yours, you can ask that it be added. (You can also ask that accounts opened prior to June 1, 1977, be listed on both your reports.) This can help you develop and maintain an independent credit record.

If you and your spouse separate or divorce, you should notify each of your joint creditors separately, in writing, asking them to remove your name from joint accounts and stating that you will not be responsible for any future debts incurred on them by your ex-spouse. You should also check with each creditor to make sure no other procedures are required to get your name off the account.

■ What should a person do if there's an error on his or her credit card statement?

You should send a written notice to the credit card company within sixty days after the first bill containing an error was mailed to you. Send it to the address for payment disputes (it will be noted on the bill), not the regular address for payments. Your letter should include

- **your name**
- **your account number**

- **a description of the error, including the date and amount of the error**
- **any corroborating information you might have, such as a receipt showing a different transaction amount (send photocopies, not originals)**

It's a good idea to send the letter via certified mail with a return receipt requested.

The credit card issuer is required by the federal Fair Credit Billing Act to acknowledge your letter within thirty days of receiving it and is required to resolve the situation in ninety days, either by

- **correcting the error and crediting your account or**
- **sending an explanation to you of why it believes that there was no billing error**

Until the billing error is resolved, you don't have to pay any portion of the bill that is in dispute. If the issuer responds that "We're right, and you're wrong," you should work your way up the creditor's chain of command. Don't rely on a clerk to resolve the problem. Call and ask to speak to the head of the disputes section. Write a letter and send it to this person and send a copy to the head of the financial institution as well.

If the creditor still fails to resolve the matter to your satisfaction and you're confident that you're right, you may consider pursuing legal action. If you still refuse to pay, however, the creditor can begin collection procedures. If you're not going to pay, you should write to the creditor within ten days of receiving the creditor's conclusive report and state why you refuse to pay the disputed amount. Then if the creditor reports you to a credit bureau, the creditor must also report that you don't believe you owe the money.

CASE IN POINT

Renting-to-Own: Costly Ventures

At first Flora Hall may have thought she was getting a good deal. Hall, a Milwaukee resident, had agreed in April 1991 to pay $77.96 a month to rent a new washer and dryer from Rent-A-Center, a company that operates stores in forty-nine states. Under her contract with the store, Hall had the option to purchase the appliances after making nineteen successive monthly payments, plus one final outlay of $161.91. The total cost: $1,643.15.

That price seemed pretty steep to Hall, who estimated that the retail value of a washer and dryer was closer to $600. Even though the rental agreement clearly stated that purchasing the property by renting it first was a more expensive option than just purchasing the appliances outright, Hall stopped making payments after forking over $1,069, arguing, among other things, that she had already paid more than the appliances were worth. She also said she had never read the various forms she signed.

Rent-A-Center sued to recover the merchandise. Hall argued that the rent-to-own transaction could be considered a sale of goods and that as such it violated Wisconsin consumer law, which requires companies involved in credit transactions to state the annual interest rate and the total cost of the merchandise under the credit agreement. Two state courts ruled in Hall's favor, and in March 1994 the state's highest court upheld those rulings.

In a similar case issued the same month, a New Jersey court also held rent-to-own companies are subject to consumer lending laws that regulate interest rates. In several states, rent-to-own companies have backed legislation that recognizes their transactions as distinct from sales — and thus not subject to interest-rate limits. The industry argues that such deals are not credit sales since most customers only rent and don't end up buying and are free to cancel the deal at any time.

Problems with Creditors

When you have disputes with a creditor or a credit reporting agency, there are several steps you can take to try to resolve it.

- First, formally register your complaint with the creditor or the credit reporting agency.

Notify the institution *in writing* of your problem. Find out the name and address of a person in authority and write directly to that person. If you are not satisfied, work your way up, writing to the company president if necessary. Your letter should explain the situation clearly and state how you would like the conflict to be resolved. Your letter should state your name, address, telephone number, and appropriate account numbers. Ask for a response by a specified date. If you have not received one, send a follow-up letter.

- Next, notify the appropriate regulatory agency, such as the Federal Trade Commision (see page 360 for numbers).

You can ask the creditor or credit reporting agency for the name of the federal and state agencies that oversee its activities. An agency probably can't intercede on your behalf, but it will monitor complaints to help determine if a creditor or credit reporting agency is violating the law. You should also send a copy of your letter to the regulatory agency for the institution with which you have the problem.

- Sue in federal court.

You can pursue this option if a federal statute has been violated. It's advisable to consult an attorney for help.

- Sue in state court.

If your state has laws governing consumer financial transactions, you may have a state case if that law has been violated. Again, you should consult an attorney for help.

Defaulting on a Loan

Jeremy and Blossom had been a couple for several years, and a pretty happy and peaceful couple at that. Even though they had never married, they often referred to each other as husband and wife in public. That's why Jeremy was so distraught after Blossom broke up with him rather suddenly. He went on a major shopping spree, taking out loans to buy a motorcycle and powerboat. Then he decided to take hang-gliding lessons. His last flight was a spectacular soar through the sunset with a band of red-tailed hawks. It came to an abrupt end when he crashed and broke twelve bones. Unable to work for several months, he stopped paying his bills.

What happens when a person can't make payments on a loan?

A person who has fallen behind in payments or has stopped paying altogether is said to be in **default.** If you're in this position, you might try contacting your creditors directly. Often, creditors just want some sort of guarantee that they will be paid, and they may be willing to help you restructure your finances in order to work out a way to pay off the debt. You'll probably need to speak to someone with more authority than the clerk who answers the phone, and if you initially get the cold shoulder, be persistent. Ask to speak to a supervisor and work your way up the chain of command. Always be polite and stress that you are trying to find the best way to meet your obligations.

If you think you have a valid reason for being in default (your payment got lost in the mail, or you were withholding payment because of a dispute over the goods), you should let your creditor know in writing. Keep records of all your communications.

One important detail to know is whether your loan is "recourse" or "nonrecourse," and your loan agreement will give you the answer. If the loan is nonrecourse, then the creditor can "satisfy" the debt only by seizing the actual asset for which you borrowed the money. Thus, if you took a nonrecourse loan to buy a car and have fallen behind on your payments, the creditor's only option is to repossess your car.

If, however, you took a recourse loan, then (as the name suggests) the creditor has other recourse and can seize nonrelated assets to pay off the debt.

If you fail to pay and don't contact your creditor or work out a satisfactory agreement, you may be sued or have your possessions seized (see page 374).

Federal Consumer Credit Laws

Some of the federal laws that protect consumers on credit matters are listed here.

- **Equal Credit Opportunity Act.** Prohibits the denial of credit because of your sex, race, marital status, religion, national origin, age, or because you receive public assistance.
- **Fair Credit Reporting Act.** Gives you the right to learn what information is being distributed about you by credit bureaus.
- **Truth in Lending Act.** Requires lenders to give you written disclosures of the cost of credit and terms of repayment before you enter into a credit transaction.
- **Fair Credit Billing Act.** Establishes procedures for resolving billing errors on your credit card accounts.
- **Fair Debt Collection Practices Act.** Prohibits debt collectors from using unfair or deceptive practices to collect overdue bills that your creditor has forwarded for collection.

The Federal Trade Commission has brochures on each of these laws. You can obtain copies by writing or calling:

Federal Trade Commission
Public Reference
Washington, DC 20580
202-326-2222

Collection Agencies

Lying in traction at the hospital, Jeremy had a lot of time to think, but he didn't spend that time worrying about his bills. After three months, they had really accumulated. In fact, most of them had been sent to collection agencies. And one — the agency trying to collect on his motorcycle — was using scare tactics. Without fail, he was getting weekly phone calls in the hospital from the collection agency trying to squeeze money out of him. Every time a friend gathered his mail and brought it to him, Jeremy found a couple of threatening letters from the agency. They'd even left messages for him on his voice mail at work.

Are collection agencies allowed to harass people continually?

No. Collection agencies are not allowed to harass, oppress, or abuse any person in connection with the collection of a debt. The federal Fair Debt Collection Practices Act and some state laws impose stringent rules under which a creditor can attempt to collect a debt. For example, a **debtor** (person who owes money) can be called only at home (not at work) between certain hours, generally between 8:00 A.M. and 9:00 P.M. Obscene or threatening language cannot be used; the collector cannot pretend to represent the government or falsely imply that you have committed a crime. In addition, the collector is allowed to speak about the matter only with

- **the debtor (you)**
- **the debtor's attorney**
- **a credit reporting agency**
- **the creditor**
- **the creditor's attorney**
- **the debt collector's attorney**

> **Getting Help with a Credit Problem**
>
> If your credit problems have gotten out of hand, low-cost (and sometimes even free) help is available from Consumer Credit Counseling Services, a nonprofit organization that has offices throughout the country in every state. The financial counselors there can help you set up a budget and may also be able to negotiate a repayment plan with your creditors.
>
> You can find out the office nearest you by calling 800-388-2227 or by writing:
>
> National Foundation for Consumer Credit
> 8611 Second Avenue, Suite 100
> Silver Spring, MD 20910
>
> Your local chamber of commerce, Better Business Bureau, or one of your creditors can also direct you to counseling programs in your area.

Any debt collector who fails to comply with the law is subject to civil liability. In other words, you can sue the debt collector for damages, including attorney's fees.

The Fair Debt Collection Practices Act protects only debtors who are being pursued by third-party bill collectors (collection agencies or law firms hired to collect the money you owe someone else). If the creditor is pursuing you directly (for example, the collections department of a hospital that you owe money), the federal restrictions do not apply. You may, however, be protected by state law.

Note: your account won't usually be turned over to a collection agency until your lender has declared you to be in default. Typically, the lender will have already made an effort to collect from you directly. If you have a written loan agreement, it usually will define when default kicks in, but it could occur even if you've missed just one payment. Once your delinquent account is turned over to a collection agency, it's probably too late to keep it from going onto your credit report. As noted above, try to keep this from happening by contacting your creditors as soon as you realize you are going to have trouble paying. Avoiding them will only lead to greater problems.

Seizure of Assets

Jeremy didn't know where to turn. He watched with horror as his medical expenses added up — especially since he had no health insurance. And then there were the bills for the motorcycle and the boat. He left Blossom a desperate message: "They're going to repossess my Harley," he moaned. "It's the bike of my dreams, and I'm going to lose it. They're also eyeing the money I have stashed in my savings account. Can you help?"

Blossom called back. "This is your idea of a 'matter of life and death'?" she asked with disgust. "Grow up, Jeremy."

■ Under what circumstances can a creditor seize a person's assets?

A creditor usually seizes your assets because you have failed to make payments (called a default) or have violated some other terms of your loan agreement, perhaps by destroying the asset that served as collateral for the loan. There are a number of different procedures the creditor can use to accomplish the seizure.

The most common method is for the creditor to sue you, get an official judgment, and then have the court's decision carried out by the local sheriff's department. If your property is seized, it will be sold, usually at an auction. The money raised from that sale is turned over to the creditor to satisfy the debt. Any excess is returned to you. Similarly, money in your bank account (up to the amount you owe) might also be seized.

If you are sued, you will receive notice by being served with papers. These papers will have information about what you need to do, including the deadline for filing an answer with the court. It is critical that you respond by the deadline. If you don't, you could automatically have a judgment entered against you that's called a default judgment. If it's possible, you should consult a lawyer. The local court clerk may also be able to give you information about the proper procedure you need to follow. If you can't afford a lawyer, a law school in your area may offer free legal advice, or you may qualify for low-income legal services. (See Chapter 30, FINDING AND USING A LAWYER).

A creditor may also seize your assets in what is called a **replevin** action. This is a relatively fast and inexpensive way for an individual creditor to seize or repossess assets (but not real estate) that

- **are leased from the creditor**
- **have been offered to a creditor as collateral**

Say you lease a refrigerator from a store and stop making the agreed-upon monthly payments. Or say a bank loaned you money to buy a car (which you offered as collateral), and then you stop making payments. In both cases you are in default and the creditors (either the store or the bank) can go to court and initiate replevin actions. In such a situation, where the creditor essentially owns a piece of property in your possession, you should be notified of impending court action against your property. If you fail to show up in court on the designated date, you may receive no further notice of the court's action. In other words, someone from the sheriff's department could show up with a court order to repossess your refrigerator and you would have no say in the matter.

Note: In a replevin action, your property can be seized before the outcome of the lawsuit. It's necessary, however, that a judge first issue an order to do so.

Are there any assets that are exempt from seizure?

Yes, although the laws vary from state to state. Usually household items, such as clothing, furniture, and appliances, are protected unless the creditor has a specific "interest" in that item. For instance, as mentioned above, if you took out a loan to buy a refrigerator and then failed to repay it, the refrigerator could be repossessed.

Other assets, such as a car you use for work, might also be exempt. You should check your state laws to find out the local rules governing your particular circumstances.

What's the best way to protect against a seizure of assets?

Pay your bills, if possible, and try not to overextend yourself with credit. When you do borrow money or buy on credit, carefully review what you sign. Check the various clauses in the contract that relate to default to see if anything seems unreasonable. Standard-form contract language normally gives the creditor the right to demand full payment of the outstanding balance if a default occurs.

If the contract is unintelligible legalese, you can ask the bank's loan manager or someone at the credit card company to explain carefully the terms to you. (If it's a credit card issuer, you might also get help from BankCard Holders of America, a nonprofit organization. Its number is 703-481-1110.) Remember, however, that in the event of a dispute, the written terms of the contract are likely to prevail — even if you didn't understand them, which is why you should clear up any uncertainties before making a commitment.

If you do fall behind in payments on a loan, your first line of defense should be to talk with your creditor. Some creditors are flexible in helping you work out a payment schedule. Indeed, you probably have numerous options available if you keep the lines of communication open and contact the creditor as soon as you realize there's a problem.

Loss of Utilities

The situation went from bad to worse. Jeremy had worked out a payment plan with his creditors, but he had forgotten a few details . . . like his phone and utility bills.

Under what circumstances can a person's phone and other utilities be turned off?

If you have not paid your phone or other utility bill, they may pull the plug on you. If you are behind on your bills or can't make a particular payment, you should contact the utility to arrange a manageable payment schedule. Each state has its own regulations about when a utility may terminate phone, gas, or electric service. In most states, you must be given seven to ten days' notice before the service is turned off. You can check with the agency that regulates utilities in your state. Also, your state may have an assistance program that helps elderly people or those with low incomes pay utility bills in emergency situations, such as during cold weather.

Are the rules the same for cable television?

No. Since cable isn't considered a vital service, there generally are fewer protections if you fail to pay the bill. Cable is regulated locally, by the government agency that awarded the franchise to your cable company. You should check with the appropriate local officials to find out the rules for cable television service in your area.

Wage Garnishment

Jeremy, who was finally back to work, found a note on his desk from his boss, Rob Vanilla: "Please see me ASAP."

"Yes, sir, you wanted to see me, sir?" (Jeremy had had a lot of practice being obsequious due to numerous dealings with his creditors.)

"Jeremy, I'm afraid we're going to have to let you go," Vanilla said blandly. "I hate to do it. You're a good worker and you've been here a long time. But it's company policy. Three different creditors are trying to garnish your wages, and we just can't afford to be involved in your problems."

"Garnish?" asked Jeremy with genuine surprise. "What does that mean? I get my wages with a sprig of parsley now?"

What does it mean when a person's wages are garnished?

It means that a portion of your compensation is paid directly by your employer to your creditor. Wages can be garnished to pay for things like delinquent loans, child support, and back taxes, but only after a judge has issued an order to do so. Federal law protects people from unfair and unreasonable garnishment. In addition, many states have enacted wage garnishment laws of their own. For instance, some states restrict it to particular types of obligations such as child support. And in many circumstances, there are limits to the percentage of your salary that can be garnished. Unemployment compensation, welfare benefits, income tax refunds, and veterans' disability and social security benefits are not subject to garnishment.

Can an employee be fired for being in debt?

Federal law says you can't be fired if only one creditor is garnishing your wages. Beyond that the rules vary from state to state, and you may not be protected if more than one creditor tries to garnish your wages. Federal law also prohibits employers from firing workers if their wages are being garnished for child support payments.

How does a garnishment work?

Your creditor must go to court seeking a garnishment, and you must be notified. The court will determine how much can be garnished based on your earnings, and will issue an order of judgment. Your employer will be notified and required to withhold the appropriate amount. When the amount owed is satisfied, the garnishment will stop.

Student Loans

Beatrice had to admit she was prejudiced against Alena's new boyfriend before she even met him. Why was a twenty-two-year-old man interested in her sixteen-year-old daughter? Alena had raved about Reed for weeks — how cool and neat he was, and really, really smart.

"We talk about philosophy and politics and stuff, Mom," Alena had attempted to assure her. "Reed has been to college. None of the guys my own age can talk about anything besides sports."

Alena invited Reed to the house for dinner. When the big night came, it was a disaster. Alena knew her mother didn't like Reed from

the moment he walked in the door. But the real trouble started when they began talking about college, and Reed confessed he had dropped out after two years.

"I wasn't learning anything," Reed asserted. "That's why I'm not going to keep paying off my student loans."

Beatrice rolled her eyes. "That's real smart," she said under her breath.

Are defaults on student loans treated differently from defaults on other loans?

Yes. Unlike most loans, a student loan gets more time before it is considered in default. It usually is not in default until it has been unpaid for six to nine months.

Once a student loan is in default, your lender (usually a bank) will turn the loan over to the government agency in charge of collecting the money owed. The agency may be able to collect a portion of your federal income tax refund or of your wages (that's called a garnishment; see facing page). In addition, your default will probably be reported to consumer credit rating agencies, which could make it difficult to obtain credit in the future.

If you make a good faith effort to repay and your lender is willing, a student loan can usually be lifted out of default by making twelve *consecutive* payments on time every month (a one-time lump payment won't get you out of default). Obviously, defaulting on student loans has serious negative consequences. If you cannot meet your payments, you should contact your lender immediately. There are a variety of arrangements that you can make to avoid default. Once you are in default, it is too late for your lender to forbear (refrain from collecting) or defer (postpone collecting) your loan, because it will have already gone to the government agency that guaranteed the loan to collect payment. Thus, it will be out of the lender's hands, and therefore the importance of contacting your lender *before* you default on your student loans cannot be overemphasized.

BANKRUPTCY

Jeremy was depressed, and for good reason. His girlfriend of many years kicked him out. He had spent three months in the hospital with compound fractures. He had lost his job, and all his creditors were after him. The only good thing happening was that after trying for years, his best friend from college was about to have a baby. In fact, he met a woman at the baby shower who piqued his interest. Consuela was smart, funny, and very nice, and it was she who suggested that he might want to declare personal bankruptcy to clean up the financial mess of his life. As for the emotional mess, maybe they could have dinner Saturday night?

"I don't even mind paying," she offered. "Trust me, I'm a doctor."

What is bankruptcy?

Bankruptcy is a process governed by federal law and overseen in federal bankruptcy court. It is intended to help when people cannot (or will not) pay their debts. The idea of bankruptcy is to help a **debtor** (the person who owes, or is in debt) get his or her financial situation in order and begin with a clean slate. The bankruptcy laws also may help creditors (the people who lent the money) recover some, if not all, of what is owed to them. Bankruptcy proceedings may be initiated either by a person in debt (voluntary bankruptcy) or by a creditor (involuntary bankruptcy).

Though there are five types of bankruptcies, the two main types of personal bankruptcy are **Chapter 7** and **Chapter 13.** You begin a bankruptcy proceeding by filing a petition with your local bankruptcy court. When you do that, it's sort of like putting up a temporary moat between you and your creditors, because an automatic stay is imposed that protects you and your assets from seizure and lawsuits.

In a **Chapter 7** bankruptcy, your assets are liquidated (collected and sold) and the proceeds are distributed to your creditors. After you have filed for Chapter 7 bankruptcy, your creditors will be notified, and much of your property will be turned

The Basic Procedure of a Bankruptcy

- You decide whether to file under Chapter 7 or Chapter 13.
- The process begins when you file a petition with the U.S. Bankruptcy Court.
- An automatic stay is imposed, which protects your assets from seizure and lawsuits.
- A trustee is appointed to oversee the procedure.
- You submit a list of all your creditors to the trustee.
- Your creditors are notified that you have filed a bankruptcy petition.
- If you have filed under Chapter 7, the trustee will "liquidate" your nonexempt assets and distribute the sale proceeds to your creditors.
- If you have filed under Chapter 13, you must submit a plan to the trustee outlining how you will repay your creditors. Your creditors are allowed to have input into your plan.
- Once your assets have been liquidated and distributed, or once you have repaid your creditors according to your plan, a hearing will be held and you will be "discharged" from bankruptcy.

Note: bankruptcy is not intended to let people escape paying debts that they are able to pay but would prefer not to, and the bankruptcy judge can reject a filing if it is determined that a person actually has the ability to pay his or her debts.

over to a court-appointed trustee, who will oversee its sale.

Not all your assets will be sold. Federal law allows a person in bankruptcy to keep certain possessions. (This is known as **exempt** property. Everything else is **nonexempt.**) In addition, states are free to allow additional exemptions. Some, like Florida and Texas, allow many more exemptions than the federal law does. For instance, in most cases these states exempt a person's principal dwelling, no matter what its value, from the reach of bankruptcy proceedings. However, if you divert your assets and buy a house in one of these states solely to keep away from your creditors, it's possible that you would not be protected.

Some of the exemptions the federal law allows are

- **your residence or personal property, up to $7,500 (which means that if your home is sold, you can keep up to $7,500)**
- **one car, up to the value of $1,200**
- **household property, including books and appliances, up to $500**
- **up to $500 worth of jewelry**
- **professional books or tools, up to $750**
- **any income from social security, disability, public assistance, unemployment, pension funds, life insurance, alimony, or veteran's benefits**

Once your assets are sold, the proceeds are used to pay your creditors. Depending on the assets available, creditors may not receive back every penny that you owe them. They each should, however, receive a pro rata share of what you owe. If you have no assets available, then none of them will receive anything. These determinations will be made by the trustee and approved by the judge and are based on an analysis of your total income and assets.

You retain more control of your possessions in a **Chapter 13** bankruptcy. The key difference between Chapter 13 and Chapter 7 is that under Chapter 13 you keep your assets but usually pay more to creditors than under Chapter 7. Generally, people filing under Chapter 13 still have a fairly regular income. Often they are trying to save their homes from foreclosure.

After you file for bankruptcy under Chapter 13, all debt collection proceedings against you stop, and a trustee is appointed to oversee your case. Within a set period of time, you must submit to the trustee a plan in which you outline how you will repay your debts over the course of three to five years. (You may be forgiven from paying interest and penalties.) Your creditors are then notified and, if your plan is approved, you must make regular payments to the trustee who will distribute the money to your creditors. If you meet your obligations under the plan, you will be discharged from debt. If you don't, your bankruptcy may be converted to Chapter 7 and your assets may be liquidated. Or the judge may decide to dismiss your petition and let your creditors foreclose and repossess your assets.

■ **Which is better, Chapter 7 or Chapter 13?**
It depends on your circumstances. If you're really overwhelmed with debt, you may need Chapter 7. If there's some realistic expectation you'll be able to repay some or all of what you owe, then Chapter 13 is better. If you have to declare bankruptcy, Chapter 13 is better on your credit report since it shows a willingness to make good on your obligations through a repayment plan.

■ **How long does it take to get out of bankruptcy?**
The proceedings can take anywhere from a few months to a few years, depending on the circumstances of your case. Generally, in the final stage of your case, there will be a "discharge hearing," in which the judge will notify you which of your debts have been excused and which have not. You then "emerge" from bankruptcy.

■ **Is a lawyer necessary?**
A lawyer is not absolutely required but is strongly recommended since bankruptcy is a very serious matter that will have an impact on your financial future for years. You can file for bankruptcy without a lawyer simply by going to the clerk of your local federal bankruptcy court and asking for the appropriate forms. And, of course, since you are filing for bankruptcy, it is possible that you don't have much money to pay a lawyer. Before going ahead on your own, however, check with your local bar association or local law schools to see what kind of legal services are available in your area to help people in bankruptcy proceedings who can't afford to represent themselves. It is a complicated procedure that can be made a lot easier with the help of an attorney.

Am I Forgiven?

Will all your debts be "forgiven" if you declare bankruptcy?

Not necessarily. Depending on your assets, income, and the type of bankruptcy you declare, you may be relieved of the obligation to pay some of your debts. These may include

- **medical expenses**
- **credit card debt**
- **some court judgments against you for personal liability or personal injury (for instance, if someone won an award after suing you because he slipped and broke his ankle in your house)**

Certain debts, however, cannot be avoided by filing for bankruptcy. These include

- **child and spousal support**
- **most taxes**
- **some student loans**
- **government fines or penalties, such as for traffic violations**
- **debts you incurred based on fraud**

Even after emerging from bankruptcy, you will still have to pay these debts.

Also, a bankruptcy filing protects you only from debts incurred *before* the date of filing. Any debts incurred *after* you file, including taxes, must still be paid.

Spending Money While in Bankruptcy

The idea of bankruptcy made Jeremy nervous. It made him think of the depression and of going to the poor house. He saw his future financial life crumbling before him and worried that he'd have to ask a judge for permission every time he wanted to buy anything.

■ Does a person have to get official approval to spend money while in bankruptcy?

Not necessarily. You may continue to pay your ordinary debts, such as living expenses, rent, and utilities. There are some spending restrictions however. You may not be allowed to purchase a new home or take a long vacation. If you wish to spend money outside the ordinary course of your business or lifestyle, you probably have to get permission. Of course, if you fail to get approval to jet off to Aruba for a long weekend or take your spouse out to a fancy dinner, you may not get caught. But if you have no credit cards, are on a budget, and have limited funds available, splurging will not be that easy.

Once the bankruptcy proceedings are completed, however, you are free to spend without permission.

■ What kind of damage does bankruptcy do to a person's credit rating?

After filing for bankruptcy, you may have difficulties getting a loan, but it depends on the financial institution to which you apply. Your credit reports generally can include your bankruptcy filing for between seven to ten years from the date the bankruptcy judgment is rendered. In addition, each individual debt can remain on your credit report for seven years from the date of last activity.

Many financial institutions reviewing your credit history may consider you to be a higher credit risk. Declaring bankruptcy is a signal to future creditors that

- **you have been unable to pay your debts in the past**
- **you may be unable to pay your debts in the future**
- **you are willing to declare bankruptcy in order to avoid debt obligations**

However, bankruptcy is not the end of the line. Obtaining a bankruptcy discharge allows you to free your future earnings from the claims of past creditors. Furthermore, you are not allowed to declare Chapter 7 bankruptcy within six years of obtaining a bankruptcy discharge, so in some ways, you are less of a credit risk to financial institutions. However, you can file for bankruptcy under Chapter 13 within that time frame.

If Your Spouse Declares Bankruptcy

Blossom didn't harbor any hard feelings against Jeremy. She just thought that she had outgrown him and that it was time to move on. She was a little embarrassed by the way he behaved at the end, getting down on one knee and begging her to marry him.

"Thank goodness I didn't take him up on his proposal," Blossom told Beatrice. "He'd be dragging me down with him."

■ If one spouse declares bankruptcy, how does that affect the other spouse?

It depends on the property laws of your state. In what is known as a community property jurisdiction, each spouse is entitled to an equal share of all property earned or purchased during the marriage, no matter whose name it's in. What that means in a bankruptcy situation is that half of all property is up for grabs unless it was owned separately by the "nondebtor" spouse before the marriage or was a gift or inheritance made only to that spouse.

In what's called an equitable-distribution or common-law property jurisdiction, the debtor's bankruptcy may have less effect on his or her spouse, since each spouse separately owns whatever he or she earned during the marriage. If the spouses own property together, that property may be used for payment to a debtor's creditors. However, before joint property can be sold by the bankruptcy trustee or distributed to creditors, the nondebtor spouse must be given the opportunity to purchase it. If the title to the property is held solely in the nondebtor spouse's name, the property will not be counted as part of the debtor's assets and will not be affected by the declaration of bankruptcy. (For more on property laws, see page 172.)

RETIRING

26

The Tech Security Division of Global World Systems International (U.S.) Inc. had been good to Gordon Goodfriend. In fact, when the Tech Security recruiting rep had come to State ("the Harvard of the Upper Midwest") that cool spring morning back in 1954, Gordon — a senior engineering major with a 3.8 average, a crew cut, and 1947 Studebaker — had leaped out of his bed at Alpha Gamma early. A big company meant big benefits and big opportunities. Gordon wanted to make a good impression. At the end of the interview, when the rep squeezed his hand and winked, Gordon knew he had the job.

But Gordon was no longer that gung-ho young man. For thirty-nine years he had worked at Tech Security, rising through the ranks to his current position — Regional Unit Manager, Aerospace Hardware (Explosive Bolts). He had made a nice living for his family and put three kids through college. But now — it wasn't that he had grown tired of his work; it was just that, well, he had been behind a desk for a long time. More and more he caught himself daydreaming about the cabin upstate and about how the river almost seemed to boil when the trout were really hitting. "I'm sixty-two," Gordon thought, "maybe it's time to retire and enjoy life."

But Gordon also wondered if he could afford to stop working. True, he and Grace had tried to save, and they both were still pretty healthy. Nevertheless, he'd heard a lot of stories about pensioners scavenging through other people's garbage and surviving on meals of cat food, and he couldn't help feeling concerned about what awaited him in old age.

■ Are senior citizens entitled to certain financial and tax protections?

Yes. Life is often difficult for people as they get older and have less income and more health problems. Of course, most senior citizens are eligible for Social Security and Medicare, complicated government programs that we do our best to explain below. In many states senior citizens may also qualify for other benefits, such as

- **protection from rent increases**
- **real estate tax exemptions**
- **financial help with utilities**
- **discounts on pharmacy bills**

Your town or county clerk can tell you if seniors in your area are entitled to protections relating to property ownership. Your state's department on aging should also have information on benefits, as will your local agencies on aging or senior centers. Many benefits may be available only if your income falls below a certain level, but some are available to everyone.

SOCIAL SECURITY

Eligibility

Over the years Gordon had never given much thought to Social Security — although he did notice the amounts taken out of his paycheck every two weeks. Now he wanted to know where that money had gone — how much of it he was entitled to get back, and when he could start collecting.

■ What is Social Security?

What Gordon knows simply as "Social Security" is more formally called Old Age, Survivors and Disability Insurance (OASDI) under Title II of the Social Security Act. It is a national program created by Congress, which pays money to retirees, survivors of deceased workers, and people who have become disabled.

While there are different types of benefits under the program, when most people refer to Social Security they are talking about money paid to older workers or retirees who have made contributions to the program from their earned income. Most employees are required to contribute, though some state and local government workers are exempt.

Social Security can seem like a nightmarish bureaucracy with a complicated morass of regulations and lots of indecipherable terminology. But basically it works like this: while you are working you are required to give a portion of every paycheck to the Social Security Administration, the federal agency that runs the program. When you retire — or if you should become unable to work — the Social Security Administration pays you. Broadly, the system is meant to work like a pension plan. While you work, you put money into the plan; when you retire, you take money out.

Who is eligible to collect Social Security benefits?

You become eligible to collect Social Security benefits based on your history of contributions to the program. You may choose to begin receiving benefits as early as age sixty-two or as late as age seventy. The age at which you begin to receive benefits and the amount of your contributions over your working years will affect the size of your monthly benefit. You may also be eligible to collect benefits if you become disabled (see page 385).

Can a person still work and collect?

Yes. But for workers under age seventy who have chosen to begin receiving benefits, there are limits to the amount of income you can earn in any year without reducing your benefits. (In 1994 it was $8,040 for workers under sixty-five and $10,200 for workers between sixty-five and sixty-nine.) Income earned above these limits will reduce your benefits by one dollar for every two dollars you earn if you are under sixty-five, and by one dollar for every three dollars you earn if you are sixty-five to sixty-nine. After you reach age seventy, earning income does not reduce your benefits.

How Is the Amount of Benefits Calculated?

The level of Social Security you get is based on how much you have paid into the program at the time you begin receiving benefits.

Anyone who has worked for forty "quarters" since 1951 is likely to be covered by the program. You will be considered to have worked four quarters in a calendar year as long as you earned a certain amount in that year. For example, in 1994 each $620 you earned represented a credit for a quarter; thus, if you earned at least $2,480 (4 x $620), you received credit for four quarters. Even if you earned the $2,480 all in one month and didn't earn anything for the rest of the year, you still get the credit. You cannot, however, get credit for more than four quarters per calendar year.

If you reached age sixty-two before 1991, you may qualify for the program even if your "earnings record" calculated by the SSA shows you have less than forty covered quarters.

Early Retirement

One of Gordon's hesitations about retiring was the thought of giving up the salary and standard of living he'd gotten used to working at Tech Security. He still had expenses to think about — kids, car payments, property taxes, the phone bill, the pool man. Gordon wanted to stop working — but he was not in any rush to become poor. Maybe, he wondered, he'd be better off waiting a few years.

■ **What is the difference in benefits if a person retires at age sixty-two instead of age sixty-five?**

Many factors affect the amount of Social Security benefits you receive, but generally, the older you are at retirement, the more you will be paid. At present, if you start receiving benefits at age sixty-two, the monthly payment will always be about 20 percent less than if you waited until age sixty-five. If you retire after age sixty-five, your monthly benefits will be slightly higher for each year that you waited.

Thinking about retirement reminded Gordon of a brush with wealth he had once had. Cecil from shipping had tried to talk Gordon and a few of the other Tech Security fellows into splitting a bunch of lottery tickets. Cecil had found no takers and wound up buying only a single ticket for himself. Gordon had muttered something discouraging about the odds.

A few days later Cecil — now a national celebrity on account of having won the biggest jackpot in state history — announced his retirement at age forty-three and his plans to relocate to Pompano Beach, Florida.

Gordon was still kicking himself.

Now and then he found some consolation in imagining the downside of Cecil's sudden wealth. "Well," Gordon announced one day to a bunch of fellow nonmillionaires in the cafeteria, "I guess he can't get Social Security." The men grunted with a kind of vague satisfaction and went back to eating.

■ **Does early retirement affect a person's ability to collect Social Security?**

No. You can still begin collecting benefits starting at age sixty-two, provided your earnings record shows that you worked at least forty quarters.

Pension Plans and Taxes

Since the day he drew his first paycheck, Gordon had been contributing to Tech Security's pension plan and was counting on collecting that money when he retired.

■ **Can a person draw a pension and still collect Social Security?**

Yes. Social Security is considered to be a basic source of income for workers in their retirement years. The amount of benefits is generally unaffected by other pension benefits. However, some government employees may receive less Social Security, depending on the kind of retirement plan they have.

■ **Is Social Security income taxable?**

Yes. Depending on your other sources of income, you may have to pay federal income tax on up to one-half of your Social Security benefits. You may also have to pay state taxes. If your income is below a set level, however, you will not have to pay taxes on your Social Security. To find out whether you need to pay taxes, you can call the Social Security Administration or the Internal Revenue Service.

Note: While the government can tax your Social Security, that income is shielded from your creditors — the people to whom you owe money.

Benefits for Unemployed Spouses

Gordon's wife Grace never had a paying job — although she frequently reminded him that cooking, cleaning, and raising four kids had not been any day at the beach. One night when they were discussing Gordon's plans for retiring and collecting Social Security benefits, Grace — a diminutive woman who seldom raised her voice — suddenly demanded, "Hey, Mr. Big Deal Entitlement Receiver, what about *my* Social Security benefits?"

■ **Are unemployed spouses able to collect Social Security benefits?**

Yes. Even a spouse who never worked is entitled to Social Security. If both of you are over sixty-five when your benefits begin, your spouse may be entitled to receive an additional amount equal to 50 percent of your benefit. Thus, if you get $100, your spouse gets an additional $50, for a total of $150 between the two of you. However, the amount of your spouse's benefit may be less if you or your spouse receives a federal, state, or local government pension.

Your spouse may begin receiving payments as early as age sixty-two, provided you are also receiving benefits at that time. If you have reached age sixty-five and are receiving benefits, but your spouse is between ages sixty-two and sixty-five, your spouse's benefits will be something less than 50 percent of yours, reflecting the discount applicable to the early commencement (before age sixty-five) of your spouse's benefits.

■ **What happens if both spouses worked?**

Each spouse either collects his or her own benefits *or* his or her share of the other spouse's benefits, depending on which is higher.

How to Verify Your Earnings Record

It is a good idea to review your earnings record every few years to make sure it is accurate.

You can do so by filing Form SSA-7004 with one of the three national Social Security offices. The form can be obtained by calling Social Security at 800-772-1213, or your local Social Security district office, and you can return it in the mail. It usually takes six to eight weeks to get a response, and if you think it's in error, you can appeal through your local Social Security office.

You are "taxed" only on your earnings up to a set amount each year (it was $60,600 in 1994). Anything you earn in excess of that maximum will not increase your benefits. Your earnings record will reflect only the amount you have earned up to the maximum of each year.

Benefits for Children

Of Gordon and Grace's four kids, three were out of the house, but the youngest, Bradley, age sixteen, was still in high school. Gordon often despaired of his grades, his taste in music, and his tattoos. But he loved him and was preoccupied with ensuring he would be as financially secure as possible.

■ **When are children entitled to collect Social Security benefits?**

A child can receive Social Security benefits after a retired parent begins receiving them *if* the child is unmarried. These benefits are generally available to children under eighteen (nineteen if still in high school) and children of any age with severe disabilities, so long as they were disabled before reaching age twenty-two. The amount of a child's benefit is usually 50 percent of your benefit rate, but since there is a limit on the total amount of benefits one family can collect, the amount per child may be less. A child is also eligible to receive benefits if the parent dies or becomes disabled.

Survivors' Benefits

Although Gordon expected (and hoped) to live to an exceedingly ripe old age, he wanted to make sure Grace and the kids would be provided for if anything happens to him. He had life insurance, of course, but he wondered if his family would be entitled to Social Security if he died.

■ **What happens to the benefits if a person dies?**

Upon your death, and even if you were not receiving benefits at the time of your death, each member of your family who meets certain requirements will be entitled to survivor's benefits. Those eligible include

- **a spouse who has reached age sixty**
- **a spouse who is caring for a child who is under age sixteen or who became disabled before reaching age twenty-two**
- **a disabled spouse who has reached age fifty and is unable to perform any substantial, gainful activity**
- **a disabled child who became disabled before reaching age twenty-two**
- **an unmarried dependent child under age eighteen (or under age nineteen if a full-time student in a high school program)**
- **parents of the deceased worker who have reached age sixty-two if the worker was paying at least half of the parents' support**

There is a limit to how much one family can collect; it varies, depending on the size of the family.

Disability Benefits

Gordon was sixty-two and in excellent health, but his old friend and bowling partner Howard recently stopped working at age sixty for health reasons.

Can someone younger than sixty-two collect Social Security benefits?

Yes. People sixty-two and older can collect **retirement** benefits, but if health reasons cause you to stop working at any time before your sixty-fifth birthday, you may be eligible for **Social Security Disability Insurance Benefits** (SSDIB). To collect these benefits you will need to prove two things:

- **that you meet the Social Security standard for disability**
- **that you are "insured" because you have worked the required number of quarters for a person your age and contributed to Social Security**

To determine if your disability qualifies you for Social Security Disability benefits, usually a state agency that handles health issues (often called Disability Determination Services, or DDS) must find that you are suffering from a physical or mental impairment that meets the Social Security Administration's criteria. First, the DDS determines if your impairment prevents you from participating in "any substantial gainful activity." Your condition must have lasted a full year or be expected to last a full year or be expected to result in your death within a year.

You will be found "not disabled" if you are working and earning over $500 per month or if your impairment is found "not severe." You may also be found not disabled if you still have the ability to work — even if it's not at the same job.

If the government rules that you are disabled, benefits can start as early as five months after you become disabled. (You may be entitled to retroactive benefits for up to one year, depending on how much time elapses between the onset of your disability and when you file an application.) The typical benefit averages between $641 and $1,092 a month.

If you want to appeal a denial of benefits, you should do so promptly, since you usually have only sixty days to appeal. An explanation of how to appeal will be provided with your denial notice, or you can visit any Social Security office.

In Case of Divorce

Gordon's older sister Mary, a retired harness racing jockey, had married a lawyer named Dean. To the surprise of no one (least of all Gordon, who had always had this thing about lawyers) Dean had taken up with one his clients, a woman just slightly too old to be his daughter. Mary filed for divorce and got a settlement that Gordon regarded as scandalously puny. He frequently irritated his sister with suggestions that she had overlooked sources of cash that rightly belonged to her. "You're probably not getting any of his Social Security, are you?" Gordon asked her once.

Mary barely looked up from her copy of the *Sporting News.* She smiled quietly to herself.

What to Do If You Are Denied Benefits

If you are not satisfied with your benefits, you have sixty days to submit a written request for a reconsideration. The request should be sent to your local Social Security district office (which should be listed in your local phone book) and should state the reasons why you disagree with the determination. Depending on the nature of the issue, either a case review, a formal conference, or a hearing may follow.

If you fail to appeal a determination within sixty days, your options are limited unless you can show you had a good reason for filing late. If you can't, you may be able to file a new application and seek retroactive collection of benefits. You can also try to reopen the claim by filing a petition with a judge who is specially designated to hear Social Security appeals.

It's not necessary to have a lawyer when making an appeal. However, there are lawyers available who handle this type of case, and if you don't have much money, you may be able to get assistance from a legal services organization that won't charge you anything. (For more, see the box on page 404 and Chapter 30, FINDING AND USING A LAWYER.)

■ **Is a person entitled to a share of an ex-spouse's Social Security benefits?**

Yes. A former spouse age sixty-two or older who is not remarried can receive Social Security benefits if the marriage lasted more than ten years. Former spouses decide on their own when to start receiving benefits after reaching age sixty-two, so long as the divorce occurred more than two years before the benefits begin. When the worker spouse retires, dies, or becomes disabled, a former spouse can often receive monthly benefits equal to 50 percent of what the worker spouse receives. Even if you both worked, you are still eligible to collect your share of your ex-spouse's benefits.

Letting Someone Else Manage the Money

Gordon's father, Carl, was in his mid-eighties and drawing Social Security benefits. He had been a precision welder (and briefly a semi-pro hockey player) before retiring and moving in with his son's family. Gordon paid all the household bills, and each month his dad laboriously itemized what he reckoned his share was and left the money in cash on the kitchen table. Gordon thought it might make more sense to have the Social Security check made out directly to him.

His father, however, was a proud man and not someone to be trifled with on the subject of money. So Gordon handled the situation the way he dealt with most family problems — by fretting quietly.

■ **Can a person be designated to receive a family member's Social Security benefits?**

Yes. You may ask the Social Security Administration to make you a "representative payee." The appointment will be granted if your family member approves or if you can show that your relative is legally incompetent (see page 322) or mentally or physically incapable of managing his or her benefits.

While any friend or "custodial institution," such as a nursing home, can be designated as "representative payee," the Social Security Administration prefers to appoint relatives who have a "strong concern" for the beneficiary. The representative payee may pay all your bills with the Social Security funds, and if there is any left over, it must be saved for you. It does not belong to the representative payee.

Supplemental Security Income

Carl had been frugal during his working years and had saved enough money (along with his pension and Social Security) to live on. His friend Burt had not been so lucky. Burt, who lost his sight in his late sixties, had worked for a company that went broke, leaving him with no pension to fall back on. "Without my Supplemental Security check," he once said to Carl, "I don't know how I'd make it."

■ What is Supplemental Security Income?

Supplemental Security Income (SSI) is a federal welfare program for adults and children with disabilities and people age sixty-five and over with low income and few financial resources (like bank accounts, stocks, or bonds). You don't have to qualify for Social Security benefits in order to get SSI, and it is possible to get both Social Security and SSI. However, if you're applying based on a disability, you must meet the same standard for disability as with regular Social Security benefits (see page 385).

People who qualify for SSI receive a check each month, and the amount will vary depending on the recipient's state of residence and level of income. (In New York, a person living at home could get as much as $532 a month in 1994.) If you qualify for SSI, you are also automatically entitled to health care coverage under the Medicaid program (see page 398).

You usually can apply for SSI and Medicaid by completing forms provided by your local welfare office, department of social services, or Social Security Administration office. If the application is approved, you will be paid benefits based on the date you filed the application. If your application is not approved, you can appeal. The procedure is similar to appealing for more Social Security benefits (see the box opposite).

PENSIONS AND RETIREMENT PLANS

It was Gordon and Grace's turn to host the monthly dinner party of On Pins and Needles, their bowling team, which had been rolling strikes together for thirty years. Grace was anxiously icing the cake — in the shape of a bowling pin — when Donna walked into the kitchen.

"Grace, just relax. It's only a cake," Donna said.

"No, it's not that," said Grace. "Gordon's retirement is coming up sooner than I expected. The time just flies by. I remember packing his lunch for his first day at Tech Security. It seems like it was last week. He had a bologna sandwich, macaroni salad, and oatmeal cookies. Homemade. Yeah, those were the days."

The two women laughed.

"But, I have to admit, Donna, I'm worried about money. How will we manage without Gordon's weekly paycheck?"

Donna looked concerned. "But what about his pension? I thought Tech Security really took care of its people."

■ What is a pension plan?

A pension plan is an employer's program for providing retirement income to eligible employees. Employers are not required to provide a pension plan, but if they do, the plan must meet certain requirements. Pension plans offered by private (nongovernment) employers are governed by the Employee Retirement Income Security Act of 1974 (ERISA) and by the Internal Revenue Code. ERISA covers all employer-sponsored pension plans except when the employer is a church or the federal, state, or local government. Plans sponsored by these entities are regulated by the Internal Revenue Code. Plans sponsored by state and local government are also subject to state law.

Different Types of Pension Plans

Generally, there are two basic types of pension plans: **defined benefit plans** and **defined contribution plans.**

In a **defined benefit plan,** the plan specifies how much in benefits the plan will pay out to a retiree. The defined benefit usually is calculated using a formula based on a percentage of your final compensation multiplied by the number of years you work for your employer. With this type of plan, you should be able to estimate from the start of your employment what your ultimate pension benefit will be.

Your employer is required to fund a defined benefit plan adequately so it will provide the promised benefits when you and other employees retire. You do not have any input into how the money in the defined benefit plan is invested.

In a **defined contribution plan** (also referred to as an individual account plan), the employer pays a specified amount of money each year, which is then divided among the individual accounts of each participating employee. Your retirement benefit is the balance of your individual account when you retire.

The amount the employer puts in varies, depending on the type of defined contribution plan. It can be

- **based on the discretion of your employer**
- **a fixed dollar amount**
- **a percentage of your compensation**

There are a wide variety of defined contribution plans, including

- **profit-sharing plans, in which the employer contributes a portion of each year's profit to the plan**
- **employee stock ownership plans (ESOPs), in which the employer's contribution is made in the form of company stock**
- **401(k) plans, in which each employee may elect to defer a portion of his or her income and place the money in an individual pension account (in some 401(k) plans, the employer also contributes to the employee's individual account)**

Some defined contribution plans allow you to choose how your money is invested. Some do not. The value of your individual account at retirement will depend on the amount of annual contributions, plus investment gains or losses.

Each plan has its own rules regarding employee eligibility to participate and the formula used for determining benefits. According to federal law, the eligibility rules must allow for participation by a broad group of workers, and the benefits formula cannot discriminate in favor of highly compensated employees.

If you work for a private employer that offers a retirement plan, you must be provided with a summary of the plan that describes, in clear, nonlegal terms, the substantive provisions of the plan. Among other things, the summary should outline

- **who's eligible to participate**
- **how benefits are determined**
- **the age at which you can start receiving benefits**
- **who administers the plan**
- **claims procedures**

Vesting

Gordon came up and rubbed Grace's shoulders. "Don't worry, honey," he said. "I met with our head of human resources, and she said I'm fully vested in the pension plan."

"What does a vest have to do with it?" asked Grace.

What does vesting mean?

Often the money your employer pays into a retirement plan may not automatically be yours if you have not yet worked for the company for a specified number of years. To be "fully vested" means that you have a nonforfeitable right to your entire pension benefit, even though payment of the benefit may not be made until some later date. (Any of your own contributions to your plan, such as through 401(k) deductions from your salary, are automatically yours.)

Each plan varies, but it often takes between five and seven years of service with your employer to become fully vested. If you leave the company or retire after becoming fully vested, your entire pension benefit is still yours. If you leave before becoming fully vested, you lose the unvested portion.

■ If a person quits a job before reaching retirement age, is the pension lost?

Not if you are vested. However, payment may be delayed until you reach retirement age. Also, you usually can be forced to withdraw your pension benefit money if you quit and your benefit is $3,500 or less.

Early Withdrawals

Bart and Allegra had sold their house and were buying a new one. Unfortunately, they had to close on the new house before getting the money for the old one. Bart hated to do it, but he broke down and asked his father for a bridge loan, to cover the gap between the two sales.

Gordon wanted to help, but he and Grace simply didn't have the cash on hand to make even a short-term loan. Grace wondered if they could borrow the money temporarily from Gordon's pension fund.

"After all, we need the money only for three weeks," she said.

■ Is it possible to borrow or withdraw pension money before retirement?

If you participate in a **defined benefit plan** (see the box opposite), it is unlikely that you can gain access to your pension money before retirement. If you are in a **defined contribution plan,** such as a profit-sharing, 401(k), or stock bonus plan, you may be able to

- **take a loan from the plan**
- **make a regular withdrawal, if the plan permits**
- **make a "hardship withdrawal"**

How Pension Payments Are Made When You Are Married

If you are married at the time you start receiving your pension benefits, ERISA requires that they automatically be paid in the form of a **joint and survivor annuity** unless you and your spouse sign a statement electing a different form of payment. That's a rule developed to protect nonworking spouses from losing all pension income after a retiree's death.

With a joint and survivor annuity, you (the participant in the pension plan) get a check every month. After your death, your spouse (the nonparticipant) continues to get a monthly check equal to one-half the benefit for the rest of his or her life.

Alternatively, you can elect to receive a lump-sum payment or a **single life annuity** with which you get a monthly check from the time you retire until you die. The monthly payment of a joint and survivor annuity is less than the monthly payment of a single life annuity. This is because the same pension benefit must be divided over two lifetimes instead of only one. The amount of the reduction will vary depending on your age and your spouse's age.

When both you and your spouse work, you each are entitled to share in the other's pension.

(See also page 186, on your right to a share of your spouse's pension when you divorce.)

A "hardship withdrawal" is limited to situations in which you have an immediate and heavy financial need. A plan may permit a hardship withdrawal for medical expenses, purchase of a principal residence, or tuition for dependents.

You also may be able to receive pension payments before normal retirement age through early retirement, disability retirement, or by taking a series of equal periodic payments based on your life expectancy.

Is there a penalty for early withdrawal?
Yes. If you take either a hardship or a regular withdrawal, you will have to pay federal income taxes. You may also have to pay state and local income tax. In addition, if you are under age fifty-nine and a half, there is an additional 10 percent federal tax on the amount of the withdrawal. There is no penalty for a loan.

Mismanaged Funds and Other Improprieties

Grace wasn't sure whether she should mention it, but she had read in the newspaper that Tech Security's head accountant was being investigated by the federal government for embezzlement. He had fled the country, and there was speculation that he had stolen at least $1 million. In fact, according to the story, the whole company could go under.

Is pension fund money protected?
Yes, in several ways. The funds must be held separately from any other company accounts and may not be used for an employer's business purposes. The funds are managed by a **fiduciary,** a person, committee, or company with a legal duty to act prudently and for the sole benefit of the fund. The fiduciary usually has the authority to invest the

CASE IN POINT

A Grand Pension Scam

Cheating workers out of their hard-earned pensions isn't a very nice thing to do. It's also not a very legal thing to do. But that's exactly what the Continental Can Company was accused of in a series of class action lawsuits initiated in 1981 on behalf of some 3,900 steelworkers.

What the workers alleged was that the company violated the Employee Retirement Income Security Act by intentionally calculating when to lay off workers to keep them from qualifying to receive their pensions. Using these calculations, it then laid off more than 3,900 people.

Suits were filed in three courts on behalf of workers at forty-five Continental Can plants across the nation. The litigation dragged on for over a decade, with the company paying an estimated $6 million to expert witnesses. One of the culminating events was a trial before federal district court judge H. Lee Sarokin in 1989 in Newark, New Jersey. The question before Sarokin was whether or not the company would have laid off some of the workers anyway, even without the illegal plan.

Sarokin's ruling in favor of the plaintiffs did not mince words: "For a corporation of this magnitude to engage in a complex, secret, and deliberate scheme to deny its workers bargained-for pension benefits raises questions of corporate morality, ethics, and decency which far transcend the legal issues posed by this matter."

Sarokin appointed a law school professor to help forge a settlement. In December 1990, after a decade of stonewalling, the company finally offered to pay $415 million. That was much more than lawyers for the workers had expected, especially since one of Continental's lawyers had previously asserted that the workers' losses probably didn't even top $20 million.

The offer was accepted.

plan's assets just like any other portfolio of assets. However, under ERISA a fiduciary must diversify the plan's investments and must avoid high-risk investments. If the fund is mismanaged or embezzled, you and any other employees can sue the fiduciary. If you win, the award will be paid to the pension plan, not to you.

Since pension funds are held separately from an employer's assets, such funds are protected if the employer enters bankruptcy. In addition, the federal Pension Benefit Guaranty Corporation (PBGC) guarantees payment of vested retirement benefits under most defined benefit plans in certain situations, such as a company's bankruptcy. (Defined contribution plans do not get this protection.) However, benefits above a set level are not insured, so you could lose part of your pension, particularly if you had a high salary or worked for the company for many years.

For any kind of plan, you are supposed to receive an annual report summarizing the status of the plan. While interpreting these reports can be a challenge, some warning signs of potential problems include a sudden huge loss in investment earnings or an employer's failure to make any contributions to the plan.

If you are concerned about the security of your pension, you may wish to contact a lawyer or the Department of Labor at 202-219-8776 (see page 404 for additional numbers). ERISA also prohibits an employer from discharging an employee for the purpose of preventing the employee from receiving a pension. If this happens to you, you may file suit in federal court. You will have to prove that interference with your pension rights was a motivating factor for the discharge. Your potential recovery includes lost wages and benefits, plus attorneys' fees.

To Register a Complaint about Your Retirement Benefits

Federal law (ERISA) usually requires that you first file a claim for benefits according to the procedure described in the summary of your pension plan. If your claim is denied, the plan will outline how to appeal. If you have followed all the specified procedures and are still unhappy, you may then sue in federal or state court. You should consult a lawyer to help you do that.

Note: some courts have limited the evidence and arguments you can present to those you raised during the administrative claims process. Therefore, you may also want to consult a lawyer to help ensure that you are informed of all the arguments you should make during that process. (See Chapter 30, FINDING AND USING A LAWYER.)

Health Benefits

Gordon's retirement party was a gala event. The entire family attended, and even his normally scruffy grandchildren looked presentable. Tech Security presented him with a gold-plated engraved bolt in addition to the traditional retirement watch.

The morning after the party, Gordon sat at the kitchen table reviewing the packet of material describing his pension plan.

"This is strange," he said to Grace.

"What?" Grace teased. "That you don't have a hangover after last night's party?"

"There's no mention here of the health insurance benefits." He felt himself getting angry. "If they think they are cheating me out of that, well, they don't know who they're dealing with."

"Gordon dear, you're sputtering."

■ Is health insurance part of a pension plan?

No. Federal law does not require an employer to offer postretirement health benefits. Health benefits (for employees and retirees) are generally provided by health plans that are separate from pension plans. If you work for a private employer (not the government), a promise to keep you on the health plan after retirement is probably unenforceable unless it's stated in the official document outlining your company's health plan. If your employer offers a retiree health insurance program, you should consult the written description of the plan to see whether it specifies that you will receive coverage for only a limited period of time or whether the employer has reserved the right to change or terminate the coverage after your retirement.

401(k) Plans

Gordon's retirement got Beatrice to thinking about planning ahead. She had always felt too young to worry about retirement and too short of cash to try to sock money away. But since Vinny and Alena were teenagers, it seemed pretty obvious to Bea that she wasn't getting any younger. She decided to set up a retirement program for herself and the employees in her consulting business. Her accountant recommended a 401(k).

■ What is a 401(k) plan?

A 401(k) plan is a defined contribution retirement plan set up by an employer for its employees. It allows eligible employees to have a portion of their compensation contributed directly to the plan instead of being paid to them in their paychecks. The employer may match all or part of the employees' contributions. The amount deposited in the plan is not taxed for federal or state income tax purposes (except in Pennsylvania, where the contribution is subject to state income tax) until it is later withdrawn from the plan. The investment earnings on the savings are not taxed either until you withdraw from the plan.

Each plan has its own guidelines about when you can withdraw. The general rule is that you begin taking money out when you retire. The money is also paid out if you die and, in some plans, if you become disabled.

You may defer paying tax on certain withdrawals from a 401(k) plan if you roll over (transfer) the money directly to an IRA or another qualified pension plan. This is what you would do, for example, if you change jobs or get laid off. Otherwise, you generally pay federal income tax on any withdrawal from a 401(k) plan, unless your withdrawal is made as a loan (which is taxed only if you fail to repay it). If you make a withdrawal before reaching age fifty-nine and a half, you will have to pay a 10 percent federal penalty tax.

Can a person contribute to an IRA for a spouse who doesn't work?

Yes, within limits. You can open a separate IRA for your spouse if he or she is under age seventy and a half and if you file a joint federal income tax return. The total *combined* contribution you can make each year to your IRA and your spouse's IRA is $2,250, or your entire taxable income for the year, whichever is less. You can divide the contribution between the two IRAs any way you want, so long as you don't contribute more than $2,000 to either one.

IRAs

After Gordon's retirement party, Bradley and his companion Peter realized they had better start thinking about their retirement. It was still a long way off, but neither of them had pension plans.

"How can we save for the future?" Brad wondered. "Whenever we have extra money in the bank, we manage to spend it. We need to be protected from ourselves."

■ What is an IRA?

An IRA (individual retirement account) is a type of account that earns investment income and allows you to defer paying tax on that income. Anyone who earns money can contribute annually to an IRA account, and many people qualify to deduct the contribution from their income taxes. Even if your company has a pension plan, you can still make an IRA contribution, but it won't be tax deductible.

Most banks, insurance companies, mutual fund companies, brokerage houses, and other financial institutions offer IRAs. Individuals can contribute $2,000 or 100 percent of their taxable compensation (whichever is less) each year to an IRA. Compensation includes wages, salaries, tips, commissions, fees, bonuses, taxable alimony, and spousal maintenance payments. If your taxable income is $1,800, you can put all of it into an IRA; if it is $18,000, you can invest only $2,000 in the IRA.

What are the rules about IRA withdrawals?

You are allowed to withdraw money from your IRA at any time. However, if you do so before turning age fifty-nine and a half, you have to pay a 10 percent federal penalty tax. You will also have to pay income tax if your contributions were tax deductible. If you have paid income tax on the money you contribute to the IRA, then the only tax you will have to pay on withdrawal is on the amount of investment income earned. That tax must be paid whenever you make a withdrawal, no matter what your age. You must begin to receive payments from your IRA by April 1 of the year after the year in which you reach age seventy and a half. If you choose not to receive payments then, you will be assessed a penalty tax equal to 50 percent of your minimum withdrawal amount.

Keogh Plans

Bradley saw how secure his father's pension made his parents feel, and he wanted a pension too. He knew that insecurity was the trade-off for the freedom of being self-employed as a private detective. Still, he didn't want to be punished in old age for that freedom.

As luck would have it, Brad had a client who was the director of human resources for a large company. Clyde had been receiving threatening blackmail letters, and he wanted Brad to track down the perpetrator. The two men had become friendly during the course of the case and had traded confidences. Clyde's dream was to own his own business, and Brad's fantasy was for a pension.

"That's no fantasy," Clyde told him. "Just set up a Keogh plan."

What is a Keogh plan?

A Keogh plan (sometimes called an "HR 10" plan) is a retirement plan that covers one or more self-employed individuals. A self-employed individual is a person who declares income from self-employment for federal income tax purposes. This income is known as "earned income." You can be an employee of one business and also have earned income from a self-employed business.

Some Keogh plans cover self-employed individuals who are considered "owner-employees." An "owner-employee" is either

- **the sole owner of an unincorporated business or**
- **a partner in a business who owns more than 10 percent of the partnership**

Any Keogh plan that covers owner-employees must also cover nonowner-employees. And it must be democratic. The plan cannot provide the owner with contributions or benefits that are more favorable than those provided for the employees. The amount you can contribute varies, depending on how the plan is set up. The withdrawal rules and penalties are the same as for an IRA.

SEPs

Peter scheduled a meeting to discuss retirement planning with the head of employee benefits at his company. She suggested he establish a SEP. As he drove home, his mind was whirling with letters — SEP, IRA. He started playing with the letters: spare, spear, aspire, pairs, sepia. He wondered how many words could he make?

What is a SEP?

SEP stands for "simplified employee pension." It is a special kind of pension plan that your employer can provide or that can be established by a self-employed person. With a SEP, your employer contributes money directly into an IRA that you establish yourself or that your employer helps you establish. You can contribute more to a SEP than to a regular IRA. The annual maximum is $30,000 or 15 percent of your earnings, whichever is lower. The withdrawal rules are the same as for an IRA.

MEDICARE

One icy winter day, Carl insisted on helping Bartholomew and Bradley shovel the driveway. The boys kept warning their grandfather to take it easy, but the old man persisted, heaving huge mounds of snow over the rosebushes with alarming vigor. Finally, though, as he was spreading salt on the front steps he lost his footing and fell hard on his right hip. He knew — even before he hit the pavement — that he would have to have surgery for an artificial joint to replace his shattered old bones. As he lay on the frozen ground, with his grandsons fussing anxiously around him, the one G-rated word the boys could make out through the tapestry of obscenities issuing from the old man was "Medicare."

What is Medicare?

Medicare is a national health insurance program for seniors and people with disabilities, regardless of income. Anyone over sixty-five who is eligible for Social Security or Railroad Retirement Benefits — a program similar to Social Security for railroad employees, their spouses, and survivors — is automatically eligible. People with disabilities who have received Social Security Disability Income for at least twenty-four months and some people who are receiving regular dialysis or have received a kidney transplant because of kidney failure are also automatically eligible. U.S. citizens are automatically eligible as are permanent legal residents who have been continuously residing in the United States for at least five years, though they must file an application.

The Medicare program is administered by private health insurance companies who contract with the federal government to process claims.

1994 Medicare Part A Hospitalization Benefits

	You Pay	Medicare Pays
Up to 60 days:	$696 deductible and nothing per day	everything else
61 to 90 days:	$174 per day	everything else
60 additional days:	$348 per "lifetime reserve day"	everything else

The Medicare program is divided into two sections. **Part A** is hospital insurance that covers hospital care as well as skilled nursing facility, hospice, and home health care. **Part B** is medical insurance that covers physicians' fees, therapy services, ambulance services, laboratory tests, supplies, and durable medical equipment, such as a wheelchair.

Part A Benefits

Anyone eligible for Social Security or Railroad Retirement Benefits is eligible for Medicare Part A benefits free of charge. Others may be eligible for Medicare if they pay a monthly premium. (In 1994 it ranged between $184 and $245 per month.)

Part A benefits include

Hospital Benefits

Entitle you to ninety days of in-hospital care for each "benefit period." A benefit period begins when you enter the hospital and ends after you have been out of the hospital (or skilled nursing facility) for at least sixty continuous days. There is a deductible for each benefit period ($696 in 1994). In addition, you have to pay a "co-insurance amount" for days 61 through 90 ($174 per day in 1994). After you have exhausted your ninety days of coverage, Medicare will pay for an additional sixty days of care in your lifetime. You will have to pay a portion during these "reserve" days ($348 per day in 1994).

For additional hospital coverage, you can purchase a "Medigap" policy (see page 397).

• Skilled Nursing Facility Benefits
Entitle you to up to 100 days of care in a Medicare-certified skilled nursing facility (SNF) per benefit period, provided you were hospitalized for at least three days during the thirty days prior to admission in the SNF and that you need and receive daily skilled services. Medicare defines "daily" as seven days a week of skilled nursing and five days a week of skilled therapy. Skilled nursing and therapy services include evaluation and management as well as observation and assessment of a patient's condition. Medicare pays for the first twenty days in full. For days 21 through 100, you pay a portion ($87 per day in 1994).

• Home Health Benefits
Medicare covers up to thirty-five hours a week of home health aide and skilled nursing services if you are homebound and require skilled services on an *intermittent* basis. Skilled nursing services include the administration of medication, tube feedings, catheter changes, and wound care. Intermittent usually means less than five days per week, but some people who receive home health care services up to seven days a week will be covered if the services are needed only for a finite and predictable amount of time.

You can also qualify for up to thirty-five hours per week of home health aide services if you are homebound and need skilled physical, speech, or occupational therapy.

You must receive any of these services from a Medicare-certified Home Health Agency (CHHA) in order to be covered. Medicare home health coverage is available indefinitely so long as you remain homebound and continue to require skilled nursing services on an intermittent basis or skilled therapy services.

There is no prior hospitalization requirement, and the benefit covers individuals with chronic illnesses as well as those who are acutely ill. The benefit is available at no cost to you, and there is no deductible or co-insurance required.

• Hospice Benefits
Available to terminally ill patients. Medicare will cover 95 percent of the cost of hospice care, and you will have to pay the remaining 5 percent. Once you elect Medicare hospice benefits, you become ineligible to receive benefits for hospital care related to your terminal illness.

• Part B Benefits
Medicare Part B covers most reasonable and necessary medical services. You can receive this coverage once you turn sixty-five, but you must pay a monthly premium ($41.40 in 1994). If you wait to enroll in Part B until you are older than sixty-five, your monthly premium may be higher, since Medicare imposes a 10 percent premium penalty for every year you delay enrollment. However, if you are working and are covered under your employer's group health plan, you may delay enrolling without a penalty until seven months after your retirement.

Medicare sets "approved charges" for all the medical services it covers. A very important thing to know is that Medicare *does not* cover many common health expenses, such as prescription drugs, routine checkups, vision and hearing care, custodial care, and dental care. It also does not cover experimental procedures. Medicare does cover biannual mammograms and triannual pap smears as well as flu vaccines.

With Part B you must pay an annual deductible ($100 in 1994), and after that Medicare generally will pay 80 percent of its approved charge for your medical care. Unfortunately, many health care providers charge substantially more than Medicare's approved charge for their services, and you must pay for any charges that are above the approved Medicare rate, which can get expensive. For example, there is no limit on what ambulance companies and durable medical equipment suppliers may charge you. The Medicare-approved portion may represent only a small part of your bill.

Some health care providers, however, "take assignment," which means that they agree to accept Medicare's approved charge as payment in full. Medicare pays 80 percent of the approved charge, and you pay the remaining 20 percent. Your local Medicare carrier has a directory that lists all doctors and suppliers in your area who always take assignment. If you want to limit the amount you pay for medical expenses, it is a good idea to ob-

If Your Medicare Claim Is Denied

For Part A (hospital) coverage, the hospital or Medicare review board must inform you in writing if your stay will not (or will no longer) be covered by Medicare. The denial notice you receive will tell you how to have the denial reconsidered. Many denials are overturned.

If your claim is reconsidered but you are still unhappy, you can appeal again. A large number of appeals are successful.

If your Part B claim is denied, you will receive an Explanation of Medicare Benefits. You then have six months to ask for the denial to be overturned. If you are rejected again, you have six months to request a hearing through your local Medicare carrier. If your claim is again denied, you have sixty days to request a hearing before an administrative law judge. Many Part B appeals are successful.

It's not necessary to have a lawyer, but if the issue is especially complex it may be helpful. For more information about Medicare, you can call the Medicare hotline at 800-638-6833. (See also "Legal Services for Older People," page 404.)

tain a copy of this directory and use it when choosing your health care providers.

Even when doctors don't take assignment federal law limits the amount that they may charge Medicare patients (other health care providers, such as ambulance companies, are not covered by this limit). The limit is 15 percent above Medicare's approved charge. Some states, including Massachusetts, Minnesota, Rhode Island, Pennsylvania, Ohio, Connecticut, Vermont, and New York, have stricter limits.

Dealing with Doctors and Hospitals

When Carl broke his hip, he saw a number of doctors about it — including an extremely well regarded orthopedist who promised him that a total hip replacement these days was no more involved than having a hangnail trimmed. The doctor assured Carl he'd be back on his feet in a few days and running the forty-yard dash again within weeks. He also described his fee for the operation as "frankly, a lot."

"You're not like these poor saps who have to count on Medicare are you, old-timer?" the doctor asked with an indulgent smile. Carl gulped.

■ Are all doctors required to accept Medicare patients?

No. Doctors are not required either to treat Medicare patients or to take assignment (accept the fees established by Medicare). But federal law prohibits doctors from charging Medicare patients more than 15 percent above the Medicare-approved charge. Some states have even stricter limits.

Even if your doctor charges more than the Medicare-approved charge, he or she must still submit a claim to Medicare on your behalf (and cannot charge you for this service). Medicare will pay you 80 percent of its approved charge, and you will be responsible for the rest of the doctor's bill up to the applicable federal or state limit.

■ Can hospitals turn away Medicare patients?

Hospitals cannot refuse patients on the grounds that their health coverage is through Part A of Medicare. Remember, though, not all hospital stays or services are covered by Medicare. It is the hospital's responsibility to inform you if something is not covered.

■ Is a person who has health insurance through an employer also eligible for Medicare?

Yes. Medicare is the primary payer if your employer has fewer than twenty employees. It's the secondary payer if your employer has twenty or more employees and provides group health insurance. In fact, because it's free, you should sign up for Part A once you are eligible, whether or not you have other insurance.

However, it may not be cost-effective to sign up for Part B if you already are covered under an employer group health plan. That's because you will have to pay Medicare's Part B monthly premium and annual deductible, and your returns will be limited. For example, if your ambulance company charges $150 and your employer plan approves $100 and pays $80 (80 percent of the approved charge), the most Medicare will pay is $20.

MEDIGAP

Carl's health insurance from the welding company he worked for — along with Medicare — paid the bills for his broken hip. But when his friend Burt was in the hospital following the most recent of several heart attacks, Carl worried that his friend wouldn't be able to afford the care. Carl was a little mystified when his friend announced, "Don't worry about me. I've got Medicare *and* Medigap."

What is Medigap?

Medigap is insurance that supplements the basic coverage provided under Medicare and pays for health care costs that Medicare does not pay for — such as deductibles and co-insurance. There are ten variations of Medigap plans available through private insurance companies. The basic benefits offered under all plans include

- **hospital co-insurance**
- **full coverage for 365 additional hospital days (to be used after exhaustion of Medicare hospital reserve days)**
- **20 percent co-payment for physician and other Part B services**
- **three pints of blood**

There are a number of additional benefits available depending upon the plan you select. These benefits include

- **coverage of the Medicare hospital deductible**
- **skilled nursing facility daily co-insurance**
- **coverage of the Part B $100 deductible**
- **80 percent of emergency medical costs outside the U.S. during the first two months of a trip**
- **payment to cover the difference when a doctor's fees are over the Medicare-approved charge**
- **at-home custodial care in addition to and in conjunction with Medicare-approved home care**
- **some prescription drug coverage**
- **some preventive medical care coverage**

There are many services a Medigap plan will not cover. These include

- **custodial care — such as feeding, bathing, and grooming — either at home or in a nursing home**
- **long-term skilled care in a nursing home**
- **unlimited prescription drugs**
- **vision care**
- **dental care**
- **private nurses**

If Medicare does not cover your medical care because it is unreasonable and unnecessary or experimental, Medigap will not cover it either.

If you can afford it, and you do not have employer retiree insurance or other insurance to supplement Medicare, Medigap is a good option. If, however, you retire but retain health insurance coverage from your employer, you may be covered for most services. The combination of Medicare and retiree insurance might be more complete than what you would receive through a Medigap policy.

It may be wise to stay in your employer's health plan after retirement, if that is an option, since any new insurance plans (including Medigap) may exclude preexisting health problems for up to six months. If you do opt to enroll in a Medigap plan, it's usually best to do so during the six months following your enrollment in Medicare Part B. During that period, insurance companies must let you sign up for the plan of your choice, without regard to your health or age.

Once you select a Medigap policy, you have thirty days to review the plan and cancel it without penalty. You also are allowed to change or cancel your policy once a year, although in most states your insurer can reject your application for more comprehensive coverage. However, if you wish to downgrade your policy, you may do so.

MEDICAID

Gordon also worried about the cost of just being old. Mostly he was afraid of running through his pension and government benefits and not having enough money to cover his medical expenses. His father, Carl, kidded him, "Don't worry about it, Junior. If you make it to my age and go broke, you'll still have Medicaid."

What is Medicaid?

Medicaid (formally known as Title XIX of the Social Security Act) covers some health care costs for certain people with low income and few assets. For people over sixty-five or who are disabled, qualification for the program is based on a review of their income and assets.

Every state Medicaid program *must* cover basic medically necessary supplies and services, including

- **physician and clinic services**
- **inpatient and outpatient hospital services**
- **lab tests and x-rays**
- **nursing home care and limited home health services for people who medically qualify for nursing home care**
- **family planning services and supplies**
- **nurse-midwife services**
- **rural health clinic services**
- **prenatal care**

In addition, states *may* provide additional services, including

- **expanded home health services**
- **prescription drugs, dentures, eyeglasses, prosthetic devices**
- **dental services**
- **hospice care**
- **home and community-based care for functionally disabled elderly individuals and community-supported living arrangements**

Medicare Benefits for Low-Income People

The Qualified Medicare Beneficiary (QMB) program, sometimes called the Medicare Buy-in Program, is a benefit for Medicare beneficiaries who live at or below the federal poverty level. If you are enrolled in this program, you will not have to pay Medicare premiums, deductibles, or co-insurance, and you will not need a Medigap policy.

If you believe you are eligible for QMB benefits, contact your local or county "department of social services" (sometimes called the Medicaid office, the department of human services, or the department of public welfare). Don't be scared off by the agency. The social services staff is there to help you; be persistent with them.

Note: You do not have to enroll in Medicaid to enroll in the QMB program. If agency staff are not familiar with the QMB program refer them to the law: Social Security Act, Section 1902(a)(10)(E) and Section 1905(p). If you cannot locate the appropriate office, contact your local Area Agency on Aging and ask where to apply for QMB benefits. You can also call the toll-free Medicare hotline at 800-638-6833 for further information.

Even if you are already enrolled in Medicaid, the QMB program may give you — at no extra cost — access to a large number of health care providers who would not treat you unless you are also a Medicare beneficiary.

Is there a charge for Medicaid services?

It depends. Many states require Medicaid recipients to pay co-payments or deductibles for certain services. These fees are supposed to be nominal. So a provider who accepts Medicaid patients is prohibited from charging you at all unless your state allows for these nominal co-payments. However, a doctor or other service provider who does not accept Medicaid may bill you for the entire cost.

Who is eligible for Medicaid?

Anyone who receives (or is eligible to receive) public assistance, including most people receiving Supplemental Security Income (see page 387), is eligible to receive Medicaid — and may even get it automatically. In addition, people age sixty-five or over or who are disabled and who can show that their income and assets do not exceed certain very minimal levels (usually less than the federal poverty level) are also eligible.

Medicaid recipients are allowed to have minimal savings and other resources. The maximum levels vary from state to state, but an individual living alone can usually have at least $2,000. Your home is not counted as an asset if you, a spouse, a dependent, or a disabled family member is living in it. Essential personal property, such as clothing, furniture, and automobiles, is also not counted. Neither are burial plots. Each person can also have a "burial fund" of $1,500, including the cash value of any life insurance.

Some states have a "spend-down" or "surplus" program. That means that you may qualify for Medicaid even if your income is *above* the monthly limit. In these states, you may "spend down" some assets and income to qualify by paying personally for certain medical expenses. For example, if your monthly income is $650 and the Medicaid income limit is $525, you may qualify for Medicaid coverage if you spend at least $125 of your income on medical expenses per month.

You may also be able to transfer some assets in order to qualify. The rules on this are tricky, though, and you should consult a lawyer or Medicaid expert (such as a geriatric social worker) before doing so. If you transfer too much within thirty-six months of an application for Medicaid nursing home benefits (and, in some states, home care benefits as well), you may have to pay privately for some of your nursing home or home care costs before Medicaid will cover them.

Signing Up for Medicaid

Application for Medicaid is made through your local welfare office or department of social services. You will have to produce documents to verify your income and assets. If your application is denied, you may appeal. Be warned, though, the rules relating to qualification are very complicated.

NURSING HOMES

Freedom of Choice

Although it was a distant prospect, Gordon was resigned to the idea of a nursing home for himself if it ever became necessary. His father Carl's response to such a suggestion, however, was a flinty "nothing doing." At a spry and wiry eighty-seven, Carl was in good shape and at times appeared likely to outlive his son and grandchildren.

Still, he had a recurring fear that his children might one day decide to ship him off to a nursing home against his will. Gordon's repeated assurances to the contrary did not pacify the old man. One evening Carl wrote out a directive (witnessed by the entire family) stating that "On no account should the party of the first part, Carl Goodfriend, ever be sent against his will to a nursing home." Gordon — who knew better than to argue with his dad when he was in a directive-drafting mood — sighed to himself and signed the paper.

Can a healthy person be forced to go to a nursing home?

No. No one can force you to go to a nursing home as long as you are capable of managing your affairs and are living in a safe environment. However, no document stating your unwillingness to enter a nursing home is binding if you are unable or unwilling to care for yourself.

Many states have rules that require health care professionals, police officers, social workers, and clergymen to report concerns they may have about an elderly person being in need of protective services. If such a report is made, it is likely that a representative of a state or local government will investigate and decide whether there is reason to change the elderly person's living situation.

If the state concludes that the elderly person needs protective services on account of abuse, neglect (including self-neglect), exploitation, or abandonment, it is likely that the investigator will file an application for the appointment of a **conservator** (also referred to as a **guardian**) of the elderly person.

It is also possible for a relative or friend to apply (against your wishes, if necessary) to have a conservator appointed.

What happens when a conservator is appointed?

If a conservator is appointed for you, you could lose the right to control any personal, financial, health care, and lifestyle decisions, including where you will live. The best way to prevent that from happening is to make plans while you are fully "capable" for the possibility that you will become unable to provide your own care. You have to be prepared to find someone to help you in your home if it is becoming a burden to do your own food shopping, bookkeeping, or housekeeping.

It is a good idea to state both orally and in writing that you do not wish to live in a nursing home, and that you want all your assets to be used to provide for your care at home. You can also name the person you want to be your guardian in the event you become incapable. Each state has laws designating how to do this. Often you can just fill out a form, but you may want to consult a lawyer, since a guardian will have an enormous responsibility for your care.

The idea is to appoint someone to take care of you and make sure you are living safely, because if your living condition is dangerous, your wishes will not prevent a conservator from making a determination that it is not possible to care for you in your home.

If you are appointed as conservator for your parent, you will be able to use your parent's money to tend to his or her needs. Even if your parent is admitted to a nursing home based on your signature as conservator, you do not assume responsibility to pay for your parent's care out of your own assets.

CASE IN POINT

Stuck in a Nursing Home

When Harry Newman, a retired printer in Texas, tried to leave the Big Town Nursing Home in Texas in September 1968, he was caught by Big Town employees and locked in a wing with disturbed, senile, and incorrigible patients. Newman didn't give up. He tried to flee several more times, but was always caught, brought back, and taped into a "restraint chair" for several hours. When he finally escaped after fifty-one days at Big Town, he had lost thirty pounds.

Newman sued the nursing home for false imprisonment, and in December 1970, the Texas Court of Civil Appeals granted him a $13,000 award. The court brushed aside the nursing home's arguments that it had not intended to oppress Newman, noting the home knew there was no court order committing Newman to Big Town. Moreover, when Newman had entered the home, Newman's nephew, who had entered his uncle in the nursing home, signed an agreement that stated Newman was not to be held against his will. Because he was not permitted to use the phone, had his clothes and suitcase locked up, and was forcibly prevented from leaving, Big Town had falsely imprisoned him, the court ruled.

How To Be Appointed Conservator

To be appointed conservator (also referred to as a guardian) for your parent (or anyone else), you generally must apply to the court in the jurisdiction where your parent lives. The court will supervise to ensure that you are acting in your parent's best interests. In many states, a public or private agency may also be able to petition for conservatorship.

When you apply to be appointed conservator, the court may first appoint an independent party, usually a lawyer, to represent the interests of your parent or loved one and to assess the need for an appointment. Then there will be a hearing during which the judge (and in some cases, a jury) will consider evidence of your parent's "competency." Usually this involves reports from physicians that the person is incapable of managing his or her affairs or is a danger to himself or others. Any stated wishes of your parent are likely to be considered, and the judge (or jury) will then decide whether the appointment of a conservator is appropriate. If you and other family members are feuding, the judge may try to appoint a more neutral guardian.

If you are appointed guardian, your duties will vary depending on the order granting you authority. You may also have to make periodic reports to the court.

It's not necessary to hire a lawyer to initiate this process, although you certainly may find it easier to have the guidance. If there is any contention about the appointment, it is highly advisable that you seek legal assistance.

Paying the Bills

Virginia, Gordon's co-worker, had come to realize she could no longer care for her elderly mother at home. The woman had a variety of real and imagined ailments and was subject to bouts of confusion and weeping. But Virginia worried that after getting her mother into a nursing home, the family would not be able to afford it. She imagined a terrible scene in which her mother was kicked out after running out of money.

Will Medicare or Medicaid pay for a nursing home if a person runs out of money?

Medicaid will pay for nursing home care in many cases so long as you have not made any property transfers that would disqualify you (see page 399). A nursing home may be allowed to discharge you to an appropriate setting if you become a Medicaid recipient after you are admitted and if the nursing home does not have a contract to treat Medicaid patients. (Most nursing homes do have such a contract.) More typically, if you have made a timely application for benefits, the nursing home usually cannot evict you for going on Medicaid unless you have failed to apply for Medicaid or simply refuse to pay your bills. Someone at the nursing home, often a social worker, should be available to help you or a family member apply for benefits.

Medicare is a different story. It does not cover custodial care in a nursing home. At most, it will cover the first twenty days in a Medicare-certified skilled nursing facility as well as part of the charge for the twentieth through one hundredth days. These costs are covered *only if* your admission was within thirty days of a hospital stay of at least three days (not including discharge day) *and* you receive skilled nursing seven days a week or skilled therapy services five days a week.

Can children be forced to guarantee payment of their parents' nursing home bills?

No. Children are not legally liable for their parents' care. However, many nursing homes will not admit

If a Nursing Home Patient Is Not Being Cared For Properly

If you are concerned that a nursing home patient is being neglected or treated improperly, you should speak to the social worker at the home. If you are still not satisfied, you should complain to the agencies in your state that oversee nursing homes — often the state department of health, the state department of insurance, and the state nursing home licensing and certification board. You may also contact your state or local department on aging and ask for intervention.

patients with limited resources unless someone (often a child) guarantees payment. If you do not want to assume liability for the bills, do not sign a nursing-home admission agreement on your parent's behalf, unless it is clear that you are not agreeing to take financial responsibility.

Refusing Treatment

Carl's friend Virgil had been in a nursing home for a number of years. Virgil had never been what you might call easygoing. Back in his hockey days he had been a ferocious (not to say dirty) defender and had led the league in total penalty minutes three years in a row. When Carl visited him at the nursing home, he noticed several orderlies with limps.

Virgil confessed that he had refused treatment (including medicine for his phenomenally high blood pressure), thrown his meal trays on the floor, and generally raised Cain with anyone on the staff who came near him.

Can a patient in a nursing home refuse medical treatment?

Yes. As long as you are mentally capable, you are in charge of the medical care you receive. Sometimes patients in a nursing home (or hospital) have to work very hard to have their decisions to refuse further medical treatment respected, but it is your right to refuse.

It helps to make your wishes known to family members and doctors before an emergency arises. You might also sign a written document such as a living will (see page 327).

Can a nursing home evict a difficult patient?

Federal law prohibits nursing homes from evicting a patient for a reason other than nonpayment of charges. (Even then the facility must hold off on an eviction if the charges are in dispute, or if the patient is appealing a denial of benefits.)

However, if a patient needs to be transferred for medical or health and safety reasons, it is possible that he or she could be evicted. Before an involuntary transfer, the nursing home must give the patient thirty days' notice as well as information about how to appeal the decision.

POWER OF ATTORNEY

As Gordon's father, Carl, had gotten older he had gradually lost patience with a lot of life's little responsibilities — writing checks, filling out and signing forms, and so on. One day as he was writing a check to renew his subscription to *Outlaw Biker* magazine he looked up at his son.

"You're supposed to be taking care of your old man in his dotage, boy," he said. "I'm going to give you my power of attorney and then you can worry about all this stuff for me."

What is "power of attorney"?

Power of attorney is the authority to act legally for another person. The power of attorney can be given for a single very specific task, such as writing checks on a single bank account, or it can cover all your affairs. When you grant someone power of attorney, he or she becomes what is called your "attorney-in-fact."

You can give someone power of attorney that remains effective if you become disabled or incompetent. That is called a "durable power of attorney."

How to Give Someone Power of Attorney

To grant someone power of attorney, you must sign a written document that states to whom you wish to grant authority to handle your affairs. While you don't need a lawyer to draw up this document, you will need to sign it before a **notary public,** a person authorized to witness the signing of documents. You may also need one or more witnesses. A notary public, town clerk, or registrar of deeds will be able to tell you the requirements in your state.

Can power of attorney be granted to more than one person?
Yes. You can designate one or more persons to act separately or together on a power of attorney, but it will be more complex, because if they are designated to act together they will both usually have to agree on how to handle your affairs. When you grant someone power of attorney, you do not give up any of your decision-making powers, as in a conservatorship. You are, however, agreeing to stand behind your designee's exercise of power. It is very important to appoint only someone you trust.

In some states, it is possible to grant someone power of attorney that goes into effect *only* if you become incapable of managing your affairs. This is called a "standby" or "springing" power of attorney. You also can grant someone, like a babysitter, temporary power of attorney to make emergency decisions for your children.

If you become mentally or physically incapable and have not designated a person to have durable power of attorney, then someone must be appointed as your conservator or guardian in order to pay your bills. (Generally, a court must determine whether appointment of a conservator or guardian is warranted.) That alternative is likely to be both complicated and expensive, since the court supervises the conservatorship and may require the conservator to post a bond.

Note: sometimes financial institutions are reluctant to rely on a power of attorney. You may need to persevere in explaining that it is in force. If a lawyer helped you grant power of attorney to someone (see the box), it may be helpful to have the lawyer speak to the person or institution that hesitates to recognize it.

Revoking Power of Attorney

"Are you really sure you want me to have your power of attorney there, partner?" Gordon asked his dad. "What if I blow your vast fortune on Girl Scout cookies or something like that?"

Carl did not kid around when the subject was money. "If you spend one nickel on those damn cookies, I'll revoke my power of attorney so fast you'll see stars," he said.

■ Can power of attorney be revoked?
Yes. You can revoke your power of attorney at any time by simply tearing up the document. You should notify any individual or institution that may be relying on the power of attorney that the person is no longer your agent. It's usually best to provide notification in writing.

Legal Services for Older People

All states are required to make funding available for free legal services on noncriminal matters for people over age sixty. Not all cases can be handled, but your state agency on aging (see listing below) can direct you to the people in your area who provide these services.

You might also get assistance from local law-school legal aid clinics and local bar association programs that provide legal services for the elderly.

Other sources of assistance and information include

American Association of Retired Persons
601 E Street NW
Washington, DC 20049
800-424-3410

American Bar Association Commission on Legal Problems of the Elderly
1800 M Street NW
Washington, DC 20036
202-331-2200

Choice in Dying
200 Varick Street
New York, NY 10014
212-366-5540

Eldercare Locator
800-677-1116

Legal Counsel for the Elderly
604 E Street NW
Building A, Fourth Floor
Washington, DC 20049
202-234-0970

Medicare Beneficiaries Defense Fund
1460 Broadway
Eighth Floor
New York, NY 10036-7393
212-869-3850

National Citizen's Coalition for Nursing Home Reform
1224 M Street NW
Suite 301
Washington, DC 20005-5183
202-393-2018

National Senior Citizen Law Center
1815 H Street NW, Suite 700
Washington, DC 20006
202-887-5280
or
777 South Figueroa Street, Suite 4230
Los Angeles, CA 90017
213-236-3890

FOR FURTHER REFERENCE

Nationwide Organizations:

National Association of State Units on Aging
1225 I Street NW, Suite 725
Washington, DC 20005
202-898-2578

National Association of Area Agencies on Aging
1112 Sixteenth Street
Washington, DC 20036
202-296-8130

National Coalition of Senior Citizens
1331 F Street NW
Washington, DC 20004
202-347-8800

State Agencies on Aging:

Alabama
Commission on Aging
770 Washington Avenue, Suite 470
Montgomery, AL 36130
205-242-5743
800-243-5463 (toll-free in AL)

Alaska
Older Alaskans Commission
P.O. Box 110209
Juneau, AK 99811-0209
907-465-3250

Arizona
Aging and Adult Administration
1789 West Jefferson, Site code 950 A
Phoenix, AZ 85007
602-542-4446

Arkansas
Office of Aging and Adult Services
Department of Human Services
P.O. Box 1437, Slot 1412
Little Rock, AR 72203
501-682-2441

California
California Department of Aging
1600 K Street
Sacramento, CA 95814
916-322-5290

Colorado
Aging and Adult Services Division
Department of Social Services
1575 Sherman Street, 4th Floor
Denver, CO 80203-1714
303-866-3851

Connecticut
Elderly Services
Department of Social Services
175 Main Street
Hartford, CT 06106
203-556-3238
800-443-9946 (toll-free in CT)

Delaware
Department of Health and Social Services
Division of Aging
1901 Norte, DuPont Highway
New Castle, DE 19720
302-421-6791
800-223-9074 (nationwide toll-free)

District of Columbia
D.C. Office on Aging
441 Fourth Street NW
1 Judiciary Square, 9th Floor
Washington, DC 20001
202-724-5626

Florida
Aging and Adult Services
1317 Winewood Boulevard
Tallahassee, FL 32311-0700
904-488-8922

Georgia
Division of Aging Services
2 Peachtree Street, 18th Floor
Atlanta, GA 30303
404-657-5258

Hawaii
Executive Office on Aging
Office of the Governor
335 Merchant Street, Suite 241
Honolulu, HI 96813
808-586-0100

Idaho
Idaho Office on Aging
Statehouse, Room 108
Boise, ID 83720
208-334-3833

Illinois
Department on Aging
421 East Capitol Avenue, #100
Springfield, IL 62701-1789
217-785-2870
800-252-8966 (toll-free in IL)

Indiana
Bureau of Aging and In-Home Services
P.O. Box 7083
Indianapolis, IN 46207-7083
317-232-7020
800-545-7763 (toll-free in IN)

Iowa
Department of Elder Affairs
914 Grand Avenue
Des Moines, IA 50319
515-281-5187
800-532-3213 (toll-free in IA)

Kansas
Department on Aging
Docking State Office Building
915 Southwest Harrison Street
Topeka, KS 66612-1500
913-296-4986
800-432-3535 (toll-free in KS)

Kentucky
Division for Aging Services
275 East Main Street
Frankfort, KY 40621
502-564-6930

Louisiana
Office of Elderly Affairs
P.O. Box 80374
Baton Rouge, LA 70898-0374
504-925-1700

Maine
Bureau of Elder and Adult Services
35 Anthony Avenue
Statehouse, Station 11
Augusta, ME 04333-0011
207-624-5335

Maryland
Office on Aging
301 West Preston Street
Baltimore, MD 21201
410-225-1100
800-243-3425 (toll-free in MD)

Massachusetts
Executive Office of Elder Affairs
1 Ashburton Place
Boston, MA 02108
617-727-7750

Michigan
Office of Services to the Aging
P.O. Box 30026
Lansing, MI 48909
517-373-8230

Minnesota
Minnesota Board on Aging
444 Lafayette Road
St. Paul, MN 55155-3843
612-296-2770
800-882-6262 (toll-free nationwide)

Mississippi
Division of Aging and Adult Services
P.O. Box 352
Jackson, MS 39205
601-359-4929
800-948-3090 (toll-free in MS)

Missouri
Division of Aging
Department of Social Services
P.O. Box 1337
Jefferson City, MO 65102-1337
314-751-3082
800-392-0210 (toll-free in MO)

Montana
Citizen's Advocate for Aging
c/o Department of Family Services
P.O. Box 80005
Helena, MT 59604
406-444-7786

Nebraska
Nebraska Department on Aging
301 Centennial Mall South
P.O. Box 95044
Lincoln, NE 68509-5044
402-471-2306

Nevada
Division of Aging Services
Department of Human Resources
340 North 11th Street
Las Vegas, NV 89101
702-486-3545

New Hampshire

Division of Elderly and Adult Services
State Office Park South
115 Pleasant Street
Annex #1
Concord, NH 03301-3843
603-271-4680
800-351-1888 (toll-free in NH)

New Jersey

Division on Aging
Department of Community Affairs
South Broad and Front Streets
CN 807
Trenton, NJ 08625-0807
609-292-4833
800-792-8820 (toll-free in NJ)

New Mexico

State Agency on Aging
228 East Palace Avenue
Santa Fe, NM 87501
505-827-7640
800-432-2080 (toll-free in NM)

New York

New York State Office for the Aging
Agency Building 2
Empire State Plaza
Albany, NY 12223
518-474-4425
800-342-9871 (toll-free in NY)

North Carolina

Division of Aging
Department of Human Resources
693 Palmer Drive
Raleigh, NC 27603
919-733-3983
800-662-7030 (toll-free in NC)

North Dakota

Aging Services Division
North Dakota Department of Human Services
P.O. Box 7070
Bismarck, ND 58507
701-224-2577
800-472-2622 (toll-free in ND)

Ohio

Ohio Department of Aging
50 West Broad Street, 9th Floor
Columbus, OH 43215
614-466-7246

Oklahoma

Aging Services Division
Department of Human Services
P.O. Box 25352
Oklahoma City, OK 73125
405-521-2327

Oregon

Senior and Disabled Services Division
Program Assistance Section
Department of Human Resources
500 Summer Street NE, 2nd Floor, South Side
Salem, OR 97310-1015
503-945-5832
800-232-3020 (toll-free in OR)

Pennsylvania

Department of Aging
400 Market Street
Market Street State Office Building
Harrisburg, PA 17101-2301
717-783-1550

Rhode Island

Department of Elderly Affairs
160 Pine Street
Providence, RI 02903-3708
401-277-2858
800-322-2880 (toll-free in RI)

South Carolina

Governor's Office: Division on Aging
202 Arbor Lake Drive, Suite 301
Columbia, SC 29223
803-737-7500

South Dakota

Office of Adult Services and Aging
700 Governor's Drive
Pierre, SD 57501
605-773-3656

Tennessee

Commission on Aging
500 Deadrick
Andrew Jackson Building, 9th Floor
Nashville, TN 37243-0860
615-741-2056

Texas

Texas Department on Aging
P.O. Box 12786
Capitol Station
Austin, TX 78711
512-444-2727
800-252-9240 (toll-free in TX)

Utah

Division of Aging and Adult Services
Department of Social Service
P.O. Box 45500
Salt Lake City, UT 84145
801-538-3910

Vermont

Department of Aging and Disabilities
103 South Main Street
Waterbury, VT 05671-2301
802-241-2400

Virginia

Department for the Aging
700 East Franklin
Richmond, VA 23219-2327
804-225-2271
800-552-4464 (toll-free in VA)

Washington

Aging and Adult Services Administration
Department of Social and Health Services
P.O. Box 45050
Olympia, WA 98504-5050
206-586-3768
800-422-3263 (toll-free in WA)

West Virginia

Commission on Aging
State Capitol
Charleston, WV 25305
304-558-3317

Wisconsin

Bureau on Aging
Division of Community Services
217 South Hamilton Street, Suite 300
Madison, WI 53703
608-266-2536

Wyoming

Division on Aging of Wyoming
Hathaway Building, Room 139
Cheyenne, WY 82002
307-777-7986
800-442-2766 (toll-free in WY)

Organizations with Pension Information:

American Association of Retired Persons
601 E Street NW
Washington, DC 20049
202-434-2277

Pension Rights Center
918 16th Street NW, Suite 704
Washington, DC 20006
202-296-3776

Department of Labor
Pension and Welfare Benefits Administration
Room N 5619
200 Constitution Avenue NW
Washington, DC 20210
202-219-8776

DYING

27

EUTHANASIA

Gordon's friend Phil had bone cancer. His condition was deteriorating quickly, and he'd been in the hospital for several weeks, suffering intense pain. Phil's wife quietly mentioned to Gordon that she had begged the doctor to give Phil "one dose too many" of morphine and put a permanent end to her husband's agony.

■ Is it against the law for a doctor to help someone die?

Yes. While it is legal for a doctor to *withhold* medical treatment if the patient refuses it, or has said that he or she does not want to be sustained by artificial means, all states ban euthanasia, in which a doctor administers a treatment in order to terminate the patient's life. In addition, many states also have banned "assisted" suicides, in which doctors have passively helped someone die by writing prescriptions for medication, such as sleeping pills, that a person can take in a large, lethal dose. Unlike the now-famous Dr. Jack Kevorkian, who has aided and been present at suicides, these doctors merely provide the means without taking an active role. As long as there was a legitimate reason to prescribe the medication, it is improbable that they would be found guilty of a crime. Many in the medical community, however, do not approve of such a practice.

Surprisingly, perhaps, unassisted suicide is also illegal in most states. Still, no one is ever prosecuted for suicide or even attempted suicide.

OF FUNERALS AND FUNERAL HOMES

While Carl was not embarrassed by the subject of death — or anything else for that matter — Gordon was more circumspect. He knew of course that his father would not live forever and he wanted to minimize the number of arrangements he would have to worry about when the time came. He wanted to have his father's funeral planned in advance, but he was too embarrassed to raise the subject directly with Carl.

■ Can a child negotiate a preplanned funeral arrangement for a parent without the parent's consent?

Yes, but make sure that your parent has not already done so. If your parent has qualified for Medicaid, it is possible that the funeral costs are covered or that your parent's funds were already used to prepay the fees. Many people on Medicaid "spend down" their resources to meet Medicaid asset requirements partly by paying for their funeral costs in advance.

■ Does a person have to abide by the arrangements a parent has made with a funeral director?

No. If your parent planned for a simple funeral, it is possible that an undertaker will allow you to do something more elaborate if you are willing to pay. (Likewise, the funeral could be *less* elaborate, but you will probably not get any money back if the funeral contract is irrevocable.) However, most ethical funeral home operators are inclined to comply with the wishes of the deceased. In fact, the funeral director will be required by law to honor any requirements that are specified in a contract even after your parent dies.

■ Are children of the deceased required to pay funeral costs?

No, unless they contract for the arrangements and the deceased's estate is too small to pay the charge. According to federal law you are only responsible for funeral charges you agree to in advance and in writing.

CASE IN POINT

Gone but Definitely Not Forgotten

People who deal with death — funeral home directors, cemetery managers, and crematorium operators, to name a few — are used to dealing with people under emotional distress. But some of the saddest cases arise when these very people are negligent and add additional distress to an already difficult time.

For example, when Kristie Ross died in 1981 at age seventeen, her mother, Francine, wanted to bury her in a dignified way that was a stark contrast to the punk rock life the girl had led. Ross advised Forest Lawn Memorial Park in suburban Los Angeles that she wanted a private burial and service and that Kristie's sleazy friends and acquaintances should be kept away.

Forest Lawn officials orally agreed to do everything they could. Yet the punk rockers came anyway, complete with white face makeup, black lipstick, and hair splashed in the colors of the rainbow. Some dressed in black leather, while one — in a look that has yet to emerge from the Paris salons — wore a dress decorated with live rats. And to further ruin an already horrible day, the uninvited guests openly drank and snorted cocaine while being verbally abusive to family members. The police eventually had to be called.

Shaken by the events, Ross asked Forest Lawn to guard Kristie's grave, for fear her "friends" would vandalize it. The cemetery agreed to do so, but the next day Ross discovered the grave had indeed been disturbed. Upon arranging for a new grave at a secret location, Ross asked if she could have a private guard present until the body could be moved. After first agreeing to her request, the cemetery balked and refused to let in the guard.

Ross sued Forest Park for negligence, breach of contract, and emotional distress. The cemetery moved to dismiss the case, arguing it had no duty or right to exclude anyone during a funeral. The California Court of Appeals ruled otherwise in 1984 and allowed the suit to continue.

The court criticized Forest Park for arguing that state law forbids a business from arbitrarily excluding a prospective customer. "Given the sensitive nature of the services offered by the cemetery, a policy permitting private funerals by which those who are not invited may not attend is a reasonable regulation . . . ," Judge Herbert Louis Ashby wrote. Ross eventually accepted a $75,000 settlement from Forest Park in 1991, ten years after Kristie died.

Unfortunately, funeral services aren't the only thing that occasionally get mishandled. So learned Ella Belle Brown when her husband, Charles, died in 1984. Ella and son Michael arranged to have the body cremated and the ashes sent home.

The ashes arrived three weeks later in a plastic box with a brown wrapper. And so they remained until one year later when Michael planned to scatter them in an area near their home. He removed the wrapper and found another man's name on the burial transfer certificate. Charles Brown, it turned out, was forever lost.

When Ella found she had had a stranger in the house for a year, she began to suffer headaches, stomach pains, and insomnia. She and Michael sued the mortuary and crematorium, but an Idaho trial judge initially dismissed their suit. Neither of them had suffered physical injury, and ordinarily, courts won't allow somebody to collect damages for emotional distress unless he or she has actually suffered a physical injury.

However, an exception has been recognized for the negligent handling of a dead body and the physical harm, such as Brown's, that could result from mental anguish, and the Supreme Court of Idaho reversed part of the lower court's ruling in 1990 and let Ella, as the surviving spouse, proceed with her suit. While the court rejected claims that the funeral director and crematorium intentionally inflicted emotional distress on Brown, it ruled that a case could be made for negligence.

Is embalming legally required?

No. States don't require embalming. You can generally decide in what style and manner you want to dispose of a body — within the realm of convention. You can cremate the body, bury it in a simple coffin, or inter it in fancy marble. State laws, however, do restrict the sites on which bodies can be buried or otherwise disposed of, so you may not be permitted to bury a loved one in your backyard or dump your husband's body in the local river where he went fishing every weekend.

DONATING YOUR BODY

Gordon also wondered if after his father's death he could have the body given to science. Carl had expressed admiration for people who became organ donors, but this — like the whole range of questions relating to death — was not the kind of subject that Gordon could easily raise with his dad.

Can a deceased person's organs be donated for transplant?

It varies from state to state, but if the deceased has said nothing on the subject, it is usually up to the spouse or children to decide. If the person has stated that no parts should be donated, the state's laws probably will not allow you to override that expressed wish. (See page 325.)

What to Do If Someone Dies

The best thing to do when someone dies is to call a doctor or registered nurse. The laws of each state determine who can officially pronounce the death.

It is not a good idea to dial 911 — unless, of course, you are not sure if the person is dead — because in many states emergency medical technicians must treat the call as an emergency and take steps to resuscitate until a doctor or registered nurse is able to pronounce the death. Any steps to resuscitate, of course, are unnecessary.

If you are unable to reach your doctor right away, you may also receive advice from a funeral home about the best way to proceed.

Is it necessary to get a death certificate?

Yes. A death certificate is needed for a variety of things, such as insurance and pension claims, and to transfer stocks and bank accounts out of the dead person's name. Death certificates are available from the "vital statistics" office of either the town or county where the death occurred.

THE LEGAL SYSTEM 28

LAWS

Sources of Law

Beatrice was on her way to a dentist's appointment, and she was in no mood for a confrontation. But there she was, facing a crowd of protesters who had blocked the entrance to the building, which also housed an abortion clinic. "Abortion is murder," shouted one demonstrator. "The Bible says, 'Thou Shalt Not Kill.'"

"The Bible's not the law of the land," retorted a woman wearing a "Pro-Choice" T-shirt. "*This* is," she proclaimed, waving a copy of the U.S. Constitution.

Where do laws come from?

There are four basic types of law in the United States:

- **the U.S. and state constitutions**
- **statutes (laws passed by Congress, state legislatures, and local councils)**
- **administrative rules and regulations**
- **case law**

The **U.S. Constitution,** which established our country as a republic and outlined the structure of the government, is considered the "supreme law of the land," and all other law must be in agreement with the principles and rights it sets forth. The Constitution's first ten amendments, known as the Bill of Rights, are the source of most of our fundamental rights, such as the freedoms of speech and religion, the right to a jury trial, and the protection against unreasonable searches and seizures. The amendments were written by the framers of the Constitution specifically to safeguard against the *federal* government interfering too much in the lives of individuals. And over the years, the U.S. Supreme Court has ruled that a number of rights are also protected from actions by *state* governments.

State constitutions establish the structure of a state's government and may also establish individual rights greater than those found in the U.S. Constitution.

Statutes are the laws passed by elected federal, state, and local legislatures. **Administrative rules and regulations** are the rules issued by regulatory agencies. For example, the Internal Revenue Service develops the rules that specify how people should comply with the tax laws passed by the U.S. Congress.

Case law, also known as **common law,** is the law created by judges when deciding individual disputes or cases. Although each judicial opinion is intended to resolve only the particular case before the court, the way judges interpret and then apply the law in each case serves as a **precedent** for courts facing similar cases in the future and is usually considered binding on that court and all lower courts in the same jurisdiction.

The principle of adhering to precedent is known as the **doctrine of stare decisis,** which is Latin for "to stand by that which is decided." Courts sometimes do, however, overrule their own precedents. When a novel legal question comes before a court, it is called a **case of first impression.**

Common law is derived from the English judicial system, in which there were few statutes at first and judges decided disputes based on social custom and on what they thought was fair. Once made, a decision became the precedent for all similar cases to follow. In our country, judges are guided by the laws passed by Congress and the state legislatures, and judicial decisions are often interpretations of those laws. If no statute specifically governs a dispute, previous judicial decisions are relied on.

The opinions issued by the highest court in a given jurisdiction set the precedent for subsequent decisions issued by all lower courts in that jurisdiction. Decisions of federal law by the U.S. Supreme Court must be followed by all other courts until either Congress passes a law modifying the ruling, or a Constitutional amendment is adopted or the Supreme Court itself modifies the ruling. Likewise, the decisions of each state's highest court prevail in that state but don't bind courts in any other state.

In the pecking order of the legal system, state law must generally yield to federal law. If there were a conflict between state and federal environmental regulations, for example, a court would likely find that the federal rules govern.

States also cannot pass laws that restrict individual rights protected by the U.S. Constitution. A state can, however, expand on those rights. For instance, the Supreme Court has ruled that it does not violate the U.S. Constitution for states to ban the use of drugs, even as part of a religious ceremony (see page 292). Nevertheless, a state court might find that such a ban interfered with the *state's* constitutional right to practice religion.

Note: All states, with the exception of Louisiana, are common-law states. Louisiana is more of a hybrid, combining elements of the common-law system with those of the civil-law systems used in many foreign countries, including most of Europe, Japan, Israel, North Africa, and much of South America. The Louisiana system is derived in part from Roman, Spanish, and French law — most particularly the Napoleonic Code, a set of rules enacted in France in 1804. In Louisiana, many of the rules are "codified," and judges are not necessarily bound by precedent as they are in common-law states. The difference between the two systems is especially notable in the areas of business law and estate planning.

Types of Law

As Beatrice debated whether or not to push through the protesters and exercise her right to have a cavity filled, someone hurled a brick through the building's front window, seriously injuring one of the nurses inside. As the police rushed to grab the culprit, Beatrice rushed to leave the scene. She later read in the paper that the brick thrower was facing two trials — a civil suit for the injuries to the nurse and a criminal case for aggravated assault.

"Criminal case? Civil case? Can't they just do it all at once?" Beatrice asked a friend.

■ What is the difference between criminal and civil law?

They are two separate bodies of law that play out on separate tracks in the justice system, although many judges preside over both kinds of cases. Criminal law involves punitive actions by the government, initiated by prosecutors, to protect people and property from the harmful acts of others. It defines what acts are criminal (such as murder, embezzlement, or dumping hazardous waste on a beach) and establishes the rules and procedures that must be followed when someone is accused of a crime. (For more on criminal law, see Chapter 13, GETTING ARRESTED.)

Civil law involves lawsuits brought by private individuals and companies (and sometimes by the government) to obtain financial compensation or court orders requiring or forbidding specified acts. It defines the rights and responsibilities that people have in all sorts of transactions. The law governing contracts and the law governing compensation for personal injury are among the many "categories" of civil law.

While a single incident can give rise to both civil and criminal cases, each must be brought separately because of some essential differences in the way civil and criminal cases proceed through the courts. First, a criminal case can be initiated only by the government. Civil cases, on the other hand, can be initiated by individuals or corporations, as well as by the government. Second, the degree of proof needed to win a civil case is not as exacting as that needed to secure a conviction in a criminal case. In a civil case, the **plaintiff** (the person who brings the lawsuit) usually only has to show by "a preponderance of the evidence" that the facts alleged are true. In a criminal case, the prosecution has the much heavier burden of proving that the defendant is guilty "beyond a reasonable doubt." (For more on proof, see page 424, and for more on reasonable doubt, see page 214.)

Another key difference between civil and criminal law is that criminal cases (other than minor offenses) typically carry the possibility of a prison sentence. A person who loses a civil case won't be sent to jail, although he or she may be ordered to:

- **pay money to the other party**
- **fulfill a contract**
- **cease a particular action, such as infringing on someone else's patent**

Does the military have a separate legal system?

Yes. Members of the armed forces are governed by the Uniform Code of Military Justice no matter where they are or whether their activities are military related or nonmilitary. Crimes under the code range from arson and murder to showing disrespect to a senior officer and being absent without leave. Military trials are known as courts-martial, with juries made up of military officers. Accused military members have the right to an attorney (civilian or military), and court-martial rulings can be appealed to the U.S. Court of Military Appeals, the military's highest court.

For incidents that occur off military property, an armed forces member could be tried in *both* civilian and military courts.

COURTS

Beatrice belonged to a group, Parents Against Porn, which was trying — unsuccessfully — to shut down Kinky Is Us, an "adult" bookstore that had opened across the street from the local junior high school. The group's members had picketed and petitioned and gotten plenty of positive publicity, but had failed to persuade the city council to act against the porn shop. Bea called an emergency strategy meeting at her house. "We need a new plan," she told the others.

"Let's show them we mean business," said her friend Brett. "I think it's time we take the case to the Supreme Court."

How Are State Court Systems Structured?

There are usually three levels: a trial court, an intermediate appellate court, and a final appellate court. However, some states have only two levels. The highest court in most states is called the supreme court. (One utterly confusing exception is New York, where the supreme court is the trial court, while the highest court is the court of appeals.)

Most states also have smaller, specialized courts that hear particular types of cases. These include

- **Family courts.** In most places, these courts hear cases involving allegations of child abuse and neglect, cases involving child support and custody, and cases involving juvenile crime.
- **Probate courts,** also known by other names, including surrogate's courts. They oversee the probate of wills and administration of estates. In some states, they also rule on applications for guardianship, adoption of minors, and questions of incompetency.
- **Traffic courts.**
- **Housing courts,** which hear landlord-tenant disputes (see page 41).
- **Small-claims courts** (for more, see page 431).

Can any case go to the Supreme Court?

No. Usually only cases that deal with questions of constitutional or federal law are heard by the Supreme Court, and generally the court accepts only a tiny percentage of the cases that have worked their way up through the lower courts (for more, see page 425). Cases that deal exclusively with questions of state law usually do not go further than a state's highest court.

What is the difference between state and federal courts?

They are distinct systems with separate sets of rules and procedures, but the main difference is in the types of cases they hear. Some matters, like divorce cases, can be heard only in state court. Others, like bankruptcy cases, can be heard only in federal court.

Generally, the type of case that can be brought in federal court is limited to:

- **cases involving issues of federal law or the U.S. Constitution**
- **cases between residents of different states when more than $50,000 is at issue (this is called "diversity jurisdiction")**
- **cases between U.S. citizens and foreigners**
- **cases involving issues of federal *and* state law**

State courts can hear all matters involving state law. They can also hear cases that assert claims under federal law or the U.S. Constitution, such as discrimination claims, unless the federal statute has conferred *exclusive* jurisdiction on the federal courts or agencies.

Is there a difference between state and federal court judges?

Yes. Federal judges are nominated by the president and confirmed by the Senate. With the exception of bankruptcy court judges, all federal judges are appointed to lifetime terms. Congress has the power to impeach a judge who is deemed to have acted improperly, but this is extraordinarily rare.

The selection of state court judges varies from state to state. In some states, judges run for election. In others, they are appointed by a government official, usually the governor. In either case, they usually serve limited terms.

How Is the Federal Court System Structured?

It's divided into three levels: trial courts, appellate courts, and a final appellate court.

- **Trial courts.** Called United States District Courts. Each state has at least one federal court jurisdiction within its boundaries. Some states have as many as four.
- **Intermediate appellate courts.** Called United States Courts of Appeals. There are thirteen, each governing a "circuit." Twelve circuits cover geographic regions of the country, including the District of Columbia circuit. One, the Federal Circuit, also based in the District of Columbia, hears only certain specialized categories of cases, including patent disputes and claims against the government.
- **The final appellate court.** The United States Supreme Court hears appeals from the U.S. Courts of Appeals, from the highest courts in the states, and (in a few rare cases) even directly from U.S. District Courts.

There are also several specialized federal courts. These include:

- **Bankruptcy Courts**
- **Tax Court**
- **Court of International Trade, which hears cases involving imports, tariffs, and customs duties**
- **Court of Customs and Patent Appeals, which hears appeals from the Court of International Trade, the U.S. International Trade Commission, and the Patent and Trademark Office**
- **Court of Federal Claims, which hears certain cases brought against the U.S. government**

SUING AND BEING SUED

29

Beatrice was feeling blue. She'd been making carrot salad for a picnic when she had a mishap with her food processor and lost two fingers on her left hand. Nearly a year later she was still reliving the accident.

"If only I had put on oven mitts when I removed the blade," Beatrice sighed to her friend Derek. "If only I had been paying attention to what I was doing."

"Stop blaming yourself," said Derek. "It's not your fault those blades are so sharp. Accidents happen, and I'll bet you're not the first person to be seriously injured by one of those things."

"Hmmm," Derek added after a long silence. "Maybe you should sue."

■ What kinds of things should a person consider before pursuing a civil lawsuit?

There are a few important legal questions you should ask. First of all, do you have a **valid claim?** A **valid claim** is one where the grievance can be resolved by legal action. For instance, say you decide to take a cruise and the ship's captain gets a little tipsy one night, running the ship aground. You are thrown from your bed, breaking your arm and suffering a concussion. You would have a pretty good negligence case against the captain and the cruise company. But say instead that it was cloudy for the whole week of your cruise, thwarting your planned dream tan. Unless the cruise company had made a specific guarantee of sunny weather (which is very unlikely), your disappointment has no legal remedy.

Next, do you have **standing?** To initiate a lawsuit you must have standing, which means you must be sufficiently affected by the matter at hand. In other words, you can't sue just because something bad happens. Also, something bad must happen *to you.* For instance, you can't sue your local paper for libeling your best friend. You also can't sue a local developer just because a building he designed is excruciatingly ugly. If, however, the building is next door to your home and would block your light or somehow directly intrude on your property, then you might have standing to try and stop the development.

Last, each state has laws, known as **statutes of limitations,** that require you to bring a suit within a certain period after an injury. The time limits vary from state to state and for different types of cases. Some limits may be as short as thirty days, and they are seldom greater than six years. In cases where the injury is not immediately apparent (for example, a person has been exposed to a substance that causes cancer many years later) the time period in which a person can bring a lawsuit usually starts when the person knew or should have known of the injury.

In medical malpractice cases, some states have absolute time limits on how long after an injury a person may sue, no matter how long it took the patient to realize the injury may have been wrongfully caused.

Once you've considered these legal questions, the most important question is whether a lawsuit can in fact solve your problem. You may have a grievance with someone, but suing won't necessarily help. Litigation can take years, and *lawyers are expensive* (though in some cases you won't have to pay up front. See "Fees," page 440). The time, money, and effort involved in a lawsuit aren't always worth it — even if you win — so you should objectively analyze your chances. Do you have evidence? Witnesses? Can you prove the other party violated some legal duty to you? Also, you should think about the personal effect of litigation. The other party will likely try to discredit you and your claims, which can be one of the more painful parts of the adversarial process. You might also consider whether your case will draw a lot of publicity, and if so, whether you want it.

Note: Although there is some overlap between the way criminal and civil cases proceed, the issues outlined in this chapter generally relate to civil lawsuits. For more details on the procedures and rules in criminal cases, see Chapter 13, GETTING ARRESTED. Also, particular considerations involved in bringing a personal injury lawsuit are addressed in Chapter 21, GETTING HURT.

Damages

Beatrice contacted a lawyer, Pete Pointer. He asked her a lot of questions to determine the exact extent of her injuries from the food processor. Beatrice told him that her medical bills alone totaled more than $6,000. Plus, she had lost at least $15,000 in wages. And not to forget, the pain in her fingers had been excruciating.

■ What exactly are damages?

Damages are the amount of money a defendant pays to compensate a victim for his or her injuries. There are two major kinds:

- **Compensatory damages.** This is money awarded to reimburse actual costs such as medical bills and lost wages. Compensatory damages can also be awarded for things that are harder to measure, such as pain and suffering. If a spouse or child is severely injured or killed, the survivor may also win damages for what is called "loss of consortium." This is to compensate for the loss of the loved one's companionship and affection. Compensatory damages are also awarded in commercial disputes, such as breach of contract cases.
- **Punitive damages.** This is money awarded to the victim that is intended to punish a defendant with the aim of stopping the person or business from repeating the type of conduct that caused an injury and setting an example to deter others from similar conduct. In theory, the *possibility* of getting hit with a large punitive damage award makes people take steps to keep accidents from happening in the first place. Courts allow punitive damages only in cases where there is intentional misconduct or where the defendant has recklessly (as opposed to negligently) placed people at risk. For example, if a manufacturer failed to conduct adequate tests on a new product or disregarded scientific or technical

CASE IN POINT

Goodbye, Dali

A famous painting by Salvador Dali that depicts the image of a melting clock is altogether appropriate to this tale of dissolving deadlines. A Washington couple named Balog, on vacation in Hawaii, visited a Honolulu art gallery in 1978 and bought a series of works by Salvador Dali. The gallery subsequently sent the Balogs mailings in 1979, 1980, 1981, 1982, and 1987 containing documents labeled "Confidential Appraisal — Certificate of Authenticity" for each work the couple had purchased. The mailings also stated that the art had appreciated in value and gave estimates of its rising value.

Ten years later, in 1988, the Balogs learned through media reports that their Dalis were probably fake, and they decided to sue the gallery to recoup the $36,200 they had spent. The Balogs' challenge was to get permission to sue so long after the alleged fraud. Even though the gallery had at one point admitted it had known the works were questionable since at least 1980, it argued that the Balogs couldn't sue because the statute of limitations had long since passed.

In a 1990 ruling that differed from the trend in other circuits, a Hawaii federal district court found that the certificates created an express warranty about the future value of the work. Thus, the court ruled, the deadline for filing a lawsuit moved to the time when the breach of warranty was discovered. The court also ruled that the statute of limitations deadline should be moved up because the gallery had fraudulently concealed the facts.

reports about the hazards of the product, and went ahead and sold it anyway, a court might consider those actions reckless if they resulted in harm to users of the product.

In almost all situations, plaintiffs cannot collect punitive damages if they do not also get compensatory damages. But compensatory damages can be as low as one penny. Some states have set limits on the amount of punitive damages and damages for pain and suffering. These limits are known as "caps."

Reaching a Settlement

Pointer wrote Slicer Dicer a letter outlining the potential case. "Now we wait," he told Beatrice. "My guess is we'll hear back from them pretty quickly and be able to reach a settlement without ever filing a complaint in court."

Don't all cases have to go through the courts?

No, not if the parties can reach a settlement. Generally, a lawyer representing a plaintiff in a personal injury case will first write to the defendant detailing the client's version of what happened and outlining the damages. Usually the defendant's insurance company will respond and, depending on the facts, may make an offer to settle the case. If the offer is unacceptable, the parties will try to negotiate a reasonable figure. If a settlement still can't be reached, then a lawsuit may be filed, and the case may go to trial. It is possible, however, to reach a settlement at any time in the process — even during a trial.

Location, Location, Location

Pointer's optimism had been unfounded, since Slicer Dicer refused to negotiate a settlement. "We've got to move forward and file a complaint," he told Beatrice. "We just have to decide where to file it."

"You mean we have a choice?" asked Beatrice.

Can a lawsuit be brought anywhere?

No, a case must be initiated in a court that has **jurisdiction,** which means that it is located in the right place and has the power to rule on the questions of law at issue in the dispute. Federal courts, for instance, usually hear only cases in which there is an issue of federal law or where the parties involved are from different states.

One thing to determine is what law applies to your situation — federal, state, or both. Another consideration is where the parties are located. Generally, you can file a case in the state in which you are a resident or in the state in which the other party is a resident or is doing business. However, the defendant (party being sued) usually must have ties to the state where the suit is brought. So if a person from California is poisoned by a hamburger she eats at a diner while vacationing in New York, she probably can't sue in California unless the diner's owner also has business in California, or lives there or enters the state long enough to be served papers there. (See page 420 on service of papers.)

You may also want to consider which laws are most favorable to you. But keep in mind that a state does not always have to apply its own law when deciding your case. In fact, its laws may compel it to apply the law of the state where the harm or dispute occurred. So getting a case in a particular court is not necessarily a guarantee that the law of that state will apply.

Also, even if you decide the best strategy is to bring your case in state court, the other party may be able to transfer it to federal court (so long as the case meets the requirements for being tried in federal court). So you may not have the final choice on which court hears your case.

Can a person pick which judge hears the case?

No. You can pick the court, but not the judge. And judges aren't usually allowed to pick the cases they hear either. Cases are typically assigned to judges at random, though there are exceptions. The parties in a lawsuit may nevertheless attempt to "judge-shop" either by filing a motion during a particular week when they know Judge X will be the one hearing motions or by trying to recuse Judge Y in a two-judge jurisdiction.

Serving Papers

Things were moving ahead. Pointer had filed the complaint, and now he had to give official notice to Slicer Dicer.

"How about leaving a message on the company voice mail," suggested Beatrice.

"Not if we ever want to see the light of day in a courtroom," said Pointer.

What is the proper way to notify the other party that a lawsuit has been filed?

It depends on the type of case and the procedures of the court in which you're filing. The act of notifying the other parties that an action has begun and informing them of the steps they should take in order to respond is known as the **service of process.** Typically, you have to deliver a copy of the **complaint** (the document that outlines the charges) and the summons (the document that states when the other parties must appear to answer the charges) to all the other parties in person. In some jurisdictions, it may be acceptable to send it via registered mail, return receipt requested. A failure to serve process properly can result in the dismissal of a lawsuit.

Discovery

I think we may be on to something here," Pointer told Beatrice over the phone. "I just went through a box of Slicer Dicer files and found a memo from an in-house engineer urging management to include a warning on blade removal with the processor."

Beatrice was confused. "I don't understand. How did you arrange this? They let you go through a box of their documents? You saw company memos?"

"This is called discovery," said Pointer. "It's part of the process."

What is discovery?

Discovery is the fact-finding process that the parties in a lawsuit go through before trial, and it can take months, even years, to complete. Each side tries to gain information through methods such as **depositions** (oral questions) and **interrogatories** (written questions), and by requesting documents and other information, such as contracts, memos, photographs, and floor plans, relating to the case. Each jurisdiction has its own rules for discovery, and judges can force unwilling parties to come forward with information if it is relevant.

CASE IN POINT

Hairpiece v. Fat Boy

A fair amount of decorum can be expected in courtroom proceedings, especially if a jury is present. Take away both the judge and the jury, though, and lawyerly instincts sometimes dominate. Consider the following exchange, which took place during a deposition in May 1992. Joseph Jamail, then sixty-six, represented the plaintiffs, who claimed the Monsanto Company had exposed them to toxic chemicals. Edward Carstarphen, then thirty-four, defended Monsanto.

Jamail: You don't run this deposition, you understand?

Carstarphen: Neither do you, Joe.

Jamail: You watch and see who does, Big Boy. . . . And don't be telling other lawyers to shut up. That isn't your goddamned job, Fat Boy.

Carstarphen: Well, that's not your job, Mr. Hairpiece. . . .

Witness: I'd like to knock you on your ass.

Jamail: Oh, you big fat tub of shit, sit down.

In July 1992, Monsanto settled the case for $39 million.

Depositions

Beatrice received a summons to appear at the law offices of Wiley, Wiley & Wiley for a deposition. "What more can they want to know?" Beatrice wondered. She'd already seen several doctors to get their opinions on the damage to her hand (as if the visible damage wasn't evidence enough), and she'd accounted for nearly every penny spent on medical treatment, physical therapy, a housekeeper to help with chores she couldn't handle, and a plane ticket for her mother, who came to help. She'd also calculated all her lost income. Now the Slicer Dicer lawyers wanted to quiz her in person. About what, she couldn't imagine.

■ What happens at a deposition?

A witness gives testimony under oath. Depositions usually take place in the office of one of the lawyers, and a witness is often represented by her own lawyer or by a lawyer for one of the parties to the lawsuit. No judge is present, but the testimony is recorded by a court reporter and possibly may be used during the trial. It also may be videotaped. If a witness is ill or otherwise unable to testify at trial, the judge may allow the transcript to be read or the videotape to be presented.

Venue

Pointer opened his newspaper, and he was furious. A front-page article announced a new little league ballpark . . . sponsored and financed by Slicer Dicer. Obviously, it was a goodwill publicity stunt in anticipation of the trial.

"Slicer Dicer owns this town," Pointer grumbled. "I'm applying for a change of venue."

■ What is a change of venue?

It's a change in the location of a trial, usually granted to avoid prejudice against one of the parties in both civil and criminal cases. A change of venue may be appropriate if a case has received so much local publicity that the judge believes potential jurors will be unable to give it fair consideration. This, however, happens only rarely.

THE TRIAL

The big day finally arrived. Beatrice and Pointer sat at one table in the courtroom. Slicer Dicer's legal team from Wiley, Wiley & Wiley sat at the other. As the potential jurors filed in, Beatrice wondered whether it was worth it to bare her private life to so many strangers.

■ Are all civil cases tried before a jury?

No. There are two types of trials: those before a jury and those before a judge, known as "bench trials." In a trial without a jury, a judge hears the case alone and rules on the facts. Usually, both parties in the lawsuit must agree to waive a jury trial, though some states do not permit jury trials in certain cases, such as divorces or probate disputes. A bench trial is often faster than a jury trial. (For more on criminal cases, see Chapter 13, GETTING ARRESTED.)

Picking a Jury

Beatrice eyed the prospective jurors nervously. She knew Pointer was going to try to pick people who would be sympathetic, but they all looked bored and one man was actually muttering to himself. Based on appearance alone, she wanted none of them on her case.

■ How does jury selection work?

It's the first thing that happens in both civil and criminal trials. Both sides have a right to participate in choosing the jury. The theory is that this process will eliminate potential jurors most likely to have a bias against one side or the other. In practice, however, each side tries to pick people it thinks will be most sympathetic to it.

At the start of the trial, the judge will call in a panel of potential jurors who will sit down in the courtroom. From this pool, a group of jurors (sometimes twelve, but sometimes fewer) and often one or two alternates will be chosen.

The potential jurors are questioned in a process called **voir dire.** Pronounced "vwa dear," it's a French phrase that means "to speak the truth." First, the judge asks general questions about people's occupations, whether they know any of the participants or lawyers in the case, or whether they have seen or heard any of the pretrial publicity about the case.

Then the lawyer for each side may question the jurors, trying to expose any biases. (In federal court, these questions are asked by the judge.) For example, a lawyer might ask, "What magazines do you read?" The prospective juror who says he subscribes to *Cigar Aficionado* might be sympathetic to a cigarette maker facing a product liability charge, and the plaintiff's lawyer might try to exclude him from the jury. Similarly, a woman whose son was killed in a car accident might be excluded from a jury in a case against a drunk driver.

Some lawyers may try to take advantage of the voir dire process to educate the jury about their case. For example, a defense lawyer might ask whether a potential juror understands the concept of "asumption of risk" and then use this line of questioning to explain the concept.

Rejecting Jurors

One of the potential jurors in Beatrice's case was asked whether she could be fair and impartial. "I don't know," she answered. "I think big corporations are pretty evil."

CASE IN POINT

Prejudice on Trial

One of the most hard-fought stages of a trial is jury selection, since the makeup of a jury is often key to a case's outcome. And race is an important factor that lawyers for both sides have sometimes used to manipulate that outcome to their advantage.

A 1986 ruling by the Supreme Court in *Batson v. Kentucky* altered the ability of prosecutors to reject jurors solely because of their race. In the case, Batson, an African-American who had been tried and convicted by an all-white jury in Kentucky on a second-degree burglary charge, had argued that the prosecutor had used his peremptory challenges (challenges for which he had to give no justification) to exclude all four black members of the group of potential jurors.

The Supreme Court ruled in favor of Batson, reversing his conviction. In a decision written by Justice Lewis Powell Jr., the court held that while "a defendant has no right to a . . . jury composed of members of his or her own race," it was a denial of equal protection for a prosecutor to use peremptory challenges on the basis of race. The court announced a new procedure, in which a prosecutor must give a race-neutral reason in order to exclude a minority from a jury.

In a 1994 decision the Supreme Court went further and banned gender-based discrimination in jury selection. Writing for the majority in *J.E.B. v. Alabama,* Justice Harry Blackmun noted that part of the Court's concern was that both race and gender discrimination can cause harm to "individual jurors who are wrongfully excluded from participation in the judicial process." Interestingly, the *J.E.B.* case was an action by the state of Alabama to prove paternity and collect child support payments from a man who objected to the state using nine of its ten peremptory strikes to remove *male* jurors.

Can potential jurors be rejected?

Yes. Each side in a civil and criminal case is given an opportunity to **challenge** (oppose) each juror. If the judge agrees, the juror will step down from the jury box and will not serve on the case.

There are two types of challenges. The first is a challenge **for cause.** A juror can be rejected "for cause" if it is revealed during questioning that he or she has prejudged the case and is apparently unable or unwilling to set aside preconceptions and pay attention only to the evidence. Sometimes jurors admit they cannot be fair or mention things that quite obviously put their ability to be fair into question. For example, in a purse-snatching case, a juror might be challenged for cause if her purse had been snatched the week before if she admits or signals that she will have difficulty being impartial. Each side can make an *unlimited* number of challenges for cause, so each side tries to find reasons to eliminate jurors that they suspect would be unsympathetic.

In addition, each side has a *limited* number of **peremptory challenges** with which they can eliminate any particular juror without stating a reason. In recent years, courts have held that peremptory challenges may not be used for the purpose of keeping members of a particular race or sex off the jury.

In major trials, particularly those that get a lot of publicity, juror questioning can take days, even weeks, and sometimes it takes more time than the rest of the trial. Generally though, it is concluded within one or two days.

Evidence

Pointer had told Beatrice that the hardest part of her case would be proving that the injury was caused by the manufacturer's negligence and was not her own fault. Fortunately, Beatrice was a compulsive saver and had all the warranties and warnings that came with the food processor. She had brought the whole file to Pointer's office.

"Is this evidence enough?" Beatrice had asked with pride. "There's no warning in here about removing the blade."

"It's a good start," he had replied.

What is evidence?

The lawyers in a civil or criminal trial may introduce many different kinds of **evidence** — testimony, documents (photocopies are usually okay in most courts, though originals are preferred), photographs, maps (of an accident scene, for example) and videotapes. The rules about what's admissible as evidence are complicated, especially when it comes to **hearsay** — statements made outside of court. Hearsay is usually excluded because it's not trustworthy, and because it's believed that a witness should personally testify in court instead of having a third person repeat his or her comments. It also deprives the accused of the right to confront the witness and challenge negative testimony. There are, however, many exceptions to the rule excluding hearsay, and often it will be allowed in for one reason or another.

During a trial, both sides may present opening statements in which they can outline the facts of their case. Nothing the lawyers say during the openings constitutes evidence. To present the facts, each side may call **witnesses,** people who come to the stand and swear to give truthful evidence. If a witness won't come voluntarily, a judge may issue a **subpoena** that orders him or her to appear. This means that you can force people to testify on your behalf in both civil and criminal cases. The courts have ruled that no one is immune from a subpoena, not even the President of the United States. However, it is possible for a subpoenaed witness to object to testifying (a reporter, for example, may claim that information he or she has is confidential), and the judge will rule on those objections.

Sometimes, both parties will hire **expert witnesses.** Often, one side's experts will be used to throw the testimony of the other side's experts into question.

The kinds of questions witnesses may be asked are critical. Each party calls its own witnesses and questions them on **direct examination.** With limited exceptions this means that they may ask only "direct questions," open-ended questions that do not suggest a specific answer. For example, "Where were you on the night of July 23, 1992?" is a direct question.

The other party then has the right of **cross-examination.** On cross-examination, the opposing lawyer may ask "leading questions." Leading questions are ones that suggest an answer. The witness often may respond only with a yes or no, so the questioner has much more control over the content of the answers. For example, "Isn't it true that on or about July 23, 1992, you smashed up a new Ferrari that did not belong to you?" is a leading question. On cross-examination, lawyers use the power to ask leading questions to reveal additional facts that might favor their client and to try to convince the jury that the witness does not know as much as the other side claimed, or that the witness is not believable, is prejudiced against the defendant, or has ulterior motives for testifying.

Cross-examination is a very critical part of any case, because it is the time when a witness's motives are questioned and doubts about the evidence are raised. Each side often gets to ask a witness additional questions in **redirect** and **recross examination.**

The party that has the **burden of proof** in a case is the one that must persuade the judge or the jury that enough facts exist to prove the allegations of the case. If, for instance, you bring a negligence case against a manufacturer, it is your burden to prove that the company was at fault. If the manufacturer wants to claim that you misused the product, then it has the burden of proving so. In a criminal case, the government always has the burden of proving that the defendant is guilty.

How much proof does it take to win a lawsuit?

It depends on the kind of case. There are three basic "levels" of proof. Most civil cases must be proved **by a preponderance of the evidence.** This means that, to prevail, the plaintiff must persuade the judge or the jury that the facts are more probably one way (the plaintiff's way) than another (the defendant's). Sometimes a civil case must be proved **by clear and convincing evidence,** a higher burden for a plaintiff to meet. (In order to have someone committed to a mental hospital, it would be necessary to show by clear and convincing evidence that the person presented a danger to him- or herself and others, for example.) The highest level of proof is required in criminal cases. In those, the government must prove a person's guilt **beyond a reasonable doubt** (for more on reasonable doubt, see page 214).

Sending the Case to the Jury

After the witnesses for both sides had been called to testify (including Beatrice, who tripped on her way to the stand, demonstrating a certain amount of clumsiness), the lawyers scheduled a meeting with the judge to discuss the jury charge. "What's that for?" asked Beatrice. "They're not on trial."

What is the jury charge?

This is legal jargon for the judge's instructions to the jury, which include an explanation of how to apply the relevant law to the evidence the jury has heard. This happens at the end of the trial, after both sides are finished presenting their cases. The attorneys will give closing arguments, often an eloquent summing-up of the evidence and the last attempt to win over the jury. The judge will then instruct the jurors on what they are to consider in their deliberations. Sometimes the jurors will be given a list of questions to answer. Jurors are supposed to consider only evidence presented at the trial, but the judge usually tells them they can use a witness's demeanor to determine if he or she is believable.

The jurors are then sent to deliberate. While the entire trial is "on the record," that is, transcribed by a stenographer or tape machine, no one is permitted to hear what is discussed in the jury room. (The jurors are usually free to discuss their deliberations after the verdict.)

Must a verdict be unanimous?

Yes, in all federal cases (although in a federal civil case, if both parties agree, a majority verdict will suffice). Some states, such as Oregon, require only a substantial majority of the jurors to agree on a verdict in civil and criminal cases. Some states, like New York, require a unanimous verdict in crim-

What Makes the Supreme Court Supreme?

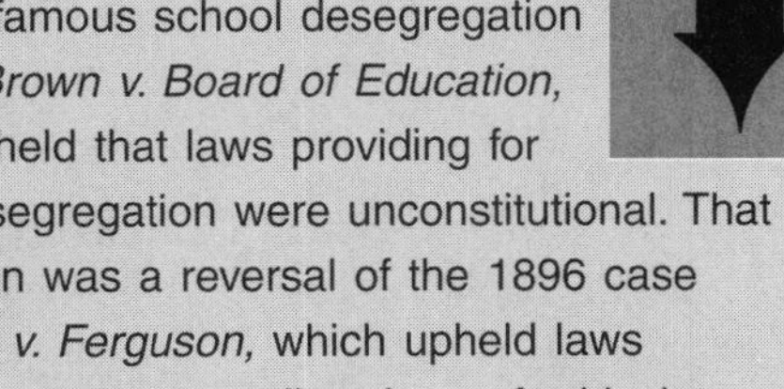

The Supreme Court is the highest federal appeals court in the country, hearing arguments and writing decisions for a selected number of cases brought to it by those who disagree with decisions of lower appeals courts.

The Supreme Court agrees to review (in legalese, it "grants **certiorari** to") very few of the cases submitted to it each year. (During the 1992–93 term, the Court accepted only 97 cases and declined to hear 6,205.) The seven men and two women now on the Court have the final responsibility for analyzing whether the questions presented to them are important enough to justify the Court's attention and, if so, whether the lower court's decision was in accordance with the Constitution and laws of the U.S. and with the Court's own **precedents** — its prior interpretations of the Constitution and laws.

Sometimes the court will reverse its own previous decisions, as it did in 1954 in the famous school desegregation case *Brown v. Board of Education,* which held that laws providing for racial segregation were unconstitutional. That decision was a reversal of the 1896 case *Plessy v. Ferguson,* which upheld laws requiring separate railroad cars for blacks and whites.

Judges who disagree with the majority may write dissenting opinions, as Justice John Marshall Harlan Sr. did in *Plessy.* A dissenting opinion carries no legal authority, but it may have moral weight, which can help later judges to overturn a previous decision or explain why the decision shouldn't be relied on as precedent. The classic example of this is Harlan's *Plessy* dissent, in which he argued that separation of the races was in and of itself unequal and unconstitutional. Harlan's dissent went on to be cited in support of scores of subsequent civil rights decisions.

inal cases, but accept a majority verdict in civil cases. More typically, however, jurors must unanimously reach a verdict; if they cannot all agree, and the jury is "hung" — incapable of reaching a decision — the judge will eventually declare a mistrial. When this happens, the prosecutor or the plaintiff must then decide whether or not to pursue a retrial.

APPEALS

The jurors did think Beatrice was a klutz. But they also thought that Slicer Dicer had failed to warn users properly about taking care with the sharp blade. They awarded $60,000 to Beatrice. One of Slicer Dicer's lawyers took Pointer aside. "You know we can tie this thing up for years on appeal and maybe get it reversed," he said. "Or we can talk now about settling. How does $25,000 sound?"

What's an appeal?

An **appeal** is a request to a supervisory court, usually composed of a panel of judges, to overturn the legal rulings of a lower court. The purpose of an appeal is to have a higher-level court review the procedures at the trial and rule whether the verdict was arrived at properly. For instance, an appellate court may find that a judge mistakenly allowed in evidence that should have been kept out or gave improper jury instructions. If the appellate court believes an error affected the outcome of the trial, the verdict may be overturned.

If a party intends to appeal, he or she usually begins the process by filing a "motion for a new trial" with the trial court, outlining the legal errors he or she believes were committed during the trial. Though it seems contradictory to appeal to the judge

Anatomy of a Civil Lawsuit

The procedures in a civil case vary slightly from state to state and between state and federal court, but the general routines are similar.

- The suit begins when the injured party, the **plaintiff,** files a **complaint.**
- The person sued, the **defendant,** is served with a **summons,** accompanied by a copy of the complaint, which sets forth the grounds for the plaintiff's contention that the defendant is liable and states when the defendant should appear in court to answer the charges.
- The defendant may choose to file a **motion to dismiss,** asserting that even if all the allegations are true, the plaintiff is not entitled to any legal relief. If that motion is denied, or if the defendant chooses not to file it, he or she must file an **answer** within a specified period of time. The answer either admits to or (more typically) denies the factual or legal basis for liability.
- Both parties engage in **discovery,** a process in which they request pertinent information from each other. For example, in a personal injury case, each side may seek out all relevant police, insurance, and medical records. If the judge allows the request, the other side must either produce the material or convince the judge of its reasons for not complying.
- Both parties may also seek assistance from experts. Medical specialists, accountants, chemists, child therapists, handwriting analysts, and engineering experts are a few of the many kinds each side may call, and often a case will pit experts in the same field against each other.
- The parties usually engage in **settlement** negotiations. Over 90 percent of all cases settle, or end without trial. Settlement discussions can happen at any point — before or during a trial, and sometimes even after a trial to avoid an appeal.

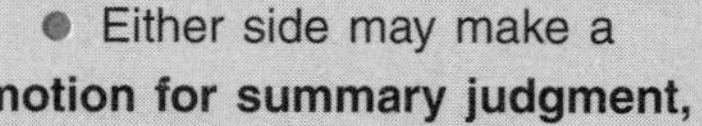

- Either side may make a **motion for summary judgment,** which asserts that the other side has raised no genuine issue to be tried and asks the judge to rule in favor of the moving party. This motion is typically made before the trial. During the trial, a similar **motion for directed verdict** can be made by either side after the other is done presenting its case.
- If the case goes to trial, each party will present evidence to a jury, which will render a **verdict,** or to a judge, who issues a **decision.** (Most negligence trials are heard by a jury.)
- The judge then enters a **judgment** for the winning party. If the judge does not believe the evidence supports the jury's verdict, the judge may disregard the verdict. (This rarely happens.)
- The losing party may make a **motion for a new trial,** asserting that the trial was unfair due to legal errors that prejudiced its case.
- The losing party may make a motion for a **judgment non obstante veredicto,** known as a judgment notwithstanding the verdict, or a J.N.O.V. This motion asks the court to rule in favor of the losing party even though the jury verdict was in favor of the other side. Usually, the argument is that the facts or law do not support the jury's verdict.
- The losing side may **appeal** — bring the case before a higher court.
- If the judge believes the damages awarded to the plaintiff are too high, they may be reduced. They may also, in some cases, be increased. Either side may appeal the amount of the damage award.
- If the plaintiff wins, he or she obtains a court order requiring the defendant to pay the amount of the judgment or allowing the plaintiff to seize specified property of the defendant.

before whom you got an unwanted outcome, legal rules give that judge first crack at correcting errors before an appeal proceeds.

Generally, the motion for a new trial will be denied. On occasion, though, a judge will recognize that he or she made a mistake and issue a reversal. If the motion for a new trial is denied, which it usually is, then the appealing party must file a **notice of appeal** with the trial court. In most states, if this document is not filed within a set time period (often thirty days of the final judgment), no appeal will be allowed. This is one deadline that is usually inflexible.

An appellate court may either uphold the trial court ruling, or it may reverse all or part of the ruling. If the court finds legal errors in the conduct of a trial serious enough, it may order a new trial, which is what usually happens when a case is "reversed." However, many legal errors are found to be "harmless errors" that did not affect the outcome of the trial. A verdict usually will be reversed only when the error can be shown to have affected the outcome. If, for example, the trial judge should have excluded some evidence, that usually will not be enough to win a reversal if the rest of the evidence pointed overwhelmingly to a defendant's guilt or liability.

Most states and the federal government have two levels of appeals — an intermediate appellate court, such as the U.S. Circuit Courts of Appeal, and a top-level court, such as the state or federal supreme courts. In the federal system, and in many state systems, you do not have an automatic right to be heard by the highest court. In the federal system, for example, the U.S. Supreme Court, with a very few limited exceptions, gets to pick and choose which cases it will hear, and in fact hears only about three percent of all the cases people ask it to hear (see the box on page 425).

Usually, you can appeal your case only to the highest level of the system under which it was tried. If you are convicted of a state crime in state court, then typically you can appeal only within the state system. However, if a state case requires interpretation of the U.S. Constitution, then it may be possible to appeal from a state's highest court to the U.S. Supreme Court. But, again, the Supreme Court will hear only a small percentage of the cases brought to it.

BEING A WITNESS

Subpoenas

During his lunch break one afternoon, Bart had seen a young woman crushed by a hit-and-run driver speeding away from a bank robbery. After a year, the victim was just beginning to walk again, and her prognosis was good. But at least once a month, Bart still woke up in a sweat from the image of the driver looking straight into his eyes and pointing a gloved finger at him.

So it was big news when the criminals finally were apprehended, and Bart read all about it with interest. But when he received a subpoena to testify at the trial, he was terrified.

■ What is a subpoena?

A **subpoena** is an order commanding a person to appear to give testimony either in court, in a grand jury (see page 208), or in a deposition (see page 421). A subpoena can also order someone to turn over relevant documents to the other side during a lawsuit. If you ignore a subpoena, you could be held in contempt of court, fined, and possibly even sentenced to jail. If you've witnessed a crime and are being called to testify about what you saw, you probably do not need your own lawyer. However, most lawyers would advise you *never* to go near a prosecutor, grand jury, or plaintiff's lawyer without legal representation. And if you don't understand why you got a subpoena, or if you believe you are the subject of an investigation, you may want to call a lawyer.

■ What is the difference between a summons and a subpoena?

A summons usually notifies the recipient that he or she is being sued and gives the deadline for filing a written answer to the complaint. A subpoena orders the recipient to appear to give testimony at a specified time and place.

If you receive a summons, you should respond as directed. It's generally a good idea to consult a

Litigation Alternatives

Some problems require outside help, but don't necessarily have to be resolved by litigating in court. There are several methods of alternative dispute resolution available. Two of the most popular options are **mediation** and **arbitration.** In mediation, a neutral third party helps the parties resolve a dispute, but the mediator does not have the power to impose a decision on the parties. If you can't reach a satisfactory resolution, you can go ahead and pursue a lawsuit.

In arbitration, the disputing parties agree (often before any dispute arises) to abide by the decision of an arbitrator. These decisions are considered **binding,** which means you are bound to abide by them, usually without the option of appealing. If you're unhappy with the results of an arbitrated dispute, you may find a pretext to file a lawsuit, but most courts will throw out such a case.

Many contracts, such as those between stockbrokers and their clients, labor union agreements, and other employment contracts, contain an arbitration or mediation clause, which means that the parties *must* submit to arbitration or mediation before litigating.

Mediation and arbitration can save both time and money, since the process generally moves faster and costs less. It's not necessary to have a lawyer, although you may want one, especially if you're trying to resolve a marital dispute or a case involving a large sum of money. If the amount of money is not too high, you might also consider small-claims court (see page 431).

Sometimes a dispute will start out in mediation and then proceed to arbitration if the problem could not be resolved. You may want to avoid using the same mediator if your case goes on to arbitration. That helps ensure an unbiased process, especially since you may want to change the way you present your case if you did not get the desired result.

Things to consider when choosing a dispute resolution program:

- What are the costs? Some are free. Others charge a fee. Often it's low and reasonable, but it could be higher for a complicated case.
- Is the decision binding?
- Do you have the option of taking the case to court if you're still dissatisfied?
- Who pays for the program? This can give you an idea how neutral it is.

Many organizations and public agencies offer dispute resolution programs. Some state and federal courts also have such programs. In fact, you sometimes may be directed to try to resolve a problem in one of these forums before litigating. You can get referrals from your local Better Business Bureau, local bar association, state consumer protection agency, or local court.

More information is also available from:

American Arbitration Association
140 West 51st Street
New York, NY 10020-1203
212-484-4000

American Bar Association
Section of Dispute Resolution
1800 M Street NW
Suite 200 South
Washington, DC 20036
202-331-2258

National Institute for Dispute Resolution
1726 M Street NW
Suite 500
Washington, DC 20036
202-466-4764

lawyer before filing an answer (or appearing in court if that's called for). If you fail to answer without justification, the judge may automatically enter a judgment against you — known as a **default judgment.**

Under what circumstances can a person who is subpoenaed refuse to testify?

If you receive a subpoena, you must show up as indicated or you may be found in contempt, and you generally must answer all questions. However, the Fifth Amendment of the U.S. Constitution gives you the right not to say anything that might be self-incriminating, so you do not have to answer a question if the answer could be used to implicate you in a crime. In some cases, though, the government will grant a witness **immunity,** which means that anything the witness says during testimony cannot be used against him or her. If you have been granted immunity, you cannot refuse to answer questions without risking being held in contempt. If you believe your testimony could be self-incriminating, you should definitely consult a lawyer.

There are also several reasons why a subpoena may be **quashed** — declared invalid. These include

- **it seeks irrelevant material**
- **it is overly broad in the material it seeks**
- **it requires an appearance at an inconvenient time or place**
- **it seeks privileged information that is protected (such as lawyer-client or doctor-patient information)**

You should definitely consult a lawyer if you want to quash a subpoena, because you will face serious consequences if you fail to comply.

Perjury

I know that the driver has it in for me," Bart told the prosecutor, who had asked Bart to come in for an interview before the trial. "I don't want to testify."

"Don't be ridiculous," the prosecutor said sweetly.

"Listen, I really didn't see anything," Bart insisted.

"That's not what the police report says," she replied more firmly. "And let me remind you, we prosecute perjurers."

What is perjury?

Perjury is a crime in which a person knowingly makes a false statement while under oath in court. In some jurisdictions, even making a false statement in a legal document could be considered perjury. The penalties for perjury vary from state to state.

CLASS ACTIONS

Bradley and Peter had been noticing a bad odor in their water. They knew that a local chemical manufacturer, Stinkbombs, U.S.A. Inc., had been dumping its waste in a vacant lot near its factory, and what they soon learned was that the chemicals had leached into the ground and could be affecting the drinking water in thousands of homes. When the discovery was reported in the local newspaper, housing prices dropped immediately. Several irate homeowners met to discuss the situation, and one insisted they take legal steps to get compensation.

What is a class action suit?

It's a lawsuit in which one or more parties file a complaint on behalf of themselves and all other people who are "similarly situated" (suffering from the same problem). Class actions are often used when a large number of people have comparable claims, and they are especially effective when the individual claims are relatively small and too expensive to try separately.

Say, for instance, that a credit card company has allegedly overcharged customers by using improper finance charges. One individual may bring a class action suit on behalf of all the people the company is suspected of overcharging. If the company is found liable, it will have to pay damages to each member of the class.

State attorney generals often bring this type of consumer class action suit, but private attorneys may also do so.

What Is the General Procedure of a Class Action?

After the suit is filed by the named plaintiffs, a class is either approved or denied by a judge (see below). Then follows a period of discovery, during which the parties exchange pertinent information. This may last years, and settlement negotiations may occur at any time. If there is no settlement, the case goes to trial.

As with regular civil trials, a judge may try it himself or herself, in what is known as a "bench trial," but only if there are no monetary damages. If the plaintiffs are seeking money damages, that portion of the case will be tried before a jury. If they are seeking a court order to restore lost jobs, for example, that portion must be tried before a judge.

Overall, the judge plays a much bigger role in a class action suit than in an ordinary lawsuit. The judge must decide several things:

- **if the class is a clearly definable group**
- **whether the harm that the class alleges can be demonstrated for all members**
- **whether most members can be identified and located**
- **whether members of the class will receive the same fair treatment they would get if they brought individual suits**

When that's done, the judge must

- **decide how the plaintiffs will give notice to other members of the class that a lawsuit in which they have an interest has been filed**
- **ensure that the best interests of all the members of a class have been adequately represented by the parties who filed the suit (the "named plaintiffs") and their lawyers**
- **approve the fairness of any settlement**
- **oversee the distribution of any award to all members of the class who can be found**

In what cases is a class action appropriate?

Class actions have been used to handle claims by groups of people injured by hazardous products, pharmaceuticals, or even environmental pollution. For example, class action settlements have provided compensation for Vietnam veterans exposed to Agent Orange and women injured by the Dalkon Shield intrauterine device. However, some lawyers believe that class actions should never be used in personal injury cases because the individual plaintiffs might not get as much money in damages as they would if each of them, acting separately, brought the case to a jury.

Giving Notice

Many of Brad's neighbors had not been at the block association meeting and were unaware that a lawsuit was in the works.

How do people learn that they are potential participants in a class action suit?

Generally, a small group of people initiate the action, filing suit as the members of the class they are trying to create. These originators of the suit are called the **named plaintiffs** because the suit is named after them, even though the class may end up including thousands of people. After they file the suit, they wait for the judge to **certify** or approve the class. If the judge approves the plan and the class obtains certification, the named plaintiffs are required to notify the other members of the class. The judge will issue specific rules about notification.

Giving notice is extremely important because many class members may not be aware that they have a claim or that their rights will be affected by the lawsuit. The preferred method of notice is a letter to each class member. If their names and addresses are not known, the court may allow the information to be published in newspapers. The notice gives members of the class the choice of whether or not to join the suit.

If you learn that you are part of a class action, the notice — whether it comes by mail or runs in the newspaper — may ask you to join the lawsuit by sending in a claim form. In many cases, you will be included automatically unless you specifically request to "opt out." This may be an important decision, because once you join the class you no longer have the right to bring your own lawsuit, and your claim will be decided by the verdict or settlement of the class action.

If you learn that you may be part of a class action suit that involves a significant amount of compensation, particularly where personal injury is involved, it is important to consult an attorney who is familiar with the litigation promptly. Class actions can be an efficient means of resolving mass claims, but it is easy to lose your "day in court" unless you are aware of your options.

Settlement of a class action must be approved by the court, generally after a hearing on the fairness of the agreement. As a class member, you are entitled to object to the terms of the settlement. After the judge approves the settlement, you are bound by it, and lose your right to object to it.

DO IT YOURSELF: SMALL-CLAIMS COURT

lossom and Jeremy's kitchen renovation was finally finished. They were happy with everything except James, the contractor, who had demanded

CASE IN POINT

Agent Orange

One of the most complex class action suits ever was filed in 1978 by a group representing Vietnam veterans and their families against several chemical companies that manufactured the herbicide Agent Orange. Agent Orange, which was sprayed by the U.S. Army to defoliate the jungle and destroy enemy food supplies during the Vietnam War, contains dioxin, a toxic byproduct.

The veterans exposed to the chemicals during the war claimed that Agent Orange caused a wide range of illnesses and disabilities, including cancer in the veterans and birth deformities in their children. Their complaint alleged, among other things, that the manufacturers had been negligent and had failed to warn of the dangers. They sought damages of from $4 to $40 billion and asked the court to establish a trust fund to pay victims.

A class action in this type of case, known as a mass tort because so many people are affected by it, was unprecedented. It was filed in federal court in New York and was actually the consolidation of many smaller, separate class action suits. Altogether, the case included some 2.4 million veterans and their family members from the U.S., Australia, and New Zealand.

The plaintiffs were represented by a network of nearly 1,500 law firms located throughout the country. The cost of preparing to defend the case at trial has been estimated at $100 million.

It never made it that far, though. Under the leadership of federal judge Jack Weinstein, a special settlement master was appointed to work out an agreement. In May 1984, after six years of litigation, a settlement was reached between the manufacturers and veterans, creating a $180 million fund to which the defendants contributed varying amounts. The Monsanto Chemical Company and Dow Chemical paid the largest percentages. A group of veterans challenged the fairness of the settlement, but it was upheld.

In November 1993, a group of veterans petitioned the U.S. Supreme Court to reopen the case, arguing that new Agent Orange–induced health problems have been discovered since the settlement. Without comment, the justices refused in February 1994 to reopen the litigation.

Some Practical Advice

Life is full of frustrations, especially for consumers facing big corporations and impersonal storekeepers. While the legal system entitles consumers to certain rights and protections, suing is rarely the most efficient way to solve a problem.

Your first step should be to contact the merchant that sold you the goods or the company that manufactured them.

If you can't resolve the problem that way, write to the person in charge of handling complaints, either at the store or the manufacturer, or both. Give detailed information about what you bought, including model and make numbers, what the problems are, and photocopies of any relevant information, such as sales receipts, warranties, contracts, and canceled checks. State specifically what resolution you would like, and give the company a reasonable time to respond.

Send copies of your complaint letter to your local Better Business Bureau, state consumer protection agencies, and appropriate federal agencies, such as the Federal Trade Commission and even the U.S. Postal Service (if you bought the product through the mail). Note on your complaint letter to the company that you have sent copies to these agencies. When confronting a possible investigation from a regulatory agency or consumer protection bureau, many companies will be anxious to reach a satisfactory solution to avoid having a complaint on record.

If the company doesn't respond within a reasonable time, write again, summarizing your first letter and asking for action or response. You may also want to contact your local media's consumer reporters.

If the company still fails to respond, you may decide to pursue a court case or try alternative dispute resolution (see page 428).

extra money before he would finish the job. Jeremy was not convinced that the money was legitimately spent, and he wanted it back. James wouldn't answer his calls, and Jeremy was at the end of his rope. He decided to take James to small-claims court.

What is small-claims court?

Small-claims courts are special state courts, authorized by state law to decide specified types of cases. Although their jurisdiction varies somewhat from state to state, small-claims courts typically hear cases where the amount in dispute is below a set limit — usually between $2,000 and $3,000. Thus, disputes involving small sums of money or property are most suitable for small-claims court. These courts may also be authorized to hear landlord-tenant disputes and other specific types of claims.

Procedures in small-claims court are much simpler and faster than in regular courts. Typically, cases are decided by a judge without a jury, and trials are held soon after the case is filed. Because of the financial limits on the disputes that the courts will hear, it does not usually make economic sense to hire a lawyer. Most parties in small-claims courts represent themselves.

Blossom tried to talk Jeremy out of the suit. After all, $2,500 was a lot of money, but it still didn't seem worth all the hassle. And frankly, she didn't want all of Jeremy's attention being diverted. She urged him to track down James and try to settle things amicably.

Is it wise to try to settle a case before going to court?

Definitely. Before filing a small-claims action, it is often best to contact the other party to determine if the matter can be resolved. Any court proceeding has risks.

- It can be time-consuming for all the parties.
- The results are unpredictable, especially if the court has little to go on other than each party's version of the facts.
- It may be difficult to collect on a judgment.

In many communities, one alternative is to use a dispute settlement center. These centers provide a mediator, whose role is to facilitate a resolution between the parties. The mediator does not decide the case, but instead helps the parties to reach an amicable agreement. If the dispute has generated intense personal feelings, settlement is usually not feasible without the assistance of a mediator or other third party.

Mediation centers are often nonprofit organizations that charge only a modest fee for their services. (The United Way funds several such programs.) You can look for listings in the yellow pages of the phone book, or ask a court clerk for a referral.

Whom Do You Sue?

Blossom and Jeremy were unable to resolve their differences with James, so Jeremy went ahead with a lawsuit. But he was unclear exactly how to proceed. Was he suing James, or James's company, Renew, Redo, Rehue?

Who should be sued — a business, an individual, a family?

In small-claims court you *must* correctly name the party you are suing. If you are suing an individual, use his or her proper name rather than a nickname. If the other party is married and his or her spouse is a co-owner in the business or was personally involved in the matter for which you're suing, be sure to name both of them as defendants. This often makes it much easier to collect a judgment.

If the other party is a business, you need to know whether the business is incorporated. If it is, you usually will have to sue the corporation, rather than an individual person. A business is generally (but not always) required to communicate that it is incorporated by using the words "incorporated" or "inc." in its name. You can find out if a business is licensed in your state as a corporation by calling the corporations division of the secretary of state's office.

In most cases involving disputes over goods and services, you may bring a claim only against the incorporated business and not against the owner. If the business is not incorporated, you should sue the owner(s) as well as the business. If the case involves fraud or negligence, however, you may sue the individual who committed the wrong as well as the business, regardless of whether or not the business is incorporated.

Sue or Be Sued

To bring an action in small-claims court, contact the local clerk of the court. Most have forms you fill out to begin the action. The required information includes the name and address of each party, the nature of the dispute, and the remedy you want. You also have to pay a filing fee (usually about $50). If you win the case, the defendant can be ordered to pay you the filing fee in addition to whatever damages you are awarded.

If you are being sued in small-claims court, you will be served papers notifying you of the suit and instructing you to appear in court. You have every right to defend your case with witnesses, and you are also free to bring a counterclaim against the person who is suing you. Say, for instance, that you are a housepainter in a dispute with a client. She says you screwed up her kitchen walls, and thus has refused to pay you the balance and has sued in small-claims court to recover the money she already paid you. You could countersue for the money she owes you. You each would present your case to the judge, who would then make a ruling.

Serving Notice

Jeremy went to the clerk of the court and began the suit: *Jeremy Jones v. Redo, Renew, Rehue, Inc., and James Askew.* But James was keeping a low profile and may even have skipped town.

■ Is it necessary to "serve papers" on the party being sued?

Yes. When you are suing, you must make sure that the other party is properly served or the action can be dismissed. "Serving papers" or "service" means that the party is given both a copy of the complaint and a summons that tells them how and when they must respond to the complaint. Every state has its own procedures, which must be carefully followed to carry out service. In most states, service can be performed by a deputy sheriff or other officer for a small fee. This is often the best and easiest method to use. All states require corporations to register the name and address where they can be served with legal papers. You can determine this so-called registered agent by contacting the state Department of Corporations or the office of the secretary of state.

Witnesses

As their court date approached, Blossom and Jeremy were nervous. Jeremy had carefully prepared his case, but neither of them had any experience with the legal system. Still, Blossom couldn't wait to take the stand and testify about how James had made their lives miserable. Jeremy thought they might be better off with a more objective witness, like the contractor who had to come in and finish the job.

■ Is it a good idea to bring witnesses to small-claims court?

Absolutely! Although the formal rules of evidence are frequently relaxed in small-claims court, these courts usually refuse to allow "hearsay" testimony. Hearsay is when one witness attempts to tell what another person said. Most small-claims courts will not even allow affidavits or other notarized statements. This is because with hearsay testimony or written statements, the other party is deprived of the right to cross-examine the witness. If the case involves a dispute over what was said or done, bringing a *disinterested* witness who can support or corroborate your testimony greatly enhances your case. Otherwise, it can be difficult for the judge to determine which of these strongly biased parties testified accurately.

■ Is it possible to appeal a small-claims court decision?

Probably. Rules for small-claims court usually allow either party to appeal, often with an entirely new trial. In many states, an additional, though modest, fee is required from the appealing party. But you should consider the extra time and expense of a possible appeal when you are deciding whether to sue someone.

Collecting Your Judgment

Blossom and Jeremy won their case. That night they toasted each other with champagne at Dinner for Two, their favorite restaurant. "Maybe you should go to law school," Blossom teased Jeremy.

Although they felt vindicated, there was still one problem: James wouldn't meet their eyes the whole time they were in court, and they were doubtful they would be able to collect their $2,500 from him.

■ What happens if the losing party refuses to pay?

When a party fails to pay, the judgment can be enforced through a judicial process called "execution." (This is a legal term that has nothing to do with killing people.) A deputy or other court official notifies the party that a judgment is outstanding against him or her and that if it is not paid, the official will seize and sell the party's property or bank accounts to pay the judgment. Usually, you will have to pay a small fee to execute on the judgment, but this amount is added to what the defendant has to pay.

Most states allow debtors to protect some property from execution, and this may prevent or delay collection of the judgment. Enforcing a judgment can be difficult, which is why it is wise to include all responsible parties as defendants in the action. That increases the odds that there will be a party against whom a judgment can be enforced.

After Blossom and Jeremy's success in court, Beatrice considered taking Max to small-claims court, since he had been remiss on his child-support payments for the last few months. If she could just see him in court, she might be able to make him face up to his responsibilities. But the clerk of the court advised her to call a lawyer.

■ What kind of case would not be appropriate for small-claims court?

Small-claims court is appealing to many people: it offers a simplified procedure to enable individuals to enforce obligations, often without the expense of an attorney. However, not all cases can be brought in small-claims court. Divorce, child-support, and other family-law cases, as well as cases that raise questions about land titles or boundaries, *must* be tried in regular courts. Other cases that involve complicated legal issues or personal injury could be brought in small-claims court, but shouldn't be because of their complexity and the seriousness of the issues at stake.

Consumers should also be wary of bringing claims against a business when the business has a possible claim against you. The defendant in a small-claims action usually has the right to bring a counterclaim. This means that the defendant can assert that it is entitled to money or other relief from the person who brought the original suit. The business can appear with its attorney, and you could end up with a judgment entered against you.

FINDING AND USING A LAWYER

30

LOOKING FOR A LAWYER

Beatrice hadn't even put 2,000 miles on her new car when she was rear-ended by that idiot in the van who obviously was color-blind, since he rammed into her while they were stopped at a red light. And wouldn't you know it? It turned out that Bea knew Bruce, the driver; she had worked with his sister Pamela at Frozen and Fabulous.

Fortunately, Bruce's insurance covered the bodywork that her car needed, but Beatrice had her own bodywork to take care of. She had been out of work for weeks since the accident, unable to turn her head. Bea's doctor recommended treatments of therapeutic massage in addition to physical therapy. Bea thought that since she had a personal connection with Bruce, he would be happy to help pay for her treatment. Instead, he had stopped returning her calls.

"What am I going to do?" Beatrice wondered. She was at her wit's end. Because she couldn't work, she couldn't pay for her treatments. Therefore she couldn't get better and go back to work.

"Am I going to have to take this guy to court?" she asked herself.

■ How does a person know when he or she needs a lawyer?

If you want to sue someone, or if someone sues you, you will probably need a lawyer. You always have the right to represent yourself, but generally it's not advisable to do so. In some lawsuits, usually those brought or defended in small-claims court, it's usually not necessary to use a lawyer. But if the amount of money involved is high, getting a lawyer is a good idea, especially if the court's procedures are confusing or if the other side has a lawyer. Most people need lawyers

- **to get divorced**
- **for estate planning (making wills and trusts)**
- **if they are the executor of someone else's estate**
- **to buy or sell houses and other real estate**
- **to enter a business contract**
- **if they are in an accident**
- **if they are charged with a crime**

People may also need lawyers if they think they are entitled to something from the government — like unemployment insurance or social security — but are unable to get it.

Specialists and Generalists

Beatrice called Evelyn, a lawyer she knew. Evelyn, it turned out, had gone on an extended trek in the Himalayas. Bea was at a loss, since Evelyn was the only lawyer she knew. Should she call that 800 number she'd seen advertised? Should she pick a name out of the phone book? She scanned the listings under "Attorneys." Justin Tyme? Eileen Dover? How should she choose?

■ Do all lawyers handle all problems?

No. The law is too complex, and there are too many different fields of law for all lawyers to be able to handle all problems. Some lawyers specialize in narrow areas, like antitrust law or banking law. Others specialize in criminal or personal injury law. On the other hand, some lawyers are general practitioners and can handle a variety of legal problems that individuals are likely to encounter.

You probably know what kind of problem you have — criminal, accident, divorce — and you should look for a lawyer who handles that kind of case. In the unlikely event that you don't know the legal category into which your problem falls, you can describe it to a lawyer, and he or she can help you figure it out. Some law firms are staffed with

Are Legal Service Plans a Good Deal?

Several organizations sell "legal insurance" for an annual fee, usually between $8 and $16 a month. Some employers and labor unions sign workers up for prepaid plans as part of their benefits package, and you may also be able to purchase prepaid legal services through your bank, credit card company, or other groups in which you are a member.

What you get from these services varies greatly, depending on the individual plan and the quality of its lawyers. Many restrict the number of "free" hours you get before extra charges kick in. The monthly fee usually covers preparation of a simple will and a review of some documents and contracts. If you need more help than the plan offers, it's usually available at a discounted hourly rate.

While these plans may be useful for answering basic legal questions, they're probably not the place to go if you have a complex problem, especially since you won't always be able to control who works on your case or be sure that that person has the appropriate expertise.

If you are thinking of joining a plan, you should check with your employer or union to see if there's an existing group you are entitled to join. When you are evaluating whether it's worth your money or not, here are some of the things to consider

- **What type of service is provided?**
- **Are you entitled to of^ace visits or just phone calls?**
- **Will the attorneys draft documents, such as wills or contracts, if necessary, or will that cost extra?**
- **If you are limited in the number of consultations or types of services, what is the fee for additional consultations?**
- **Can you choose your own lawyer?**
- **What is not covered?**

For a listing of organizations that offer prepaid legal services, you can contact:

National Resource Center for Consumers of Legal Services
P.O. Box 340
Gloucester, VA 23061

American Prepaid Legal Services Institute
541 North Fairbanks Court
Chicago, IL 60611-3314
312-988-5751

a variety of specialists. So while one lawyer may not be able to handle your problem, someone else at the firm possibly can.

Word of Mouth

"There's got to be a better way," Beatrice sighed after randomly calling a couple of lawyers from the phone book. The first one she spoke with said that her case sounded like "a pain in the neck." The second one seemed to be speaking gibberish (it was legalese), and when Bea asked for a translation, the lawyer told her it was too complicated for a "nice lady like yourself to understand." Beatrice hung up immediately.

How does a person find the right kind of lawyer?

Since each state has its own licensing and practice requirements, you usually will need to find someone in your own state. The best way is to get recommendations from friends and relatives who have hired lawyers in the past. In addition to getting names and phone numbers, you should ask your friends these questions:

- **What kinds of legal problems did they have?**
- **Were they satisfied?**
- **Did the lawyer do what he or she promised?**
- **Did the lawyer return phone calls?**
- **Was the fee reasonable?**

Aside from word of mouth, you can also ask your local bar association for recommendations, since many maintain lawyer referral lists by area of practice. To get on these lists, lawyers usually have to show the bar association that they have adequate experience in that practice area. A lawyer who ill served clients would not likely stay on the list for long. (For bar association listings, see page 449.)

You might also try contacting any law schools in your area, since many have clinics that provide some legal services. And if you belong to a union or other professional organization, you may be entitled to legal counseling as a benefit of your membership. Last, every state provides some noncriminal legal services for low-income people. However, you may only be able to use them if your income falls below a very minimal level. For names of legal aid groups in your state, look in your phone book under "legal services" or "legal aid." Or, you can contact:

Legal Services Corporation
750 1st Street NE
Eleventh Floor
Washington, DC 20002-4250
202-336-8800

"You Don't Want My Case?"

Armed with a short list of recommendations, Bea scheduled her first meeting with a lawyer named Parker Drew (or was it Drew Parker?). After telling Parker/Drew about the accident and all that followed, she actually liked the guy and was all set to hire him. He was a sympathetic listener and asked intelligent questions.

"I'm sorry, I just don't have time for you right now," he said gently. "I've got too much on my plate."

"Wait a second, Mr. Drew or Mr. Parker, or whatever your name is!" Bea sputtered. "I'm the one who's supposed to be hiring you. Or not, as the case may be. And that is the case!"

Drew Parker led Beatrice out of his office by the elbow.

■ **Is a lawyer required to accept every case?** No. Just as a client can choose not to retain a lawyer, a lawyer can turn down a client, unless the lawyer was assigned by the court, which usually happens only in criminal matters. Lawyers turn down clients for many reasons. The lawyer may be too busy to accept a new case. Or he may not be competent in the particular area or law. Or he simply may not be interested.

Is She Really Worth $200 an Hour?

When Beatrice regained her composure, she crossed Drew off her list and called the next candidate. Angela Solomon had a strong reputation and even a national profile. When Bea met her, though, there was something about the woman that made her uncomfortable.

"But everyone talks about how brilliant she is," mused Beatrice. "What should I do? How do I know?"

■ **How can a person tell if a lawyer is good?** Judge lawyers in the same way that you have learned to judge other people, whether in your job or personal life. Trust your instincts. If you don't like someone, keep looking. Interview at least two, preferably three, lawyers before choosing one. A lawyer worth hiring is one who won't charge you for an initial meeting to hear your problem and discuss it preliminarily.

Solicitations

As she did every day, Beatrice quickly sorted her mail into two piles: "Open" and "Throw Away." But this day, an envelope she had tossed on top of the "Throw Away" pile caught her eye. The return address was from a lawyer's office. When she opened it, she was amazed to see that it was a personal letter to her soliciting her business.

"A lawyer, advertising?" Bea said to herself with disgust. "Is that legal?"

■ **Under what circumstances, if any, are lawyers allowed to advertise or solicit business?**

Lawyers have a constitutional right to inform prospective clients of the availability of their services. As long as they are honest in what they say, they can advertise. Some states require lawyers who send solicitation letters to mark them with words like "Advertising Material," especially when the lawyer knows that the recipient needs a lawyer. (Perhaps the lawyer has learned from a police report that the recipient was in a car accident.) There are many variations among jurisdictions about what lawyers may or may not say in advertisements and letters, and how they may say it. As a rule, however, lawyers *may not* solicit business in person or by telephone unless a prospective client is a friend, family member, or former client.

Your First Meeting

Third time's the charm," Beatrice muttered under her breath. For this interview with a lawyer, she had a list in hand — a list of questions to help her make a rational judgment about the suitability of this attorney. Going into the meeting, Beatrice had her doubts. A lawyer named Daisy Steer?

■ **What questions should a person ask a lawyer before deciding whether to hire him or her?**

There are a number of questions you should ask, including these:

- **How long has he or she been in practice?**
- **What kind of experience does the lawyer have, especially in the area of your problem?**
- **Has his or her practice been in the same community?**
- **The names of a couple of former clients to check with as references. (The lawyer will have to get the clients' permission to do this.)**

Good lawyers will be willing to discuss their experience with you. They should also be willing to answer specific questions about structuring a working relationship with you, including these:

- **Will you return my phone calls within a day or two?**
- **Will you describe your fee structure in a written retainer agreement?**
- **Will your bills specify the work done, when, and by whom?**
- **Will you give me at least monthly progress reports?**
- **Will you consult me on all important decisions in my matter?**

Fees

Beatrice really liked Daisy, and also liked the fact that nearly all the other lawyers in her firm were women. They agreed in principle that she would retain Daisy's services, but they still had a few details to hammer out. Bea was a little taken aback when Daisy asked if she had her checkbook with her.

"My checkbook?" she asked with puzzlement.

"Of course your checkbook. Unless you have cash. So you can pay me a retainer," she responded without missing a beat.

■ **What is a retainer?**

The word "retainer" usually refers to the up-front payment a client gives a lawyer to accept a case — the client is paying to "retain" the lawyer's services. It needn't be the entire fee, which can be greater than the retainer. Usually a retainer is paid in advance, but it may sometimes be paid in installments during the early part of the relationship. A "retainer agreement" is the contract between the lawyer and the client that defines the work the lawyer will do and the compensation (or method of determining the compensation) that the lawyer will receive. It is best to have this retainer agreement in writing and have it be as detailed as possible. If a lawyer asks for a retainer when you have a contingency fee arrangement, the retainer agreement *must* be in writing.

Your Legal Bill

Does your lawyer have to give you a detailed bill?
As with many other aspects of the lawyer-client relationship, it is best to resolve billing issues before retaining your lawyer. Specify at the outset if you want to receive a detailed bill, and how often you want to receive it. The bill should note

- **the amount of work every lawyer at the firm has done**
- **each lawyer's hourly rate**
- **the specific type of work done, such as research, brief writing, or witness interviews**

If the lawyer is charging you for "disbursements," expenses for things like long-distance calls and photocopying, these also should be detailed. Even if you don't request a periodic, detailed bill at the outset, you can do so later. When you make such a request, your lawyer should provide you with one.

What if you think you're overcharged?
Your lawyer has an obligation to discuss the bill with you if you believe it is too high. (You might ask whether the lawyer will be available to discuss problems with the bill without charging you for the time spent doing so.) The lawyer should be willing to explain all the charges on the bill. If you are still unsatisfied, you can ask for an adjustment. If you're still unsatisfied, you should find out if there is a procedure in your jurisdiction for mediating or arbitrating fee disputes between lawyers and clients. Many jurisdictions have these procedures. It's also likely that there's someone at your state or local bar association who handles complaints from clients. (See bar association numbers on page 449.)

If a person decides not to pursue a legal case, does the retainer (or part of it) have to be refunded?

Not always. Most courts — but not all — allow nonrefundable retainers, as long as they are not unreasonably high. (Certain types of cases, like divorces, are sometimes excluded.) So if a lawyer's fee is \$100 an hour, and you pay a \$500 retainer but then decide to drop your case after the lawyer has worked two hours, the lawyer can keep the \$500, as long as you were specifically told that the retainer was nonrefundable. The reasoning is that by accepting your case, the lawyer may have turned down other business, expecting that she would be spending time working on your case. But if the retainer was very large and the matter was ended very quickly, a court could find it unreasonable for the lawyer to keep the whole thing.

Whether a retainer is nonrefundable, and in what amount, are appropriate subjects for negotiation before you hire the lawyer.

Are lawyer's fees negotiable?

Absolutely. Lawyer's fees are very rarely set by law. You can bargain with a lawyer just as you can bargain for anything else you might purchase. That doesn't mean that the lawyer will agree to reduce a quoted fee, but you should feel free to ask. You should also ask whether the quote is based on an hourly rate or is a flat fee.

Clients can also negotiate for the way in which the fee is paid. The lawyer may want to get a large retainer in advance, but you can ask if the lawyer would be willing to take part in advance and part later.

Beatrice just didn't have the kind of cash the lawyer quoted as her hourly rate. She told Daisy the fee was more than she could afford. "Of course it is," said Daisy. "But that doesn't matter, because I'd be willing to take your case on a contingency basis."

What is a contingency fee?

A contingency fee usually gives the lawyer a percentage interest in a client's case. For example, if you were injured and are suing the person who caused the injury, the lawyer's fee might be 25 percent of any money you recover. The entire fee is not always contingent. Some lawyers charge a retainer plus a percentage of any recovery. Again, these are appropriate subjects for negotiation between lawyer and client.

Some contingency fees are on a sliding scale. This means that the lawyer gets a higher percentage of a specified amount and a lower percentage of any additional money recovered. For instance, the lawyer may get 40 percent of the first $10,000 she recovers for the client and 25 percent of anything above $10,000.

When a lawyer charges on a contingent fee basis, she takes a risk that the client will recover nothing, in which case the lawyer also recovers nothing. While this fee structure enables you to hire a lawyer without risking your own money, it also means that if the lawyer is successful, she will probably get a higher fee than she would have earned if she charged strictly on an hourly basis.

■ Is there a limit to what percentage the lawyer can take?

It depends on the type of case. All jurisdictions limit the contingency percentage in personal injury cases, and some also limit it in medical malpractice cases. These limits vary widely. However, it is unusual (except in cases involving small sums) for contingent fees to be more than one-third of the total recovery.

The laws do not set the contingency fees. Rather, they merely limit how high the fee can be. You can always negotiate for a lower contingent rate. You should not hire a lawyer who tells you that the law specifies that she is *entitled* to a one-third contingency. What the lawyer should say is that the law specifies that she is not allowed to charge *more than* a one-third contingency. There is no rule that says she cannot charge less.

In cases other than personal injury or medical malpractice, the law does not generally limit the amount of the contingency, and it is up for negotiation between lawyer and client. In choosing an acceptable contingency, a lawyer will consider the risk that the client will recover nothing and the lawyer will have worked for nothing. The greater the risk, the higher the contingency percentage the lawyer will want.

■ Can a person fire a lawyer who took a case on contingency?

As always, if you are not happy with your lawyer, you can fire her even if she is working for you on contingency. However, if the case has already been filed in court, you will have to get the judge's authorization. The judge will usually grant permission unless the case is very close to trial.

If you fire a lawyer who has taken your case on contingency, he or she is still entitled to a fee for the work done. In some places, the lawyer has a right to a portion of the client's ultimate recovery. In other places, the fee is measured by the reasonable value of the lawyer's services up until the time of firing, regardless of the ultimate outcome of the case. If, however, you had good reason to fire the lawyer (perhaps he or she failed to do any work on your case), then the lawyer has no right to a fee.

■ Are there cases that can't be taken on a contingency basis?

Yes. The most prominent examples are divorce cases, child-custody cases, and criminal cases. A lawyer cannot agree to a fee contingent on his or her ability to secure a divorce, custody, or an acquittal for the client.

"What a relief to have chosen a lawyer and to know that my case is in good hands," Beatrice told her friend Derek over brunch one Saturday morning. On Daisy's advice, Bea had resumed her massage treatments and felt well enough to go back to work.

"I hope you got that fee agreement in writing," Derek warned. "My cousin had a bad experience with that once, where his lawyer all of a sudden upped his rates."

Attorney's Liens

If you have a fee dispute with your lawyer, he or she may be able to institute a claim against your money or property, called a **lien**. There are two types.

- A **retaining lien** gives a lawyer the right to hold onto your money or property (such as a deed) until you pay the bill. The attorney does not have to go to court to institute this lien. He or she just keeps the property until you pay or go to court asking a judge to order a release. The judge would probably hold a hearing to determine whether the lawyer had good reason to keep your possessions.
- A **charging lien** entitles a lawyer who has sued someone on your behalf the right to be paid from the proceeds of the lawsuit, if there are any, before you receive those proceeds. The lawyer is entitled to payment for the amount of services rendered even if you fired the lawyer. However, if you fired the lawyer "for cause," such as the failure to do the promised work on your case, then he or she would not be entitled to any portion of the proceeds.

Some jurisdictions recognize one or the other lien. Some recognize neither, and some recognize both.

Before hiring a lawyer, you can ask whether he or she would be willing to waive the retaining lien, if it is recognized in your jurisdiction. This lien can seriously hamper a client who wants to change lawyers before a case is over, because the original lawyer can refuse to turn over your files to the new lawyer if he or she believes you still owe money. If the attorney agrees to waive the lien, you should ask that it be put in writing.

If a lawyer charges a set fee for a service, can additional costs be added later for the same service?

No. A deal is a deal. Unless the lawyer was misled, he or she cannot raise the fee. However, lawyers who charge by the hour may periodically raise their hourly rates for all clients. A lawyer should tell you when he or she raises the hourly rate in the midst of representing you. But even before taking your case, a lawyer should alert you if he or she expects to raise the hourly rate before your case is completed. You should feel free to discuss this possibility with a lawyer before retaining him or her.

Beatrice assured Derek that she didn't have to pay anything, because her lawyer took her case for a contingency fee.

"I wouldn't be so sure about that," Derek said. "There can be all sorts of hidden costs with lawyers."

"Like what?" asked Beatrice, looking worried.

"Oh, you know, expenses, phone calls, stuff like that."

"Aren't those just business expenses?" asked Beatrice. "Part of being a lawyer, running an office?"

Can a lawyer charge the client for expenses incurred while working on a case?

It depends. When a lawyer takes a case on a contingency basis, the rules vary from state to state. In many states, a lawyer can "advance" the client the money to cover the costs for things like court filing fees and expert witnesses, so long as the client remains ultimately liable for the full amount. In other states, you and your lawyer can agree that you will reimburse the lawyer only if you win the case and recover enough money to pay back the expenses. Even in states that require the client to be ultimately liable, most lawyers will not ask for reimbursement if they lose the case.

What are typical expenses?

Some pass-along charges are easy to understand. For example, if your lawyer has to pay a court filing fee in connection with your case, he or she will ask you for reimbursement. But you may be charged for other, less obvious expenses, such as

- **long-distance telephone calls**
- **overnight mail**
- **messenger services**
- **out-of-town travel if it is needed**
- **photocopying**
- **computerized legal research**
- **other office costs, such as the use of a fax machine**

Sometimes when lawyers charge for office expenses, they bill you for more than what it actually costs them to provide the service. For example, they may charge you twenty cents a page for photocopies even though their cost is less. You should not hesitate to discuss these additional costs with a lawyer you are interviewing. You should ask the lawyer what "disbursements," as lawyers call them, will be charged to you and at what rate. You should specify that any such disbursements must be detailed in your bills. What you don't want is a bill that says simply: "Disbursements — $100." No magic rule says which disbursements can be properly passed along to the client and which cannot. This is negotiable. But unless you say something, it's very possible that the lawyer will pass along such costs.

CONFIDENTIALITY

Bart was contemplating running for a seat in the state senate. His wife, Janet, was supportive, as long as she didn't have to do any campaigning. But when Bart reflected privately on the matter, he realized that he had a personal liability that could become an explosive campaign issue: he was still married to his first wife, Allegra. When he and Allegra split up, everyone assumed that they would divorce, and so did Bart. But somehow they just never did. And then he fell so deeply in love with Janet that he forgot about everyone and everything else, and the next thing he knew, they were married.

At least that's the way Bart told the story to Julius, the lawyer he consulted to see if he could discreetly remedy the situation.

Are things a person tells to a lawyer confidential?

Rules about confidentiality vary from state to state, but certain basic principles hold true in most places. Information you give your lawyer, his colleagues, and assistants (including clerical staff) to help him represent you is considered "privileged" information. This means that your lawyer won't reveal the information except to help solve your legal problem and that no court can force him to reveal the information.

Information that your lawyer learns from other people in connection with his work for you is also protected, but is considered "confidential." When information is confidential (but not privileged), your lawyer cannot reveal it except to help you. However, if your lawyer is asked by a court to reveal confidential (but not privileged) information, he may have to do so.

There are some exceptions to this. The circumstances are varied, but basically they fall into two categories. If your lawyer has information that shows that you plan to commit a criminal act, especially if the crime will cause someone bodily harm, he or she may (and in some places **must**) take steps to protect the victim. This exception applies only if your lawyer concludes that you are going to commit a crime in the future. If you go to a lawyer for help because of a crime you have already committed in the past, the exception doesn't apply. The lawyer can't reveal your confession.

The other exception arises if you and your lawyer get into a dispute about whether he did a good job. In that case, the lawyer may be able to use your confidential or privileged information to defend himself. That dispute could arise, for example, if

- **you refuse to pay your lawyer's fee**
- **you sue your lawyer for malpractice**
- **you file a complaint with a lawyer's disciplinary body**

WHEN A LAWYER QUITS

Bart slammed down the phone in anger. Julius had learned that an old law school classmate was going to be Bart's biggest opponent in the state senate race, so he decided he didn't want to represent Bart. "I'm sending your retainer back immediately," Julius said apologetically. "Along with a couple of names of other people who might be able to help you."

■ Under what circumstances can a lawyer drop a case?

Generally, a lawyer is obligated to keep a case once it has been accepted. However, lawyers may sometimes withdraw from representing a client if

- **the client has not paid the lawyer's fee**
- **the client wants the lawyer to do something illegal or unethical**
- **the client has lied to someone and refuses to correct the lie. (In most states, if the client has lied in court, the lawyer may be obligated to tell the judge.)**
- **the client is making it unreasonably difficult for the lawyer to represent him or her (refusing to return phone calls, for example, or not giving the lawyer the information needed to conduct a thorough investigation)**
- **the lawyer discovers a conflict of interest**

A lawyer cannot, however, drop a case just because he grows tired of the matter or because, through no fault of the client, it is taking longer than the lawyer anticipated. Nor, ordinarily, can the lawyer withdraw because the case is not as financially rewarding as it had originally appeared, or because the lawyer wants to free up time to take a more lucrative assignment.

If a lawyer is representing a client in a matter that has been filed in court, the lawyer cannot withdraw for *any* reason unless the judge agrees. However, if the lawyer has a good reason, and the matter is not about to go to trial, the judge will usually agree.

MALPRACTICE

Bart's anger with Julius turned to rage. Bart had refused to let Julius back out of their agreement because he didn't want to have to tell his secrets to another lawyer. So Julius told a reporter from the local paper about Bart's bigamy, and the reporter called Bart for confirmation. "Off the record, my friend," the reporter advised Bart, "I would sue Julius for malpractice."

■ What is legal malpractice?

A lawyer is guilty of malpractice if he or she does not exercise the same degree of care, skill, and judgment as do other lawyers practicing in your community. A lawyer who claims to have expertise in an area of law must bring a higher-than-average level of skill to your matter, and a lawyer could be liable for neglecting your matter or revealing your confidences improperly.

If you believe a lawyer has mishandled your case, the first thing you should do, if feasible, is to talk to the lawyer about it. He or she may be able to satisfy you that your suspicions are wrong. The problem may be only a failure of communication. However, if you cannot talk to your lawyer about it (perhaps he won't return your calls) or if talking about it doesn't satisfy you, you may want to consult a second lawyer about whether you have a claim against your first lawyer. You can also file a complaint with the local disciplinary agency that governs lawyers (for more, see page 448), and you can notify the state or local bar association (for listings, see page 449).

CONFLICTS OF INTEREST

Bradley had become good friends with another private investigator, Natasha, with whom he frequently had lunch to discuss case progress. After months of informal collaboration, they decided to join forces, combine their businesses, and work as a team. They scheduled a meeting with a lawyer to help them draw up the documents for forming a partnership. But when they told the lawyer

what they wanted, he shook his head. "I can represent only one of you," he said. "Otherwise it's a conflict of interest."

What is a conflict of interest?

A lawyer has a conflict of interest if his professional or personal obligations to other people, or his own personal or financial interests, will make it difficult for him to handle a case. For example, it would be a conflict of interest for a lawyer to represent both a husband and a wife in the negotiation of a separation agreement. Similarly, it would be difficult for a lawyer to represent both the seller and buyer of real estate.

A lawyer would have a conflict of interest if a client asked the lawyer to represent her in suing one of the lawyer's former clients in a case where the new lawsuit dealt with the same matter as the prior representation. For example, a lawyer who has represented a tenant in negotiating a lease with the landlord could not later represent the landlord seeking to evict the tenant for violating the same lease.

A lawyer's own interests can also create a conflict. For instance, it would be a conflict for a lawyer to represent someone challenging a will if the lawyer's friend or close relative is a beneficiary under the will.

Sometimes a conflict of interest can be waived, and the lawyer can represent both parties, but only if the client is fully apprised of the conflict and the dangers it creates, and then agrees to hire the lawyer anyway. So if two people like Brad and Natasha want to go into business together, they might like to hire a single lawyer to prepare a contract because it would be cheaper than hiring two lawyers. A single lawyer ordinarily can do the job, but only after fully explaining the limitations that arise from representing both parties. For example, the lawyer could not advocate a provision that would significantly benefit one party but disadvantage the other. On the other hand, if both people are in virtual agreement, or if they are prepared to resolve any differences themselves and are relying on the lawyer only as a source of information and technical assistance, they can agree to waive the lawyer's conflict.

Some conflicts of interest are so serious that they cannot be waived. For example, if two people are charged with a crime and each wants to claim that the other is primarily responsible, they will obviously need separate lawyers.

ESCROW ACCOUNTS

Natasha and Bradley's first few months together were tremendous. They located a woman's long-lost sister and recovered a valuable painting that had been stolen from a local gallery. Both cases brought in hefty fees, and the publicity brought in several new clients. They needed more office space, and they put down a deposit to buy a small, rundown building (being sold for a small, affordable price). The seller's lawyer took their check. "Don't worry," she said. "Your money's safe in my law firm's escrow account."

What is a lawyer's escrow account?

An escrow account is a special bank account in which a lawyer deposits money that does not belong to him or his firm. For example, a firm may handle a client's funds or receive money to be paid to the client. Or if you are buying a house, you may give the seller's lawyer a down payment to hold in an escrow account. Only when the sale goes through will the money be paid to the seller; until then, the money will sit in escrow, where no one can touch it.

The firm cannot mix up client money with its own funds; it has to deposit client's money in an escrow account. Money for numerous clients can be in the same escrow account. The point is to keep the funds separate from those of the lawyer and the firm.

When a lawyer has your money in an escrow account, he or she must give it to you on demand. If your lawyer claims she has a right to some of the money, because she has not yet been paid her fee, she cannot take what she thinks is hers without your consent. If you and your lawyer disagree, the money must stay in escrow until you come to terms.

A lawyer who improperly takes money from an escrow account (even with the honest intention of repaying it) can be seriously disciplined and possibly disbarred.

DISAGREEING WITH YOUR LAWYER

After celebrating her fifth year in business, Blossom threw a party for all the employees who helped Made in America become such a success. And what better place to do it than around the pool in her backyard? She went all out, even doing some of the cooking for the party herself.

Blossom felt bad when her personnel manager Deirdre had to be rushed to the hospital because she was stung by a bee. (Deirdre was allergic.) But not nearly as bad as she felt when she found out that Deirdre was suing her for damages.

Blossom called her lawyer to put her on the case. After listening to Blossom's description of what happened, Janice spoke in measured tones. "I'll be frank with you," she said. "As your lawyer, my advice is to settle out of court. The last thing you need is a lawsuit on your hands."

"No," retorted Blossom. "The last thing I need is to be taken to the cleaners by an employee. A former employee."

■ Does a person have to take a lawyer's advice?

Some decisions are clearly for the client to make. These include

- **whether to settle a civil claim**
- **whether to plead guilty**
- **whether to testify in a criminal case**
- **whether to accept proposed contract terms in a negotiation**

You can always defer to your lawyer's recommendations and sometimes even give him or her the authority to make these decisions. But you don't have to.

Other types of decisions are for the lawyer, though of course the client can participate. These include

- **how to draft a court document**
- **what witnesses to call**
- **how to write a contract in a way that best protects the client's interests**

Generally, the lawyer decides what *means* to use, and the client decides on the *ends*. But even that distinction is not entirely accurate. For example, if your lawyer believes that your case will be significantly enhanced if you spend $5,000 for a particular expert witness, that is a question about the *means* of running your case, but it is a decision that you have to make.

If your lawyer receives a plausible offer of settlement from the other side (or a plea bargain offer in a criminal case), he or she has an obligation to discuss it with you. This is true even if the lawyer would advise you to reject the offer. Ultimately, these decisions are for the client; the lawyer cannot deprive you of the right to make the decision by failing to inform you of the offer. You can, however, authorize your lawyer to settle a civil case without consulting you if the lawyer believes the offer is fair.

When you interview a lawyer, you should discuss decision making. If you want to participate in all significant decisions in connection with your case (even if they are about means and not ends), you should say so and see whether the lawyer is willing to agree. A lawyer who is not willing to agree may not be a good lawyer for you.

WHO WORKS ON YOUR CASE

Blossom was resolute. She wanted to fight this case in court, and she told her lawyer so in no uncertain terms. She had never been sued before and was afraid that settling out of court would make her vulnerable to further lawsuits.

"Well, if you insist, we'll work with you on it," Janice told Blossom. "But my schedule is full right now. I'll have to let one of my colleagues handle it for you."

■ Can a lawyer pass a case on to other lawyers at the same firm?

Yes. When you hire a lawyer who works in a firm, you actually hire the firm. If you want to specify the kind of attention a particular lawyer will give to your case, you should do it at the outset. At the very least, you may want to get the lawyer's assurance that he or she will closely review the work of any other lawyers involved on your matter. You can also ask to meet the lawyers who will work on your case.

A lawyer's freedom to assign work to others does not extend outside the firm. A lawyer can't ask someone who is not in the firm to work on a matter unless the client agrees.

DATING YOUR LAWYER

Blossom wasn't thrilled that Janice wouldn't be handling her case; after all, the two women had a longstanding professional relationship. But she had to admit that the lawyer assigned to her case seemed extremely smart and capable. Not to mention his drop-dead good looks. After their second meeting in his office, Dick suggested that they discuss the case further over dinner on Friday night.

■ Can lawyers and clients date each other?

It's not a good idea to date your lawyer while he or she is still representing you. In many states, it is actually improper for a lawyer to begin an intimate relationship with a client in a criminal or matrimonial case before the matter is over. There are many reasons for this.

- The very fact of an intimate relationship with your lawyer could hurt your chances of winning a custody battle for a child.
- Being in an intimate relationship with you can make the lawyer less effective as your advocate. (Of course, it could work the other way, too, but the law tries to guard the client.)
- It may become unclear whether communications between you and your lawyer are protected as confidential or are merely part of your personal relationship and thus not protected from disclosure.

There have been cases in which lawyers have demanded sexual favors from clients in exchange for the lawyer's help, most frequently in matrimonial matters. It is improper for a lawyer to accept sex in exchange for legal help, even if the client is willing to agree to that exchange.

DEALING WITH IMPROPER BEHAVIOR

Blossom didn't think any harm would come from having dinner with Dick, her new lawyer. And it turned out that they had a lot more in common than her case. Things were progressing well both with Blossom's case and with her friendship with Dick until she discovered that he was married. Blossom immediately called a halt to the nonprofessional facet of their relationship. In retaliation, Dick stopped returning her calls about the case and seemed to be neglecting his professional obligations.

■ What should a person do if a lawyer has acted improperly?

If a lawyer has acted improperly and you have been damaged as a result, you should consider suing him for legal malpractice (see page 445). In addition, every jurisdiction has its own rules of ethics that govern lawyers, and those rules are adopted by the courts of the jurisdiction. It is the courts that license lawyers to practice. Thus if a lawyer violates a rule of ethics, he or she can be disciplined. Discipline can lead to censure, suspension from practice, or even disbarment.

In every jurisdiction there is a disciplinary authority that receives complaints about lawyers. If you believe your lawyer has acted improperly, you should consider complaining to this authority, usually listed in the phone book under state government offices. Or you can call your state or local bar association to get the number (see listings opposite). Complaints are easy to make. You don't need a lawyer to complain about a lawyer. Although disciplinary authorities cannot order lawyers to pay you damages caused by their negligence, some are empowered to order lawyers to return money wrongfully withheld from a client.

■ What are some common complaints about lawyers?

One of the most frequent complaints to disciplinary authorities is that a lawyer has neglected a client's matter. Once a lawyer accepts a matter, he is obligated to pursue it diligently, regardless of whether he is being paid for the matter or whether the payment is on a contingency basis. When a lawyer neglects a matter, it can cause the client great anguish even if the client doesn't ultimately lose any money. If a lawyer's neglect causes a client to lose a case, the client may have a claim for malpractice.

Clients also complain about lawyers who fail to keep them informed about what is happening in their case — even though the lawyers may not be neglecting their cases. A lawyer is obligated to keep a client informed of a case's status. Another common (and legitimate) complaint is that a lawyer has recovered money for the client but has failed to turn it over.

FOR FURTHER REFERENCE

State Bar Associations

Alabama
Alabama State Bar
415 Dexter Avenue
Montgomery, AL 36104
mailing address:
P.O. Box 671
Montgomery, AL 36101
205-269-1515

Alaska
Alaska Bar Association
510 L Street No. 602
Anchorage, AK 99501
mailing address:
P.O. Box 100279
Anchorage, AK 99510
907-272-7469

Arizona
State Bar of Arizona
111 West Monroe
Phoenix, AZ 85003-1742
602-252-4804

Arkansas
Arkansas Bar Association
400 West Markham
Little Rock, AR 72201
501-375-4605

California
State Bar of California
555 Franklin Street
San Francisco, CA 94102
415-561-8200

Colorado
Colorado Bar Association
1900 Grant Street, No. 950
Denver, CO 80203
303-860-1115

Connecticut
Connecticut Bar Association
101 Corporate Place
Rocky Hill, CT 06067-1894
203-721-0025

Delaware
Delaware State Bar Association
1225 King Street, 10th Floor
Wilmington, DE 19801
302-658-5279
302-658-5278 (lawyer referral service)

District of Columbia
District of Columbia Bar
(mandatory organization for all DC attorneys)
1250 H Street NW, 6th Floor
Washington, DC 20005
202-737-4700

Bar Association of the District of Columbia
(voluntary organization)
1819 H Street NW, 12th Floor
Washington, DC 20006-3690
202-223-6600

Florida
The Florida Bar
The Florida Bar Center
650 Apalachee Parkway
Tallahassee, FL 32399-2300
904-561-5600

Georgia
State Bar of Georgia
800 The Hurt Building
50 Hurt Plaza
Atlanta, GA 30303
404-527-8700

Hawaii
Hawaii State Bar Association
1136 Union Mall
Penthouse 1
Honolulu, HI 96813
808-537-1868

Idaho
Idaho State Bar
P.O. Box 895
Boise, ID 83701
208-334-4500

Illinois
Illinois State Bar Association
424 South Second Street
Springfield, IL 62701
217-525-1760

Indiana
Indiana State Bar Association
230 East Ohio Street
Indianapolis, IN 46204
317-639-5465

Iowa
Iowa State Bar Association
521 East Locust
Des Moines, IA 50309
515-243-3179

Kansas
Kansas Bar Association
1200 Harrison Street
Topeka, KS 66601
913-234-5696

Kentucky
Kentucky Bar Association
514 West Main Street
Frankfort, KY 40601-1883
502-564-3795

Louisiana
Louisiana State Bar Association
601 St. Charles Avenue
New Orleans, LA 70130
504-566-1600

Maine
Maine State Bar Association
124 State Street
P.O. Box 788
Augusta, ME 04330
207-622-7523

Maryland
Maryland State Bar Association
520 West Fayette Street
Baltimore, MD 21201
410-685-7878

Massachusetts
Massachusetts Bar Association
20 West Street
Boston, MA 02111
617-542-3602
617-542-9103 (lawyer referral service)

Michigan
State Bar of Michigan
306 Townsend Street
Lansing, MI 48933-2083
517-372-9030

Minnesota
Minnesota State Bar Association
514 Nicollet Mall
Minneapolis, MN 55402
612-333-1183

Mississippi
The Mississippi Bar
643 North State Street
Jackson, Mississippi 39202
601-948-4471

Missouri
The Missouri Bar
326 Monroe
Jefferson City, Missouri 65102
314-635-4128

Montana
State Bar of Montana
46 North Main
P.O. Box 577
Helena, MT 59624
406-442-7660

Nebraska
Nebraska State Bar Association
635 South 14th Street, 2nd Floor
Lincoln, NE 68508
402-475-7091

Nevada
State Bar of Nevada
201 Las Vegas Boulevard
Las Vegas, NV 89101
702-382-2200

New Hampshire
New Hampshire Bar Association
112 Pleasant Street
Concord, NH 03301
603-224-6942

New Jersey
New Jersey State Bar Association
One Constitution Square
New Brunswick, NJ 08901-1500
908-249-5000

New Mexico
State Bar of New Mexico
121 Tijeras Street NE
Albuquerque, NM 87102
mailing address:
P.O. Box 25883
Albuquerque, NM 87125
505-843-6132

New York
New York State Bar Association
One Elk Street
Albany, NY 12207
518-463-3200

North Carolina
North Carolina State Bar
(mandatory organization)
208 Fayetteville Street Mall
Raleigh, NC 27601
mailing address:
P.O. Box 25908
Raleigh, NC 27611
919-828-4620

North Carolina Bar Association
(voluntary organization)
1312 Annapolis Drive
Raleigh, NC 27608
mailing address:
P.O. Box 12806
Raleigh, NC 27605
919-828-0561

North Dakota
State Bar Association of North Dakota
515½ East Broadway, Suite 101
Bismarck, ND 58501
mailing address:
P.O. Box 2136
Bismarck, ND 58502
701-255-1404

Ohio
Ohio State Bar Association
1700 Lake Shore Drive
Columbus, OH 43204
mailing address:
P.O. Box 16562
Columbus, OH 43216-6562
614-487-2050

Oklahoma
Oklahoma Bar Association
1901 North Lincoln
Oklahoma City, OK 73105
405-524-2365

Oregon
Oregon State Bar
5200 SW Meadows Road
P.O. Box 1689
Lake Oswego, OR 97035-0889
503-620-0222

Pennsylvania
Pennsylvania Bar Association
100 South Street
P.O. Box 186
Harrisburg, PA 17108
717-238-6715

Puerto Rico
Puerto Rico Bar Association
P.O. Box 1900
San Juan, Puerto Rico 00903
809-721-3358

Rhode Island
Rhode Island Bar Association
115 Cedar Street
Providence, RI 02903
401-421-5740

South Carolina
South Carolina Bar
950 Taylor Street
P.O. Box 608
Columbia, SC 29202
803-799-6653

South Dakota
State Bar of South Dakota
222 East Capitol
Pierre, SD 57501
605-224-7554

Tennessee
Tennessee Bar Association
3622 West End Avenue
Nashville, TN 37205
615-383-7421

Texas
State Bar of Texas
1414 Colorado
P.O. Box 12487
Austin, TX 78711
512-463-1463

Utah
Utah State Bar
645 South 200 East, Suite 310
Salt Lake City, UT 84111
801-531-9077

Vermont
Vermont Bar Association
P.O. Box 100
Montpelier, VT 05601
802-223-2020

Virginia
Virginia State Bar
(mandatory organization)
707 East Main Street, Suite 1500
Richmond, VA 23219-0501
804-775-0500

Virginia Bar Association
(voluntary organization)
701 East Franklin Street, Suite 1120
Richmond, VA 23219
804-644-0041

Virgin Islands
Virgin Islands Bar Association
P.O. Box 4108
Christiansted, VI 00822
809-778-7497

Washington
Washington State Bar Association
2001 Sixth Avenue
500 Westin Building
Seattle, WA 98121-2599
206-727-8200

West Virginia

(mandatory organization)
West Virginia State Bar
2006 Kanawha Boulevard East
Charleston, WV 25311
304-558-2456

West Virginia Bar Association
(voluntary organization)
904 Security Building
100 Capitol Street
Charleston, WV 25301
304-342-1474

Wisconsin

State Bar of Wisconsin
402 West Wilson Street
Madison, WI 53703
608-257-3838

Wyoming

Wyoming State Bar
500 Randall Avenue
Cheyenne, WY 82001
mailing address:
P.O. Box 109
Cheyenne, WY 82003
307-632-9061

GLOSSARY

A-B trust See **bypass trust.**

Actual malice To win a defamation suit, public officials or prominent people, such as political candidates or movie stars, must prove that the offender made a false statement with actual malice. This means that the statement was made with knowledge that it was false or with serious doubts about whether it was true.

Adjournment in contemplation of dismissal See **pretrial diversion.**

Administrator Person appointed to oversee the handling of an estate when there is no will.

Advance directive See **living will.**

Affidavit A written statement made under oath.

Age of majority The age when a person acquires all the rights and responsibilities of being an adult. In most states, the age is eighteen.

Alimony Also called maintenance or spousal support. In a divorce or separation, the money paid by one spouse to the other in order to fulfill the financial obligation that comes with marriage.

Alternative dispute resolution Methods for resolving problems without going to court.

Amicus curiae Latin for "friend of the court." Refers to a party that is allowed to provide information (usually in the form of a legal brief) to a court even though the party is not directly involved in the case at hand.

Annulment A legal decree that states that a marriage was never valid. Has the legal effect of wiping out a marriage as though it never existed.

Answer In a civil case, the **defendant**'s written response to the **plaintiff**'s **complaint.** It must be filed within a specified period of time, and it either admits to or (more typically) denies the factual or legal basis for liability.

Appeal A request to a supervisory court, usually composed of a panel of judges, to overturn the legal ruling of a lower court.

Arbitration A method of alternative dispute resolution in which the disputing parties agree to abide by the decision of an arbitrator.

Arraignment The initial appearance before a judge in a criminal case. At an arraignment, the charges against the defendant are read, a lawyer is appointed if the defendant cannot afford one, and the defendant's plea is entered.

Articles of incorporation A document that must be filed with a state in order to incorporate. Among the things it typically must include are the name and address of the corporation, its general purpose, and the number and type of shares of stock to be issued.

Assignment The transfer of legal rights, such as the time left on a lease, from one person to another.

Assumption of risk A defense raised in personal injury lawsuits. Asserts that the plaintiff knew that a particular activity was dangerous and thus bears all responsibility for any injury that resulted.

Asylum seeker A foreigner, already in the U.S. or at the border, who seeks refuge, claiming an inability or unwillingness to return to the home country because of a well-founded fear of persecution.

At-will employment An employment relationship where the employer has the right to fire a worker for any cause at any time — usually without any notice.

Bad faith Dishonesty or fraud in a transaction, such as entering into an agreement with no intention of ever living up to its terms, or knowingly misrepresenting the quality of something that is being bought or sold.

Bail The money a defendant pays as a guarantee that he or she will show up in court at a later date. For most serious crimes, a judge sets bail during the arraignment.

Bail schedule The list that sets the amount of bail a defendant is required to pay based on what the charge is. A judge may be able to reduce the amount.

Bailment A legal relationship created when a person gives property to someone else for safekeeping. To create a bailment the other party must knowingly have exclusive control over the property. The receiver must use **reasonable care** to protect the property.

Bankruptcy Insolvency; a process governed by federal law to help when people cannot or will not pay their debts.

Bench trial Also called court trial. A trial held before a judge and without a jury.

Beneficiary Person named in a will or insurance policy to receive money or property; person who receives benefits from a trust.

Beyond a reasonable doubt The highest level of proof required to win a case. Necessary to get a guilty verdict in criminal cases.

Bifurcation Splitting a trial into two parts: a **liability phase** and a **penalty phase.** In some cases, a new jury may be empaneled to deliberate for the penalty phase.

Bill of Rights The first ten amendments to the U.S. Constitution.

Binder An outline of the basic terms of a proposed sales contract between a buyer and a seller.

Board of directors The group of people elected by a corporation's shareholders to make major business decisions for the company.

Bond A document with which one party promises to pay another within a specified amount of time. Bonds are used for many things, including borrowing money or guaranteeing payment of money.

Booking Part of the process of being arrested in which the details of who a person is and why he or she was arrested are recorded into the police records.

Brief A written document that outlines a party's legal arguments in a case.

Burden of proof The duty of a party in a lawsuit to persuade the judge or the jury that enough facts exist to prove the allegations of the case. Different levels of proof are required depending on the type of case.

Buy-sell agreement An agreement among business partners that specifies how shares in the business are to be transferred in the case of a co-owner's death.

Bylaws A corporation's rules and regulations. They typically specify the number and respective duties of directors and officers and govern how the business is run.

Bypass trust Also called a marital life estate or an A-B trust. A trust designed to help couples with combined assets over $600,000 save money on estate taxes. A bypass trust allows each member of a couple to use the $600,000 estate tax exemption.

Capital gain The profit made from the sale of a capital asset, such as real estate, a house, jewelry, or stocks and bonds.

Capital loss The loss that results from the sale of a capital asset, such as real estate, a house, jewelry, or stocks and bonds. Also the loss that results from an unpaid, nonbusiness (personal) loan.

Case law Also known as common law. The law created by judges when deciding individual disputes or cases.

Case of first impression A novel legal question that comes before a court.

Caveat emptor Latin for "buyer beware." This rule generally applies to all sales between individuals. It gives the buyer full responsibility for determining the quality of the goods in question. The seller generally has no duty to offer warranties or to disclose defects in the goods.

Certiorari Latin that means "to be informed of." Refers to the order a court issues so that it can review the decision and proceedings in a lower court and determine whether there were any irregularities. When such an order is made, it is said that the court has granted certiorari.

Chapter 7 bankruptcy A type of bankruptcy in which a person's assets are liquidated (collected and sold) and the proceeds are distributed to the **creditors.**

Chapter 13 bankruptcy A type of bankruptcy in which a person keeps his assets and pays **creditors** according to an approved plan.

Challenge for cause Ask that a potential juror be rejected if it is revealed that for some reason he or she is unable or unwilling to set aside preconceptions and pay attention only to the evidence.

Change of venue A change in the location of a trial, usually granted to avoid prejudice against one of the parties.

Charging lien Entitles a lawyer who has sued someone on a client's behalf the right to be paid from the proceeds of the lawsuit, if there are any, before the client receives those proceeds.

Child abuse Defined by state statutes. Usually occurs when a parent purposefully harms a child.

Child neglect Defined by state statutes. Usually arises from a parent's passive indifference to a child's well-being, such as failing to feed a child or leaving a child alone for an extended time.

Children's trust A trust set up as part of a will or outside a will to provide funds for a child.

Circumstantial evidence Indirect evidence that implies something occurred but doesn't directly prove it. If a man accused of embezzling money from his company had made several big-ticket purchases in cash around the time of the alleged embezzlement, that would be circumstantial evidence that he had stolen the money.

Class action suit A lawsuit in which one or more parties file a complaint on behalf of themselves and all other people who are "similarly situated" (suffering from the same problem). Often used when a large number of people have comparable claims.

Clear and convincing evidence The level of proof sometimes required in a civil case for the plaintiff to prevail. Is more than a **preponderance of the evidence** but less than **beyond a reasonable doubt.**

Closing In a real estate transaction, this is the final exchange in which the **deed** is delivered to the buyer, the **title** is transferred, and the agreed-on costs are paid.

Codicil A supplement to a will.

Cohabitation agreement Also called a living-together contract. A document that spells out the terms of a relationship and often addresses financial issues and how property will be divided if the relationship ends.

Collateral An asset that a borrower agrees to give up if he or she fails to repay a loan.

Collective bargaining agreement The contract that spells out the terms of employment between a labor union and an employer.

Comity A code of etiquette that governs the interactions of courts in different states, localities, and foreign countries. Courts generally agree to defer scheduling a trial if the same issues are being tried in a court in another jurisdiction. In addition, courts in this country agree to recognize and enforce the valid legal contracts and court orders of other countries.

Common law Also known as case law. The law created by judges when deciding individual disputes or cases.

Common-law marriage In some states, a couple is considered married if they meet certain requirements, such as living together as husband and wife for a specific length of time. Such a couple has all the rights and obligations of a traditionally married couple.

Community property Property acquired by a couple during their marriage. Refers to the system in some states for dividing the couple's property in a divorce or upon the death of one spouse. In this system, most property a husband and wife acquire while married is owned equally (fifty-fifty) by both of them, regardless of who provided the money to purchase the asset or whose name the asset is held in.

Comparative negligence Also called comparative fault. A system that allows a party to recover some portion of the damages caused by another party's negligence even if the original person was also partially negligent and responsible for causing the injury. Not all states follow this system.

Compensatory damages Money awarded to reimburse actual costs, such as medical bills and lost wages. Also awarded for things that are harder to measure, such as pain and suffering.

Complaint In a civil action, the document that initiates a lawsuit. The complaint outlines the alleged facts of the case and the basis for which a legal remedy is sought. In a criminal action, a complaint is the preliminary charge filed by the complaining party, usually with the police or a court.

Concurrent sentences Criminal sentences that can be served at the same time rather than one after the other.

Conditional dismissal See **pretrial diversion.**

Conflict of interest Refers to a situation when someone, such as a lawyer or public official, has competing professional or personal obligations or personal or financial interests that would make it difficult to fulfill his duties fairly.

Consecutive sentences Criminal sentences that must be served one after the other rather than at the same time.

Conservator Person appointed to manage the property and finances of another. Sometimes called a guardian.

Consideration Something of value that is given in exchange for getting something from another person.

Contempt of court An action that interferes with a judge's ability to administer justice or that insults the dignity of the court. Disrespectful comments to the judge or a failure to heed a judge's orders could be considered contempt of court. A person found in contempt of court can face financial sanctions and, in some cases, jail time.

Contingency fee Also called a contingent fee. A fee arrangement in which the lawyer is paid out of any damages that are awarded. Typically, the lawyer gets between one-fourth and one-third. If no damages are awarded, there is no fee.

Contract An agreement between two or more parties in which an offer is made and accepted, and each party benefits. The agreement can be formal, informal, written, oral, or just plain understood. Some contracts are required to be in writing in order to be enforced.

Contributory negligence Prevents a party from recovering for damages if he or she contributed in any way to the injury. Not all states follow this system.

Copyright A person's right to prevent others from copying works that he or she has written, authored, or otherwise created.

Corporation An independent entity created to conduct a business. It is owned by **shareholders.**

Creditor A person (or institution) to whom money is owed.

Cross-examination The questioning of an opposing party's witness about matters brought up during **direct examination.**

Custodian Under the Uniform Transfers to Minors Act, the person appointed to manage and dispense funds for a child without constricting court supervision and accounting requirements.

Damages The financial compensation awarded to someone who suffered an injury or was harmed by someone else's wrongful act.

Debtor Person who owes money.

Decision The judgment rendered by a court after a consideration of the facts and legal issues before it.

Deed A written legal document that describes a piece of property and outlines its boundaries. The seller of a property transfers ownership by delivering the deed to the buyer in exchange for an agreed-upon sum of money.

Defamation The publication of a statement that injures a person's reputation. **Libel** and **slander** are defamation.

Default The failure to fulfill a legal obligation, such as neglecting to pay back a loan on schedule.

Default judgment A ruling entered against a defendant who fails to answer a summons in a lawsuit.

Defendant In criminal cases, the person accused of the crime. In civil matters, the person or organization that is being sued.

Defined benefit plan A type of retirement plan that specifies how much in benefits it will pay out to a retiree.

Defined contribution plan Also called an individual account plan. A type of retirement plan in which the employer pays a specified amount of money each year, which is then divided among the individual accounts of each participating employee. Profit-sharing, employee stock ownership, and 401(k) plans are all defined contribution plans.

Deposition Part of the pretrial **discovery** (fact-finding) process in which a witness testifies under oath. A deposition is held out of court with no judge present, but the answers often can be used as evidence in the trial.

Direct evidence Evidence that stands on its own to prove an alleged fact, such as testimony of a witness who says she saw a defendant pointing a gun at a victim during a robbery.

Direct examination The initial questioning of a witness by the party that called the witness.

Directed verdict A judge's order to a jury to return a specified verdict, usually because one of the parties failed to prove its case.

Disbursements Legal expenses that a lawyer passes on to a client, such as for photocopying, overnight mail, and messenger services.

Discovery Part of the pretrial litigation process during which each party requests relevant information and documents from the other side in an attempt to "discover" pertinent facts.

Dismissal with prejudice When a case is dismissed for good reason and the plaintiff is barred from bringing an action on the same claim.

Dismissal without prejudice When a case is dismissed but the plaintiff is allowed to bring a new suit on the same claim.

Double jeopardy Being tried twice for the same offense.

Due process The idea that laws and legal proceedings must be fair. The Constitution guarantees that the government cannot take away a person's basic rights to "life, liberty or property, without due process of law." Courts have issued numerous rulings about what this means in particular cases.

Duty to warn The legal obligation to warn people of a danger. Typically, manufacturers of hazardous products have a duty to warn customers of a product's potential dangers and to advise users of any precautions they should take.

Easement Gives one party the right to go onto another party's property. Utilities often get easements that allow them to run pipes or phone lines beneath private property.

Elective share Refers to probate laws that allow a spouse to take a certain portion of an estate when the other spouse dies, regardless of what was written in the spouse's will.

Emancipation When a minor has achieved independence from his or her parents, often by getting married before reaching age eighteen or by becoming fully self-supporting.

En banc French for "by the full court." When all the members of an appellate court hear an argument, they are sitting en banc.

Encumbrance Any claim or restriction on a property's title.

Equal Access Act A law passed by Congress in 1984. It requires public schools to allow students to meet before and after classes for religious purposes, including prayer, if they want to do so. If all extracurricular activities are prohibited by a school, it can also nix the prayer meetings. Otherwise, it has to allow them.

Equal Protection Clause Portion of the Fourteenth Amendment to the U.S. Constitution that prohibits discrimination by state government institutions. The clause grants all people "equal protection of the laws," which means that the states must apply the law equally and cannot give preference to one person or class of persons over another.

Equitable distribution In a divorce, one of the ways in which property is divided. In states with equitable distribution systems, property acquired during a marriage is jointly owned by both spouses. But equitable distribution does not necessarily mean *equal* distribution, and ownership does not automatically split fifty-fifty. Rather, the distribution must be fair and just (equitable).

Escrow Money or documents, such as a deed or title, held by a third party until the conditions of an agreement are met. For instance, pending the completion of a real estate transaction, the deed to the property will be held "in escrow."

Escrow account A special account in which a lawyer or escrow agent deposits money or documents that do not belong to him or his firm.

Escrow agent In some states, this person conducts real estate closings and collects the money due the parties.

Establishment Clause Portion of the First Amendment to the U.S. Constitution that prohibits government from "establishing" a religion.

Estate All the property a person owns.

Evidence The various things presented in court to prove an alleged fact. Includes testimony, documents, photographs, maps, and videotapes.

Executor Person named in a will to oversee and manage an estate.

Exempt employees Workers not entitled to overtime, generally workers in executive, administrative, or professional positions.

Exempt property In a bankruptcy, the possessions that a person is allowed to keep.

Exigent circumstances Emergency conditions.

Ex parte A Latin phrase that means "by or for one party." Refers to situations in which only one party (and not the adversary) appears before a judge. Such meetings are often forbidden.

Expert witness A witness with a specialized knowledge of a subject who is allowed to discuss an event in court even though he or she was not present. For example, an arson expert could testify about the probable cause of a suspicious fire.

Express warranty An assertion or promise concerning goods or services. Statements such as "This air-conditioner will cool a five-room house" or "We will repair any problems in the first year" are express warranties.

Fair use The use of a portion of copyrighted material in a way that does not infringe the owner's rights. The use of a portion of material for educational purposes, literary criticism, or news reporting is often considered a fair use.

Fault auto insurance system Refers to a system in which the party that bears the blame (fault) for an accident is liable for any damages.

Felony Serious crime punishable by incarceration for a year or more. Includes rape, murder, robbery, burglary, and arson.

Fiduciary duty An obligation to act in the best interest of another party. For instance, a corporation's board member has a fiduciary duty to the shareholders, a trustee has a fiduciary duty to the trust's beneficiaries, and an attorney has a fiduciary duty to a client.

Fixtures All things that are attached to property, such as ceiling lights, awnings, window shades, and doorknobs. Fixtures are automatically included in a sale, unless specifically mentioned in the contract as going to the seller.

Foreclosure When a borrower cannot repay a loan and the lender seeks to sell the property.

Foreseeability A key issue in determining a person's liability. If a defendant could not reasonably have foreseen that someone might be hurt by his or her actions, then there may be no liability.

Franchise A business relationship in which an owner (the **franchisor**) licenses others (the **franchisees**) to operate outlets using business concepts, property, trademarks, and trade names owned by the franchisor.

Garnishment Also known as wage execution. A court-ordered method of debt collection in which a portion of a person's salary is paid to a creditor. Often used to collect child-support payments.

General partner One of two kinds of partners in a limited partnership. A general partner has the right to participate in the management of the partnership and has unlimited personal liability for its debts.

Good faith Honest intent. An agreement might be declared invalid if one of the parties entered with the intention of defrauding the other.

Grand jury A group of citizens convened in a criminal case to consider the prosecutor's evidence and determine whether probable cause exists to prosecute a suspect for a felony.

Grantor The person who sets up a trust.

Green card An immigrant visa. Allows an alien to become a lawful permanent resident of the U.S. and to work legally, travel abroad and return, bring in a spouse and children, and become eligible for citizenship.

Gross negligence Failure to use even the slightest amount of care in a way that shows recklessness or willful disregard for the safety of others.

Grounds for divorce The legal reason (or reasons) a divorce is granted. There are two kinds of grounds: fault and no-fault.

Guardian Person assigned by the court to take care of minor children or incompetent adults. Sometimes called a conservator.

Guardian ad litem Latin for "guardian at law." The person appointed by the court to look out for the best interests of a child during the course of legal proceedings.

Habeas corpus A Latin phrase meaning "you have the body." Prisoners often seek release by filing a petition for a writ of habeas corpus. A writ of habeas corpus is a judicial mandate to a prison official ordering that an inmate be brought to the court so it can be determined whether or not that person is imprisoned lawfully.

Health care proxy Someone designated to make a broad range of decisions for a person who is not able to give **informed consent.**

Hearsay Secondhand information that a witness heard about from someone else and did not see or hear himself. Hearsay is not admitted in court because it's not trustworthy, though there are many exceptions.

Heirs Persons who are entitled by law to inherit the property of the deceased if there is no will specifying how it's divided.

Holographic will An unwitnessed handwritten will. A few states allow such documents to be admitted to probate, but most courts are very reluctant to accept them.

Hostile environment sexual harassment Where a person is subject to unwelcome sexual advances, requests for sexual favors, or other verbal or physical conduct of a sexual nature to such an extent that it alters the conditions of the person's employment and creates an abusive working environment.

Hung jury A jury that is unable to reach a verdict.

Immigrant visa See **green card.**

Immunity Exemption from a legal duty, penalty, or prosecution.

Impairment When a person's faculties are diminished so that his or her ability to see, hear, walk, talk, and judge distances is below the normal level as set by the state. Typically, impairment is caused by drug or alcohol use, but can also be caused by mental illness. Even if a person's alcohol level is lower than the legal intoxication level, he can still be convicted if the state can show his abilities were impaired.

Implied consent laws (also called express consent) Laws adopted by all states that apply to testing for alcohol in the blood, breath, or urine (most states have such laws that apply to testing for the use of drugs). The principle underlying these laws is that any licensed driver who operates a vehicle has consented to submit to approved tests to show intoxication.

Implied warranty A guarantee imposed by law in a sale. Even though the seller may not make any explicit promises, the buyer still gets some protection.

Implied warranty of fitness for a particular purpose Warranty that exists when a seller should know that a buyer is relying on the seller's expertise.

Implied warranty of habitability Law that exists in most states which governs residential rentals and asserts that regardless of what a lease says, the landlord must provide premises that are safe and livable (habitable) at some basic level. Problems with essential building services and cleanliness are often breaches of the implied warranty and the landlord will be required to correct them.

Implied warranty of merchantability Warranty that guarantees that goods are reasonably fit for their ordinary purpose.

In camera Latin for "in chambers." Refers to a hearing or inspection of documents that takes places in private, often in a judge's chambers.

Indictment A formal accusation of a felony, issued by a grand jury after considering evidence presented by a prosecutor.

Indigent Lacking in funds; poor.

Information A formal accusation of a crime, issued by a prosecutor. An alternative to an indictment.

Informed consent Except in the case of an emergency, a doctor must obtain a patient's agreement (informed consent) to any course of treatment. Doctors are required to tell the patient anything that would substantially affect the patient's decision. Such information typically includes the nature and purpose of the treatment, its risks and consequences, and alternative courses of treatment.

Infractions Sometimes called violations. Minor offenses, often traffic tickets, which are punishable only by a fine.

Infringement Unauthorized use, typically of a patent or copyright.

Interlocutory order Temporary order issued during the course of litigation. Typically cannot be appealed because it is not final.

Interrogatories Part of the pretrial **discovery** (fact-finding) process in which a witness provides written answers to written questions under oath. The answers often can be used as evidence in the trial.

Intestate To die without a will.

Irrevocable living trust A trust created during the maker's lifetime that does not allow the maker to change it.

Joint and survivor annuity A form of pension fund payment in which the retired participant gets a check every month. If and when the participant dies, the spouse continues to get a monthly check equal to one-half of the benefit for the rest of his or her life.

Joint custody When both parents share custody of a child after a divorce. There are two kinds of custody: **legal custody** and **physical custody.** Either or both may be joint.

Joint property Sometimes called joint tenancy. Property that names a co-owner on its deed or title. Co-owners retain ownership of the property upon the death of a co-owner. A co-owner in a joint property arrangement cannot give away his or her share of the property.

Judgment A court's official decision on the matters before it.

Judgment non obstante veredicto Known also as a judgment notwithstanding the verdict. A decision by a trial judge to rule in favor of a losing party even though the jury's verdict was in favor of the other side. Usually done when the facts or law do not support the jury's verdict.

Jurisdiction A court's authority to rule on the questions of law at issue in a dispute, typically determined by geographic location and type of case.

Jury charge The judge's instructions to the jurors on the law that applies in a case and definitions of the relevant legal concepts. These instructions may be complex and are often pivotal in a jury's discussions.

Just cause A legitimate reason. Often used in the employment context to refer to the reasons why someone was fired.

Legal custody In a divorce, one of two types of child custody. A parent who has **legal custody** has the right to be involved in all the decision making typically involved with being a parent, such as religious upbringing, education, and medical decisions. Legal custody can be either sole or joint. Compare with **physical custody.**

Legatee Also known as a **beneficiary.** Person named in a will to receive property.

Lemon laws Laws that require manufacturers to repair defective cars. If the repairs are not made within a reasonable amount of time and number of attempts, the manufacturer is required to refund the purchase price, less a reasonable amount for the use of the car.

Lesser included offenses Charges that contain elements of the most serious charge against a defendant. For instance, a person charged with first-degree murder (which requires premeditation) could be convicted of second-degree murder (a killing done without premeditation) or manslaughter (a killing done in the heat of passion).

Liability Any legal responsibility, duty, or obligation.

Libel Defamatory (false and injurious) written statements or materials, including movies or photographs.

Lien A claim against someone's property. A lien is instituted in order to secure payment from the property owner in the event that the property is sold. A mortgage is a common lien.

Limited-liability company A business structure that is a hybrid of a partnership and a corporation. Its owners are shielded from personal liability, and all profits and losses pass directly to the owners without taxation of the entity itself.

Limited partner One of two kinds of partners in a limited partnership. Is personally liable for the debts of the partnership only to the extent of his or her investment in it and has little to no voice in its management.

Limited partnership A partnership with two kinds of partners: **limited partners,** who provide financial backing and have little role in management and no personal liability, and **general partners,** who are responsible for managing the entity and have unlimited personal liability for its debts.

Liquidated damages The amount of money specified in a contract to be awarded in the event that the agreement is violated.

Living-together contract See **cohabitation agreement.**

Living trust A trust created during the maker's lifetime. Some living trusts are set up so that they can be changed during the maker's lifetime. These are called "revocable." Others, known as "irrevocable," are set up so that they can't be touched.

Living will Also known as a medical directive or advance directive. A written document that states a person's wishes regarding life-support or other medical treatment in certain circumstances, usually when death is imminent.

Maintenance See **alimony.**

Malpractice Improper or **negligent** behavior by a professional, such as a doctor or a lawyer. The failure of a professional to follow the accepted standards of practice of his or her profession.

Mandatory sentence A criminal sentence set by a legislature that establishes the minimum length of prison time for specified crimes and thus limits the amount of discretion a judge has when sentencing a defendant.

Marital life estate See **bypass trust.**

Mediation A method of alternative dispute resolution in which a neutral third party helps resolve a dispute. The mediator does not have the power to impose a decision on the parties. If a satisfactory resolution cannot be reached, the parties can pursue a lawsuit.

Medical directive See **living will.**

Minor A person who does not have the legal rights of an adult. A minor is usually defined as someone who has not yet reached the age of majority. In most states, a person reaches majority and acquires all the rights and responsibilities of an adult when he or she turns eighteen.

Miranda warning The statement recited to individuals taken into police custody. It warns of their right to remain silent and to have an attorney.

Misdemeanor Crime that is punishable by less than one year in jail, such as minor theft and simple assault that does not result in substantial bodily injury.

Mitigating factors Information about a defendant or the circumstances of a crime that might tend to lessen the sentence or the crime with which the person is charged.

Motion A request asking a judge to issue a ruling or order on a legal matter.

Motion for a new trial Request in which a losing party asserts that a trial was unfair due to legal errors that prejudiced its case.

Motion for directed verdict A request made in a civil case. Asserts that the plaintiff failed to present a **prima facie** case or that the defendant failed to make an adequate defense. It asks the judge to rule in favor of the moving party. Typically made after the plaintiff is done presenting his or her case.

Motion for summary judgment A request made by either side in a civil case asking a judge to decide an issue based on the argument that there is no genuine factual dispute to be considered by a jury. Typically made before the trial.

Motion to dismiss In a civil case, a request to a judge by the **defendant,** asserting that even if all the allegations are true, the **plaintiff** is not entitled to any legal relief and thus the case should be dismissed.

Motion to suppress evidence A request to a judge to keep out evidence at a trial or hearing, often made when a party believes the evidence was unlawfully obtained.

Named plaintiffs The originators of a class action suit.

Negligence A failure to use the degree of care that a reasonable person would use under the same circumstances.

No-fault auto insurance system Under a no-fault system it doesn't matter which driver made the mistake that caused an accident. Each individual recovers from his or her own insurance carrier, regardless of who caused the accident.

No-fault divorce A divorce in which it doesn't matter who did what to whom that caused the marriage to break down; all that matters is that there is no reasonable prospect of reconciliation.

Nonexempt employees Workers who are entitled to overtime pay after working more than forty hours in a five-day workweek. Generally includes secretaries, factory workers, clerical workers, and anyone paid by the hour.

Nonexempt property In a bankruptcy, the possessions of a person that can be sold.

Nonimmigrant visa Visa granted to a foreigner who does not intend to stay in the U.S. permanently.

Notary public A person authorized to witness the signing of documents.

Notice of appeal The document a person must file with the trial court in order to pursue an appeal.

Officers of a corporation Those people with day-to-day responsibility for running the corporation, such as the chief executive, chief financial officer, and treasurer.

Open adoption An adoption in which the birth mother may retain some visitation privileges.

Own recognizance Sometimes called personal recognizance. A person who promises to appear in court to answer criminal charges can sometimes be released from jail without having to pay bail. This person is said to be released on his or her own recognizance.

Parens patriae Latin for "parent of his country." Used when the government acts on behalf of a child or mentally ill person. Refers to the "state" as the guardian of minors and incompetent people.

Parole A system for the supervised release of prisoners before their terms are over. Congress has abolished parole for people convicted of federal crimes, but most states still offer parole.

Partition A court action to divide property. Typically taken when a property is jointly owned and a dispute arises about how to divide it.

Partnership An association of two or more people who agree to share in the profits and losses of a business venture.

Patent A document issued to an inventor by the United States Patent and Trademark Office. Contains a detailed description of what the invention is and how to make or use it and provides rights against infringers.

Penalty phase The second part of a bifurcated trial, in which the jury hears evidence and then votes on what penalty or damages to impose.

Pension plan An employer's program for providing retirement income to eligible employees.

Peremptory challenges A limited number of challenges each side in a trial can use to eliminate potential jurors without stating a reason. May not be used to keep members of a particular race or sex off the jury.

Perjury A crime in which a person knowingly makes a false statement while under oath in court. In some jurisdictions, making a false statement in a legal document can also be considered perjury.

Personal guardian Person appointed to take custody of children and provide for their care and upbringing. Distinguished from property guardian.

Personal recognizance Sometimes called own recognizance. A person who promises to appear in court to answer criminal charges can sometimes be released from jail without having to pay bail. This person is said to be released on his or her personal recognizance.

Personal representative A person who manages the legal affairs of another, such as a power of attorney or executor.

Petit jury The jurors empaneled to hear a civil or criminal trial. Distinguished from a grand jury.

Petition A written application to the court asking for specific action to be taken.

Petition for probate The document that summarizes a will's provisions and names the heirs.

Petty offenses Minor crimes, such as traffic violations, which are generally punishable by a fine or short jail term.

Physical custody In a divorce, one of two types of child custody. A parent who has physical custody lives most of the time with the child. Compare with **legal custody.**

Piercing the corporate veil A legal concept through which a corporation's shareholders, who generally are shielded from liability for the corporation's activities, can be held responsible for certain actions.

Plaintiff The person who initiates a lawsuit.

Plea bargain A negotiated agreement between the defense and the prosecution in a criminal case. Typically the defendant agrees to plead guilty to a specified charge in exchange for an oral promise of a lower sentence.

Pleadings In a civil case, the allegations by each party of their claims and defenses.

Power of attorney The authority to act legally for another person.

Precedent A previously decided case that is considered binding in the court where it was issued and in all lower courts in the same jurisdiction.

Preliminary hearing Legal proceeding used in some states in which a prosecutor presents evidence to a judge in an attempt to show that there is probable cause that a person committed a crime. If the judge is convinced probable cause exists to charge the person, then the prosecution proceeds to the next phase. If not, the charges are dropped.

Preponderance of the evidence The level of proof required to prevail in most civil cases. The judge or jury must be persuaded that the facts are more probably one way (the plaintiff's way) than another (the defendant's).

Presentencing report A report prepared by a probation department for a judge to assist in sentencing. Typically contains information about prior convictions and arrests, work history, and family details.

Pretrial diversion Also known as adjournment in contemplation of dismissal or conditional dismissal. A program in which a defendant essentially is put on probation for a set period of time and his or her case does not go to trial during that time. If the defendant meets the conditions set by the court, then the charge will be dismissed.

Prima facie Latin for "at first view." Refers to the minimum amount of evidence a plaintiff must have to avoid having a case dismissed. It is said that the plaintiff must make a prima facie case.

Privileged communication Conversation that takes place within the context of a protected relationship, such as that between an attorney and client, a husband and wife, a priest and penitent, and a doctor and patient. The law often protects against forced disclosure of such conversations.

Pro se (pronounced pro say) A Latin phrase that means "for himself." A person who represents himself in court without the help of a lawyer is said to appear pro se.

Probable cause A reasonable belief that a person has committed a crime.

Probate The legal process in which a court oversees the distribution of property left in a will.

Probation The release into the community of a defendant who has been found guilty of a crime, typically under certain conditions, such as paying a fine, doing community service, or attending a drug treatment program. Violation of the conditions can result in incarceration. In the employment context, probation refers to the trial period some new employees go through.

Promissory note A written document in which a borrower agrees (promises) to pay back money to a lender according to specified terms.

Property guardian Person appointed to oversee property left to a minor in a will. Distinguished from a personal guardian.

Prosecutor The government lawyer who investigates and tries criminal cases. Typically known as a district attorney, state's attorney, or United States attorney.

Protective order In litigation, an order that prevents the disclosure of sensitive information except to certain individuals under certain conditions. In a domestic dispute, an order that prevents one party from approaching another, often within a specified distance.

Public defender A lawyer who works for a state or local agency representing clients accused of a crime who cannot afford to pay.

Punitive damages Money awarded to a victim that is intended to punish a defendant and stop the person or business from repeating the type of conduct that caused an injury. Also intended to deter others from similar conduct.

Quash To nullify, void, or declare invalid.

Quid pro quo A Latin phrase that means "what for what" or "something for something." The concept of getting something of value in return for giving something of value. For a contract to be binding, it usually must involve the exchange of something of value.

Quid pro quo sexual harassment Where an employee is threatened with a demotion (or promised a promotion) in exchange for "sexual favors." It usually comes from a supervisor or other person in a position of authority.

Quitclaim deed A deed that transfers the owner's interest to a buyer but does not guarantee that there are no other claims against the property.

Real property Land and all the things that are attached to it. Anything that is not real property is personal property, and personal property is anything that isn't nailed down, dug into, or built onto the land. A house is real property, but a dining room set is not.

Reasonable care The level of care a typical person would use if faced with the same circumstances.

Reasonable doubt The level of certainty a juror must have to find a defendant guilty of a crime.

Re-cross examination Questioning a witness about matters brought up during re-direct examination.

Re-direct examination Questioning a witness about matters brought up during cross-examination.

Refugee A person who applies to enter the U.S. from outside the country, claiming an inability or unwillingness to return to (or remain in) the home country because of a well-founded fear of persecution.

Remand When an appellate court sends a case back to a lower court for further proceedings.

Replevin Repossession. Action taken by a **creditor** to seize assets of a debtor.

Residuary estate Also known as residue of the estate. Portion of the estate left after bequests of specific items of property are made. Often the largest portion.

Residuary legatee The person or persons named in a will to receive any residue left in an estate after the bequests of specific items are made.

Res ipsa loquitur A Latin phrase that means "the thing speaks for itself." Refers to situations when it's assumed that a person's injury was caused by the negligent action of another party because the accident was the sort that wouldn't occur unless someone was negligent.

Retainer Refers to the up-front payment a client gives a lawyer to accept a case. The client is paying to "retain" the lawyer's services.

Retaining lien Gives a lawyer the right to hold onto your money or property (such as a deed) until you pay the bill.

Revocable living trust A trust created during the maker's lifetime that can be changed. Allows the creator to pass assets on to chosen beneficiaries without going through probate.

Right against self-incrimination Granted by the Fifth Amendment. Allows a person to refuse to answer questions that would subject him or her to accusation of a criminal act.

Right of eminent domain The government's right to acquire private property for public use.

Right of survivorship In a joint tenancy, the property automatically goes to the co-owners if one of the co-owners dies. A co-owner in a joint tenancy cannot give away his or her share of the property.

Security agreement A contract between a lender and a borrower that states that the lender can repossess the property the borrower has offered as **collateral** if the loan is not paid as agreed.

Self-proving will A will accompanied by a sworn statement from witnesses and signed before a notary public. Many states accept such wills in order to avoid the cumbersome process of requiring an executor to track down the witnesses.

Separation agreement In a marital breakup, a document that outlines the terms of the couple's separation.

Service of process The act of notifying the other parties that an action has begun and informing them of the steps they should take in order to respond.

Settlement An out-of-court agreement by the parties that ends a civil lawsuit.

Shareholder An owner or investor in a corporation.

Single life annuity A form of pension plan payment in which the retired person receives a monthly check from the time of retirement until death.

Slander Defamatory (false and injurious) oral statements or gestures.

Sole proprietorship A form of business organization in which an individual is fully and personally liable for all the obligations (including debts) of the business, is entitled to all its profits, and exercises complete managerial control.

Spendthrift trust A trust designed to keep money out of the hands of creditors. Often established to protect someone who is incapable of managing his or her financial affairs.

Spousal right The entitlement of one spouse to inherit property from the other spouse. The right varies from state to state.

Spousal support See **alimony.**

Standard of care The degree of care a reasonable person would take to prevent an injury to another.

Standing The legal right to initiate a lawsuit. To do so, a person must be sufficiently affected by the matter at hand, and there must be a case or controversy that can be resolved by legal action.

Stare decisis A Latin phrase meaning "to stand by that which is decided." Refers to the principle of adhering to **precedent** when deciding a case.

Stationhouse bail Bail that some defendants accused of misdemeanors may be allowed to pay at the police station. This allows them to be released prior to appearing before a judge.

Statutes of fraud Laws in most states to protect against false claims for payment from contracts that were not agreed upon. The specific laws vary from state to state, but most require that certain contracts be in writing.

Statutes of limitations Laws setting deadlines for filing lawsuits within a certain time after events occur that are the source of a claim.

Strict liability Liability even when there is no proof of negligence. Often applicable in product liability cases against manufacturers, who are legally responsible for injuries caused by defects in their products even if they were not negligent.

Sublet When a party agrees to rent a space from the main tenant for a portion of the time remaining on the lease.

Subpoena An order compelling a person to appear to testify or produce documents.

Summation The closing argument in a trial.

Summons A legal document that notifies a party that a lawsuit has been initiated and states when and where the party must appear to answer the charges.

Tangible personal property Anything other than real estate or money, including furniture, cars, jewelry, and china.

Tenancy in common A type of joint ownership that allows a person to sell his share or leave it in a will without the consent of the other owners. If a person dies without a will, his share goes to his heirs, not to the other owners.

Testamentary trust A trust created by the provisions in a will. Typically comes into existence after the writer of the will dies.

Testator The person who makes a will.

Title Ownership of property.

Title search A review of the land records to determine the ownership and description of the property.

Tort A civil wrong that results in an injury to a person or property.

Totten trust A bank account in your name for which you name a beneficiary. Upon the death of the named holder of the account the money transfers automatically to the beneficiary.

Trademark A word, name, or symbol used to identify products sold or services provided by a business. Distinguishes the products or services of one business from those of others in the same field. A business using a trademark has the right to prevent other businesses from using it and can get money to compensate for its infringement.

Trade name The name used to identify a business.

Trust Property given to a trustee to manage for the benefit of a third person. Generally, the beneficiary gets interest and dividends on the trust assets for a set number of years.

Trustee Person or institution that oversees and manages a trust.

Uniform Commercial Code A model statute covering things such as the sale of goods, credit, and bank transactions. All states have adopted and adapted the entire UCC, with the exception of Louisiana, which adopted only parts of it.

Uniform Reciprocal Enforcement of Support Act Law that allows an order of child support issued in one state to be enforced in another state.

Unjust taking When the government acquires private property and fails to compensate an owner fairly. A taking can occur even without the actual physical seizure of property, such as when a government regulation has substantially devalued a property.

Valid claim A grievance that can be resolved by legal action.

Verdict The formal decision issued by a jury on the issues of fact that were presented at trial.

Vested right An absolute right. When a retirement plan is fully vested, the employee has an absolute right to the entire amount of money in the account.

Vicarious liability When one person is liable for the negligent actions of another person, even though the first person was not directly responsible for the injury. For instance, a parent sometimes can be vicariously liable for the harmful acts of a child and an employer sometimes can be vicariously liable for the acts of a worker.

Visitation right The right granted to a parent or other relative to visit a child on a specified basis. Usually occurs during a divorce proceeding.

Void marriage One of two types of marriages that can be annulled. A void marriage is one that is void and invalid from its beginning. It is as though the marriage never existed and it requires no formality to terminate it. For instance, an incestuous marriage would likely be considered void.

Voidable marriage A valid marriage that can be annulled if challenged, but that otherwise remains legitimate. For instance, if one of the parties was a minor at the time of marriage, the marriage could be annulled if challenged. If it's never challenged, the marriage is considered valid.

Voir dire A French phrase that means "to speak the truth." The process of interviewing prospective jurors. Pronounced "vwa dear."

Wage execution See **garnishment.**

Warrant An official order authorizing a specific act, such as an arrest or the search of someone's home.

Warranty A promise about a product made by either a manufacturer or a seller.

Witness Person who comes to court and swears under oath to give truthful evidence.

Workers' compensation A benefit paid to an employee who suffers a work-related injury or illness.

Writ A judicial order.

Wrongful discharge When an employee is fired for reasons that are not legitimate, typically either because they are unlawful or because they violate the terms of an employment contract.

THE CONSTITUTION OF THE UNITED STATES OF AMERICA

The Constitution was drafted in 1787 and became effective in 1789. The text is reprinted below. We have added material in brackets to summarize various provisions, and those words are not part of the Constitution.

We the people of the United States, in order to form a more perfect union, establish justice, insure domestic tranquility, provide for the common defense, promote the general welfare, and secure the blessings of liberty to ourselves and our posterity, do ordain and establish this Constitution for the United States of America.

ARTICLE I

Section 1.

[Legislative powers of Congress]
All legislative powers herein granted shall be vested in a Congress of the United States, which shall consist of a Senate and House of Representatives.

Section 2.

[The House of Representatives]
The House of Representatives shall be composed of members chosen every second year by the people of the several states, and the electors in each state shall have the qualifications requisite for electors of the most numerous branch of the state legislature.

No person shall be a Representative who shall not have attained to the age of twenty five years, and been seven years a citizen of the United States, and who shall not, when elected, be an inhabitant of that state in which he shall be chosen.

Representatives and direct taxes shall be apportioned among the several states which may be included within this union, according to their respective numbers, which shall be determined by adding to the whole number of free persons, including those bound to service for a term of years, and excluding Indians not taxed, three fifths of all other persons. The actual enumeration shall be made within three years after the first meeting of the Congress of the United States, and within every subsequent term of ten years, in such manner as they shall by law direct. The number of Representatives shall not exceed one for every thirty thousand, but each state shall have at least one Representative; and until such enumeration shall be made, the state of New Hampshire shall be entitled to choose three, Massachusetts eight, Rhode Island and Providence Plantations one, Connecticut five, New York six, New Jersey four, Pennsylvania eight, Delaware one, Maryland six, Virginia ten, North Carolina five, South Carolina five, and Georgia three.

When vacancies happen in the representation from any state, the executive authority thereof shall issue writs of election to fill such vacancies.
The House of Representatives shall choose their speaker and other officers; and shall have the sole power of impeachment.

Section 3.

[The Senate]
The Senate of the United States shall be composed of two Senators from each state, chosen by the legislature thereof, for six years; and each Senator shall have one vote.

Immediately after they shall be assembled in consequence of the first election, they shall be divided as equally as may be into three classes. The seats of the Senators of the first class shall be vacated at the expiration of the second year, of the second class at the expiration of the fourth year, and the third class at the expiration of the sixth year, so that one third may be chosen every second year; and if vacancies happen by resignation, or otherwise, during the recess of the legislature of any state, the executive thereof may make temporary appointments until the next meeting of the legislature, which shall then fill such vacancies.

No person shall be a Senator who shall not have attained to the age of thirty years, and been nine years a citizen of the United States and who shall not, when elected, be an inhabitant of that state for which he shall be chosen.

The Vice President of the United States shall be President of the Senate, but shall have no vote, unless they be equally divided.

The Senate shall choose their other officers, and also a President pro tempore, in the absence of the Vice President, or when he shall exercise the office of President of the United States.

[Impeachments]

The Senate shall have the sole power to try all impeachments. When sitting for that purpose, they shall be on oath or affirmation. When the President of the United States is tried, the Chief Justice shall preside: And no person shall be convicted without the concurrence of two thirds of the members present.

Judgment in cases of impeachment shall not extend further than to removal from office, and disqualification to hold and enjoy any office of honor, trust or profit under the United States: but the party convicted shall nevertheless be liable and subject to indictment, trial, judgment and punishment, according to law.

Section 4.

[Elections; meetings of Congress]

The times, places and manner of holding elections for Senators and Representatives, shall be prescribed in each state by the legislature thereof; but the Congress may at any time by law make or alter such regulations, except as to the places of choosing Senators.

The Congress shall assemble at least once in every year, and such meeting shall be on the first Monday in December, unless they shall by law appoint a different day.

Section 5.

[Judging elections and qualification of members; rules and records of proceedings]

Each House shall be the judge of the elections, returns and qualifications of its own members, and a majority of each shall constitute a quorum to do business; but a smaller number may adjourn from day to day, and may be authorized to compel the attendance of absent members, in such manner, and under such penalties as each House may provide.

Each House may determine the rules of its proceedings, punish its members for disorderly behavior, and, with the concurrence of two thirds, expel a member.

Each House shall keep a journal of its proceedings, and from time to time publish the same, excepting such parts as may in their judgment require secrecy; and the yeas and nays of the members of either House on any question shall, at the desire of one fifth of those present, be entered on the journal.

Neither House, during the session of Congress, shall, without the consent of the other, adjourn for more than three days, nor to any other place than that in which the two Houses shall be sitting.

Section 6.

[Congressional compensation; incompatible offices]

The Senators and Representatives shall receive a compensation for their services, to be ascertained by law, and paid out of the treasury of the United States. They shall in all cases, except treason, felony and breach of the peace, be privileged from arrest during their attendance at the session of their respective Houses, and in going to and returning from the same; and for any speech or debate in either House, they shall not be questioned in any other place.

No Senator or Representative shall, during the time for which he was elected, be appointed to any civil office under the authority of the United States, which shall have been created, or the emoluments whereof shall have been increased during such time: and no person holding any office under the United States, shall be a member of either House during his continuance in office.

Section 7.

[Revenue bills originate in House]
All bills for raising revenue shall originate in the House of Representatives; but the Senate may propose or concur with amendments as on other bills.
[Presidential signing/vetoing of bills; override of vetoes]

Every bill which shall have passed the House of Representatives and the Senate, shall, before it become a law, be presented to the President of the United States; if he approve he shall sign it, but if not he shall return it, with his objections to that House in which it shall have originated, who shall enter the objections at large on their journal, and proceed to reconsider it. If after such reconsideration two thirds of that House shall agree to pass the bill, it shall be sent, together with the objections, to the other House, by which it shall likewise be reconsidered, and if approved by two thirds of that House, it shall become a law. But in all such cases the votes of both Houses shall be determined by yeas and nays, and the names of the persons voting for and against the bill shall be entered on the journal of each House respectively. If any bill shall not be returned by the President within ten days (Sundays excepted) after it shall have been presented to him, the same shall be a law, in like manner as if he had signed it, unless the Congress by their adjournment prevent its return, in which case it shall not be a law.

Every order, resolution, or vote to which the concurrence of the Senate and House of Representatives may be necessary (except on a question of adjournment) shall be presented to the President of the United States; and before the same shall take effect, shall be approved by him, or being disapproved by him, shall be repassed by two thirds of the Senate and House of Representatives, according to the rules and limitations prescribed in the case of a bill.

Section 8.

[General powers of Congress]
The Congress shall have power to lay and collect taxes, duties, imposts and excises, to pay the debts and provide for the common defense and general welfare of the United States; but all duties, imposts and excises shall be uniform throughout the United States;

To borrow money on the credit of the United States;

To regulate commerce with foreign nations, and among the several states, and with the Indian tribes;

To establish a uniform rule of naturalization, and uniform laws on the subject of bankruptcies throughout the United States;

To coin money, regulate the value thereof, and of foreign coin, and fix the standard of weights and measures;

To provide for the punishment of counterfeiting the securities and current coin of the United States;

To establish post offices and post roads;

To promote the progress of science and useful arts, by securing for limited times to authors and inventors the exclusive right to their respective writings and discoveries;

To constitute tribunals inferior to the Supreme Court;

To define and punish piracies and felonies committed on the high seas, and offenses against the law of nations;

To declare war, grant letters of marque and reprisal, and make rules concerning captures on land and water;

To raise and support armies, but no appropriation of money to that use shall be for a longer term than two years;

To provide and maintain a navy;

To make rules for the government and regulation of the land and naval forces;

To provide for calling forth the militia to execute the laws of the union, suppress insurrections and repel invasions;

To provide for organizing, arming, and disciplining, the militia, and for governing such part of them as may be employed in the service of the United States, reserving to the states respectively, the appointment of the officers, and the authority of training the militia according to the discipline prescribed by Congress;

To exercise exclusive legislation in all cases whatsoever, over such District (not exceeding ten miles square) as may, by cession of particular states, and the acceptance of Congress, become the seat of the government of the United States, and to exercise like authority over all places purchased by the consent of the legislature of the state in which the same shall be, for the erection of forts, magazines, arsenals, dockyards, and other needful buildings;

—And To make all laws which shall be necessary and proper for carrying into execution the foregoing powers, and all other powers vested by this Constitution in the government of the United States, or in any department or officer thereof.

Section 9.

[Importation of slaves prior to 1808]
The migration or importation of such persons as any of the states now existing shall think proper to admit, shall not be prohibited by the Congress prior to the year one thousand eight hundred and eight, but a tax or duty may be imposed on such importation, not exceeding ten dollars for each person.

[Habeas corpus]
The privilege of the writ of habeas corpus shall not be suspended, unless when in cases of rebellion or invasion the public safety may require it.

[Bills of attainder; ex post facto laws]
No bill of attainder or ex post facto law shall be passed.

[Taxation; interstate shipping]
No capitation, or other direct, tax shall be laid, unless in proportion to the census or enumeration herein before directed to be taken.

No tax or duty shall be laid on articles exported from any state.

No preference shall be given by any regulation of commerce or revenue to the ports of one state over those of another: nor shall vessels bound to, or from, one state, be obliged to enter, clear or pay duties in another.

[Drawing money from treasury; financial records]
No money shall be drawn from the treasury, but in consequence of appropriations made by law; and a regular statement and account of receipts and expenditures of all public money shall be published from time to time.

[Titles of nobility]
No title of nobility shall be granted by the United States: and no person holding any office of profit or trust under them, shall, without the consent of the Congress, accept of any present, emolument, office, or title, of any kind whatever, from any king, prince, or foreign state.

Section 10.

[Limits on power of states]
No state shall enter into any treaty, alliance, or confederation; grant letters of marque and reprisal; coin money; emit bills of credit; make anything but gold and silver coin a tender in payment of debts; pass any bill of attainder, ex post facto law, or law impairing the obligation of contracts, or grant any title of nobility.

No state shall, without the consent of the Congress, lay any imposts or duties on imports or exports, except what may be absolutely necessary for executing its inspection laws: and the net produce of all duties and imposts, laid by any state on imports or exports, shall be for the use of the treasury of the United States; and all such laws shall be subject to the revision and control of the Congress.

No state shall, without the consent of Congress, lay any duty of tonnage, keep troops, or ships of war in time of peace, enter into any agreement or compact with another state, or with a foreign power, or engage in war, unless actually invaded, or in such imminent danger as will not admit of delay.

ARTICLE II

Section 1.

[Office of the President]
The executive power shall be vested in a President of the United States of America. He shall hold his office during the term of four years, and, together with the Vice President, chosen for the same term, be elected, as follows:

[Appointment of electors]
Each state shall appoint, in such manner as the Legislature thereof may direct, a number of electors, equal to the whole number of Senators and

Representatives to which the State may be entitled in the Congress: but no Senator or Representative, or person holding an office of trust or profit under the United States, shall be appointed an elector.

[Old method of electing President, Vice President]

The electors shall meet in their respective states, and vote by ballot for two persons, of whom one at least shall not be an inhabitant of the same state with themselves. And they shall make a list of all the persons voted for, and of the number of votes for each; which list they shall sign and certify, and transmit sealed to the seat of the government of the United States, directed to the President of the Senate. The President of the Senate shall, in the presence of the Senate and House of Representatives, open all the certificates, and the votes shall then be counted. The person having the greatest number of votes shall be the President, if such number be a majority of the whole number of electors appointed; and if there be more than one who have such majority, and have an equal number of votes, then the House of Representatives shall immediately choose by ballot one of them for President; and if no person have a majority, then from the five highest on the list the said House shall in like manner choose the President. But in choosing the President, the votes shall be taken by States, the representation from each state having one vote; A quorum for this purpose shall consist of a member or members from two thirds of the states, and a majority of all the states shall be necessary to a choice. In every case, after the choice of the President, the person having the greatest number of votes of the electors shall be the Vice President. But if there should remain two or more who have equal votes, the Senate shall choose from them by ballot the Vice President.

The Congress may determine the time of choosing the electors, and the day on which they shall give their votes; which day shall be the same throughout the United States.

[Qualifications to be President]

No person except a natural born citizen, or a citizen of the United States, at the time of the adoption of this Constitution, shall be eligible to the office of President; neither shall any person be eligible to that office who shall not have attained to the age of thirty five years, and been fourteen Years a resident within the United States.

[Filling Presidential vacancies]

In case of the removal of the President from office, or of his death, resignation, or inability to discharge the powers and duties of the said office, the same shall devolve on the Vice President, and the Congress may by law provide for the case of removal, death, resignation or inability, both of the President and Vice President, declaring what officer shall then act as President, and such officer shall act accordingly, until the disability be removed, or a President shall be elected.

[President's compensation]

The President shall, at stated times, receive for his services, a compensation, which shall neither be increased nor diminished during the period for which he shall have been elected, and he shall not receive within that period any other emolument from the United States, or any of them.

[Oath of office]

Before he enter on the execution of his office, he shall take the following oath or affirmation:—"I do solemnly swear (or affirm) that I will faithfully execute the office of President of the United States, and will to the best of my ability, preserve, protect and defend the Constitution of the United States."

Section 2.

[Presidential powers]

The President shall be commander in chief of the Army and Navy of the United States, and of the militia of the several states, when called into the actual service of the United States; he may require the opinion, in writing, of the principal officer in each of the executive departments, upon any subject relating to the duties of their respective offices, and he shall have power to grant reprieves and pardons for offenses against the United States, except in cases of impeachment.

[Treaties; judicial and other appointments]

He shall have power, by and with the advice and consent of the Senate, to make treaties, provided two thirds of the Senators present concur; and he shall nominate, and by and with the advice and consent of the Senate, shall appoint ambassadors, other public ministers and consuls, judges of the Supreme Court, and all other officers of the United States, whose appointments are not herein otherwise provided for, and which shall be established by law: but the Congress may by law vest the appointment of such inferior officers, as they think proper, in the President alone, in the courts of law, or in the heads of departments.

The President shall have power to fill up all vacancies that may happen during the recess of the Senate, by granting commissions which shall expire at the end of their next session.

Section 3.

[Presidential information to Congress; power to convene or adjourn]
He shall from time to time give to the Congress information of the state of the union, and recommend to their consideration such measures as he shall judge necessary and expedient; he may, on extraordinary occasions, convene both Houses, or either of them, and in case of disagreement between them, with respect to the time of adjournment, he may adjourn them to such time as he shall think proper; he shall receive ambassadors and other public ministers; he shall take care that the laws be faithfully executed, and shall commission all the officers of the United States.

Section 4.

[Impeachment]
The President, Vice President and all civil officers of the United States, shall be removed from office on impeachment for, and conviction of, treason, bribery, or other high crimes and misdemeanors.

ARTICLE III

Section 1.

[Judicial powers; compensation]
The judicial power of the United States, shall be vested in one Supreme Court, and in such inferior courts as the Congress may from time to time ordain and establish. The judges, both of the supreme and inferior courts, shall hold their offices during good behaviour, and shall, at stated times, receive for their services, a compensation, which shall not be diminished during their continuance in office.

Section 2.

[Jurisdiction of federal courts]
The judicial power shall extend to all cases, in law and equity, arising under this Constitution, the laws of the United States, and treaties made, or which shall be made, under their authority; to all cases affecting ambassadors, other public ministers and consuls; to all cases of admiralty and maritime jurisdiction; to controversies to which the United States shall be a party; to controversies between two or more states; between a state and citizens of another state; between citizens of different states; between citizens of the same state claiming lands under grants of different states, and between a state, or the citizens thereof, and foreign states, citizens or subjects.
[Jurisdiction of Supreme Court]

In all cases affecting ambassadors, other public ministers and consuls, and those in which a state shall be party, the Supreme Court shall have original jurisdiction. In all the other cases before mentioned, the Supreme Court shall have appellate jurisdiction, both as to law and fact, with such exceptions, and under such regulations as the Congress shall make.
[Trial of crimes by jury]

The trial of all crimes, except in cases of impeachment, shall be by jury; and such trial shall be held in the state where the said crimes shall have been committed; but when not committed within any state, the trial shall be at such place or places as the Congress may by law have directed.

Section 3.

[Treason]
Treason against the United States, shall consist only in levying war against them, or in adhering to their enemies, giving them aid and comfort. No person shall be convicted of treason unless on the testimony of two witnesses to the same overt act, or on confession in open court.

The Congress shall have power to declare the punishment of treason, but no attainder of treason shall work corruption of blood, or forfeiture except during the life of the person attainted.

ARTICLE IV

Section 1.

[Respect by states for each other's acts]
Full faith and credit shall be given in each state to the public acts, records, and judicial proceedings of every other state. And the Congress may by general laws prescribe the manner in which such acts, records, and proceedings shall be proved, and the effect thereof.

Section 2.

[Privileges of citizens]
The citizens of each state shall be entitled to all privileges and immunities of citizens in the several states.
[Extradition between states]
A person charged in any state with treason, felony, or other crime, who shall flee from justice, and be found in another state, shall on demand of the executive authority of the state from which he fled, be delivered up, to be removed to the state having jurisdiction of the crime.
[No emancipation of escaped slaves]
No person held to service or labor in one state, under the laws thereof, escaping into another, shall, in consequence of any law or regulation therein, be discharged from such service or labor, but shall be delivered up on claim of the party to whom such service or labor may be due.

Section 3.

[Admitting new states]
New states may be admitted by the Congress into this union; but no new states shall be formed or erected within the jurisdiction of any other state; nor any state be formed by the junction of two or more states, or parts of states, without the consent of the legislatures of the states concerned as well as of the Congress.
[Regulation of U.S. territory]
The Congress shall have power to dispose of and make all needful rules and regulations respecting the territory or other property belonging to the United States; and nothing in this Constitution shall be so construed as to prejudice any claims of the United States, or of any particular state.

Section 4.

[Republican form of government]
The United States shall guarantee to every state in this union a republican form of government, and shall protect each of them against invasion; and on application of the legislature, or of the executive (when the legislature cannot be convened) against domestic violence.

ARTICLE V

[Amending the Constitution]
The Congress, whenever two thirds of both houses shall deem it necessary, shall propose amendments to this Constitution, or, on the application of the legislatures of two thirds of the several states, shall call a convention for proposing amendments, which, in either case, shall be valid to all intents and purposes, as part of this Constitution, when ratified by the legislatures of three fourths of the several states, or by conventions in three fourths thereof, as the one or the other mode of ratification may be proposed by the Congress; provided that no amendment which may be made prior to the year one thousand eight hundred and eight shall in any manner affect the first and fourth clauses in the ninth section of the first article; and that no state, without its consent, shall be deprived of its equal suffrage in the Senate.

ARTICLE VI

[Debts predating Constitution]
All debts contracted and engagements entered into, before the adoption of this Constitution, shall be as valid against the United States under this Constitution, as under the Confederation.

[Supreme laws]

This Constitution, and the laws of the United States which shall be made in pursuance thereof; and all treaties made, or which shall be made, under the authority of the United States, shall be the supreme law of the land; and the judges in every state shall be bound thereby, anything in the Constitution or laws of any State to the contrary notwithstanding.

[Constitutional Oath]

The Senators and Representatives before mentioned, and the members of the several state legislatures, and all executive and judicial officers, both of the United States and of the several states, shall be bound by oath or affirmation, to support this Constitution; but no religious test shall ever be required as a qualification to any office or public trust under the United States.

ARTICLE VII

[Ratification of Constitution]

The ratification of the conventions of nine states, shall be sufficient for the establishment of this Constitution between the states so ratifying the same.

Done in convention by the unanimous consent of the states present the seventeenth day of September in the year of our Lord one thousand seven hundred and eighty seven and of the independence of the United States of America the twelfth. In witness whereof we have hereunto subscribed our names.

G. Washington, President and deputy from Virginia; New Hampshire: John Langdon, Nicholas Gilman; Massachusetts: Nathaniel Gorham, Rufus King; Connecticut: Wm. Saml. Johnson, Roger Sherman; New York: Alexander Hamilton; New Jersey: Wil. Livingston, David Brearly, Wm. Paterson, Jona. Dayton; Pennsylvania: B. Franklin, Thomas Mifflin, Robt. Morris, Geo. Clymer, Thos. FitzSimons, Jared Ingersoll, James Wilson, Gouv Morris; Delaware: Geo. Read, Gunning Bedford jun, John Dickinson, Richard Bassett, Jaco. Broom; Maryland: James McHenry, Dan of St Thos. Jenifer, Danl Carroll; Virginia: John Blair, James Madison Jr.; North Carolina: Wm. Blount, Richd. Dobbs Spaight, Hu Williamson; South Carolina: J. Rutledge, Charles Cotesworth Pinckney, Charles Pinckney, Pierce Butler; Georgia: William Few, Abr Baldwin

[The first ten amendments to the Constitution, known as the Bill of Rights, were ratified in 1791. The date of ratification of subsequent amendments is indicated at each amendment.]

AMENDMENT I

[Freedom of speech, religion, press, and assembly]

Congress shall make no law respecting an establishment of religion, or prohibiting the free exercise thereof; or abridging the freedom of speech, or of the press; or the right of the people peaceably to assemble, and to petition the government for a redress of grievances.

AMENDMENT II

[Right to bear arms]

A well regulated militia, being necessary to the security of a free state, the right of the people to keep and bear arms, shall not be infringed.

AMENDMENT III

[Quartering of troops]

No soldier shall, in time of peace be quartered in any house, without the consent of the owner, nor in time of war, but in a manner to be prescribed by law.

AMENDMENT IV

[Search and seizure]

The right of the people to be secure in their persons, houses, papers, and effects, against unreasonable searches and seizures, shall not be violated, and no warrants shall issue, but upon probable cause, supported by oath or affirmation, and particularly describing the place to be searched, and the persons or things to be seized.

AMENDMENT V

[Grand juries; double jeopardy; self-incrimination; due process; compensation for property]
No person shall be held to answer for a capital, or otherwise infamous crime, unless on a presentment or indictment of a grand jury, except in cases arising in the land or naval forces, or in the militia, when in actual service in time of war or public danger; nor shall any person be subject for the same offense to be twice put in jeopardy of life or limb; nor shall be compelled in any criminal case to be a witness against himself, nor be deprived of life, liberty, or property, without due process of law; nor shall private property be taken for public use, without just compensation.

AMENDMENT VI

[Speedy trial; juries; confronting witnesses; assistance of counsel]
In all criminal prosecutions, the accused shall enjoy the right to a speedy and public trial, by an impartial jury of the state and district wherein the crime shall have been committed, which district shall have been previously ascertained by law, and to be informed of the nature and cause of the accusation; to be confronted with the witnesses against him; to have compulsory process for obtaining witnesses in his favor, and to have the assistance of counsel for his defense.

AMENDMENT VII

[Jury trial in civil suits]
In suits at common law, where the value in controversy shall exceed twenty dollars, the right of trial by jury shall be preserved, and no fact tried by a jury, shall be otherwise reexamined in any court of the United States, than according to the rules of the common law.

AMENDMENT VIII

[No excessive bail; cruel, unusual punishment]
Excessive bail shall not be required, nor excessive fines imposed, nor cruel and unusual punishments inflicted.

AMENDMENT IX

[Reserved rights of people]
The enumeration in the Constitution, of certain rights, shall not be construed to deny or disparage others retained by the people.

AMENDMENT X

[Powers not delegated belong to states]
The powers not delegated to the United States by the Constitution, nor prohibited by it to the states, are reserved to the states respectively, or to the people.

AMENDMENT XI [1795]

[Federal judicial power and suits against states]
The judicial power of the United States shall not be construed to extend to any suit in law or equity, commenced or prosecuted against one of the United States by citizens of another state, or by citizens or subjects of any foreign state.

AMENDMENT XII [1804]

[Current method of electing President and Vice President]
The electors shall meet in their respective states and vote by ballot for President and Vice President, one of whom, at least, shall not be an inhabitant of the same state with themselves; they shall name in their ballots the person voted for as President, and in distinct ballots the person voted for as Vice President, and they shall make distinct lists of all persons voted for as President, and of all persons voted for as Vice President, and of the number of votes for each, which lists they shall sign and certify, and transmit sealed to the seat of the government of the United States, directed to the President

of the Senate; The President of the Senate shall, in the presence of the Senate and House of Representatives, open all the certificates and the votes shall then be counted; the person having the greatest number of votes for President, shall be the President, if such number be a majority of the whole number of electors appointed; and if no person have such majority, then from the persons having the highest numbers not exceeding three on the list of those voted for as President, the House of Representatives shall choose immediately, by ballot, the President. But in choosing the President, the votes shall be taken by states, the representation from each state having one vote; a quorum for this purpose shall consist of a member or members from two-thirds of the states, and a majority of all the states shall be necessary to a choice. And if the House of Representatives shall not choose a President whenever the right of choice shall devolve upon them, before the fourth day of March next following, then the Vice President shall act as President, as in the case of the death or other constitutional disability of the President. The person having the greatest number of votes as Vice President, shall be the Vice President, if such number be a majority of the whole number of electors appointed, and if no person have a majority, then from the two highest numbers on the list, the Senate shall choose the Vice President; a quorum for the purpose shall consist of two-thirds of the whole number of Senators, and a majority of the whole number shall be necessary to a choice. But no person constitutionally ineligible to the office of President shall be eligible to that of Vice President of the United States.

AMENDMENT XIII [1865]

Section 1.

[Ban on slavery]
Neither slavery nor involuntary servitude, except as a punishment for crime whereof the party shall have been duly convicted, shall exist within the United States, or any place subject to their jurisdiction.

Section 2.

Congress shall have power to enforce this article by appropriate legislation.

AMENDMENT XIV [1868]

Section 1.

[U.S. citizenship; due process; equal protection]
All persons born or naturalized in the United States, and subject to the jurisdiction thereof, are citizens of the United States and of the state wherein they reside. No state shall make or enforce any law which shall abridge the privileges or immunities of citizens of the United States; nor shall any state deprive any person of life, liberty, or property, without due process of law; nor deny to any person within its jurisdiction the equal protection of the laws.

Section 2.

[Apportionment of Representatives]
Representatives shall be apportioned among the several states according to their respective numbers, counting the whole number of persons in each state, excluding Indians not taxed. But when the right to vote at any election for the choice of electors for President and Vice President of the United States, Representatives in Congress, the executive and judicial officers of a state, or the members of the legislature thereof, is denied to any of the male inhabitants of such state, being twenty-one years of age, and citizens of the United States, or in any way abridged, except for participation in rebellion, or other crime, the basis of representation therein shall be reduced in the proportion which the number of such male citizens shall bear to the whole number of male citizens twenty-one years of age in such state.

Section 3.

[Disqualification for office]
No person shall be a Senator or Representative in Congress, or elector of President and Vice President, or hold any office, civil or military, under the

United States, or under any state, who, having previously taken an oath, as a member of Congress, or as an officer of the United States, or as a member of any state legislature, or as an executive or judicial officer of any state, to support the Constitution of the United States, shall have engaged in insurrection or rebellion against the same, or given aid or comfort to the enemies thereof. But Congress may by a vote of two-thirds of each House, remove such disability.

Section 4.

[Cancellation of Confederacy claims and debts]
The validity of the public debt of the United States, authorized by law, including debts incurred for payment of pensions and bounties for services in suppressing insurrection or rebellion, shall not be questioned. But neither the United States nor any state shall assume or pay any debt or obligation incurred in aid of insurrection or rebellion against the United States, or any claim for the loss or emancipation of any slave; but all such debts, obligations and claims shall be held illegal and void.

Section 5.

The Congress shall have power to enforce, by appropriate legislation, the provisions of this article.

AMENDMENT XV [1870]

Section 1.

[Right to vote]
The right of citizens of the United States to vote shall not be denied or abridged by the United States or by any state on account of race, color, or previous condition of servitude.

Section 2.

The Congress shall have power to enforce this article by appropriate legislation.

AMENDMENT XVI [1913]

The Congress shall have power to lay and collect taxes on incomes, from whatever source derived, without apportionment among the several states, and without regard to any census of enumeration.

AMENDMENT XVII [1913]

[Election of Senators]
The Senate of the United States shall be composed of two Senators from each state, elected by the people thereof, for six years; and each Senator shall have one vote. The electors in each state shall have the qualifications requisite for electors of the most numerous branch of the state legislatures. When vacancies happen in the representation of any state in the Senate, the executive authority of such state shall issue writs of election to fill such vacancies: Provided, that the legislature of any state may empower the executive thereof to make temporary appointments until the people fill the vacancies by election as the legislature may direct. This amendment shall not be so construed as to affect the election or term of any Senator chosen before it becomes valid as part of the Constitution.

AMENDMENT XVIII [1920]

Section 1.

[Prohibition on sale of alcoholic beverages]
After one year from the ratification of this article the manufacture, sale, or transportation of intoxicating liquors within, the importation thereof into, or the exportation thereof from the United States and all territory subject to the jurisdiction thereof for beverage purposes is hereby prohibited.

Section 2.

The Congress and the several states shall have concurrent power to enforce this article by appropriate legislation.

Section 3.

This article shall be inoperative unless it shall have been ratified as an amendment to the Constitution by the legislatures of the several states, as provided in the Constitution, within seven years from the date of the submission hereof to the states by the Congress.

AMENDMENT XIX [1920]

[Right of women to vote]
The right of citizens of the United States to vote shall not be denied or abridged by the United States or by any state on account of sex. Congress shall have power to enforce this article by appropriate legislation.

AMENDMENT XX [1933]

Section 1.

[Terms of President, Vice President, Congress]
The terms of the President and Vice President shall end at noon on the 20th day of January, and the terms of Senators and Representatives at noon on the 3d day of January, of the years in which such terms would have ended if this article had not been ratified; and the terms of their successors shall then begin.

Section 2.

[When Congress meets]
The Congress shall assemble at least once in every year, and such meeting shall begin at noon on the 3d day of January, unless they shall by law appoint a different day.

Section 3.

[Filling presidential vacancies]
If, at the time fixed for the beginning of the term of the President, the President elect shall have died, the Vice President elect shall become President. If a President shall not have been chosen before the time fixed for the beginning of his term, or if the President elect shall have failed to qualify, then the Vice President elect shall act as President until a President shall have qualified; and the Congress may by law provide for the case wherein neither a President elect nor a Vice President elect shall have qualified, declaring who shall then act as President, or the manner in which one who is to act shall be selected, and such person shall act accordingly until a President or Vice President shall have qualified.

Section 4.

The Congress may by law provide for the case of the death of any of the persons from whom the House of Representatives may choose a President whenever the right of choice shall have devolved upon them, and for the case of the death of any of the persons from whom the Senate may choose a Vice President whenever the right of choice shall have devolved upon them.

Section 5.

Sections 1 and 2 shall take effect on the 15th day of October following the ratification of this article.

Section 6.

This article shall be inoperative unless it shall have been ratified as an amendment to the Constitution by the legislatures of three-fourths of the several states within seven years from the date of its submission.

AMENDMENT XXI [1933]

Section 1.

[Repeal of Prohibition]
The eighteenth article of amendment to the Constitution of the United States is hereby repealed.

Section 2.

[Transportation of liquor and state laws]
The transportation or importation into any state, territory, or possession of the United States for delivery or use therein of intoxicating liquors, in violation of the laws thereof, is hereby prohibited.

Section 3.

This article shall be inoperative unless it shall have been ratified as an amendment to the Constitution by conventions in the several states, as provided in the Constitution, within seven years from the date of the submission hereof to the states by the Congress.

AMENDMENT XXII [1951]

Section 1.

[Presidential term limit]
No person shall be elected to the office of the President more than twice, and no person who has held the office of President, or acted as President, for more than two years of a term to which some other person was elected President shall be elected to the office of the President more than once. But this article shall not apply to any person holding the office of President when this article was proposed by the Congress, and shall not prevent any person who may be holding the office of President, or acting as President, during the term within which this article becomes operative from holding the office of President or acting as President during the remainder of such term.

Section 2.

This article shall be inoperative unless it shall have been ratified as an amendment to the Constitution by the legislatures of three-fourths of the several states within seven years from the date of its submission to the states by the Congress.

AMENDMENT XXIII [1961]

Section 1.

[Electors for District of Columbia]
The District constituting the seat of government of the United States shall appoint in such manner as the Congress may direct: A number of electors of President and Vice President equal to the whole number of Senators and Representatives in Congress to which the District would be entitled if it were a state, but in no event more than the least populous state; they shall be in addition to those appointed by the states, but they shall be considered, for the purposes of the election of President and Vice President, to be electors appointed by a state; and they shall meet in the District and perform such duties as provided by the twelfth article of amendment.

Section 2.

The Congress shall have power to enforce this article by appropriate legislation.

AMENDMENT XXIV [1964]

Section 1.

[Ban on poll taxes]
The right of citizens of the United States to vote in any primary or other election for President or Vice President, for electors for President or Vice President, or for Senator or Representative in Congress, shall not be denied or abridged by the United States or any state by reason of failure to pay any poll tax or other tax.

Section 2.

The Congress shall have power to enforce this article by appropriate legislation.

AMENDMENT XXV [1967]

Section 1.

[Succession of Vice President to Presidency]
In case of the removal of the President from office or of his death or resignation, the Vice President shall become President.

Section 2.

[Filling Vice Presidential vacancy]
Whenever there is a vacancy in the office of the Vice President, the President shall nominate a Vice President who shall take office upon confirmation by a majority vote of both Houses of Congress.

Section 3.

[Vice President as Acting President]
Whenever the President transmits to the President pro tempore of the Senate and the Speaker of the House of Representatives his written declaration that he is unable to discharge the powers and duties of his office, and until he transmits to them a written declaration to the contrary, such powers and

duties shall be discharged by the Vice President as Acting President.

Section 4.

Whenever the Vice President and a majority of either the principal officers of the executive departments or of such other body as Congress may by law provide, transmit to the President pro tempore of the Senate and the Speaker of the House of Representatives their written declaration that the President is unable to discharge the powers and duties of his office, the Vice President shall immediately assume the powers and duties of the office as Acting President. Thereafter, when the President transmits to the President pro tempore of the Senate and the Speaker of the House of Representatives his written declaration that no inability exists, he shall resume the powers and duties of his office unless the Vice President and a majority of either the principal officers of the executive department or of such other body as Congress may by law provide, transmit within four days to the President pro tempore of the Senate and the Speaker of the House of Representatives their written declaration that the President is unable to discharge the powers and duties of his office. Thereupon Congress shall decide the issue, assembling within forty-eight hours for that purpose if not in session. If the Congress, within twenty-one days after receipt of the latter written declaration, or, if Congress is not in session, within twenty-one days after Congress is required to assemble, determines by two-thirds vote of both Houses that the President is unable to discharge the powers and duties of his office, the Vice President shall continue to discharge the same as Acting President; otherwise, the President shall resume the powers and duties of his office.

AMENDMENT XXVI [1971]

Section 1.

[Voting age lowered to 18]
The right of citizens of the United States, who are 18 years of age or older, to vote, shall not be denied or abridged by the United States or any state on account of age.

Section 2.

The Congress shall have the power to enforce this article by appropriate legislation.

AMENDMENT XXVII [1992]

[When Congressional pay raise takes effect]
No law, varying the compensation for the services of the Senators and Representatives, shall take effect, until an election of Representatives shall have intervened.

INDEX

A

C

H

I

J

K

L

U

V

W

Y

Z